BUKOVINA

# Bukovina

## THE LIFE AND DEATH OF AN EAST EUROPEAN BORDERLAND

CRISTINA FLOREA

PRINCETON UNIVERSITY PRESS
PRINCETON & OXFORD

Published by Princeton University Press

41 William Street, Princeton, New Jersey 08540
99 Banbury Road, Oxford OX2 6JX

press.princeton.edu

GPSR Authorized Representative: Easy Access System Europe - Mustamäe tee 50, 10621 Tallinn, Estonia, gpsr.requests@easproject.com



ISBN 978-0-691-27680-9
ISBN (e-book) 978-0-691-27681-6

Library of Congress Control Number: 2025940314

British Library Cataloging-in-Publication Data is available

Editorial: Priya Nelson and Emma Wagh
Production Editorial: Kathleen Cioffi
Jacket Design: Karl Spurzem
Production: Erin Suydam
Publicity: William Pagdatoon

Jacket images: Courtesy of the Romanian Academy Library and the National Library of Poland

This book has been composed in Arno

Printed in the United States of America

10 9 8 7 6 5 4 3 2 1

To my father,
who taught me how to learn

## CONTENTS

# CONTENTS

# ACKNOWLEDGMENTS

A SAYING I heard often growing up in Romania was, "Every kick in the behind is a leap forward." Over the many years it took to research and write this book, I experienced both kicks and leaps, and every leap was because of the many wonderful people who stood by my side and urged me forward. I am delighted to be able to thank them now.

I owe this book's existence to the fabulous Priya Nelson and her wonderful editorial assistant, Emma Wagh. I will always be grateful to Natasha Wheatley for introducing me to them. I cannot thank the crew at Princeton University Press enough for taking an interest in my work and guiding it to publication with professionalism and humanity. Kathleen Cioffi moved the manuscript seamlessly through the various production stages and Francis Eaves copyedited it with infinite care and patience. I am forever indebted both to them and to the three reviewers who read my work and offered such generous and thoughtful feedback. Two of them have since revealed themselves. I give my heartfelt thanks to Joachim von Puttkamer, to Kathryn Ciancia, and also to the anonymous reader for their diligent reading and invaluable suggestions for improving the manuscript.

The book originated from a dissertation I wrote at Princeton University. My amazing advisor, Stephen Kotkin, completely changed my understanding of the past and taught me the value of taking risks and pursuing ambitious projects. I will always be grateful to him for encouraging me to find my path and trust my voice. At Princeton, I also benefited tremendously from the mentorship of Jan Gross and the late Andy Rabinbach. Andy, in particular, sustained my work with his good humor and humanity, and reminded me of why I wanted to be doing it in the first place. It would be remiss of me not to mention too Michael Gordin, Katya Pravilova, Yair Mintzker, Katja Günther, and Irena Grudzińska-Gross. They all helped shape who I am as a scholar. Many Princeton colleagues and friends gave me invaluable advice and supported me over the years. I am especially indebted to Will Schultz, Marc Volovici, Reut Harari, Marcia Schenck, and fellow Soviet history survivors Elidor Mëhilli, Franziska Exeler, Kyrill Kunakhovich, and Mayhill Fowler.

I was lucky to benefit from generous institutional support while researching and writing this book. An ACLS Eastern Europe grant (a type of grant no longer in existence) let me travel to archives and libraries in Austria, Germany, Israel, Romania, and Ukraine. The American Friends of Marbach supported my research trip to Marbach, and the Center for Jewish History in New York granted me a summer research fellowship to work in their collections. Archival staff on three continents made the research process manageable. Special thanks are due to Maria Guțu and the staff of the State Archives of Chernivtsi Oblast, who put up with my endless requests for documents despite tough work conditions. I am also grateful to Wolfgang Maderthaner and Susanne Kühberger at the Austrian State Archives in Vienna and Miriam Caloianu at the Center for the Study of Romanian Jewry. Everywhere I went, generous people invited me into their homes and kept me company during my archival trips. I am extremely grateful to Hanna Volovici in Jerusalem and Natalya Mikhailovna Frunchak , Oksana Ivasiuk, and Nelly Pavlovna in Chernivtsi. I thank Nancy Wingfield for providing indispensable contacts in Chernivtsi and encouraging me to continue my work. Svitlana Frunchak, Natalya Lazar, and Hanna Skoreiko, all excellent scholars and natives of Chernivtsi, gave me invaluable tips on handling the local archives. Tamara Scheer helped me navigate the archives in Vienna.

I began reworking my dissertation into a book while a postdoctoral fellow at the Harvard Academy of Scholars. Kathleen Hoover and Bruce Jackan made the house on 1727 Cambridge Street the best work environment I could hope for. Along with time and resources, the Academy gifted me new friends, colleagues, and mentors. Chris Gratien, Rishad Choudhury, Lina Britto, Małgorzata Kurjanska, and Zach Howlett helped me rethink my project and made my year at the Academy unforgettable. My manuscript workshop at Harvard was an incredible experience. I am hugely thankful to Pieter Judson, Mark Kramer, Odd Arne Westad, Michael David-Fox, and Serhii Plokhy for reading and commenting on my work. My colleagues at SUNY Albany, especially Maeve Kane, Ryan Irwin, Nadieszda Kizenko, Patrick Nold, and Federica Francesconi, welcomed me into their department and offered much-needed encouragement and good cheer.

I like to say—only half in jest—that I went to graduate school twice: once at Princeton and a second time at Cornell. I arrived in Ithaca knowing little about teaching and even less about how to write a book. My colleagues taught me everything. I am grateful to my mentors and friends, Claudia Verhoeven, Durba Gosh, Maria Cristina Garcia, Isabel Hull, Tamara Loos, and Aaron Sachs for all the time they invested in me. Robert Travers and Mostafa Minawi read an earlier version of my manuscript and gave me wonderful suggestions. I was also fortunate to be part of a cohort of brilliant young scholars who have enriched my experience at Cornell beyond measure. I am grateful to Casey Schmitt, Ruth Lawlor, Mayor Juni, Nick Mulder, Kristen Roebuck, Mara Du, Rachel Sandwell,

Paraska Tolan-Szkilnik, and Camille Suarez for their astute comments on my work, as well as their friendship and camaraderie.

I also owe thanks to the East European Research Pod at Cornell. Sophie Pinkham, Leila Wilmers, Maria Taylor, Lori Khatchadourian, and Patricia Young gave terrific feedback on my introduction. I am deeply thankful to Sophie for introducing me to the joys of non-academic writing and for keeping me supplied with wonderful reading recommendations. I am indebted to Patricia for standing by me while we plotted how to put Cornell on the Eastern Europe studies map. The Junior Faculty Colloquium, European History Colloquium, Reppy Institute Seminar, Comparative History Colloquium, and German Studies Colloquium at Cornell provided excellent venues for presenting my work. I learned immensely from many graduate students and friends, especially Duncan Maclean Eaton, Kaitlin Findlay, Madeleine Lemos, Christopher Mingo, David Rubinstein, and Emre Susamci. They have all been a great source of inspiration and fulfillment.

One semester at the Cornell Center for Social Science and a year at the Society for Humanities gave me the time I desperately needed to revise my manuscript. Paul Fleming and the Society fellows made my work productive and enjoyable. Through the European History Colloquium and the Institute for European Studies at Cornell, I also got to know scholars who have influenced me greatly: Natasha Wheatley, Dominique Kirchner Reill, Giuliana Chamedes, and Kathryn Ciancia, to name just a few. Dominique changed my life when she put me in touch with her copyeditor, Martha Schulman. Working with Martha has been transformative. She is one of the most astute and generous readers I have known, and extremely fast to boot. Thanks to the writing buddies I made at Cornell, writing no longer feels lonely. I am thankful to Lauren Monroe, who made writing at five in the morning something to look forward to. I am also grateful for feedback and encouragement from colleagues I met at various conferences and workshops outside Cornell, especially Tara Zahra, Peter Holquist, Máté Rigó, Iryna Vushko, Holly Case, Fran Hirsch, Philippe Blasen, Mirna Zakic, Tarik Cyril Amar, Gaëlle Fisher, Vejas Gabriel Liulevicius, Irina Livezeanu, Anna Muller, Claire Morelon, and Marco Bresciani.

Bringing this book into the light was a nerve-wracking process. Margo Irvin and the editors of the East European history series at Stanford, Norman Naimark and Larry Wolff, generously shared their readers' reports with Princeton University Press. Ali Garbarini, my thesis advisor at Williams College, supported me during this difficult time with endless patience, care, and humanity. I am so grateful to her for her time, kindness, and wisdom. My Cornell friends Irina Troconis and Imane Terhmina cheered me on as I tried to figure out a path to publication. Maki Matsui provided much-needed distraction and encouragement. Claudia Verhoeven offered me her friendship and company during the final push. Friends both human and canine—Katy Noonan and Mookie, Jane Mt. Pleasant and Becka, and Mary Beer and Molly—brought me joy and sustained me through writing this book. Pam Johnson kept me sane, helped me gain confidence, and taught me how to make time.

If I could give out medals for both brilliance and humanity, three people in particular would deserve them. One of them is my Princeton colleague and friend Kyrill Kunakhovich, who has read pretty much everything I have ever written. I have known him for over a decade and am still awed by his brilliance and generosity. Another is Will Schultz, whom I met on my first day of graduate school at Princeton. Becoming his friend was the smartest thing I have ever done: I am so grateful for the patience and affection he has shown me. Finally, Kathryn Ciancia did the heroic job of reading my manuscript in its entirety in record time. Whether she knows it or not, she has been my inspiration and model.

My Ithaca family has given me strength and joy while writing this book. Its feline members, Joey and Willie (known as Cozonac and Marmeladă in Romanian), have been a constant source of amusement and comfort. My golden retriever, Rosika, changed my life vastly for the better. I owe most of my friendships in Ithaca to her—as well as my sanity and physical health. Jay Alipour has been by my side throughout this long process, lighting the way with his unmistakable humor, kindness, and love and giving me the home I always wanted. I thank him for never doubting that I could do this, and reminding me not to take myself too seriously.

My greatest debt goes to my parents and grandparents. My mother and father, Nadia and Mircea, have put up with my prolonged absence and tried their best to help me as I worked through weekends and holidays. My father has been my most passionate supporter, taking endless joy in each of my accomplishments, no matter how small. I owe so much to him for instilling in me a love of books and for modeling curiosity, persistence, and moral integrity. Nor would I ever have written this book if it had not been for my grandparents, especially Omama and Otata. They are the reason I became a historian of Eastern Europe. Although their lives were torn apart by nationalism, imperialism, Nazism, and Communism, they lived with fortitude and decency. This book is my attempt to understand the world they came from—the world my parents and I inherited.

# NOTE ON PLACE NAMES AND SPELLING

AS A result of repeated regime changes and territorial reconfiguration, places and people in Bukovina changed names often. In multilingual Bukovina, a place could have many different names, with different spellings, at any one time depending on who was speaking or writing. For the sake of clarity, I refer to Chernivtsi as Czernowitz in chapters on the pre–World War I period. In chapters focusing on the period between 1918 and 1940, I refer to it as Cernăuţi, using the Romanian spelling. I call the city Chernovtsy in 1940, when it came under Soviet occupation, and it was once again renamed. Readers fluent in Romanian may thus be surprised to find Rădăuţi sometimes spelled as Radautz.

My choice of spellings is not meant as any kind of statement about the national or ethnic character of different places or people. I simply refer to them as they appear in the documents cited in this book.

All translations in the book are my own.

# BUKOVINA

# Introduction

IMAGINE A DISTANT place, barely within a traveler's reach, "where once there was forest upon forest and marshes and moors,"[1] and "beautiful highlands [. . .] with narrow and wide river beds, dark forests, also with flourishing villages and friendly towns." The deeper you travel into this breathtaking landscape, the more you forget the busy streets of Europe's capitals, and "the more wonderful the magic of this small Carpathian world" seems.[2] This was how the authors of the *Kronprinzenwerk*, an encyclopedia of the Austro-Hungarian lands commissioned by the Crown Prince and published between 1886 and 1902, described Bukovina, a place most readers would not have been to or known. A few might have learned about it from reading Karl Emil Franzos's travel sketches, published in May 1876 under the title *Aus Halb-Asien*, "From Half-Asia."

Though born into a German-speaking Jewish family in the Galician town of Czortków, Franzos was not an outsider in Bukovina. Shortly after his father's death, the young Karl Emil had moved to Czernowitz, then Bukovina's provincial capital, to study at the city's German-language *Gymnasium* (secondary school; plural *Gymnasia*). Here he finally felt "like a German among Germans."[3] He read Goethe and Heine and became deeply enamored of German humanism. He dreamed of studying philosophy, but he was poor, and would have had to convert to Christianity to be eligible for a government stipend. Franzos ultimately decided to follow in his father's footsteps and study law in Vienna. He returned to Czernowitz in the summer of 1868 and wrote his first novella, *Das Christusbild*, about a Jewish ghetto.[4] A few years later, he gave up law to continue writing, despite being repeatedly rejected by publishers.

In 1874 he had a breakthrough: the *Neue Freie Presse*, Austria's most prestigious newspaper, began publishing his travel sketches of the monarchy's easternmost territories and south Russia and Romania, the borderlands he called "Halb-Asien." Little did Franzos know what staying power that name would have. Bukovinans would come to think of themselves and their province as balancing uneasily between worlds, always on the verge of sliding out of Europe and back into the presumed backwardness of the East.

In *Aus Halb-Asien*, Franzos painted the portrait of Bukovina as a traveler approaching by train would have seen it. From a compartment window, the province would have appeared neat and charming. After many hours of travel through Galicia's dark and muddy expanses, Bukovina gave Franzos the impression that he was "in the West, where *Bildung*, good manners, and white tablecloths could be found" once more.[5] It looked like a flourishing little piece of Europe, like a mirage "in the middle of the Half-Asian cultural desert." In this "blessed land," Franzos wrote, "the soil is better cultivated and the cottages are friendlier and cleaner." More astonishingly, people here "wore the clothing and spoke the language [. . .] customary between the Kinzig and Neckar" in Germany.[6]

But the mirage lasted just fifteen minutes, the time it took to descend from Czernowitz's center into the lower city. In the so-called Judenviertel, the city's oldest quarter, the Western-looking cafes and hotels gave way to "small and pathetic houses" inhabited by "people in caftans and women with curious headgear." Here the city reminded Franzos of a "Podolian ghetto"—not a term of endearment, for he was an acerbic critic of life in Eastern Europe's Jewish ghettos.[7] A few streets on, the city changed faces yet again, with onion-domed Orthodox churches replacing the synagogues, and Russian baths and straw-covered huts surrounded by corn fields, brown heathlands, and forest. One could be forgiven for thinking oneself in the middle of Ukraine, although, as Franzos reassured the reader, "we are still in a district of the city of Czernowitz and still a good distance from its boundary."[8]

Atop the hill called Habsburgshöhe, the visitor would come face to face with one of Czernowitz's most prominent and awe-inspiring edifices: the Greek-Oriental archbishop's residence. Built in Moorish style, decorated with colorful mosaics and crenelated towers reminiscent of minarets, the *Residenz* transported viewers to Spain, the Arab lands, or the Byzantine empire. Farther down, along the shores of the Prut river, Czernowitz morphed again, now evoking the landscapes of industrial Britain with "stone buildings and smoke coming out" of its factories, the "air heavy with coal smoke." At the city's farthest end, by the Austriaplatz, the urban landscape gave way to the "uninhabited steppe which stretches for miles upon miles." Here Bukovina resembled the American prairie, untamed by pioneers.[9]

When I visited Chernivtsi (as Czernowitz is now called) in the fall of 2013, the journey was as long and arduous as Franzos's had been over a century earlier. Traveling there, whether by bus from Kyiv or Lviv, or Kishinev in neighboring Moldavia, or by train from Bucharest or Moscow, feels like journeying to the end of the world. When you get off the train and make your way into the old Austrian-built railway station, you think you have arrived in the middle of an ordinary Central European town, no different from Graz or Linz. But as you

FIGURE 0.1. Czernowitz's formerly majestic synagogue (see Figure 2.4), located in the city center, is now a cinema. Locals call it the "kinahoha" in jest. Photo by author, 2013.

walk up the hill, into the city proper, you are greeted by apartment buildings that seem to have been lifted straight out of interwar Bucharest or Paris.

Walk past the city hall, and you come upon an imposing building painted white and pale blue with a large clock above its entrance. On either side of the door posters advertise Hollywood's latest productions, which you can watch there. Once a synagogue with a cupola and imposing towers in Moorish Revival style, the building now looks strangely incomplete without them. The Soviets converted it into a cinema (*kinoteatr*), and locals call it "kinahoha." Further out, this Austro-Romanian city becomes a Soviet provincial town, with ornate administrative buildings and residences giving way to Khrushchev-era prefabricated apartments, lined up like rows of matchboxes. Just feet from a prominent monument to Bukovina's liberation by the Soviets is a life-size statue of Emperor Franz Joseph, who has a new lease on life these days as young Ukrainian residents look to Chernivtsi's Habsburg imperial past to distance themselves from Russia.

A patchwork of architectural styles and symbols, Bukovina bears the marks of repeated regime change. Successive attempts to remake the province, from its emergence as a self-standing entity in the late eighteenth century to its partition during World War I and again in 1944–45, have created a confusing yet marvelously complex landscape that seems to inhabit multiple epochs and spaces simultaneously. Caught in successive geopolitical transformations, Bukovina was repeatedly annexed and lost by different states. Again and again, it found itself in the middle of disputes for regional supremacy between competing empires or their successor states: at first Poland, Hungary, and the Ottoman Empire; then Romania and Ukraine, then the Soviet and Nazi empires. Handed from one polity to another, Bukovina underwent several revolutions and counterrevolutions, becoming, as historian David Rechter writes, "a conduit for transmitting all manner of ideas, goods, and people between Central and Eastern Europe, Eastern and Southeastern Europe, and even between Europe and Asia."[10]

This book tells the story of the successive attempts to integrate Bukovina into different polities, remaking it in the process, and of the people who lived there amid transformation and reinvention. The chapters to come explore how state officials, urban elites, and villagers in Bukovina made sense of the ideologies handed down from the centers of power, and how they participated in and were shaped by changing governance practices.

Bukovina may seem like a "faraway country" inhabited by people "about whom we know nothing"—as Neville Chamberlain said of Czechoslovakia in 1938. Arguing for its significance is less difficult today, when the war in Ukraine has once again focused the world's attention on Eastern Europe. Through the little-known story of Bukovina, this book seeks to explain how Eastern Europe got to such a point, and what might come next. Moreover, however small or insignificant Bukovina may seem, its story is also very much the story of many other contested borderlands across the globe, from Kashmir and Manchuria to the Bay of Bengal, and from the Caucasus to Alsace-Lorraine.[11] These regions have been laboratories of experimentation with different forms of statehood, governance, and ideologies, from imperialism, to nationalism, to socialism. They have experienced multiple attempts to reimagine not only the world, but time itself. This book invites readers to view the past three centuries from the perspective of a European periphery whose story highlights how central competition is to modern statehood, the endurance of empires and their legacies, and the unexpected convergence of the various ideological projects that shaped the modern world.

## A Multivalent History

The following pages aim to offer an overarching, perhaps even, in a sense, a "total" history of Bukovina, constituting the first *longue durée* study of the province in the English language. The narrative does not, as one might expect from Fernand Braudel's use of that term, extend past human memory or trace changes in climate, landscape, or environment over the long term.[12] But it does look at one region over the course of almost two centuries. This extended temporal perspective has two main advantages. First, it sheds light on mutual influences and connections between regimes and polities separated not only by different ideologies, but by time. The reason for these connections, I argue, is that the different states and political actors in Bukovina ended up shaping each other through competition, emulation, and absorbing each other's legacies.[13] Second, a long-term perspective allows us to better understand a region profoundly shaped by polities that left complex cultural and intellectual legacies. The long view lets me underscore the asynchronous nature of change in the East European borderlands, where the end of a state's political existence rarely meant the end of its cultural and institutional life. At the same time, state-led projects often remained unfinished, or were carried out halfheartedly and on the cheap.[14]

This is a history decompartmentalized across not only time, but space. It follows in the footsteps of Gaëlle Fisher, Mariana Hausleitner, Kurt Scharr and other historians whose works combine the histories of rural and urban populations in Bukovina in one narrative.[15] Some of the richest literature on Bukovina focuses on Jewish urban life, and especially on its provincial capital, Czernowitz. In part, this is because urban Jews left behind more written sources and are more visible than other communities in newspapers, memoirs, and institutional archives, especially from the Austrian period. They were deeply involved in municipal affairs and unusually powerful economically and politically, particularly before World War I.[16] They helped transform Czernowitz into an urban center with great ambitions—if not plentiful resources. They were the city's coachmen, merchants and store owners, and professionals. Their stores—bearing their owners' names, "Leon Fuhrmann," "Ehrlich," "Leon Wagner"—lined Czernowitz's main street, the Hauptstrasse, which connected the train station to the city center dominated by the elegant *Rathaus* with its tall clock tower.

Descendants of Czernowitz Jews still visit Chernivtsi today and participate in projects to preserve the memory of Bukovinan Jewish life, such as the rehabilitation of the Jewish cemetery and the foundation of a Jewish museum in the city center. Marianne Hirsch, a literary scholar and descendant of a Jewish family from Czernowitz, wrote with Leo Spitzer one of the best books on the city: *Ghosts of Home: The Afterlife of Czernowitz in Jewish Memory* (2011), a mélange of history and memoir with ruminations on nostalgia and homecoming. But though Czernowitz looms large in memory and imagination, it was actually a small part of the province. Most Bukovinans lived in the countryside—a perpetual source of fear and fascination for city dwellers who

FIGURE 0.2. Postcard (1910) showing the main street in Czernowitz, Hauptstrasse, featuring the *Rathaus* (city hall) in the background, and Jewish shops. Public domain.

struggled to draw sharp limits between their city and the surrounding villages.[17] Bukovina's Romanians, Ukrainians, and Germans were predominantly rural.

In merging Bukovina's rural and urban histories, the present volume also seeks to overcome the ethnic fragmentation that prevails in the existing literature on the region. In Bukovina, as elsewhere, history writing was central to the forging of competing nationalisms.[18] From the mid-nineteenth century onward, Ukrainian and Romanian historians worked to prove that their respective ethnic and national groups had settled Bukovina first and were therefore entitled to the territory. More recently, a new generation of historians from the region have begun questioning nationalist myths and traditional interpretations of the region's history. Even so, a Romanian-authored two-volume encyclopedia of Bukovina published in 2000 barely mentions any non-Romanians. The tendency is still either to focus on one's own national group or, at the other extreme, to sentimentalize Bukovina's multicultural past to demonstrate the Europeanness of its present-day inhabitants. By contrast, this book portrays Bukovina as a site of entanglements and interactions between different ethnic groups, without taking sides or uncritically depicting it as a kind of multinational paradise lost.[19]

To do so, the book draws on a vast and diverse body of materials in a variety of languages (Romanian, Ukrainian, Russian, German, French, Yiddish), mined from archives and libraries in six different countries. Since the administrations and people who came to and went from Bukovina often took pieces of its past with them, researching the region's history is a painstaking process akin to reconstructing a broken glass pane from hundreds of shards scattered across the world. The only sensible approach to studying Bukovina's tangled past is transnational and comparative, since traditional historiographical boundaries do not adequately represent Bukovinans' experiences. Bukovina's most prominent late nineteenth-century historian, Raimund Friedrich Kaindl (1866–1930), knew this: "we will have to go first to the east and north, and then back to the west and across the Danube to the south to gather all the historical facts which concern our Bukovina, which influenced it and continue to do so. No local history can be separated from the history of neighboring regions and this is all the more so in the case of Bukovina's history."[20]

Since this state of affairs is hardly unique to Bukovina, this book moreover makes an argument for studying Eastern Europe and Europe as a whole across traditional chronological and geographical boundaries. Although historians are now exploring cross-border and transnational phenomena in Europe, most historiography remains siloed and fragmented between different areas of specialization.[21] Trained either as Ottomanists or Habsburg historians, as Russianists or Sovietologists, historians tend to stick to their own turf. But this option was not available to Bukovinans, who had to become specialists in multiple empires and polities over the course of one lifetime. Historians of the region need to do the same.

Although it is not a global history in the usual sense of the term, this study shares with global histories the desire to shift attention from capitals and power centers to see how small and apparently remote places were embedded in larger contexts and interactions. It deliberately focuses on the story of a political and economic periphery to make an argument for the significance of small, seemingly marginal places.[22] Yet much of what we call "global history" aims to chip away at stories of Western exceptionalism, or "provincialize" Europe, as Dipesh Chakrabarty memorably put it.[23] Here, I show that we need not leave Europe to find complexity and difference. Power differentials structured relationships among European actors too: Europe was a continent of great powers and small states, of economic giants and countries that lagged behind, of rulers and the ruled.[24] Places like Bukovina remind us of the multiperspectival, complex nature of European history, a history made up of a multiplicity of stories, often clashing.

As global historians and practitioners of micro-history have observed, foregrounding small, marginal places presents several advantages. Such places offer new angles of vision from which to observe the great powers anew and notice phenomena that may not be visible elsewhere.[25] Moreover, marginal places have often been central to the development of states and the global order's overall evolution. "What Europe has been and done since the second half of the nineteenth century," historian Holly Case writes, "has hinged on how marginal states interpreted its role and function in international relations."[26] Even peripheries that struggled economically have made key contributions to the cultural and intellectual lives of imperial heartlands.[27] Peripheries have always been important to empires' expansion and survival,[28] especially during transitional periods when political and cultural systems were reinvented and revamped.[29]

In fact, Bukovinans' intellectual and moral universe revolved around a deep preoccupation with peripherality and marginality that shaped virtually everything, from their interactions with the states that governed them to their interpretation of ideologies and experience of change.[30] Many of them felt marginal not merely because they lived far from the center of power, but because, coming from a place that straddled multiple worlds, they did not feel they truly belonged anywhere.[31] In her memoir, Pearl Fichman, a former resident of Czernowitz, recalled that she felt "fake" her entire life. Though born on Romanian soil in interwar Romania, Fichman came from a German-speaking Jewish family who kept Austrian traditions. They lived in Romania but "ate Wiener Schnitzel and drank spritz," "listened to German classics," and read "Schiller, Goethe, Heine."[32] This failure to be completely integrated, whether into a polity, nation, or culture, became a defining feature of many Bukovinans' lives.

Sometimes, anxieties about peripherality translated into an overwhelming fear of being left behind and forgotten, of dropping out of history. At other times, these feelings gave rise to a sense of superiority and exceptionalism. Some Bukovinans came to believe that because they were located on the margins of states, they had privileged insight into those states. Bukovinan Germans felt more German than their counterparts in Berlin. The writer Gregor von Rezzori (1914–1998), who built his entire literary identity around his Bukovinan origins, claimed that they made him a "free man" who "thinks every ideology stupid."[33] Philipp Menczel, a local journalist, could never forget or forgive the man he met visiting a spa resort in Germany, who asked him if Czernowitz was anywhere near "Kattowitz," a Polish town over four hundred miles away.[34] Such encounters reminded Bukovinans that power inequalities persisted between residents of a small province and metropolitans, even if the latter were in reality the more provincial, and the former the more cosmopolitan.

As people like Menczel knew only too well, being marginal did not mean being static, backward, or disconnected from the rest of the world.[35] Bukovina's location on a geopolitical fault line ensured that it was always connected to people and places far beyond its borders, and meant too that it was located at the epicenter of the revolutions and transformations that eventually encompassed all of Europe. In highlighting these aspects of its history, I join other historians of Eastern Europe in their efforts to "de-provincialize" Bukovina. Many have done this by tracing the various forms of exchange and circulation that tied it to the rest of the world.[36] I argue instead that we can see it as a microcosm of Europe, and a lynchpin between that continent and the world beyond. Precisely because of its marginality, Bukovina's history offers a parable about the modern age, a time defined by bold aspirations for change coupled with a perpetual feeling of loss and homesickness.

## A Short Biography of Bukovina

Bukovina was a product of empire, a completely new geopolitical entity or, as Larry Wolff writes about the neighboring province of Galicia, a "new world [...] invented in the rational spirit of enlightened statecraft."[37] There was nothing predetermined or inherently logical about Bukovina's boundaries: in fact, the province emerged as a self-standing entity through an unexpected turn of events. When it came into being, Austria was buttressing its position in East Central Europe after regaining Hungary from the Ottomans in 1699.[38] The Habsburgs conceived of their empire as a bastion of civilization and protector of Christianity against the Ottomans, a "bulwark and guardian of Europe against Asiatic elements of every kind."[39] In the east, a new expansionist power was on the rise: Russia, whose empress Catherine the Great hoped to reach Constantinople, clashing with the Ottomans in a series of wars. The war of 1768–74 ended with the Ottomans' defeat, marking a "quantum leap in Russia's international position."[40]

Although Austria did not directly participate in the war, it gained something: in return for Austria brokering the peace, the Ottomans ceded to it the northwestern corner of the principality of Moldova, then under Ottoman suzerainty. A small, fragile state, Moldova bordered the Polish-Lithuanian Commonwealth and the Ottoman Empire. Austria's new territorial conquest, located at the converging tips of three clashing empires, in a *triplex confinuum*, would be called Bukovina.

At its annexation by Austria in 1775 the territory was sparsely populated and thickly forested. It measured 10,440 square kilometers (4,030 square miles) and counted between seventy thousand and seventy-five thousand residents, mostly speakers of Moldavian (Romanian) or Ruthenian (Ukrainian).[41] It had no obvious physical delimitations other than the river Dniester in the north and the river Prut in the east, and the bulk of its population raised cattle in the valley between the two rivers. More than half of the territory was covered with forests ripe for exploitation. Agriculture was relatively underdeveloped due to

Bukovina's scarce arable land, most of it the property of the Orthodox Church, the province's largest landowner. Empress Maria Theresa's son and (officially) co-ruler Joseph II believed this northwestern corner of Moldova, though not especially large or rich, had strategic value, and that annexing it would facilitate transportation and movement between Austrian-ruled Hungary and Galicia, which the Habsburgs had taken from Poland a few years before. And so, Bukovina came under Habsburg rule. Initially under temporary military administration, it was incorporated into Galicia-Lodomeria in 1786. It took local elites more than fifty years to persuade the Habsburgs that Bukovina deserved its own administration. They finally succeeded in 1860, when the province was granted a separate administration and provincial parliament.

Bukovina remained under Austrian rule until World War I, when it was successively occupied and liberated by the armies of the Russian and Austrian empires. Shortly after the Austrians definitively recovered it, Austria-Hungary collapsed, and Bukovina once more became the object of territorial contestation. Ukrainian and Romanian politicians both claimed it, arguing that the province was indispensable to their respective nation-states. The dispute was resolved in the Romanians' favor, and Bukovina was incorporated into Greater Romania in the fall of 1918, an outcome made possible by the simultaneous collapse of the Russian and Austro-Hungarian empires. Leaders of the newly created successor states, including Romania, were confident that history was on their side. They all sought to tie their newly incorporated provinces to new national centers and metropoles, an especially difficult task in Bukovina because of the Habsburg Empire's enduring legacies. By the 1930s, the Romanian authorities in Cernăuţi were losing patience with Bukovina, which refused to look and feel Romanian. Meanwhile, Bukovinans of all ethnicities, Romanian and non-Romanian, were feeling increasingly alienated from an administration they believed did not adequately represent their interests.

In accordance with a secret provision of the Ribbentrop–Molotov pact signed in August 1939 by Nazi Germany and the Soviet Union, Romania lost Bukovina's northern half to the Soviet Union in 1940. The almost one year that northern Bukovina spent under Soviet rule proved truly transformative, as the Soviets implemented more drastic changes than the Romanians had achieved over two decades. The Soviets came armed with an ideology and state apparatus designed to bring about revolution "from abroad."[42] As soon as they landed in Cernăuţi, renamed Chernovtsy and then Chernivtsi in Ukrainian, they launched collectivization and mass literacy campaigns, reenacting, decades later, the Bolshevik revolution of 1917. They disseminated propaganda across the province, including the deep countryside that had eluded the reach of previous administrations. Wielding the weapons of total war, the Soviets set into motion demographic transformations that would continue through the war and postwar years, completely transforming the province's northern half.

When Adolf Hitler launched Operation Barbarossa in June 1941, it caught the Soviets in Chernivtsi by surprise. Backed up by their German allies, Romanian troops entered northern Bukovina and reclaimed it, along with most of the territories they had lost to the Soviets the previous year. Having experienced occupations in World War I, some Bukovinans felt they knew what to expect. But as they painfully discovered, Nazi Germany and its Romanian ally, as well as the Soviet Union, were completely new entities, with totalizing ambitions the likes of which Bukovinans had never experienced. The returning Romanian administration came to northern Bukovina poised to achieve what they had failed to do earlier: namely, to tie the province to the nation-state for good and remove any chance of losing it again. This was a tragedy many attributed to the machinations of ethnic minorities, above all the Jews, who had allegedly invited the Soviet troops into Bukovina in 1940.

This time around, the Romanians could use war circumstances to achieve nationalization on an unprecedented scale, implementing previously unthinkable policies. Taking advantage of Nazi Germany's patronage, they carried out the wholesale deportation of Bukovina's Jewish population. But as the tides of war changed again in the Soviets' favor in 1944, the Romanians lost northern Bukovina once again. The Red Army reincorporated it into Soviet Ukraine, where it remained until the Soviet Union's collapse in 1991. Since then, the province once known as Bukovina has been divided between independent Ukraine and Romania.

Although the specifics of Bukovina's story are unique, some readers may find striking similarities between its history and Galicia's.[43] Both provinces, though poor and marginal, gave birth to tremendous cultural riches. Devoid of material and political power, they were nonetheless symbolically significant, looming larger in the imagination than they ever did physically. They were both at the center of endless myths and legends through which different states and political actors told stories about themselves. There are perhaps as many stories about Bukovina as there ever were people living there. Nationalists—Ukrainian and Romanian above all—were prolific writers of legends and creators of "invented traditions" in Bukovina.[44] Dreaming of a pristine, ethnically authentic Bukovina buried beneath the surface of the present, they chased chimeras in hopes of recapturing what had allegedly been lost through denationalization.[45] With every political rupture and takeover, moreover, state administrations also took the opportunity to rewrite Bukovina's history. Such recasting of the province's past and future was indispensable to these regimes' efforts to reimagine it as an integral part of their own polities.

But in other respects Bukovina is quite different from Galicia. First, its ethnic landscape was considerably more variegated than Galicia's; for much of its history, many ethnic groups inhabited its relatively small space. Austrian statistics recognized six different ethnic groups (*Volksstämme*) living in Bukovina, classified by their languages of daily use (*Umgangssprachen*): Ruthenians, Romanians, Germans, Poles, Magyars, and "others."[46] Unlike in Galicia, whose population was pretty evenly split between Poles and Ruthenians, Bukovina's *Volksstämme* had "an uneasy balance of power with none able realistically to claim political or cultural dominance in the manner for example that Poles managed in Galicia."[47] Romanians and Ruthenians together constituted the bulk of Bukovina's rural population (74.41 percent). Romanians, unlike Ruthenians, were well represented among the landowning, educated elite.[48] Like Galicia's Poles, Bukovina's Romanians were recognized by the Habsburg administration as the more powerful group and were recruited into the imperial administration.

Although the ethnic composition of Bukovina's population changed over time, its chronic diversity remained a source of concern for all its subsequent administrations. The Austrians were the only ones to take pride in it, likening the province to a "microcosm of the Danube monarchy."[49] Austrian poet Ludwig Simiginowicz-Staufe (1832–1897), born in Bukovina to a German mother and Ukrainian father, believed that Bukovina's diversity was one of its main selling points.[50] Since "Romanians, Russians, Israelites, Germans, Magyars, Poles, Great Russians, Slovaks, Armenians, Gypsies are all represented here," he insisted, any resident of the Habsburg monarchy would feel at home in Bukovina.[51] The head of Bukovina's Austrian gendarmerie Eduard Fischer reflected that people who "develop on such soil will not easily be able to maintain their racial purity, and under these circumstances there arise mostly mixed types, often entire groups change their languages and customs, and through this living together and in each other's midst the unique characteristics of different races become diminished."[52] For the nationalists, as we will see, this was a serious problem. To their exasperation, the inhabitants of Bukovina proved all but impossible to categorize according to national-ethnic criteria.[53] The high degree of cultural intermixing that prevailed there defied nationalists' most basic assumptions about the world.

Like Galicia, Bukovina was home to a large Jewish population, but Bukovinan Jews were generally more urban and acculturated, and occupied more politically and economically prominent positions, than their Galician counterparts. Prior to World War I, Jews accounted for 33 percent of Czernowitz's population, making Bukovina's capital the empire's fourth largest Jewish city after Vienna, Lemberg (modern Lviv), and Kraków.[54] Jews played an especially important role in Czernowitz in the 1870s and 1880s, after Austria became a constitutional monarchy.[55] The city—a symbol of imperial modernity—grew alongside them, its history impossible to disentangle from theirs. Bukovinan

Jews owed their success in part to their fluency in German, the language of culture, administration, and socio-economic mobility.

Some Bukovinan Jews, like the poet Paul Celan's mother, for example, took pride in their impeccably pronounced *Hochdeutsch*.[56] But most spoke a dialect affectionately called "Bukowienerisch," a linguistic mélange that combined the Viennese lilt with Romanian, Ukrainian, and Yiddish inflections and alluded to their ambitions of turning Czernowitz into a miniature Vienna. Thanks to Bukovina's German-speaking Jews, the German language retained its prominent position in the province long after its use had dropped in Galicia and elsewhere in the empire. This was why the young Karl Emil Franzos, whose father had been a German patriot, left Galicia to pursue a German-language education at the *Gymnasium* in Czernowitz. For as long as he lived, he viewed Czernowitz as the "antechamber to the German paradise," a cultural island where "European *Bildung* [culture, education] and Asian barbarism, European love of progress and Asian indolence" came face to face.[57]

Even today, Bukovina is known mainly through the prose and poetry of its German-language writers, most of whom were Jewish. It remains anchored in German cultural space as the symbol of a lost Germanophone Atlantis. The German-Jewish poet Rose Ausländer, born in Czernowitz in 1901 (d. 1988), claimed she owed her writerly sensibility entirely to Czernowitz and "that special landscape. The special people. Fairy tales and myths were floating in the air, one breathed them in. The four-language Czernowitz was a musical city, which sheltered many artists, poets, lovers of art, literature, and philosophy."[58] In exile in Germany and living out of suitcases in a hotel, Ausländer remembered her native city as "both beautiful and ugly," as "architecturally in bad taste and uninteresting, but in its landscape lovely and with an idiosyncratic allure." Above all, she remembered Czernowitz as a cultural paradise where literature and philosophy were discussed "with ardor," a city filled with disciples of "philosophers, political thinkers, poets, artists, composers, or mystics," where people read "in the streets, in parks, in forests, and by the shores of the Prut."[59] The German writer Georg Heinzen echoes Ausländer, describing Czernowitz as a city steeped in intellectual discourse, where "a new aesthetic theory was invented every morning," where "dogs bore the names of Olympian gods and hens scratched verses by Hölderlin in the sand."[60]

## Borderlands and States

In the mid-eighteenth century, sovereignty became associated with territory and political control came to be seen as bounded. As a result, borders became markers of modern state sovereignty, helping to "determine the nature of the state"[61] and marking "the actual power of states over societies."[62] By contrast, early modern states were typically "non-territorial, not exclusive or fixed," with no "clearly designated geographic limits to authority."[63] Spaces of empire were traditionally demarcated by "irregular and porous borders" and contained "enclaves and irregular zones and areas of partial or shared sovereignty." Once sovereignty was defined along territorial lines, the "uneven, disaggregated, and oddly shaped" political geographies of early modern empires gave way to a new constellation of clearly bounded territorial modern states.[64] Sovereign border control became the marker of being "a civilized country."[65] With the emergence of nationalism, borders took on additional significance as markers of homeland territoriality, a new way of thinking about land that deepened its symbolic value by investing it with "both material and invented properties."[66]

Bukovina's existence as a frontier district of the Habsburg Empire began in the late eighteenth century, about the same time as the emergence of the concept and practice of modern state sovereignty. Throughout its history, it remained a border province, located on the edge of territorially bounded states. After World War I, Bukovina became Greater Romania's northernmost district, bordering Poland and the Soviet Union. During World War II, a new frontier between two empires, Nazi and Soviet, ran straight down the middle of Bukovina, turning the province into the site of a colossal ideological battle and separating the newly expanded Communist world from the capitalist one. That border still splits the territory once known as Bukovina, separating the European Union from non-EU Eastern Europe, a border some have described as Europe's last Iron Curtain.

For each state that ruled Bukovina, the frontier province played a special role, both for security reasons and because it was a site of mutual observations and encounters, where states showcased their policies and ways of life. To rule Bukovina, each polity adopted a version of "frontier governmentality," a set of governmental norms, administrative practices, and legal regimes peculiar to frontier areas across the world.[67] Even the Soviets, whose revolutionary, internationalist ideology aspired to make borders redundant, were preoccupied with their westernmost frontier. Like their tsarist predecessors, they wanted to delimit and defend state frontiers, which now had new ideological meaning.[68]

Given the significance of borders to modern states, it is unsurprising that borderlands have generated a wealth of historiography. Although this literature is vast and varied, it revolves around a few general tropes and themes.[69] Most historians seem drawn to borderlands histories because they allow them to overturn narratives that may otherwise seem self-evident or set in stone.[70] In other words, borderlands histories are alluring because they show what might have emerged had history taken a different turn. Histories of borderlands often highlight failure, especially that of modern states to carry out their projects and impose their visions of "territorial and social control."[71] Books in this genre often highlight the way in which modern states, initially confident in their ability to exercise complete sovereignty and render political space uniform, discover that they lack the muscle and resources needed to establish hegemony over territories far distant from the metropole.[72] Or, as anthropologist James Scott put it, modern states fail because "the state simplifications" they require to operate fail to represent "the actual activity of the society they depicted."[73] Borderlands histories highlight the complexity of the societies modern states attempted to rule. They emphasize intermingling and hybridity, presenting borderlands as zones of "contact and transition"[74] that give rise to "malleable identities" and "syncretic cultures"[75]—and inhabited by people highly skilled in disputing state control.[76]

At first sight, this narrative of state powerlessness in the face of social complexity appears to describe Bukovina's experience well. In some respects, the province always remained outside the polities that governed it, challenging their claims to legitimacy and repeatedly failing to conform to their expectations. Upon closer examination, however, this interpretation barely scratches the surface. First, it fails to account for important differences between modern states.[77] By emphasizing their uniform failure, these narratives reduce modern states to monolithic, static entities whose actions have a predetermined outcome. But states were seldom homogeneous entities; they were diverse, and they evolved over time. There could be no coherent, unitary Habsburg imperial or national Romanian project in Bukovina, for instance, as these polities themselves kept changing, not least in response to encounters with the province's diverse population.

Moreover, although failure was indeed common, it is important to note that not all failures were equal. Not all states failed in the same ways, and even when they did, they often left behind far from negligible legacies. These legacies are especially striking in Bukovina, where regimes that followed each other in quick succession left their marks on the province's landscape long after their political demise. Beyond the appearance of constancy and circularity suggested by the "failed modernization" trope lay a reality defined by constant change.

Therefore, this book views Bukovina (and by extension the East European borderlands) as an ideal site to study the evolution of modern states' ambitions and instruments of governance comparatively. The chapters that follow highlight the great extent to which modern states were shaped by their entanglements with each other and with the populations of the border regions those states took turns at ruling. These entanglements, which could take the form of competition, emulation, or conflict, were, as historian Michael David-Fox writes, important regardless of whether they were positive or negative.[78] Borderlands like Bukovina functioned as vehicles by which different states and political regimes shaped each other directly or indirectly, through physical encounters or the legacies they left, including assumptions about what governance ought to look like, what constituted legitimate authority, and so forth.[79]

The encounters that took place in Bukovina against the backdrop of interstate competition help explain why modernizing states occupying ideologically opposite ends of the spectrum often converged in their aspirations and practices. One might attribute this convergence to the shared modernizing impulse of states that originated in the Enlightenment. Yet Bukovina lets us see another, equally important reason: different modern states took turns ruling the same border regions. Entanglements at the border thus helped to create "a world of semblances and likenesses, recognitions and misrecognitions at the very same time."[80] In Bukovina, Austrian governance practices and ideologies of rule were shaped by the Russian Empire's proximity—and vice versa. When the Russian troops occupied Czernowitz in World War I, they immediately began cleaning the city's streets to demonstrate that Russia was cultured—and to imitate what they thought the Austrians had been doing. Similarly, the Romanian nation-state that ruled Bukovina after 1918 ended up incorporating administrative bodies and cultural practices it inherited from Austria, even as it tried to differentiate itself from its imperial predecessor. Later the Soviets, though ostensibly dismissing nationalism as backwardness, found themselves paying homage to national self-determination, accomplishing in Bukovina what some nationalists had dreamed of but had never had the resources for.[81]

The interplay between states in Bukovina also shaped local nationalisms and the ways national differences were articulated. During World War I, previously weak nationalists gained a new lease on life from the great powers' efforts to channel nationalist energies toward their projects in the region. Ukrainian nationalists, for instance, benefited from Habsburg and German patronage. Romanian nationalists in Bukovina found favor with the Russian occupation authorities. The inter-imperial conflict thus reinforced the conflict between opposing national groups and injected it with new vitality and meaning.[82]

The perspective presented here highlights the importance to modern statebuilding of local cooperation, and challenges the view that modernizing states and borderland populations were inevitably locked in conflict. Even when they declared a total break with the past, states needing local participation and knowledge ended up incorporating preexisting local elites into their structures.[83] This dynamic was not exclusive to Bukovina; it was an indispensable feature of the modern state, where populations became "members of the state, not just objects of state policies."[84] The "strength and inescapability" of the modern state, as Yanni Kotsonis writes, lay in the fact that "the population comprised it."[85]

In turn, Bukovinans had ambitions and visions of their own that they pursued through and alongside states.[86] Locals pressed state officials to implement the policies they desired and thought would advance local interests. They sometimes championed state initiatives when state officials had lost interest in them, often appealing to states as an antidote to marginalization or to claim a space for themselves within domestic and international politics. The loudest advocates of modernizing reforms were often people on the periphery. Likewise, radicalizing impulses and a willingness to use violence to achieve the aims they implied did not always come from the center, but could originate in marginal places like Bukovina, where locals' dreams of becoming modern were repeatedly frustrated. Locals had limited choices, but choices, nonetheless. They were not simply swept up by impersonal forces, but tried to meld their own goals and ambitions, rooted in local circumstances, with the goals and ambitions of states that competed for influence over the region.

## Modernity and Culture

Modernization was perhaps the most important point of convergence and mutual influence among the different states that ruled Bukovina. All of them, from the Habsburg Empire to the Soviet Union, wanted to modernize the region and had in common assumptions about what modernity was: economic prosperity, literacy, the absence of ethnic and national strife, civilized government. They all viewed Bukovina as a testing ground to showcase the superiority of their respective paths to modernity. Even nostalgic regimes that harked back to an idyllic, premodern past aspired to modernity.[87] Romanian nationalists in Bukovina, for instance, hailed the countryside as the source of pristine national identity but ultimately focused their energies on the city of Czernowitz, aspiring to nationalize it and wrest it from the hands of people they denounced as "foreign" to the province. The Soviets, whom many locals dismissed as uncivilized and backward, also engaged in this "quest for modernity," asserting the need for a different way of achieving it: an anti-capitalist path.[88]

The modernizing states that tried their hand at governing Bukovina thus competed to demonstrate their civilizational superiority. One by-product of this competition was the assumption—which all regimes, whether liberal or illiberal, imperial or national, came to share—that civilized states could transform society and exercise authority by cultural means rather than through exploitation and force. Modernity was very much a "cultural program."[89] States legitimized themselves in the eyes of locals and to each other through their promise to deliver Bukovina from poverty, backwardness, and underdevelopment via reform schemes centered on education, urbanization, and hygiene.[90] One regime after another touted its efforts to build schools and hospitals and clean up and expand Bukovina's cities. As an antidote to the province's alleged backwardness, they invoked a "normative concept of culture."[91] They all paid lip service, at least, to the idea that government should seek to improve society and that the contest over territories and populations could not be justified unless it brought a civilized, just system of governance to places lacking it.[92] Local non-state actors also bandied about the idea of civilization, sometimes using it interchangeably with notions of modernity and progress.

Governance through culture was a key aspect of enlightened Habsburg rule. The concept of *Kultur*, frequently invoked under Austrian rule, had its origins in the German Enlightenment, which rejected revolutionary change in favor of "fus[ing] continuity and change."[93] Unlike their French counterparts, adepts of the German Enlightenment hoped to enact transformations through and with the state. The focus on *Kultur* thus signaled a preference for reform from within and above, as well as a reliance on the state.[94] The appeal made by all of Bukovina's rulers to "culture" to justify their rule derived to an extent from the pattern initiated by the Habsburgs that continued to set the terms for what successor regimes imagined and deemed possible. At the same time, the general preference for cultural reform shared by all polities in Bukovina was also the product of scarcity: repeatedly, states with inflated ambitions found themselves overstretched and without the necessary resources to transform the periphery economically.

Although "culture" was frequently invoked to justify rule and offer a vision of how Bukovina could achieve modernity, it meant different things to different political actors. Vejas Liulevicius has shown how Eastern Europe became an "experimental domain" for *Kultur* and was thus also key to the emergence of a German national identity defined by *Kultur*, in contradistinction to Eastern Europe's alleged poverty, misery, and dirt.[95] After a separate German nation-state emerged in 1871, the Eastern European borderlands further facilitated Austria's efforts to differentiate itself from Germany and justify its own continued existence. Increasingly, Austrian Germans conceived of Austria as a *Kulturstaat* whose mission was to bring enlightenment and civilization to the diverse peoples inhabiting its empire. Austrophiles such as the Bukovinan historian Raimund Friedrich Kaindl argued that Austria accommodated a more expansive form of German identity, one defined primarily along cultural lines and thus uncontainable within state borders.[96] German-speaking elites in the province avidly supported Austria's so-called cultural mission in the East, hoping to channel more of the state's resources and attention to the province.

The liberal bourgeois model of culture upheld by Austrian liberals in Bukovina gave rise to what locals called *Bildungsdrang*: a thirst for *Bildung*, or self-cultivation.[97] The *Gymnasia* and university of Czernowitz produced a generation of local elites fluent in the language of Goethe and Schiller and raised to believe that "the task of humanity is culture."[98] Bukovina's nationalists emerged from this "culture of culture,"[99] inheriting the Habsburg-German ideal of *Kultur*, even as they reinterpreted it as pluralistic and unique to each people rather than universalist.[100] Rather than rejecting culture altogether, they fought to ensure that their respective national groups were not left without it.[101] The cultural institutions that had prestige under imperial rule—the *Gymnasia* and the university, for example—were the most contested among nationalists. In this sense, nationalists were as much products of the liberal imperial state as they were its adversaries.

Nationalists' infatuation with culture persisted into the interwar period. Romanian nationalists in Bukovina appealed to culture to differentiate themselves from their co-nationals in the Old Kingdom and criticize the Old Kingdom's "politicianism": a synonym for corruption and superficiality.[102] In its most extreme form, this distaste for Bucharest's politics and preference for culture eventually found fulfillment in the Romanian Legionary Movement, and the other right-wing movements that were popular among Bukovina's Germans and Ukrainians. These all drew a good deal of inspiration and energy from borderlands like Bukovina, feeding on the frustrations of provincials and their antagonism toward the central government.

During World War II, Bukovina found itself in the middle of a confrontation between two rival conceptions of culture: Soviet *kul'turnost'* and Nazi *Kultur* and its Romanian version, embodied in and upheld by Ion Antonescu's racial state. The Soviet concept of *kul'turnost'* had roots in the Russian intelligentsia tradition, whose "missionary idea of transmission of education and culture to the backward masses" was in turn inspired largely by German Romanticism and Idealism. Translated into campaigns to disseminate culture to the masses, it shared with the German humanist tradition of *Kultur* and *Bildung* the impulse for "enlightened self-transformation" and the assumption that self and society could be completely remolded.[103] In a sense, *kul'tnurost'*, which put the human being and society at the center of history, resembled the classical humanist concept of *Kultur* more than Nazi Germany's racially defined *Kultur* did. In practice, it meant the Soviets founded libraries and reading rooms in remote villages and obsessively measured Bukovinian literacy levels. At the same time, they deported entire pockets of populations that supposedly stood in the way of revolution, to Siberia and Kazakhstan. This too was part of the Soviet repertoire of power.

## Time and Revolution

The onset of modernity was marked by changes in everything "from morals to law, religion, economy, states."[104] During the *Sattelzeit* (saddle period), as Reinhard Koselleck described the period between the late eighteenth and early nineteenth centuries, people's conceptions and experiences of time radically shifted. Once predetermined, the future was now changeable. Hand in hand with this new historically immanent definition of time came an inclination toward "historicity" or "historicism,"[105] and the idea that radical change was both possible and desirable.[106] This newborn revolutionary impulse could take different forms. It could be expressed as the desire to free oneself from the past or from the chains that kept one mired in a state of economic or political backwardness.[107] It could also take the form of restorative ambitions powered by the idea that a historical trajectory could be reversed.[108]

The need to distance oneself from the past and the feeling of loss that came with progress were deeply intertwined and integral to the modern experience. Walter Benjamin captured the tension between the two through the memorable image of the Angelus Novus, pushed into the future by a storm "blowing from Paradise" that "has caught his wings" so that "he can no longer claim them." Even as he moves into the future, the angel's face is "turned towards the past." This storm is "what we call progress."[109] In the modern conception of time, the present's rush toward the future was inevitable and unstoppable, but its seemingly unquenchable drive brought with it a deep nostalgia for the pile of debris left behind.

The dynamic so beautifully described by Benjamin in his *Theses on the Philosophy of History* perfectly encapsulates Bukovinans' experiences as they got caught in a maelstrom of successive modernizing projects. The appetite for change gave rise to deep and conflicting anxieties: about remaining mired in the past, and simultaneously about losing one's bearings. As Arno Mayer defined it, revolution is a moment when "a nation's or a society's traditional ground rules crumble, and willy-nilly man has to reconstruct human relations himself."[110] It is an epoch of its own.

Yet in Bukovina and much of Eastern Europe the crumbling of ground rules and reconstruction of human relations occurred repeatedly, even continually, especially during the first half of the twentieth century. Revolution was not neatly bookended, since locals experienced border shifts, regime changes, and rapid population fluctuations over and over again. Bukovinans lived always on the cusp of transformation. With every new collapse in state authority, a new regime and local actors took it upon themselves to remake Bukovina and the world. As a result, nothing ever felt stable. Reform projects were often left unfinished, and new borders were contested before the ink had even dried on new maps.

Though revolution was a more or less permanent reality in Bukovina, change did not always take the same forms. It followed a variety of cadences and rhythms, seldom uniform, simultaneous, or even complete. Nonetheless, the pendulum swing of Bukovina's history could make it seem as if the province was going through a set of revolving doors, moving through an endlessly repeating cycle of invasions and occupations followed by liberations, with the old forces coming from the east and west under different guises, but always essentially the same. Yet the illusion that nothing ever changed was just that: an illusion. It was exacerbated by the fact that so many elements of the past inscribed into the province's landscape endured almost untouched. "For the historically conscious observer," one memoirist from Bukovina wrote, "it is ghostly to pass through the center of Czernowitz today [in the 1990s]: here the past has been preserved in the facades—an Austrian past, to which the current population seems to have little connection."[111] Elements of Czernowitz's palimpsest are not simply allowed, but sometimes invited, to resurface and be re-inscribed into the urban landscape. Consider a house from Czernowitz's former Jewish quarter, once the workshop of Isak Eisikowicz, a sign painter. According to the sign running below the eaves, the workshop was founded in 1910, under Austrian rule. Yet the signage is in Romanian, not German, and dates back to the interwar period when Czernowitz became Cernăuţi, under Romanian rule. The building's current owners, residents of Ukrainian Chernivtsi, painted the building's walls in a garish turquoise that is now peeling off and revealing the original dark yellow. At the top, however, the original Romanian-language sign, formerly turquoise, has a new coat of yellow and dark green. Such gestures have become increasingly common as Ukrainians in Chernivtsi seek to distance themselves from their Soviet heritage and envision a new European future for the city.

The changes that left the deepest imprint on Bukovinans were often drawn out, incomplete, almost invisible. Slow changes could have more staying power than abrupt breaks with the past, which could just as easily and quickly be undone. Under Habsburg rule, for instance, changes happened at a demoralizingly slow pace and were often underwhelming. Locals impatient with the province's lack of progress anxiously tried to discern whether Czernowitz had become a modern *Grossstadt* yet.[112] But a hundred and fifty years after the province's incorporation into the Habsburg Empire, when that empire was no longer to be found on any map, the changes it had set into motion no longer seemed slight. Makeshift, incomplete changes had a cumulative effect, quietly producing a legacy of insurmountable mass that all future regimes had to contend with. Not only did the successor regimes have to grapple with Bukovina's persisting Habsburg legacies, but they also found themselves unwittingly borrowing, absorbing, or replicating bits and pieces of its imperial heritage.[113] They continued practices that empires had put in place: for example, promoting culture and enlightenment to integrate the periphery into the state and keep social and political unrest at bay.[114]

Empire provided an important continuity across repeated political ruptures. It was a constant presence in Bukovina, but not only, as it may seem at

FIGURE 0.3. Writing in Romanian resurfacing from underneath the peeling paint on a house in Chernivtsi, former Jewish quarter. Photo by author, 2013.

first, because the region was trapped in an endless cycle of imperial conquests. Empires endured, as legacies, cultural norms and values, and institutions, because of their enormous capacity to absorb both revolution and reform, to be "revitalized by finding a new balance between their different components."[115] Thanks to recent literature on European empires, we now know that the Ottomans, Habsburgs, and Russians—once dismissed as decrepit—were rarely as hopeless as they were made out to be. They tended to navigate repeated challenges to their authority successfully and to weather most crises intact. When collapse came, it was due not to their long-standing, irreconcilable antagonism with nationalists, but to the qualitative transformation in their relationship with nationalism brought about by total war.[116]

Bukovina's story thus calls into question chronologies that assume empires are out of the picture as soon as they collapse. As more and more historians are now showing, empires persisted in various forms well after their demise. Interwar Romania, which governed Bukovina from 1918, itself became a mini-empire by incorporating territories with highly variegated populations. It also inherited a key dilemma of imperial rule: how to manage multiethnicity, especially across large distances. Interwar nation-states such as Romania and neighboring Poland were like empires in another way, too: they pursued "colonization and civilizing missions," invoking the notions of superiority that empires before them had long used to justify their territorial claims.[117] As Jane Burbank and Frederick Cooper have argued, imperial repertoires of rule delimited what "leaders could imagine and could carry off" long after empires were extinct.[118] For all their struggles to dismantle imperial legacies, post-imperial states often ended up perpetuating them. The Soviet Union, for instance, an entity whose very existence was predicated upon anti-imperialism and anti-colonialism, ended up reconstituting empire by other means, maintaining a "sophisticated imperial policy when empire was becoming redundant."[119]

Such continuities across period ruptures gave rise in Bukovina to a profoundly variegated temporal landscape. Unlike many cities in East Central Europe that were repeatedly razed to the ground, Bukovina's capital Czernowitz was reinvented through addition, with new elements piled on top of preexisting structures. Chronically short of resources and time, political regimes tended to recycle elements of the province's heritage to build new systems of rule and ideologies, creating new universes out of scraps of old ones. To describe this multilayered landscape, one might adopt Alfred Rieber's metaphor of the "sedimentary society," which he deemed typical of the Eurasian borderlands.[120] In such places, Rieber argued, "a successive series of social forms accumulated, each constituting a layer that covered all or most of society without altering the older forms lying underneath the surface."[121]

But even this description fails to convey the complexity of temporalities that characterized life in Bukovina. Legacies did not simply lie on top of each other like so many layers of cake, but interacted and recombined periodically, giving rise to a "multiplicity and conflict of temporal regimes."[122] The concept is more aptly described as "chronocenosis," highlighting the "complex and volatile interaction of competing temporal regimes" in which "power and time interface amid intensely competitive temporal formations, not simply parallel or layered ones."[123] Bits and pieces of Bukovina's past were constantly being reincorporated into the present and taking on new meanings. This process was part and parcel of state-building and regime change in the province. To describe this experience, the Bukovinan writer Gregor von Rezzori coined a new term: *Epochenverschleppung*, meaning "epoch delay," or protraction, or the "anachronistic overlap of elements of reality that belong to a past epoch with a following one."[124]

The people who inhabited this temporal landscape developed profoundly modern sensibilities. Their cultural affinities and worldviews were permeated by a feeling of displacement in terms of both location and time. If modernity was characterized, as Marshall Berman wrote, by "the struggle to make ourselves at home in a constantly changing world," then Bukovinans were moderns *par excellence*. Their lives were defined by a "will to change—to transform both themselves and the world—and by a terror of disorientation and disintegration, of life falling apart," as well as by the "thrill and the dread of a world in which all that is solid melts into air."[125]

Von Rezzori captured these feelings best when he described himself as a living anachronism, a person fallen out of time and forced to dwell in an epoch in which he did not belong.[126] Like him, many Bukovinans in the twentieth century experienced time as lumpy, fragmented, or broken. Their lives seemed to consist of puzzle pieces that could not be made to fit together without doing violence to the individual parts. Take the family of Dmytro Yakoviichul, from the Bukovinan mountain village of Putyla: "the older children had Romanian education, the younger ones—Soviet, and our parents—Austrian [. . .]; each one of us had his own, very different views of life under the influence of different educational systems."[127] The history of one Bukovinan family was the history of three different regimes.

## Chapter Outline

The beginnings and endings of the chapters that follow are marked by wars, revolutions, and regime changes. I have adopted this structure both for clarity's sake and because so much of the book is about the importance of legacies of multiple state-building projects to the experience of living in Bukovina and Eastern Europe. A traditional chronological narrative allows us to grasp both what changed radically in the process and what stayed the same. It reveals that different regimes often set out to build new worlds out of the same material—materials they inherited from each other. Characters who appear under one guise under one administration in one chapter may reappear in a completely different guise in another. The order in which regimes occurred matters, as they often shaped their policies in response to what had come before. Proceeding chronologically allows me to highlight the accumulated effect of repeated regime changes and revolutions that, piled on top of each other, created new combinations.

The book begins by showing how Habsburg officials in late eighteenth-century Bukovina sought to transform the local population's relationship with the state as well as the nature of state authority and sovereignty in the province. Chapter 1 argues that the changes they brought about proceeded slowly and with difficulty, and shows the Habsburgs incorporating Ottoman and Moldavian legacies into their structures and then repurposing them. Though changes were slow and makeshift, by the 1870s, a hundred years after Bukovina's incorporation into the Habsburg Empire, the territory and its population had been deeply transformed.

After 1867, when the Austrian Empire split into Austrian and Hungarian halves, Bukovina was an autonomous crown land of the empire's Austrian half, called Cisleithania. Chapter 2 traces the empire's projects in Bukovina in this period, the heyday of Austro-Hungarian liberalism. I show how the Austrian liberal state sought to civilize Bukovina's countryside through an infusion of culture and literacy. Once again, their project was largely a failure, and peasants, seeing few benefits in cultural policies that presented no immediate economic advantages, emigrated overseas *en masse*. At the same time, an urban, middle-class society, highly educated and espousing liberal ideas, emerged in Czernowitz, where modernization meant paved roads, new buildings, public parks, monuments, *Gymnasia*, and the German-language university founded in 1875.

By guaranteeing equality for all ethnic groups in public institutions, the state both facilitated the rise of national intelligentsias and laid the foundations for national conflict by altering the balance of power in the province. Chapter 3 argues that Bukovina's imperial government unwittingly invested nationalism with a meaning and strength it would never have developed on its own. In turn, nationalists—though always grumbling about Austria's policies toward their respective national groups—depended on imperial institutions and structures to survive and succeed. Nationalist disputes took on new dimensions in Bukovina between 1914 and 1918, when the province came under repeated occupation by Russian, Austro-Hungarian, and German troops. Chapter 4 traces how the belligerent powers aligned their goals with those of different groups in Bukovina, promoting some and persecuting others. As a result, Bukovinan society emerged from the war torn and fractured along new lines, with those who had been on opposite sides of the barricades eager to settle scores with each other.

When Austria-Hungary collapsed in 1918, Bukovina was disputed territory, with both Ukrainian and Romanian nationalists convinced they were entitled to the province. Chapter 5 tells the story of Bukovina's uneasy incorporation into the Romanian nation-state in the 1920s, when the national administration discovered that the province's imperial make-up made it nearly impossible to renationalize. Hard as they tried to set themselves apart from their imperial predecessors, the Romanian administration in Bukovina inherited a landscape profoundly shaped by Austrian rule.

By the 1930s it was increasingly evident that the Romanian administration's efforts to integrate Bukovina into the nation-state had failed. Chapter 6 shows how, largely because of this failure, the region became a weapon in the arsenal of democracy's critics in Romania. By the end of the 1930s, all ethnic groups in the province had come to embrace integral forms of nationalism, largely as a result of mutual imitation. The chapter traces the emergence and interplay of four nationalist movements in Bukovina: the Romanian LANC and Legion of Archangel Michael, the Ukrainian moderate nationalists and the OUN, the Zionists, and the National Socialist Germans.

Chapter 7 shows how the Soviets set out to transform northern Bukovina into an outpost of Soviet civilization after incorporating it in the spring of 1940, allegedly to liberate ethnic Ukrainians from Romanian oppression. Although Bukovina had no sizable working class, the Soviets found a so-called "surrogate proletariat" in its Ukrainians, mapping the revolutionary Soviet project onto preexisting ethnic tensions.[128] The chapter argues that the Soviets were uniquely able to enact revolutionary changes in occupied Bukovina because they used extraordinary wartime measures.

Chapter 8 takes the story to 1941, when the Romanians returned to northern Bukovina to find it completely altered. Their goal was to remove all traces of Soviet rule and finalize the national unification process begun in 1918. The chapter examines how Romanian officials under General Ion Antonescu's military administration Romanianized Bukovina and purged it of its Soviet legacies. It argues that the war years permanently changed not only Bukovina's demographics, but also the way different elements of society interacted—with fatal consequences for the Jewish community, which never recovered from the devastation it suffered during these years.

Finally, the Epilogue explains what became of the land known as Bukovina once it vanished from the map in 1944, when the Soviets reclaimed the province's northern half and incorporated it into Soviet Ukraine while southern Bukovina remained under Romanian rule. It charts Bukovina's shift from the real world into nostalgia and its transformation into a borderland between the EU and Russia's so-called European backyard.

As one legend has it, inside Mount Cecina outside Czernowitz lived an old man who sat and wrote all day, surrounded by buckets of gold and coins, each guarded by a hen. Every time a hen clucked, the old man got up and tore everything he had written to pieces, then started anew. Writing the history of a place such as Bukovina often felt like that. Like the residents of this wondrous place, I found myself starting anew, over and over, searching for a way to tell Bukovina's story logically and coherently, without robbing it of its mystery or complexity. What follows is the imperfect outcome of those efforts.

# 1

# The Enlightened State

IN 1823 a Londoner made a bet that he could sleep in three different states in one night without leaving his bed. He won the bet by going to Czernowitz, a little town on the Habsburg Empire's easternmost frontier, twelve kilometers from the Turkish border and eighteen from the Russian border. The Englishman loaded his bed onto a carriage and drove to the Austro–Ottoman frontier. His servants unloaded the bed, with their master lying in it, and crossed the border into Turkish Moldavia, where the Englishman rested for an hour before packing everything up again and driving to the Turkish–Russian frontier half an hour away. After adding a Russian stamp to his travel papers, the Englishman slept on Russian soil for an hour. In the middle of the night, he and his servants crossed the border back to Austria. In Czernowitz, they unpacked and checked in to the Zum Goldenen Löwen inn.[1]

At that time, Bukovina was a relatively new Habsburg possession, annexed in 1775 barely two years after the first Polish partition whereby Austria, Prussia, and Russia had divided up the Polish-Lithuanian Commonwealth.[2] Maria Theresa, who had succeeded her father to the Habsburg throne in 1743, claimed to find the whole business despicable but, as her Prussian counterpart Frederick the Great put it, "the more she cried, the more she took."[3] Having already lost Silesia to Frederick, Maria Theresa understood that if Austria did not participate in this "act of international piracy" it could lose its status as a great power, displaced on the international stage by Prussia and Russia.[4] When Austria next proceeded to annex the northwestern corner of the principality of Moldavia, soon to be called Bukovina, the empress was again displeased and again acquiesced, deeming the annexation necessary for her empire's security on its vulnerable eastern border with Russia, a power on the rise.

Bukovina became indispensable to the Habsburgs precisely because it was located on the hinge of a changing international system, or, as a Viennese map from 1789 put it, on the "stage of the five parts of the world." Incorporating Bukovina, a fairly small and seemingly insignificant territory, meant gaining a foothold in the region where the new balance of power on the continent was

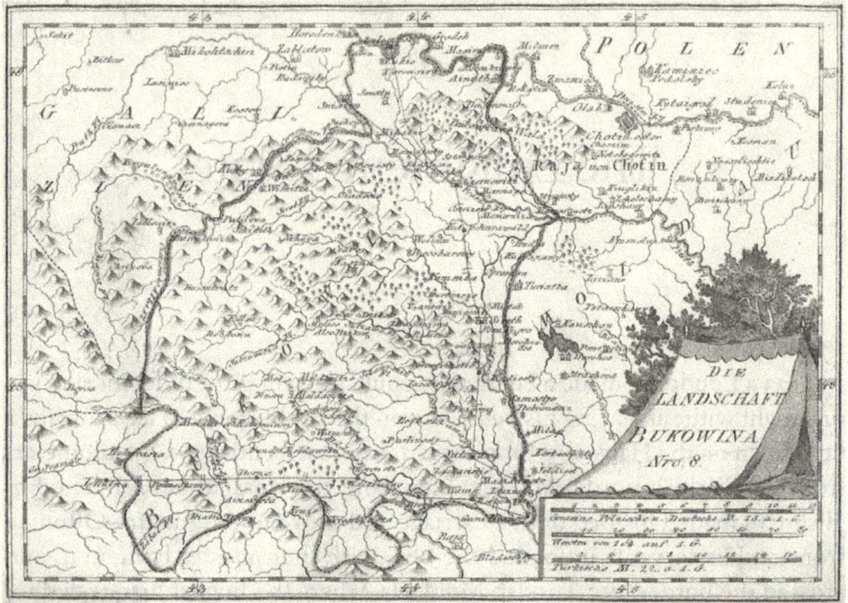


FIGURE 1.1. Pictorial map of Bukovina, from Franz Johann Joseph von Reilly, *Schauplatz der fünf Theile der Welt [. . .]; Erster Theil* (Vienna, 1789). Such early maps were indispensable to the cameralist state's efforts to put their new territorial acquisitions to good use through rational administration.

being decided. It told the great European powers competing for influence over this region that the Habsburgs, though no longer at the peak of imperial expansion, were nothing to sneer at. At the same time, Bukovina's incorporation marked the beginning of a process of internal redefinition and reform aimed at transforming the old empire into a modern territorial state. The Habsburgs saw Bukovina as a place where they could experiment with a new vision of enlightened governance that would eventually emanate to the rest of the empire.

The Habsburgs believed Bukovina, after centuries of mismanagement by the Ottomans, was essentially a blank slate. They started drawing borders around the newly annexed territory and consolidating them, since in this new age of territoriality, loose, porous borders were signs of weakness. They set up their administration as the beginning of a new era of enlightened governance, the opposite of what the Ottomans had allegedly stood for. At the same time, they found themselves absorbing Bukovina's Ottoman-era elites, resources, and institutions into their structures and repurposing them. Despite what many enlightened reformers thought, change did not proceed linearly: reforms had at times to be rolled back and reversed. Changes were far from perfect or complete. Even so, the new administration managed to set the newly acquired province on a completely new path of development. By the mid-nineteenth century, it no longer resembled a piece of the Moldavian principality under Ottoman suzerainty. It was a Habsburg creation.

## Bukovina's Annexation

Though formally allied with Russia in its fifth war with the Ottomans (1768–74), Austria had concluded a secret agreement with the Ottoman Porte in 1771, vowing to help stave off Russia by intervening in the Porte's favor during the peace negotiations. In return, the Porte promised Austria concessions, including the small territory of Little Wallachia. Meanwhile, Austria promised its official ally Russia that it would keep up a "threatening attitude" toward the Porte.[5] At Küçük Kainarca in 1774, the Ottomans signed an extremely unfavorable peace with Russia.[6] The treaty opened up avenues for further Russian involvement in the Balkans and Black Sea region, giving Russian ambassadors in Istanbul the right to make representations on the Danubian principalities' behalf,[7] confirming that, as Catherine the Great put it, "Orthodoxy is henceforth under Our imperial guardianship in places of its upspringing, protected from all oppression and violence."[8] The Russians also demanded the fortress of Azov, freedom of navigation in the Black Sea, and an independent Crimea, in exchange for which they would withdraw their troops from Moldavia and Wallachia and reaffirm the principalities' tributary relationship with the Porte.

Though its contribution to the peace negotiations was dubious, Austria demanded that the Porte deliver the promised territorial concessions—with one change: instead of Little Wallachia, Austria demanded "that corner that bumps up against Transylvania, Marmarosch, and Pocutia," a territory whose strategic importance Maria Theresa's co-ruling son Joseph II had noted on his 1773 tour of the region.[9] Like his mother, Joseph came to the conclusion that Wallachia and Moldavia were undesirable: "unhealthy and bankrupt" and "not to our advantage."[10] Little Wallachia, in particular, was impoverished and likely to present more liabilities than advantages.[11] The territory Joseph favored belonged to the principality of Moldavia, then under Ottoman suzerainty. A fifteenth-century treaty between Sigismund of Hungary and the Polish king Władysław Jagiełło had referred to this territory as "Bukovina,"[12] a name present on several early maps of the region, though without clear borders. Dimitrie Cantemir, the last native prince to rule Moldavia, mentioned Bukovina in his *Descriptio Moldaviae* (1716) as an extremely rich place where in the mountains "the most beautiful butter" collected on leaves and flowers, such that "if sheep were driven into pastures at the time this buttery dew was there, they would in a few days become so fat they would die of suffocation."[13]

What interested the Habsburgs was that Bukovina formed a natural bridge between two of their existing possessions: Galicia-Lodomeria, recently annexed from Poland, and Transylvania, which Austria had seized from the Ottomans in 1699.[14] The small protrusion of territory could save the state from having to build an expensive road through mountain passes to connect the two provinces. Emperor Joseph II concluded during his visit that Bukovina was best suited for military administration, "for it connects Transylvania with Galicia and fills the corner which Moldavia used to protrude into, and moreover it covers completely the Marmaros and shares a border with a Turkish province."[15]

Chancellor Anton Wenzel von Kaunitz agreed with Joseph about the territory's strategic importance, and pushed for direct annexation, even though many at court doubted the wisdom of this move. The Austrian ambassador to the Porte, Johann Amadeus von Thugut, warned that annexing Bukovina would "renew ancient reproaches regarding our failure to observe our conventions," amounting to a "stain on Habsburg honor."[16] Describing the peace of Küçük Kainarca as "proof of Russian skill and Turkish imbecility," Thugut believed Russia posed a much greater threat to Austria than the Ottomans did, and was wary of alienating the Porte.[17] He also feared that annexing Bukovina would invite more territorial demands from Russia and Prussia and further destabilize an already fragile international system. Nonetheless, Austria went ahead with the annexation, sending troops into the territory soon to be known as Bukovina in August 1774.

The Austrian military expedition was headed by Lieutenant Colonel (*Oberstleutnant*) Friedrich von Mieg, who was charged with mapping the territory and penning its first topographical description.[18] Bukovina was initially placed under military administration headed by General Gabriel Anton Freiherr Splény von Mihâldy, a German Protestant from Upper Hungary who reported directly to the Hofkriegsrat (Court War Council) in Vienna.[19] Splény and his successor Karl Freiherr von Enzenberg continued mapping the territory, taking stock of its population and resources to figure out how Bukovina might contribute to the state's prosperity and what kind of governance was suited for it. Sent to Bukovina for reconnaissance, von Enzenberg, head of the Austrian Second Infantry Regiment in Wallachia, spent six weeks studying the territory. The detailed report he produced concluded that the province would "facilitate our communications and commerce as well as win for us a passageway for our troops, which would otherwise have to make a vast detour to link up from one of our provinces to the other in case of war."[20]

What Austrian officers found in Bukovina provided them with the perfect justification for annexation. They saw the territory as half wild, devoid of civilization and history, a place of "cultural otherness" in need of the reform the Austrians justified as "acts of civilization against barbarism."[21] Bukovina, like

Galicia, was seen as "an ideal place to implement the vision of enlightened statecraft,"[22] ripe for transformation through enlightened reforms.[23] However, again like Galicia, Bukovina's past could not be completely abolished. Radically transforming this territory would come at a price that Habsburg officials could not always afford. At any rate, their reform program was seldom as coherent as it sounded on paper.[24] Some imperial officials charged with reforming Bukovina resisted transformations. General Splény, for one, believed that sudden changes would alienate the local population, many of whom had already left for Moldavia. Unsure of how to best integrate Bukovina into the empire's structures, imperial officials left the territory in a limbo that ended up lasting over a decade.

## The Cameralist Enlightened State

Bukovina's annexation was among a series of foreign and domestic policy changes that the Habsburg Empire underwent between the 1740s and 1780s in an effort reclaim great power status on an increasingly unstable international stage. Having suffered repeated defeats in wars that "accentuated the inadequacy of the monarchy's military establishment and its fiscal weakness," Austria experienced the ensuing shifts in the balance of power on the continent as involving a direct threat to its existence.[25] With the Ottoman Empire in retreat and Prussia and Russia on the rise, the Habsburg monarchy seemed to be at the end of its continuous expansion to the south and west.[26] These new circumstances, Chancellor von Kaunitz understood, required a reorientation in foreign policy. The ensuing changes, later known as "the diplomatic revolution," included a new French–Habsburg alliance against Prussia and the replacement of the Ottomans by Russia as Austria's main adversary in the east.[27] This new foreign policy paved the way for the Seven Years' War, which brought Austria into conflict with Prussia and left the Habsburgs defeated and depleted.

Military defeat drove home the notion that Austria was falling behind and needed urgent reforms.[28] Unlike Prussia, a modern fiscal-military state that owed its meteoric ascent to a high degree of centralization, Austria was still an early modern state. A "hotchpotch of lands," in one historian's words, its composite, decentralized structure looked increasingly obsolete.[29] Austria could only mobilize armies or collect money through the mediation of local aristocracies, who used this power to negotiate new privileges. To survive in a competitive international environment where modern centralized states had an advantage, the monarchy needed to give up indirect rule and forge direct links with its subjects.[30] Thus the Habsburg Empire became "one of several European states striving for centralization and unification yet to be achieved."[31]

By the 1770s, the Austrian Empire had become the site of some of the boldest, most expansive reforms in Europe.[32] Although set in motion by military concerns and foreign policy needs, the reforms encompassed the administrative, financial, legislative, and cultural realms.[33] They had begun in the 1740s, with Chancellor Friedrich Wilhelm von Haugwitz's restructuring of the administration and army to facilitate tax collection and strengthen central governance.[34] Next came a series of educational reforms that removed schools from Jesuit supervision and placed them under the state's control while making public primary education compulsory, so that subjects could receive "the requisite moral and economic training to become productive and orderly members of society."[35]

As head of the State Chancellery, Haugwitz's successor von Kaunitz continued the reforms, forming a United Chancery and Council of State to coordinate internal policy.[36] Though committed to modernizing the monarchy, Maria Theresa preferred moderate reform and compromise. Co-regent Joseph II, on the other hand, pressed for increasingly radical transformations, which sometimes—as when the emperor advocated reusable, open-bottomed coffins to minimize waste—bordered on the absurd.[37]

Informed by a functionalist state ideology,[38] Joseph's reforms broadened the sphere of state intervention, as seen in the multiplication of state edicts issued annually—from a hundred or so under Maria Theresa to around seven times that number under Joseph.[39] The emperor spent much of his reign traveling the realm incognito, gaining direct knowledge of the places and people he ruled, collecting petitions, and acting as "the first servant of the state."[40] Committed to forging direct links between the state and its subjects and to strengthening the monarchy's finances, the emperor introduced a new taxation system based on modern cadastres and maps.[41] Though not always coherent, his reform program envisaged "reducing corporate privileges, encouraging prosperity, promoting welfare, harnessing church resources to more rational and secular purposes, [and] inculcating values of efficiency, commitment, loyalty."[42]

Underpinning these reforms was the cameralist principle that the state's task was to increase its subjects' welfare through wisely managing population and resources. Imported into the Habsburg monarchy from the Protestant north-German universities, cameralism gave the Austrian Enlightenment a distinctive flavor. Combined with mercantilist and Italian reformist principles, cameralism displaced Counter-Reformed Catholicism as the dominant state ideology, leaving a strong imprint on the enlightened absolutist state.[43] Unlike the French Enlightenment, the cameralist-inflected Central European *Aufklärung* reinforced the state's authority by asserting its role as the main architect of reforms. It had a utilitarian and pragmatic character, concerned not only with ideas but practical approaches to governance.[44]

Cameralists such as Joseph Sonnenfels and Johann Heinrich Gottlob von Justi believed that maximizing societal happiness would increase the wealth of the state.[45] They did not differentiate between economy and state, seeing them as fundamentally interconnected and growing in tandem. For this reason, they favored population growth (even through immigration if managed properly) and advocated religious tolerance and land reforms.[46] The cameralist ideal was the "well-ordered police state," modeled on the well-ordered mine,[47] completely self-sufficient and capable of achieving great prosperity through regulation.[48] Bent on "remaking the human and natural worlds through science and discipline," cameralists believed the administration's role was to "intervene, regulate, help, protect, order, restrict."[49] They charged the state with far-reaching responsibilities: maintaining public order, regulating property and resources (land and forests), maintaining schools and churches, sorting out public finances, building and maintaining roads, repairing bridges, and instituting sanitation measures.

Bukovina's annexation happened during this process of rebuilding Austria into a centralized state capable of intervening at the local level, voluntaristic, and equipped with a well-developed state apparatus that could handle greater responsibilities.[50] The annexation also occurred in the midst of Austria's bureaucratic revolution, as it was redefining itself as a modern state run by an impersonal, professional bureaucracy.[51] In Bukovina, on Austria's easternmost periphery, the Habsburg authorities believed, "centralization and administrative reform could assume their purest forms."[52] Seen as a blank slate, Bukovina was imagined as the place where the well-ordered state could come into its own.

## Ordering Bukovina

The enlightened Habsburg state first made its presence in Bukovina felt by collecting information about the territory and representing it through maps and topographic descriptions. Here, too, cameralism played a role, as the cameral sciences taught that detailed knowledge of land, people, and resources was indispensable to good governance. Every piece of land, pasture, and building had to be measured, mapped, classified, and numbered.[53] Habsburg officials' preoccupation with mapping was shared by all enlightened states seeking to assert territorial hegemony. As historian Steven Seegel has shown, similar cartographic projects were underway in Prussia and Russia.[54] Many of the individuals involved in mapping Galicia after the partition were also employed in drawing maps of Bukovina.[55] The first cartographic representation of Bukovina was completed in September 1773. Another map, issued exclusively for military use, appeared in 1777.

Along with maps, early descriptions of Bukovina emphasized what set this territory, whose borders remained blurred, apart from Moldavia and Galicia. General Splény's military reports waxed almost sentimental about the beauty of Bukovina's natural landscape and undisturbed wilderness. Covered in forests of oak, pine, and fir, the countryside teemed with foxes, wolves, hares, and wild boar. Its "healthy air, the best waters, the abundance of arable land and meadows, the richness in wood" made it a real asset.[56] Decades later, the German traveler Georg Kohl also remarked that Bukovina's "soil yields twelvefold for all that is sown, the pastures in the valleys are extremely fine and rich, the very clouds of heaven rain honey and butter on this land of abundance." Bukovina, he wrote, was "home to the greatest delicacies throughout the Austrian Empire." There were "turkeys and capons [. . .] fattened on Turkish maize," and "every house in Bukovina was surrounded by [. . .] dirty but delicate grunters [pigs] and every village swarms with them."[57] These descriptions made clear that Bukovina's extraordinary riches were being squandered and its promise of prosperity lay unfulfilled. Splény was less enamored of the province's population, describing it as semi-nomadic and primitive.[58] The people were lazy and immoral, happy to share their mud residences with beasts and even dance with them: eighteenth-century Transylvanian historian Franz Josef Sulzer noted Bukovina's annual festivals where "forty bears danced a ballet, accompanied by tambourines, drums, and the songs of their teachers."[59]

Early topographic and ethnographic descriptions of Bukovina were also meant to help Habsburg officials delineate the annexed territory's precise boundaries. Officials collected first-hand observations about the terrain and folklore to try to discern the province's "original" borders. Friedrich von Mieg noted that in his travels around Bukovina he encountered "an old Jew" who claimed to know "an old stone near Fontana Sauchi which had been the former border between Poland and Moldavia."[60] He also met a nobleman who claimed to be in possession of a seventeenth-century diploma indicating that the former Polish–Moldavian border had been somewhere between Czernowitz and Hotin. Officials like von Mieg were eager to emphasize that the territory Austria had just carved out of Moldavia would not "make a significant and completely new acquisition, but rather, it would restore former borders." Chancellor Kaunitz's declaration that "the imperial decision is to take control of the well-known district of Moldova, as a former part of Pocutia usurped by the Turks, over which we have rights given the cession of a part of the Polish republic to the royal house of Habsburg," made this theory official.[61]

Major General (*Feldmarschal-Leutnant*) Joseph von Barco was consequently named head of an Austrian border commission that would convene with its Ottoman counterpart in September 1775 in the Moldavian town of Baia to negotiate Bukovina's new borders.[62] The negotiations were long drawn out, and Bukovina's frontiers fluctuated for years, as Habsburg troops on the ground pushed farther and farther into Moldavian territory. In the end the Porte gave in, and Kaunitz, who had advocated an uncompromising attitude, was praised for this "most successful single move" in all his foreign policy service.[63]

Even after Habsburg border markers (*Grenzadler*) were installed along Bukovina's frontier with Moldavia in November 1774, however, the border remained permeable.[64] A shortage of personnel and resources meant that the Habsburg authorities could not enforce it (especially in difficult terrain). People and cattle crossed at will, giving Habsburg sovereignty an improvised, temporary feel. This shaky, penetrable frontier was not only dangerous, given the Russian threat in the east, but was incompatible with Austria's aspirations to become a centralized, modernized state.[65] A strong frontier signified firm control over people and territory. The Habsburgs increased security along Bukovina's borders with Moldavia and the Russian Empire, diverting money from the cameral fund to pay for "wire entanglements, trenches, bridges for patrols, clearing of underbrush, establishment of border posts."[66] Governor Enzenberg made the frontier more visible by means of entrenchments and barricades "in order at least to prevent [people] from crossing the border arbitrarily by horse or by cart." By 1787 Habsburg military authorities had set up 180 border posts (*Tschardacken*) staffed by forty-three soldiers and 117 guards (*Landwächter*). By 1811, there were 205 border posts, thirty-two along Bukovina's border with Bessarabia and 137 along the border with Turkish Moldavia.[67] By the time Johann Georg Kohl traveled to Bukovina in the 1840s, crossing the Austro–Russian frontier could take weeks: "if the traveler does not have a consul-general visa, his passport is sent to Lemberg or Vienna, and he must wait a week or two imprisoned within the Russian frontier line." The gates to the "Austrian paradise" were closed to all but the few who managed to gather "myriad seals [. . .] stamps, signatures," although as Kohl soon discovered, a few well-placed bribes worked miracles.[68]

Bukovina's military administration was meant to be temporary, but multiple local actors were invested in making it last as long as possible. The Hofkriegsrat's official position was that Bukovina should be kept intact to win the local population's trust.[69] Military authorities in the territory, particularly General von Splény, insisted that its character was distinctive enough to warrant a separate administration. Splény advised placing Bukovina under a "Grenz Generalrat" (general border council) and favored gradual reforms: "this land cannot in any way be compared with the other hereditary lands and there would be almost unsurmountable difficulties from the very outset if one were to introduce administrative reforms similar to those in other provinces."[70] He stressed that "the people were too uneducated and too inexperienced" to navigate sudden reforms. Graf Heinrich Kajetan von Blumegen, the Bohemian-Austrian

FIGURE 1.2. General Karl Freiherr von Enzenberg. Brush portrait by Wilhelm Hecht, from the "*Kronprinzenwerk*" (*Die österreichisch-ungarische Monarchie in Wort und Bild [. . .]*, Vienna, 1886–1902), *Bukowina* volume (1899), 129. ÖNB Bildarchiv und Grafiksammlung. Courtesy of the Österreichische Nationalbibliothek (ÖNB, Wien).

chancellor, agreed that "Bukovina should not be unified with other provinces by any means, but should be treated as a completely separate territory as far as possible, in line with existing customs and traditions."[71]

General Enzenberg also pleaded with the central administration to allow him to staff Bukovina's institutions with Moldavians or, at least, with Habsburg military officials who spoke the local languages. Enzenberg, like bureaucrats in Galicia, came to believe that the local population could only be won over to "the rule of law and legal compliance" if they were addressed in their own language. The central authorities, however, were primarily concerned with minimizing expense. As a result, Bukovina's administration was very sparse, counting only twenty officials across the territory in 1780, plus two hundred "court constables and ushers."[72]

In 1786, after Emperor Joseph II made his second tour of the region, Bukovina's military administration was dismantled. The emperor noticed that over a decade of Habsburg governance, the territory had increased in population and become more diverse. It now boasted thirty thousand families and a more diversified economy, in part thanks to the government-sponsored immigration of handworkers, tradesmen, and merchants. "I have decided to unify Bukovina with Galicia completely," he wrote, "in such a way that the former should be treated in all political, public, and economic matters as an administrative district [*Kreis*] of Galicia by the Gubernium there."[73]

In August 1786 Bukovina indeed became a *Kreis* of Galicia, its military administration replaced by a *Kreisamt* (district office) with its seat in Czernowitz, headed by a *Kreishauptmann*: Joseph Beck, who reported directly to the Galician governor in Lemberg, Josef von Brigido.[74] Bukovina's native Moldavian nobility were recognized as "members of the Galician estates" and given seats in the Galician Landtag (parliament). Most of them opposed this new arrangement, which increased the distance between Czernowitz and Vienna and turned Bukovina into the periphery of a periphery. Bukovina was now governed by professional civil servants with a limited knowledge of local conditions—cosmopolitan, multilingual individuals whose bureaucratic rotations moved them across thousands of miles.[75]

## The Old and The New

The Austrian takeover was not the first time the territory had changed sovereignties. Located on a "geopolitical fracture zone" at the epicenter of imperial competition, the region had experienced repeated occupations over the previous centuries, most recently by Russia.[76] The Ottoman Empire's wars with Russia (1710–11 and 1768–74) had devastated the region and left its economy depleted.[77] The Moldavian principality had become a tributary to the Ottoman Porte back in the fifteenth century, following several Ottoman incursions into the Danubian principalities. Its status was established by treaties (*ahd*) that placed Moldavia between the "house of war" and the "house of Islam," which meant Moldavia had to pay the Porte an annual tribute and pursue contact with other European states only through Constantinople.[78] In return, the sultan promised to defend Moldavia against foreign attacks and prohibit Muslims from settling permanently there.[79] Even as the Ottomans tightened their grip on the region in the seventeenth century, Christian powers—Poland (under its kings Casimir and Jan III Sobieski), the Kingdom of Hungary, the Cossack Hetmanate of Bohdan Khmelnytsky, and the Russian and Habsburg empires—coveted it.[80] With the waxing and waning of Ottoman power during the seventeenth and eighteenth centuries, the region entered another era of instability.

Moldavia never came under direct Ottoman governance; it never became a *pashalik*, and initially, it enjoyed a fair amount of autonomy. But as the Porte tightened its grip on the Danubian principalities after losing Hungary and Transylvania to the Habsburgs, the region's autonomy diminished.[81] Hoping to stabilize the volatile border region, the Porte took away the native nobility's freedom to elect their own leaders, reserving its right to appoint and dismiss princes (*voyvoda* or *hospodars*) at will, choosing from a group of trustworthy individuals who were treated as high-ranking Ottoman functionaries. The decision came after the Moldavian prince Demeter Cantemir (Dimitrie Cantemir), raised in Constantinople and intimately familiar with all things Ottoman, turned against the Porte during its first war with Russia, defecting to St. Petersburg after Russia's defeat in 1711.[82]

Cantemir's defeat marked the beginning of what is called the Phanariot period in Moldavia: so named because the aspiring princely elite lived in the Phanar neighborhood in Constantinople (that is, the Greek quarter).[83] Facing financial difficulties, the Ottoman Empire sought to increase revenue by repeatedly changing hospodars, since the "princely throne had become the object of spirited bidding, and the sums offered by those in the running often reached enormous proportions, as much as seven times the annual tribute."[84] Appointments thus became shorter and shorter, averaging two and a half years.[85] To collect the money needed for the gifts required by the sultan and high Ottoman officials, the appointed princes in turn put offices up for sale.[86]

The Phanariots belonged to "trans ethnic and trans regional families," typically Albanians, Bulgarians, Vlachs, Serbs, and other "hellenized non-Greeks."[87] As the Porte's dealings with Christian powers in the Balkans increased, the Phanariot elites—Christian like the Porte's adversaries and fluent in multiple European languages—became increasingly indispensable. They served as interpreters in the Porte's campaigns against Russia and Austria, and as leaders of the frontier principalities of Moldavia and Wallachia they were expected to provide the Porte with strategic information.[88] Agents and products of Ottoman governance, the Phanariots were both useful and dangerous to the Porte, which feared that their foreign contacts, Christian religion, and knowledge of foreign languages might lead them to cooperate with foreign powers. These fears were not entirely unfounded.

Like his native predecessor Cantemir, the Phanariot Grigore Ghika III turned out to be exceedingly friendly with Russia. Though appointed by the Porte, Ghika acquired his position during the Russo–Ottoman war of 1768–74 when Russian troops were present in Moldavia. Faced with the imminent loss of Moldavia's northwestern corner, Bukovina, in 1774, Ghika tried to secure the territorial integrity of his principality by turning to Russia and simultaneously opening channels of communication with Austria. In the end, all three powers suspected him of disloyalty. Ghika lost not only Bukovina, which the Porte formally ceded to Austria in May 1775, but eventually, his head.[89]

FIGURE 1.3. The *Türkischbrunnen*: the former Turkish fountain, one of the few surviving relics of Ottoman rule in Bukovina. © Dmytro Stoliarenko / Dreamstime.com.

The Habsburg military administrators in charge of Bukovina dismissed the region's Ottoman-Phanariot period as an era of despotism, lawlessness, and abuse. Though supposedly by nature healthy and courageous, handsome and strong, Moldavians under Ottoman rule had allegedly degenerated into a "lazy and ignorant people" whose efforts "do not go beyond the indispensable needs of life." They had become indolent and prone to dishonesty and crime. "Theft is nothing out of the ordinary for them," Splény wrote, adding that Moldavians in Bukovina were "more a barbarian than a moderately civilized European people."[90] In typical cameralist fashion, he attributed Moldavians' lack of civilization to the "destructive influence of oppressive and barbaric governance."[91] Particularly harmful, in Splény's view, was Bukovina's feudal property regime, which concentrated most land in the hands of boyars (local landowners) and the Church, while peasants did not have even "one hand's width of land of their own."[92] Splény attributed their semi-nomadism to their lack of property: "even the love of fatherland, that prejudice which otherwise puts even the most miserable land before the best, means nothing to these people consisting mostly of Polish, Transylvanian, Wallachian, and as it might be Moldavian emigrants, therefore accustomed to wandering around."[93] To bring civilization to Bukovina, Splény implied, the traditional Ottoman structures of governance would have to be completely dismantled.

In practice, of course, much survived the transition to the era of enlightened absolutist governance.[94] The Josephine state absorbed and repurposed old structures, changing their function, but also prolonging their existence. This happened both because elements of traditional society provided Bukovina's new governors with indispensable local knowledge, and because the resources for a complete transformation of local institutions and society were lacking. Though less powerful and organized than their Polish counterparts in Galicia, Bukovina's Moldavian nobility kept their positions under Habsburg rule. While some boyars fled to Moldavia after the annexation, those who stayed had no qualms about cooperating with the new administration, which recognized their status by giving them administrative assignments and Austrian noble titles. The Moldavian Vasile Balş, a member of an old Moldavian boyar family with estates in Bukovina, placed himself at the Habsburg administration's disposal, and echoed Spleny's assessments of the local population's low level of civilization, writing that "the Moldavian is unmannered, inclined to cheat and even steal, is vengeful, frivolous, and eager for change; to the vices that may be considered the reaction of an oppressed people one should also add drunkenness [. . . ;] though open, they are mired in the gravest ignorance."[95]

Like Spleny, Balş blamed all this on the feudal Phanariot regime that had left Bukovina "without industry [and] almost without agriculture." He pleaded with the territory's new rulers to make their new subjects "equal to those fortunate citizens of this world, who have the Austrian state to thank for their wellbeing."[96] With his loyalty to the Habsburgs, Balş is a perfect example of the "self-orientalizing" native elites who adopted the Habsburg "discursive scheme" of civilization and barbarism to "legitimate themselves and their actions under the new banner." By this adoption elites turned themselves from potentially obsolete elements of traditional society into a "part of the imperial apparatus."[97]

In any event, Balş's enthusiasm for the Habsburg regime is unsurprising given the position of boyar families like his own in Phanariot-ruled Moldavia. Moldavian society was divided between a small secular and clerical elite, on the one hand, and the rest of the population, which was predominantly rural, on the other. Under Phanariot rule, the boyars remained the backbone of the state financially, but lost their political influence and autonomy. Many tried to improve their situation by negotiating with the foreign powers competing over the region. Countless boyar delegations presented the Russian tsarina with appeals for patronage before Russia began formalizing its protectorate over the Danubian principalities after the peace of Küçük Kainarca.[98] These nobles never acted in unison, however, as different boyar factions chose different patrons, thus exacerbating rivalries and divisions.

Balş's choice to cooperate with the Habsburgs was thus a continuation of a much older pattern. It was not only politically expedient, but in line with his convictions as an educated man of the Enlightenment who peppered his conversations with impromptu translations of Voltaire and Montesquieu into Greek.[99] Already fluent in Moldavian, French, Latin, and Greek, Balş added German to his list after Emperor Joseph II paid to have him educated in Vienna. Balş was no more self-serving than the emperor, who believed that appointing a local nobleman to the position of *Kreishauptmann* (district commissioner) of Bukovina provided the perfect opportunity to build a new administration on the cheap by recycling preexisting structures.[100] Although Austrian law was officially introduced to Bukovina in 1782, older Moldavian officials continued dispensing justice at the district level, and customary law was kept in place. The new Habsburg rulers kept old administrative divisions, leaving old village and district borders almost intact.[101]

## Managing Land and People

One early Habsburg reform in Bukovina did strike at the heart of the native nobility's power. Measures to regulate property relations and ensure the proper use of cultivable land shook to the foundations Bukovina's old economic system, which was based on the nobility's exploitation of peasant labor. Peasants in Moldavian Bukovina were subject to a harsh regime of labor duties that worsened as the principality entered its Phanariot period and the Porte increased the financial burden on its Danubian principalities. With administrative positions being sold for exorbitant prices, the boyar elite pressured hospodars to let them increase peasants' already crushing obligations. By the early eighteenth century the Moldavian peasantry's standard of living had declined so much that the Phanariot hospodar Constantin Mavrocordat felt compelled to introduce reforms to try to end a peasant exodus.[102]

But even after the reforms, Moldavian peasants still labored for free for their landowner many days a year and paid landlords a percentage of their yield.[103] Prince Grigore Ghika's regulations of 1766 show that local nobles were required to redistribute land among the peasants on their estates annually.[104] This meant that peasants were tenants, not themselves landholders, and had to perform compulsory unpaid work (*Robot*) in return for working the land allotted to them. This situation was not unique: In Galicia, peasants performed *Robot* as many as six days a week. Hungary's and Bohemia's economies were also grounded on serf labor.[105] In Bohemia, conditions were so appalling, especially after the famine of 1771–72, that the countryside erupted in violent rebellions, affording Emperor Joseph II, then touring the country, a first-hand glimpse into the disaster.[106]

Serfdom was incompatible with the cameralist state's commitment to increasing revenues by maximizing the welfare of the agricultural revenue-generating population. As cameralist thinker Justi put it, the state's purpose was to "increas[e] state wealth in rational, prudent ways," and serfdom was neither rational nor prudent.[107] Peasants who worked for themselves, cameralists believed, would be more productive; otherwise, "the estate manager must stand over them with a whip, something a well-ordered state cannot allow. Labor services are extremely harmful to the state and landlord alike."[108] Fearing that an excessively oppressive labor regime would mean that "peasants wouldn't be able to shoulder taxes," Maria Theresa had already taken measures to impose limits on the labor peasants were required to perform.[109] Although noblemen across the realm often bypassed these regulations, they eventually led to marginal improvements. Joseph II's emancipation patents accomplished more: a serfdom patent issued in 1781 allowed serfs to move, learn a trade, and marry—though not to own property.[110] The *Robot* reforms were extended to Galicia in 1782, though many noblemen ignored them.

These efforts to regulate the relationship between landlords and tenants were part of a broader process of regulating property relations in preparation for introducing a modern taxation system. Traditionally, land in Moldavia belonged either to the prince or to the nobility, clergy, or free peasantry.[111] Czernowitz, Sereth, and Suczawa once belonged to princely domains. Many villages, especially between the Prut and Dniester rivers, were owned by boyars with high positions at the princely court in Jassy. The few free peasants were concentrated in villages in the northern part of Bukovina, between the Prut and Czeremosh rivers.[112] One of Bukovina's Habsburg government's first steps was to introduce land surveys and cadastral regulations to get the lay of the land, collect information for determining taxes, and confirm the legal boundaries of locally owned property. Launched in Bukovina in 1782–84, the land survey was part of a monarchy-wide effort to strengthen the military and fiscal capacity of the state.[113] Civil engineers came to Bukovina to carry out cadastral measurements. Landowners, whether they resided in Bukovina or Moldavia proper, had to appear before a commission and provide details of their properties. In exchange, they were given official records confirming their ownership of land, which Habsburg authorities hoped would end the chronic boundary disputes and violations that took up so much of the military Auditorium's time.[114] Land was now classified into "dominical" and "rustical" property—manorial and farmers' land—so it could be taxed appropriately. Repeatedly delayed by a lack of resources and personnel and by recurrent cholera outbreaks, the cadastral regulation project was not completed until the 1850s, however.[115]

Since the cameralist state's purpose was the "maximum utilization of resources," cadastral regulation was accompanied by regulation of the use of the province's natural resources, especially the forests that covered over half of Bukovina.[116] Military authorities took responsibility for the forests, placing them under the state's stewardship—literally: the forests were now protected by military guards who ensured that limited quantities of wood were harvested, issuing "each landlord who owns forests a certain number of permits," each corresponding to one cartful of firewood. Regulations covered what kind of wood peasants could remove from the forest. Peasants were also forbidden to let their cattle graze on the forest floor. The regulations, like the cadastral system overall, were designed to minimize waste: "since the forest can be irreparably damaged if some several hundred trees are used for one fence, this abuse needs to be punished all the more, as such posts can be manufactured with only a little more effort from different wood."[117]

The cameralist Habsburgs also believed that population size and state wealth were directly proportional, leading them to try to increase Bukovina's productivity by repopulating the province with "colonists."[118] As Splény never tired of emphasizing in his reports, Bukovina was severely depopulated. By the Habsburg authorities' estimates, between 57,000 and 75,000 people lived there: around 17,000 families, scattered across 260 villages and three large towns, Czernowitz, Sereth, and Suczawa. Of those families, 15,000 were peasants, 240 belonged to the upper and middle nobility, 500 were families of priests or church singers, 280 were officials' families, and 45 were merchants.[119] The disadvantages of underpopulation were not just theoretical for Splény and his staff, who struggled to secure food for themselves and their horses, especially after the Russian occupation troops "had mowed and taken away so much hay."[120] And Bukovina's population appeared to be diminishing—a fact that Splény and Enzenberg attributed to the harsh conditions for serfs. To keep even more people from fleeing the province, Habsburg officials tried imposing fines on those who left, but these were ineffective.[121] Splény believed that a concerted effort had to be made to repopulate Bukovina, preferably with Moldavians, in order to ensure an increase in the food and cattle supply on which the territory's military administration depended. In the meantime, he promised favorable conditions to Moldavians who crossed the border into and out of Bukovina, hoping to convince them to return and settle there for good.

While Emperor Joseph II agreed that "increasing the population in this territory is the most important thing," he favored bringing settlers from the empire's heartlands—farmers and artisans, preferably German-speaking—over resettling Moldavians.[122] Although nationalists would later attribute this choice to the Habsburg Empire's larger project of Germanizing the province, the emperor's preference was not ethnically or civilizationally motivated.[123] He believed that German-speaking settlers would diversify the province's economy and improve productivity through superior methods of working the land and exploiting resources. Colonists arrived from across the empire, especially neighboring Galicia, over the next few decades.[124] Their immigration, however, was never part of a consistent, concerted, state-led campaign, but reflected individual choices. The new settlers included "an assortment of German bureaucrats, teachers, farmers, artisans, and merchants, and last but most certainly not least, Jews."[125]

The emperor did not hesitate to extend special privileges to non-German, non-Catholic colonists he believed would contribute to Bukovina's wealth, including Lipovenians, a Russian Old Believer sect who resettled in Bukovina from the Black Sea region.[126] Impressed by their diligence and agricultural skills, especially their innovations in fruit production, the emperor had an Old Believer priest brought to Bukovina so colonists could celebrate mass in their own language and by their own rite.[127] Although Catholicism remained the Austrian monarchy's official religion, the state had grown detached from religion in this age of so-called counter-Counter-Reformation, and productivity and the maximizing of wealth increasingly trumped religious prejudice. Maria Theresa's firm stance against Protestants and Jews gave way to Joseph II's policy of religious tolerance. The Tolerance Patent of 1781 gave the right of worship to Calvinists, Lutherans, and Greek-Orthodox believers—but not Jews. As late as 1780, Governor Enzenberg called for strict measures to reduce the number of Jews in Bukovina, calling them "idlers living from the sweat of Christians."[128] There was a ban on Jewish immigration and settlement in Bukovina until 1789, when religious tolerance was extended to Jews, but only if they demonstrated that they could be productive.[129]

## Church and School

The largest owner of property in Bukovina was the Orthodox Church (Greek-Oriental, in Habsburg parlance). With its myriad dioceses and monasteries employing thousands of monks, nuns, and priests, the Orthodox Church played a key economic and social role in the province: monks copied and preserved manuscripts, organized schools, and kept hospitals.[130] The Josephine state, however, viewed churches and monasteries in Bukovina and elsewhere with suspicion. Early Habsburg officials were taken aback by the priests' low level of education, as well as the overall ignorance of the population, whose beliefs—officials opined—were closer to superstition than faith. "Few people know the laws of God," a worried Splény reported.[131] Ferdinand Dans, a Galicia-based official charged with reporting on Bukovina, wrote in 1803 that priests relied on parishioners for their income, which, due to the high tax and *Robot* duties peasants had to bear, put them in a conflicted position. To make a living, clergymen did all kinds of work on the side, including "plowing their own lands," which "takes away all respect before their community."[132]

Another official noted that peasants in Bukovina mistook fasting for religion and had no qualms about bigamy, which was unusually common there. Albert von Kugler, cameral director in a Bukovinan village between 1793–98, was astonished that "robberies, murders, thefts and so on, in Bukovina have devolved into such everyday affairs that one speaks about them with the greatest indifference."[133]

Habsburg officials blamed the Orthodox Church not only for the population's indolence and loose morals, but for Bukovina's abysmal economic level. That the Church concentrated vast expanses of cultivable land in its own hands without contributing to the productive economy was, from a cameralist point of view, wasteful. Ferdinand Dans, among other officials, believed that the state needed to intervene to "do something more useful than these obstinate and ignorant monks can."[134] And intervene it did: in 1782, all but five of Bukovina's monasteries were dissolved. By 1790, the number of monasteries across the Austrian empire as a whole had gone from two thousand previously, with forty thousand monks, to twelve hundred and fifty, with twenty-seven thousand monks.[135] The administration also severed the link between Bukovina's churches and the Moldavian metropolitanate in Jassy by creating a separate bishopric for Bukovina, with its seat in Czernowitz, and subordinating the Bukovinan Church to the metropolitanate of Karlowitz, the highest Eastern Orthodox authority in the empire.[136] Rather than send yearly contributions to Jassy, as they had previously, Bukovinan churches could now use their funds locally. With the creation of the "Greek-Oriental Religious Fund" in 1786, the Church's wealth was entrusted to the state, who used it to support clergymen and sponsor a public school system.[137] By 1853 more than 58 percent of erstwhile church property in Bukovina was owned by the state, accounting for almost one third of state revenues there.[138]

The secularization of education in the empire, and thus in Bukovina, also diminished church authority. Maria Theresa, though a devout Catholic, set this process in motion through a series of school reforms issued in the 1770s and 1780s that made elementary schooling public, obligatory, and uniform.[139] Children between the ages of six and twelve would be formally registered and school attendance enforced through fines. The reforms resulted in a rapid expansion of the school system, which numbered six thousand schools and two hundred thousand students by the end of Maria Theresa's reign.[140] The dissolution of the Jesuit order in 1773 opened spaces for state-appointed teachers and gave the state new resources that it could use to overhaul the educational structures.[141] Rather than having their sons study abroad, noble families could now send them to state-regulated institutions that trained future civil servants, such as the Theresianum—which Governor Spléný himself had attended.

One of the Habsburg administration's first tasks in Bukovina was thus to bolster the province's school system. At the time of annexation Bukovina had six Moldavian schools, all subsidized by the Church through a schools fund instituted by Prince Grigore Ghika.[142] The Habsburg authorities used church funds to construct new public schools staffed by teachers from Transylvania, who could speak Romanian (Moldavian).[143] The Habsburgs prioritized Moldavian-language schools as these would help locals to access positions in the local administration. Next, the authorities opened German-Latin schools for the families of officers stationed there and, in 1808 in Czernowitz, a German-Latin *Gymnasium*.[144] These schools were designed to prepare a new generation of elite, well-educated civil servants recruited from the local population. Schools were to be, above all, useful: in the words of Joseph II, "nothing must be taught to the young people which they will later need only rarely, or [that is] not in the interest of the state, since university studies are essentially for the training of civil servants, not of scholars."[145] Another marker of a good education, Habsburg officials believed, was that it forged subjects who were capable of appreciating the benefits of enlightened governance. In an 1803 report Ferdinand Dans recommended improving public education in Bukovina because "one needs to be a man to feel what good governance can achieve for the good of mankind."[146]

After 1786, when Bukovina was incorporated into Galicia, many early measures to provide the population with an obligatory, public, secular education were reversed. Schools were placed under the Catholic Church's supervision, subordinated to the Lemberg Gubernium, and instruction was increasingly in Polish.[147] Fearing their children would be Catholicized, Orthodox families hesitated to send them to school. Literacy levels sank again, and Bukovina's school system once more became symbolic of failure and backwardness.[148]

---

The French Revolution and the Napoleonic wars permanently altered Habsburg rule in Bukovina and elsewhere in the empire. The pace of reform slowed, and many Josephine radical changes were rolled back. Emperor Francis II focused on containing the threat of revolution by strengthening censorship and banning potentially subversive societies. But Napoleon entered Vienna in 1804, and by 1806 Francis found himself presiding over the final dissolution, after a millenium, of the Holy Roman Empire. Nevertheless, and despite losing four successive wars with Napoleonic France, the monarchy survived to participate in the reconstitution of pre-Napoleonic Europe at the Congress of Vienna in 1814, where the Austrian chancellor Prince Metternich worked hard to restore the continent's previous balance of power.

An administrative district of Galicia-Lodomeria since 1786, Bukovina experienced a attempt, backed by Napoleon, to revive an independent Polish state in French-occupied Galicia in 1809. Although nothing came of this, "some Austrian officials," writes Iryna Vushko, "responded to the Napoleonic crisis by advocating more local self-administration and greater participation of Poles in Austrian administrative structures."[149] The Moldavian nobility in Bukovina resented having to speak Polish and answer to Lemberg, and resisted further integration into a Galicia increasingly dominated by Poles. The Habsburg authorities' efforts to foster the development of a Galician provincial identity thus had the unintended consequence of crystallizing a distinct Bukovinan provincial identity. In contrast to the Polish nobility in Galicia who pushed for more autonomy from Vienna, the Moldavian nobility in Bukovina called for a restoration of the pre-1786 Habsburg order that had recognized their traditional privileges.

By the early 1800s, when the Viennese police commissar Joseph Rohrer traveled to Bukovina, the province was more similar to the rest of the monarchy than to Moldavia. In Moldavia, Rohrer had attended dinners hosted by boyars who washed their beards and picked their teeth in front of their guests. In Bukovina, he found himself "back in a place where a friend of music has the chance to encounter the works of Mozart, Haydn, Clementi every day." In a civil servant's house in Suczawa, Rohrer saw a *fortepiano*: an apparition that left him feeling "strengthened, one could even say, enraptured." Rohrer sighed with relief once he could "forget the Gypsy riffraff who buzzed around my ears so lamentably in Moldavia."[150]

By the time Georg Kohl arrived in Czernowitz in the 1840s, the city "seemed at once to have brought us some hundred versts nearer to Germany, Vienna, Berlin, nay, even to Paris, Spain, and Italy." On seeing Czernowitz, Kohl effused, "the whole west of Europe seemed to be lying before our eyes and we fancied ourselves close to Vienna, the Alps, and Italy." Like those of the Viennese suburbs, Czernowitz's shops "were filled with Vienna wares and large gaudy inscriptions" that "invited passers-by to enter and purchase wines, trinkets, cakes, and other goods within."[151] By the late nineteenth century, Czernowitz had become a symbol of the enlightened absolutist state's success in transforming a "heap of clay huts" into a "friendly, civilized German city."[152] In his 1908 jubilee edition of *Geschichte von Czernowitz*, historian Raimund Friedrich Kaindl recounted how eighteenth-century Habsburg officials removed cattle herders from the city, brought in tradesmen, paved roads, and built bridges to tame the Prut's unruly waters. They regulated water use, captured stray dogs, and turned the city's confusing layout into a modern grid.[153]

By the late nineteenth century, Austrian liberals who traced their origins to the Josephine enlightenment viewed Bukovina as the most successful example of Josephine state-building. They credited it not to the improvised policies of a cameralist state, but to a consistent Austrian-German civilizing mission, and imagined Bukovina as a symbol of a larger Habsburg imperial mission that became more important as Austria's position on the continent grew increasingly insecure. The monarch Joseph II's "inspired idea to make out of Austria a German *Culturstaat*," wrote Galician-born writer Karl Emil Franzos, "was achieved only in Bukovina."[154] Though much changed over the course of decades of Habsburg rule in Bukovina, one thing—it was insisted—had been consistent: the state "still recognized official, governmental responsibility for culture, that source of so many opportunities and liabilities in the future."[155]

# 2

# Liberal Empire

WALKING DOWN a street in Czernowitz on a Sunday afternoon at the turn of the twentieth century, you could have run into any of the following types. A man wearing a top hat, clean-shaven and sporting a perfectly waxed mustache, a watch chain hanging from his pocket. A pious lady who only went out on Sundays to attend mass. A young lady and her friend, who "trot from the Catholic Church to the Herrengasse and if they haven't conquered anyone, they hang their heads and go home to dream of potential new conquests next Sunday afternoon." You could have seen a dandy walking from Cafe Habsburg to Cafe l'Europe, the brim of his straw hat turned backward according to the latest fashion. Or a "suburbanite" from Roscha or Kaliczanka near Czernowitz, followed "at a respectful distance by his wife whose Sunday duty is to follow her husband from one bar to another so he doesn't fall over."[1] Passing by one of Czernowitz's numerous cafés, you could see young people enjoying *Kremeschnitten* and sipping *mélange*.[2]

This was Czernowitz's *Bildungsbürgertum* (educated middle class), a byproduct of the liberal reforms originating in the revolutions of 1848, which put liberalism, championed by urban citizens and the new middle classes, on Europe's political map.[3] Although most of the reforms conceded by the monarchy in 1848–49 were temporarily rolled back in the 1850s, liberal ideas and projects eventually became permanent fixtures of the Austrian political landscape. Defeat in wars with Prussia and France in the 1860s prompted Emperor Franz Joseph to concede to liberal demands for constitutionalism. In 1867 the monarchy split into two: Austria (Cisleithania) and Hungary (Transleithania), autonomous states united by a shared monarch and several common ministries. The Austrian half adopted a constitution that extended equal rights to all citizens and granted all peoples the right to use their own languages in schools and governmental administration. It also abolished press censorship and guaranteed freedom of speech and instruction.[4] Since the foreign policy blunders that led Austria to lose its dominant position in Germany and Italy had also prompted questions about Austria's position on the continent, the liberal politicians and ideologues at the helm turned to the empire's eastern crown lands to redefine Austria through its alleged civilizing mission in the east. Once again, Bukovina—along with Galicia and later Bosnia-Herzegovina—became the object of reforms through which the crisis-beset empire attempted to reinvent itself.[5]

Like their counterparts in Britain and Germany, Austrian liberals set themselves apart from "the shadowy forces of reaction" represented by the past.[6] They contrasted liberal Austrian governance, defined by law and progress, with Ottoman misrule in the region,[7] thus putting a new spin on the old notion of Austria as a "bulwark of the Christian West against the Ottoman Empire."[8] Yet Austrian liberals' relationship with the past was complicated, and their ideals were not without contradictions. Even as the liberal *Bildungsbürgertum* defined its interests against those of the nobility and the state bureaucracy, it imitated the nobility and depended on the Josephine state bureaucracy to enact its liberal vision of citizenship. It "resented the incursions of bureaucracy" but ultimately wanted, as historian Pieter Judson writes, not to destroy or bypass the state, but to reform it.[9]

Liberals' preference for state-led reform reflected a further contradiction: between their egalitarian impulses and their distaste for political extremes. Liberals were skeptical of the bureaucracy but terrified of the mob. Although they advocated equal citizenship rights, this equality was not a given; rather it was earned through education and culture. As a result, liberals invested heavily in educational projects: convinced that the state had the duty to "conquer ignorance" and that they could overhaul society through education and the rule of law, they reorganized Austria's educational system.[10] Liberal politics was in essence the politics of the *Bürgertum*, of "homogeneous, meritocratic middle-class society."[11]

Liberals celebrated the empire's cultural and ethnic diversity and genuinely believed that harmony among its different ethnic groups was simply a matter of the right legal and institutional reforms. At the same time, they believed that German culture was more developed than others and that the German language could be a vehicle of universal humanistic values and "economic development, rule of law, and the cultural treasures of Western civilization."[12] In liberals' eyes, Austria was not building an empire for empire's sake but to fulfill its historic duty to bring *Kultur* to allegedly benighted lands so they could absorb the fruits of "German spiritual education."[13] Underpinning the notion of an Austrian cultural mission was an egalitarian, assimilationist impulse that implied that anyone, irrespective of ethnicity or religion, could achieve enlightenment by assimilating into German culture.[14] At the same time, as culture became a yardstick of worth, it justified inequalities and often translated into exclusivist, elitist policies.[15]

Although it did not always lead to the intended outcomes, the liberal project to transform Austria into a *Kulturstaat* left a deep imprint on Bukovina.

Provincial elites who embraced the liberal creed took it upon themselves to advocate progress and development through rational, civilized governance and closer ties to German *Kultur* and language. It was these native elites who built the infrastructure of the liberal *Kulturstaat* in Bukovina. Whether they agreed with Austrian liberals who pleaded for greater centralization or with conservatives who argued for federalization, Bukovinan elites sought to achieve their goals through a greater rapprochement with Vienna. Ironically, it was their direct ties with Vienna that helped secure provincial autonomy, thus allowing them to better preserve their interests.

Ultimately, the legal and institutional infrastructure liberals put into place changed the balance of forces in the province for good by paving the way for the province's modernization. By instituting municipal autonomy, the constitution of 1867 allowed cities like Czernowitz to develop very differently from the neighboring countryside. The constitution also recognized Austrian Jews as equal citizens, facilitating the emergence of a German-speaking Jewish bourgeoisie in Bukovina. Concentrated in towns and cities, especially in Czernowitz, acculturated Bukovinan Jews championed the state's *Kulturmission* and the universalist conception of German culture to which they owed their emancipation. Thanks to their devotion to the German language, Bukovina kept its German-speaking character long after that language was forced to retreat from Galicia or Bohemia, among other places.

The benefits of liberal *Bildung* and *Kultur* were uneven, and unequally distributed. Liberal elites who believed education could provide the best antidote to poverty managed to convince Vienna to allow a new German-language university to open in Czernowitz. But literacy levels in Bukovina remained low, and the province's predominantly rural population, mostly Romanian- and Ruthenian-speakers, remained poor. For a state that justified its existence "in terms of its ability to promote the development of its constituent nations," this was a serious problem.[16] Thanks to Austrian-sponsored modernizing reforms, Bukovina became better connected with the rest of the empire and the world, which afforded Bukovinan peasants an opportunity to look beyond the province and the empire for solutions to their plight. Meanwhile, although educational reforms did not make deep inroads into the countryside, they created the conditions for the emergence of an educated native class whose energies liberalism made possible, but could not fully contain.

## The Revolutions of 1848

Although constitutionalism turned out to be one of the 1848 revolutions' most important legacies, it was not the desire for greater representation that was the impetus for the events of that year. Economic crisis, poor harvests, and crop disasters leading to bread and potato riots laid the groundwork for revolution in the countryside.[17] Across Europe, 1848 brought rural uprisings and disputes over agricultural land, as peasants occupied forests and, in some cases, placed landowners' estates under siege. Living conditions were especially dire in rural Bukovina and Galicia, where land was overwhelmingly concentrated in the hands of the Church and the hereditary aristocracy.[18] Matters were worsened by cholera, drought, and locust infestations,[19] which provoked frequent uprisings in the countryside in 1843–44 and then again in 1848.[20]

Bukovina's experience of the revolution of 1848 led one historian to conclude that the province "may be said to have vegetated for the first half of the nineteenth century."[21] In Czernowitz, the revolution announced itself via broken windows and vandalism against local authorities, including a Roman Catholic priest, a police commissar, and a *Gymnasium* professor.[22] The insurgents were, for the most part, high school students who met at Czernowitz's Hotel de Russie.[23] They decided to chase out the mayor and city commissar and form a civilian and student guard on the Viennese model.[24] "The guards," wrote Bukovina's foremost historian R. F. Kaindl, "were overly eager and zealous, although among them there was also a night patrol which got lost in a tavern, giving spirited speeches about 'freedom' and 'the constitution' around the table instead of watching over the peace of the city."[25]

Due to its proximity to Transylvania, the epicenter of a revolution that culminated in Hungary's declaring independence from Austria, Bukovina was a base for government troops. In April 1849 imperial officials across the province were instructed to prepare for the arrival of Russian troops, sent by the tsar to help quash revolution. In May, Russian soldiers crossed into Bukovina through the frontier town of Nowosielitza, taking up quarters in residential homes in Czernowitz. By September, they were all gone, and Czernowitzers, after many unpleasant encounters with Russian troops, reclaimed their space.[26]

To calm rural unrest in Austria's easternmost crown lands, the government initiated reforms. Emperor Ferdinand I issued a constitution in March 1848 which introduced a parliament (Reichsrat) in which peasants were now also granted representation.[27] In the new Reichsrat, Bukovina was represented by a body of delegates now including seven peasants: five Ruthenian- and two Romanian-speakers.[28] Among the delegates was one named Lukian Kobylytsia, a Ruthenian peasant born a serf in the mountain district of Putyla, who had been imprisoned for instigating rural uprisings.[29] Kobylytsia was supposed to travel to Kremsier, where the first parliament would convene in October 1848, to join fellow peasant delegates in sitting awkwardly with notables to whom they, who could not follow the German-language speeches, no doubt appeared deaf and dumb.[30] Instead, he headed back to the mountains of Bukovina and sparked off an armed rebellion protesting at the fact that serfdom had been abolished in Galicia but not in Bukovina. Kobylytsia proclaimed himself "king" and told peasants that the emperor had sent him to Bukovina to urge them to revolt against their landlords.[31] He was re-arrested, but serfdom was never reinstituted, the only Austrian achievement of 1848 that was not rolled back during the restoration period.

Across Europe, the rural uprisings that culminated in the abolition of serfdom were only one of several parallel revolutions in 1848. The middle classes also revolted, entering upon the political stage for the first time to demand a break with the "civil servant state" (*Beamtenstaat*) that governed without the consent of the governed.[32] Though favoring greater representation, the middle classes remained suspicious of the peasantry and lower classes, supporting the "rule of the people" more in theory than in practice. They insisted that elections to parliament be indirect and that voters be represented according to the class or "curia" to which they belonged. What the local notables, the aristocracy, and the bourgeoisie wanted was full autonomy for Bukovina, which had been a district or *Kreis* of Galicia since 1786. Though often included on Galicia's list of nobility and given seats in the Lemberg parliament, Bukovinan notables felt poorly served by the current administration, which favored the Galician Polish (and therefore Catholic) nobility.[33]

Eager to reclaim autonomy, a delegation of Bukovinans headed by Bishop Eugen Hakman and including Romanian landowners such as Georg Wassilko, Jakob Mikuli, and Doxaki Hurmuzaki, and Austro-German notables such as Anton Kral, went to Olmütz in January 1849 to petition the emperor, whose court had relocated there, for autonomy. Although several counter-petitions were made in the Reichsrat arguing that the masses did not share this desire,[34] the province was granted its autonomy by the constitution of March 1849, which proclaimed it a hereditary duchy of the house of Habsburg.[35] From then on, Bukovina had its own provincial government, with headquarters in Czernowitz.

The Romanian aristocracy and German-speaking notables who agitated for Bukovina's autonomy in 1848 were the first representatives of an emerging provincial consciousness. They were also the first to institutionalize this sense of a distinct Bukovinan provincial identity, through newspapers, cultural associations, and organizations conceived as serving the province's population overall rather than any one ethnic or religious group. A *Landeskulturverein* (provincial cultural association), *Landesbibliothekverein* (provincial library association) and *Landeswirtschaftlicher Verein* (provincial agricultural association), as well as a new provincial public library, were established with the financial support of local noble and landowning families.[36] The Hurmuzaki brothers, sons of Doxaki Hurmuzaki who spearheaded the quest for provincial autonomy in 1848, launched the province's first newspaper in October 1848, titled *Bucovina: Gazetă Românească pentru politică, religie și literatură*

(Bukovina: Romanian gazette for politics, religion, and literature).[37] Although the newspaper was framed as a Romanian enterprise, it featured articles in both Romanian and German. In parallel, Ernst Rudolf Neubauer, a Moravian poet who had participated in the revolution of 1848 before fleeing to Bukovina, started a German-language newspaper, also named *Bukowina,* that promoted the province as unique because of its multiculturalism, diversity, and harmony, as did one of Neubauer's odes to his adopted home:

> You quiet place, that fifty years ago
> Was covered still in brush and forest green,
> Inhabited but by cheerful flocks of birds,
> What are you now, where lining your pastures
> Fine house and steep alley draw their boundaries?
> All around is mute and dead! The people here,
> Of varying race and faith, how they dream on fluff and straw,
> A medley in this land as in no other.[38]

The same local elites mobilized eleven years later, when Bukovina lost its autonomy and was reincorporated into Galicia. A new *Emancipationsruf der Bukowina,* signed by 250 petitioners, landed on the emperor's desk, pleading that Bukovina's undeniable individuality and desire for autonomy be recognized and respected. "She cannot subdue this desire [for autonomy]," the petitioners wrote, for "the feeling of a separate political individuality is so powerful and deep-rooted that the elimination of [Bukovina's] own provincial government is here seen by all as merely a transitory, unsustainable measure." The petitioners argued that Bukovina was perfectly capable of paying for its own administration and that employing local civil servants to staff its institutions was both cheaper and more practical, since Galician authorities in Lemberg operated on second-hand information. Moreover, staffing the civil service with native Bukovinans who could speak the local languages (i.e., Romanian) was desirable because "the majority of the governed did not understand the language of the *Gemeinde* [municipal authority] and provincial administration" and therefore did not understand their "benevolent intentions." The petitioners also asserted that granting Bukovina autonomy and placing it directly under Vienna's supervision would cure it of its greatest affliction: marginality. "Lying on the outermost periphery of the wide-reaching crown land of Galicia," they complained, Bukovina was "only weakly touched by the warming rays of a wholesome administration."[39]

When the central parliament was reconvened in 1861, Bukovina regained its autonomy and was again allowed representation through a provincial parliament or Diet consisting of thirty members. Initially presided over by Bishop Eugen Hakman, the province's new *Landeshauptmann* (provincial captain), it

FIGURE 2.1. Map of the mid-nineteenth century Habsburg Empire. In *Vollständiger Hand-Atlas der neueren Erdbeschreibung über alle Theile der Erde in 82 Blättern*, edited by Dr. K. Sohr, revised edition expanded and corrected by Dr. Heinrich Berghaus, with *Supplementband, 32 Blättern* (Glogau and Leipzig, 1855). By the time of the map's publication Bukovina had gained autonomy and was marked as a crown land separate from Galicia. Courtesy of David Rumsey Map Collection, Stanford Libraries.

was led from 1864 through 1874 by Eudoxiu Hurmuzaki, son of Doxaki.[40] He stood at the helm of the province's parliament, where (just as in the upper echelons of the administration) Romanian landowners and notables were in the majority: twenty-nine out of thirty-one seats in the provincial Diet were held by Romanians. With Bukovina's links to Galicia severed, Romanian elites established a monopoly on power. Almost all the presidents of the Diet and the *Landesausschuss* (provincial commission) over the next decades spoke Romanian.[41] Romanian elites in Bukovina ensured that theirs was the sole language of instruction at the theological institute in Czernowitz. They effectively turned the Orthodox Consistory into a Romanian institution, fiercely defending their right to appoint Romanian bishops and priests to church leadership positions.

## Making the *Großstadt*

Once Bukovina regained its autonomy, the locus of political and administrative power shifted to Czernowitz, which would soon be transformed into a modern administrative and cultural center. The city's development was aided by the extension of transportation and communication networks into the empire's eastern periphery in the 1860s. In 1866 Bukovinans could board a train in Czernowitz and arrive in Vienna seventeen hours later (compared to twenty-eight today).[42] The city was now connected to other provincial capitals and the imperial capital. Even more important was the liberal legislation that granted municipalities complete autonomy. The communal legislation of 1862 (*Gemeindeordnung*) created municipal councils (*Gemeinderäte*) across the monarchy, elected by all the male taxpayers in a city, entrusting decision-making to certain privileged members of the community.[43] Czernowitz gained municipal autonomy in March 1864, putting it on a developmental path very different from the surrounding countryside.

From the 1860s onward Czernowitz witnessed a construction frenzy that rendered it a near-replica of every other Austrian provincial capital. This was not because the imperial state imposed a style, but because local bourgeois elites wanted to signal their *Kultur* and their liberal values through monuments, street names, concert halls and theaters, and administrative buildings in the Neo-Baroque style.[44] As early as 1848, local engineers finished a new town hall on the Ringplatz, a handsome building with a fifty-meter (160-ft) clocktower. In 1864, work began on a residence for Bukovina's Greek-Oriental archbishop, the so-called *Residenzgebäude*, an architectural curiosity designed by the Czech architect Joseph Hlavka that combined Moorish, Byzantine, Romanic, and Gothic elements. On the initiative of a local Jewish politician and notable, Benno Straucher, a new train station was built in the lower city between 1906 and 1909. This new Hauptbahnhof, designed in the then fashionable *Jugendstil* (a Germanic counterpart to *art nouveau*), greeted visitors to Czernowitz: with its twenty-meter (65-ft) high cupola, statuary of the Greek goddess of peace Irene, and flower-holding cherubs, the central station was meant to convey "the hospitality and temperament of Bukovina."[45] The former Fischplatz, where on market day, peasant women with "white turbaned heads" and "colorful crowds" haggled, was cleaned up and renamed Elisabethplatz. Gone were the smells of "onion, garlic, cheese, herring." Jumping into the Prut without a swimming suit or wandering the streets drunk was now cause for arrest.[46]

The model for this new Czernowitz was distant, radiant Vienna, whose beauty and wonders local elites were determined to reproduce. If someone should introduce himself to a Czernowitzer as a "Wiener," they would respond, "And I am a Buko-Wiener!"[47] They were partly right, since Czernowitz's streets

FIGURE 2.2. The Ringplatz in Czernowitz, ca. 1860. Lithograph by Franz Xavier Knapp (1809–1883), an artist from Austrian Bohemia, published in the album *Illustrierte Bukowina* (Vienna, 1874). At this period Czernowitz was beginning to grow as an urban center. This square in front of the city hall hosted a weekly market. ÖNB Kartensammlung. Courtesy of the Österreichische Nationalbibliothek (ÖNB/Wien), WK1/ALB088/25685.

were named after Viennese avenues and its coffee houses and taverns imitated their counterparts in the capital.[48] Walking down Czernowitz's main street, predictably named Hauptstrasse, one arrived at the Ringplatz, where urban society convened, walked, visited taverns and cafes, and where all the luxury hotels were located.[49] Free to design a new theater for Czernowitz, *Gemeinderat* (municipal council) members sent a committee to Vienna to meet with the renowned architect Ferdinand Fellner (1847–1916). In May 1904, he traveled to Czernowitz to select the construction site: the former Fischplatz. Fellner noted that the city "reminded him of an old Austrian city which unfortunately many Austrian cities no longer felt like."[50] That was precisely the effect the *Gemeinderat* had hoped for.

The liberal-minded middle classes spearheaded the urbanization process, organizing and funding the expansion of the city's infrastructure. They nurtured *Kultur* in their ballrooms and homes, hosting Czernowitz's first music and literary societies. Local notables collected the money needed for their city to be included on the empire's cultural map, arranging guest performances by the likes of Franz Liszt, who performed at the Hotel de Moldavie in Czernowitz in 1867.[51] So many people filled the hotel's hall that evening that "the loges were in danger of collapsing," while a Romanian prince was said to have torn his gloves while applauding.[52] Sadly, such visits were rare, since traveling to Czernowitz was difficult and the city lacked a dedicated concert hall. Czernowitz elites considered raising the price of meat to help fund the construction of a new concert hall (the Musikverein).

The liberal state's *Kulturmission* in Bukovina, as in neighboring Galicia, was paid for by local elites.[53] This was due in part to a scarcity of resources in Vienna and also to Viennese prejudice and ignorance of the empire's eastern periphery. Although Bukovina's image began to improve in Vienna after the 1840s, many still saw it as "the most distant corner of civilization," a "kingdom of wolves and bears," and "Austrian Siberia."[54] Hard as its residents tried, Czernowitz could not rid itself of its reputation for "misery, moral degeneracy, ignorance, and corruption."[55] If the Viennese press mentioned the faraway city at all, it tended to be on account of some outrage or corruption, such as the scandal of 1871 when Czernowitz's newly completed railway line collapsed, revealing Bukovina once more as a "site of corruption, of arrogant chicanery, and worst of all, of downright failure."[56] These concerns were also aired in the local Czernowitz press, which took off during the 1880s, newspapers doubling in number by 1900 with titles such as the *Bukowinaer Rundschau, Bukowinaer Nachrichten,* and the dailies *Czernowitzer Tagblatt* and *Czernowitzer Allgemeine Zeitung,* widely read not only by native German-speakers but by most educated Bukovinans.[57] Like their counterparts in Kraków, Czernowitzers imagined themselves to be residing on the "cusp between European civilization and Asiatic barbarism."[58] Signs of provincialism such as "lack of manners, a boorish attitude towards art and artists, and a propensity for cheap pleasures" were documented and lamented by local journalists and feuilletonists.[59] Equally worrying was evidence of incompetence, nepotism, and corruption in the municipal administration.

In his 1908 imperial jubilee biography of Czernowitz, the historian Kaindl praised the imperial administration for all things good and modern in the city. He noted how, from the very outset, Austrian military officials in Bukovina had introduced urban institutions and features typically found in Western cities, such as a public safety apparatus and measures to prevent the spread of disease. Military authorities offered locals incentives to build homes of stone rather than wood and straw, thus checking the frequent fires and floods that had devastated the city. They paved the streets and stopped locals from littering and leaving dead cattle around. Concealed behind this image of perfect harmony and gratitude toward the imperial administration, however, was a good deal of anxiety about that administration's intentions where Bukovina was concerned.

Czernowitz's newspapers still lamented that city streets, although equipped with electric lights, were always dark. Tap water still came out brown and "heaps of trash lie around all over, emblematic of Asiatic culture."[60] A look beyond Czernowitz's main streets would reveal "a pile of trash and rubble, among it a large pit of stinking sewage, the surviving marker of Old-Czernowitz."[61] Urban elites internalized the notion that civilization in Czernowitz was fragile; they feared that as soon as they lowered their guard the city would again become the "playground of nomads."[62] Straw-covered huts would rise out of the earth. Naked children would play in empty fields. The specter of "Halb-Asien," as Karl Emil Franzos had dubbed this region between Europe and Asia, lurked behind the scenes, always threatening to reclaim Bukovina.

The *Czernowitzer Tagblatt* and *Czernowitzer Allgemeine Zeitung*, both edited by acculturated, German-speaking Jews, celebrated Austria's *Kulturmission* in the East. But by the late nineteenth century, as liberals lost their hold on the imperial government, they increasingly criticized the imperial state for failing to deliver on its promises: "They think it is enough for all threads to come together in Vienna," the *Czernowitzer Tagblatt* complained in 1903, "but this is not so. The threads must also go from the center to the remote north, south, west, and east. Especially to the east."[63] Vienna's reluctance to invest in Czernowitz left the empire's promise "to bring light and enlightenment to the land's furthest province" unfulfilled. The liberal press in Czernowitz agreed with Franzos when he said, "We are a country plunged into obscurity, a marsh in an enlightened Europe, a country that is neither loved nor hated, a country with no future, a sort of shame."[64] Instead of complaining that the imperial state was denying them the autonomy they deserved, the liberal bourgeoisie lamented the imperial state's remoteness. Czernowitz's liberals increasingly referred to themselves as "stepchildren" of the empire, devoted to their negligent parent, yet always forgotten. "Does the provincial capital really need to be so pressed against the wall every step of the way? [. . .] In Austria one has to yell to get anything done or to keep it from happening in the first place!"[65]

## The Jewish Bourgeoisie

In the words of Aharon Appelfeld, in Bukovina Jews were "the yeast that created the ferment" of modernization and urbanization.[66] They formed the bulk of the urban bourgeoisie and left a deep imprint on Czernowitz's urban landscape, so much so that contemporaries called it "Jerusalem on the Prut."[67] Jewish life and urban life developed in tandem in Czernowitz largely because the city and the community gained their autonomy around the same time. When Czernowitz became an autonomous municipality in March 1864, the city's population increased as people flocked in from Galicia and elsewhere to take up positions in the civil service and administration and benefit from new economic opportunities.[68] As Czernowitz grew, so did its Jewish population, which quadrupled from 4,678 in 1850 to 14,440 in 1880.[69] The Fundamental Rights, or Constitution, proclaimed by Emperor Franz Joseph on December 21, 1867 for Cisleithania (the empire's Austrian half) extended equal citizenship rights to Jews, paving the way for the era dubbed "the Golden Age of Bukovina Jewry."[70]

This was the culmination of a series of reforms going back to the eighteenth century, when Emperor Joseph II's edict of tolerance gave Jews permission to "carry on all kinds of trade without the right to citizenship and mastership from which they remain excluded." But in exchange for being tolerated, the emperor had expected Jews to acquiesce in his cameralist centralizing project. Jews were required to take German names and "send their children to the Christian primary and secondary schools so that they have at least the opportunity to learn reading, writing, and arithmetic."[71] Jewish communities could no longer keep their autonomous administration (the kahal) but came under the purview of the state through a new administrative body, the Kultusgemeinde.[72] Before the 1840s, most Bukovinan Jews were religious and Yiddish-speaking, much like Galician Jews. Hasidism took off in Bukovina late, in the 1840s, when a Rabbi Friedmann, fleeing the Russian authorities, opened a Hasidic court in Sadagora.[73] A vibrant Hasidic culture developed not just there, but in Wischnitz (Vyzhnytsia in Ukrainian), nurtured by the inflow of Orthodox Jews from Galicia. When Bukovina's links with Galicia were severed in 1849 and 1861, its Orthodox Jewish community became increasingly isolated from Galicia's Hasidic world. The segment—initially small—of Bukovina's Jewish population that began adopting German names and going to German-language schools was increasingly at an advantage over Orthodox Jews.[74]

The Jewish community formally split into two branches—Orthodox and progressive—when two different rabbis were elected in 1871–72. Only the progressive rabbi was recognized as a grand rabbi, a sign that acculturated Jews enjoyed higher legitimacy and greater state support. Bukovina's Jewish community was also divided spatially. Separated from the capital by the river Prut, the Hasidic community was confined to the city's outskirts. Within Czernowitz, divisions emerged between the wealthier, assimilated Jews who lived in the city center and the lower classes crowded into the "lower city," also known as the Judenvertiel. Not quite a ghetto in the traditional sense, the Judenviertel was a world of its own, crowded and loud in the early morning, when men rushed to the synagogue and women to the market. Jewish homes, historian Hermann Sternberg recalled, had basements from which "women sold bread, pretzels, and other baked goods and sweets."[75]

Jews who left the Judenviertel and made their way up the hill to the city center did so through the schools. German-language public schools were the

FIGURE 2.3. With this late nineteenth-century postcard one could send "Greetings from Bukovina," Austria's most multiethnic crown land. The image highlights Bukovina's diversity by displaying different ethnic groups side by side: Romanians, Hutsuls, Lipovenians, Ruthenians—and an Orthodox Jew in the center, who remains unnamed and marginal. Courtesy of the Biblioteca Națională a României.

Jewish community's ticket to bourgeois respectability, transforming them from quintessential outsiders into allies of the imperial administration and urban powerbrokers.[76] By 1914, about 95 percent of Bukovinan Jews had declared German their official language.[77] The Bukovinan poet Paul Celan's friend and biographer Israel Chalfen recalled that "everywhere in the city one could hear their Bukovinan German, with its Austrian informality and Slavic breadth, and interwoven with Yiddish idioms."[78] Because middle-class Jews who educated their children in German schools were so numerous in Czernowitz, German became the dominant language in the city.[79] The Austrian census counted German-speaking Jews in Bukovina among the province's German population, since Jews were not recognized as a separate ethnicity, and as far as the census was concerned the most important category was "language of daily use" or *Umgangssprache*.

From having been objects of Germanization policies in the eighteenth century, Bukovinan Jews thus turned into agents of Germanization and champions of German culture and language in a province whose ethnic German population was too small to justify or sustain German's status as a lingua franca and *Staatssprache*. Reflecting on the enduring love of Jews for the German language, Bukovinan Zionist Mayer Ebner later wrote that "the Jews have not felt such love and loyalty for any other people in the world as they did for the German people [. . .]. They took the German language with them into exile and they elevated and cultivated it and turned it into a language of the Jewish people and these Jews were the ones who turned the German language into a world language [. . .] and even the poorest caftan-wearing Jew in Barnow loves and respects Schiller as though he were part of the canon of Biblical writings."[80]

*Pace* Ebner, this love of German was not a love for "the German people." In Bukovina, as elsewhere, Jews embraced German language and *Kultur* for their promise of economic success and mobility. They did not view the German language as the exclusive possession of one ethnic group, but rather, as Austro-German liberals did, as a vehicle for humanist, universal values that any group could access. Their attachment to German was also an attachment to the monarchy, since it was the unofficial language of the imperial state and the emperor, whom Bukovinan Jews saw as their patron and protector. As Rabbi Josef Brodfeld said in his speech on the emperor's sixtieth jubilee at the reformed temple on Elisabethplatz, "the emperor has elevated us from slaves into state citizens with full rights, has put us on the same level with our beloved Christian brothers from a legal and economic point of view (and) is watching over the safety of our persons and possessions through wise laws, and has graciously opened up all state offices and honors to us."[81]

Acculturated Jews took their German identity very seriously. In 1908 Benno Straucher, the leader of Czernowitz's Jewish community, and a shrewd politician, rejected a request to host the world's first International Yiddish Language Conference in the newly built Jewish National Home on Elisabethplatz.[82] The conference's mastermind Nathan Birnbaum, a Viennese-born journalist and champion of "cultural autonomism" for Jews, had selected Czernowitz because the city had a reputation for multilingualism and tolerance.[83] What better place to convene all the luminaries of Yiddish language and literature than Czernowitz, where all languages—as Birnbaum naively thought—were equal? "In the evening we stroll through the street and the sounds of various languages emerge from the windows," wrote Yiddish writer Leib Peretz; "we want to have our own window, our own independent theme in the symphony of peoples."[84]

Unfortunately for Birnbaum, Straucher wanted nothing to do with a conference trying to elevate the Yiddish "jargon" into a national language of the Jewish people. The Jewish National Home, "designed to reflect the refined, modern imperial sensibility, with four massive Atlantes, giant nude male statues [. . .] positioned as if supporting the weight of the four-story structure," was an expression of Czernowitz Jews' desire to part with their Yiddish heritage and signal their full membership in the "civilized" world.[85] The conference rented rooms in the Ruthenian National Home.

Karl Emil Franzos, whose father read him Schiller and Lessing, shared Straucher's disgust for Yiddish, associating it with the Orthodox Jewish masses untouched by *Kultur*.[86] In the book, discussed above, for which he was most famous, *Halb Asien*, Franzos depicted Orthodox Jews as smelly and dirty, an eyesore, with their "caftans and earlocks, arguing, cajoling, yelling, whispering, bumping and tugging at each other, so incredibly dirty that it is hard to believe they wouldn't stick together as soon as they collided."[87] The author of this anti-Semitic slander was himself Jewish, but he had only discovered this accidentally, when a neighbor's child pointed at him: "Look at the little Jew!" To this, Franzos responded, "Liar! I am German!"—for, as he later wrote, the only Jews he knew were "dirty people in caftans whose language I didn't understand."[88]

Czernowitz became a symbol of German–Jewish symbiosis and a major center of Jewish acculturation in Eastern Europe,[89] with its sizable Jewish population (33 percent of the city's population by 1890) representing a wide variety of bourgeois professions,[90] and making it the fourth largest Jewish center in the monarchy after Vienna, Lemberg, and Krakow. Czernowitz Jews worked building trams and trains, in taverns and coffee houses, as producers and sellers of furniture, and in the building trade. They ran hotels and sugar factories and mineral oil refineries.[91] They owned small shops, worked in the food and wood industries, and among them were both skilled and unskilled laborers. They formed over one third of Czernowitz's industry and trade sector and constituted the majority of employees in commerce and transportation services. They played key roles in financing and carrying out Czernowitz's urbanization from the 1860s onward, helping run its municipal structures, where they mixed and mingled with Romanians and Austrian-Germans, and developed new political careers.

Nowhere was the intertwining of Jewish and urban life in Czernowitz more clearly to be seen than in Czernowitz's *Gemeinderat*, where acculturated Jews (the chair David Rothman, the councilors David and Naftali Tittinger, Bernard Baltinester, and others) played leading roles.[92] The influential position occupied by Czernowitz's Jewish bourgeoisie is demonstrated by the election of two Jewish mayors, Eduard Reiss (1905–8) and Salo von Weisselberger (1913–14),[93] and in the urban landscape, featuring such monuments to Jewish acculturation as the Schiller Theater on Elisabethplatz, the concert hall (Musikverein), the centrally located Moorish-style synagogue built in 1877, and the Jewish National House overlooking the theater.[94]

FIGURE 2.4. Postcard (1910) of the "Israelite Temple" in Czernowitz, built in 1873, and home to the city's large reformed Jewish congregation. Compare this with the same synagogue—or what is left of it—today (see Figure 0.1). *Source*: http://czernowitz.ehpes.com/czernowitz7/new-sternberg/image17.htm.

## Illiteracy and "Study Fury"

Bukovina was one of Austria's most impoverished crown lands, the economic periphery of an empire that was increasingly integrated. Along with Galicia and Dalmatia, Bukovina had the lowest GDP per capita in the 1880s: 319 crowns as opposed to 850 crowns in Bohemia. The economic disparities between Bukovina and other parts of the empire reflected distance and topography.[95] Its location at the empire's easternmost extremity meant that its economy was connected more closely with Congress Poland's, Hungary's, and Romania's than with the rest of Cisleithania's.[96] Ernst Mischler, the head of the province's Statistical Office, pointed out in 1892 that Bukovina was the third lowest contributor to the empire's budget (Salzburg and Dalmatia were even lower): providing just 1.1 percent in 1870. Compare this with how much it cost: 4.1 percent of the empire's budget went to cover the province's administrative expenses.[97] But Mischler also emphasized that the empire was investing much less in the province than was in fact needed: state institutions were spread thin and "both in the domain of river regulation and other hydraulic structures, as well as in that of rural management, there is still an enormous amount to be done in Bukovina." Moreover, Mischler thought that the imperial state should adjust its expectations to Bukovina's realities instead of demanding the same things from it as from other provinces, "irrespective of whether [Bukovina] has the financial means necessary for this."[98]

Like Galicia and Dalmatia, Bukovina had a primarily agricultural economy that was deeply shaped by centuries of feudalism. The abolition of serfdom in 1848 brought peasants both advantages and drawbacks. Though they could own property, they no longer had direct access to landowners' pastures and forests, instead renting them or sub-leasing them from other tenants.[99] Land remained concentrated in the hands of a few landowners, primarily the Greek-Oriental, or Orthodox, Church. By the turn of the twentieth century, the Orthodox Church in Bukovina owned over three hundred large estates, numerous villages, and forests worth over 16 million florins. Putna Monastery alone owned fifty-nine villages and 267 estates and employed over seven thousand peasant families. The enduring tradition of partible inheritance, in which property was divided equally among all heirs rather than being passed down to a single successor, had fragmented peasant-owned land into small strips that could not sustain much more than subsistence agriculture. Over 90 percent of the portions of land owned by private individuals in Bukovina were under five hectares in extent, and in the Kotzman district and other areas, over 98 percent of peasant households owned little or no land at all.[100]

Unlike Galicia, which developed a booming oil industry in the nineteenth century, Bukovina accommodated only small industrial enterprises and most of its limited revenue came from the export of raw materials to industrial centers further west.[101] In 1902, over 4,500 of Bukovina's 9,360 registered industrial enterprises had only one employee.[102] While Lower Austria boasted 2,228 factories by 1902, Bukovina counted only ninety-eight, most producing spirits and beer. Although Bukovinan wood, pigs, and cattle were in demand in Bohemia, Moravia, Silesia, and Germany, the transportation costs from the remote province made these goods less competitive.[103]

The liberal government of the 1860s and liberals in the province attributed Bukovina's economic afflictions to its population's low educational level and assumed the problem could be fixed by increasing school attendance and raising literacy rates. Although the relationship between economic development and literacy levels was arguably more complicated than that, the two were indeed correlated. In 1880, only 9.1 percent of Bukovina's population could read and write, compared to 49.9 percent in Austria-Hungary overall.[104] By 1910 literacy rates had increased, but still only 58 percent of its population could read and write, compared to 83.5 percent in the rest of the empire.[105] Illiteracy primarily affected the rural, Christian population: by one estimate, over 75 percent of Bukovina's Ruthenian-speaking population and over 71 percent of its Romanian-speakers were illiterate.[106]

An empire-wide school law issued in 1869 (the *Reichsvolksschulgesetz*) opened all state-supported schools to all confessions and made school attendance for children aged from six to fourteen compulsory.[107] Individual provinces bore the costs of expanding the school system, and they could decide whether a new school would open and in what language its students would study. To accommodate Bukovina's lower level of economic development, a new law was issued in 1873, especially for the province, that transferred the financial burden from individual communities to the *Landesschulfond*—the provincial school fund. The one exception was Czernowitz, whose municipality was expected to cover the costs directly.[108]

The laws increased the number of public schools in Bukovina: from fifty in 1850 to 252 in 1885, a higher growth rate than anywhere else in Cisleithania (22.3 percent as opposed to 5.6 percent).[109] These numbers obscured the fact that most schools were makeshift institutions that were poorly equipped to attract a rural population already hostile to them. Many schools had only one classroom and one teacher. According to a report from 1871, in some villages students shared space with cattle, and one inspector noted that "[i]n the few cases where I found school houses with brick walls, the water seeped through the walls, so they were covered in dry mold."[110] Three decades later, in a speech before Bukovina's Diet, Jewish politician Benno Straucher noted that some schools were housed in former morgues or community jails, "or in stables covered in fungus [. . .] so that when children come home they can't do their homework but need to be cleaned up by their parents first."[111] The girls' school in Suczawa served as the town council headquarters, and classes were often interrupted by noises from the cattle market down the street.

Most schools existed, as the *Czernowitzer Tagblatt* noted, "only on paper and they are also treated as such." Of 306 public schools recorded in Bukovina in 1891–2, only seventy-one ran on a full schedule, and eighty-two were in too poor a state to accommodate students.[112] Although the school laws of 1869 said no student could be forced to learn a second language in school, in reality many students in Bukovina's public schools had no choice but to learn a variety of languages, due to the mixed-language character of many schools.[113] A shortage of resources forced children who spoke different languages into the same classroom, where teachers would have to "present each explanation, indeed each sentence in three different languages."[114] That was the least of the teachers' problems. When a new school was built in the village of Woloka, the first teacher to take up residence there was chased out with stones. Ten years later, he reported that the school "never had many children except for the children of relatives [of the teacher], the priest, or the village forester."[115]

Perhaps the greatest obstacle to raising literacy levels in Bukovina was overcoming the rural population's resistance to schooling. Fewer than 11 percent of school-age children attended regularly in 1871.[116] Since children were an important source of labor in this deeply agricultural society, school was regarded not just as an inconvenience, but as "an evil that Beelzebub himself shrewdly concocted for the misery of the people."[117] If peasants could not be persuaded to send their children to school, perhaps, imperial officials thought, they could be coerced. First, the Hofkriegsrat (Court War Council, in Vienna) encouraged local officials to reward school attendance with prizes such as clothing and medals. When this failed, they introduced fines or several days of imprisonment for parents of truants.[118] Teachers, school principals, and community leaders were urged to implement the school regulations without compromise.[119] Local notables and intelligentsia had diverging opinions on the *Schulzwang* (compulsory school attendance). Some thought that "without *Schulzwang* there is no *Kultur*," and that fining the peasantry was an "act of culture" like any other.[120] Without it, they feared that Bukovina's population would never be anything but a "raw people who lives by wild instinct and fills the prison cells."[121]

When school attendance levels increased (from below 11 percent in 1871 to 88 percent in 1902–3), this did not mean that the rural population had been convinced of the importance of educating their children.[122] It was the urban, predominantly Jewish population that flocked to schools, turning Czernowitz's *Gymnasia* into the most overcrowded in the whole Austrian monarchy.[123] In 1864, those attending the No. 1 Staatsgymnasium in Czernowitz had to be split into four parallel classes. As many as 980 students were enrolled in 1899, and by 1903 this number had soared to 1,750.[124] The *Czernowitzer Tagblatt* predicted that Bukovina would soon be "flooded with students."[125] In 1906, over 56 percent of the student body were German-speakers, of whom over 40 percent were Jewish.[126]

Feeding into this *Studierwut*, or "study fury," as contemporaries called it, was the dearth of economic options in Bukovina. Without industry, the best option was to join the ranks of the province's civil servants, lawyers, or professors. "If there were workers' demonstrations for the intellectual professions," the *Tagblatt* quipped in July 1914, "our *Doktoren* would be marching in a long, long line."[127] By the turn of the twentieth century, Jews made up over 40 percent of the student body at Czernowitz's Francisco-Josephina university, inaugurated in 1875.[128]

## A German University

In 1879, the first Austrian conservative constitutional government came to power, and liberals moved into the opposition. Increasingly on the defensive, they had to recalibrate their ambitions. Some reaffirmed their faith in Austria's *Kulturmission* in the East, while others, their liberal faith shaken, embraced a narrower conception of Germanness, as nationalist conflict came to the fore in Austrian domestic politics. Having pushed for greater autonomy from Vienna, Galician Poles now dominated their province's cultural and political institutions. Lemberg University, once a German-language institution, now taught only in Polish. Prague University split into two sections: one German, the other Czech.[129] By 1875, petitions from universities in Zara, Trieste, and Küstenland asking to split into separate language sections had reached the emperor's desk.[130]

Then came Bukovina's petition, the last in a series of petitions the notables in various localities forwarded to the emperor over more than a decade. In 1851 there had been talk of opening a law school in Bukovina, for sons of the Moldavian landowning nobility. Members of the provincial aristocracy who helped found a provincial public library had hoped to lay the foundations for a larger institution of higher learning in the province.[131] For many, having a university in Czernowitz was the logical follow-up to Bukovina's new autonomy. In 1868 Bukovinan elites again appealed to the parliament in Vienna for permission to open a university in Czernowitz—to no avail.

Remarkably, given developments elsewhere in the empire, in 1875 Bukovina petitioned again—this time specifying that the university would use German.[132] As the Romanian-Ruthenian liberal politician Constantin Tomaszczuk put it, "Bukovina's non-German sons also strive for a German university because German education has universal significance."[133] Now Bukovina lagged behind the rest of Austria in a new arena: that of nationalism. Nationalism was on the rise in the province, but without the intensity and clout it had elsewhere. Ruthenian nationalism was in its early stages, as Bukovina's Ruthenians did not yet include a solid educated class. Romanian national politics was still young, confined to a small circle of notables and landowners focused on cultivating Romanian poetry and literature, not party politics. Men like Tomaszczuk, born of Romanian and Ruthenian parents, still spoke German and could be described by members of the United German Left (Vereinigte Linke) in Bukovina as "so replete with German *Bildung* that he could represent our interests just like a German."[134]

A staunch liberal, Tomaszczuk deployed the most persuasive liberal rhetoric he could muster to argue that it was in the imperial state's interest to respond favorably to Bukovina's petition.[135] He said that building a new

FIGURE 2.5. Dr. Constantin Tomaszczuk, "Reichsraths-Abgeordneter" (member of the imperial parliament) (n.d.). ÖNB Bildarchiv und Grafiksammlung. Courtesy of the Österreichische Nationalbibliothek (ÖNB/Wien), PORT_00070358_01.

university was like building a "spiritual lighthouse in the midst of these multilingual peoples, giving them all the same light," and added that using German as the main language of instruction would buck the trend toward "provincialization" seen in other Austrian institutions of higher learning, where German had been replaced by "lesser" languages.[136] "Ever since the Polish language was introduced as the language of instruction," Tomaszczuk complained of his alma mater in Lemberg, that university and Kraków's had "become provincial institutes, without the possibility or desire to establish contact with other universities and cultural movements in the monarchy."[137] Educated in law, philosophy, and history, Tomaszczuk had moved to Hermannstadt in Transylvania to take up a civil service position. When he discovered that civil servants there were required to speak Hungarian (since 1867), he resigned and returned to Bukovina, where he could speak German undisturbed. Convinced of the German language's universalism and capacity for bringing people together, he wanted to ensure it retained its privileged position in Bukovina.

Tomaszczuk and other liberals believed that a German-language university would make Bukovina a microcosmic model of the liberal Austrian empire. The province would exemplify what Austria was all about: the *Kulturarbeit* through which it had transformed this territory and others "from a desert into the protected province of a civilized state."[138] Or, as the Jewish future mayor of Czernowitz Eduard Reiss put it, the university in Bukovina would help carry "the Promethean spark of human culture and education eastward."[139] Opening a university this far east would promote the "consolidation of Austrian state unity."[140] "Austrian universities," Tomaszczuk believed, "have contributed more than any other institutions to fostering the consolidation of Austrian state unity," which rested "on the shared educational path [*Bildungsgang*] of all those who go beyond the level of the popular masses in their education." *Bildung*—education—and *Kultur*, Tomaszczuk argued, were "at the heart and soul of loyalty to the state": "if the state, this great social community, rests on a unity of wills [. . .] then the social community will be all the more powerful and the state will be more likely to achieve its goals." Austria's unity, in other words, had to be created and cultivated through "the most intensive, homogeneous *Bildung*, especially on the monarchy's farthest eastern border."[141]

To everyone's surprise, the emperor approved Bukovina's petition in the spring of 1875. Though many liberals in the Reichsrat doubted the viability of an institution of higher learning so far from Vienna, their qualms were ignored. The university would be inaugurated in October as a gift from Emperor Franz Joseph to Bukovina on the anniversary of 150 years of Austrian governance, "the most beautiful and the best of gifts [. . . ,] a nursery of intellectual work, a cradle of free scholarship, a temple of science!"[142] The university was presented as the culmination of Austria's *Kulturmission* in Bukovina, and unity and harmony through *Kultur* were the leitmotif of the anniversary festivities.[143] As the province's Croatian-born, Italian-speaking governor Gieronimo Freiherr von Alesani said in his speech, "in Bukovina any kind of difference disappears and the Bukovinan knows only one nationality which is called 'Austrian,' because the Bukovinan is above all simply an Austrian."[144] Officials pointed to the "Romanian and Ruthenian, German, Hungarian, and Slovak peasant boys and girls, Lipovenians and Gypsies" participating in the festivities to underline that "the most varied languages and nationalities are represented here and yet the harmony with which the entire province celebrated this significant day is not typical of this day only."[145]

Thus Bukovina, one of the empire's most illiterate provinces, where primary schools were housed in former morgues and cattle barns, came to have a university. Imperial officials found it expedient to approve Bukovina's petition because it reinforced the notion of Austria's civilizing mission in the east at a time when the empire badly needed to shore up this old notion. "The university of Czernowitz," Tomaszczuk effused, "has entered the circle of Austrian universities to apply here in the East everything that Germany has taught and to convey here the spiritual richness that comes from Germany. This is how the much-maligned Austrian cultural mission in the East is to be understood."[146] At the same time as the Austrian *Kulturmission* was being maligned by non-German nationalists, however, Austria's relationship with Germany, which Tomaszczuk took for granted, was being called into question. After 1871, with the emergence of Prussia, Austria was no longer the hegemonic German power in Europe.

With uncertainty growing for Austria internationally and domestically, Bukovina's anniversary was a chance underscore the imperial state's purpose. Czernowitz's mayor Anton Freiherr von Kochanowski declared that with the university's inauguration, Austria had fulfilled its promise to bring Bukovina into the circle of *Kulturstaaten*. Friedrich Schuler von Libloy, the university dean and professor of law, contrasted the Austrian administration's achievements in Bukovina with those of its predecessors. Unlike the Ottomans, Austria ruled not through force, but through "humanity, tolerance, work, and loyalty to the royal house of the monarchy." Rather than build churches, Libloy noted, Austria had built schools and roads and bridges so that "love of truth, and a spirit of duty, lit up and led by the torch of science, which casts its light over these lands, have replaced slavish obedience."[147]

Important as it was in providing Austria with a sense of purpose, Bukovina's university project succeeded for a more mundane reason: because it promised to be cheap. Bukovina's public library could be repurposed as a university library. Its *Gymnasia* could become lecture halls. Here, as elsewhere, the rhetoric of *Kultur* sought to compensate for the absence of resources. It was surely not a good sign that the emperor declined to attend the festivities for budgetary reasons, writing that "although it is my most ardent wish to visit the land of Bukovina I cannot exceed the budget [. . .] given current economic conditions."[148] When the university opened in the fall of 1875, it had no dedicated building, and students and faculty wandered between temporary locations. There was limited space for storing equipment and books, which often remained exposed to the elements. The library lacked a reading room, so students huddled in crowded spaces, some reading standing up. Water and gas light were scarce, and professors used sheets of cardboard as desks.[149]

Because homegrown educated elites were sparse, faculty had to be imported from across the empire and beyond. This proved a challenge, since many viewed the remote university as an "academic penal colony," where serious research was impossible due to the months-long wait for books to be delivered.[150] When the Galician-born professor of English literature Leon Kellner was preparing to take up a university position, his colleague Matthias Friedwagner, a teacher of Romance languages, warned him "to bring a maid from Vienna because the only ones available here are Ruthenian women who have nothing but a shirt and coat and who celebrate all holidays together with you, in addition to their own holidays."[151] The university did not become the cultural magnet optimistic liberals had envisioned. Students from Galicia and Moldavia continued to study at home or in France. Its only major asset was its school of theology, the only place that offered Greek-Oriental (Greek Orthodox) law, theology, and Church Slavonic classes, which attracted students from Serbia, Bosnia, Romania, Bulgaria, and Greece.[152]

Despite its many shortcomings, the university came to play a crucial role in the province—just not the anticipated one. It became an incubator for a new generation of local intellectuals, non-German-speakers, many of rural origin, who would soon challenge the liberal consensus. It thus embodied one of the liberal state's key ironies: liberalism's tendency to dig its own grave by laying the foundations for anti-liberal critique. The preconditions were already present in 1875, when Romanian federalists in Bukovina refused to participate in the anniversary celebrations.[153] Romanian landowner Alecu Hurmuzaki challenged the project, noting that only one tenth of Bukovina's population was fluent in German.

What Tomaszczuk and his allies had failed to anticipate was that German forms could be vehicles for non-German content—that universalism could further particularism. Thoroughly German institutions such as the student dueling societies (*Burschenschaften*) were adopted by non-Germans at the university in Czernowitz, but perpetuated differences rather than eliding them.[154] The Romanian society "Arboroasa," a German-style *Burschenschaft* founded by a former member of the Romanian student society in Vienna, became a center of Romanian irredentism in Bukovina. Its members met in September 1877 in the Orthodox Metropolitan's residence in Czernowitz and decided to send a letter of condolence to the Moldavian capital of Jassy, commemorating Prince Grigore Ghika, who lost Bukovina to the Habsburgs and was then assassinated by the Ottoman Porte.[155] When governor Alesani got wind of this, he ordered that Arboroasa's headquarters be searched and the society dissolved. Some members, among them the Romanian composer Ciprian Porumbescu, then a student in Czernowitz, were arrested. Later pardoned for writing the incendiary letter, which the defense called a "children's game," the Arboroasa society would play a crucial role in forging ties between ethnic Romanians in Bukovina and their co-nationals in the Old Kingdom.

Not long after, the Francisco-Josephina found itself following the trend established at other universities in the empire: although German endured much longer there than elsewhere, by the 1880s departments representing different ethnicities were proliferating. In 1881 the Romanian intelligentsia founded a separate chair in Romanian language and literature. Four years later, a similar chair in Ruthenian language and literature was established, to appease the Ruthenian intelligentsia. The department of history soon split in two: East

European history, whose chair was occupied by a Ruthenian, and South-Eastern European history, whose occupant, Professor Ion Nistor, would become the poster child of Romanian irredentism in Bukovina.[156]

## Recession and Emigration

The "current economic conditions" Emperor Franz Joseph had referred to in excusing himself from a visit to Bukovina were the consequence of one of the largest economic recessions Austria had ever seen. The collapse of the Creditanstalt bank in Vienna pushed the country into a decade of financial trouble that hit agricultural regions like Bukovina especially hard.[157] Though better off than their counterparts in Moldavia and Russian-ruled Bessarabia, Bukovinan peasants earned half the daily income and had higher rates of infant mortality and disease than other Austrian peasants. In 1910, for instance, over half the newborn babies in Bukovina died shortly after birth, which was perhaps hardly surprising since the province had only six general physicians, and poor hygiene and nutrition were endemic.[158] As the Ruthenian newspaper *Hromadyanin* reported in July 1910, most Bukovinan peasants lived on "borscht with beans and a lump of polenta," while children survived on watery soup and potatoes.[159]

As the recession began to take a hold in the countryside, conditions worsened as cash-strapped peasants took out loans they were unable to repay. Peasants usually borrowed from tavern keepers and informal lenders, many Jewish, although by the 1890s new credit societies and village cooperatives had been founded, largely by nationalist politicians, to protect peasants from usury.[160] As it turned out, however, these institutions only aggravated the problem, because loans "were too expensive due to costly formalities" and peasants were "wrongly induced to take out more money than they needed to."[161] As late as 1911, according to the Ruthenian-language newspaper *Ruskaya Pravda*, the Ukrainian association Selyanska Kassa had pushed one peasant to give up his cow as interest on a loan and then sell his land to pay off a debt of 2,000 crowns. "As well as me," the peasant complained, "the Ukrainian Kassa in Rostok emptied the bags of many other people."[162] In the year 1908 alone, over 674 peasant holdings in Bukovina, most of them under five hectares, were sold off to repay debts.[163]

This was the backdrop for Bukovina's largest rural emigration wave, which peaked in the 1890s, when imperial officials reported that in some villages "only the few, most prosperous people" stayed put.[164] The mass exodus continued into the early twentieth century. Between 1901 and 1910, almost 5 percent of Bukovina's population emigrated.[165] The exodus surprised imperial officials both because of its epic proportions and the way it revealed peasants to be less predictable and harder to reach than the authorities had thought. As one official noted, Bukovinan peasants had never been "characterized by an enterprising spirit, but always by a notorious attachment to their *Heimat*."[166] Helpless to prevent the emigration, imperial officials blamed "foreign agents" who infiltrated the countryside and manipulated uneducated, volatile peasants into selling their possessions to purchase tickets for Canada, the United States, or Brazil.[167]

When the authorities caught an "agitator" in Bukovina in 1897, he turned out to be a local Ruthene who had "concluded an agreement with the general agencies in Bremen, Kaarez and Stocki, and in Hamburg, von Karlsberg, to increase the number of emigrants."[168] Peasants who returned from America with stories of success did more than anyone else to increase emigration. One emigrant returned to Rosch after working in America for a few months, and when he left again, several other families went with him.[169] Locals also helped translate advertisements issued by international travel bureaux in Bremen, London, and Hamburg into local languages. The Austrian police found pamphlets from emigration agencies such as Zeppelin, Compass, Columbus, and Sirecky with "headers in Ruthenian and Romanian languages. The Ruthenian letterhead describes the bureau as 'the Ruthenian Agency,' the Romanian one as a 'Christian Bureau.'"[170]

Through rural emigration overseas, the remote province of Bukovina became plugged into global labor markets and responsive to global economic shifts.[171] After 1866, when the Austrian railway system was extended east to Czernowitz, Bukovinans could travel to Vienna and Germany, where many peasants did seasonal labor. The railway connected Bukovina with the rest of the world by putting port cities like Bremen, Hamburg, and Trieste, from where transatlantic liners departed for the Americas, within its reach. Bukovina's modernization did not bring the province immediate prosperity, but it offered Bukovinans a new solution to local economic problems: emigration.

Once again, a problem originating at Austria's periphery spurred reflection and hand-wringing at the center, where officials and the public began questioning the monarchy's mission and position on the international stage. Imperial officials, as Tara Zahra has shown, were anxious about Austria's place in global civilizational hierarchies, since Austrian emigrants to the Americas often ended up doing the work of former slaves.[172] In places like Brazil, state governments prized Bukovinan and Galician emigrants because they were white. In their new homes, peasant emigrants who had been considered backward and uncivilized back home were now seen as representative of European civilization. Although they were not explicitly instructed to do so, Austrian consuls often treated Bukovinan emigrants as extensions of the empire overseas. In Brazil, Austrian consuls worked hard to maintain emigrants' ties to their homeland, paying regular visits to their settlements and mediating between them and the Brazilian authorities to improve living standards.[173] They sometimes took it upon themselves to provide emigrants with last-resort assistance should they need to return home. This view of the emigrants as agents of an informal Austrian empire overseas was shared by contemporaries who thought Austria should follow the example of Italy and Spain, states that treated mass emigration as a kind of informal empire-building.[174]

Ironically, rural emigration from Bukovina accelerated the province's modernization, though not along the lines the imperial administration had anticipated and in ways it could not fully control. Peasants who emigrated wanted a traditional life that they could not afford at home, where an individual's worth continued to be measured in acres. Most emigrants hoped either to acquire land overseas or, after the American frontier closed, to work there for a few years, then return to Bukovina to purchase land with their savings. Emigrants transformed village economies in Bukovina through infusions of money, which drove up land prices, pushing more peasants overseas.[175] Even more importantly, peasants who went abroad channeled new ideas through the "rich two-way traffic" between them and their villages of origin, sustained through webs of "communication, travel, employment assistance, social control, and household management."[176] Transplanted into new environments, the emigrants developed new attitudes toward authority.[177] For many, emigration was also their first serious exposure to nationalism, through nationalist-run diaspora organizations that helped emigrants with their daily needs.[178] With the money and experience they gained overseas, Bukovinan emigrants transformed the countryside arguably more than the army of teachers and administrative officials eager to bring *Kultur* to the masses ever had.

---

From the 1890s through the 1910s, a series of electoral reforms radically expanded the franchise in the monarchy, bringing new groups into the political process and giving rise to a new generation of politicians who appealed primarily to this new constituency.[179] In Bukovina, most of them were products of the university in Czernowitz, profoundly shaped by liberal ideas and institutions—which they now criticized as elitist and oppressive. Instead, these new politicians advocated a more democratic politics, which as we shall see in the following chapters, took nationalizing and anti-liberal forms. In Bukovina too, the new professional politicians of the 1890s and 1900s helped precipitate a growing nationalization of social and political life. Initially, these new men defined their movement in opposition to the politics of the older landowning class that had dominated Bukovina's parliament since 1848. But anti-Semitism quickly began to provide their otherwise fragmented political agenda with a sense of direction and unity.

And yet, the nationalists who sought to reshape the imperial state in Bukovina at the turn of the century did so by continuing to use, in historian John Boyer's words, "traditional liberal political techniques."[180] Anti-liberals, while creating a new "social imagination,"[181] recycled liberal concepts and principles they inherited from institutions (courts and schools) that continued to uphold and propagate liberal values.[182] Although they no longer recognized German *Kultur* as a universal good, nationalists in Bukovina retained the liberal belief in culture as the preferred solution to economic and political conflict. They imbued the old concept of culture with new meaning, yet the critique of liberalism they offered, as Andrew Sartori writes about Bengali "culturalism," came "from within liberal modes of universalism."[183] The "new political men" were committed to the pursuit of modernization, which they hoped to achieve through literacy and education—and imperial state institutions.

# 3
# National Dreams

DEEPLY FASCINATED by the Byzantine empire and its afterlife, Nicolae Iorga traveled to Bukovina in 1905 to study the relics of Moldavia's golden age.[1] Born in the northeast of Moldavia, Iorga had moved to Bucharest, where he taught history at the university and led the "Liga pentru unitatea culturală a tuturor românilor" (League for the cultural unity of all Romanians). Founded in 1891, the Liga had become "one of the most important avenues for constructing national ideals in the cultural realm and connecting them to a political agenda."[2] In the summer, Iorga organized schools in the Romanian mountain town of Vălenii de Munte, with lectures on Romanian history and literature and networking events to connect Romanians from the Old Kingdom with their co-nationals in Transylvania, Bukovina, and Bessarabia.

To nationalists like Iorga, Bukovina was first and foremost the home of the relics of Stephen the Great, the medieval Moldavian prince they considered "the founder of our people."[3] Because it contained a large number of Orthodox monasteries, the province symbolized what nationalists saw as Romanian civilization's European mission: defending Christianity from barbarism. By the late nineteenth century Austrian Bukovina had become a destination for Romanian nationalist pilgrimages. In 1871, four years before the anniversary of the province's centennial under Austrian rule, Romanians gathered at Stephen the Great's grave in Putna to commemorate the four hundredth anniversary of the monastery's founding. The Bucharest paper *Românul* reported, "In this wonderful, charming place, where each hill has a legend and a *doina* [folk melody] sighs in every river; where every corner is bound up with memory of past deeds; in this place university youth are celebrating the memory of Stephen the Great, the builder of Putna monastery."[4] Naturally, Iorga could not travel to Bukovina without paying his respects to Putna. But what he found there filled him with bitterness and despair.

He began his journey through Bukovina in Suczawa, once medieval Moldova's capital, but now, it seemed, conquered and subdued by "the people of Israel." The former princely city was in ruins, haunted by stray dogs, a place not of memory, but of forgetting. Disgusted by the city's foreign-looking streets and public gardens, Iorga sought out the only living relics of Suczawa's Moldavian past: its churches. But here, too, he was disappointed. St. George's church was now "painted in blue and yellow stripes"—a sign of the growing prominence of Ukrainians in Bukovina's Orthodox Church. To Iorga, this was an abomination, a "profanation of our national colors if you think about who painted them and with what sentiments."[5] Who had painted the church at Miroutz? The Austrian administration, as part of its historical preservation and renovation efforts in Bukovina. The princely fortress in Suczawa, Putna monastery, the "Chilia de piatră"—the stone-carved cave that was once home to Stephen the Great's counselor, the legendary monk Daniil Sihastrul—all had been renovated by teams headed by the Austrian architect Karl Romstorfer. Without these preservation efforts, Romanian nationalists in Bukovina might have had no monuments left to celebrate. Chilia de piatră, for instance, had been in danger of disappearing, as locals were "breaking stones off" from its structure, likely for home-building projects.[6]

Iorga was unimpressed by the renovation and preservation. For him, the "shiny shingles, smooth stones, and Viennese saints" were signs of the empire's fake generosity toward its peoples. "Through the new sparkles and colors," he lamented, "the triumphant church will bear witness to the goodness of a government that the old one had nothing to do with, of a civilization that does not understand the former one, of an epoch in which this corner of Moldova was uplifted by the Jew and the civil servant." His only solace was among the cracked tombstones, yellowed walls, and shattered pillars behind the renovated churches, where sixteenth-century inscriptions in Latin and Church Slavonic had escaped Austria's modernizing hand. Leaving behind this desolate landscape over which "ravens, many ravens" flew, "croaking in foreign tongues about emptiness, winter, death," Iorga returned to Putna to pay his respects to "our true emperor" Stephen the Great—"not Franz Joseph I."[7]

Though discouraged by his visit to Bukovina, Iorga believed Austria-Hungary was doomed to extinction, because it rested on the unfeasible premise that fundamentally different cultures could be merged or replaced by a shared non-national culture. Such a culture, Iorga argued, necessarily lacked tradition.[8] Later, certain nationalists in Bukovina were to echo Iorga's claims. Ion Nistor, a Romanian university professor and founder of the literary society "Junimea literară" in Czernowitz, was an especially vocal critic of Austria's professed civilizing role in Bukovina. Nistor stood the liberal Austrian narrative on its head, arguing that enlightenment and culture had preceded Austrian rule in Bukovina. The Austrian school system, rather than enlightening Bukovinans, had alienated them from their "ancestral Byzantine-Slavic cultural

FIGURE 3.1. Painting of Suczawa fortress (1810), by the Austrian artist Franz Jaschke (1775–1842). Jaschke shared Romanian nationalists' fascination with Moldovan ruins in Bukovina. ÖNB Sammlung von Handschriften und alten Drucken. Courtesy of the Österreichische Nationalbibliothek (ÖNB/Wien).

origins" and confused them by exposing them to multiple languages and causing an overall drop in their educational level.[9]

The poet Gavril Rotică, a member of the Junimea circle, agreed with Nistor. Yet when he traveled to Vălenii de Munte to attend Iorga's summer school, he began having doubts. His fellow Romanians from the Old Kingdom treated him and other Bukovinans with reserve and suspicion. Rotică felt especially "hurt by the very withdrawn, glacial attitude of our brothers from Ardeal towards Bukovinans."[10] He would have been even more shocked to read what Iorga had to say about Romanians in Bukovina: he called them snobbish and disloyal, adding that the province was "foreign," like a "thorn thrust into the flesh of independent Romania." Iorga particularly resented Romanians in Bukovina for speaking their language "only when they don't want others to understand" and for being ashamed of their national origins because for them Romania was "a backward country where there is nothing to see and nothing to learn, a country with strange laws and traditions." "I never saw anyone's face light up here upon hearing the words 'from Romania,'" Iorga wrote in his Bukovinan travelogue. "Here, on the contrary, even the best of us carry our Romanian origins as a stain."[11]

By the late nineteenth century, Romanian nationalism could be felt in Bukovina but, as Iorga sensed, it bore a distinctively imperial and Austrian mark. By virtue of inhabiting a small multiethnic province of a larger empire, nationalists in Bukovina, whether Romanian, Ruthenian, German, Jewish, or Polish, often adopted ideas and tactics their co-nationals elsewhere frowned upon. Ardent nationalists in Bukovina insisted on the political necessity of empire. Those who advocated education in the national languages often preached their message in the language of empire: German. Rabid anti-Semites promoted Jewish national rights because to do so was politically expedient. Moreover, nationalisms in Bukovina evolved in both content and form, adapting to the institutional and legal frameworks of the state in which they operated. Early nationalism took the form of cultural initiatives, and until the late nineteenth and early twentieth century, nationalism barely touched the peasantry and lower bourgeoisie. This began to change once the franchise was expanded in Austria and a new generation of populist nationalists began appealing to new constituencies by championing anti-Semitism and economic reforms.

The rise of populist nationalisms in Austria—what cultural historian Carl Schorske called "politics in a new key"—coincided with the decline of liberalism.[12] In 1879, a conservative coalition of aristocrats and Czech nationalists came to power in Vienna, under Count Eduard von Taaffe.[13] Liberals lost key ministries, while non-German nationalists took advantage of the situation to push for greater language rights.[14] Through successive electoral reforms, the Taaffe administration expanded the franchise to include segments of the population that liberals had excluded or alienated.[15] Although Taaffe's government fell in 1893, the franchise continued to be expanded to include the lower urban classes and peasantry.[16] In this new climate, language politics became increasingly divisive. When Count Kasimir Badeni issued his language decrees in 1895, proclaiming Czech as well as German an official language in Bohemia and Moravia, Germans took to the streets, mobilizing "in ethnic defense."[17] The language crisis reached Bukovina too, although its impact was somewhat moderated by the province's distance from the epicenter of national conflict.

Nationalism first emerged in Bukovina among the Romanian-speaking boyar elites in the province. It came later to the Ruthenians, who took longer to develop a national intelligentsia. Until the late nineteenth century, Romanians monopolized leadership positions within the Orthodox Church and dominated provincial politics. Their positions remained secure for as long as the old curial system of elections that privileged property owners was in place.[18] The balance of power began to shift in the 1880s, as nationalists on all sides started to mobilize around language rights, with Ruthenians and Romanians defending their right to proportional representation in the Church and in schools. But nationalist politics in Bukovina was plagued by factionalism, and national communities remained deeply divided by social estate or class interests. Nationalists found themselves compelled to make deals and strike compromises with both the imperial administration and each other. As elsewhere in the monarchy, nationalists appealed to imperial institutions and laws to enforce hopelessly impractical ideas. These legal and institutional instruments facilitated national conflict, but also limited what nationalists could achieve.

## Nationalism and Language

In Bukovina, nationalism was initially limited to a narrow group of intellectuals and scholars who cultivated their respective national languages and cultures. It moved into the sphere of politics when national activists began organizing to achieve political and economic recognition. Then, finally, nationalists launched mass movements, broadening their constituencies to include peasants and workers.[19] Bukovina's early nationalists came from old Moldavian landowning families, who were multilingual and well educated, mostly by private tutors. Some, such as the Hurmuzaki family from Cernauca, sent their sons to study at the universities in Vienna and Berlin. If Alexandru, Eudoxiu, and Nicolae encountered the writings of Fichte and Herder during their university years, as is likely,[20] they would have learned that languages were not merely instruments for communication, but the reflection of a people's essence.[21] In Vienna, the multilingual Eudoxiu Hurmuzaki developed a new appreciation for his native Romanian. He spent hours in the archives, researching the history of Romanians and reflecting on what made the Romanian language and culture unique.

Eudoxiu limited his activities to research and scholarship until 1848, but when revolution broke out in Austria, he poured all his energy into demanding provincial autonomy for Bukovina, at the time an administrative district of Galicia.[22] He produced a petition that was signed by most Bukovinan landowners, both Romanian and non-Romanian. It demanded that the province be separated from Galicia and granted separate representation through a provincial parliament of its own. For Hurmuzaki, obtaining provincial autonomy was the first step toward securing greater cultural autonomy for Romanians living in the monarchy. In February 1849 he drafted a second petition, repeating his earlier demands. This time, he also pressured the head of Bukovina's Orthodox Church, Bishop Eugen Hakman, to demand that the Orthodox Church in Bukovina be unified with the Romanian Orthodox Church in Transylvania. Nothing came of this plan, since Hakman, as we shall see, turned down the request.

While Bukovina's landowning class mainly spoke Romanian and German, Ruthenian-speakers in Bukovina were predominantly peasants. Their representatives, including peasant leader Lukian Kobylytsia, opposed Hurmuzaki's petition for provincial autonomy. In Galicia, Ruthenians had mobilized in May 1848 against Polish claims to autonomy, forming a Ruthenian Supreme Council and calling for Galicia's division along ethnic and linguistic lines. In Bukovina, Ruthenian nationalism was still in its incipient stage, and Ruthenian representatives feared that if they were separated from Galicia, the nationalist movement would suffer a severe setback.

At this point, however, most nationalists in Bukovina were more interested in cultural and linguistic matters than in administrative or political ones. They founded reading clubs, academic societies, and ballrooms. In 1862 Alexandru Hurmuzaki helped found the "Reuniunea română de lepturǎ" (Romanian reading union), which provided the Bukovinan public with magazines and newspapers in the Romanian language. A few years later the organization was renamed "Societatea pentru cultura şi literatura română" (Society for Romanian culture and literature), and in 1865, it launched a Romanian periodical and began offering stipends to Romanian students in Bukovina to study at the university in Vienna.[23] At the society's inauguration, Alexandru defined its purpose as ensuring that "the Romanian nation should not remain before the other, more civilized nations in the empire a multitude bereft of the consciousness of its individuality, brute matter without a soul, despised by some, tortured and used by others."[24] Still, as noted in the previous chapter, *Bucovina*, a "gazette for politics, religion and literature," Bukovina's first, which the Hurmuzaki brothers founded in 1848, contained matter in both German and Romanian.[25]

The Hurmuzakis' nationalism was milder than that of their co-nationals in Transylvania, where Romanians faced far worse economic and political conditions. Yet Transylvanian Romanian nationalism, like that of Galician Ruthenians, left its mark on Bukovina through an influx of Transylvanian Romanians into the province. Among them was the linguist Aron Pumnul, who moved to Czernowitz after the revolution of 1848, starting a teaching career at the city's prestigious German-language *Gymnasium* in Czernowitz. Pumnul counted among his students the German-Jewish writer Karl Emil Franzos, as well as the Romanian poet Mihai Eminescu. Pumnul and other intellectuals influenced by the Daco-Roman movement in Transylvania emphasized the Romanian people's Latinity and insisted that Romanians exchange the Cyrillic alphabet for the Latin one.[26] His efforts succeeded. After 1869 a commission was formed in Bukovina to rewrite Romanian-language textbooks using the Latin script.[27]

Ruthenian intellectuals launched similar initiatives in Bukovina, though with some delay. Bukovina's Ruthenian "national awakeners" were mostly priests, sons of priests, and seminarians educated in Austrian primary school and *Gymnasia*. Though the province was no longer a part of Galicia, these intellectuals moved easily between Czernowitz and Lemberg, establishing connections with Ruthenians who were inspired—by "Karadžić, Kopitar, Šafárik, Kollár, Dobrovský, Schlözer, Herder, the *Lay of Igor's Campaign*, the Polish romantic poets, Russian, Ukrainian, and Polish history, and Ukrainian ethnography"—to cultivate a literary Ruthenian language and canon.[28] Drawing on their Galician counterparts for support, educated Ruthenian elites in Bukovina launched a cultural renaissance. They founded cultural societies, organized literary and musical events, and celebrated the writers who constituted the new Ruthenian literary canon: Taras Shevchenko, Markiian Shashkevych, Yurii Fedkovych.

Like their Romanian counterparts, early Ruthenian nationalists in Bukovina prioritized cultural organization. In 1869 they founded the province's first Ruthenian cultural society, the Ruska Besida, to cultivate "the knowledge and education of the Ruthenian people." The Besida published "works in the Ruthenian language" and organized "musical and theater events," as well as supporting teachers, writers, and youth with "stipends, prizes, and by other means." New student organizations emerged, seeking to foster national consciousness among Ruthenian youth in Bukovina through "musical and theatrical evenings." With the money they made selling tickets to performances of works such as Ivan Kotliarevsky's *Natalka poltavka*, a play written in the Ukrainian vernacular and showcasing Ukrainian folk traditions, the student organization bought more books for the Besida's library.[29]

In both Galicia and Bukovina, Ruthenian nationalists were preoccupied with seemingly arcane language matters related to orthography and spelling, which were in fact tied to deeper questions about who belonged to the Ruthenian nation. At first, most educated Ruthenians in Bukovina favored close ties with Russia. The Besida society was sponsored by the Russian consulate in Austria. Russophile Ruthenians believed that because all Eastern Slavs were related, they should use a shared written language: Slaveno-Rusyn. In the 1880s, a new generation of nationalists challenged these views. The Young Ruthenians or so-called Ukrainophiles advocated writing in the Ruthenian vernacular using phonetic spelling. In 1885 the Hutsul poet Osyp Yurii Fedkovych launched Bukovina's first periodical in the Ruthenian vernacular. The elite of Young Ruthenian politics in Bukovina were all associated with the magazine: Omelian Popovych, Erotey Pihuliak, and the Galician-born academic Stepan Smal-Stotskyi.[30] The last of these blended his political and academic work, taking great pains to prove that the language his party called Ukrainian was distinct from both Russian and Polish. Omelian Popovych, another Ruthenian-speaking intellectual, put these views into practice by writing grammar books for Bukovinan schoolchildren in vernacular Ruthenian.[31]

FIGURE. 3.2. Woman in traditional costume from the Prut river area (1897). Photographic study by the Galician photographer Juliusz Dutkiewicz (1834–1908) for the chapter "The Ruthenians," by A. Manastyrski, in the "*Kronprinzenwerk*" (*Die österreichisch-ungarische Monarchie in Wort und Bild [. . .]*, Vienna, 1886–1902), *Bukowina* volume (1899), pp. 288ff. ÖNB Bildarchiv und Grafiksammlung. Courtesy of the Österreichische Nationalbibliothek (ÖNB/Wien), KWR 20,55.

By the 1880s, there was also a new generation of Romanian nationalists in Bukovina. They were no longer members of the landowning elite, but the sons of priests and teachers, members of the urban and rural middle classes for whom the Austrian schools opened new career paths and economic opportunities. Ion Sbiera, who as a teenager had worked as a private tutor in the Hurmuzaki household and later used a stipend from the Hurmuzaki-founded Societatea pentru cultura şi literatura română to go to university, was one of these nationalists. Like his patrons, Sbiera was deeply interested in language,

FIGURE 3.3. Stepan Smal-Stotskyi (*left*) with Mykola Vasylko (previously Nikolai von Wassilko) (n.d.). *Source*: https://www.encyclopediaofukraine.com/.

which he believed "draws together the people who speak it and turns them into brothers." For him, language was a great equalizer, for "no matter their origin, if people speak one and the same language they feel and consider themselves to be like brothers, just as the members of a closely bound family feel and consider themselves to be the direct descendants of a single pair of people."[32] Growing awareness of the connections between national consciousness and language led to the founding of school societies such as Şcoala română. Established in 1883 in Bukovina, this society offered stipends to prospective gymnasium students, opened a bookstore, and acquired a printing press to produce the cultural material needed to educate a new generation of Romanian intellectuals in Bukovina—above all, future teachers.[33]

Men of Sbiera's generation were increasingly critical of multilingualism, especially as practiced in Bukovina's schools and public institutions. Multilingualism might even be, as one nationalist from Bukovina put it, "the most disgusting phenomenon of our modern life."[34] Across Europe during the second half of the nineteenth century, nationalists advocated monolingualism for both pedagogical and moral reasons.[35] Bukovinan nationalists blamed bilingualism for national opportunism, which they linked to immorality: "now you are a Romanian, if it is in your interest, now you are a good German, if that's more convenient. This duplicity of language is a tragedy for the moral progress of a people and entails its spiritual death." Nationalists insisted that people forced to speak multiple languages were condemned to ignorance, for "it is well known that only those people who were raised and developed in their own language produced amazing things for human culture."[36] Romanian nationalists blamed the low literacy rates among Bukovinan Romanians on the omnipresent German language. They warned that unless urgent measures were taken to redress the situation, Romanians in Bukovina might never develop a middle class.

Nationalists' obsession with language was not merely a reflection of Herderian ideas: it was a by-product of the institutional and legal culture they inhabited.[37] Article 19 of the constitution of 1867 for Cisleithania guaranteed all peoples (*Volksstämme*) in Austria the right to preserve and cultivate their languages as a basic citizenship right. Unlike in Transleithania, where Hungarian became the official state language, in Austria no one language had favored status.[38] Paragraph 2 of Article 19 guaranteed Austrian citizens the right to study in their own language provided that it was legally recognized as *landesüblich*—customary in their respective provinces.[39] Paragraph 3, also known as the *Sprachzwangsverbot,* decreed that no Austrian citizen should be forced to learn a second language. Initially formulated to absolve German-Austrian delegates in Bohemia from having to learn Czech, the provision implied that children should be guaranteed access to schooling in their respective national languages.

The *Reichsvolksschulgesetz* of May 1869 built the principle of *Gleichberechtigung* (national equality) into Austria's school system. This empire-wide general school law removed the schools from the Church's purview and put them under the state's supervision, setting up school districts from the provincial to the local level, along with school councils that carried out regular school inspections. The law charged the provincial school authorities with choosing the language of instruction of the schools under their supervision. According to Article 59, a community could open a new school in a specific language if over the course of five years it counted more than forty children who spoke that language and who would otherwise need to travel over four kilometers to attend a school in their native language.[40] This general law was complemented by separate provincial school laws. After 1873 Bukovina's *Landesschulgesetz* created a provincial school fund to cover the schooling costs, drawing in part on the resources of the Greek-Oriental religious fund. It also made school attendance obligatory for Bukovinan children between seven and thirteen years of age.[41]

Whether a language was represented or not in the schools, church, and administration of a province depended on how many people spoke it.[42] The first census to measure language use in the empire was carried out in 1880. It did not ask individuals about their "nationality," since in Austria this was not a juridical category. Instead, it recorded languages "of daily use," or *Umgangssprachen.*[43] There were several problems with this system and nowhere were they more visible than in Bukovina. Although most Bukovinans were at least bilingual, the census did not allow them to report more than one language of daily use. The 1880 census recorded the following

*Umgangssprachen* for Bukovina: German (19.14 percent of the province's population), Polish (3.21 percent), Ruthenian (42.16 percent), Romanian (33.43 percent), Magyar (1.74 percent), and others (0.32 percent).[44] Yet as one city magistrate from Czernowitz reported, many Bukovinans struggled to decide which *Umgangssprache* to report: "the majority of the population does not understand what is actually being asked at all. Some consider the *Umgangssprache* to be the language spoken at home, thus more or less their mother tongue; others consider it the language the individual uses in their professional life; and finally, a third group—the most numerous—see in it an expression of their nationality." Other officials in Bukovina insisted that the census complement the *Umgangssprache* with other identity markers to give a more accurate picture of a population whose language use was far from stable.[45]

Moreover, the language rights spelled out in the constitution of 1867 were often difficult to put into practice. In theory, no one could be forced to study in a non-native language. In practice, everyone in Bukovina had to learn a second language, and German was the lingua franca in middle schools, *Gymnasia*, and public institutions.[46] This was both because building multiple schools was expensive and communities could not afford it, and because native and non-native German-speakers in Bukovina held the German language in high regard. Aurel Onciul, a lawyer turned nationalist politician, studied the language question in Austria closely. He concluded that in Bukovina, which counted not just two recognized languages, as in Bohemia, but six (German, Romanian, Ruthenian, Russian, Polish, Hungarian), it was inevitable that the German language should play a mediating role. "The diversity of languages to be used by the administration is so great," he argued, "that a common language of mediation is indispensable [. . .]. German is the only language that can function as such."[47] That said, Onciul believed that it was unacceptable for civil servants in Bukovina to default to German purely on account of the "inconvenience suffered by officials who have to learn extra languages."[48] The courts generally agreed with Onciul. In one case, the Ruthenian Association in Bukovina submitted a complaint to the Reichsgericht (imperial court of justice) against local legal authorities who had been turning down Ruthenian-language petitions. Since Ruthenian was recognized as *landesüblich* (locally customary) in Bukovina, the imperial court ruled in the petitioners' favor, requiring the provincial court to accept petitions in Ruthenian and issue their responses in Ruthenian, too.[49]

Another reason that German was used by most civil servants was the prejudices many Habsburg bureaucrats had against so-called lesser languages. Nikolai von Wassilko, the descendant of an old Romanian landowning family who made a career as a Ruthenian politician, complained that the language

FIGURE 3.4. Nikolai von Wassilko, later Mykola Vasylko (1868–1924), one of Bukovina's most prominent politicians, was born in a Romanian family but became a Ruthenian nationalist. Courtesy of Derzhavnyi Arkhiv Chernivetskoi Oblasti.

situation among official circles in Bukovina was the worst in all of Austria. Officials made vague promises to learn the local languages, but then applied for language exemptions for their children, offering reasons ranging from ill health to intellectual exhaustion. Some admitted that they doubted the local languages would "reward the effort of learning them."[50] After all, while German had a rich cultural heritage, Ruthenian "had separate words for branches that had fallen from a tree and branches that were broken off but still attached," but lacked the words "to express the scientific, technological, and political advances that had been made in Europe"; and while "Poles played the piano, Ruthenians [played] the handmade hurdy-gurdy."[51]

To Wassilko's ire, civil servants' linguistic competence was never fully verified or enforced. Vague professions of fluency in local languages passed for evidence. Statements like "We had a cook at home and the two of us spoke in the local language" qualified candidates for civil service positions.[52] Romanian nationalist Ilie Toroutiu shared Wassilko's sentiments, complaining that officials who came to Bukovina looked down on "our little land as one dark corner that could never be penetrated by culture because it was inhabited by a people that doesn't even deserve to exist."[53]

To the distress of nationalists like Wassilko and Torouţiu, many Romanians and Ruthenians felt the same way about Bukovina's lesser languages. Educated Romanians, another nationalist complained, "believe that a Romanian cannot live and progress" without a German-language education: "they say that it is good and useful that in so-called Romanian high schools they study in German, such that Romanian students can learn more and better German, which will be useful to them insofar as they will be sought after for civil service jobs and promoted more quickly."[54] This state of affairs meant that even the best-intentioned civil servants did not feel compelled to learn the local languages. Military officers stationed in Czernowitz noted that it was impossible to learn Romanian in a city where everyone spoke German. According to Governor Graf von Meran, even qualified candidates "born in the province and raised here only rarely master a language other than German in both writing and speaking."[55]

## Nationalism and the Church

The wealthy and powerful Orthodox Church became one of the main arenas of language conflict in Bukovina. Disputes over language use and representation within the Church illustrated both the obstacles that nationalists confronted there, and how the imperial administration unwittingly aided them. Early Habsburg officials in Bukovina viewed the Orthodox Church as a relic of the old feudal order.[56] The Church was the single largest landowner in the province but, according to cameralist officials, it did not administer its great riches well. In 1781 Emperor Joseph II cut the Bukovinan Church's ties with Moldova and the metropolitanate of Jassy and moved the Bukovinan Orthodox bishop's residence from Radautz to Czernowitz.[57] He also decreed that all church property be brought under the state's purview. With a few exceptions, all monasteries in Bukovina were dissolved and their revenues and land (over 260 estates) were consolidated into a new institution directly supervised by the state: the Greek-Oriental religious fund. Established in 1783, the fund was supposed to further "the good of the clergy, religion, and humanity."[58]

Unlike in Serbia or neighboring Transylvania, in Bukovina the Orthodox Church was ethnically mixed (predominantly Ruthenian and Romanian), and Bukovinan Orthodox clergy traditionally held services in multiple languages.[59] The Church's leaders were more preoccupied with theological matters and the Church's own economic interests than with national and ethnic concerns.[60] This became evident in 1848, when the Bukovinan Orthodox bishop Eugen Hakman rejected Hurmuzaki's proposal to create a joint Orthodox Church for all Romanians in Transylvania and Bukovina. Born into an ethnically mixed peasant family in Wasloutz, Hakman was trained at a school for clergy in Czernowitz and then the university in Vienna. Unlike his Transylvanian counterpart Andrei Şaguna, who believed the Church would have to embrace nationalism to stay relevant, Hakman believed Bukovina's Orthodox Church was inherently supra-ethnic.[61] In a letter he wrote local clergy in May 1868, chastising them for getting mixed up with nationalist movements, he insisted that "the kingdom of Christ was not of this world."[62]

When Bukovina became definitively autonomous in 1860, Hakman was named *Landeshauptmann* and marshal of the provincial diet.[63] Czernowitz became the religious capital of the Orthodox Church in the region—a status symbolized by the newly built Bukovinan archbishop's palace (the Erzbischöfliche Residenz), a grand architectural complex combining Byzantine, Gothic, and Romanesque styles. At the same time, Bukovina's Orthodox Church was subordinated to a new synod for all Orthodox bishops in the empire, led by the patriarch of Karlowitz.

Hakman began pushing for Bukovina's removal from the Serbian patriarchate's jurisdiction, asking that the province be granted its own metropolitanate.[64] Şaguna took the opportunity to plead again for the union of Bukovina's Orthodox Church with the Romanian Church in Transylvania. Hakman again rejected the proposal, arguing that "we Bukovinans are not like all Romanians because some of our brethren are Ruthenians. If we have to choose between Karlovci and Alba Iulia we could not decide amongst us." The imperial administration granted Hakman's wish, naming him head of a newly independent metropolitanate of Bukovina and Dalmatia in 1873. Hakman traveled to Vienna to receive his formal appointment but died a few days before being officially granted the title.[65]

Imperial legislation and policies dating back to the 1780s reinforced the Bukovinan Orthodox Church's supranational character. Habsburg officials wanted to ensure that Romanian and Ruthenian interests were adequately represented in the Church, especially after the constitution of 1867 granted all peoples (*Volksstämme*) in the empire equal rights. In 1873 Romanian and

FIGURE 3.5. Private chapel in the archbishop's residence in Czernowitz, 1917. Built between 1864 and 1882 on the basis of designs by the famed Czech architect Josef Hlavka, the Erzbischöfliche Residenz was the headquarters of Bukovina's Eastern Orthodox metropolitan bishop. ÖNB Bildarchiv und Grafiksammlung. Courtesy of the Österreichische Nationalbibliothek (ÖNB/Wien).

Ruthenian were both recognized as official languages of the Orthodox Church in Bukovina, which gave Ruthenian nationalists a legal basis for disputing the traditional predominance of Romanian clergy within the Church's leadership.[66] While the measure was meant to ensure proportional representation for the two largest groups of believers in the Bukovinan Church, Romanian elites increasingly perceived these policies as evidence of the imperial administration's bias toward Ruthenians. Romanians worried that the Orthodox Church was being denationalized or "slavicized": that "Bukovina's entire governmental politics is [. . .] under the influence of a bureaucracy persuaded of Austria's Slavic mission."[67]

In turn, Ruthenian nationalists complained that Romanian clergy and activists were forcing their language upon Ruthenian parishioners. They also claimed that their co-nationals were victims of denationalization attempts. Both sides mobilized historical sources to assert their respective groups' long-held rights to the province and its Church. Romanian nationalists pointed to documents produced by early Habsburg officials in Bukovina to prove that

Romanians came before Ruthenians. If Ruthenians now outnumbered them, this was only because "Romanians not only do not Romanianize [others] but are losing their language in favor of other idioms."[68] Ruthenians invoked even older sources such as church manuscripts and Moldavian court documents to prove that Ruthenians preceded Romanians in Bukovina. They claimed that Bukovina had been part of the old kingdom of Kyiv and that its monasteries had been built and painted by "Little Russian" monks.[69]

But the Orthodox Church presented challenges to both groups of nationalists. Traditionally, this church was defined by its anti-Catholic and anti-Polish stance, not by ethnic tensions between Ruthenian and Romanian parishioners and clergy. Many Bukovinans, whether they spoke Romanian or Ruthenian at home, identified with the so-called "Wallachian" confession (meaning Orthodox).[70] For Ukrainophile nationalists, however, the Orthodox Church was not only an obstacle to Ukrainian nationalism, but an unwelcome vehicle for Russian influence over Ruthenians in Bukovina. "It is self-understood," the Ruthenian parliamentary delegate Erotey Pihuliak argued, "that these priests do their best to present in the worst possible light the Ruthenian intelligentsia who wish to show the people the path to salvation."[71]

Nationalist conflict over the Orthodox Church reached fever pitch in the years leading up to World War I. Ruthenian nationalists began demanding that the Church be divided into two dioceses: one Ruthenian, the other Romanian. Romanian elites brushed off the request as "tendentious politics," claiming it was in the Orthodox Church's best interest to remain whole.[72] To conciliate the Ruthenians, the imperial administration appointed two Ruthenian counselors to the Konsistorium and two Ruthenian professors of theology at the university of Czernowitz. A Ruthenian delegation to Vienna demanded that the emperor approve the creation of a separate Ruthenian bishopric for Bukovina in March 1900. Three years later, a group of Ruthenian delegates marched past the residence of Metropolitan Vladimir Repta, whom Romanian nationalists considered one of their own, and refused to follow the custom of removing their hats before him.[73]

Bukovina's governor Karl Freiherr von Bourguignon tried to prevent the Church's division by appointing Ruthenians to leadership positions within it. From his perspective, dividing the Church would present endless "complications," especially "given the border position of the crown land."[74] In 1913 Governor Bourguignon appointed a Ruthenian, Artemon Manastyrski, to the general vicar's seat that became vacant when Vladimir von Repta was named metropolitan of Bukovina.[75] To placate the Romanians, Bourguignon also named Eusebie Popovych general vicar. In 1911 Popovych had petitioned for a separate Ruthenian bishopric to be created in Bukovina to prevent a Young Ruthenian candidate from being named archbishop.[76] Other Romanians agreed that the

Orthodox Church should be divided "as long as this equality is a real one and not a so-called equalizing justice, through which an artificial and mechanical balance would be created between the two nationalities."[77]

As it turned out, von Bourguignon's attempt to balance Romanian and Ruthenian interests in Bukovina left pretty much everyone dissatisfied. Romanians protested at the measure as an "assault on the historical continuity of the church and its national Romanian character." In a new petition to the emperor, they complained that "in our time we have had to make great sacrifices as far as the historic character of our Church was concerned for the sake of constitutional rights and peace within the Church."[78] Metropolitan Repta also contested the governor's decision, accusing the administration of violating the *Gleichberechtigung* (equality) principle by selecting a general vicar by nationality when "there is no mention of nationality either in the religious regulation plan or the internal regulations of the Consistory. The regulations demand only that members of the Consistory be able to speak both languages."[79] Ruthenian priests took to the streets, demanding that the Church be divided "in the interest of peacekeeping."[80] Governor von Bourguignon never had the chance to work out a solution, since World War I broke out a few months later.

## The Competition for Schools

Nationalists criticized the imperial administration's efforts to enforce equal representation for Romanians and Ruthenians within the Orthodox Church as an unwelcome interference in Bukovinan affairs. Where schools were concerned, however, they were happy to co-opt imperial institutions and officials to help them make Bukovinans more invested in their national languages. Since nationalists made little headway without the element of compulsion that state institutions and legislation could provide, they tried to enroll state institutions into their effort to turn constitutional provisions of citizenship rights into obligations. Across the Habsburg monarchy during the late nineteenth century, nationalist organizations focused on education as an instrument to nationalize people who did not primarily think of themselves in national terms. Nationalist activists launched a veritable assault on people who were "nationally indifferent," especially rural populations who resisted history's supposed march toward nationalism.[81] Here was nationalism's supreme irony. As Pieter Judson writes, although nationalists extolled the village as a repository of national consciousness and virtue, they realized that consciousness and virtue could not be found there naturally, but had to be taught.[82] In many respects, peasants in Bukovina were nationally indifferent, meaning that they had no national loyalties or switched sides opportunistically, and tended to greet nationalists' initiatives with apathy.[83]

As we have seen, multilingualism, which was promoted by both the Church and the school system, was widespread in Bukovina. Although Paragraph 3 of the constitution provided that no one should be forced to learn a second language, this was difficult to enforce in Bukovina, whose student body, including Romanians, Ruthenians, Jews, Poles, Armenians, Gypsies, Slovenes, Hungarians, Serbs, Croats, and Italians, was multilingual. To accommodate these varied language needs, the teachers' institute in Czernowitz required future teachers to take exams in three provincial languages (*Landessprachen*): Romanian, Ruthenian, and German.[84] Multilingual schools were the default in Bukovina, because lumping speakers of different languages together was cheaper than opening separate schools for each group. In Klokuczka, primary school staff explained that they were unable to create uniform language sections, because the student body consisted of unequal numbers of speakers of different languages. As a result students were grouped into bilingual sections. By the end of 1885 there were as many as sixty-eight mixed-language schools in Bukovina and fifteen schools that taught in four languages: German, Romanian, Ruthenian, and Polish.[85] Teachers in mixed-language classes practiced "utraquism," using two languages of instruction side by side,[86] sometimes having to "repeat each explanation, indeed each sentence, in three different languages."[87]

Even when instruction in the national languages was an option, many students did not take advantage of it. Cultivating the national languages in school took additional class time and more resources than most people were willing to invest. In 1867 little over 9 percent of the Greek-Oriental *Oberrealschule*'s student body attended Romanian language classes, and only 4 percent were enrolled in Ruthenian classes. Teachers at the *Oberrealschule* worried that they would lose their jobs due to low enrollment in optional classes in local languages—a phenomenon they attributed partly to "ignorance about the law" and partly to "indifference."[88] In response, nationalists appealed to the imperial administration to make instruction in their native languages compulsory for Romanian and Ruthenian children in Bukovina. Their petition was rejected on the grounds that no students could be forced to learn a specific language, allowing most schools to continue privileging German. In another instance, a group of Ukrainophiles appealed to the Ministry of Education to reprimand a Ruthenian theology professor at the university in Czernowitz, Eugen Kozak. A Russophile, Kozak was denounced for testing students in an "incomprehensible" mix of Church Slavonic and Russian, while disparaging the Ukrainian language as "a Galician dialect that needs to be eradicated." The appeal claimed that he had behaved "in a way that was offensive not only to both candidates examined, but also to the entire Ukrainian nation."[89]

That German remained the dominant language of instruction in Bukovina was not the result of the imperial administration's efforts to denationalize or

Germanize the population, as nationalists later claimed. The reality was that local people often preferred to enroll their children in German-language schools to increase their chances at better paying jobs and civil service positions. This behavior frustrated nationalists. Some explained it by saying that Romanians, for instance, were by nature talented at learning languages and receptive to foreign influences. They warned that Romanian children coming from the countryside to Czernowitz to study would rent rooms in foreign homes and lose their national identities while speaking foreign languages. In fact, most individuals did not abandon their native languages, but switched as needed between languages in their daily interactions. The Ruthenian nationalist Omelian Popovych came from an upwardly mobile family whose ticket to economic success was the German language. His mother spoke Ruthenian at home but wrote in German, while his father, "fascinated by the German language, was nationally indifferent." Popovych grew up speaking a mixture of languages: German and a Hutsul dialect of Ruthenian, which resulted in unheard-of feats of syntax and sentences combining Ruthenian and German vocabulary such as "*Mamochko*, er hat meine *mysochka* genommen und sie hat mein *hornyatko* zerschlagen." (Mommy, he took my bowl and she smashed my cup.)[90]

To advance their agendas, nationalists competed for imperial patronage and support, reinforcing the value of imperial institutions in the process.[91] In Bukovina they pushed for greater representation for their respective groups within existing schools, especially at the higher-levels such as *Gymnasia* and the university. At the same time, they demanded that schools be separated by national language. To out-compete others in schooling was every nationalist's dream. To that end, they were willing to push more German-language instruction onto their co-nationals. To increase the number of Romanian-speakers at the *Obergymnasium* in Czernowitz, for instance, nationalists argued that Romanian students should receive better German-language instruction in the lower grades.

Romanian nationalists especially resented German-speaking Jews for allegedly monopolizing Bukovina's most prestigious schools. In 1909 the *Bukowiner Volksblatt* (a Christian Social periodical) reported with alarm that Czernowitz's state *Gymnasium* had "become a purely Jewish school."[92] Jewish students were numerous not only at the German-language *Gymnasia* but also in institutions especially created for Orthodox students. In 1891, 154 students of "Mosaic religion" were attending the Greek-Oriental *Oberrealschule* in Czernowitz, compared to only thirty-seven "Greek-Oriental" students.[93] "I do not think it was the founders' last wish," the nationalist Vasile Greciuc wrote, "that from the fortune they bestowed upon the monasteries almost four hundred people foreign to their religion, more than half of them Jews, should be brought up and taught in their mother tongue year by year."[94]

Convinced that they could overturn established economic and cultural hierarchies in Bukovina through education, nationalists resented any suggestion that they should adapt their demands to the specific economic needs of their respective groups. In the opinion of Eugen Ehrlich, later a famous legal scholar, then teaching at the university in Czernowitz, nationalists in Bukovina were profoundly misguided. Their obsession with claiming seats within prestigious institutions led to the overcrowding of *Gymnasia* and the neglect of economic problems. "It is most peculiar," he reflected, "that both peoples [Romanians and Ruthenians] should first and foremost think about founding as many *Gymnasia* as possible. Do they really believe that a people become or can become great through *Gymnasia*? I am not of this opinion and wish to hear as little as possible about *Gymnasia*, which are still so highly attended, and which aim to create so many civil servant positions."[95] Others agreed, advocating school curricula for Romanians and Ruthenians that focused on instruction in agriculture and trades. Nationalists would not hear of it. When a German deputy in the Landtag suggested that students in Bukovina pursue practical education instead of crowding into the *Gymnasia*, Nikolai von Wassilko snapped that "while [the Germans] eat the apple, they want the Romanians and Ruthenians to eat the peel only [. . .]. We are supposed to remain a nation of shoemakers and tailors who feed the foreign civil servants!"[96]

Indeed, as elsewhere, poverty and illiteracy were directly correlated in Bukovina. Although the provincial school law of 1873 made schools more accessible, illiteracy rates remained high and school attendance rates low among the rural population.[97] Nationalists who believed bilingualism impaired cognitive development blamed the situation on students having to study in non-native languages. Here, as elsewhere in Austria under the Taaffe administration, nationalists demanded more schooling in non-German languages.[98] The imperial administration responded by opening parallel classes within existing institutions, often with mixed-language instruction: German with Ruthenian or Ruthenian with Polish, for example. Eventually, these parallel classes split off and formed separate *Gymnasia*. Even the teachers' institute in Czernowitz eventually splintered into separate language sections. As soon as Ruthenians got their own *Gymnasium* in Wiznitz, Romanians demanded that mixed German–Romanian *Gymnasia* be converted into exclusively Romanian institutions.[99]

Over time, Bukovina's school system became increasingly nationalized. As we shall see, in 1909–10 Bukovina's parliament adopted a "national compromise" on the Moravian model, which institutionalized separation by nationality first in electoral politics and then in education. Bukovina's once common four-language schools gradually disappeared.[100] Local officials and members of the provincial diet repeatedly rejected calls to nationalize all schools in the province: Czernowitz's municipal school council insisted that "the differentiation of city schools by language and their re-establishment as purely national schools is frowned upon by the community."[101] The most the school council would accept was the introduction of Romanian-language instruction in suburban schools where "non-Romanian elements of the population are weakly represented."[102]

## Fragmentation and Compromise

The nationalization of Bukovina's schools was the pet project of a new generation of nationalists who made their way into the Landtag in the early twentieth century, making Bukovinan politics both more democratic and less liberal. To appeal to a new peasant and petty bourgeois constituency, nationalists changed their political repertoire and practices, focusing increasingly on economic matters and championing a politics of national defense and survival. They sought to break the power of older political elites through new institutions such as agricultural and cooperative societies and popular banks. But as they tried to restructure Bukovinan politics, nationalists ran into unexpected obstacles. First, they discovered that divisions within their national communities were more pronounced than they had imagined. Even in moments of crisis, nationalists found themselves fighting not so much their national adversaries as others in their own national camps, with whom they disagreed about almost everything. Populist nationalists deepened existing rifts even further by pitting one interest group against another: landowners against peasants, teachers against village priests. Internecine warfare became common not only at the level of party politics, but among nationalist activists working in local communities.

In Bukovina, much like neighboring Galicia, this new political landscape was the outcome of peasant emancipation and electoral reforms. After serfdom was abolished in 1848, peasants in both provinces became increasingly politicized through the school system, which gave rise to a new village intelligentsia that challenged priests' traditional authority.[103] In Galicia, priests, urban intellectuals, and landed gentry started going into villages in the 1870s to promote cultural and economic reform, and mobilize peasants into nationalist movements that were now transformed to make the nation "familiar to [peasants] in their own terms."[104] Teachers and civil servants, themselves of rural origins, returned to the village to bring the enlightenment and modernization that the imperial administration had failed to provide.[105] In the 1890s nationalists in Bukovina began mobilizing this new rural intelligentsia to push for further electoral and economic reforms aimed at improving peasants' lives. This was the mission of Aurel Onciul's Democratic Peasants Party (Partidul Țărănesc Democrat). Capitalizing on mutual resentments among "boyars and clergy" and teachers and peasants, the party embraced a populist egalitarian vision of national renewal and blamed the miserable conditions in the countryside on

Jewish usurers. Onciul and his party presented themselves as saviors of the downtrodden masses who were "getting poorer" and emigrating *en masse* because "the bloodsuckers were grabbing their wealth with their talons."[106]

By the early twentieth century, all the major nationalist movements in Bukovina were divided into factions representing different economic interests. To challenge older national elites whose politics did not reflect the needs of new constituencies, newly founded parties did not hesitate to cooperate across national divides. In May 1903, for example, Aurel Onciul and Nikolai von Wassilko founded the Progressive Union (Freisinniger Verband).[107] They were soon joined by politicians from other national camps who shared their commitment to electoral reforms: Benno Straucher from the National Jewish Party and Stefan Stefanowicz from the Armeno–Polish Alliance. Together, they organized a common electoral campaign for the Landtag elections of July 1904, running on a platform of democratization and appealing primarily to the lower and middle classes. Although they won the elections, they did not have the majority needed to push through their desired electoral reforms. Soon after, the alliance dissolved.[108] At no point did alliance members renounce their nationalist agendas, even when they conflicted with those of their allies. They simply put national conflicts on hold to achieve their shared goals before turning against each other again.

Instances of political cooperation across ethnic and national lines were common in Bukovina. Compromise was a key element of nationalist political culture, but not necessarily a sign of tolerance. National adversaries often came together to pursue non-progressive, illiberal political goals. To Iancu Flondor, a landowner and prominent Romanian nationalist in Bukovina, it seemed as though Romanians were cursed to "devour each other. One barely manages to create some unity among them and immediately there emerges a new faction."[109] Aurel Onciul tried to cure Romanians of divisiveness by bringing them into a cross-national alliance of Christian parties bound by their shared animosity toward Jews. He urged his national adversaries to put their shared political and economic interests first and set aside national hatreds that profited the Jews. As a member of the Christian Social Party in Bukovina wrote in the Viennese *Reichspost*, "exclusive nationalism used to be nothing but a whip in the hands of the Jews who sat and watched the battle of all against all with great satisfaction." Anti-Semitism would thus become "the form through which the oppressed among all nationalities can get along."[110]

Nationalists in Bukovina used these tactical alliances to institutionalize national differences as well. Ironically, to achieve their desired goal of nationalizing the schools and provincial politics, they needed to cooperate with each other. The result was the Bukovinan Compromise of 1910, modeled after the Moravian

Compromise of 1905, which turned nationality from a matter of personal choice into a concern of the state.[111] While working as an insurance attorney in Brünn (modern Brno), Aurel Onciul had the chance to observe how the Moravian Compromise introduced new election rules for the local diet and new laws that regulated which languages were used in local schools.[112] A similar compromise was later introduced in Budweis, where nationalists redrew electoral districts, dividing citizens by nationality rather than territory.[113]

Nationalist politicians in Bukovina began proposing similar reforms for elections to their Landtag in July 1909. In October most delegates in Bukovina's Landtag voted to adopt a compromise on the Moravian model. In Bukovina's case, voters would be separated into five national cadastres: Romanian, Ruthenian, German, Polish, and Jewish.[114] In May 1910 the emperor sanctioned this *Ausgleich* (compromise) with only one caveat: that Jews should not be awarded a separate national cadastre, but would continue to be counted as Germans. All voters in Bukovina were to be registered by nationality, beginning in June 1910. Local officials would assign voters the appropriate national categories. Although voters could contest this assignment, officials would have the final say.[115]

During the negotiations that led up to this point, anti-Semitic politicians in Bukovina found themselves championing Jewish national rights, while the imperial government denied Jews national recognition. Officials in Vienna rejected the demand for a separate Jewish cadastre as "racist" and insisted that Jews were a religious rather than national group.[116] Benno Straucher, a former German-Jewish liberal turned Jewish nationalist protested that denying Jews their own curia was the real act of hatred and racism. Together with the young Bukovinan Zionist Mayer Ebner, Straucher had formed a Jewish national party in 1900, the Jüdischer Volksverein. As a member of the so-called "Jewish Club" in the Vienna parliament, Straucher agitated for national and linguistic recognition for Jews in the census of 1910.[117] When Nathan Birnbaum, a former Zionist turned Yiddishist, requested permission to hold an international Yiddish language conference in Czernowitz in 1908, Straucher had turned him down. He wanted nothing to do with the Yiddish language and was equally uninterested in Zionist plans for emigration to Palestine.[118] Straucher doggedly pursued his own brand of Jewish nationalism, insisting that Jews in Bukovina and Galicia were in fact a nationality even if they had no distinctive national language of their own.[119] In a great twist of irony, Straucher found support in his quest for Jewish national recognition among Bukovinan politicians, including the anti-Semite Aurel Onciul. Granting Jews national autonomy, non-Jewish nationalists in Bukovina thought, would help splinter the German electoral cadastre and make it easier for them to gain leverage over key political institutions in the province.

## Imperial Nationalisms

Not only did nationalists in Bukovina employ imperial institutions to carry out their goals, but the tactics they deployed were specific to the province. They all had to grapple with Russia's physical proximity to Bukovina, as well as the reality of Austrian–Russian imperial competition. All were shaped by interactions with other nationalists both within Austria and across the border in Russia. Russia's proximity explains why so many Ruthenian nationalists in Bukovina (including the Ruska Besida's founders) came under Russia's influence. Especially after 1867, when Poles gained cultural autonomy in Galicia, Russophile Ruthenians in Bukovina argued that Ruthenian was a dialect of Russian and that Ruthenians' interests were best protected by the tsar. Grigorii Kupchanko, the editor of a Russophile journal in Bukovina sponsored by Russia, insisted that Ruthenians should not pick fights with fellow Orthodox believers, because it would distract them from the more dangerous Polish–Ruthenian conflict. Only the Russian tsar, Kupchanko told Ruthenians, could liberate them: "the time will come [. . .] and is not too distant now, when Moscow will lift itself up and free you; it will by no means let you perish at the hands of the evil Catholics or under the weight of the heavy Polish yoke."[120]

Initially, Romanian nationalists were favorably disposed toward Russophile Old Ruthenians, as they felt similarly threatened by Polish expansionism and Catholic proselytism. As soon as Bukovina gained provincial autonomy from Galicia, however, their priorities changed. Romanian nationalists now frowned upon both Old Ruthenians and Young Ruthenians who aligned themselves not with Russia but with the Austrian administration. "A true national standpoint," one "Bukovina Romanian" wrote in 1900, "should in any case be directed toward neither one nor the other Ruthenian party, which carries only ephemeral significance," but "needs to fight only the Ruthenization of Romanians."[121] Though opposed to the Old Ruthenians, Young Ruthenians or Ukrainophiles also tried to defend Ruthenians' national interests by placing these in the larger context of inter-imperial competition. Ruthenians, they insisted, were naturally on Austria's side. Such assurances of loyalties were sometimes mixed with veiled threats that, should Austria fail to support them, Ruthenians in Bukovina would have no choice but to turn to Russia.

Nationalists in Bukovina looked to each other for inspiration even—or especially—when tensions between them ran high. Romanian and Ruthenian nationalists went from coexisting uneasily to colliding head on, especially after the census revealed that Ruthenians now outnumbered Romanians in Bukovina. While warning about the dangers of "slavicization," Romanian nationalists closely observed and even emulated their Ruthenian adversaries. Alarmed by Ruthenian efficiency, Romanians rushed to create replicas of institutions the Ruthenians were founding in Bukovina (which were in turn replicas of institutions founded by Ruthenians in Galicia). Similarly, Germans in Bukovina (much as in Bohemia) mobilized in reaction to the national mobilization of non-German groups.[122] In 1897 a group of German politicians founded the Verein der christlichen Deutschen in der Bukowina (Bukovina Association of Christian Germans), an ethnic defense party, *völkisch* (nationalist and populist) in orientation, seeking to foster national (*Stamm*) consciousness among Germans in Bukovina through German reading rooms and by encouraging German agriculture, trade, and commerce.[123] Unlike Georg von Schönerer's Pan-Germans, who emerged around the same time, the Verein did not challenge the monarchy's territorial integrity. Instead, it claimed its achievements for the German ethnic group. It redefined Emperor Joseph II, for instance, as a proto–German nationalist who had carried out Germany's civilizing mission in the east. His figure was of such importance to them that Christian Germans in Czernowitz placed his statue in front of the German National Home building.[124]

The historian Raimund Friedrich Kaindl was one of the Verein's foremost members. Born into a German-speaking family in Bukovina and educated at the university in Czernowitz, Kaindl considered himself a German nationalist. Yet he strongly disliked von Schönerer's ideas when he first encountered them at the university. Von Schönerer's movement was centered upon anti-Semitism and anti-Catholicism and advocated that the predominantly German Austrian heartlands be separated from the rest of the empire to be united with the German nation-state. When Pan-German students in Czernowitz took to the streets singing "Die Wacht am Rhein" to protest von Schönerer's arrest, Kaindl stayed put.[125] In his view, Pan-Germans did not understand what made Germans German: that is, *Kultur*, or their civilizing mission in the east. This mission, he believed, was best furthered by the Habsburg monarchy, not the German nation-state founded in 1871. In his academic work Kaindl sought to demonstrate that Germans could not be confined within a nation-state that truncated the organic ties binding together different branches of the German people. He was also concerned that, after 1871, Germans in the nation-state had become indifferent to their co-nationals in the east. These latter Germans, Kaindl insisted, were not extraneous, but indispensable to the nation, as they had transformed a place like Bukovina from "a wild, empty land where not even the highest clergy could read and write" into a bastion of civilization.[126]

Anti-Semitic populist Aurel Onciul shared Kaindl's conviction that the Habsburg monarchy was necessary for the survival of his nation. His view of the monarchy was far from sentimental, however. In *Das österreichische Problem* (The Austrian Problem), published in 1905, Onciul argued that "among the nation-states of Europe the polyglot Austro-Hungarian monarchy is a puzzling creation of times gone by." Nations had existed from time immemorial, but had been superseded by the supranational formation of Austria-Hungary. Austria, he argued, had emerged naturally, through the "voluntary unification" of the many small peoples that inhabited the Danube valley. By defending them from foreign encroachment, the monarchy had made it possible for these smaller peoples to enjoy "several hundred years of uninterrupted cultural development."[127]

Bukovina's multiethnic character, a product of imperial rule, left a deep imprint on nationalists' imaginations. In such an environment, political success depended on adaptability: exclusionary forms of nationalism remained on the fringe. Much as they grumbled about Bukovinans' indifference to national issues, nationalists saw an opportunity in the fact that "nothing is so consolidated that it cannot be opened up again."[128] If national identities were not fully consolidated, national activists could still try to draw people into their respective communities. A scandal broke out in 1908 when a Romanian delegate in the Landtag revealed that students in a school in the village of Ceahor were being shifted around to increase enrollments in the school's Ruthenian-language section. A special commission was sent to Ceahor to investigate the matter, which was ultimately resolved in the Ruthenians' favor. Romanian activists never reconciled themselves to the decision.[129]

Another way to draw people into national communities was through displays of cultural superiority. The result was a proliferation of national or cultural "homes" in Czernowitz, one for each national community. These "home" buildings provided physical cohesion to nations and manifested their power in physical space. Because Romanians lacked a "national palace," writer Elena Niculiţă-Voronca complained in 1894, they only convened as a national community every two or three years. "We barely look at each other any more," she complained; "feelings aren't made of iron, they become blunt and numb and along with them dies all desire for action and life." The solution was a national center that would provide the national community with a "nucleus" and "serve as a magnet" for the nation.[130]

Since nobody in Bukovina "dares say that their blood is not mixed," many nationalists preferred to assimilate ethnically and linguistically impure elements than to reject them.[131] The nationalist society Răzeşii şi mazilii (Free peasants and minor nobility) followed similar principles, assuming that most Ruthenian-speakers in Bukovina were actually Romanians who had forgotten their language and who "out of ignorance or confusion think they are Russians and even speak or fight the Romanians, who are nevertheless their brothers from long ago."[132] Trying to ascertain what nationality Bukovinans were was a waste of time because, as the old saying went, "Father is Russian, mother is Russian, but Ivan is Moldavian."[133] To recover allegedly lost co-nationals, the

Răzeşii şi mazilii society published magazines and booklets, often in both Romanian and Ruthenian. Readers were told their ancestors had been members of the lower Romanian nobility who had forgotten their native language.[134] But while it was unfortunate that a Romanian could become Ruthenian by forgetting his or her native language, the good news was that he or she could presumably be re-Romanianized by re-learning it. If that were to happen, Romanian nationalists hoped they could "turn this into what it used to be, a Romanian country."[135]

When exclusionary forms of nationalism emerged in Bukovina, they splintered nationalist groups. The Verein der christlichen Deutschen, for instance, defined Germans along racial and ethnic lines. This caused it to split with the German National Party (Deutsche Nationalpartei), which had traditionally included many Jews. Now calling themselves the German Progressive Party (Deutsche Fortschrittspartei), the remaining members of the latter worried that if Jews were rejected, they would run into the arms of the Slavs, who were already too numerous. And if Jews were no longer Germans, the German language would suffer a major blow in Bukovina. A contributor to a 1900 issue of the *Bukowinaer Post* blamed "the decline of German-language education in the Ruthenian parts of Bukovina" on negligence toward German-speaking Jews. "It cannot be in the interest of [Germans] when the schools replace the current German mother tongue of Jews who are living among Ruthenians with a Slavic language." The writer insisted that Jews had as much of a cultural role to play in Bukovina as Germans did: "there are by the way areas where Jews have a cultural mission to fulfill and everyone who knows our province will have to admit that specifically in the Wiznitz-Putila mountains the Jewish population is literally the only cultured element [. . . and] if they suddenly disappear, then the entire area will immediately be plunged into a state of utter unculturedness."[136]

Jewish politics in Bukovina fractured as well, mirroring the split within the German National Party. Traditionally, educated Jews in Bukovina favored assimilation into German culture. In 1883 a Jewish merchant and politician from Czernowitz named Leon Rosenzweig argued that Jews would only overcome discrimination by letting go of their differences: "then we will no longer have to suffer as Jews for the simple reason that we will no longer be Jews, Jews who want to set themselves apart from all other peoples through their particular religion and origin." Rosenzweig believed Bukovinan Jews should not only maintain their ties with Germans, but learn from their example that ethnic and racial mixing were recipes not for national extinction, but for success. Germans, he believed, "stood at the epicenter of civilization" precisely because they were not afraid to move around taking their culture with them and mingling with other peoples.[137]

By the late nineteenth century, a new Jewish politics was on the rise in Bukovina. It emerged first at the university in Czernowitz, among academic societies modeled on German *Burschenschaften*. In 1891 Jewish students formed the academic society Hasmonea, which urged Jews to defend their national honor. By 1910 a group of Jewish students in Czernowitz was gathering to demand that Jews be registered as a separate nationality even if they declared German their "language of daily use." They also demanded the founding of a special chair for Jewish history and literature at the university. Yet even the most uncompromising Jewish nationalists could not rid themselves entirely of German influence. The Hasmonea's members, though Zionists, spoke German with each other and carried on German traditions. Their organization was in every way a typical German *Burschenschaft*: its members wielded shiny swords, wore colorful uniforms, and engaged in duels. To celebrate the anniversary of the society's foundation, the Hasmonea convened at a traditional German beer hall in Czernowitz.[138]

---

Squabbles over national politics were an integral part of daily life in Bukovina during the late nineteenth and early twentieth centuries. Yet later the province would be remembered as a haven of peaceful coexistence, a place where cultural pluralism was seen "as a benefit rather than a disadvantage" thanks to people and institutions that mediated between cultures.[139] The German-language poet Georg Drozdowski described Bukovina in his memoir of life in Czernowitz as a place where "one lived and let live," where people formed "that Austrian mix, which creates unity out of differences" because "no demon had yet inoculated intolerance [into society] and no one was less worthy because of his language or race."[140] With typical sarcasm, the Bukovinan writer Gregor von Rezzori noted that in Czernowitz "you can find a dozen of the most disparate nationalities and at least half a dozen bitterly feuding faiths—all living in the cynical harmony that is built on mutual aversion and common business dealings."[141]

Less urbanized than Bohemia and Moravia, where nationalist tensions reached fever pitch in the 1880s and 1890s, Bukovina gave rise to a variety of nationalisms that bore the imprint of the province's multinational character. Nationalist movements there remained poorly organized and highly fragmented, even at their peak. Like elsewhere in the monarchy, in Bukovina nationalists dealt in irreconcilable contradictions. They idealized the peasantry and dreamed about a golden age in the past. Yet rather than reject modernity, they proposed quicker and better paths to it. Nationalists disapproved of national indifference but also saw it as an advantage that allowed them to re-nationalize the province more easily. They were, as John Connelly says about nationalists in Eastern Europe more generally, deeply afraid that their respective nationalities would perish or be swallowed by foreign cultures. Yet they did not always believe that their national existence was best secured through national statehood; they trusted the empire, seeking to keep their national cultures alive not so much through anti-imperial struggle, as by profiting from inter-imperial competition and leveraging imperial resources.[142] The shape and content of their activity was a function of the imperial state that nationalists inhabited. Yet that state's very existence, which so many took for granted, would soon come under threat.

# 4
# Between Worlds

ON AUGUST 5, 1914 the head of Bukovina's gendarmerie General Eduard Fischer received orders to "begin war with Russia early on August 6."[1] The last days of August found Czernowitzers perched on elevated points around the city, observing the Russian troops crossing the border. Alois Regius, a city notable, watched these developments through his opera glasses.[2] Bukovinans like him had front seats for the massive conflagration that would reshape Europe and bring about Austria-Hungary's demise. After bringing Bukovina's governor to safety in Dorna-Watra, in southern Bukovina, General Fischer took matters into his own hands, forming his own volunteer units to wage a guerrilla war on the Russian troops. In late August, after several incursions into enemy territory, Fischer's troops took the Russian border town of Nowosielitza. On August 25 the Viennese received with their morning coffee the news that "an attack on Bukovina by Russian troops was countered near Nowosielitza."[3]

But soon the tables were turned. Only a week later, Czernowitz was awoken by a deafening blast. Austrian troops in retreat had exploded the bridges over the river Prut, which connected the city with the villages now under Russian occupation. "I hurried into the city hall," one Czernowitzer remembered, "on the Ringplatz and in the streets the whole of Czernowitz had gathered. I found out that after our great railway bridge [over the Prut] exploded, our troops had retreated."[4] On September 2 the victorious Russian troops entered Czernowitz and planted a Russian flag atop the city hall tower. Mayor Salo Weisselberger had little option but to hand over the city keys to a Russian commander, for the Russians threatened that Czernowitz "would be made one with the earth if the people do not give themselves up."[5]

The first two years of the war were disastrous for Austria-Hungary. Russian troops occupied both Galicia and Bukovina in late August 1914. By the end of September the Russians were triumphant on the Galician front, capturing Lemberg.[6] Austria briefly recovered parts of Bukovina that fall, but on October 27 Russian bombardments resumed. Cossack divisions crossed the Prut and took back Czernowitz. The second Russian occupation of Bukovina lasted until February 1915, when the Austrians again returned. In June 1916 Russian troops organized the Brusilov offensive, again setting fire to the bridges over the Prut and raining down shells upon the city.[7] All Austrian gendarmerie units not in service were rounded up to help with the evacuation. As General Fischer noted in his diary, "trains [were] hauled, horses saddled up, the chancellery packed," and officers' wives were put on trains headed west.[8] All means of transportation were mobilized to evacuate people and property, including city trams. Refugees streamed south, filling the streets of Radautz, while Fischer frantically drove around frontier villages, ordering the deportation of Lipovenians: Russian Old Believers now deemed unreliable.

In the spring of 1917, however, the Russian army began disintegrating as news of revolutionary turmoil back home ripped through the front. Banditry and desertions by the rank and file became common, and soldiers who had targeted only certain groups of people for violence now began indiscriminately assaulting locals. The Russian Provisional Government, which had assumed power after the tsar's abdication, tried to remedy the situation by launching a new offensive in the summer of 1917. When the Central Powers counterattacked, the Russian army collapsed and began retreating from Galicia and Bukovina.[9]

The returning Austrian authorities attempted to restore order, but they could not hold on to the province for long. Plagued by poor infrastructure and equipment, the Austro-Hungarian war effort wasted immense amounts of human resources and energy. Barely a few months into the war, Austria-Hungary had suffered as many as 189,000 dead, 490,000 wounded, and 278,000 captured in a series of dreadful winter battles in West Galicia and the Carpathians. Over time, it became increasingly dependent on its German ally, recovering from successive defeats only with Germany's help. In 1916 Austro-Hungarian troops had been smashed again by the Russians, with over one third of them falling into enemy hands.[10]

The war in Bukovina was nothing like the war soldiers experienced in the trenches of Verdun or on the battlefields of Somme. For one thing, the eastern front was four times longer than the entire western front, and the war here was one of movement rather than attrition, punctuated by regime changes and revolutions.[11] Populations shifted as a result of mass deportations and expulsions, creating a huge refugee problem.[12] The war brought state institutions to the brink of collapse and changed the balance between military and civilian authorities.[13] Wartime violence on the eastern front was often amplified by ethnic diversity, with belligerents waging war against not only external enemies, but suspected internal ones, usually entire ethnic groups who were treated as potential spies. And unlike in the west, war on the eastern front continued long past the Armistice in November 1918, albeit carried out by other means.[14]

FIGURE. 4.1. Street in Czernowitz, August 1, 1917. Taken by the returning Austrian authorities, the photograph records the destruction Czernowitz's infrastructure during the war. Austrian soldiers are chatting with locals and keeping an eye on the street. ÖNB Bildarchiv und Grafiksammlung. Courtesy of the Österreichische Nationalbibliothek (ÖNB/Wien).

As the front line shifted and the Austrian and Russian armies each conquered and lost Bukovina repeatedly, the province became a point of overlap between them, with belligerents interacting on the battlefield, confronting each other, but also competing. Each occupation regime in Bukovina inherited a social landscape profoundly transformed by previous occupations that in turn shaped the policies of the occupations that followed. War and occupation permanently altered Bukovinans' relationship with the imperial state and with each other.

Rather than a period of interregnum, the war was a foundational experience in the region's history of statehood. State–society relations were transformed by both deliberate attempts to create new forms of statehood and frequent regime changes. Hoping to muster support, both the Austrian and Russian empires sponsored national revivals and mobilized local ambitions. Their interests and those of local groups thus became entangled in a relationship that combined oppression and concession. Repeated cycles of retribution and purges following each change in occupation meant that Bukovinans experienced the war not only as a conflict of empires, but as an existential struggle.

## First Encounters

Somewhere near a ravine to the east of Czernowitz, two pillars stood facing each other. A wooden board nailed into the black and yellow pillar read "Austrian Empire." Perched above the Gothic inscription was the double-headed Habsburg eagle. Barely ten steps away, another eagle looked it "threateningly in the eye." This was the Russian eagle, towering above the Cyrillic inscription spelling out "Russian State." Just miles from Bukovina's capital, the two empires thus came face to face.[15] To the south, Bukovina bordered on Romania—a small state with growing ambitions. Bukovina's frontiers with Russia and Romania were porous, allowing the province to become a conduit for Russophile and Greater Romanian irredentist propaganda in the years leading up to the outbreak of World War I.

In 1913 and early 1914, a group of Ruthenians charged with leading a pro-Russian irredentist movement were put on trial in Marmaros, Sziget, and Lemberg.[16] The first trial pointed to Czernowitz as the headquarters of "the heads of a highly treasonous group with networks all over Austria-Hungary." Among the accused were Alexei and Georgii Gerovskii, two Russian nationalist brothers from Bukovina. In January 1914 the Gerovskiis were arrested for distributing Russophile propaganda in the province. But before they could be tried and sentenced they escaped the criminal court building where they were held in Czernowitz. A friendly prison guard lent them new clothes, let them out the front door, and drove them across the border to Russia.[17]

Romanian irredentist propaganda also flowed into Bukovina, especially after the Second Balkan War (1913), which "filled Romanians with an exaggerated consciousness of their power."[18] In 1913 Czernowitz officials noticed that Romanian intellectuals in Bukovina were visiting Romania with suspicious frequency. Theater companies had been giving performances in Bukovina, and Romanian personalities had been coming to Czernowitz to give lectures. But it was rare that Romanian nationalists in Bukovina expressed themselves "in a manner that broke the law or political decorum."[19] Austrian officials kept an especially close eye on Romanian teachers and Orthodox priests, but could seldom find compelling evidence against them. In the spring of 1914 they put a Romanian priest from a village bordering on Romania under surveillance and dismissed him from his post for allegedly imposing the Romanian language upon his parishioners.[20] The Austrian authorities knew that Romanian irredentism, although increasing, was limited to educated circles in Bukovina. Even so, they feared that it would spread to peasants, who were "easy to influence because of their lack of education and naivety."[21]

In August 1914 Czernowitzers encountered the enemy for the first time in the flesh. Philipp Menczel, a local journalist and Zionist who would soon be deported to Siberia, recalled seeing a Cossack swimming across the Prut, "so drunk that he completely lost consciousness."[22] Julius Weber, a journalist who fled with the Austrian administration to Dorna-Watra, recalled how the Russian troops burst into the university library "tearing the costly classics into paper shreds," stealing and breaking objects, turning the gymnastics room into a "butchery" and using sports equipment as a support "for the cut up meat."[23] Menczel noted that while the Russian officers tried "to appear civilized," the Cossacks and "Asiatics" gave the occupation the character of a "Tatar invasion."[24] Increasingly, he viewed the war as an existential conflict between civilization and barbarism, culture and savagery.

By chronicling the devastation the Russians wrought upon Bukovina, Menczel and Weber hoped to persuade Austria to pay greater attention to the fate of this land, otherwise little known and neglected. Bukovina, Menczel insisted, was "the fulcrum of a cultural front, the cultural conscience of Central Europe." Austria's great achievement, now under threat, had been to transform this "wild Turkish corner" into a "supple hoop whose purpose was to keep tightly together the seemingly loose pieces of the Danube basin and Carpathian foothills."[25]

The Russian troops directed their brutality above all against the Jewish population of Bukovina, with Valerian Nikolaevich Murav'ev, the Russian Foreign Ministry's attaché to the southwestern front, playing a decisive role.[26] When touring Bukovina in October 1917, the Austrian governor noticed that while the Russians had largely spared peasant houses, the homes of Jews who had fled during the war had been burnt to ashes.[27] One reason for this brutality was that Jews were suspected of spying for Austria and blamed for the Russian troops' failures at the front. Russian soldiers were given a free hand to rob and brutalize Jews they encountered in occupied territories. In the Kotzman district of Bukovina, the Russian army took "some Jewish families from certain communities and chased them like a herd toward the firing line which ran right outside Szypenitz."[28]

Hundreds of Jews fled the invading Russian troops, running toward the Romanian border in winter with little more than the clothes on their backs. A Bucharest representative of the Alliance israélite described the "innumerable women, old men, and children shaking from cold [and] begging to be let in across the frontier to take refuge in Romania."[29] Their pleas were in vain, as the Bucharest authorities only accepted refugees who could prove that they had plans to leave the country as soon as they had arrived.

Given the first Russian occupation's brutality, Austrian patriots in Czernowitz (many of them German-speaking Jews like Menczel and Weber) found it outrageous that the Russians tried to persuade locals that they had "a sense of order and justice, spirit of hygiene and welfare, humanity, and culture." After the Austrians liberated Czernowitz for the third time, the *Czernowitzer Allgemeine Zeitung* related how the Russians had tried to pretend they were *Überkulturmenschen* and equal to Austrians by cleaning the city five times a day and fining barbers who failed to wear white robes, which the *Zeitung*'s editors compared to "covering up a crust of dirt with French perfume."[30]

Just as the Austrians played up the Russian army's brutality and barbarism, the Russian authorities never tired of talking about the atrocities the Austrians committed against alleged Russian collaborators in Bukovina. Locals were encouraged to make declarations about how they had been persecuted and to finger Austrian collaborators in return. Alexander Strelchuk, a thirty-four-year-old Orthodox peasant from Glubokaya, blamed Jews and Germans for the more than 150 "Russian peasants" arrested by the Austrian gendarmerie in October 1914 (four were hanged). According to Strelchuk, their motive had been to repay the peasants for welcoming the Russian troops and pointing them toward Jewish homes.[31]

## Denunciation and Collusion

Most people experienced Bukovina's successive occupations and liberations as a mixture of disasters and unexpected blessings. For many, the breakdown of state authority brought enormous losses, whether of life, limb, property, or all three, especially during the first months of Russian occupation. One evening two Cossack soldiers knocked on the door of Dmytro Ladygin, a priest from the village of Berhometh, asking if a Jew lived there. Failing to find any Jews, the Cossacks took his supply of butter;[32] in another village the Russians "stripped the priest Strilczuk's boots from his feet."[33] Many Christian women in Bukovina's northern districts, meanwhile, were raped and infected with "syphilis or gonorrhea or both."[34] Ladygin's wife and daughter spent the first nights of the Russian occupation hiding in the forest.

Bukovinan Jews, as the Russian-Jewish writer and activist S. An-Sky wrote of Austrian Jews in general, went from "enjoying civil rights under Austrian rule to being ruthlessly murdered."[35] Suspecting Jews of treason and espionage, the Russian authorities deported them from the combat zone.[36] Caught in a wave of spy hysteria, the Russian authorities imagined that Jews were communicating with Germans by telephone—or by sneezing, a technique which they supposedly used to tell the enemy where to bombard. The humiliations to which Bukovinan Jews were subjected by the Russians terrified their Christian neighbors, who began wearing crosses or lockets with Jesus Christ's portrait for protection.[37] In some instances, the Russians used Jews as living shields, pushing them against the barrage of fire that rained down from the opposite side. In a village near Czernowitz, Cossack soldiers grabbed "four bearded Jews, drove them across the frozen river, tied their beards together, forcing one of them to play the fiddle and the other one to dance."[38] The humiliations inflicted could be truly appalling, as in a story recounted by one of Nikolai von Wassilko's correspondents in Bukovina:

> On the Seletyn bridge a Jew meets a Huzul, holds him back, and talks to him. Behind the Jew a Cossack comes quietly and hears the Jew saying to the Huzul, "Bad man!" The Cossack then grabs both of them, asks them what they were both saying. His anger seems to concentrate on the peasant, the Jew stands by speechless and the Huzul excuses himself, says he said nothing. Before long they are surrounded by grinning Cossacks. The Cossack orders the Huzul: "Drop off your pants!" "Sir, I am innocent." "Drop your pants immediately. Good: now bend forward." Then the Cossack grabs the Jew by his beard, pulls his head towards the peasant's naked behind and orders the Jew on the one hand to "kiss" and the peasant on the other hand to "break wind."[39]

Although anti-Semitism was widespread in the Russian army, the military and civilian authorities did not agree on a concerted Jewish policy for the occupied territories. Military officials were generally harsher. For Murav'ev and the supreme commander-in-chief Grand Duke Nikolai Nikolaevich, a Russian western borderland purged of Jews was part of their vision of a reformed postwar Russian empire. Civilian governors were more moderate, but since the military had the upper hand in Bukovina, it could institute ruthless anti-Jewish measures: it deported Jews, confiscated their property, extorted money from them, and took hostages.[40] When the Russian troops returned to Bukovina after being briefly repelled by the Austrians in November 1914, Governor S. D. Evreinov accused local Jews of "celebrating the withdrawal of Russian troops from Czernowitz, burning the Russian flag, mocking Russian institutions." He punished them by demanding the Jewish community pay 50,000 rubles and took six Jewish representatives hostage to guarantee payment. The committee formed to collect the money failed: since "all the wealthier Jews left Czernowitz," they could only gather 1,000 crowns. When the Jews did not pay, another thirty people were taken hostage. Jews also made up the bulk of deportees from Bukovina.[41] Of the 446 people deported from the Kotzman district during the second Russian occupation, 331 were "Israelites," sixty-seven Greek Orthodox, and forty-eight Roman-Catholic.[42]

These policies were partly motivated by the Russian occupation authorities' desire to secure the support of Christian peasants in Bukovina.[43] Some peasants did perceive Russian actions as repairing injustices suffered under Austrian rule, for the Russians "persecuted the rich, especially the Jews, and spoiled the masses, in that they gave them gifts (of stolen property) and distributed among them land."[44] In January 1915 Galicia's Russian governor Georgii Bobrinskii visited Czernowitz and promised to distribute to the peasant population goods expropriated from landowners and Jews who had fled the province. A week later, peasants turned up to claim the goods. The Ukrainophile politician Erotey Pihuliak was surprised to discover that Ruthenian peasants were only too happy to accommodate the Russian authorities in exchange for small gifts. People, he reported, "to our deepest regret, are prejudiced in the enemy's favor."[45]

Once the Austrians left, nobody forced peasants to send their children to school. Also gone were the fines for violating school attendance laws. Tsarist officials encouraged peasants to help themselves to property abandoned by fleeing landowners. A Russian commander who set up headquarters on Georg von Wassilko-Serecki's estate in Berhometh tried to incite peasants on the estate against the Wassilko family by asking "how much they have to pay the Baron."[46] When they left the estate, the Russians took all the furniture and belongings (including Wassilko's dog), then set the property on fire.[47]

Merchants and smugglers in Bukovina enriched themselves during the Russian occupations by trading on the black market. The inflow of almost 150,000 Russian officers and soldiers into Czernowitz led to a commercial boom, with handworkers, tailors, and shoemakers making good money catering to Russian officers and "their frivolous wives," in General Fischer's words. Eau de cologne sales apparently boomed, as the Russian soldiers used it "as a replacement for alcohol."[48] Sugar, flour, and coffee poured into the city, leaving locals who hadn't seen these goods since the start of the war "staring with astonishment."[49] Through trade and smuggling, some people acquired powerful patrons among the Russian officials. One tax official in Seletyn, a German named Anton Zachmann, provided Cossack troops with clothing and wood. In return, the Russian army gave him various goods and "horses stolen from peasants." Zachmann told anyone he came into conflict with that "he would bring a Cossack over."[50] Some local women, impressed by "Russian officers' gentlemanly behavior and rich gifts," took Russian lovers. As many as 292 women left Czernowitz with the Russians in 1915—a fact that General Fischer attributed to "the easy morals that were typical of this place in peacetime too."[51]

Like the Russians, the Austrian authorities elicited locals' participation and support in securing control over the province. Since the start of the war, locals had been encouraged to engage in surveillance.[52] People listened in on each other's conversations and kept an eye on each other, particularly in inns, taverns, and coaches. The chain of denunciations that started in the fall of 1914 grew longer and longer as people who were denounced to the Austrians turned their denouncers in to the Russians, and vice versa. When the Russian troops who had retreated from Bukovina in February 1915 returned, they wanted those who had collaborated with the Austrians to be made to pay for their actions; and in March that year the tsar instructed subordinates that "those nationalities that are hostile to us will have to answer for atrocities [. . .] against the Slavic and Romanian population of Bukovina."[53]

Returning Austrian officials had the same idea, collecting information about people's actions under the Russian occupation. A certain Hostiuc, the director of the magistrature in Czernowitz under the first Russian administration, was denounced for having used Russian protection to form a city mafia of sorts, trafficking property "left behind by citizens who had fled Czernowitz."[54] The Austrians used information collected from local denouncers to arrest people, organize treason trials, and confine suspects in internment camps.[55]

## Losing Trust in the State

The brutal first Russian occupation strengthened many Bukovinans' bonds with the Austrian state. In the mountain districts of Bukovina, where the Russians set fire to houses, "tore [clothes] apart in front of [locals'] eyes and burnt expensive, irreplaceable goods," local women began holding secret masses for the Austrian emperor. But as the war went on, Bukovinans increasingly lost trust in Austria, now a military dictatorship where military officials and the gendarmerie wielded arbitrary power over civilians.[56] "In the streets during the day, but above all at night," a Bukovinan Romanian historian recalled, "soldiers, patrolling up and down with ttheir rifles and sharp bayonets, ordered that [everyone] be quiet and at crucial moments that all lights be turned off."[57]

General Fischer's gendarmerie arrested and executed suspected collaborators on little or no evidence, and the returning Austrian and German armies treated the areas they liberated almost as enemy territory. In June 1915 the Ukrainian politician Erotey Pihuliak reported that "Hungarian, Croat, Polish legionaries, and even Germans from the Reich outdo each other in damage, destruction, and bullying." In the northern districts inhabited mostly by Ruthenians, returning troops burned fences, trampled meadows, stole everything down to the last cow and horse. By 1915, in the once prosperous Hutsul village of Moldawa, only one man still owned a wagon and two horses. Pihuliak held the Austrian *Etappenoberst* in Moldawa responsible for all this, claiming that he was "very angry and cares about nothing at all but giving the Jewesses who work at the post office diamond rings as gifts."[58]

Locals who suffered losses during the war often complained that Jews sat around doing nothing, shirking their responsibilities or taking advantage of martial law to enrich themselves.[59] A teacher named Hordiichuk recalled how many "innocent Ukrainians" had been deported to Hungary after a group of Jews had supposedly presented the Austrian military authorities in Wizenka

FIGURE 4.2. "Waiting for construction to begin for this destroyed home." Photograph from Suceava, 1920–21, for the American Jewish Joint Distribution Committee (JDC, or "Joint"), which provided support for the reconstruction of Jewish homes. The image is from an album documenting the JDC's work in Bukovina: the man featured here received a loan to rebuild his home. Courtesy of the Joint Distribution Committee Archives.

with a list of "our poor people, explaining that the Ukrainian population is friendly to the Russians and fraternized with them, the best proof of this being that they took soup, meat, and potatoes from the Russians." To Hordiichuk, this was the height of hypocrisy, since some Jews had also done business with "the thousands of sacks of stolen goods they bought from the Russians." The teacher predicted that "it is not impossible that the people should soon have a reckoning with the 'patriots,' as they well deserve."[60] "When our troops are here," a local from Hadikfalva lamented, "then all the confidential informers are there, they eat and drink and sleep well and take lots of money for their stupid insinuations. But as soon as the Russians were here not even one of these informers could be seen, precisely when they were most needed."[61]

Romanian and Ruthenian nationalists in Bukovina increasingly viewed the monarchy as an instrument of Jewish domination. In a letter to the Austrian War Ministry, a Bukovinan Romanian who had fled to Romania wrote that he did so in order to "escape the Jewified monarchy."[62] The Romanian politician

Gheorghe Serbu, put under surveillance in 1915 for "unpatriotic activities and espionage," deeply resented the "Jewish speculators—so-called high patriots" who had supposedly spread rumors about his activities under Russian rule. In his biting letter to Bukovina's governor von Meran, Serbu went on to say that if the authorities did not immediately free him, he would "have nothing left to do but follow my brave, self-sacrificing colleagues [Jews] to Vienna to play 'war *Tarok*' there in the coffee houses."[63]

The Austrian authorities made the situation worse by making the monarchy look both exceptionally brutal and extremely incompetent. Thanks to poor planning and leadership, the Austro-Hungarian army was exhausted before it even saw combat. Soldiers' boots and clothes were worn out after a long and senseless march across Galicia. Laden with over twenty-five kilograms (55 lbs) of equipment that they carried on muddy roads, with swollen feet, soldiers wondered why they were there.[64] After 1916, as Austria became increasingly dependent on German support, the lesser partner in an unequal alliance, the Austrian army was unable to keep its German allies from terrorizing the local population. Arbitrary requisitioning led peasants to stop cultivating their lands as "their efforts and worries which they put into working the soil were in vain because everything was taken away from them by German soldiers over the course of a few days and destroyed." German soldiers tore down announcements posted by the Austrian authorities and in some places forbade the local population from selling food to Austrian troops. Caught between the squabbling allies, Bukovinans became suspicious of both, not knowing "who governs today: the Austrian officials or the German commanders."[65]

That fatal mix of ruthlessness and incompetence was especially evident in how the Austrian authorities treated those suspected of collaborating with the enemy. People were arrested and held captive for years without evidence. While in captivity, they were often mistreated and subjected to abuse. In July 1914, for instance, the gendarmerie in Bukovina arrested a Romanian "theologian" on suspicion of espionage. His travel companions and the owner of the inn where he stopped reported that he looked out the window too often and asked too many questions about the army's activities at the front. The man had spent half a year in prison before the authorities decided that "officials without a juridical education" but "preoccupied by the good of the state had arrested him entirely by mistake."[66]

Among the arrested was one man who had apparently been overheard saying "Romania is for Russia and against Austria, and Russia promised Bessarabia to Romania and we must go and save our brothers in Transylvania."[67] He was pardoned, since no evidence was found against him (though he lost his job). The arrested were not always treated well: a Romanian priest suspected of irredentism was chained up with "a Gypsy," which Romanian onlookers

FIGURE. 4.3. World War I refugees from Bukovina crowded together inside an electric train (n.d.). ÖNB Bildarchiv und Grafiksammlung. Courtesy of the Österreichische Nationalbibliothek (ÖNB/Wien), WK1/ALB104/31876.

considered the height of humiliation.[68] In October 1914 Governor von Meran reported to the Ministry of Interior that a great number of Romanians had been arrested on military orders, but their precise number was unknown.[69]

It was not just those punished for sympathizing with the enemy who lost their trust in the state; the feeling was also common among refugees fleeing the incoming Russian invasions. From the start, Bukovinans were struck by how poorly prepared Austrian officials were to handle the masses of people displaced by the war in the east. To Eduard Fischer, who took great pride in defending Bukovina from the Russians, civilians seemed like an afterthought. During the evacuations, he prioritized food, cattle, and trains. When the Russian army approached Bukovina again in June 1916, desperate locals assaulted Fischer's trains, hoping to save themselves. While civil servants were transported to Prague, where they were assigned apartments until it was safe to return to Bukovina, most Bukovinans who made it out of the crown land did so crowded into cattle cars.

Once they reached safety, Bukovinan refugees found that their fellow citizens reacted to their plight with indifference and even hostility. Bukovinan refugees who stopped in Hungary on their way west met locals who refused to sell them food or boarded up their wells, hoping thirst would force the refugees to leave sooner. Hungarian merchants grabbed horses and cattle from refugees and resold them at exorbitant prices. In July 1916 a gendarmerie watchman from Dornavölgy, "despite the pouring rain," evicted refugees "and put their things into the open air in the mud. The families were interned in barracks and remained without food all day long."[70] In Bohemia and Moravia, Bukovinan refugees—especially Jews—were accused of engaging in illegal trade and usury and of lying about their situation to obtain alms. Bukovinans, like other refugees from the east, were also unwelcome in Vienna, where merchants refused to sell them food, and locals would not rent them apartments.[71] The Viennese were especially prejudiced against Jews from Galicia and Bukovina, whom they regarded as uncivilized.

After being sworn at and insulted, most refugees could hardly wait to return to Bukovina. The years they spent away from home took a severe economic and personal toll: their families were broken up, and many could not find employment in crown lands whose languages they did not speak. A veritable outpouring of petitions for repatriation from Bukovina's refugees reached the Ministry of Interior in Vienna in 1916. In May that year one man who had managed to return to his native village of Czudin in Bukovina while his family remained in Vienna wrote that "it is possible to live in peace here and to continue working, there is no shortage of milk and eggs, no shortage of meat, things are more expensive but not like in Vienna."[72] Another refugee who had been scraping together an existence in Eipel (Úpice) in Bohemia since December 1914 complained that he had applied for permission to return to Bukovina numerous times and had been consistently rejected because the province was still part of the combat zone. Even well-off individuals such as Elias Wender, who owned several enterprises, printing presses, and the newspaper *Czernowitzer Tagblatt*, feared bankruptcy since "most employees have been mobilized" and their families were not allowed to return to Bukovina to help with the business for as long as the province was part of the front.[73]

In addition to eroding Bukovinans' faith in the monarchy and their fellow citizens, the refugee experience reified their ethnic differences. The Austrian authorities contributed to this by insisting that the refugees be assigned separate housing by ethnicity "in order to maintain their feeling of *Heimat*."[74] Refugees were processed in inspection centers and sent to specially created refugee camps or barracks. Well-off refugees, including German-speaking Jews from Czernowitz, went to Vienna. Others were assigned to locations based on their nationality, everywhere from Bohemia, Moravia, Upper Austria, Styria, Silesia, to Salzburg. Germans from Bukovina were scattered between Baden, Kottingbrunn, and Leesdorf bei Wien. Most Jewish refugees from the eastern crown lands ended up in eastern Bohemia and Moravia, concentrated in three large camps in Mikulov, Kojetin, and Pohořelice.[75] Once assigned to a camp or community, refugees had to go there to receive state support, which most desperately needed. One of the largest refugee camps was in Gmünd, a barrack town built to accommodate thirty thousand Ukrainians. It had a hospital with eleven hundred beds, two hospitals for infectious diseases, special stalls for horses, cattle, and pigs, a reserve guard of two hundred men, and a branch of the gendarmerie.[76]

## Nationalism and Patriotism

By and large, Bukovinans remained loyal to the Austrian monarchy to the very end. However, repeated cycles of violence and retribution invested ethnic differences with new meanings. By the end of the war, moreover, radical nationalism had moved from the fringes of local politics closer to the center. At the war's outbreak, a group of Romanian nationalist irredentists crossed the border into Romania and formed a Bukovinan refugees' committee. Exiled in Bucharest, they contributed to Romania's war effort by writing propaganda articles denouncing Austria's crimes against Romanians in Bukovina—the greatest of these being, they insisted, their denationalization.[77] Emilian Slușanschi, a Romanian lawyer from Bukovina, spoke before the Romanian Congress in Bucharest, condemning the Germanization and Ruthenization of the province's Romanian schools. Ion Nistor developed this idea further in publications accusing the Austrian administration of plotting with Ruthenian nationalists to erode Bukovina's Romanian character. Ilie Torouțiu, another Bukovinan lawyer, warned the Romanian public about the Jews' dominant role in Bukovina.[78] The Romanian teacher Ion Grămadă, who died at the front, penned explosive articles documenting atrocities the Austrian gendarmerie had committed in the province, mostly, he said, against Romanians.

Romanian notables in Bukovina, including nationalists like Aurel Onciul, discounted these allegations. One Romanian delegate in the Landtag dismissed the Romanian Cultural League's propagandistic campaign against the monarchy as a tactical error based on a misguided understanding of Romanian interests. Romanians under Austrian rule, he insisted, were anything but persecuted: "During my three-year service as delegate, I turned in many Romanian petitions to the state administration and it never happened that such a petition was not accepted."[79] In the *Bukowinaer Post* Aurel Onciul wrote that "the existence of our entire nation depends on the existence of a powerful Austria-Hungary." Moreover, Onciul argued that "for us Bukovinan Romanians, any intervention of the Cultural League in our affairs is absolutely undesirable."[80]

Irredentists hoping for Bukovina's future unification with the Kingdom of Romania dismissed such avowals of loyalty to the monarchy as fabrications "written with the gendarmes behind one's back."[81] But most Romanians in Bukovina did not envision a national destiny shared with their fellow Romanians across the border. Governor Rudolf Graf von Meran noted that "the people in the Romanian parts of the province are patriotic, they have faith and hope in the emperor and speak with him with great respect and childlike love."[82] Reflecting on the relationship between Romanians on both sides of the Austro-Romanian border, Ilie Grămadă, a Romanian irredentist, had to admit that "we do not know each other, and we make no effort to get to know each other either."[83]

Loyalist nationalists like Onciul had more clout than the irredentists who fled Bukovina, both because they stayed behind and because they had more political capital—capital they used to mobilize their respective nationalities to contribute to Austria's war effort. Onciul organized massive demonstrations of loyalty, including a rally in the old Moldavian city of Suczawa in November 1914, when five thousand Romanian peasants from all over Bukovina came to proclaim their loyalty to the emperor. The gathering took place in the courtyard of the Johannes Novi monastery, a pilgrimage site for Orthodox Romanians because it supposedly contained the relics of Saint John. A Romanian peasant delegate insisted that "the gentlemen in Bucharest should not concern themselves about us." Bukovinan Romanians, he claimed, "feel very good as Austrian citizens because they are treated in the same way as other peoples in the monarchy." Protesting against the Kingdom's claims to represent Romanians everywhere, the delegate declared that Bukovinan Romanians "already have a fatherland that we love and wish to defend with our last drop of blood." Onciul suggested that Romania join the war on Austria-Hungary's side since "we have learned from our parents that the most dangerous enemy of the entire Romanian people are the Russians, and against them only powerful Austria can protect us."[84]

Onciul's former partner in the Progressive Alliance of 1904, Nikolai von Wassilko, similarly argued that the interests of Ukrainians in the monarchy were perfectly aligned with Austria's. Amid anti-Russophile campaigns prior to the outbreak of war, Wassilko had reassured the Austrian authorities that Ukrainians in Bukovina had no desire to "exchange the good Austrian administration [. . .] for tsarist slavery."[85] At the same time, he noted that Austria was partly to blame for Russophile sentiment among Ukrainians, noting in a 1912 speech in the Reichsrat that Austrian policies of "neglect, contempt, and oppression of the Ruthenian people" had practically thrown Ruthenians into Russia's arms.[86] Wassilko spent the war years in Vienna, where Ukrainian nationalist institutions and organizations promised to recruit Ukrainian volunteers to join the imperial and royal troops at the front in exchange for financial support.[87] In turn, the Austrian government hoped to benefit from the propaganda these organizations disseminated among Ukrainians under Austrian rule, on enemy territory, and among prisoners of war.[88]

One of these organizations was the Ukrainian National Council (Ukrainska Natsionalna Rada), formed in Vienna with Wassilko as its deputy head. In May 1915 the Council called for territorial autonomy for all Ukrainians under Austrian rule.[89] Later, in a document composed in June 1916 on "the Ukrainian question," the Council noted that "Galicia and Bukovina must be tied to the state even more profoundly and tightly than before."[90] The Ukrainian National Council's vision of a postwar Ukraine centered on a Galicia divided into two distinct sections: one Polish, one Ukrainian. Together with Ukrainian Galicia, Bukovina would be part of a large Ukrainian entity under Austrian rule. Though committed to working with Austria, the Council lamented that the monarchy had neglected Ukrainians and that "the third largest people in Austria is as a result lagging far behind the smallest [peoples] in its national-cultural development."[91]

Both the Austrian and Russian armies and civilian authorities tried to secure a foothold in the region by sponsoring nationalist causes they believed could help them further their interests. In September 1914 Russia's Grand Duke Nikolai Nikolaevich issued a manifesto to the peoples of Austria-Hungary, promising to fulfill all their "national desires."[92] His appeals were heard and circulated across Austria-Hungary, in Bohemia, Moravia, Bukovina, and Galicia. The Central Powers, meanwhile, as soon as they occupied a part of Poland,—largely in response to Russian efforts to court Poles—sponsored a Polish state-building project that helped lay the foundations for the postwar resurrected Poland.[93] In Bukovina, the tsarist authorities courted Romanians, in large part because Russia wanted Romania to join the war effort on the Entente's side. The Russian Foreign Ministry's attaché Murav'ev advised the Russian authorities to proceed "tactfully" where Romanians in Bukovina were concerned.[94]

In deference to the Romanians, the tsarist administration staffed Bukovina's new government with cadres from neighboring Bessarabia, who spoke Romanian.[95] They named Bessarabia's former vice-governor S. D. Evreinov head of Bukovina's civilian administration, directly subordinate to Galicia's governor Georgii Bobrinskii. The night Evreinov arrived in Czernowitz, its mayor Salo Weisselberger was awoken from his slumbers, told to take "warm clothes and money," and deported to Siberia. On Evreinov's instructions, the former municipal council was replaced with a city administration consisting mostly of Romanians, among them Titus von Onciul and Modest Scalat, along with men by the names of Hackmann, Welehorski, and others. The new mayor was also Romanian: Themistocle Bocancea, a middle-aged lawyer who had fled to Russia with Alexei Gerovskii, whom he had defended during his high treason trial in 1914.[96]

The Austrian authorities saw Romanians' attempts to ingratiate themselves with Russian authorities in Bukovina as opportunistic rather than motivated by nationalist convictions. An Austrian report noted that Bocancea had been inspired by "no means by political convictions, but rather by material reasons [...] and in order to maintain his position, he became a spineless instrument of the Russian government and a terror for the population."[97] Yet opportunism and nationalism became increasingly inextricable. The very act of siding with one occupier against another gave national identities in Bukovina new coherence and strength. In 1912, Modest Scalat had protested against the oppression of Romanians in the Russian Empire, declaring that "Romanians in Bukovina are in the best position, for their full national freedom and development are guaranteed by law."[98] In 1914, that same Scalat, now a Russian-appointed city magistrate, threatened that Bukovina would soon "go over to Romania and the Romanians would be in charge." "You hope the Austrians will come back," he warned, "but that is out of the question. Austria is in tatters, Austria is lost, now we (Russians together with Romanians) will rule here."[99] First Austrophile, then Russophile, Scalat ended up a victim of his own flexibility. As soon as the Austrian authorities returned to Czernowitz, they tried him for collaborating with the Russians.

At first, Ukrainian nationalists in Bukovina were firmly on the monarchy's side, an obvious choice since the Russian government had banned the Ukrainian language, forcing Ukrainian nationalists into exile.[100] But then in the Russian Empire the February revolution of 1917 brought about the tsarist administration's collapse and its replacement by a Provisional Government. This had consequences for Bukovina too. In March 1917 the province's Russian governor Aleksandr Trepov was replaced with a new regional commissar appointed by the Provisional Government: Dmytro Doroshenko, a Ukrainian nationalist who believed the Ukrainian question could be solved within the framework of a reformed Russian empire. Romanian notables in Bukovina who had been appointed by the tsarist administration were replaced by Ukrainian activists. Valerian Nikolaevich Murav'ev, who had been responsible for deportations and hostage-taking in Bukovina, was arrested.[101] Doroshenko intended to put Czernowitz's administration in Ukrainian hands and make Ukrainian Bukovina's official language.[102]

Although his plan never came to fruition, Ukrainians now enjoyed a privileged position. Ukrainian activists who arrived in Bukovina urged their conationals to "join their brothers in Russia to fulfill the ideal of a free Ukraine."[103] According to the Austrian police director, "urban Ruthenians" remained indifferent. Moreover, the Russian Provisional Government lacked a firm grip on power. Governor Doroshenko tried importing the February revolution into Bukovina, but as late as August 1917, Alexei Gerovskii was back in Czernowitz demanding that tsarist rule be restored.[104] Soon Doroshenko was gone and so was the Russian army, which had been disintegrating since the unsuccessful offensive of summer 1917.

## National Self-Determination

Emperor Karl, the great nephew and heir of Emperor Franz Joseph, who died in November 1916, visited Czernowitz in August 1917 and instructed the returning Austrian authorities to restore order in Bukovina. But too much had changed, and these authorities could not turn back the clock. Some areas of the province had been completely devastated by the war. While retreating, the Russian army had employed its infamous scorched earth policy, plundering and destroying entire villages. Property had been redistributed in Bukovina during the war and the individuals who had acquired it were unwilling to relinquish their gains. Peasants, tired of having the fruits of their labor confiscated, opposed the Austrian troops' attempts to requisition their grain and animals. After multiple occupations, many people had learned to be circumspect and mistrustful of state authorities. They knew better than to volunteer information, lest the province change hands again.

Indeed, many Bukovinans thought this was entirely possible, especially when news of Emperor Karl's attempts to negotiate a secret peace with the Entente leaked. Rumors spread that at the Brest-Litovsk peace in March 1917 Emperor Karl had agreed to unite Bukovina and East Galicia into an autonomous Ukrainian province as a concession to Ukraine, whose grain Austria desperately needed.[105] Bukovina's new governor Josef Graf von Ezdorf feared that if the emperor did unify Bukovina's Ukrainian part with East Galicia, there would be street demonstrations in Czernowitz.[106]

When Emperor Karl's attempts to conclude a separate peace treaty with the Entente became public, Austro–German antagonisms reached the point of no return. Bukovinans, too, grew increasingly hostile toward German soldiers in the province. In reoccupied Bukovina, German soldiers were sworn at and given to understand they were not welcome. "My basket with official mail," one of them complained, "was thrown out by a civilian. [. . .] This is already the second case in which we are insulted while traveling by train. [. . .] Such words of derision as 'marmalade,' 'marmalade soldier,' and expressions such as 'war prolonger' have been heard even in Czernowitz in the Volksgarten and on busy streets."[107]

Hoping to restore people's faith in the monarchy, Emperor Karl re-instituted constitutional rule in May 1917.[108] On October 17, 1918 he issued a manifesto to Austria's nationalities, laying the groundwork for a federal reorganization of the monarchy: "Austria shall become a federal state in which each national

FIGURE. 4.4. Austrian soldier in dog-drawn cart (dogs may have been used to substitute for horses, once these were no longer available for requisitioning), in Bukovina near the border with Romania, ca. 1917; photograph from the K.u.k. Kriegspressequartier Lichtbildstelle (Imperial and Royal War Press Office Photograph Section), Vienna. ÖNB Bildarchiv und Grafiksammlung. Courtesy of the Österreichische Nationalbibliothek (ÖNB/Wien), WK1/ALB105/32261.

component [*Volksstamm*] will form its own state organization in its area of settlement [. . . and] this reorganization, which in no way touches the integrity of the lands of Hungary's holy crown, guarantees every national [. . .] state its independence."[109] Though meant to preempt revolution, the manifesto had the opposite effect. Groups with strong nationalist movements formed national councils and quickly moved from demanding autonomy to proclaiming their independence.[110]

As nationalists asserted their right to national self-determination, the Austrian military began to fall apart. Governor Ezdorf watched helplessly as order broke down in Bukovina, and Czernowitz succumbed to chaos. "In the streets during the day soldiers roam around aimlessly and haphazardly," the *Czernowitzer Morgenblatt* reported in November 1918. Officers could be seen walking around "in civilian clothes," "without rosettes and without caps" while "the strangest figures can be seen with white armbands and weapons" in an impromptu citizens' guard, trying and failing to restore order. In the meantime, "in the lower city" homes were plundered while "soldiers and the

FIGURE 4.5. Emperor Karl on the eastern front, December 1917. This photograph by the Austrian photographer Heinrich Schuhmann the Younger (1888–1963) shows locals, mostly peasants holding religious icons and symbols, welcoming the emperor to Bukovina. ÖNB Bildarchiv und Grafiksammlung. Courtesy of the Österreichische Nationalbibliothek (ÖNB/Wien), 211.826-C.

light-shunning rabble, joined also by Italian prisoners, took advantage of the whole confusion and carried out multiple thefts."[111]

Few politicians in the monarchy—nationalist or not—contemplated Austria-Hungary's actual demise, however.[112] Moreover, nationalists who proclaimed their respective nationalities' right to self-determination had little idea of what this might mean in practice. The Romanian National Council (Consiliul Naţional Român) in Vienna, consisting of Romanian delegates in the Austrian parliament, was still imagining an Austrian Bukovina.[113] They headed back to Bukovina in October 1918, but their train had to turn around near Przemysl, where a bridge over the San river had been blown up by Ukrainians, now fighting with Poles over Galicia.[114] The delegates spent the rest of the year in Vienna, disconnected from events in the province. Meanwhile, nationalist politicians on the ground took a very different path.

Two different national bodies claimed Bukovina: the Romanian National Council and the Ukrainian National Council. Romanian representatives in the Reichsrat and Landtag, along with Romanian mayors from across Bukovina, gathered in Cernowitz on October 17 and proclaimed that "the Romanian people in Bukovina establishes the right to decide its own fate."[115] The gathering proclaimed solidarity with co-nationals in Transylvania and Hungary and demanded the creation of a joint representative body for all the empire's Romanians. It also created a Constituent Assembly whose task was to form a de facto provisional government. The Constituent Assembly first convened on October 27, proclaiming itself a National Council which "will represent us [Romanians] through mandatories also at the peace conference." The participants declared furthermore that they did not "recognize the right of anyone else to make decisions or debate the [fate of] the Romanian people in Bukovina. The Constituent [Assembly] decisively rejects any attempt at undermining Bukovina's [integrity], but it also wishes to come to an understanding with the peoples with whom [the Romanians] coexist."[116] On October 28 Iancu Flondor, effectively the Assembly's leader, asked Governor Ezdorf to hand over Bukovina's administration to the Romanian Council.

Meanwhile, a Ukrainian National Council (Rada) had formed in the Galician capital of Lemberg on October 15. The Council's Bukovinan branch, headed by Omelian Popovych, called itself the "Bukovynskyi Kraiovyi Komitet" (Ukrainian Provincial Committee of Bukovina). On November 1 the Ukrainian National Council's troops (formerly part of the Habsburg army) occupied Lemberg. They voted to draw a demarcation line through Bukovina based on the last Austrian census, effectively partitioning the province. By November 6, Ukrainians had laid claim to parts of Bukovina and occupied most public and administrative buildings in Czernowitz. On November 9 the Rada proclaimed the independence of the West Ukrainian Republic, which claimed areas of the monarchy inhabited by Ukrainians, including Bukovina. Omelian Popovych came to an understanding with Aurel Onciul to divide Bukovina into Ukrainian and Romanian halves. Romanians Alexandru Hurmuzaki, president of Bukovina's Diet, and Gheorghe Grigorovici, president of the Social Democratic Party, also supported the partition. But Iancu Flondor firmly rejected it and invited the Romanian army to cross the border into Bukovina to restore order.[117]

Romanian troops arrived in Czernowitz on November 11, 1918.[118] Onciul rushed to Jassy to persuade the Romanian government to stay out of Bukovina, but was arrested on the way. With the Romanian army watching, Flondor organized a General Congress on November 28 to determine Bukovina's future.[119] Since the Romanian military had already imposed martial law on Bukovina, the Congress was little more than a formality. By the time it convened, the gendarmerie in Czernowitz was sweeping up suspected Ukrainian sympathizers. Officially, however, the status of non-Romanians in the recently reconfigured territory was not yet decided. While Flondor promised extensive rights to non-Romanians, more radical nationalists insisted that minorities should not receive any special consideration.

Most non-Romanian representatives at the Congress supported Bukovina's unification with Romania. Ukrainian representatives, however, boycotted the Congress, continuing to claim at least part of Bukovina for a Greater Ukrainian state. Members of the Jewish National Council refused to take sides, which the Romanians interpreted as implicit support for the Ukrainian claims. Polish and German representatives aligned themselves with the new ruling nationality in the hope of securing good conditions and extensive rights under Romanian rule. Stanislaus Kwiatkowski, representing Bukovina's Poles, argued that Poles should be recognized because they had "fulfilled their historic mission to defend Christianity and culture in Eastern Europe" by "shedding their blood in these parts," beginning with the Polish knights of the Middle Ages and ending with their sacrifices in the recent war.[120]

Soon after the West Ukrainian Republic seized Lemberg, a war broke out between the Republic and the new Polish state, which also claimed Galicia. Ukrainian volunteers and troops were shifted from Bukovina to Galicia to fight the Poles, leaving the local Rada understaffed and the Romanians effectively in charge. Although it no longer had troops on the ground, Ukraine did not renounce its claims to Bukovina. Nor was Bukovina's official status settled. At the Paris peace conference, the Ukrainian Republic's delegation insisted that its claims deserved recognition because of its "long history of striving for independence."[121] The delegation appealed to the Western Allies' anti-Bolshevik sentiments by emphasizing Ukraine's commitment to fighting Bolshevik Russia. Since the Ukrainian Republic had not formally renounced its claims to northern Bukovina, as late as April 1919 some locals heard rumors that their province would fall into Ukrainian hands.

## Bukovina in Paris

The Romanian delegation, headed by Prime Minister Ionel Brătianu, arrived in Paris on January 13, 1919 claiming to represent not only the Romanian kingdom but also

> the Romanians of the region snatched away 150 years ago from Moldavia and linked together with the Austrian Crown under the name of Bukovina, Transylvania, and the regions of Marmarosch and Crishana—of the Banat of Temeshvar—who before 1914 had always demanded their separation from the Austro-Hungarian Empire and have since then, as soon as they were able to do so freely, shown their will to be reunited with the Romanians in the Kingdom of Bessarabia.[122]

Taking advantage of Romania's strategic position, Romanian politicians had been pressing both the Entente and the Central Powers for territorial concessions since the war's beginning—at first in return for neutrality and later in exchange for entering the war on the Entente's side.[123] By 1916, as Russia launched the Brusilov offensive, pushing the Central Powers west of the Carpathians, the Entente powers felt that Romania's contributions to their war effort could definitively tilt the balance in their favor. The Romanian government expanded its demands to include not only Transylvania, the Banat, and Bukovina, but also several Hungarian counties along the Tisza river.[124]

Brătianu's strategy had been to bide his time, observing the situation at the front and calibrating Romania's position accordingly. He put off committing troops and resources to the war effort until the very last minute and then only in return for concessions that would in normal circumstances have been unthinkable. When Romania entered the war in August 1916, Article 6 of the agreement it signed with the Entente provided that Romania's rights at the postwar peace negotiations would be rights equal to those of the other powers.[125] In December, Bucharest fell to the Germans, and in early 1917 the government and royal family fled to Jassy. The following year, Romania was forced to sign a humiliating peace with the Central Powers. Since the Allies did not view Romania as a full partner, due to its quick defeat, they were taken aback when the Romanians showed up in Paris with a comprehensive list of demands. Nonetheless, Britain and France felt that Romania's safety was necessary to successfully contain Bolshevism. As the French Marshal Foch put it, it was imperative (especially once revolutionary fervor had spread to Budapest, resulting in the formation of a Hungarian Soviet Republic in March 1919) to "build on Romania, for there you have not only an army but also a government and a people."[126]

Romanian delegates in Paris argued that their demands were actually modest. Were they to take the principle of national self-determination to its logical conclusion, they claimed, "Romania would have to claim without any possible contestation the union of hundreds of thousands of Romanians by their language, habits, and heart, who live in compact groups on the left bank of the Dniester and on the other side of the Bug as far as the Dnieper."[127] As a successor to the Moldavian principality that Bukovina had been a part of when Austria had annexed it, Romanian delegates insisted, their country had historic rights to the province.

Moreover, they claimed that Romanians in Bukovina were the victims of a denationalization process even more severe than Romanians in Transylvania had suffered. In a 1918 publication on the 'national problems' of Austria-Hungary, Romanian diplomat Dimitrie Drăghicescu (who was part of the Romanian delegation at the Paris peace conference) claimed that while

Transylvanian Romanians had tasted "the brutality of Hungarian oppression," their Bukovinan counterparts had lived under the more subtly oppressive "cold and calculated perfidy of the Austrians, so refined in the art of robbing or suppressing the national life of peoples who had the misfortune of falling under their yoke." Indeed, in Drăghicescu's view, "[t]he Habsburg and Austrian administration who always flatter themselves that they civilize the people they conquer were by no means superior to Russian tsarism."[128]

Discounting Austria's professed civilizing role in Bukovina did not keep the Romanian delegation from claiming a similar role for a Greater Romanian state. They argued that only a powerful Romania could serve as what Nicolae Petrescu-Comnen, a Romanian diplomat, called a "Latin sentinel on the border of the eastern world." Petrescu-Comnen, who had spent World War I in Switzerland publicizing the Greater Romanian cause, went to great lengths to convince the Allies that this Latin sentinel "strong and conscious of its own power, on the banks of the Danube, is an imperious necessity."[129] The Romanian delegation proclaimed that "through its adhesion to the act of unification proclaimed by Bukovina, Romania proceeds to reconstitute this province, to ensure its security, stopping at the frontier with the Dniester the expansion of anarchy which menaces that whole part of Europe. At the cost of military sacrifices which haven't yet come to an end, Romania looks after Bukovina and thus affirms its solidarity with the general interests of civilization."[130]

Notwithstanding such assertions, however, Bukovina was not high on Romania's list of territorial priorities. Romanian nationalists in the Old Kingdom were more concerned with Transylvania, "the fresh-flowing wound" and birthplace of Romanian nationalism—indeed, it was Romania's commitment to freeing Transylvania that had had the most influence on its 1916 decision to enter the war on the Entente's side.[131] In contrast, Bukovinan irredentists in Bucharest—among them the historian Ion Nistor—insisted that Bukovina was absolutely indispensable to Romania. "It cannot be doubted," he wrote, defending Romania's claims to the northern half of the province, also claimed by Ukrainians, "that a small part of Bukovina, which would secure Romania's borders, should have greater significance for the future of a country of Romania's size than for the Russian government."[132] For Romania, he insisted, Bukovina was a site of national memory and myth-making, akin to an "open-air museum." "There is no other corner of territory in all the Romanian lands," the Romanian diplomat Drăghicescu agreed, "where such varied and precious historical memories have accumulated in so great a number."[133]

Bukovina's unification with Romania, in practical terms accomplished in Czernowitz under the watchful eye of the Romanian troops, was enshrined in Article 95 of the peace treaty of Saint Germain with Austria. Romania also obtained Transylvania, the Banat, and Bessarabia. All this came at a price, however. In exchange for achieving international recognition, the newly expanded Romanian state was required to sign a minority protection treaty. Insulted by the implication that Romania could not be trusted with running its own government as it saw fit, Prime Minister Brătianu stormed out of the conference. His impetuousness impressed Sir James Wycliffe Headlam-Morley, a British historian and government advisor who helped draft the Versailles Treaty. In his memoir, he recalled Brătianu complaining that "the Allies pledged that small states should be treated on complete equality with large states" but that "the proposed procedure [the minority treaty] [. . .] was an infringement of their sovereignty."[134] Brătianu felt the treaty essentially assigned Bukovina not to Romania, but to the great powers, as minorities could appeal to the League of Nations if they felt mistreated.

---

"When the clock strikes a happy hour there [in the west], it does for us too. We no longer live in the East European time zone," the Czernowitz press had written hopefully in the summer of 1914.[135] The war, they hoped, would finally put Bukovina on Austria-Hungary's mental map, showing how important this seemingly insignificant land was to the monarchy. The next months and years proved disappointing. The Austrian authorities in Bukovina hurriedly withdrew, leaving it completely undefended, three times. Many saw the authorities' behavior as indicative of the empire's general negligence and indifference to the eastern borderlands. But more held on to the vision of an Austrian civilizing mission in the east, a concept that framed their experience of the war as a massive confrontation between civilization and barbarism. This was especially true of Czernowitz's German-speaking Jews, the liberal bourgeoisie who formed the backbone of the Austrian liberal state in Bukovina.

Although both the Austrian and the Russian military authorities in Bukovina launched deportations, carried out executions, and used violence to keep the territory under control, they were open to collaboration with locals. From the very outset, they recruited protégés—often entire ethnic groups. They had no qualms about exchanging collaborators as needed. This situation was distinctly different from was to happen in World War II. For now, it was still possible for an ethnic Romanian in Bukovina to seek Russian patronage, then Austrian, then Russian again. Some individuals became expert in changing hats. But most of Bukovina's population identified themselves with one great power or another: Romanians with the Russian Empire (during Bukovina's first two Russian occupations), Jews with Austria, Ruthenians/Ukrainians first with Austria, then post-revolutionary Russia. Moreover, the series of occupations gave each group at different times opportunities to pursue its own goals. Nationalists of all stripes benefited from the confrontation, because they could mobilize imperial conflict to advance their own vision of Bukovina.

As the imperial army began unraveling in the summer of 1918, local actors mobilized to lay claim to Bukovina. While all championed the notion of national self-determination, the concept central to of US President Woodrow Wilson's vision of a new international order, they disagreed about what this might entail. Its practical implications were especially obscure in Bukovina, an imperial by-product with an extraordinarily diverse population. Visions of a postwar Bukovina jostled each other: a Ukrainian vision of a partitioned Bukovina, divided along ethnic lines (which some Romanians also backed) and a Romanian vision of an intact Bukovina to be returned to its rightful owner, the Romanian nation-state.

In the end, the Bukovinan question was resolved on the ground by local developments, particularly Iancu Flondor's appeal to the Romanian troops to liberate the province. When the time came for the great powers in Paris to arbitrate territorial disputes, the Romanians—taking advantage of the war's geopolitical reversals—presented the world with a *fait accompli*: a Romanian Bukovina. The small, half-forgotten province, they insisted, was the key to the integrity of the Romanian nation-state. The great powers, albeit skeptically, agreed, and Bukovina became a provincial region of Greater Romania. But instead of cementing Romania's integrity and sovereignty, the little province was to prove troublesome, denting the nation-state's sovereignty rather than boosting its prestige.

# 5

# "Returning" to Romania

OF ALL the Allies' partners in World War I, Romania made the most expansive territorial claims and scored the greatest victories. It acquired Bessarabia after signing a separate peace with Germany in 1917. In 1918 it annexed Transylvania, the Banat, Southern Dobrogea, and Bukovina. All these acquisitions were internationally recognized in 1920, thanks largely to France's conviction that an enlarged Greater Romania would be a bulwark against the expansion of Bolshevism from the east.[1] But once the euphoria of expansion and unification subsided, unease set in. On paper, Romania was a unitary nation-state. In practice, the government had not started unifying the newly incorporated territories with the Old Kingdom and each other. Unification proved time-consuming and expensive: the necessary resources were in short supply after a war that had ravaged the country's economy and devastated its infrastructure. The newly annexed provinces contributed new resources and capital, but integration into the nation-state was costly. A new infrastructure was needed to connect transportation and legal systems, currencies, and institutional infrastructures in which the newly incorporated territories were embedded.[2] Moreover, regional elites eager to preserve the privileges they had enjoyed under imperial rule resented and resisted Bucharest's centralizing ambitions.[3]

As one of Greater Romania's most ethnically variegated territories, Bukovina posed special challenges to the national consolidation, state-building, and unification project.[4] A British Foreign Office report drafted in preparation for the Paris peace conference described the province as "inhabited by a strange mixture of races, even at the present day," thanks to its location "on the great highway of migrations from the east to the west."[5] This was largely why nationalists in the Old Kingdom disdained it, associating it with national indifference, opportunism, and arrogance. The eminent nationalist historian Nicolae Iorga did everything he could to perpetuate this image, insisting that Bukovina lacked a distinctive culture. He described it as "deformed" and developmentally "stunted." "Austrianism," he insisted, "was a thing that withered [everything] away, that dried [everything] up."[6] For this reason Iorga wanted

Bukovina to be incorporated into Romania as soon as possible, and all traces of its regional autonomy erased: "Bukovina has no reason to continue as Bukovina. It must first begin by being very Bukovinan within Romania in order to end up not being Bukovinan at all." The Bukovinan Romanian nationalist Ion Nistor agreed with Iorga that everything of value in Bukovina "emanated from the vigor of the creative spirit of our Moldavian ancestors" while "Habsburg rule was and remained eternally foreign to this land, to its ancient cultural and artistic traditions."[7]

The next few years would prove Iorga and Nistor wrong, as Austria's legacies in Bukovina turned out to be remarkably resilient. Whether artificial or not, Bukovina's imperial heritage did not wither away to reveal the province's unchanged national essence. Romanian officials who stepped into their new administrative roles in Cernăuţi (as Czernowitz now became) discovered Bukovinans with Romanian names who could not speak or read a word of Romanian.[8] Peasants in the Cernăuţi region were "disfiguring" their national costumes with foreign clothing or "abandoning them altogether."[9] The Austrian empire lived on in the minds of Romania's new Bukovinan subjects, many of whom experienced the transition from imperial to national rule as an abrupt decline in their living conditions. Taken aback by what they perceived as their new rulers' apparent cultural inferiority, many Bukovinans came to resent their loss of autonomy to Bucharest.[10] Ironically, the Romanian government's aggressive centralization measures contributed to the crystallization of a regional identity in Bukovina in the 1920s, one that transcended ethnicity and was deeply rooted in Bukovina's imperial past.

Over the 1920s, as non-Romanians in Bukovina progressively lost the rights they had enjoyed under Austrian rule, Ukrainians and Jews aired their grievances before the League of Nations. Ukrainian organizations in exile denounced the Romanian government's nationalization policies targeting areas of Bukovina predominantly inhabited by Ukrainians. They brought minority rights violations to the League's attention and disputed Romania's right to northern Bukovina. The League rejected all petitions that questioned the post-Versailles territorial settlement, but the steady flow of petitions was bad for Romania's image, as the government had to repeatedly justify its minority policies before the international community.[11] As in neighboring Transylvania, in Bukovina non-Romanian economic elites managed to retain their positions much longer than Romanian nationalists had anticipated. To counter this, the National Liberal administrations that governed Romania for the better part of the 1920s sought to promote the formation of a Romanian middle class in Bukovina through language decrees and school policies that put Romanian-speakers at an advantage.

Romanian officials and nationalists in Bukovina believed that Jews presented the most serious obstacle to the province's Romanianization: a

Romanian middle class would never come into being if Jews retained their positions of privilege. But the real trouble with Bukovinan Jews was that they provided a living link to the province's imperial past. As Jewish memoirist Pearl Fichman recalled, Jews in interwar Bukovina nurtured Austrian traditions "in the home as if Romania was only an incidental whim of history."[12] Jews in Cernăuţi kept speaking German, and, as elsewhere in Europe, they were suspected of harboring Communist sympathies. Though bound by the minority protection treaties to extend citizenship rights to all Jews in the newly annexed territories, the Romanian government gradually disenfranchised them by amending its citizenship laws. Many Bukovinan Jews lost their Romanian citizenship as a result, becoming stateless. Defenseless in the face of growing anti-Jewish violence, some Bukovinan Jews indeed put their hopes in Communism, which promised equality for people of all religions and races. Some joined the Communist movement which, after 1924, was banned and forced underground.

Bukovina's physical proximity to the Soviet Union exacerbated fears of Communist infiltration, as did its strong Social Democratic tradition. By the early 1920s a Communist movement developed there as a radical offshoot of Social Democracy. Though Communists were only a small fraction of the left in Bukovina, the Romanian authorities viewed all leftist factions, Communist or not, as dangerous, especially since their members were predominantly Ukrainian and Jewish. To prevent the eruption of a Bolshevik revolution on the Russian model at home, Romanian policy makers launched a controlled revolution from above. Between 1919 and 1921, the National Liberal Party implemented one of Eastern Europe's most radical land expropriation and redistribution reforms.[13] But both Romanians and non-Romanians in Bukovina disliked the agrarian reform's implementation. Ukrainians denounced it as a discriminatory measure designed to promote the Romanianization of ethnically Ukrainian territories; Romanian nationalists protested that it had not gone far enough.

National Liberal policymakers felt conflicted about the peasantry and its role within the nation-state. As nationalists, many looked to the peasantry as a repository of national consciousness and authenticity, a "symbol of the nation and ally of the state."[14] As modernizers, they believed peasants had to be educated, improved, and eventually transformed into a Romanian middle class. The land reforms were part of this modernization program. So was a series of reforms instituted during the 1920s, including the opening of new schools and rural reading societies and "homes of culture" in the countryside. Much like their Austrian counterparts, Romanian officials discovered they lacked the means radically to transform the countryside. Rural inertia, much like Bukovina's stubborn "foreignness," frustrated their state-building and modernization project.

## Imperial Legacies

Coming out of the war, Romania was eager to exercise its hard-won sovereignty over the newly annexed territories and claim a place for itself in the postwar international order. This should not have been hard in a world in which principles of democracy and national self-determination were to reign supreme. Yet as Romanian representatives in Paris soon discovered, despite the rhetoric of autonomy and self-determination, old hierarchies persisted. As historian Eric Weitz put it, the post-Versailles order developed "the imperial civilizing mission into a comprehensive program."[15] The Allied powers, it turned out, felt entitled to make decisions on successor states' behalf and to force their hands through ultimatums or by threatening to withdraw international recognition. The minority protection treaties, imposed on the successor states but not on the Allies themselves, reflected enduring power inequalities. "For us Romanians," the Bukovinan Vasile Grecu wrote in 1922, "this treaty [the Minority Protection Treaty] was useless and somewhat offensive as well, for we consider it to be a mark of honor for our race not to oppress anyone."[16] The age of empires was, in other words, not quite over.

Moreover, nation-states built on the wreckage of old empires had, in the process of absorbing former imperial territories, become mini-empires in their own right.[17] Romania was a patchwork of territories and populations inherited from the Austro-Hungarian and Russian empires, inhabited by an ethnically diverse population steeped in differing administrative and political traditions. In some parts of Romania ethnic Romanians were numerically a minority. Former imperial possessions such as Bukovina, once they had been incorporated into Romania, forced the nation-state to reckon with the old imperial dilemma of governance amid diversity. The Romanian government found itself in a position long familiar to Austrian authorities in Bukovina: having to arbitrate between different national groups clamoring for rights and resources.[18] Moreover, though Austria-Hungary was gone, its offices, churches, museums, and schools did not disappear in 1918. Nor did the people staffing them.[19]

Bukovina's imperial inheritance as a former periphery of Austria-Hungary might have been more modest than other imperial provinces', but it was no less tangible. With its "ubiquitous stuccoed yellow" Habsburg administrative buildings, its German-language *Gymnasia,* and its statues of Habsburg emperors and empresses, Bukovina's former provincial capital Cernăuţi, *née* Czernowitz, had a decidedly Austrian look.[20] Relics of Bukovina's Austrian past filled public and private spaces. Many roads were flanked by "wooden poles painted in the Austro-Hungarian colors," while "in the buildings of various authorities and in cafes there [were] no portraits of the [Romanian] royal family."[21] Cernăuţi's cafes displayed "paintings representing the victories of the

Central Powers' armies" and passers-by wore "emblems representing the former emperors Wilhelm and Carol with the German-Austrian national colors."[22] "Life-sized portraits of the former emperor Franz Joseph" adorned teachers' homes in Cernăuţi, while "the portraits of their Majesty the King and Queen [of Romania] are completely absent."[23] "One said Ferdinand, Carol, and Mihai, and thought Franz Joseph," the poet Georg Drozdowski recalled. "In my room," he added "there hung a silver emperor in relief, from my father, and no king as wall decoration."[24] To Romanian nationalists, these omnipresent relics of empire reminded Romanians in Bukovina of their former enslavement and signaled the nation-state's impotence.[25]

To remedy the situation, the new administration in Cernăuţi began dismantling the most inconvenient and offensive relics of the city's Austrian heritage. They started by removing monuments and changing street names. A decree issued in January 1919 ordered that all Austrian emblems displayed "on the edifices of offices or in their interiors" be promptly removed.[26] Nationalist hotheads began vandalizing public monuments. Old stones crumbled; bronze heads rolled to the ground; imperial eagles were caged behind museum windows.[27] A beloved statue of Friedrich Schiller was removed from Cernăuţi's Theater Square in 1922. Shortly afterward, the secretariat for internal affairs decided that "today names of squares, parks, streets, etc. reminding of this [imperial] rule can no longer be maintained" for "traces of this rule [. . .] insult the sentiments of every true Romanian."[28] Beginning in February 1919, all German place names in Cernăuţi were converted to Romanian ones. Franzjosefsgarten became Arboroasa, Austriaplatz became Grigore Ghica-Vodă, while the Hauptstrasse was renamed Strada Regele Ferdinand (King Ferdinand Street).[29]

These quick and cheap measures were largely ineffective. People still referred to streets and buildings by their old names. When businesses in Cernăuţi were required to change their foreign nameplates to Romanian ones within two weeks, the owners protested that "it is out of the question that nameplate painters, six in number, should finish the nameplates of several thousand business owners and merchants in such a short time."[30] To save money, shopkeepers crossed out bits and pieces of foreign names, such that "what is left of the text is either names or signs in the Romanian language."[31] A similar fate befell the administration's measures to remove all Austrian crowns from circulation. Bukovinans began to "show up at the ticket office with crowns; crowns are not accepted so they have to look for lei. At the ticket office they immediately find a vendor who for four or five crowns sells them one leu."[32] The resulting economic chaos meant that Romanian authorities had no choice but to allow both currencies to circulate in Bukovina.[33] Without the money or personnel to give Cernăuţi a total makeover, the empire's material relics kept on going, like old pieces of machinery to which the key had been lost.

FIGURE 5.1. The former Herrengasse in interwar Cernăuţi, shown here, was renamed "strada Iancu Flondor" after the leader of the General Congress who voted for Bukovina's union with Romania. Courtesy of the Biblioteca Naţională a României.

The Romanian administration's appetite for removing all traces of empire soon gave them a reputation as the "enforcers of a curse flung by world history [. . .] upon the Habsburgs and their empire."[34] Since purely destructive policies were highly unpopular and largely ineffective, the authorities tried to put a more creative imprint on urban space. A monument to unification was inaugurated in Cernăuţi on November 11, 1924 on the city's former Ringplatz.[35] It depicted a bison, an old symbol of the Moldavian principality, trampling under its hooves the Austrian eagle that "had torn from [Moldova's] body its most beautiful part and the richest in precious memories one hundred and fifty years ago, to keep it in the darkest and most oppressive slavery."[36] The Romanian royal pair Queen Mary and King Ferdinand came for the monument's unveiling, and attended a festive mass at the Orthodox cathedral in Cernăuţi, visited the war heroes' cemetery, watched a performance at the National Theater, then dined, it was reported, on salmon mayonnaise, hare cutlets, French salad, and "giardinetto" (fruit salad), to the accompaniment of music by Beethoven, Schubert, and Boccherini.[37]

When the time came to foot the bill, the city had an unpleasant surprise. In addition to the "preparation and arrangement of the celebrations," Cernăuţi was expected to pay for the monument: one which turned out, moreover to be

FIGURE 5.2. Locals posing with the "Monumentul Unirii" bison in interwar Cernăuţi. Mark Goldberger Photo Collection.

highly unpopular with locals.[38] The Zionist Philipp Menczel thought it displayed a "tasteless brand of patriotism." The Catholic press in Cernăuţi remarked on the monument's "lack of tact, and absurdity," while the popular Jewish press described it as "a perfect symbol of these years of transition" and "days of illness" marked by the "boiling over of nationalism [and] paroxysms of anti-Semitism."[39] As an allusion to Romania's poverty, a group of students in Cernăuţi tied a bag of hay around the bison's head, in keeping with the then popular saying "România mare, mămăligă n'are" (Greater Romania has no polenta).[40]

A cheaper and more convenient way to deal with Cernăuţi's Austrian heritage was to recycle as much of its cultural and material infrastructure as possible. Reclaiming former bastions of imperial culture such as the city theater, popular with former imperial elites and the German-speaking public, had symbolic and political significance for the Romanian nation-state. As Irina Livezeanu writes, "cultural institutions produce and project the public images of a society to itself and to the outside world. They also generate society's elites."[41] Four years after Bukovina's unification with Romania, the theater in Cernăuţi was still staging plays in German. In September 1922 a group of Romanian nationalist students took the theater by assault during a German-language performance of Schiller's *The Robbers*. "The famous actor Moissi was chased by *Hakenkreuzler*, and the Vienna troupe were unable to play as the police refused to be responsible for order, in other words, they could not keep the order for the sake of the Jews," wrote the Zionist Israel Cohen.[42]

By the end of the month the theater had been renamed "Teatrul Naţional." The nationalist newspaper *Glasul Bucovinei* was jubilant: "having to conquer a Romanian national theater for the Romanians in Bukovina's capital in Greater Romania may seem odd, even impossible. And yet, this national theater in Cernăuţi had to be reconquered."[43] The theater's newly appointed Romanian director exclaimed with relief that "real cultural work can be done" now.[44] The *Czernowitzer Morgenblatt* protested in vain that "[t]he theater is the property of the entire city's population," not just Romanians.[45]

That Romanian officials and nationalists coveted places like the Schiller Theater in Cernăuţi was, of course, deeply ironic. These were bastions of imperial culture that drew their prestige from their association with Habsburg rule. Rather than dismiss them altogether, Romanian nationalists claimed them for their own nationality, thus reasserting their symbolic value.

## Regionalism

Bukovinans' experiences under Austrian rule shaped their expectations and attitudes toward the Romanian administration. Measured with an Austrian imperial measuring stick, the Romanian nation-state fell short. Romania's troops looked shabby; its civil servants appeared ignorant and uncultured. The Bukovinan Jewish poet Alfred Kittner recalled how, as a teenager at the time of Austria's collapse, he had watched with tears in his eyes as "the pathetic Romanian troops" made their entrance into Czernowitz and "the beloved Austrian army withdrew."[46] Locals in the predominantly Ukrainian village of Zastavna did not think the Romanian administration worthy of respect, because Romanian soldiers walked around "in torn clothes" and worked for money "on the estates of Jewish proprietors around there." The Austrians, they said, "had not allowed [...] imperial soldiers to become slaves to the Jews."[47]

These attitudes persisted throughout the 1920s. Increasingly, Bukovinans associated Romanian rule with disorder, corruption, and lawlessness. Many Bukovinans viewed their new metropole Bucharest as the realm of "Byzantine barbarians and Orientals."[48] Some even demanded the institution of a "cordon sanitaire" to keep out Old Kingdom vices such as "corruption, demagogy, politicianism, Balkanism."[49] "In railway stations and especially on trains," one

Bukovinan deputy in the Romanian parliament complained in 1919, "thefts are the order of the day. Due to the crowdedness caused by the fact that anyone can climb into a car, whether they have paid for it or not, trains have become a real bane for those who have no choice but to travel."[50] "Damn you all," blurted an exasperated policeman of "uncertain Ukrainian or Polish" nationality in Cernăuţi. "There are still Austrian laws here, Austria still exists!"[51] Many Bukovinans came to regret the passing of Austrian rule for, as one resident of Zastavna put it, "in Austria it was better and there was more justice."[52]

To nationalists like Nicolae Iorga or Bukovina's Ion Nistor, Bukovinans' nostalgia for Austrian rule made no sense. Iorga felt confident that "Austria cannot be regretted any more than Don Quixote's [old horse] Rosinante, who passed away with her long tongue sticking out [. . .] by the side of the road."[53] Nistor similarly insisted that Habsburg rule had left only a superficial veneer in Bukovina, behind which the province's real national essence hid. Habsburg rule, he said, "remained eternally foreign to this country, to its old artistic traditions."[54] In other words, as an imperial creation, Bukovina had no logic. It remained a "shapeless amalgam" inhabited by a "species of bipeds developed in the political greenhouse of the former Austrian regime."[55] "Everything that has been preserved in Bukovina in terms of monuments of art," Nistor wrote, "emanated from the vigor of the creative spirit of our Moldavian ancestors [. . .]. Habsburg rule was and remained eternally foreign to this land."[56]

The reality was that many Bukovinans were as nostalgic for Austrian as they were dissatisfied with Romanian rule. For one thing, as a remote province of a small nation-state, Bukovina felt even more marginal than before. Now that the vast space of empire was traversed by multiple national borders, people used to being able to travel more or less freely were stopped repeatedly and kept waiting for hours while "one nation-state represented through the person of a sergeant assumes the right to confiscate a traveler's schnapps and tobacco."[57] Money could no longer be transferred across the former Austrian–Romanian border. Unable to receive remittances from home, Bukovinan students at the university in Bucharest fell on hard times.[58] Many wondered "how it can be that when Bukovina was moaning under foreign yoke and was separated [from Romania] by the Austrian border, they could cross into the Old Kingdom to buy bread and today when the border has fallen, they can no longer pass to buy this bread in the Old Kingdom."[59] Bukovinans complained that Bucharest failed to compensate them for the losses they had suffered during the war. In December 1919 Bukovinan deputy Ion Zelea Codreanu warned the Romanian parliament that his compatriots were "threatening to come into the capital, all of them, and demand justice for everything they should have been given."[60]

Bucharest's National Liberals took these expressions of discontent as signs of separatism, and responded by removing all traces of regional autonomy from Bukovina, one by one. The centralization process culminated in 1925 with

FIGURE 5.3. Iancu Flondor (1865–1924), January 1, 1919. History and Art Collection / Alamy Stock Photo.

a new administrative law that dissolved communal councils and restructured the nation-state around a new administrative unit: the *judeţ*, headed by a prefect appointed directly by the Ministry of Interior.[61]

As centralization proceeded apace, even Romanians who were initially enthusiastic about Bukovina's unification with Romania began grumbling. Among the first to protest was Iancu Flondor, the very man who had invited the Romanian army into Bukovina in the fall of 1918 and then orchestrated the General Congress that sanctioned unification. Bucharest rewarded Flondor by appointing him minister-delegate of Bukovina—a position he shared with Ion Nistor. But Flondor had his own ideas about unification: he believed the newly annexed provinces had something important to contribute to Greater Romania, and he hoped Bukovina and Transylvania would help the Old Kingdom break "the power of the political clientele" and move Old Kingdom politics away from "petty conflict and corruption."[62]

In March 1919, when one of Flondor's envoys arrived in Bucharest to discuss plans for Bukovina, he was told the administration should work "so that Bukovina may fuse with the Old Kingdom as soon as possible."[63] Flondor insisted that "the country's administration be entrusted to objective persons who are qualified" and that no legislative reforms be instituted in Bukovina "without consulting the country's representatives." When the government decided to take a different path to unification, Flondor resigned in protest.

By contrast, Flondor's fellow minister-delegate Ion Nistor, head of the Democratic Party of Unification (Partidul Democrat al Unirii) in Bukovina, declared his "complete trust in the heads who are now leading the country's destiny." His supporters countered Flondor's objections, insisting that "Romania is a nation-state and it cannot tolerate an autonomous province at its margins."[64] Capitalizing on his wartime connections in Bucharest, Nistor became sole minister of Bukovina after Flondor's resignation in April 1919. He used his position to push the National Liberal government's centralization agenda in Bukovina. Once the National Liberals lost their monopoly on government in the late 1920s, however, Nistor started voicing his own complaints. By 1930 he found himself in the position of his old rival Flondor, defending Bukovina's interests before a government bent on replacing all Bukovinans in important administrative positions with Old Kingdom Romanians. Once a beneficiary of centralization policies that facilitated his political advancement, Nistor now criticized the administration for violating Bukovinans' rights. "A Bukovinan," Nistor's newspaper *Glasul Bucovinei* wrote in September 1931, "can no longer become either a financial administrator, or an agricultural counselor, or a director of a secondary school, or a school inspector."[65] A further article lamented that "[t]his Bukovina, with its abundance of specialized intellectuals in all administrative branches, with its national traditions and battles, with its progressive cultural and economic life has ended up being treated in the worst ways."[66]

At the opposite end of the political spectrum from Nistor's party, a group of leftists in Bukovina promoted regionalism in their newspaper *Viața Bucovinei*. Comparing Bukovina with Switzerland, the editors argued that the province's ethnic diversity was its most distinctive trait, to be protected and preserved.[67] Because Bukovina's population "was superior to that in many other regions of our country," the newspaper's editor Titu Cristureanu insisted that the province's "geographic and economic distinctiveness" be recognized and accommodated. Cristureanu blamed Bucharest's "obsolete" approach to governing Bukovina for the province's poor state. "The culture that flows abundantly from the center, sometimes as a product of [. . .] abstract mentalities," he explained, "cannot and should not be allowed to be imposed as a universal recipe."[68]

## The Minorities Question

The product of one hundred and fifty years of imperial rule, Bukovina's ethnic diversity was one of its most distinctive traits. In some areas Romanians were outnumbered by non-Romanians, mostly Ukrainians and Jews. Yet Romanians were now the titular nationality, and other groups were classified as ethnic minorities. At the Paris peace conference, the Allied powers required successor states like Romania and Poland that had large minority populations to sign minority protection treaties as a precondition for achieving international recognition.[69] The treaties gave non-titular nationalities a way to be "vocal in the international arena" through the League of Nations, the official guarantor of minority rights.[70] Minorities could report rights violations to the League's Minorities Section. The League would first assess a petition's "receivability," then decide whether the complaints fell within its sphere of responsibility. Then it submitted the complaint to representatives of the accused government.[71] When possible, the Minority Department tried to resolve grievances through "informal mechanisms and procedures," avoiding territorial revisions at any cost.[72]

Due to its intricate "internal mechanisms" and a rapidly declining international situation, the League made only "modest progress" in addressing the grievances submitted to it.[73] Its effectiveness was also diminished by the fact that the successor states resented intrusions into their internal affairs. These states used the designation of minorities as agents of the League and of foreign powers to justify treating them as second-class citizens rather than "partners in the state-building process."

Starting in 1920, petitions concerning the status of Bukovina's Ukrainians began piling up on the Minority Department's desks in Geneva. The petitions referred to Romanian rule in northern Bukovina as a "regime of occupation" and argued that Romanian sovereignty there was temporary, as Bukovina's northern borders had yet to be settled. The Bukovinan Delegation of the Ukrainian National Council demanded in 1921 that the Liquidation Commission charged with distributing Austria-Hungary's gold reserves among its successor states suspend its activities until northern Bukovina's status was definitively decided: "sovereignty over these territories according to the Treaty of St. Germain belongs to the great powers of the Entente." Evidently, the Delegation believed there was still a chance Ukrainians could gain representation, or even a nation-state of their own.[74]

In 1924 the Political Committee of Bukovina, a local branch of the Ukrainian National Council, submitted another complaint to the League, this one disputing Romania's claim to northern Bukovina as a violation of Ukrainians' rights to national self-determination.[75] Northern Bukovina, they argued, had been claimed by the National Republic of Western Ukraine, and Romanian representatives had agreed to the province's partition when the Romanian Aurel Onciul signed a convention with the Ukrainian Omelian Popovych on November 6, 1918.[76] Romania, the Committee argued, imposed its rule upon northern Bukovina by force. Iancu Flondor, after inviting the Romanian troops in, "immediately began organizing gatherings of bandits to give the

Romanians a reason to reinsate order and occupy the territory."[77] Romanian rule in northern Bukovina was therefore illegitimate and, the Ukrainian National Council's head Ilie Semaka insisted, Ukrainian youth in Bukovina thus could refuse to join the Romanian military: "the Romanians are only the occupiers of the Ukrainian part of Bukovina and as such they do not have the right to recruit Ukrainians into the army, which they are doing illegally by forcing our youth to serve the Romanian state."[78]

Ukrainians' status as a nationality without a nation-state complicated matters. League officials were often unsure whether various self-proclaimed representatives of the Ukrainian nation were legitimate or not. In 1927, for instance, the League rejected a petition by the Ukrainian National Council on the grounds that it did not legitimately represent Ukrainians in Sub-Carpathian Russia and Bukovina, as those territories had been allocated to Czechoslovakia and Romania. The Minorities Section's president Erik Colban thought the Ukrainian National Council's "representative character with respect to the population is highly doubtful, if not non-existent," and that its petition suggested the Council "hasn't adjusted to the new status quo."[79] The Ukrainian National Council had been established on October 18, 1918 by Ukrainian deputies in the former Austrian parliament and various local diets who hoped to establish a West Ukrainian Republic on former territories of Austria-Hungary inhabited by a predominantly Ukrainian population.

Colban was right: in 1927, those territories had long since been distributed among successor states, but the Council had not reconciled itself to the new status quo—nor did it intend to.[80] The Political Committee of Bukovina asserted that "being a nation alien and hostile to Romania [. . .] the Ukrainian people in Eastern Europe does not wish by any means to renounce its rights to independence as a state." "On account of this unparalleled state of subjection and oppression," the petitioners continued, "the Ukrainian people feels a deep hatred toward the Romanian regime [. . .].The idea of removing the Romanian yoke through a rebellion and uniting with the people of its race into Soviet Ukraine will persist until [the Ukrainian people] attains its national ideal."[81] The petition was rejected because its signatories had not renounced their ambition for an independent Ukraine.

Although League officials rejected most petitions submitted on behalf of Bukovina's Ukrainians, they paid close attention to the information petitioners provided. This was how they discovered that "the entire power over the Ukrainian territory of Bukovina is in the hands of the military municipality and in those of the gendarmerie commanders in small towns and villages."[82] Northern Bukovina was, in other words, under a state of siege that allowed the Romanian government to suppress Ukrainian institutions and arrest prominent Ukrainians without trial.[83] Under martial law Romanian authorities could "carry out a merciless policy of denationalization" as "no meetings of any kind may be held, not even those of educational and cooperative associations."[84] "We live in a country of order and this is why they issue proclamations, register, identify, arrest, and punish continuously," the Social Democratic newspaper *Vorwärts* remarked sarcastically in September 1924.[85] Ioan Rudnicki, president of the Political Committee of Bukovina, reported that over 3 percent of Ukrainians in Bukovina had been "arrested for no reason" by January 1919. Prominent Ukrainians had been imprisoned for over six months, including Erotey Pihuliak (the Ukrainian nationalist we met in chapters 3 and 4), Teophile Bryndzan, director of the Ukrainian *Gymnasium* in Kitsman (Kotzman in German; Coţmani in Romanian; previously Cozmeni or Chiţmani) Kassian Bryndzan, preacher at the cathedral in Cernăuţi, and historian Myron Corduba.[86]

The Romanian Siguranţa (secret police) brought the reign of terror into the countryside through its agents, who were scattered across villages such that "nobody in the district knows if he isn't suspected or if his name isn't written down in the Siguranţa's black book." Kosty Bozan, a Ukrainian peasant who declared that "Bukovina should belong to the Ukrainians up to the river Siret" received "fifty baton blows." In predominantly Ukrainian Kitsman one "peasant woman from a neighboring village [. . . was] captured and beaten with twenty-five blows of baton" for ignoring the curfew.[87] Two gendarmes in the village Luca caught a peasant they suspected of theft (later proved innocent), tied him to two horses, and dragged him to a nearby village; "on the way they kicked him and struck him on the head with a whip."[88] In another village, a Romanian gendarme confiscated a peasant's fruit, taking the best for himself and throwing the rest to the pigs.

Petitioners frequently complained about the Romanian government's denationalization and centralization policies in Bukovina which, they argued, overwhelmingly affected Ukrainians in the province's north. The Ukrainian National Council's Bukovinan Delegation reported in 1921 that Ukrainian clergy in northern Bukovina were banned from reciting the liturgy in Ukrainian. At the cathedral in Cernăuţi, Kassian Bryndzan still spoke Ukrainian, but "only dares to preach after dusk in the Ukrainian language."[89] Ukrainians who did not submit to the new language regime, the Bukovina Delegation reported, were no longer admitted to the Orthodox Consistory where they had enjoyed equal representation under Austrian rule.[90] In addition, Ukrainian schools to the south of the Prut were being converted to the Romanian language. One of the first institutions to fall victim to the Romanianization campaign was the Ukrainian *Gymnasium* in Kitsman which was declared Romanian state property and converted into a Romanian-language *lycée*.[91] In his petition to the League, Ioan Rudnicki also complained that Ukrainian associations, clubs, and reading circles had been suppressed in Bukovina, while the university's Ukrainian literature department had been dissolved.[92] From 1924 Ukrainian primary schools in northern Bukovina were Romanianized; no formal decree had been issued, but oral instructions sufficed, as local teachers were afraid to disobey.

Hoping for minority votes, the National Liberal Party relaxed its Romanianization offensive slightly before the elections of 1926, only to resume it afterward. In June 1926 they formalized the Romanianization of Bukovina's primary schools, requiring them to teach exclusively in Romanian. Numerous Ukrainian-language schools in northern Bukovina were converted into Romanian ones.[93] Ukrainian representatives immediately protested. A Senator Lukaszewicz warned that "unlawful, unjust" policies of this kind damaged Romania's standing in the eyes of its own people and its rapport with the local Ukrainian population.[94] "Through a forced and accelerated Romanianization," he insisted, "one can end only with cultural decline, creating a population which cannot read, [. . .] altogether inferior from a cultural point of view, a population which cannot ever achieve economic prosperity, which is contrary to the state's interests."[95]

In Bukovina, the Ukrainian lawyer Vasyl Duchak submitted a petition to the Cernăuţi tribunal on behalf of the parents of sixty-three children in the village of Bărbeşti, requesting that Ukrainian instruction be reintroduced in their school.[96] The petitioners justified their request by invoking the rights they had previously enjoyed under Austrian rule; the Romanian Ministry of Education rejected their petition.[97] Minister Constantin Angelescu insisted that the law of 1926 was designed to provide denationalized Romanians in northern Bukovina with access to instruction in their original native language, referring to an idea supported by historian Ion Nistor that most Ukrainians in northern Bukovina were Romanians who had been Ukrainianized under Austrian rule. "We desired that Romanians in origin, who became foreigners and who were constrained by circumstances to adopt a different language, should be led to resume using their own national language," Angelescu explained. He also justified brushing the request aside on the grounds that the government had barely enough resources to build schools for Romanians: "how can I contract such an obligation when we can't even create schools in places where children are Romanian?"[98]

Duchak did not give up. In May 1928 he submitted another petition to the League of Nations, rebutting the Romanian government's arguments in support of the school law of 1926 and accusing them of further discriminating against Ukrainians in the census of 1927. The census listed people according to their "national origins" rather than their "language of daily use," as the Austrian census had, which, Duchak insisted, allowed Romanian officials to classify Ukrainian-speakers as ethnic Romanians against their will. Like Constantin Angelescu, Duchak justified his claims by appealing to history. He argued that

Ukrainians in Bukovina were entitled to cultural rights under Romanian rule because they had historic rights to the territory. Reversing Nistor's arguments about the primacy of Romanians in Bukovina, Duchak argued that Ukrainians were the first to settle there: Romanians had migrated to Bukovina in the thirteenth century, while Ukrainian tribes had been there since at least the tenth.[99]

In response to Duchak's May 1928 petition, the Romanian government submitted a memorandum to the League arguing that Bukovina had always been an integral part of Moldova. "It was in this corner of territory that the country's first capital was located, the metropolitan seat as well, the most ancient and beautiful monasteries, veritable jewels of oriental religious art erected through the piety of the most ancient princes, defenders of the faith, to serve as their place of burial." Romanian officials responded by pointing to Governor Enzenberg's writings and Friedrich von Mieg's maps (see chapter 1 above) to argue that Ukrainians had arrived to Bukovina later, from Galicia. To blame Austria for allegedly denationalizing and "Ruthenianizing" Bukovina's Romanian population, the Romanian authorities used Austrian sources to prove that Romanians pre-dated and had outnumbered Ukrainians in Bukovina.[100] How could one deny it when the Austrians acknowledged it too?

## Old Elites, New Elites

Not only did non-Romanians outnumber Romanians in some parts of Bukovina, but many still enjoyed social and economic privilege, in part because in Greater Romania minorities had too great a "demographic and economic weight" for the authorities to be able to contemplate their expulsion without putting the economy at risk.[101] Bukovina's prewar urban bourgeoisie was predominantly Jewish. A 1911 study by a Romanian nationalist showed that eighty-two of the ninety-six lawyers registered in Czernowitz were Jewish.[102] Visiting Cernăuţi in 1920, the Anglo-Jewish secretary of the World Zionist Organization Israel Cohen remarked that "if one took a stroll along the principal street one could find hardly more than one or two names of non-Jews over the long array of shops on either side."[103] The most widely read newspapers in Cernăuţi after 1918 were the *Allgemeine Zeitung,* founded by Zionist Philipp Menczel, and the *Czernowitzer Morgenblatt,* run by two Jewish editors, Julius Weber and Elias Weinstein. This did not sit well with the Romanian administration. Continued Jewish economic dominance suggested that Romanians were in charge only on paper and ran counter to the Romanian National Liberals' doctrine of economic nationalism and goal of forging a new Romanian commercial bourgeoisie. To upend existing socio-economic hierarchies, Romania's National Liberal governments targeted Bukovina's secondary schools and civil service for reform. The schools were the producers of elites, while the civil service was highly visible and remained dominated by elites whose training and socialization had taken place under Austrian rule.

To make schools more accessible to Romanian students, the government launched a series of language regulations that gave the Romanian language a prominent role in education. Beginning in 1920, non-Romanian secondary schools in Bukovina had to conduct all official and internal communication in Romanian, such that "no official paper or note will be written in any language other than Romanian."[104] That fall, minority high schools in Bukovina were informed that they needed to start offering more Romanian-language classes.[105] By 1924, all minority schools in Bukovina were required to teach the Romanian language, as well as history and geography in Romanian.[106] A ministerial order stipulated that "if a student knows a discipline well but makes mistakes in the Romanian language, the grade he will receive must correspond to his deficiencies in the Romanian language."[107]

Romanian nationalists in Bukovina were especially concerned about the large number of Jewish students enrolled in Bukovinan schools. They believed that Jewish domination of the schools had led to Jewish domination of the liberal professions and the relegation of ethnic Romanians to inferior positions. Nationalists in the Old Kingdom agreed: like the nineteenth-century Romanian philosopher Vasile Conta, many believed that "if we do not fight against the Jews, we will die as a nation."[108] But how was one to "fight against the Jews" with the minority protection treaties in force? The treaties required postwar successor states to provide all national minorities with schooling in their respective national languages. The Romanians found a loophole: most Jewish parents in Cernăuţi insisted that their children study in German; thus, as *Glasul Bucovinei* saw it, they "diabolically persisted in using a foreign language that is not even the language of their nationality but also not the language of the state in which they live."[109] Beginning in the fall of 1921, Jewish schools in Bukovina were required to teach exclusively in Romanian.[110] "The fact that Jews are divided between Hebrew and Yiddish supporters," the *Czernowitzer Morgenblatt* protested, "does not give the administration the right to claim Romanian as their mother tongue."[111] When the Jewish Council finally opted for Hebrew as a language of instruction, Romanian officials objected that "the Hebrew language is just like Latin, a dead language."[112]

To speed the transition to all-Romanian instruction, the government required Bukovinan teachers to take Romanian language exams. Local author Franz Porubsky taught German and Latin at the second state *Gymnasium* in Cernăuţi. When he failed his first language exam, he was allowed to keep his job, likely thanks to a lack of qualified teachers. When a new round of harsher language policies was issued in the 1930s, Porubsky was warned that he could lose his post unless he passed the language exam. Seeing no way out, and chronically depressed, he took his life in August 1934.[113] Others, still young and able to adapt, went along with the Romanian administration's policies. Non-Romanian teachers from Bukovina were relocated to the Old Kingdom to encourage cultural and linguistic assimilation. In turn, teachers from inner Romania were invited to come to "territories where national consciousness has been lost or is endangered" in return for higher salaries.[114]

The university was nationalized even faster. All non-Romanian professors, most of them Jews and Germans, were given two years to learn Romanian, too short a time span, as some protested: "it is impossible to master the language to the point that we can teach it in just a few months."[115] In addition to passing the language exams, the professors were required to swear an oath of loyalty to Romania. Most chose not to do so. In the fall of 1919 they boarded a train to Vienna, never to return. The two old-timers who remained, Eugen Ehrlich and Adolf Last, were eventually chased out by nationalist students who vowed never to "admit at any price the reinstitution of the old Austrian spirit to Cernăuţi university."[116]

But old habits die hard. The strict new language regulations did not mean the sudden disappearance of non-Romanian languages from public and private space. Many Jews in Cernăuţi continued speaking German. "Until first grade, at the age of six and a half," Pearl Fichman, who grew up in a Jewish family in Cernăuţi, said, "I had no concept of anything Romanian, although I was born in Romania."[117] After studying Romanian in school, the Jewish poet Ilana Shmueli, a friend of Paul Celan, could "understand almost everything" but could "not utter one word [. . .]. I remember only one poem and one song."[118] Students and teachers in "fully Romanian" as well as ethnically mixed schools tended to "speak and write Romanian with great difficulty" even after switching to Romanian-language instruction.[119] Teachers, many native speakers of Ukrainian and German, spoke their native languages both "at home and in the teachers' room."[120] "Due to the culture and education they received in the German language," they spoke Romanian awkwardly, "translating into [it] constructions [typical] of the language in which they received their education."[121] German remained the lingua franca of Cernăuţi's university, too. One visiting inspector reported that he "did not even hear ten Romanian words" during his entire visit, as "almost all students speak German, Ruthenian, Polish, or Judaic jargon." Students walked down corridors "in German medieval costumes of the former corporations from the Austrian era," "German uniforms that offend our national feeling."[122]

The baccalaureate exam, introduced in 1925 as a prerequisite for admission to university, was intended to remedy this situation. The Ministry of Education appointed "external commissions" to evaluate baccalaureate candidates' exams, allegedly to ensure fairness. In Bukovina, this meant a largely Jewish student body was evaluated by a small group of Romanian professors, often committed nationalists. Only 15 percent of the Jewish students who took the exam in Cernăuţi that first year passed. The results were even more disastrous in 1926: fifty-one of sixty-eight Jewish candidates and twenty-six of twenty-nine Ukrainian candidates failed, while all Romanian students passed. This time around, a group of student protesters physically assaulted the baccalaureate commission members.[123] Nine were put on trial in November 1926 and charged "according to the law that bans Communist activity."[124] During the trial, Romanian nationalist student Nicolae Totu shot and killed David Fallik, a Jewish student who had accused a Romanian professor during the protest of coming "from the Old Kingdom to ask tricky questions so the students will fail. But we know more than all the students from the Old Kingdom put together, and even more than the teachers."[125] Over thirty thousand Jews attended Fallik's burial in Cernăuţi, grieving his death and horrified that his assassin had been acquitted. Across the city, Jewish homes and businesses flew black flags.

Fallik's murder and Totu's acquittal confirmed what many Jews already suspected: that they were no longer safe in Bukovina. In a memorandum to the League of Nations, the Joint Distribution Committee noted that in Bukovina "Jewish travelers on railways are assaulted and forced to leave the trains; Jews are driven out of cafes and theaters, and are set upon in the streets; Jewish schoolchildren are attacked in schools, and students in the universities, and synagogues have been desecrated." The perpetrators were usually students, often the first generation in their families to go to university. Many had fallen under the spell of an anti-Semitic professor in Jassy, A. C. Cuza, founder of the National-Christian Defense League (Liga Apărării Naţional Creştine), who demanded that the number of Jewish students admitted to Romanian universities be limited by a *numerus clausus*. Cuza's anti-Semitism was legendary: when a Jewish carter asked him for directions, Cuza apparently was so "indignant that a Jew should have ventured to speak to him that he struck the carter. The carter hit back, and was sentenced to three months imprisonment, fined, and forced to pay damages. The incident was followed by anti-Semitic riots in Bucharest, Jassy, and Focşani." The Romanian government did not officially condone anti-Semitic violence, but they did little to curb it. University professors, high school teachers, and priests felt free to wear the swastika, the symbol of A. C. Cuza's League, on their lapels and to openly disseminate anti-Semitic propaganda.[126]

Non-Romanians—especially Jews—employed in Bukovina's civil service were subject to similar Romanianization policies. Beginning in 1919, the Romanian administration required proof of fluency to be awarded or retain a position in the civil service. The language exam for civil servants consisted of "free essays or translations [. . .] without a dictionary" and an oral exam in which "the examiners may choose what questions to ask."[127] Lawyers who "are not Romanian by birth" had to pass a Romanian exam to retain their right to practice.[128] By 1922 court rooms across Bukovina were rejecting petitions drafted in German.[129] Lawyers who could not speak Romanian fluently stuttered and stumbled, frantically looking up words in pocket dictionaries while judges sat "practically barricaded with dictionaries, Romanian grammar books, and textbooks." "For many lawyers," the *Czernowitzer Morgenblatt* objected, "this decree amounts to the end of their career, because if one takes away their language, one also takes away their livelihood."[130]

Minorities who had graduated from a Romanian *Gymnasium* or "were known" to speak Romanian fluently were exempted from the language exams. Non-Romanian civil servants tried to use this loophole to obtain exemptions. "In my childhood, I had the best opportunity to learn Romanian," pleaded one candidate.[131] Non-Romanian lawyers mobilized to demand "a longer transition time for the language switch."[132] The strict language policies did not keep civil servants from using German and other languages at work. A steady stream of official correspondence "in foreign languages, unknown to the authorities in the Old Kingdom" flowed from the newly annexed provinces to Bucharest.[133] The administration ordered "all chiefs of departments and services" in Bukovina to "start carrying out their internal and external correspondence only in the official language."[134]

Yet civil servants from Bukovina continued writing their correspondence with Bucharest in German, on Austrian stationery sealed with Habsburg double-headed eagle stamps.[135] A new order suspended all paperwork from the newly incorporated provinces until "it has been translated into the Romanian language."[136] Civil servants in the provinces were instructed to eliminate "the language, inscriptions, effigies, and stamps reminiscent of the old regime."[137] The state's capacity to reshape practices on the ground remained limited, however. As late as 1937, Bucharest threatened functionaries "who conduct correspondence or use seals with different symbols or a language different from the official ones of the Romanian state" with "merciless disciplinary sanctions."[138]

It was not just that Bukovinans rejected Bucharest's rules. The Romanian state was forced to compromise because it lacked the capital and expertise to bring about the changes it desired. State authorities in Bukovina closed their eyes to the shortcomings of non-Romanian civil servants who were, for the time being at least, irreplaceable. Prime Minister Alexandru Averescu's appointed minister-delegate for Bukovina, Dori Popovici, declared in June 1920 that "we must admit that we have very good functionaries who know the Romanian language insufficiently and whom we cannot otherwise use unless we let them work for now in the German language."[139] Civil servants whose Romanian skills were modest at best passed the exam anyway. Of the thirty-nine candidates who took the Romanian language examination in October 1924 in Cernăuţi, only one failed.[140] Minority civil servants were given several opportunities throughout the 1920s to retake the language exam and "reclaim their posts if they pass."[141] The administration even organized language classes in Cernăuţi to prepare "public, administrative, and juridical functionaries who do not know the state language."[142] Local officials often intervened on behalf of their non-Romanian employees, especially if they knew them well and could claim they were indispensable. In 1935, when the time came to fire six firefighters who had repeatedly failed their language exams, their superiors insisted that they were "irreplaceable" because they knew the city "in its smallest details."[143]

## Statelessness

Back when the great powers were working out the breakup of empires between 1918 and 1920, Jewish organizations in Paris had put pressure on the decision-makers to ensure that Jews in the East European successor states would be protected against violence.[144] Romanian Jews submitted memoranda demanding complete civic and political equality. When Articles 3 and 7 of the Minority Treaty for Romania gave Jews in Romania's newly incorporated territories full citizenship rights, Romania's National Liberal prime minister and key representative in Paris Ion I. C. Brătianu resigned in protest. His successor Alexandru Averescu signed the minority protection treaties, albeit unwillingly.

This was not the first time that pressures to resolve the "Jewish question" had put Romania in a humiliating position internationally.[145] At the Congress of Berlin in 1878, the great powers had agreed to recognize Romania's independence from the Ottoman Empire on the condition that Romanian Jews be fully enfranchised. Before then, Romanian Jews had occupied a legally ambiguous category: although denied full citizenship rights, they were expected to fulfill citizenship duties. After the 1870s their access to various professions was increasingly limited as economic and citizenship rights became more interlinked.[146]

It was no secret that Bukovinan Jews had, in the words of Marsha Rozenblit, "assumed and hoped for the continuity of Austria-Hungary" to the very end.[147] The Bukovinan-Israeli historian Zvi Yavetz recalled in his memoirs how his grandmother thought of Emperor Franz Joseph as "an angel in human form," while Romanians were traitors who "disappointed the emperor when he relied on them."[148] Many Cernăuţi Jews agreed with Yavetz's grandmother that Romania was inferior to Austria and, by extension, Bukovina. To them, Romania was "the poorest and dirtiest country."[149] "Beatings were formerly unknown here," complained the *Morgenblatt*'s editors in 1927; "today, unfortunately there are beatings here far too often."[150] "Bucharest is not as dull as Belgrade, not as frowsy as Sophia," one Jewish resident of Cernăuţi told Israel Cohen; "but can you compare it with Vienna, at least with the Vienna that once was?"[151] This hostility to Romanian rule, the authorities feared, would contaminate other Bukovinans, sowing the "seed of mistrust [. . .] inside the tortured souls of its Bukovinan subjects toward everything Romanian and especially toward the Romanian state."[152] Police officials even suspected Jewish merchants of deliberately raising food prices to make Romanians "suffer the consequences of their reckless wish" to unify Bukovina with Romania.[153]

Pressure from the Allies on Romania meant that the government had no choice but to award Jews in Bukovina full citizenship rights by the Romanian constitution of 1923. But already on February 23, 1924 a new law "concerning the acquisition and loss of Romanian nationality" required individuals in the newly annexed provinces to prove that they were legally registered there before November 18, 1918 to retain their citizenship rights.[154] They had to show that they had "possessed the *Heimatrecht* in those provinces" and that "up to the date of the promulgation of this law, have not opted for any other nationality."[155] Across former Austria-Hungary, successor states used the Habsburg legal system of *Heimatrecht* or *pertinenza* as a basis to grant or deny national citizenship to former imperial citizens and to decide who was entitled to "social benefits, work, and to remain in their place of residence."[156]

Many Bukovinans were unable to provide the required documents. Under Austrian rule, pertinency or *Heimatrecht* had little meaning beyond allowing communities to deny welfare and poor relief to individuals not legally registered there. It was "not actually related to individuals' connections to communities," and it was quite common for people to work their whole lives in places where they were not legally registered.[157] But, as a report issued by the Joint Foreign Committee indicated, "during the war public archives were destroyed on a very large scale, and even those who possessed the local *Heimatrecht* are now, in many cases, unable to prove it." All these people now risked losing their Romanian citizenship. By 1924, the period during which individuals in ethnically mixed territories could opt for citizenship in a different successor state had long expired. As a result, the people in question had "lost their old nationality without gaining a new one."[158] Yet the Romanian government insisted there was nothing out of the ordinary about its requirements for citizenship, since in Austria-Hungary too "only *Indigenat* [citizenship] conferred Austrian or Hungarian nationality while domicile conferred no right at all."[159]

By the Joint's estimate, over thirty thousand Bukovinan Jews were in danger of losing their nationality. "Not only will the limitation of the new Nationality Law exclude large numbers of persons from Romanian nationality," the Joint warned the League, "but, owing to the circumstances in which it has been promulgated, it will actually have the effect of transforming these persons into what is known as *Heimatlosen*: that is, persons without any nationality whatever."[160] In 1924 the Joint Foreign Committee reported that over sixteen thousand Jews from Bukovina and Transylvania had become *Heimatlosen*, and many more would soon be relegated to this "abnormal status."[161] Losing Romanian citizenship could have disastrous consequences, including no longer being allowed to practice one's profession and losing legal protection where one lived.

Among those who became suspended in this legal limbo was a group of pensioners, former Austrian civil servants and employees from Bukovina and their dependents, now residing in Vienna. Most had taken refuge in Vienna during World War I and had never returned to Bukovina, whether because the journey was too dangerous or because they had nowhere to go back to. Until April 1923, they received their pensions from Romania. But even then, after taking pains to prove that they were entitled to a pension by means of a medical certificate "which costs 40,000 Austrian crowns and a new authorization [which] costs 70,000 Austrian crowns," the pensioners received "just enough to buy twenty-five loaves of bread per month" and were as a result "living today in the utmost misery, suffering cold and hunger." Many were widows and orphans of former civil servants who, "if they are not to starve must allow themselves to be supported by their Austrian relations. These persons, who have seen better days, are now absolutely destitute and have to spend days and weeks applying for relief to various charitable organizations and literally beg for their bread."[162]

The Bukowiner Zentralverband in Vienna, formed to represent these pensioners' interests, first appealed to the Romanian king for help. "It is surely right," Zentralverband heads A. M. Ehrlich and Friedrich Kleinwächter wrote, "that the successor states of the former Austro-Hungarian monarchy should take over the duties implied in the contracts concluded between that monarchy and its state officials."[163] Yet in April 1923 the Romanian government stopped paying their pensions altogether, following a new pensions law that said that only individuals residing on the territory of Romania could receive pensions from the Romanian state. Most of the pensioners represented by the Bukowiner Zentralverband were too old and frail to go back to Bukovina and too poor to cover the costs of relocating there.[164]

At this point, the pensioners took their case to the League of Nations, sending four petitions to its Minority Section between 1923 and 1925. At first, they protested against the Romanian government's requirement that they relocate to Romania. Then they complained that the Austrian government had denied them citizenship because of their religion.[165] The Finnish diplomat Aarne Wuorimaa, serving in the Secretary General's Office at the League, was confused by the petitioners' confusion: "in the first letter, the petitioners frankly regarded themselves as Romanian subjects; in the second letter it would seem that they regarded themselves as a minority in Austria and as such claimed the right to enjoy the status of Austrian citizens. In their third letter they would appear to have altered their minds [*sic*] and to have determined to secure more favorable treatment from the Romanian government and Romanian nationals. In the fourth letter, their position from a nationality point of view seems to be wholly undefined, and one has the impression the petitioners themselves are at a considerable loss to decide what direction they should turn."[166]

As a result of rapidly changing citizenship regulations, the petitioners had found themselves suspended between two states, neither of which wanted responsibility for their welfare. Moreover, League officials could not ascertain what the petitioners' complaint was really about: whether it was "a complaint by Jews who claim a right of option for Austrian nationality in preference to the nationality given them by the peace treaty, or a badly expressed complaint of having been prevented from obtaining Austrian nationality as a direct consequence of the peace treaty." In the end, they concluded that there was not enough evidence to support the petitioners' claim that the Romanian and Austrian governments' measures targeted Jews specifically.[167] They acknowledged that the "unfortunate Jewish group" was in a miserable condition that had worsened between 1923 and 1925, but decided that their care did not fall within the competence of the League's Minority Section.[168]

In 1928 the League received a new set of petitions from another Bukovinan pensioners' organization in Vienna, whose members were "former Austrian functionaries who do not have Romanian nationality and who, originating in the former Great Austria, exercised their functions in Bukovina and, after their retirement, did not remain in the country but returned to Austria, their veritable country of origin."[169] The petitioners hadn't received their pensions in five years and had become "completely impoverished and are not at all capable of bearing the costs, enormous for them, which would be required to return to the country."[170] Austria refused to help the Jewish retirees, citing its pension law which affected all Bukovinans. Article 1 of the Austrian pensions law of March 18, 1920 "restricted the application of the laws of option to retirees who have *Indigenat* in a locale of the Austrian republic on the condition that the last post they occupied is on the territory of the Austrian republic." As a result, the pensioners were now "passed over by both Austria and Romania."[171] In August 1929 Angel María Céspedes, a member of the League's General Assembly, visited the Romanian Legation in Geneva to investigate the pensioners' problem. Nothing could be done to improve their situation, he concluded, since "the legislation applies to all liberated provinces as does the right of the Romanian state to adopt different legislative dispositions for different provinces of the kingdom."[172]

Such was the confusion created by the transition to a new international system in which sovereignty was connected to "populations conceived in national and racial terms."[173] Tragically, this confusion became an argument against assisting the people left stranded by these changes.

## *Socialism and Communism*

Nearly every aspect of Romania's governance of Bukovina in the 1920s was shaped by an all-encompassing fear of Bolshevism. Since Bukovina shared a border with the Soviet Union, Bucharest deemed the province especially vulnerable to Communist infiltration. This was especially true for its northernmost districts, inhabited predominantly by non-Romanians. After a Soviet Ukrainian state emerged in the north, Romanian officials feared Ukrainians in Bukovina would also fall under the Soviet Union's spell.[174] There were signs of pro-Bolshevik sentiments among Bukovinan Ukrainians as early as 1920, when the pro-unification newspaper *Unirea* reported that "Ruthenians from across the Prut are mocking our administrative organs and our national sentiments" while "dozens of them are crossing the river Dniester to fraternize with the Bolsheviks."[175] As elsewhere in interwar Eastern Europe, in Romania Jews were assumed to be pro-Communist. As Paul Hanebrink writes, anti-Semites at the time "won audiences for their views by unmasking different Communist revolutionaries as Jews."[176] In this regard, too, Bukovina posed problems, since its urban population included many Jews.

While likely exaggerated, these anxieties about the spread of Bolshevism into Romania were not entirely unfounded. The early postwar years were ripe for revolution: people worn out by war and displacement had to endure food and housing shortages. Prices went through the roof, leading the *Czernowitzer Tagblatt* to declare in 1919 that "the misery in this land is very great, and the population is desperate because of the rise in prices and the impossibility of continuing commercial relations with the West."[177] During Cernăuţi's "bread crisis," legions of Bukovinan women traveled hundreds of miles to Moldova to find bread.[178] In 1919, the Red Cross rescued Bukovinans with emergency supplies of flour, sugar, meat, and condensed milk.[179] A lack of materials, money, and labor aggravated the housing shortage in Cernăuţi. Locals who had construction materials hoarded them "in order to obtain higher prices" so that "everything, beginning with the nails" had to be imported.[180] Some Bukovinans were forced to live in trenches and improvised tents, even in winter. Somewhere in the province, the Bukovinan deputy Ion Zelea Codreanu discovered eight children whose parents had died in the war, huddled together in a hut made of fir tree branches.[181] "Thousands of peasant families" in Bukovina lived "for the third winter in a row in underground huts, exposed to typhus and tuberculosis."[182] The first few years of Romanian rule brought few if any improvements. In 1921 a general strike broke out in Bukovina, stopping trains, stores, cinemas, and restaurants from functioning for days at a time.[183]

Panicking, Romanian officials tightened security measures at Bukovina's borders. Refugees returning to Bukovina were not allowed back in unless they could prove that they had lived in Bukovina before the war, while foreigners coming on business would "not be received under any circumstances."[184] Border guards were ordered to "observe all persons who are working against our Romanian national interests and who might have ties with countries hostile to us or who are instigating people to Bolshevism and revolt."[185] The administration imposed martial law and a state of siege on Bukovina, "from the Prut to the Dniester and the districts Vijniţa, Văşcăuţi, Siret, Rădăuţi, and Storojineţ," exacerbating the province's economic troubles and slowing down an already difficult recovery process.[186] Because travel was allowed only after six in the morning, peasants who sold their goods at the market in Cernăuţi "preferred to stay home with their goods for fear of in some way infringing the state of emergency and being fined." Cafes and restaurants closed, and "many loyal customers, who used to rush into coffee houses early in the morning to have their breakfast found the doors closed and wandered around the streets hungry and frozen."[187]

Romanian officials then arrested and interned suspected Bolshevik sympathizers in Bukovina. They especially targeted individuals with Ukrainian names, much as Austrian officials had tracked down suspected Russophiles during World War I. "We will have to continue arrests," said Bukovina's new minister-delegate Iancu Flondor. "If Bolshevik bands invade Bukovina, [. . .] in rebellious localities all men between eighteen and forty-five years old will be picked up and placed in internment camps."[188] The suspects and their families were whisked away to the city of Târgu Neamţ and kept under surveillance. "Those who wish to leave the country for Galicia, for example, will be allowed to do so only if they give up for good their right to return," Bukovina's minister Ion Nistor announced in March 1919.[189]

Bukovina's leftist political spectrum was more complex than Romanian officials guessed. The Social Democratic Party, active in Austrian Bukovina since the 1890s, considered the province an ideal place to carry out socialist politics due to the relative weakness of nationalist movements there. Its Jewish branch was especially strong. Its members were opposed to both assimilation and Zionism and advocated national autonomy for Jews.[190] After 1918 the Jewish branch of Bukovina's Social Democratic Party resurfaced under a new name: "Bund," chaired by Jakob Pistiner. Its agenda included "close cooperation with the international socialist movement in every activity [and] full autonomy in Jewish questions." Following negotiations with Jewish socialists in

FIGURE 5.4. Children and adults pose for a group photograph for the Jewish Educational Children's Colony in Vizhenka, Bukovina (1920). Notice the Yiddish-language signs at the back. Yiddish was the preferred language of Jewish socialists in Bukovina. Courtesy of the Joint Distribution Committee Archives.

the Old Kingdom and Bessarabia, the Bukovinan Bund joined the all-Romanian Bundist organization in January 1923. Although some Bundists considered Yiddish a "jargon," the party used Yiddish in its political propaganda and pushed to have Yiddish recognized as a legitimate national language.[191] The Bund thus contributed to the blossoming of a Yiddish-language cultural scene in interwar Bukovina.

By the early 1930s Cernăuţi was one of Eastern Europe's major Yiddish cultural centers, an unexpected consequence of Bukovina's incorporation into Greater Romania. With former imperial borders dissolved, many Yiddish-speaking Jews relocated from formerly Russian Bessarabia to Bukovina to take advantage of its relative prosperity. Among the new arrivals was Eliezer Shteynbarg, a Yiddish schoolteacher and writer who set up the Yidisher Shulfareyn, an organization which had ties to Bessarabia and the Old Kingdom. Its members aimed to "go to the people to raise national consciousness and elevate it through their own language."[192] Organizations like the Shulfareyn made Cernăuţi a destination for "Jewish youth blessed with talent, who brought with them love for Yiddish."[193] Among them were Jacob Shternberg, Mosche Barasch, and Itzik Manger. In 1928 Galician writer Shmuel Aba Soyfer, who came to Cernăuţi to study history at the university, launched the "first tribune for free Jewish speech in Romania": the periodical *Tshernavitser Bleter.*

The Morgenroyt, a *Bildungsfareyn* (educational organization) for Jewish workers set up by the Jewish branch of the Social Democratic Party in 1908, was part of this scene. After 1918 it offered evening classes for Jewish youth whose education had been interrupted by the war and adult training in a variety of trades. Members had access to a "library of modern Jewish literature" consisting of six thousand volumes and a workers' kitchen, all free.[194] The classes were initially held in the primary school on Landhausgasse. When this was forbidden, the Morgenroyt bought a plot of land in the center of Cernăuţi and "proceeded to construct the Morgenroyt Haus."[195] The Bukovinan Bundist Joseph Kissman collected donations for the Morgenroyt through the Yiddish newspaper *Forverts* in New York City with the help of his friend the editor, Abraham Cahan. By 1936 the Morgenroyt had set up a "professional school for seamstresses and tailors, a school for carpenters, an evening school for young apprentices working in workshops in the city, with 350 students, professional courses for adults, a library with an enormous amount of materials on Jewish culture, [and] a music and theater section"—all with donations from abroad.[196]

In 1922, a group of radical leftists split with the Social Democratic Party of Romania and formed a Communist Party. Unlike the Socialists and Social Democrats, who formed a federation in 1921 and operated independently of the Soviet Union, the Communists officially joined the Comintern in 1922. Following Moscow's line, they advocated self-determination for all minorities in Romania and called for the secession of Bukovina and Bessarabia, a position that resulted in them being deemed a security threat.[197] Proclaimed illegal on April 11, 1924, the Communist Party never grew beyond "a small group of sectarian intellectuals, predominantly Jews and minorities."[198] In Bukovina, Communists dismissed Social Democrats such as Jakob Pistiner of the Bund as having outlived their relevance, since they were "the same as they used to be in the Austrian parliament, and after all we are in the midst of the revolutions of 1924, not in 1914."[199] Unable to operate in broad daylight, Bukovinan Communists hid behind the Party of Ukrainian Workers, "Vyzvolennia": a revolutionary-national organization that aimed to combat economic and national discrimination against Ukrainians. The party's official publication *Borets* traced "the national economic destruction and the destruction of minority cultures by social fascists" and complained about the administration's efforts to abolish teaching in students' native languages.[200] For Romanian officials, however, Communism remained associated primarily with Jews. "If one's hair

FIGURE 5.5. "Finished" part of the Jewish Cultural House, "Morgenroyt," Bukovina, ca. 1920. Courtesy of the Joint Distribution Committee Archives.

was curly and unruly," Pearl Fichman recalled, "the teacher would call you a Communist."[201]

Some, though by no means all, Bukovinan Jews arrived at Communism via the Yiddish cultural movement. Born in 1902 in the village of Zadowa, Prive Friedjung was the daughter of a kosher butcher in Bukovina. In 1915 the family were forced to evacuate their home, staying in in a village near Linz until the end of the war. Soon after returning to Bukovina, now under Romanian rule, Friedjung discovered the organization Morgenroyt. She joined it to speak and read in her native Yiddish: "a cultural movement opened up before me which I could naturally not have experienced in my village, and Yiddishism—which was my foundation—came into connection with the revolutionary movement."[202] In the Morgenroyt library Friedjung encountered the works of Marx, Engels, and Karl Kautsky, as well as pamphlets praising Soviet Russia.[203] She soon joined the illegal Communist Party. While trying to deliver a message to another member, she was arrested by the Siguranţa and released only when her Orthodox Jewish father paid a bribe. When she was arrested again later, she was sentenced to half a year in prison. After her release, Friedjung moved to Vienna, where she immediately reported to the local party organization and continued distributing Communist newspapers and pamphlets.

The Siguranţa's brutal treatment of real and suspected Communists radicalized young leftists like Prive Friedjung. The Siguranţa did not differentiate between Communists and Social Democrats, between Bolsheviks and national irredentists. "Using the state of siege, which continues on the other side of the Prut, as a pretext, the authorities are carrying out a systematic persecution of all opposition parties, especially the Social Democrats," the Bukovinan Social Democratic *Vorwärts* announced in January 1927.[204] As rumors spread about "illegal newspapers and organizations in Bukovina," the Siguranţa carried out house searches and arrests, confiscating newspapers and locking up those seen carrying them. These tactics persisted even after the National Liberals lost their grip on power in 1928. Faced with a new wave of workers' strikes in the early 1930s, the National Peasant Party (Partidul Naţional Ţărănesc) cabinet shut down trade unions and put down strikes by force.

## The Peasant Question

Ever since the mid-nineteenth century, the "peasant" had been the subject of impassioned debate in Romanian intellectual and political circles. Since Romania was a predominantly agricultural country (78 percent of its population was rural), the peasant question and the national question were intertwined.[205] Western-educated Romanian National Liberals who believed Romania should follow the Western European model of development saw peasants as an obstacle to the country's modernization. Backward, illiterate, and impoverished, they had to be educated and reformed so that the peasantry would stop being peasants and become part of a new Romanian middle class.[206] Nineteenth-century Romanian "poporanists," or populists, on the other hand, argued that Romania should follow a special path to development, retaining rather than transforming its rural economy. Like their Russian counterparts the *narodniki*, these Romanian intellectuals held "the peasant" up as a bastion of moral purity against the city's corruption.[207]

By the mid-1920s, young nationalists of peasant background, the first to go to university, were entering the political scene by the back door of riots and anti-Jewish violence. Their intellectual leaders championed the peasant cause and denigrated the city as polluted by foreign influences. Historian Nicolae Iorga, highly admired in these circles, believed that "the village was the place where the laws of social change operated in their purest form, [. . .] a preserver of a way of life built over the centuries."[208] By contrast, wrote the interwar poet Lucian Blaga, "the city-dweller lives in fragments, in relativity, in mechanic concreteness, in a sober sadness and lucid superficiality."[209]

The reality of Romanian peasants was far from these idyllic images. They lived in terrible conditions, especially in the Old Kingdom. Crowded into huts made of clay, they had limited access to schools or health care.[210] Following the abolition of serfdom in the Russian Empire, peasants in the United Principalities had been allowed to own land privately, but the best land remained in landowners' hands and the plots allotted to peasants were too small to make a difference.[211] Numerous large estates were owned by absentee landlords and run by tenants who sublet the land to peasants, often at exorbitant prices.[212] Though deeply dissatisfied with their lot, peasants were completely disenfranchised and had no outlet for their anger but rebellion. The largest revolt, in 1907, resulted in the death of over a thousand people and caused "enormous destruction of property." More large properties were divided among peasants after the revolt, but overall too little changed hands. Romania remained the Eastern European country with the largest disparity between the number and size of smallholdings and large estates.[213]

During World War I, the land question in Romania became a ticking time-bomb. The immediate danger came from Russia where, after the revolution of February 1917, peasants seized landowners' estates and divided the land between themselves. Peasant soldiers deserted their units and joined the land grab, leading to the army's rapid dissolution. It seemed entirely possible that the revolution would spread into Romania, given that Russian and Romanian troops had direct contact with each other on the Moldavian front, and because events in the Russian Empire always had repercussions for Romania.[214] To spare the Romanian army the fate of its Russian counterpart, King Ferdinand promised the troops that they would be rewarded with land as soon as they returned home.[215]

The National Liberal Party (Partidul Naţional-Liberal), called to power in December 1913, elected a constituent assembly whose task was to revise the 1866 Romanian constitution's provisions regarding expropriation and franchise. This assembly appointed two commissions to launch the land reform. In March 1918, however, Romania was forced to sue for peace, and Bucharest came under German occupation. The newly appointed government of

FIGURE 5.6. "Bukowina: Bauern aus Klosterhumora" (1894): Romanian peasants at Humor monastery, shown wearing traditional dress, against the backdrop of the monastery wall. Likely taken to further ethnographic knowledge (*Volkskunde*) of Bukovina, the image presents Romanian peasants as a type in much the same way as Romanian nationalists would later think of them. ÖNB Bildarchiv und Grafiksammlung. Courtesy of the Österreichische Nationalbibliothek (ÖNB/Wien).

Alexandru Marghiloman dissolved the constituent assembly and announced a new agrarian reform. When the Central Powers collapsed and Romania reentered the war in the fall of 1918, this too was suspended. Yet on November 13, 1918 King Ferdinand issued a new proclamation of land reform, followed by several laws in the form of decrees for each of Romania's newly incorporated provinces.[216] General Alexandru Averescu's government, formed in March 1920, issued a second land reform law in July 1921.[217]

Between 1917 and 1921 Romania implemented the most radical land reform in Eastern and Central Europe.[218] "One might put it paradoxically," wrote historian David Mitrany in 1930, "and say that it was just the extreme violence of the Russian revolution that saved the peace in Romania," by leading "the rulers and landlords hastily to surrender their shirts, when in less stormy times they might have bargained hard for a button."[219] Through a controlled agrarian revolution from above, the Romanian government prevented peasants from seizing land violently and falling into Communist hands.[220]

In Bukovina, the land reforms were initiated by a decree of September 7, 1919, then modified under Averescu's government in July 1921.[221] The land reforms marked for expropriation mortmain estates (lands held inalienably by ecclesiastical corporations), estates of absentee landlords and individuals who had lost their civil rights, estates farmed out during nine consecutive years before 1919 by absentee landlords, and all estates larger than 250 hectares.[222] A decree enacted in July 1921 modified the land reform in the landowners' favor, allowing them to continue using their land until it was transferred to its new owners. Landowners were to be compensated for their losses, with the state bearing up to 50 percent of the cost.[223] Over 76,000 hectares of land were expropriated in Bukovina.[224] The whole procedure was placed in the hands of different local commissions, each formed of two intellectuals, a mayor, landowners, and two peasants, and coordinated by the Regional Bank in Cernăuți. Some land in "undeveloped regions" was set aside for colonization by Romanian national peasants with little or no land, through a Central Resettlement Office.[225] These reforms, though comprehensive, proved inadequate, however. Peasants still lacked the equipment and knowledge necessary to reform the agricultural economy. Many were still without land or had too little to support their families.[226]

By the mid-1920s both non-Romanians and Romanians in Bukovina were complaining about the land reforms' outcome. Ukrainian politicians believed the Romanian government had used the land reforms to Romanianize predominantly Ukrainian territories in the north. The Ukrainian senator Kost Krakalia complained before the Senate in December 1926 that Romanians who did not qualify to receive land (priests, teachers, state employees)[227] were getting it anyway, while Ukrainian peasants were passed over.[228] Ukrainian lawyer Vasyl Duchak similarly noted that ethnic Romanian state employees were awarded land in Bukovina at the expense of poor Ukrainian peasants, even though the law "does not allow assignment of expropriated land to priests, teachers, officials, and state functionaries and in general to persons who do not practice agriculture as their principal occupation."[229] The government was taking advantage of a loophole in the agrarian law for Bukovina: Article 79 allowed it to "portion out areas destined for purposes of general interest, hygiene, or state interest."[230] It justified its actions by invoking the concept of "state utility."

By the Romanian government's count, up to 21,803 non-Romanian peasants in Bukovina had received plots of land, including some who had "served in Ukrainian legions in 1918–1920 and who fought the Romanian troops." Romanian officials insisted that everyone, including the Ukrainian minority in

Bukovina, "is being treated on a basis of perfect equality with the Romanian majority in the province."[231] Writing in 1930, historian David Mitrany argued that nationalization was not the primary driver behind the Romanian land reforms, but a consequence of them. In Transylvania, for instance, most large estates were in non-Romanian hands. To redistribute this land to the peasants meant transferring it from non-Romanians to Romanians. In Bukovina, the situation was more complex, because Romanians were better represented among the landowning class. Still, the Bukovinan politician and landowner Iancu Flondor believed land reforms were necessary as a form of national retribution and historic justice for Romanian peasants in "nationally endangered" territories who had safeguarded Romanian culture and traditions.[232] But as the Romanian delegate to the League Nicolae Petrescu-Comnen admitted, many Romanian peasants in Bukovina did not receive land, since all that had been available was gone.[233] In Rădăuţi district, for example, many properties "ended up in the hands of Germans, Jews, and even Hungarians," and "peasants not included on lists for the distribution of land revolted."[234]

In parallel with land redistribution, the Romanian administration set out to reform the countryside through a strong infusion of culture. Bucharest believed that rural illiteracy and poverty provided fertile ground for Communism, since uneducated, impoverished peasants were easily manipulated by Bolshevik agents. A contributor to Ion Nistor's *Glasul Bucovinei* wrote in 1922 that "in our country, large masses of people, the peasantry above all, and manual laborers are in a great state of cultural inferiority compared to the cultures of the West." "The propagandists of utopias impossible to achieve," the author continued, "find their best allies in the ignorance and lack of knowledge of the masses."[235] Moreover, peasant poverty and illiteracy made a mockery of Romania's claims to embody European civilization at Europe's eastern frontiers. The desire to alleviate rural misery was closely bound up with concerns about national prestige.[236]

To alleviate cultural and educational disparities between Romanians and non-Romanians in Bukovina, the National Liberal governments of the 1920s launched literacy campaigns. The Romanian Ministry of Education tried to provide the countryside with new schools and village reading rooms.[237] Drawing on his experience leading educational initiatives for Romanians in Austrian Bukovina, ex-teacher George Tofan drew up plans for a new round of school reforms. "The school system," he insisted, "must stem from the life of these people, from the depths of its being."[238] To "guide the people down the path of work and progress" and help them "maintain national consciousness through the power of national culture," the authorities set up "homes of culture" (*cămine culturale*) in the countryside. These organized "festivities with conferences, songs, fireworks, theater, cinema," and hosted Sunday lectures by "honest speakers, learned people, priests, and teachers." They were also supposed to educate peasants politically by collecting and passing on to Bucharest information about "the needs of the masses, or any kind of social danger."[239] Some of these initiatives were modeled directly on other nationalities' efforts to build "mass culture." The Cultural League (Liga culturală) in Bucharest admitted that Romanians had much to learn from their Hungarian neighbors, who had developed "a mass culture that is well above our own."[240]

These efforts faced considerable material deficiencies and peasant resistance. In parts of northern Bukovina severely damaged by World War I, the infrastructure required to support such initiatives had to be built from scratch. In one village in northern Bukovina, local officials struggled to set up a public library, as only three buildings remained standing after the war.[241] Moreover, there was a perpetual shortage of books in Romanian. One high school reported that its library, stuffed with materials from the Austrian period, had "no Romanian books at all." Teachers from rural Bukovina inundated Bucharest officials with petitions for book donations and other resources, claiming that they were "the only institution of Romanian culture in this alienated part of the country that is successfully propagating the idea of state and nation."[242] The Romanian authorities on the ground also discovered how deeply rooted were Bukovinan peasants' prejudices against teachers and schools. Switching the official language of instruction to Romanian, it turned out, did not draw more peasant children into schools. Parents continued sending them to work in the fields, and as a result "school attendance is good during the winter months but in summer it is absolutely terrible."[243] Romanian officials in Bukovina, like their Austrian predecessors, found themselves having to coerce peasant families into sending their children to school. There were even proposals to impose a "school tax" on all adults who had not learned to read and write by a certain age.[244]

Bukovina's villages were still struggling as late as 1928. School inspectors found village schools in a sorry state, lacking heating and teaching materials. Schools and churches could not compete with taverns. Romanian peasants had taken to wearing "Jewish clothes" and dancing "tango and other modern dances" at parties and balls, such that "the following day, on Sunday, drunken locals sleep until the afternoon and the church preaches to nobody." In Bukovina's mountain districts, visiting Romanian officials met Hutzuls who "think the loss of a cow much greater than the loss of a woman" and "exchange wives amongst themselves and rent them out for a few months."[245] Everywhere they looked, officials found signs of moral degradation.

---

Across Europe, state-forming processes in the 1920s were conducted "over a topography of mass death and collapsed states."[246] The National Liberal architects of Romania's unification had to integrate the nation-state's newly incorporated provinces while simultaneously rebuilding a country devastated by war. These twinned state-building and unification processes took place against the backdrop of revolutionary unrest and chaos, as imperial administrations fell apart and Eastern Europe descended into paramilitary violence and pogroms.

The recently expanded Greater Romania defined itself as an anti-imperial and anti-revolutionary state, Europe's defender against the Communist threat in the east. It narrowly escaped the fate of Russia and Hungary, where Bolshevik revolutions brought Communists to power, by enacting a controlled social revolution of its own. Romania's National Liberal governments, which remained in power for the greater part of the 1920s, sought to preempt social unrest and legitimize their state as "the superior alternative to the now defunct empires which they replaced."[247] They did this through centralization, modernization, and nationalization policies aimed at binding the newly incorporated territories to the nation-state, giving them a national Romanian character that reaffirmed Romania's status as a civilized European state.

These policies were not immediately effective, however. The people who implemented them were usually appointed by Bucharest and lacked both local knowledge and resources. As a result, they often compromised and deviated from their avowed goals. Bukovinans compared them with their Austrian predecessors and found them uncultured, poor, destructive, and inefficient. Many Bukovinans looked upon Romanian rule as temporary and voiced the hope that it would soon come to an end. In turn, Romanian authorities and their supporters in Bukovina grew increasingly frustrated by the state's inability to erase traces of Austrian rule. The empire's shadow followed the province's new rulers everywhere as they struggled to lay the foundations for a new, unified nation-state.

The Romanian National Liberal governments' most glaring failure in Bukovina was their incapacity to remedy the province's "foreign" character. By 1930 many Bukovinans were blaming this failure on "democracy"—even though they had never experienced a truly democratic regime. On paper, the Romanian state was democratic, and in the aftermath of the war, the Romanian government allowed democratic reforms such as expansion of the franchise and land redistribution. But these democratization measures were always half-hearted and incomplete. National Liberals held on to the financial and industrial oligarchy that kept them in power.

Faced with growing dissatisfaction, the National Liberals maintained their monopoly on Romanian politics by using fears of Bolshevik revolution to stifle reformist movements and criticisms of their own policies.[248] This changed when the National Peasant Party (Partidul Naţional-Ţărănesc; hereafter NPP), formed in 1926 through the merger of the Peasant Party (Partidul Ţărănesc) and the National Romanian Party (Partidul Naţional Român) of Transylvania, won a resounding victory in the elections of 1928.[249] The NPP promised to repair the constitutional regime the National Liberals had damaged by election-rigging, ruling through the police and gendarmerie, and using loopholes in the constitution to evade civil rights guarantees.[250] It promised greater civil and political rights for all citizens, including minorities.[251] Across interwar Eastern Europe, peasant governments similarly pledged to fight "rampant corruption, cronyism, trafficking, militarism," and urban political culture by reasserting the peasantry's potential as a source of political renewal.[252]

Only a year later, however, Romania was plunged into an economic crisis of unprecedented proportions. The Great Depression hit agricultural countries like Romania especially hard. The prices of oil and agricultural goods plummeted, and unemployment rates rocketed as factories closed one after another.[253] The NPP could do little to alleviate the crisis.[254] Facing unemployment, workers across Romania launched a new wave of strikes, the largest being in the Jiu Valley mines in August 1929.[255] The Peasant Party government's crackdown on the strikers killed some miners, which lost it the support of its main constituency. By 1930 the NPP had become a "peasant party with no peasants."[256] It was during this crisis that King Carol II, who had renounced his throne in 1926 in favor of his son Michael and gone into exile, returned to Romania. The NPP prime minister Iuliu Maniu agreed to Carol's return on the condition that he renounce his illicit relationship with Elena Lupescu—the cause of his previous abdication.[257] Carol consented, but when he invited Lupescu back to Bucharest, Maniu resigned in protest in October 1930. Thus began a three-year period of instability during which nine different governments ruled Romania.[258]

Bukovina came out of its first decade of Romanian rule with a new experience and conception of government. The loss of its former regional autonomy made many Bukovinans feel that as a province of a second-rate nation-state, they were more marginal and isolated even than before. Moreover, most of Bukovina's non-Romanian population found itself increasingly disenfranchised. What the National Liberal state had been able and unable to do during the 1920s in Bukovina shaped Romanian and Bukovinan politics during the decade that followed. Its anti-Communism, driven by an all-consuming fear of Bolshevik revolution, stifled the left and paved the way for the radical right's rise. The National Liberal governments of the 1920s also laid the foundations for the ever more authoritarian state of the 1930s through policies that affirmed the state's role as the driver of economic and cultural progress. Moreover, the implementation of the land reforms shifted common understandings of property from a liberal individualist conception to a collectivist-nationalist one. Thus the bourgeois champions of industrialization laid the foundations for the property rights violations Bukovinans would soon experience under Soviet rule.

# 6
# Decade of Extremes

BY THE EARLY 1930S, across Europe, "the almost universal acceptance of democracy" at the end of World War I was giving way to a growing rejection of democratic values.[1] Most Romanians, too, were becoming disenchanted with parliamentary democracy. Mircea Eliade and Emil Cioran, of later international fame, equated democracy with "politicianism," corruption, and inefficiency.[2] They saw the democratic order inaugurated in Paris in 1920 as hypocritical and blamed it for consigning Romania to a position of inferiority.[3] And by the end of the decade, respectable Romanian politicians beyond these radical circles had rejected democratic values and moved further to the right.[4]

Authoritarianism and fascism owed their growing appeal in Romania in large part to the successes that Nazi Germany, Fascist Italy, and the Soviet Union were enjoying when the remaining European democracies were struggling. Many concluded that only a powerful state built on totalitarian foundations could achieve national unity, modernization, and economic development. The idea of a total authoritarian state appealed not only to the radical intellectual circles frequented by Eliade and Cioran, but more broadly to policy makers who were hoping thereby to eliminate illiteracy, remove corrupt political elites, and regenerate the country.[5] Eugenicists such as Iuliu Moldovan, whose ideas gained wide currency during the 1930s in Romania, envisioned a new Romanian nation-state with greatly expanded responsibilities and prerogatives, including the social engineering of its population.[6]

Romanians agreed that the new nation-state should be truly national, with ethnic Romanians in dominant positions. Even the moderate progressive Iuliu Maniu believed that the national state was "the most perfect human organization." As we have already seen, breaking the monopoly of "foreigners" on Romania's economy and culture, especially in newly annexed provinces like Bukovina, was a goal of the National Liberal governments that ruled the country in the 1920s. Yet, as Vladimir Solonari writes, "commitment to democracy meant that the rights of minorities could not be openly violated."[7] With the ongoing collapse of democracy, the Romanian government, no longer bound by this concept, was free to experiment with increasingly daring nationalization policies.[8]

Bukovina, with its stubbornly foreign character, became a weapon in the arsenal of those eager to point out democracy's failures. It showed how democracy had made a mess of the Romanian nationalization project: that the nation-state was national only on paper, with "foreigners" still in economically prominent positions while Romanians constituted the underclass.[9] Visiting Cernăuţi in 1922, Mircea Eliade wrote that "Cernăuţi is a beautiful city, situated on hills; and only 2 percent of its Romanians know Romanian [. . .]. You can't imagine what pleasure it gave me to hear two peasants speaking Romanian. It was the first time I was hearing [the language] in Cernăuţi."[10] As late as 1930, Cernăuţi's population included only 27 percent Romanians, and over 38 percent Jews.[11] Almost a decade after the province's incorporation into Romania, a school inspector reported that "progress toward Romanianization, beginning with Cernăuţi, a revoltingly alienated city, and up to the northern shore of the Dniester, proceeds at the pace of a tortoise."[12]

Not only did foreigners retain their dominant role in Bukovina, but the province continued to resist integration into Romania. Many Bukovinans, including ethnic Romanians who had advocated for the province's unconditional unification with Romania, mourned their loss of autonomy, feeling that Bucharest disregarded their interests in favor of its own. By the mid-1930s, even Ion Nistor, an avid supporter of centralization in the early 1920s, had become a regionalist. Bukovina thus provided grist to the mills of those who insisted that "democracy was supposed to have unified the nation; instead, it seemed to have divided it."[13]

Moreover, during the 1930s, Bukovina became an epicenter of increasingly radical nationalist projects, boosted, in part, by its frontier position and ethnic diversity. The province's proximity to the border meant that Bukovinans had relatively easy access to the outside world and became vehicles for the circulation of radical ideas and propaganda to and from Nazi Germany, the Soviet Union, and neighboring Poland. For the Romanian establishment, which had only a limited capacity to control who went in and out of the country, Bukovina's international connections were a liability. As Nazi Germany and the Soviet Union grew bolder, Romanian authorities feared Bukovina's large minority populations would become a fifth column, paving the way for foreign aggression and the unraveling of the country's already fragile sovereignty.

That Bukovina was home to an ethnically diverse population also meant that different nationalist projects rubbed up against each other, radicalizing each other in the process. In the 1930s, Ukrainian, Romanian, and Jewish nationalists became suspicious of "foreigners" and wanted firmer borders around their respective national groups. They shared not only a disposition and set of ideas, but also practices; ironically, integral nationalists who preached separation from other national groups were the by-product of continued Bukovinan transnational exchange.

## "Slaves to a Faith": The Legion of Archangel Michael

It was the fall of 1923. A delegation of thirty Bukovinan peasants arrived in Bucharest to complain about two problems: Bucharest's excessive centralization measures and Bukovina's Jews, whom they accused of "turning hard-working Romanian peasants into drunkards."[14] The delegates came directly from Câmpulung, where the National-Christian Defense League (Liga Apărării Naţionale a Creştinilor; hereafter LANC), an organization formed in March 1923 and headed by the Jassy law professor A. C. Cuza, had just held its first congress. Cuza was a close friend of Ion Zelinski, a Bukovinan born in the Storojineţ district in 1878, who had relocated to Jassy to work as a German language teacher. Zelinski's son (and Cuza's godson) Corneliu was a university student in Jassy when he joined his godfather's party. In February 1923 he stopped by Bukovina on his way back from Berlin to agitate on LANC's behalf. The following year, he joined his father Ion Zelinski and sister Irredenta(!) on another agitational trip to Bukovina. Their work paid off. By 1926 LANC had a branch in Bukovina and its own newspaper: *Gazeta poporului*.[15]

In Cernăuţi, as in Jassy, Cuza's party gained a following among Romanian students, many of them impoverished youths, the first in their families to attend university. Romanian youths in Cernăuţi, the historian Zvi Yavetz recalled, "practically stormed the doors of nearly all faculties," but places in dormitories and classrooms were limited. Rent was high and government scholarships few. Jewish students were, by contrast, generally better off and better educated.[16] To its constituency of students, LANC presented itself not as a party but as a "brotherhood" of Christian self-defense that called on its members to "battle against the Jewish population as an attempt to prevent the spread of the Bolshevik revolution."[17] Beyond the university, LANC found supporters among Bukovinans living on the border with the Soviet Union, and later on among rural populations whose conditions of living deteriorated further during the depression. LANC's claim that the Jews were to blame for the peasantry's plight resonated with voters, as did its calls to expropriate Jewish property.[18] At the height of its success, in the elections of 1931, the party won 22 percent of Bukovina's votes.[19] While some Ukrainians and Germans also voted for LANC, it was underrepresented in areas with large minority populations.[20]

LANC left a deep imprint on interwar Romanian politics, in large part because it served as an incubator for an even more radical right-wing movement: the Legion of Archangel Michael (Legiunea Arhanghelului Mihail). The

Legion came into being when a group of youths, again led by Cuza's godson Corneliu Zelinski, who had changed his foreign-sounding name to the Romanian Zelea Codreanu, split from LANC in 1927. The Legion's name harked back to Codreanu's time in Văcărești, where he and his companions were imprisoned between 1923 and 1924 for plotting the assassination of several National Liberal politicians and Jewish personalities, and he had been inspired by "a large icon of the Archangel Michael in the prison chapel" to form the movement.[21] The cover of the first issue of *Pământul Strămoșesc* (Ancestral land), the Legion's publication, displayed Archangel Michael hovering over a map of Romania "with black dots showing everywhere that there were Jews."[22]

Ideologically, Codreanu's movement was hard to pin down. Romania, he assured his followers, "is suffering from a lack of men, not of programs."[23] Other Legionaries, too, echoed Codreanu's claim that the movement was supra-political. Ion Moța, soon to be martyred in the Spanish Civil War fighting against the Republic, insisted that Legionaries "do not do politics, and we have never done it for a single day in our lives"; instead, "we are slaves to a faith." "People as they are today," Moța argued, "raised on politicianism and infected by Jewish influence will compromise even the best programs."[24] The Legion combined "in a self-styled blend anticommunism, antisemitism, and xenophobia" with "mystical Orthodox spirituality, the passionate cultivation of rural traditions, and the rejection of liberal institutions and democratic politics."[25] They promised "equity to the peasantry, a new world to the youth, order to the bourgeoisie."[26]

Codreanu's Legionaries believed the solution to Romania's problems could not be found in traditional politics. What was required was a complete revolution "in the human condition," a general rebirth and moral regeneration[27]—or, as Mircea Eliade argued, a transformation through "Christianity, Renaissance, Reformation."[28] Like other movements on the right, the Legion was aggressively anti-Semitic and had a general dislike of minorities or "foreigners," as they were now called.[29] The Legion disliked traditional elites as much as it did foreigners, blaming corrupt and spineless politicians for succumbing to foreigners and facilitating their infiltration into Romanian society.[30] Needless to say, the Legionaries believed parliamentary democracy was irredeemable, as it allowed foreigners and good-for-nothing politicians to grab power.[31]

Having grown out of the student movement of the 1920s and LANC, the Legion appealed above all to students and the young: the disoriented, frustrated, alienated, and lost who had nothing but their youth to feel good about. Nichifor Crainic, the poet and theologian who called for the remaking of Romania into an "ethnocratic state,"[32] effused that "our era is the era of the youth. An old world is collapsing, a new one seeks its form. Its pulse seethes in the arteries of youth."[33] Youth would bring about the anti-democratic revolution the Legion called for. Appropriately, among the Legion's most avid supporters were members of the "generation of 1927," young intellectuals who felt called upon to bring about a social revolution. Too young to have participated in World War I, these men were disillusioned with Romania's political class and its brief experiment with democracy. As the philosopher Emil Cioran wrote, "the democratic regime of Romania had no other mission than to defend the Jews and Judeo-Romanian capitalists."[34] His generation, in contrast, had a historic mission to create a new national elite, incorruptible and inoculated against greed, untainted by association with the establishment, and completely independent of foreign influence.[35]

For the likes of Eliade and Cioran, Legionarism also promised finally to pull Romania out of its provincialism and backwardness. Eliade saw integral nationalism as the way to end Romania's failing efforts to imitate the West and instead assert its own civilization.[36] "I wanted to oppose our cultural dependence on France," he wrote, "a dependence that I regarded as proof of intellectual sloth. I demanded from the 'provincial,' as I demanded from myself, a superhuman effort to learn and do everything that our forebears had not had the leisure to learn and do."[37] Cioran believed a violent revolution was needed to shake Romania out of its slumber. His frustrations with Romanian culture's parochialism and "nothingness" found expression in *Schimbarea la faţă a României* (*The Transfiguration of Romania*) (1936), in which he claimed that "our whole life for the last century has been the process through which we have come to realize that we have done nothing [. . .]. The comparison with what has been done in other parts of the world has revealed the nothingness of our past, and the non-existence of our culture."[38] For intellectuals of this stamp, these problems were not theoretical; the nation's very existence was at stake: "if we do not concentrate our forces, we will surely disappear like an ephemeral image, from the surface of history."[39]

In Bukovina, the Legion recruited its followers primarily among students, priests, lawyers, and educated professionals, at first ethnic Romanians, then increasingly also Ukrainians and Germans. The first Legionary formations emerged there in 1929, after Codreanu visited to tour the monasteries. By 1933 the Legionaries boasted 140 *cuiburi* (nests) in the Bukovinan towns of Rădăuţi and Suceava.[40] Here too, the Legion's promises appealed to impoverished intellectuals like Iulian Vesper, born in 1908 in a village near Rădăuţi, the first in his family to go to university. He recalled how Romanian students like him would "sneak into the dining hall in the morning or during lunchtime before tea and before the first course was served, when little baskets with slices of bread were displayed in a row. They would pass by them in a hurry, throwing into their half-open bags a few slices, exiting sneakily—and in this way they alleviated their hunger that day."[41]

Legionary youth at the university in Cernăuţi gravitated to Traian Brăileanu, one of the protagonists of the baccalaureate incident of 1925 and a sociology professor. Born in Bukovina in 1882, the ninth son of a schoolteacher,[42] Brăileanu had studied philosophy at the university in Cernăuţi and earned a doctorate in sociology in 1909.[43] In March 1921, he returned to teach in the department of ethics, sociology, and politics. He experimented with various kinds of politics before arriving at Legionarism. At first, he was a National Liberal and a supporter of Ion Nistor's Democratic Party of Unification (Partidul Democrat al Unirii).[44] Then he joined Alexandru Averescu's People's Party (Partidul Poporului). Growing increasingly radicalized, he shifted to LANC and finally to the Legion in 1930, in solidarity with the student protests which, in his view, were "not a matter of conspiracy and revolts, of turbulent demonstrations, of political revolution," but the hallmark of "the birth of a new world of Romanian culture."[45] Before long, Brăileanu became a spiritual mentor to Legionary youth in Cernăuţi, presiding over student congresses and promoting Legionary ideals through "dances, lectures, cultural evenings." One such event at Putna monastery in September 1929 was attended by four hundred students from across Romania. At a similar gathering in 1935, Brăileanu won his audience's hearts with a speech lamenting that Romanian students had to go overseas because Cernăuţi university was "filled with Jews."[46]

Beyond the university, Legionary youth in Bukovina convened regularly to attend propaganda meetings and congresses and engage in manual labor. Through a system of "work camps," the movement sought to provide its members with "citizenship education" aimed at developing both their spiritual lives and their "physical nature."[47] One such work camp was set up on the Storojineţ estate of Neagoe Flondor, a member of the famous Bukovinan landowner family and a Legion sympathizer. Legionaries boasted that participants in Flondor's work camp included "professors, doctors, lawyers, teachers, students, and some workers."[48] A similar work camp in Rădăuţi in 1936 devoted itself to building a church, named after the Legion's patron saint Michael, while in the Cernăuţi suburb of Mănăstirişte, Legionaries built roads.[49]

The camps' role was to strengthen Legionaries' bodies through work and reshape them into new men devoted to "work, religiousness, discipline, heroism, the cultivation of all Christian virtues." Graduates of this new school of citizenship would be ready to lay the foundations of a new kind of state, "totalitarian, energetic, moral, Christian."[50] The work camps' other goal was to bridge the deep social and regional rifts that separated Romanians by forming "a work community in which Romanians of all social classes and from all regions should come together."[51] Chirilă Ciuntu, a Bukovinan youth who joined the Legionaries in 1936, attended a work camp in Mănăstirişte and effused that "all distinctions of social class and nationality were erased, which were in Bukovina a very difficult problem to solve."[52]

While the camps educated Legionary youth in virtue, publications such as Traian Brăileanu's *Însemnări sociologice* expounded Legionary ideas.[53] The journal spoke to the Legionaries' key preoccupations: Communism and Marxism, foreign domination and the Jewish threat, the faults of democracy, and the superiority of village life over urban civilization. Its contributors, many of them students and mentees of Brăileanu, wrote at length about the existential threat foreigners posed to Romania. This danger, they believed, was especially acute in Bukovina. In April 1935 *Însemnări* reported that in Cernăuţi only 104 of 643 lawyers were Romanian while 475 of them were Jews. In Suceava, fifty-five of sixty-eight lawyers were Jewish. This explained why Bukovina "looks like a Jewish colony into which a few Romanians have strayed." It was also why the province gave "the impression of [being] a foreign territory temporarily ruled by the Romanian state, which forgot that Bukovina was until recently a completely Romanian territory."[54]

"The state," Brăileanu wrote, "has the duty to intervene and establish a just proportion between Romanians and minorities in all free professions."[55] Yet the state could not fulfill that duty if its political elites were dependent on foreigners. "Our leading class," the Bukovinan Legionary George Macrin wrote, "depends on forces foreign to the interests of our Romanian nation, such as Judaism and freemasonry."[56] As Brăileanu saw it, democracy was at fault because it "does not temper the pretensions of the political class, its thirst for wealth and luxury."[57] The solution was simple. "All social categories," Brăileanu wrote, "priests, philosophers, poets, industrialists, will have to become integral nationalists, hence Legionaries."[58] This new generation of youth "born and developed under the burden of insurrection and persecutions"[59] would form a new political elite, one made up of "soldiers and ascetics," untainted by association with the establishment and independent of all foreign influence.[60]

By "foreigners," *Însemnări sociologice* almost always meant "Jews," who were responsible for "Communism, liberalism, democracy, individualism, corruption, poverty, alcoholism, promiscuity, social inequality, cultural backwardness, immorality, atheism, rationalism, intellectualism, humanitarianism, cosmopolitanism."[61] How could Jews possibly be involved in all these things at the same time? For Brăileanu, again the explanation was simple. Communism was an instrument of Jewish world domination, which was why Jews, despite being so well represented among the capitalist class, also spearheaded the international proletarian revolution.[62] It was also why they mobilized minorities against the state by intervening with the League of Nations.[63] To make matters worse, Jews defied the basic nationalist assumption that nations had territories of their own. Jews not only lacked a territory, but were also, so Brăileanu explained, fundamentally unassimilable.[64] When they adopted the language and cultural practices of other people, they did so only superficially and instrumentally, infiltrating and compromising them in the process. To counteract their influence, it was necessary to create "an exclusivist national political organization" impermeable to Jews.[65]

Brăileanu's *Însemnări* also dismissed "civilization" and democracy as the by-products of Jewish domination. Civilization, the journal wrote, "brought with itself a considerable weakening of religious and moral feeling,"[66] and resulted in an artificial state that did not reflect the community's values and needs.[67] It was this artificiality that Legionary thinkers like Brăileanu blamed for Romania's political and economic crisis. Barbu Slușanschi, a member of Brăileanu's group and frequent contributor to *Însemnări,* argued that "only the moral world of the peasant can be the foundation to the spiritual unity decisive for the structure of the state."[68] This was a popular opinion among Legionaries, who went on pilgrimages into the countryside, promising peasants the moon. Corneliu Zelea Codreanu's entire mystique was built around an idealized image of the peasant. He toured the countryside dressed in national garb, "riding a white horse, accompanied by several lads [. . .] who get off the horse, kiss the earth, and then leave without a word."[69] The Legionaries who went with him held giant crosses in their hands and, in Codreanu's words, "passed in song with horses trotting, on the crests of the hills beside the Prutwhere our forefathers had passed and fought so many times."[70]

In Bukovina these ideas were also expressed aesthetically. A group of young intellectuals who called themselves the "Iconar" group published a magazine of the same name, with "faith in God, respecting popular art, distaste for material life" as its key values.[71] Ironically, given Legionaries' commitment to overcoming class and regional divisions, the Iconar helped perpetuate these differences. In its efforts to translate the Legionary worldview into an aesthetic and literary position they claimed was distinctively Bukovinan, the group rejected the imposition of Old Kingdom culture on Bukovina after its unification with Romania. Bukovina, they said, had the right to an aesthetic and cultural expression of its own, and it would be superior to "the bourgeois pragmatic spirit, the Balkan coterie, the taste for rapid wins, advancing on the social scale as a result of all kinds of compromises" that Bucharest brought to Bukovina. Bucharest, in turn, looked upon Iconar with distrust and contempt. The famous literary critic George Călinescu dismissed the group as amateurish and insignificant. "The effect of an exceedingly brusque contact with that which isn't suited to Bukovina's rural structure," he wrote, "is a confused, mottled verbosity, a rush for neologisms by one party and for archaisms by another."[72]

How Legionaries in Bukovina, as elsewhere in Romania, fared depended a good deal on what the authorities in Bucharest thought of the Legion and above all, whether the king perceived them as a threat or a group he could work with. In 1933, in its final year in power, Alexandru Vaida-Voevod's Peasantist government looked to the Legionaries for support against the Communist threat.[73] The National Liberals, who returned to power in 1933 with A. G. Duca as prime minister, began clamping down on the movement, banning it altogether in December. The Legionaries retaliated later that month by assassinating Duca, which led the next cabinet of Constantin Angelescu to introduce new repressive measures, including a state of siege and increased censorship.[74] After Gheorghe Tătărescu's government put Legionaries on trial in 1934, the Legion resurfaced under a new guise: the "Everything for the Country" (Totul pentru Ţară) party.[75] This was when Bukovinan Chirilă Ciuntu, who later wrote a memoir about his experiences in the Legion, first joined the Legionaries. Although the organization technically no longer existed, in Cernăuţi Legionaries continued meeting illegally in the German National Home building.

Though driven underground, the organization carried on largely undisturbed. On Sundays Legionaries went to Cuciurul Mare, Boian, and Mămăeşti on marches. Sometimes gendarmes got in their way, but "the peasants encouraged us with music and Legionary songs and shouted at us to go on past the gendarmes, since they would defend us with their own lives."[76] The Siguranţa and border guards in Bukovina suspected the Legionaries received funding and support from Nazi Germany.[77] While this was not in fact the case, border authorities kept a close eye on trains crossing the border and rummaged through passengers' suitcases looking for German-language literature. Ciuntu was not worried, however. He felt confident that "the Legionary avalanche could no longer be stopped by any power in the world," as it gave everyone in Bukovina, including the thieves who roamed Cernăuţi's suburbs, a mission: "to build a new country, side by side with the Legionaries."[78]

## Searching for Zion

The most immediate consequence of the establishment of LANC and the Legion's growing influence on Romanian youth was the rapid growth in anti-Semitic violence in 1930s Bukovina. In 1930 several gendarmerie battalions from Cernăuţi and Rădăuţi came to Borşa and Bălăceana to quieten the unrest that broke out during a fire targeting Jewish property. Jews could no longer take the authorities' protection for granted, however. The police and justice system increasingly treated them as though they were outside the law's protection. In 1933 young nationalist hotheads associated with LANC broke the windows of Jewish stores in Cernăuţi and attacked customers. Then they smashed

FIGURE 6.1. The old theater, now the Romanian National Theater in Cernăuţi, in the 1930s. It was the site of bitter disputes between Romanian nationalists and German-speaking Jews in the interwar period. Courtesy of the Biblioteca Naţională a României.

the windows of the theater in Cernăuţi when Jewish actors were performing, throwing rotten eggs and tear gas.[79] Both in Cernăuţi and Suceava, countless Jewish stores and synagogues came under assault.[80] Students beat up their Jewish colleagues on their way to class.[81]

LANC, which merged with Octavian Goga's National Agrarian Party (Partidul Naţional Agrar) to form the National Christian Party (Partidul Naţional Creştin; hereafter NCP) in 1935, was behind much of this violence. Bukovinan peasants and intellectuals traveling to the NCP's congress in Bucharest "insulted, robbed, and even beat up Jews as they boarded the trains."[82] A group of peasants from Rădăuţi got off the train in Roman and "rushed to the restaurant of Ilie Sticlaru, a Jew, [. . .] behind the station, and asked him to give them bread. As the merchant was closing up, the peasants smashed the windows and doors, went inside, and began beating up the staff and the owner."[83] The group's leader was Nichifor Robu, soon to be prefect of Cernăuţi. Nor did Robu's new position of authority change his approach. He threatened Jews with beatings and insisted that "the kikes need to be chased out of their homes and their wealth will be divided among the adherents of the Cuzist party."[84] "The stick's too good for you [Jews]," he said, "it's a bullet you need."[85]

Bukovinan Jews did not take this lying down. One July evening in 1936 Edi Wagner, a twenty-year-old member of the Jewish Bund and the Morgenroyt, where he led a balalaika orchestra, entered Cernăuţi's public garden with a group of friends. When they ran into a group of Romanian Legionary youth, a fight broke out that culminated with the Jewish student Isidor Koschmann stabbing Gheorghe Gligor, the Romanian Legionaries' leader, in the heart.[86] Immediately after Gligor's death, Professor Ţopa, head of the Legionary organization in Bukovina, issued a threat to "those who haven't learned to respect the laws of hospitality of the Romanian people."[87] That night, over thirty young Bundists were arrested. Edi Wagner was, according to Joseph Kissman, tortured to death, though the police "claimed that he had thrown himself out the window." Wagner died that night in hospital and was buried secretly in the Jewish cemetery in Cernăuţi.[88]

Anti-Semitic excesses of this sort and government-initiated anti-Jewish measures bolstered yet another nationalist movement in Bukovina: Zionism. The first Zionist organizations in the province emerged from the same incubator that gave birth to Romanian, German, and Ukrainian nationalist movements there: the university in Cernăuţi.[89] As we saw in chapter 2, students joined academic dueling societies modeled on German *Burschenschaften*—initially ethnically mixed, by the 1890s these were increasingly segregated along ethnic lines. The first Zionist student society in Cernăuţi was Hasmonea, founded in October 1891 by Josef Bieber and Siegmund Neuberger, who also belonged to the Jewish national academic society Kadimah in Vienna.[90] Kadimah's members learned to fence and devoted themselves to studying Jewish history, discussing Jewish questions, and turning "Jewish youth into fighters for Jews and Jewry."[91]

Hasmonea shared many of these goals, and quickly developed too a reputation for combativeness.[92] Its members challenged members of non-Jewish societies, and fellow Jews who frequented German academic societies such as the Akademische Lesehalle, to duels.[93] Mayer Ebner, one of Hasmonea's key founders, seemed never to miss a fight. On one occasion in the later 1890s, while sitting with fellow Hasmonean Isak Schmierer at the Café Korso on Cernăuţi's Herrengasse, Ebner had been approached by a member of the Arminia society and one from a similar *Burschenschaft*-style student association, the Bukese—none other than the young Traian Brăileanu. Brăileanu and his friend demanded that Ebner hand over the newspaper he was reading. When Ebner refused, Brăileanu started spouting anti-Semitic invective. Max König, another Hasmonean, showed up and a fight broke out. The Arminia member fled the café, while Brăileanu straggled behind after taking a beating.[94]

Hasmonea was only the most prominent of several academic societies in Austrian Bukovina that wanted Jews to be recognized as a distinct nationality.[95] Many of these organizations resurfaced after Austria-Hungary's collapse. Members of Dror, an association of Bukovinan Jewish refugee children in

FIGURE 6.2. Members of the Jewish Hasmonea fraternity in Czernowitz, ca. 1934. United States Holocaust Memorial Museum, courtesy of Lotte Gottfried Hirsch.

Vienna, returned to Bukovina after the war and formed a new youth organization: Hashomer Hatzair.[96] By 1922, it was the largest Jewish youth movement in Romania, with members from Bukovina, Bessarabia, Transylvania, and the Regat.[97] Hashomer youth marched in knee-length trousers and shirts opened at the neck, laughing "at those who fled from the rain or sat by the stove on cold winter days." They went on "excursions in the forest and fields on weekends" to prepare for the "future life of simplicity in Eretz Israel." Members had to abide by ten commandments, including "love of truth" and "loyalty to the people, language, and land." Alcohol, tobacco, and sex were all off-limits. The organization cultivated its members' knowledge of Jewish history through conversation and classes that taught students about "the tiniest particularities of the land [of Palestine]." Students could be found reading Martin Buber's writings on Hasidic literature, and Theodor Herzl, Achad Haam, and revolutionary writers such as Kropotkin and Landauer.[98]

Hashomer Hatzair's practices were shaped by its ties with Zionist youth organizations abroad. Its leaders corresponded with Jewish youth who went to Eretz Israel to drain marshes, build streets, work in ports, and study "sociology and pedagogy even when their stomachs ached with hunger."[99] These ties were not always to Hashomer Hatzair's advantage. The few Jewish youths who left Bukovina for Palestine wrote back complaining about poor living conditions, and Zionists back home had to work to dispel this bad news.[100] Few

Hashomer members seriously considered leaving Bukovina for Palestine.[101] Most joined the movement because it offered them space to breathe and membership in a community that cultivated camaraderie, physical work, and intellectual exchange. Eli Rottner, who moved from Polish Galicia to Cernăuţi after the war and joined Hashomer Hazair there, recalled that neither he nor his fellow members "took [politics] seriously even when they talked about it." In Colomeea (formerly Kolomea), where Rottner and his friends started a pioneer group in the spring of 1919, the Hashomer set up shop on the premises of the Jewish Colonization Association. They spent their days working in the garden and forest and their nights reading biographies of Zionist pioneers and philosophical and scientific works such as Spinoza's *Ethics* and Marx's *Das Kapital*.[102] When organizing became difficult in Bukovina due to strict censorship laws and the state of siege, Hashomer's ties with other organizations provided young Jewish men and women in Bukovina with an indispensable social and political outlet.

But Zionist organization in Bukovina still struggled. For one thing, the central Zionist bureau in Cernăuţi had "no more means than a territory ten times smaller."[103] In May 1923 the Bukovina Zionist committee reported that the "Schekelaktion in Czernowitz is very weak, just like any other organizational activity." This was strange, given that there was "generally a very lively economic life in Bukovina thanks to the good situation of the province and its great potential for export, and thanks also to the fact that in Austrian Bukovina economic conditions were always more stable and orderly than in Romania." Condemned to struggling on a perpetually low budget, Zionists accused Bukovinan Jews of "pseudo-nationalism." "Zionists limit their activity to criticizing Straucher but not much else"—that is to say, their political life in Bukovina was apparently consumed by petty rivalries and disputes.[104]

Mayer Ebner, who by the turn of the twentieth century had become the key Zionist activist in Bukovina, played no small part in this squabbling. He spent much of the 1910s and 1920s battling local Jewish personalities, especially Philip Menczel and Benno Straucher.[105] Born in 1872 to a Jewish merchant father and a pious Jewish mother, Ebner went to the *cheder* and then a Jewish primary school. As an eighth grader he helped found Hasmonea, and in 1897 he accompanied Isak Schmierer and Leon Picker as delegates of the Zionist association in Czernowitz to the first Zionist congress in Basel. After graduating law school, Ebner worked side by side with Benno Straucher as a legal intern. He also wrote for Menczel's newspaper *Jüdisches Echo*. In 1904 he broke with Straucher to pursue his own brand of Jewish politics, authentically nationalist and much less willing to compromise than Straucher's.[106] Next, Ebner parted ways with Menczel over emigration to Palestine: Menczel believed Zionists should direct their efforts toward emigration, while Ebner argued for the primacy of local politics (*Landespolitik*).[107] "Zionism is not limited to the question of who wants to go to Zion," he insisted. Rather, it resembled "glasses through which we see all other questions." By the same logic, dreaming of Palestine and being loyal to Romania were not mutually exclusive. "Many of us will dream of the palm and cedar trees of Lebanon, but we also feel good in the shadow of northern spruces. Palestine is spatially and spiritually too narrow for a people spanning the entire world."[108]

Ebner preached these ideas in the *Ostjüdische Zeitung*, published by his Jewish Unity Party (Jüdisches Einheitspartei), founded in 1919.[109] The newspaper's contributors denounced the Romanian administration's violations of Jewish and minority rights, especially in the realm of education.[110] Ebner also used the newspaper to criticize the Romanian citizenship regime introduced through the 1924 "Laws on Acquiring and Losing Romanian Nationality," also known as the Mârzescu Laws. These laws required non-naturalized minorities to obtain "Romanian nationality," as certified by local authorities who drafted official "nationality lists," before they could apply for Romanian citizenship. As historian Chris Davis notes, "anyone who happened not to be home at the time the authorities prepared these lists, or who for any other reason was not counted, could not later add their name. These persons—including their descendants—were subsequently regarded as foreigners before the law."[111] The law had disastrous consequences for Bukovinan Jews who had opted for Romanian citizenship after Bukovina's annexation by Romania, but who were now told they were no longer entitled to citizenship rights because they did not qualify as Romanian nationals.

Ebner aired his concerns before the Romanian Senate too, warning in April 1930 that "for a few weeks now the state police [in Cernăuţi] has been asking these so-called stateless persons to prove within a certain period of time that they have become Romanian citizens or they can present foreign passports, or else they will be expelled."[112] This, Ebner insisted, was not right, since "the stateless" had not acquired citizenship in other successor states either and their "expulsion from Romania is physically impossible, simply because no other state will take these stateless persons."[113] More than thirty thousand Bukovinans who had lost their citizenship asked the Romanian Ministry of Justice to intercede and restore their citizenship rights. By 1932, when the *Ostjüdische Zeitung* reported on the case, four years had passed, and their petitions were still unresolved.[114]

The *Ostjüdische Zeitung* called for unity among Bukovinan Jews but resisted their assimilation into Greater Romanian Jewish organizations. After becoming a delegate in the Romanian Senate in 1926, Ebner joined an electoral alliance with Zionists from Transylvania and Bessarabia, forming the first Jewish National Club in the Romanian parliament.[115] The club ran its own list of candidates, separate from the Regat Jewish organization the Union of Romanian Jews (Uniunea Evreilor Români, or UER), led by Wilhelm Filderman. An "acculturationist without being assimilationist," Filderman embraced the vision of Jewish politics known as *doikeyt*, or "hereness."[116] In Ebner's eyes, however, Filderman was happy to let Jews become completely disenfranchised because he felt more Romanian than Jewish. "For us it is very clear," it was stated in the *Ostjüdische Zeitung*, "that the UER is only the Jewish section of a Romanian party, and the Jewishness of this association is only on a secondary plane. Filderman is in reality a nationalist Romanian of Mosaic religion."[117] Ebner contested Filderman's claim to speak on behalf of all Jews in Greater Romania, above all Bukovinan Jews, whom Ebner deemed more nationally conscious as Jews than their counterparts in the Old Kingdom. Max Diamant, another Bukovinan Zionist, shared the view that "the Jews of the Regat were completely without rights not too long ago" and as a result did not "dare say anything other than what the authorities are saying."[118]

Ebner insisted that the UER should be emulating Bukovinan Jewish organizations rather than the other way around. "It is not proper for us Bukovinan Jews to assume the nationally weak mentality of the Union of Romanian Jews," he wrote, adding that "we should rather bring Old Kingdom Jews to our national idea."[119] Moreover, Ebner resented Filderman for taking credit for the emancipation of Romanian Jews after World War I while underplaying the key role that the Jewish representatives Chaim Weissman from Transylvania, Jacob Kohan-Bernstein from Bessarabia, and Max Diamant from Bukovina had played at the Paris peace conference.[120] Sparks flew when Filderman visited Cernăuţi in April 1929 to urge its Jewish community to join hands with Jews in the Old Kingdom, "shoulder to shoulder, against the enemy of Jewry as a whole." When Filderman told his audience, "I come now for the second time in order to speak to Jews as a Jew," they booed him. He then tried flattery: "We consider this part of Romania the most high-standing intellectually in the entire country. We hope we are not wrong about that. We are intellectuals and we wish to speak to intellectuals." The next day, Ebner summoned his followers to the Jewish National Home for a protest meeting. "These practices of Old Kingdom Jewry," one speaker said, "cannot and should not be allowed to penetrate here [. . .]; we need no assimilation, we will fight for the rights we deserve."[121]

While resisting incorporation into the UER, Ebner's Zionists assured the Romanian administration that their politics aligned perfectly with the Romanian government's goals. They likened their efforts to promote the Hebrew language among a predominantly German and Yiddish-speaking Jewish community to the Romanian administration's efforts to promote Romanian among a multilingual population. "That we are resurrecting the Hebrew language as our old national language, which was never dead," it was asserted in the

*Ostjüdische Zeitung*, "the Romanians will understand, since they too have a feeling for the historical."[122] Bukovinan Zionists hoped Romanian officials would recognize Hebrew as the Jewish national language, "the language of life, family, and the street" and, in accordance with the Minority Treaty, let it therefore become the main language of instruction in Jewish schools in Bukovina.[123] Hebrew, Zionists hoped, would strengthen the national consciousness of Bukovinan Jews and cure them of their tendency to throw "their Jewishness overboard on the first occasion that it becomes uncomfortable to them."[124] This, the *Ostjüdische Zeitung* assured Romanians, was "the spiritual change [also] wanted by the Romanian state."[125]

First, it was necessary to wean Bukovinan Jews off speaking Yiddish and German. When the Jewish National Council rejected a petition to introduce Yiddish as the main language of instruction in Bukovina's Jewish schools in August 1919, Mayer Ebner remarked that "Yiddish is not yet a language of its own; it can develop into a language but only on a confined territory with a predominant Jewish majority."[126] Bukovinan Zionist Mendel Kinsbrunner went a step further, dismissing Yiddish as "a German [language] at an earlier level of development, augmented by a considerable number of Hebrew and Slavic expressions."[127] By Zionist logic, German was an even greater obstacle to attaining national consciousness, since most educated Jews in Bukovina spoke it as their mother tongue. "We can no longer be pioneers of *Kulturdeutschtum*," Mayer Ebner declared in 1921, "since everywhere we hear Hebrew being spoken and German will soon disappear from the Jewish home."[128] When accused of abandoning "the cause of German culture," Ebner replied that "we have not abandoned the Germans, for we never belonged to them, just as they never were ours."[129] But Ebner spoke German and used it even to promote his Zionist convictions. On the anniversary of 150 years of German life in Bukovina, in 1932, Ebner wrote in the *Ostjüdische Zeitung* that "the world should know that Bukovina is the blessed spot of land where Germans and Jews for over one and a half centuries have lived in harmony side by side, peacefully and in friendship and that they will—God willing—continue living so further."[130]

After 1933, Ebner and other German-speaking Zionists in Bukovina underwent an existential crisis. Hitler's rise to power and Bukovinan Germans' subsequent shift to the right prompted Zionists to reconsider their relationship with German culture.[131] Meier Teich, a Zionist from Suceava who had tended to wax sentimental about the universal appeal of Schiller and Beethoven, now urged Jews to distance themselves from all things German.[132] "We no longer want to be German *Kulturträger* [transmitters of cultural values]," he wrote; "politically and culturally we leaned too much toward Germany. The head and the heart have to unlearn. It is our tragedy that many of us still have to say this in the German language."[133]

## Stateless Nation

Ukrainian nationalism in Bukovina also shifted to the right in the 1930s, as increasingly radical ideas gained ground. Nevertheless, the moderate current within the province's Ukrainian politics remained dominant. The Ukrainian Nationalist Party (Ukrainska Natsionalna Partiia, or UNP), formed in 1927 and headed by Volodymyr Zalozetskyi, was active until 1938.[134] Its goal was to defend the cultural and political rights of Ukrainians in Bukovina through electoral politics. To increase Ukrainian representation in parliament, the UNP made electoral alliances with Romanian parties such as the NPP, which promised minorities greater autonomy.[135] Some of the UNP's demands were met by the NPP government that came to power in the elections of 1928.[136] Teofil Sauciuc-Săveanu, the NPP prefect of Bukovina, gave Zalozetskyi and two other Ukrainian delegates his word that "in all Ukrainian villages the Ukrainian language will be taught" and told them that "if this is not the case then he would hand in his resignation."[137]

Under the NPP government, Ukrainians in Bukovina were again able to publish textbooks and teach in their language, although parents who wanted their children to study in Ukrainian had to write a special petition stamped by a notary, a costly and time-consuming procedure. "We will bring the last egg to the market to help the children, we will bring the last hen, we will bring something from the house and buy the stamp, for we don't want our children to be blind": so the Ukrainian nationalist newspaper *Chas*, launched in 1928, ventriloquized its readers.[138] But when the National Liberals returned to power in 1933, they reinstated their harsher minority policies. The UNP then devoted itself to denouncing these measures and trying to counter them through endless memoranda and petitions.[139]

Zalozetskyi's nationalists tried to tread a fine line between denouncing the Romanian authorities and courting them. Zalozetskyi wanted to persuade the Romanian government that Ukrainians were their natural allies, since "Ukrainians are today a nation without a state, since they do not recognize the fiction of state independence the Communists created for them under the name of Soviet Ukraine [. . . and] all the authorities in Kiev know that the union with the Romanian state is the natural conclusion, for Romania has an interest in ensuring that there is a free Ukrainian state beyond the Dnieper [. . .]. [O]ur Cossacks fought more than once shoulder to shoulder with the Romanians against all kinds of enemies. We have the same faith and the same God."[140] Sometimes, Ukrainian nationalists combined these appeals with covert threats, such as when *Chas* warned that Ukrainian reading rooms should not be closed down because "it is in the state's interest to make sure that peasants are educated so they can defend themselves against anarchist elements without scruples"—a reference to Bolshevik or Communist influence from across the border.[141]

Ukrainians were indeed strongly represented within the Communist movement in Bukovina. Its leaders were former members of the Communist Party who had been driven underground and who called for Bukovina's liberation and annexation by the Soviet Union.[142] The Ukrainian Communists Ivan Stasiuk, S. Halytskyi, T. Kozak, and V. Rusnak, among others, emerged from the Ukrainian branch of the Social Democratic Party of Bukovina. In July 1929 they founded a revolutionary organization of their own: the Vyzvolennia, which agitated for the "social and national liberation of Ukrainian workers." Unlike the Communist Party, which the Mârzescu law of 1924 proclaimed illegal, the Vyzvolennia could operate freely. It recruited its supporters from predominantly Ukrainian districts in Bukovina such as Zastavna, Vyzhnytsia (Vijnița), Sadhora (Sadagura), and Kitsman (Coțmani).[143] At the peak of its activity, the organization numbered nine thousand activists in Cernăuți district and three thousand in Storojineț.[144] The Vyzvolennia's press organ, the *Borets*, reported on the conditions of workers and peasants in Bukovina, and denounced Romanian authorities' abuses. But when its editor-in-chief Ivan Stasiuk was arrested and sentenced to three years in prison in 1930, the *Borets* ceased to exist,[145] and in 1934 the Vyzvolennia itself was banned.[146]

Zalozetskyi's nationalist party stood at the opposite end of the political spectrum. Its newspaper *Chas*, published between 1928 and 1938, was firmly anti-Soviet. Its editors denounced Soviet claims to have brought liberation to Ukrainians as hypocritical. They noted that Ukrainians under Soviet rule were "alienated from their national traditions and raised as internationalists and anti-religious people,"[147] while Russians held privileged positions.[148] At the same time, *Chas* sought to foster greater national consciousness among Ukrainians in Bukovina. It relentlessly demanded Ukrainian-language schooling, complaining that "the majority of our children remain illiterate because they aren't learning in the language they learned at home, for all classes in school are in the Romanian language which is complicated for these children and confusing."[149] The editors also urged readers to stop speaking foreign languages, something that many apparently found difficult: "here in Bukovina Ukrainian is only used within the household" while "amongst ourselves and with gentlemen it is not proper to speak Ukrainian. First, because the German language is a lordly language and second, because if someone overheard us, they might think we don't know German. Oh, what shame!"[150] Instead, readers were to "keep the language clean and pure,"[151] and parents were to "make sure that their children learn how to read and write in their native language even if this requires paying someone to teach them."[152] Readers were also urged to boycott non-Ukrainian establishments and distance themselves from "foreigners": "So foreigners don't swindle our people, we must take all commerce into our own hands." Ukrainians were encouraged to learn from the Czechs, "who have very adroitly dispensed with foreigners."[153]

But *Chas* was only a newspaper, and a struggling one at that. Ukrainians outside elite circles seemed uninterested: "our peasants read very little, even fewer of them actually pay for their newspapers."[154] The paper survived on donations from Ukrainian nationalists abroad. Bukovinan Ukrainians in Canada sent contributions to the Ukrainian *Kultfond,* a fund meant to facilitate investment in "the defense of Ukrainian culture."[155] Before long, *Chas*'s secretary Yurii Serbiniuk was urging donors to stop sending money because the Romanian Siguranţa was confiscating the donations. Students played a crucial role in forging ties between Ukrainian nationalists in Bukovina and nationalist organizations abroad. Many traveled to Prague, home to the largest community of Ukrainian exiles in Europe, and linked Ukrainian student associations there with those in Bukovina.[156] The Austrian-Ukrainian politician Stepan Smal-Stotskyi, whom readers may recall from chapter 2, lived in Prague and maintained an active correspondence with Ukrainians in Bukovina through *Chas.*[157] But the Siguranţa began denying Ukrainian students in Cernăuţi and neighboring districts visas to travel to Prague as early as the 1920s, and it collaborated with the Polish police in Lwów (previously Lemberg) to track down people connected to Ukrainian irredentist centers in Berlin, Warsaw, and Prague.[158]

Ukrainian irredentism did not have much appeal beyond a small group of elites: "intellectuals, lawyers, teachers, professors, students, *Gymnasium* pupils, doctors, Greek Catholic and Orthodox priests."[159] Yet as Romanian officials well knew, the rural intelligentsia was not without influence. When the Ministry of Education announced a reduction in the number of Ukrainian-language classes taught in the schools of Cernăuţi district, peasant delegations went to Cernăuţi to protest. Local officials concluded this was "as a result of the movement on the part of teachers and Ukrainian priests who agitate the population, showing that they were deprived of a right the previous government had given them."[160] Officials worried that the rural intelligentsia was using cultural organizations as a front for irredentist propaganda. Ministry of Education officials reported that reading rooms and the premises of cooperatives and choir societies in Bukovina had been converted into national shrines "with a purely Ukrainian aspect": "on the walls hang pictures of Ukrainian scholars, and here and there are little paper flags with the yellow and blue Ukrainian national colors."[161] In northern Bukovina, Ukrainian cultural societies such as Narodnyi dim and Chetalnya Ruskoi Besidy were organizing "theater performances with allegorical scenes showing Ukraine in chains being saved by the Cossacks," and distributing "candy in the Ukrainian national colors" to the audience. As far as Romanian officials were concerned this was no longer "just cultural propaganda, but a subversive activity that undermines not only the Romanian element as an ethnic entity but the actual structures of the political state." "In northwestern Bukovina," one school inspector warned, "Ukrainian propaganda has become a real danger to the state."[162]

By the late 1930s, however, the Ukrainian nationalists Romanian officials feared had begun losing ground to more radical, right-leaning groups that capitalized on the UNP's failures and limited popularity. This new radical movement emerged out of student underground societies such as Zaliznyak,[163] the Legion of Ukrainian Revolutionaries (Lehion ukrainskikh revolutsioneriv), and the Avengers of Ukraine (Mesnyki Ukrainy), whose members called for a national revolution and a total break with nationalist traditions plagued by an "excessive commitment to democratic and parliamentary procedures."[164] Across western Ukraine, youth groups like these provided the Organization of Ukrainian Nationalists (Orhanizatsiia ukrainskykh natsionalistiv, or OUN), founded in 1929 in Vienna, with its base of support. Influenced by Dmitri Dontsov, a former Marxist and Social Democrat who later moved toward "militant integral nationalism," OUN members and sympathizers glorified the Ukrainian nation and called for a national revolution to "discard the democratic and socialist baggage." At its founding congress, the OUN declared the Ukrainian nation "the starting point for all activity and the end goal of every undertaking of a Ukrainian nationalist."[165]

What set the OUN apart from other Ukrainian nationalisms was its revolutionary nature and penchant for "a corporate state and a nationalist developmental dictatorship, modeled on Fascist Italy."[166] Over time, the OUN took on increasingly pronounced fascist ideas,[167] such as "the glorification of the nation and the state, eternal conflict as the essence of life, the exaltation of militarism and imperialism, will and faith as the motive forces of history, action as the solution to all problems, the nation as a living organism"; at the same time, the OUN insisted on its originality, describing its beliefs as "the nationalism of a stateless nation that lives only by irredentism and is ready to sacrifice everything and everybody for the destruction of the cult of those states that do not allow it to live."[168]

By 1934 the OUN had a branch in Bukovina, led by Orest Zybachynskyi. Its weekly *Samostiinist*, along with its other journal the *Moloda Bukovyna*, were platforms to criticize moderate Ukrainian politicians such as Lev Kohut or Kost Krakalia.[169] The group remained on the fringe of Bukovinan life until 1938, when the international context changed radically, opening avenues for the OUN to take on a more central role.

## Royal Dictatorship

By 1937, Romanians had lost faith in the National Liberal party, as the elections that year proved. Led by Gheorghe Tătărescu, the National Liberals in power failed to achieve a majority despite forming an electoral alliance with Vaida Voevod's Romanian Front, the German Volksgemeinschaft, and Nicolae

Iorga.[170] King Carol invited the politician Ion Mihalache to form a Peasant Party government, but he refused. Carol's most acerbic critic, Iuliu Maniu, went so far as to form an electoral non-aggression pact with Corneliu Codreanu and Gheorghe Brătianu's Young Liberals. Banned in 1934, Codreanu's Legion had resurfaced under a new guise, as "Everything for the Country" (Totul pentru Ţară).[171] It garnered 15.6 percent of the vote in the elections of 1937, turning from a fringe party into a non-negligible, though still not dominant, political force.[172]

In Bukovina, Codreanu's party won 22.8 percent of the vote—a higher percentage than the national average. In predominantly Romanian districts such as Rădăuţi and Câmpulung, Everything for the Homeland took over 30 percent of the votes,[173] capitalizing on "rising dissatisfaction with Romanian public life among peasants, workers, the middle class element."[174] "People who had been manipulated for their votes," the Bukovinan Legionary Chirilă Ciuntu claimed, "put their faith in the Legionary movement" because Legionaries "were not coming to them with any promises, only with songs and the desire to build."[175] After the funeral procession of Vasile Marin and Ion Moţa, Legionaries killed in the Spanish Civil War, passed through Cernăuţi, the Bukovinan Israeli historian Zvi Yavetz recalled that "my Romanian, Polish, and Ukrainian neighbors, whose names and addresses I can still remember, joined the Iron Guard with great fervor and started to appear proudly in their green shirts."[176]

Feeling threatened by the growing popularity of Codreanu's movement, the king charged Octavian Goga and A. C. Cuza's NCP with forming a cabinet even though they had secured just 10 percent of the vote.[177] Established in 1935 through the merger of LANC and Goga's National Agrarian Party, the NCP was firmly on the right, poised against "politicianism, economic ruin, and exploitative democracy."[178] It was committed to ending "Jewish exploitation" and ensuring that ethnic Romanians attained dominant roles in the spheres of culture and the economy.[179] Goga's avowed goal was to "rid the industry, commerce, and the professions of the foreign monopoly which has pushed aside our own nationals" and to "clear [the Jews] out and to re-establish Romanians in their jobs."[180] Goga specifically called out the "towns in Bukovina, Bessarabia, or Moldova where tens of thousands of Yids with eyes filled with sickness zoom around like a hornet's nest, tens of thousands of Yids with their eyes filled with conjunctivitis, with dark hatred for our nation."[181] The "birth certificate of the new cabinet," as Goga put it in his inauguration address, was "Romania for the Romanians!"[182] These words could have come straight out of Corneliu Codreanu's mouth. Unlike Codreanu, however, Goga was a monarchist. And so, by putting him in charge, the king was throwing the radical right a bone while retaining a firm grip on power.

Neither the NCP's anti-Semitism nor their commitment to Romanianization were new. As we saw in chapter 5, National Liberals had begun to Romanianize the state through cultural policies aimed at creating new Romanian educated elites while removing minority civil servants and functionaries from their positions.[183] Goga's government continued these anti-Jewish policies and implemented others. To ensure the Romanianization of the industries and civil service, the new administration introduced a *numerus valachicus*, legally obliging all public and private enterprises to employ at least 75 percent Romanians.[184] It also banned Jews from selling state-monopoly products and expropriated agricultural enterprises and properties owned by Jews. In January 1938, for instance, the Jewish Home in Cernăuţi's center was confiscated and transferred to Bukovina's Orthodox Religious Fund.[185]

On January 22, 1938 the government issued a new decree on citizenship rights, requiring naturalized Jews to submit their papers for "verification" within forty days.[186] The new law, Goga said, targeted Jews who, having obtained citizenship rights through "corrupt and fraudulent means," had "flooded the country in their hundreds and thousands and have remained there out of greed for grain."[187] To prove he was a Romanian citizen, one Moritz Blum, born in the Cernăuţi district in 1888, provided a "birth certificate, a school certificate, a certificate from the imperial commission pronouncing him apt for military service." But the Romanian court counselor who reviewed his file told him that "all the documents are useless because they proved that he had been born there [in Bukovina] but not also that he had lived there without interruption."[188] Blum was one of some ten thousand Jews in Bukovina who were deprived of their citizenship over the course of that year.[189] By one estimate, a third of Bukovina's Jews were stateless by 1939.[190]

During its forty-four days of rule, the Goga-Cuza government achieved by legal means much of what revolutionary Legionaries had long dreamed of. By appointing the NCP to government, the king had hoped to outmaneuver and neutralize the Legionaries; instead, the NCP normalized aspects of Legionary culture and practices. With the swastika now displayed on all public buildings in Cernăuţi, hooligans broke into Jewish homes and beat up Jewish passers-by confident they would go unpunished. It got so bad that "Jews no longer dared to go into the streets," Leopold Hessing recalled. The city was "barely recognizable and commerce, which had been almost completely Jewish, was completely incapacitated."[191]

By January 1938 rumor had it that Goga was negotiating with Codreanu behind the king's back. Fearing a rapprochement between the NCP and Codreanu, Carol forced Goga to resign as prime minister and replaced him with a government of national unity headed by the Orthodox patriarch Miron Cristea.[192] Ironically, this new attempt to outwit the Legionaries pushed the government further to the right. In February 1938 Romania became a royal dictatorship in which "civilian prefects were replaced with military ones, royal powers were extended, the legislature emasculated."[193] The king abrogated the constitution of 1923, dissolved all political parties, and reinstituted the state of siege.[194] Then he shifted his attention to the Legionaries, charging his newly appointed prime minister Armand Călinescu with destroying the movement once and for all. During April 1938, dozens of high-profile Legionaries were accused of high treason based on a law "on the maintenance of order" issued on April 15. Codreanu was arrested on April 16 and sentenced to ten years of hard labor.[195] According to Chirilă Ciuntu, many Legionaries in Cernăuţi were spared because the local authorities protected them. This changed, however, when the Iron Guard (that is, the Legionaries) assassinated prime minister Călinescu in September. Ciuntu was tracked down by the police, his house was searched, and he was arrested along with three hundred other Legionaries in Bukovina.[196] Legionary students who had escaped arrest barricaded themselves inside the university building in protest in October. They later handed themselves in to the police and were put on trial, found guilty, and each condemned to two years in prison.[197]

In the rest of the country, Legionaries carried out acts of terrorism. As soon as he returned from an official visit to France and Germany, the king ordered the execution of Codreanu and thirteen other Legionaries on the night of November 29–30.[198] Instead of destroying the movement, these executions made martyrs of the Legionaries, who now enjoyed the sympathy of previously indifferent people.[199] It also unleashed another orgy of Legionary violence. The night Codreanu was killed, two synagogues in Cernăuţi were set on fire. Factories and stores owned by Jews were looted in Cernăuţi, Câmpulung, Rădăuţi, and Boian. In December 1938 the World Jewish Congress reported that prefects in Bukovina were openly calling for massacres and promising peasants "homes and boutiques belonging to Jews," while in Cernăuţi every "concierge who denounces a meeting of Jews" was promised a monetary reward of two hundred lei.[200]

With the Guard's top leadership eliminated, the king instituted a new regime whereby only one political party was allowed to exist: the Front of National Rebirth (Frontul renaşterii naţionale, or FRN), formed on December 16, 1938.[201] The Front pursued "the elevation of the country to reinforce the national idea, the cult of the monarchy and the solidarity of its sons, reinforcing the family as a social cell, creating a spiritual life through the development of the Christian faith and autochthonous culture."[202] Hoping to lure youth from the Iron Guard, the king also founded Straja Ţării (Sentinel of the Motherland) in October 1937, a scout organization modeled on the Hitler Youth, whose members wore uniforms and used the fascist salute.[203] A lover of "parades and grandiose festivals" who "wore garish uniforms with medals" and "whose true passions were [his mistress] Lupescu, hunting, and cards,"[204] Carol nonetheless envisioned his rule as a "great cultural epoch in Romanian history"[205] and saw himself as a *Kulturträger*, or bearer of culture to his people.[206]

Carol's modernizing and "civilizing" ambitions extended to the country's administration, which was still plagued by regional divisions. A new administrative law in August 1938 merged Bukovina with two districts of Bessarabia, Hotin and Dorohoi, to form a new unit: the Suceava region.[207] Heading the region's administration was a new royal resident, directly appointed by the king: Gheorghe Alexianu, professor of comparative law at the University of Cernăuţi and co-author of the new law.[208] Alexianu's successor, Gheorghe Flondor (a member of the famous Flondor landowner family), began his term in February 1939 by vowing to "contribute with all my strength to fortifying the Romanian element by re-establishing its rights." Flondor's goals reflected the values enshrined in the February 1938 constitution, which asserted "firmly the primacy of the Romanian nation, which, through its sacrifices and its faith has created the national state."[209]

Different minority groups were treated differently, depending on internal political goals and increasingly volatile international circumstances.[210] With no state and nobody to protect them, Jews in Bukovina remained a target. Royal resident Alexianu passed a new order in December 1938 requiring the province's Jews to keep their stores open daily, including Saturdays (the Jewish sabbath, or day of rest). A new language ordinance issued on December 1, 1938 banned the use of languages other than Romanian in public spaces and mandated that all stores, factories, banks, and offices display a sign warning customers that "Romanian shall be spoken."[211] In Bukovina this law disproportionately affected Jews. A liquor store in Cernăuţi was shut down for three days in January 1939 when the police caught its owners speaking Yiddish.[212] As Edith Silbermann recalled, "one would be reported by informers, given fines, among other things, even taken to the police station" for failing to speak Romanian.[213] Following these measures, the number of Jewish students enrolled at the university in Cernăuţi dropped significantly: in 1919–20, Jewish students had comprised 50.3 percent of the university's student body; by 1938–39 their percentage had dropped to 8.9.[214]

Where other minorities were concerned, the government was less consistent. For instance, between 1938 and 1939 it went from persecuting Ukrainians suspected of irredentism to harboring Ukrainian nationalist refugees fleeing Czechoslovakia. Ukrainian nationalists in Bukovina were brought before military courts and put on trial twice in 1937. In April, a number were arrested for heckling while the Romanian anthem was played during a festival celebrating poet Taras Shevchenko. Among these were Orest Zybachynskyi, leader of

FIGURE 6.3. Identity card photograph of Orest Zybachynskyi, October 30, 1931, while he was a student at the law school in Cernăuți. Courtesy of Derzhavnyi Arkhiv Chernivetskoi Oblasti

Bukovina's the OUN branch,[215] and Ivan Hryhorovych, the editor of the OUN's journal *Samostiinist*.[216] When Ukrainian nationalists in Carpatho-Ukraine took advantage of Czechoslovakia's debacle at Munich to form an autonomous region in November 1938, Bukovina immediately witnessed a spike in Ukrainian nationalist propaganda and the Romanian government became more concerned. Ukrainian peasants who believed that Bukovina would soon become part of a Greater Ukrainian state refused to buy land from Romanians.[217]

After Hungary occupied Carpatho-Ukraine in mid-March 1939, however, Ukrainian nationalism no longer seemed an immediate threat to the Romanian authorities, who were now more preoccupied by Hungarian revisionism. When Ukrainians fleeing Carpathian Ukraine were allowed to take refuge in Bukovina, Ukrainian politicians there began ramping up their demands for more Ukrainian language classes.[218] The government invited Yurii Serbiniuk to Bucharest in September 1939 to begin negotiations. Serbiniuk assured the king of the Ukrainian minority's loyalty to the Romanian state, but also presented him with a list of twenty requests.[219] Although only some of these were met, Serbiniuk and other leaders of the Ukrainian minority in Romania signed an agreement to join the Front of National Rebirth.[220] This was exactly what Romanian officials had been hoping for. By joining the FRN, Ukrainian representatives were essentially agreeing to give up "their project for a Ukrainian state under the aegis of a foreign power, encompassing Romanian territories." The government's accommodationist policy toward Ukrainians lasted through September 1939 when the Soviet Union invaded eastern Poland on the pretext of liberating its Ukrainian and Belorussian minorities. This revived Romania's worries, as it feared that alienated and dissatisfied Ukrainians might support a Soviet invasion.[221]

## The Crisis

Throughout the 1920s Romania's foreign policy makers had sought to preserve the country's borders and resist the territorial revisionism of neighboring Hungary, Bulgaria, and the Soviet Union. At that point, France was Romania's main investor and creditor and, in the words of R. G. Waldeck, "no other people in Europe had such a passion for France as the Rumanians."[222] Romania signed a treaty of friendship with France in 1926 and forged regional alliances with Yugoslavia and Czechoslovakia in 1920–21, and with Greece, Turkey, and Yugoslavia in 1934.[223] The Soviet Union remained a thorn in the flesh, refusing to recognize Bessarabia's incorporation into Greater Romania.[224] During his tenure as foreign minister, Nicolae Titulescu had tried to solve the problem by joining France's non-aggression pact with the Soviet Union.[225]

By the late 1930s all that had changed. The French-backed collective security system into which Romania had embedded itself was rapidly eroding. Romania lost faith in France after it failed to respond to Hitler's remilitarization of the Rhineland. Moreover, the Munich agreement, whereby Great Britain and France essentially handed over Czechoslovakia's Sudetenland region to Germany, made it clear that Germany was now the hegemonic power in central and southeastern Europe, while the Western powers could no longer be relied upon to protect Romania. King Carol adjusted to these changes by pursuing a policy of informal neutrality,[226] combining rapprochement with Germany with measures to ensure continued Western involvement in his country.[227]

Throughout the 1930s Germany worked to reorient the economies of southeastern European countries, especially Romania and Yugoslavia, toward fulfilling its own needs. Nazi officials such as Hermann Göring believed the economies of these countries perfectly complemented Germany's, because they could supply its military-industrial machine with much-needed raw materials.[228] Romania was of great interest as a supplier of petrol, oil-seed crops, and wheat,[229] all resources without which Germany had no hope of surviving a war in the east.[230] Through various forms of "soft power" such as cultural diplomacy and economic development schemes, German business elites, academics, and state officials therefore set about binding Romania ever more closely to Germany.[231] They gradually persuaded traditionally hostile Romanian elites to overcome their suspicions and place their bets on Germany's success.[232] And indeed, by 1940, Romania's economy was completely dependent on Germany's.[233]

Germany's involvement in Romania was primarily, but not only, economically motivated. Romania had a large ethnic German minority population, some of whom resided in Bukovina, predominantly small landholders and peasants. Of the 75,533 Germans numbered in Bukovina in 1930, two thirds lived in the Câmpulung and Rădăuţi districts or in the suburbs of Cernăuţi.[234] The community consisted of both Catholics and Protestants, each originally with its own organization and representatives. A unified German organization had emerged in Bukovina only in 1918, after the province was annexed by Romania. The German National Council (Deutsche Volksrat) voted for unification with Romania and in 1919 was absorbed by an all-Romanian ethnic German organization, the Verband der Deutschen in Rumänien.[235] In 1935, the organization was restructured along Nazi lines and renamed "Volksgemeinschaft der Deutschen."

At first, Germans in Bukovina were ambivalent about Hitler's rise to power.[236] By the mid-1930s, however, many of them had come under his spell.[237] Hitler's most vocal apostle in Bukovina was Erwin Landwehr, who organized Nazi groups, went on propaganda tours around the province, and connected Bukovinan Germans with their co-nationals in Transylvania.[238] Landwehr often traveled to Germany and brought back to Bukovina Nazi publications such as the *Völkischer Beobachter*, *Junge Front*, *Deutsche Press*, and *Der Stürmer*.[239] A letter titled "Unser Program" (Our program), discovered in the luggage of one Erwin Millanich, who was returning from Germany to Cernăuţi by train in January 1935, urged Germans to follow a comprehensive fourteen-point program: they were to aspire to "the total Germanizing of the globe" and be "totally loyal toward the state and spiritually tied to our motherland." Point six demanded that "all people of German nationality in Romania be encompassed by professional groups and incorporated into national German organizations."[240]

Nazi ideas were also circulated by Bukovinan students who studied in Berlin and by youth organizations such as the Wandervogel and the Deutscher Jugendbund.[241] Local Nazi propagandists enticed German youth to enroll in the Deutscher Arbeitsfront and fostered epistolary friendships between Bukovinan Germans and Berliners.[242] These efforts were evidently not in vain: in May 1939, the Romanian police reported that Germans in the Bukovinan village of Luisenthal were "celebrating Hitler's successes and hoping that Bukovina would become a German protectorate."[243]

The police kept a close eye on Nazi sympathizers. As friendly as Romania was to Germany, the government regarded all minorities as potential fifth columns. This was especially the case after Munich, when Romanian officials feared that dissatisfied ethnic Germans might provide justification for German aggression as Sudeten Germans had done in Czechoslovakia—after all, ethnic Germans in Romania also complained about discrimination. Germany's consul in Bukovina, Fritz Schellhorn, noted in May 1938 that German schoolchildren in Bukovina often came into conflict with Romanian teachers, and that ethnic German firms had to pay higher taxes.[244] German teachers who had not passed their language exams were fired, leading to a sudden drop in the number of schools offering German-language classes.[245] In June 1938 the Volksgemeinschaft demanded autonomy "on the basis of the national cadastre."[246]

To avoid a fate like Czechoslovakia's, Romania issued a new minority statute in July 1938, vowing to accommodate "minorities living in Romania as Romanian citizens who identify with the interests and aspirations of their adoptive country."[247] A new institution created earlier that summer, the General Commissariat for Minorities (Comisariatul General al Minorităţilor), was charged with implementing the statute.[248] In January 1939 the ethnic German community joined the Front of National Rebirth, but, in defiance of the Front's provisions, the Volksgemeinschaft continued operating independently, forming political and paramilitary organizations of its own.[249]

By the fall of 1939, Romanian officials, initially alarmed by the Volksgemeinschaft's brazenness, had much greater worries. With Soviet troops knocking at Romania's doors, it appeared that securing Germany's protection might be the only way for Romania to avoid the fate of Poland, which was swiftly occupied in September by Nazi Germany from the west and the Soviet Union from the east.[250] King Carol tried to persuade Wilhelm Fabricius, head of the German Legation in Bucharest, to commit to a political agreement between Germany and Romania. Fabricius replied that Romania could rely on Germany's goodwill where the Soviet Union was concerned—but made no further commitments.[251] When the Soviet Union issued Romania an ultimatum in June 1940, demanding that it cede Bessarabia and northern Bukovina, German officials in Bucharest advised the king to go along with Soviet demands to avoid a war.[252]

The loss of Bessarabia and northern Bukovina strengthened Carol's resolve to obtain territorial guarantees from Germany. Shortly after the Soviet annexation, he invited the Germans to send a military mission to Romania and issued a new round of economic and political concessions.[253] In July 1940 he named pro-Nazi Ion Gigurtu prime minister and formed a new cabinet that included Iron Guard members whom he had formerly kept at arm's length.[254] Shortly afterward, Romania left the League of Nations and formally joined the Axis powers. Yet Hitler's support for Romania was contingent on the country's willingness to solve its territorial disputes with Hungary and Bulgaria. After some resistance, Romania agreed to hand over southern Dobrogea to Bulgaria in August 1940.[255] Later that month, Romanian and Hungarian representatives met to discuss their respective claims to Transylvania. Since they could not agree, Romania appealed to Germany to arbitrate, hoping Hitler would reward the Romanian government's generosity to Bulgaria by supporting Romania against Hungary. To everyone's shock, Hitler insisted Romania hand over northwestern Transylvania to Hungary. Enforced by the second Vienna Diktat of August 30, 1940,[256] this arrangement deprived Romania of over forty thousand square kilometers of territory and 2.5 million people, more than a million of whom were ethnic Romanians.[257]

---

Most nationalist movements in 1930s Bukovina had a strong anti-establishment and regionalist dimension that made them adversaries of the Romanian state and monarchy. The king's main priority was to retain full control over the country's domestic and foreign policy. From his point of view, all radical nationalists were dangerous. To put down perceived threats, Carol was willing to use repressive measures against both Romanian nationalists he could not fully control (the Legionaries) and non-Romanians. But in reckoning with radical nationalisms, the establishment adopted some of their trappings.[258] It not only incarcerated and executed Legionaries, but borrowed from their repertoire of cultural practices and ideas in the hope of neutralizing their movement.

The territorial losses Romania suffered in the summer of 1940, especially in Transylvania, brought the country to the brink of collapse.[259] Not just Guardists, but moderate politicians too believed the king had betrayed the country by handing over its prized possessions without a fight.[260] Faced with an angry mob rioting at the Crown Palace and green-shirted Guardists inciting people to revolution, King Carol charged Ion Antonescu, who had recently been recalled from house arrest in Predeal, with forming a new cabinet of national unity.[261] "Simple, honest, and very much in earnest," as the German-American journalist Rosie Goldschmidt Waldeck described him in her autobiographical account *Athene Palace*,[262] Antonescu accepted on the condition that the king grant him "all necessary power."[263] On September 4, 1940 he became "Conducător" (equivalent to German "Führer" or Italian "Duce"), and immediately demanded the king's abdication, warning Carol that "he wouldn't take responsibility for the king's safety."[264] On September 6, the king abdicated and left Romania.[265]

Romania became a National Legionary State on September 14, 1940.[266] The new government appointed Horia Sima, Codreanu's successor as head of the Iron Guard, vice-president. Traian Brăileanu, the mentor of many of Bukovina's young Guardists, became minister of education. Although they were in power for only five short months, the Legionary State wasted no time. Beginning in December 1940, Jews were required to pay military taxes and were conscripted for obligatory labor.[267] Guardists appointed commissars of Romanianization, raided Jewish shops and houses and subjected Jews to arbitrary confiscations.[268] Legionaries went on violent rampages, killing officials they deemed responsible for Codreanu's death. In November 1940 two prominent personalities, the economist Virgil Madgearu and the historian Nicolae Iorga, were brutally murdered.[269] Then, while Antonescu was visiting Hitler in January 1941, the Legionaries staged an uprising that threw the country into total chaos. The German military mission in Bucharest, present in the capital since October 1940, was instructed to remain neutral and lend Antonescu a helping hand if things should get out of control.[270] The Legionaries' revolutionary zeal was too much for Hitler, who preferred a stable regime that would not threaten Germany's economic interests in Romania. Antonescu put down the Legionary rebellion and proclaimed Romania a military dictatorship.

# 7

# Soviet Utopia

WHEN THE red army reached Cernăuţi on June 28, 1940, it had been raining for days, and "the roads were soaked and the water in the Prut had gone black."[1] Slogging up the hill, Soviet tanks were greeted by crowds "happily, with flowers," and with revolutionary banners that locals had allegedly prepared "while waiting for many years for their liberation."[2] As in eastern Poland in the fall of 1939, in northern Bukovina Soviet authorities were sent ahead to organize "friendly receptions for the incoming Soviet army."[3] Two women who happened to be walking down a street were stopped and given a bouquet of flowers and a red flag to hold while a military correspondent took their photograph to be published in the local newspaper as evidence of the Soviet regime's popularity.[4]

Such expressions of enthusiasm were indispensable to the Soviet "scenario of power" in the newly annexed East European borderlands.[5] The Soviets felt they could not build their regime until they had proved that, as Jan Gross writes, "the political justification of the invasion was correct."[6] In their first reports on the newly annexed province, Soviet officials logged all local demonstrations of support. They noted, for instance, that an old Ukrainian woman had welcomed a Soviet lieutenant thus: "Comrade, I am already old, I am not embarrassed, allow to me to kiss you!"[7] Others allegedly kissed Soviet tanks in gratitude for their liberation.[8] Whether or not these are reports of genuine incidents is hard to tell; what is certain is that the Soviets found no shortage of collaborators in northern Bukovina. With their help, within months, if not indeed weeks, of their arrival, they managed to leave an indelible imprint on the province.

The Soviet Union's annexation of northern Bukovina was enabled by the Nazi–Soviet non-aggression treaty of August 1939, whereby the Soviets were enabled to incorporate territories from Romania, Poland, Finland, Latvia, Lithuania, and Estonia.[9] Following this territorial enlargement, the Soviet Union's European frontier shifted westward, now passing through the middle of Bukovina. The border separating the newly expanded socialist world from the capitalist one was for the Soviets a boundary "between good and evil."[10] They therefore approached northern Bukovina with both trepidation and excitement, their ambivalence toward the province reflecting their general ambivalence toward the West.[11] On the one hand, they feared that Bukovina swarmed with enemies who could easily infiltrate the Soviet Union. On the other, they were drawn to its relative material abundance and beauty that let them experience "the West" without leaving the Soviet Union.[12] The Soviets had no doubt that Bukovina was "Western," but that was not necessarily a compliment. They defined themselves in contrast to lands still burdened by the "survivals of capitalism," seeing themselves as superior in culture, education, modernity. To the Soviets, places like northern Bukovina were "both marginal and central, backward and crucial."[13]

Following this imperial expansion, the Soviets looked upon themselves as ambassadors of a civilization that boasted "a superior version of modernity, resting on Marxist doctrine."[14] They came to northern Bukovina as civilizers, proud of having overcome their poverty and backwardness by "telescoping modernity and thus surpassing the Western system." In Bukovina they saw themselves as competing with the West to prove the superiority of their "cutting-edge modernity" and their civilizing mission,[15] premised on the idea that rational economic organization and "advanced cultural practices" could speed up progress.[16]

Of course, the Soviets were neither the first nor the last of Bukovina's rulers to make such claims. Like the other modern states that had tried their hands at governing the province, the Soviet Union was inspired by enlightened ideas of modern governance and the belief that an ideal social order could be attained by working through and with the state.[17] The Soviets also shared a predilection for using "cultural technologies of rule" to enact their transformational vision.[18]

Yet the Soviet Union was in many regards altogether new. Its ambitions were more radical than those Bukovinans had experienced before, for the Soviets aimed at no less than the total transformation of society.[19] The Soviet "civilizing mission" aspired to a new totality.[20] They could not admit that anyone might refuse to partake in their revolution. Nor did they tolerate alternative visions.[21] Moreover, forged in war and revolution, the Soviet state boasted an unusual structure. It was a party state, equipped with powerful instruments to pursue revolutionary goals, not least its acceptance of violence as a necessary, indeed indispensable, element of revolutionary governance. Soviet officials in northern Bukovina had no qualms about using coercion to reforge local society, although, as we shall see, they were capable of ideological compromises and tactical decisions as well.

Most unusual of all was the Bolsheviks' approach to the nationality question. They sought to tame difference, ironically, by institutionalizing it. They

FIGURE 7.1. In this photograph, Bukovinans are shown welcoming the Red Army, June 28, 1940. Such displays of enthusiasm, whether real or orchestrated, became a source of self-legitimation for the Soviets. Courtesy of Derzhavnyi Arkhiv Chernivetskoi Oblasti.

transformed the former Russian Empire into a modern federation, an ethno-territorial unit that guaranteed all members full national cultural autonomy.[22] Even more, the Soviet Union was an "anti-imperial empire." It was animated not solely by empires' traditional concerns with self-preservation and strategic expansion, but by a commitment to extending the socialist revolution. It was, in short, an "ideological empire" that aimed to transform modern nationalities into socialist nations to be fully assimilated into the Soviet state.[23]

While the Russian occupation authorities who had come to Bukovina in 1915–16 had been poised to assimilate the province's Ukrainians into the Russian nation (by claiming they were effectively the same thing), the Soviets encouraged a sense of national distinctiveness among Bukovinan Ukrainians. (Soviet newcomers, however, spoke Russian despite clear instructions to switch over to Ukrainian.) They settled decades of territorial contestation between Romanians and Ukrainians by declaring the province's northern half to be "the last part still missing from unified Ukraine."[24] At the same time, they set out to rebuild the Ukrainian nation in northern Bukovina by eliminating relics of its bourgeois past, using techniques for building socialism that had been tested elsewhere.

## Seizing Bukovina

On September 17, 1939 the Red Army moved into Poland, after the German Wehrmacht had invaded from the west on September 1. They claimed they were coming to liberate their "Belorussian and Ukrainian brothers" who were "threatened by the German advance."[25] In June 1940 the Soviet Union also grabbed Lithuania, Estonia, and Latvia; Bessarabia and northern Bukovina came next.[26] With one sweep, the Soviet Union thus expanded beyond the borders imposed on it in the 1920s, following the treaties of Brest-Litovsk and Riga, when it had lost most of the former Russian Empire's western borderlands.[27] Now these lost territories were recovered, and new land added, at minimum expense. The newly annexed territories brought nearly thirteen million additional inhabitants, seven million of whom were Ukrainian-speakers.[28]

The Soviets owed these gains to the Ribbentrop–Molotov pact, a nonaggression treaty between the Soviet Union and Nazi Germany initiated by Germany in early August 1939. Friedrich-Werner Graf von der Schulenburg, the German ambassador to Moscow, met with the Soviet commissar of external affairs Vyacheslav Molotov on August 17 to discuss Germany's offer. Two days later, Stalin declared himself ready to accept it, as he believed it would further the Soviet Union's goal of breaking out of capitalist encirclement by having the capitalists wage war on each other for as long as possible. "Our task," he explained in a speech before the Central Committee on August 17, "consists in making sure that Germany can continue waging this war. Biding its time, the USSR will help Germany, supplying it with raw materials and food. We must do everything to ensure this war lasts as long as possible."[29]

Germany and the Soviet Union signed the treaty during the night of August 23–24 in Moscow. The Nazi minister of foreign affairs Joachim von Ribbentrop flew in from Germany in Hitler's personal Condor plane. Swastikas were rushed in from Moscow's film studios (where they had been used as props in anti-Nazi propaganda films) to decorate the airport.[30] The nonaggression treaty also included a secret protocol that established a mutual demarcation line between Nazi Germany and the USSR in the event of conflict in Poland. In exchange for Stalin's neutrality in such a conflict, Hitler agreed that "the better part of Poland," as well as Estonia, Latvia, Lithuania, Finland, and Bessarabia would remain under Soviet influence.[31]

Neither the treaty nor the protocol mentioned Bukovina. The Soviets insisted on Bessarabia, a bone of contention over which they had broken diplomatic relations with Romania in 1924.[32] Bukovina was first mentioned in a Soviet note to Berlin of June 23, 1940, in which Molotov notified Germany of the Soviet Union's intention to annex the province. Surprised, the Nazis protested that Bukovina had never belonged to the Russian Empire and had a markedly German character. The Soviets then agreed to limit their claim to the province's northern half, including Cernăuţi. This, Molotov calculated, was the minimum of territory necessary to advance Soviet strategic interests in the area—namely, to establish a direct railway link between Bessarabia and western Ukraine.[33]

With the Germans pacified, on June 26 Molotov sent the Romanian ambassador in Moscow, Gheorghe Davidescu, a note demanding that the Romanians immediately evacuate northern Bukovina and Bessarabia. The ultimatum presented the Soviet Union's claim to Bessarabia as restoring the historic justice that the Romanians had violated when they annexed the province from Russia in 1918. The Soviet Union also claimed northern Bukovina as a form of compensation for the "heavy losses" that Bessarabians had suffered "during twenty-two years of Romanian rule." They insisted that northern Bukovina was organically tied to Soviet Ukraine by its "shared historic fate, as well as its community of language and national composition." Restoring it to Russia, Molotov wrote, would make it possible to "solve peacefully the prolonged conflict between the USSR and Romania."[34] The Romanian government had until the end of June 27 to respond. Because it took the Romanian delegation in Moscow until the morning of June 27 to transmit the text to Bucharest, the Romanians actually had only about sixteen hours to make up their minds.[35]

Romania was in a truly unenviable position. It had received guarantees of the "inviolability of its borders" from France and Great Britain in April 1939, yet these were in the event of an attack by Germany, not the Soviet Union.[36] In any case, as the Soviet diplomat Ivan Maiskii later recalled, the former British prime minister Lloyd George viewed Britain's involvement in Eastern Europe skeptically: "We are giving guarantees to Poland and Romania, but what can we do with them in the case of an attack by Hitler? Almost nothing! Geographically these two countries are situated in such a way that you can't reach them."[37] Romania's only hope was that Germany, which had strong economic interests in a country it viewed as a "gas station for German troops," would intervene on Romania's behalf.[38] But the Germans told the Romanians that they could not offer any assistance and urged them to accept the ultimatum to keep the peace in Europe.[39] In the likely event that Hungary and Bulgaria also made territorial claims on Romania, the country's Balkan allies moreover gave the Romanian government to understand that it should not rely on their support.

Under these desperate circumstances, an emergency Crown Council convened on June 27 in Bucharest. To oppose the ultimatum would have been, in the Romanian prime minister Gheorghe Tătărescu's opinion, "the easiest decision: it would have been a decision made on instinct, a manly decision [. . .]. But opposition would have meant not only an unequal war, but also a war in which our army could not throw in all of its forces [. . .]. [I]t would signify in the best case, a waste of our armed forces."[40] The General Staff agreed with Tătărescu, as did the majority of Crown Council participants, who voted to accept the ultimatum. In its reply to Moscow, the Romanian government noted that it was ready to initiate "friendly talks" about the Soviet Union's claims with regard to Romania.[41]

The Soviets, lacking patience for such equivocations, dismissed Romania's reply as inadequate and issued a final ultimatum. They gave the Romanian authorities four days to evacuate northern Bukovina and Bessarabia completely and warned that Soviet troops would occupy major cities like Chişinău, Cetatea Albă (Akkerman), and Cernăuţi on the following day, June 28. The Romanians were instructed to refrain from destroying railways, telegraph and telephone lines, factories, and locomotive depots during their retreat.[42]

Contrary to the evacuation terms spelled out in the ultimatum, Soviet mechanized troops rolled into Bessarabia and northern Bukovina right away, throwing the Romanian authorities and troops in these provinces into utter panic. The first Soviet divisions in Cernăuţi surrounded the Romanian 8th division's headquarters and seized the train station.[43] Although the occupation was supposedly timed such that the two armies would not meet, the Soviets clashed with the Romanian troops in retreat.[44] Soviet soldiers opened fire on Romanian troops, robbed Romanian officers of their horses, and humiliated them by forcing them to salute the red flag. Although they were technically not at war with Romania, the Soviets even took one Romanian general prisoner.[45] These experiences were especially humiliating for Romanian soldiers, as their officers instructed them not to shoot back.[46]

The Romanian General Staff had been preparing for this moment for some time.[47] From mid-June to June 26, the Soviets had been concentrating their troops on the border with Romania and flying their planes along the Romanian frontier,[48] prompting the Romanians to dig trenches along the border and requisition the local population's horses.[49] Yet when it happened, the evacuation was nothing like the Romanian military command had imagined. They were shocked to discover that soldiers from Bessarabia and Bukovina deserted *en masse*.[50] The Romanian authorities attributed this behavior to Soviet propaganda, disseminated by "tanks provided with loudspeakers, which go around villages and when they meet the retreating troops, shout at the Bukovinan and Bessarabian soldiers to drop their weapons and go home."[51] Even so, it was difficult not to conclude—as many Romanian military officials did—that most Bessarabians and some Bukovinans "did not have solid ties to their people and the patriotism they showed did not rise above narrow family and land interests."[52] Romania's state-building efforts in these two provinces had been tested, and had failed.

Military authorities and Romanian refugees from the two provinces singled out local Jews and Ukrainians as having fraternized with the Red Army and assisted them in "persecuting" the Romanian troops.[53] Rumors circulated of locals who stopped Romanian officers to insult them and steal their property. In one village, a civilian addressed one of the evacuating officers thus: "Shut up, do you think you're still an officer? You are a rag!"[54] Romanian refugees who made it to Romania brought chilling stories about Communist Jews who had allegedly set the Orthodox cathedral in Cernăuţi on fire—or, as another rumor had it, taken down the cross on the cathedral's spire and replaced it with a red flag and portrait of Stalin.[55] Sergiu Flondor, a descendant of the illustrious family of Romanian landowners and politicians that had produced Bukovina's first Romanian minister-delegate after 1918, recalled that his family "were met by a sufficiently large group, formed in its majority by rebellious Jewish youth but also hooligans with threatening looks, waving red flags, shouting insults, and singing the Internationale."[56] Similar reports came from Vijniţa, where Jews allegedly tore down Romanian flags and took evacuee trains by assault: "a group of them disarmed and took the clothing off a group of Romanian soldiers who were fleeing, leaving them only in their shirts and underwear and spitting at them while everyone looked on."[57]

A former royal resident (*rezident regal*) reported that a group of Jewish youths had gathered in Cernăuţi's Unification Square on June 28, singing revolutionary songs and vandalizing Romanian monuments.[58] The demonstrators included old Jewish and Ukrainian Communists freshly released from the city's jail, among them Sarah Grinberg, A. J. Valach, and D. M. Rusnak, who had joined the movement in the 1920s. With the Romanian police and troops on the run, these Communists formed provisional committees to guard city property during the evacuation and prepare for the Red Army's arrival.[59] The royal resident also described Ukrainian Communists from Cernăuţi's suburbs coming to welcome the Soviet troops in a column headed by a red flag and followed by two Communists who were "carrying a hammer and sickle made of wood and cardboard."[60]

All this went to confirm the Romanian authorities' belief that Jews were turncoats and Communists.[61] Humiliated and outraged by the "cowardly betrayal of the Jewish population" in northern Bukovina, retreating Romanian soldiers plundered and murdered Jews in the Herţa region and in southern Bukovina, still under Romanian control. On June 28–30 Romanian soldiers shot at people attending the funeral of a Jewish soldier, killing nineteen.[62] In a village in the Herţa region they murdered sixteen Jews and threw their bodies on a refuse dump. Similar atrocities took place in Suceava and Rădăuţi counties.[63] The gruesome attacks shocked even the Romanian military commanders, who ordered that the violence cease immediately lest the Soviets intervene to end it.[64] The Soviets contributed a good deal to the state of generalized panic by refusing to define the southernmost border of the territory they claimed.[65] Rumors about Soviet tanks crossing into southern Bukovina made the rounds of the Romanian military, throwing soldiers into despair. Many abandoned their units and fled for their lives, shouting "Run, the Russians are coming in their tanks!"[66]

In the meantime, Cernăuţi's Unification Square had turned into a "sea of red flags" which "even the most reserved people ended up pulling out of their pockets and waving above their heads."[67] Having documented the Red Army's friendly reception in northern Bukovina, the Soviet authorities fed it back to the population through the Soviet press and special screenings of films such as "Bukovina is a Ukrainian Land," directed by the wife of the famous Soviet Ukrainian director Alexander Dovzhenko.[68] Both in their communication with the local public and in internal reports, the Soviets dwelt on the celebratory mood at the beginning of Soviet rule in northern Bukovina.[69] The stories they spun made its annexation to Soviet Ukraine on August 2, 1940 look like a foregone conclusion.[70] Not content simply to incorporate the territory and move on, the Soviets sent a delegation of Bukovinans to Moscow to ask Stalin directly that northern Bukovina be formally incorporated into Soviet Ukraine.[71] The Soviet Union obliged, incorporating the province first by decree and then through a series of administrative reforms that introduced the Soviet administrative system of *oblasti* ("oblasts": regions) and *raiony* ("raions": districts within a region).[72] Now northern Bukovina's "Sovietization" could proceed apace.

## Modernization and *kul'turnost'*

To "Sovietize" northern Bukovina was to integrate it into the allegedly superior form of modernity the Soviet Union had achieved at home and was now ready to export to the capitalist world.[73] Here, as elsewhere, "Sovietization" took the form of cultural revolution: the all-encompassing transformation required to build socialism and the new revolutionary Soviet order. Culture, culturedness, and cultural revolution were all "an integral part of a broader vocabulary of transformation that encompassed everyday life, behavior, and the new Soviet person."[74] At the root of the Soviet notion of cultural revolution was a belief in the radical "plasticity of man" that allowed for the reinvention of human beings to achieve a new order that was "progressive, rational, and beautiful in contrast with pre-Revolutionary society."[75] For the Bolsheviks, who inherited the impulse to bring "culture" to the masses from the radical Russian intelligentsia of the nineteenth century, *kul'turnost'* became a kind of "secular religion."[76] It was not only about boosting cultural levels by traditional methods, but about mobilizing as though for combat, to uplift the masses by waging "cultural war."[77] In the 1920s the Bolsheviks also saw "cultural revolution" as a way to overcome their own—and Russia's—cultural backwardness. As Lenin himself memorably put it, it was imperative to "plow the local soil with a cultural tractor."[78]

The penchant for cultural revolution remained important under Stalin, reaching its peak during the collectivization and industrialization campaigns of the 1930s.[79] At the height of Stalin's "Great Break," backwardness effectively became illegal, as "economic underdevelopment would translate into economic poverty, political inferiority, military impotency, unequal relationship with the developed world, dysfunctional dependency."[80] Soviet officials admitted that Russia "had always been considered a backward state in an economic and cultural respect when compared to the Western states and America."[81] Now, having overcome their own backwardness, the Soviets denounced Bukovina's as a legacy of capitalist rule that could be remedied through *kul'turnost'*.

As a catchword for Soviet modernity, *kul'turnost'* was rather blurry, tied vaguely to the idea of bringing culture to the backward masses, reaching prosperity through "efficient work," and achieving superiority over the West.[82] It was in this latter form that *kul'turnost'* made its appearance in newly incorporated Northern Bukovina in 1940. What would it look like? Mass literacy, cleanliness, and efficiency, "proper conduct in everyday life, including bodily hygiene, domestic order and labor efficiency, as well as a demonstrative appreciation of high culture." This "cultured life" could be found on collective farms and in modern factories, embodied by highly productive workers, clean, smart, efficient, ambitious, and politically conscious.[83] To achieve *kul'turnost'* the Soviets had myriad institutions that reached into the deepest recesses of daily life, including theaters, village reading rooms, libraries, cinemas, and reading cabinets.[84] They vowed not to rest until "there were clubs and reading rooms in all villages."[85]

The Soviet authorities measured the success of their cultural revolution by compulsively checking literacy levels and school attendance rates in the province. They tallied the numbers of presentations given, performances organized, volumes accumulated in provincial libraries. By June 1941 they proudly counted "8 raion homes of culture, 6 raion clubs, 217 village clubs, 78 reading homes, 16 mass libraries, and 206 village club libraries."[86] They boasted that school attendance in the Chernivtsi oblast had increased to 92.2 percent, "while under Romanian rule, during better times, it was only 73 percent."[87] The ultimate goal was political enlightenment: workers and peasants needed to be able to read Stalin's and Lenin's biographies and Stalin's Constitution. But Soviet officials also made it a point to demonstrate that "high culture" was no longer the prerogative of the upper classes. Instead, "the Revolution had expropriated high culture for the benefit of the working classes."[88]

Eradicating backwardness was as much about destroying an old way of life as building a new one.[89] Everything that stood in the way of modernization was to be removed: in Bukovina's case, as in all Soviet Ukraine, the countryside presented the greatest obstacle. During the 1930s Soviet Ukraine had been the site of the infamous "grain collections," a ruthless campaign to further industrialize at the countryside's expense.[90] The collections were meant to bring class struggle and revolution to the countryside, ending rural backwardness while subduing the hostile or indifferent peasant population, while the institution of the collective farm—*kolkhoz,* or *kolgosp* in Ukrainian—was meant to end the shoddy practices that had condemned peasants to a life of misery, improving productivity by applying modern, scientific methods to agriculture. In reality, forced collectivization resulted in a catastrophic famine (the *Holodomor*) that killed millions of Ukrainians.

The Soviets also hoped for total collectivization in Northern Bukovina, but for strategic reasons they decided to move gradually. "In the question of collectivization," *obkom* (abbreviating *oblastnoi komitet,* the highest Communist Party authority in an oblast) first party secretary Ivan Samuilovych Hrushetskyi said, "we have to carry out work more boldly, though we shouldn't allow any forced endeavors." The "task of the party organization" was "to help those who wish to join the *kolgospy.*"[91] In other words, Bukovinan peasants were expected to join the collective farms voluntarily.

The Soviet authorities laid the foundations for collectivization by importing "the revolutionary transformations of October 1917" into Bukovina's countryside.[92] To acquaint the peasantry with the notion of class struggle, they divided peasants into three categories: *kurkuli* (or *kulaki*: rich peasantry), *serednyaki* (middling peasants), and *bednyaki* (poor peasants). What these categories meant varied. A *kurkul* could be anything from a peasant who employed workers outside his family to someone who owned a couple of cows or a large plot of land. The category included some peasants who had saved money while working in Canada and the United States in the early 1900s and returned to Bukovina to buy land they could not otherwise have afforded.

Next, the Soviet authorities confiscated land from the rich and redistributed it to the poor.[93] By October 20 they had appropriated and collectivized over 175,000 hectares of land, water, and forests, as well as livestock and agricultural equipment from large landowners, including the Orthodox Church. By January 1941, according to Communist party reports, poor peasants in Northern Bukovina had received 49,819 hectares of land and seeds, 1,177 head of cattle, 790 horses, and 5,394 sheep.[94] The *bednyaki,* the beneficiaries of this windfall, were reportedly thrilled. In the village of Zadubrivka, peasants showed up at party headquarters before the crack of dawn on land redistribution day. They paid the Soviets back by helping them track down *kurkuli* and locate hidden property and so-called "saboteurs."[95]

Though discouraged, some forms of private property were initially allowed in Northern Bukovina, but onerous taxes in kind made the lives of property-owning individuals impossible. According to Dumitru Nimigeanu, the head of a peasant household in Tereblecea, peasants who owned cattle were required to pay up to forty kilograms of meat per head of cattle (about one tenth of a cow's weight).[96] The state also required deliveries of grain, oats, and corn proportional to the size of the land owned. As one peasant later recalled, the usual norm for a village in Northern Bukovina was eighteen wagons of grain per year, but Communist village authorities would frequently try to get twenty-five wagons instead, to impress their superiors.[97]

Some of the property the Soviets confiscated from landowners and from those they deported provided the raw material for Northern Bukovina's first collective farms. The first *kolgosp* opened in January 1941 in a village in Kelmenetskyi raion; by April 1941 the Soviets had opened sixty-two collective farms. Hoping to persuade peasants to join collectives voluntarily, the Soviets unleashed over twelve thousand agitators into the countryside,[98] charged with familiarizing peasants "with the successes of building socialism in the USSR, the Soviet Constitution, and the achievements of the *kolgospy* in Ukraine."[99]

So that Bukovinan peasants could see the blessings of collective agriculture directly, Soviet officials sent local delegations to visit agricultural exhibitions in Moscow and Kyiv. On their return, the delegates were required to speak to their neighbors about the superior way of life they had witnessed on Soviet collective farms. Some dutifully reported that they had seen things "which we had never seen before and could never see under Romanian rule," such as planes and tanks, whole villages where peasants "lived like kings and like educated people without a care in the world." Others effused that the *kolkhozniki* lived like *kulaki*—apparently a highly desirable way of life, "with cattle and birds of which we could only dream" and "clean sheets and carpets" and radios that played "making you want to dance all night." "We now know what the Romanians told us about Soviet power being all hunger and toil and fatigue was a lie," one delegate proclaimed. "Whoever lies to us about Soviet power, we will spit in their face."[100]

However, efforts to make collective farming appealing faced serious obstacles. The *kolgospy* suffered from negative publicity, and peasants, suspicious of what they did not experience first-hand, feared the collectives were another ruse to extract more labor from them. It was said that peasants on collective farms had nothing to eat: "wherever there are *kolkhozy* there is not a piece of bread left," and collective farm members "stand in line for borscht." People coming to Northern Bukovina from areas that had already been collectivized said, "I am coming here because over there it's very bad," "work is hard and there is nothing to eat, there is nowhere to buy [food], everything is expensive. In Russia people are suffering very much, there is nothing, they only work day and night in vain, and then they receive only one kilogram of bread and those who work, their children die of hunger."[101] In one case, a peasant who had recently joined a collective showed up before the raion authorities demanding to withdraw, allegedly because his wife disapproved: "my wife didn't know that I entered the *kolkhoz*, I tricked her, the woman wasn't at the meeting and does not want to enter the *kolkhoz*."[102]

A similar campaign unfolded in the cities, where Soviet officials vowed to bring culture and literacy to the working classes by freeing them from an exploitative capitalist regime. The decree of August 15, 1940 redistributing land and agricultural property in Northern Bukovina also made industrial enterprises, factories, and commercial institutions that employed more than twenty workers the property of the state.[103] The change, the Soviet authorities boasted, meant that living conditions were improving substantially and workers' purchasing power was growing so they could emerge from the "dark basements" to which the bourgeoisie had confined them and take over the former bourgeoisie's luminous apartments.[104]

The newly socialized factories were meant not only to bolster productivity by adopting Soviet production methods (namely, economic planning), but to serve as sites of cultural revolution. Workers were expected both to fulfill production quotas and work on their own education and political enlightenment by attending evening school, music circles, language clubs, and lectures about "what Communism and Socialism are, what Lenin and Stalin have to say about youth, the foundations of the Marxist dialectic method [. . . and] the October socialist revolution."[105] To this end, factories were to be supplied with cafeterias, workers' clubs, "red corners,"[106] and theatrical and musical circles.[107] Officials gauged their success by counting the growing number of Stakhanovite workers in the province,[108] identifying almost three thousand of these by February 1941.[109]

The Soviets' insistence that they were civilizers conflicted with the prejudices of Bukovinans, who saw them as poor, unrefined, and backward. Bukovinans happily contributed to the ever-expanding repertoire of stories that made the rounds of the newly incorporated territories in 1939–40, featuring Soviets in the role of savages. Pepe Georgescu, a Romanian actor and staunch anti-Bolshevik, recalled seeing Soviet soldiers running down Cernăuţi's streets, "biting on a piece of salami and one of chocolate," their rucksacks stuffed with stolen "candy and cakes." "While eating," Georgescu wrote, "they would constantly spit, blow their noses, and cough disgustingly onto the plates."[110] In eastern Poland the Soviets were similarly reported to be "falling off bicycles,

FIGURE 7.2. "The Bolsheviks set houses in Cernăuţi on fire" (1941?). Once the Romanians reclaimed northern Bukovina in 1941, their propaganda ministry carefully documented the acts of destruction carried out by the Soviets in Bukovina; photograph from M.C.G. Secţia Propagandă Serv. Fotografic. Courtesy of the Biblioteca Naţională a României.

eating toothpaste, using toilets as sinks, wearing multiple watches, or bras as earmuffs or lingerie as evening gowns."[111] Even to Bukovinan peasants, whose civilized status had always been in dispute, the Soviets appeared barbaric. "We only saw the faces of foreigners, who did not even resemble people," Dumitru Nimigeanu wrote about his first encounter with the Red Army. "There was no difference between soldiers and officers. You could see all of them always scratching their armpits. We laughed, but they were very proud, saying it was an honor to be dirty!"[112]

Painfully aware of their poor reputation, Soviet officials were keen to dispel locals' prejudices. Red Army soldiers, for instance, were told never to take food from locals if offered. Instead, they were to persuade Bukovinans that the Soviet Union was a land of abundance. As one peasant woman from Northern Bukovina recalled, "we wanted to give the Red Army food, we brought them milk, but they told us, 'We don't need anything, we have plenty of everything and can even feed you with it.'"[113] Some Soviet soldiers took these instructions to heart more than others, sometimes with ridiculous effects. One Bukovinan railway worker tried to befriend a Soviet sentinel who had been sent to guard his locomotive by offering him some of his oranges for lunch and asking if "there were such fruits in Russia too." The sentinel reassured his interlocutor: "We have it, in Moscow, two whole factories that make them." The railway worker concluded that "they were illiterates. And such people were claiming to bring us culture. . . ."[114]

The Soviet cultural revolution in Northern Bukovina was constantly undermined by the opportunism, materialism, and ignorance of many Soviet cadres.[115] Across the oblast, Soviet employees abused their power to confiscate property. Officials collected taxes from "households which by law should have been exempted from the grain delivery." They incorrectly registered poor peasants as *kurkuli*. Others stole in broad daylight, claiming, in the words of one official, "I am responsible for the entire village, and I work for everyone and I have the right to take [. . .] whatever I like."[116] Thefts made a mockery of the socialization and collectivization processes. Among the "socialized" property, officials included a "trench coat, a carpet, two gold rings, gold watches, a gold necklace," and "old women's shirts, six teaspoons, one pair of stockings, bedsheets."[117]

## The Party State

Nowhere was the Soviet Union's novelty better reflected than in how they approached state-building in a province whose population had until recently lived under a capitalist-bourgeois system of the worst kind: a royal dictatorship. Unlike the other regimes Bukovinans had lived through, the Soviets brought a ready-made script that allowed them to set up their party state practically overnight, however imperfectly. This was a prefabricated regime, with a plan not just for the economy, but everything else too.

The Soviets immediately began creating organs of Soviet power at all levels, from the village and city soviets to the village-, raion-, and oblast-level party organizations. They measured, divided, and distributed land as a necessary step toward liquidating the legacies of Northern Bukovina's Romanian past. Moreover, they announced that their state rested on an unprecedented level of "moral-political unity" that allowed people to become fully integrated into the state rather than merely subordinated to it, ensuring total participation and consent.

Even though Soviet authorities took it for granted that Bukovinans would participate in the state-building process, as a frontier population with ties to the capitalist world, they were suspect. The Soviets thus sought to walk a fine line between incorporating locals into the state-building process and keeping dangerous elements out of it. The conspiratorial mindset built into the Soviet system was especially acute on the frontier. For this reason, high-level positions were usually entrusted not to locals but to Communists who, like *obkom* first secretary Ivan Samuilovych Hrushetskyi, had come to Northern Bukovina from the eastern oblasts of Soviet Ukraine, where they had proved their loyalty.[118] Yet *obkom* party officials feared that Soviet cadres, brought there to convert locals to socialism, were going native: picking up locals' bad habits and colluding with them rather than educating them. Hrushetskyi warned that "we need to have the highest communist vigilance [. . . , for] over a cup of tea, over a glass of wine, these people try to influence our communists."[119] Northern Bukovina's damaging effects on Soviet newcomers were reflected in the "outrages" Communists committed there. Soviet newcomers' children, as Svitlana Frunchak relates, habitually engaged in hooliganism and threatened their classmates with arrest.[120]

At the same time, the Soviets were wary of alienating locals by giving the impression that this was just another foreign occupation regime. Hrushetskyi warned party authorities against treating locals, particularly those among them who had "waited for Soviet power," with excessive mistrust: "we do not work with them, do not notice them [. . . ; our] trade workers are often rude to locals while they are much nicer to newcomers. Often a local would make a mistake and get punished for it by getting fired."[121] Local authorities were instructed to compromise even on ideology to foster local partnerships. *Obkom* members admitted local youth into the Komsomol even if they were religious, including individuals "who wore crosses on their chests." "In the future they will stop praying," the Soviets reassured themselves, noting that "what counts are social origins rather than ideology, so these people shouldn't be driven away."[122]

The elections to the local soviet and the supreme soviets of the USSR and Ukrainian SSR, organized in December 1940 and January 1941, provided locals with their first lesson in participatory socialist state-building, a form of "participation without political power."[123] Some local voters understood they weren't really deciding anything. One school principal from Khotyn, charged with carrying out pre-electoral propaganda, complained, "Look how they torture us to carry out propaganda. As though anyone will fulfill it and pay any attention to it! Everyone knows the Party sets its own candidates and each person goes and votes for them so they won't be under suspicion!"[124] The elections' role was to bolster the regime's legitimacy by involving locals directly in its construction since, as Hrushetskyi put it, "our power is in our relationship with the masses and that is what we must cultivate."[125]

The pre-electoral campaign, beginning in October 1940, was more important than the elections themselves, as it let the Soviets rapidly increase the size of their party-state apparatus in Northern Bukovina while providing locals with an educational experience. Over the course of the three months or so preceding the elections of January 1941, the Soviets set up institutions, from agitational collectives to Komsomol organizations at the village, city, and oblast level. In October 1940 Chernivtsi oblast had 216 first-level party organizations and 2,400 party members and candidates. By June 1941 there were 319 first-level party organizations and 3,500 members and candidates.[126] The elections provided the Soviet authorities with an opportunity to build the regime practically out of thin air, in record time—albeit imperfectly.

In reality, most of the institutions created overnight were poorly equipped and utterly inadequate. Chernivtsi's house of propaganda, the oblast's main center "of political-educational work" had only one copy of Lenin's works and no copies of the Soviet encyclopedia, though "it could have been bought even in Kyiv at the bazaar."[127] Study circles were "working poorly or are not working at all because we don't have adequate leaders."[128] Lower-level officials had to figure things out on their own, provided with instructions but rarely with material support. When officials in one raion petitioned the Chernivtsi authorities to help them set up a cinema, they were issued with "theoretical instructions" rather than money. "The party *obkom* has every right to expect things from us," one *raikom* official complained, "but it must also help us practically."

Rarely in their offices and unreachable by phone, Soviet officials were seldom accessible or helpful to those subordinated to them. Agitators in one raion shared their workspace with pigs—and that wasn't even the worst. Many Soviet cadres were extremely uninformed politically. One Communist Party member in the oblast confessed to having "only looked through the first chapter of the short course history of the CPSU two years ago." When asked to give his opinion on the Petersburg Union for the Liberation of the Working Class, one of the earliest Marxist organizations in the Russian Empire, whose members included V. I. Lenin and Georgii Plekhanov (the father of Russian Marxism), he shook his head: "There are so many different unions, how can one tell them apart?"[129]

This ignorance was problematic, as the Soviet propaganda apparatus played an especially important role in the state-building process leading up to the elections. Its task was to teach locals, especially the peasants and lower classes, about the Soviet party state. Under Soviet rule, one agitator insisted, elections would no longer be like in the past, when "the bourgeoisie would chase after us to vote as though we were cattle." To make the point, *obkom* first secretary Hrushetskyi did the rounds of electoral commissions in the oblast, taking by surprise locals who "did not expect him to simply walk in like that but to drive a car with security behind him and music."[130] Agitators selected from among trustworthy locals and trained to carry out propaganda flooded the oblast with posters, brochures, and books about the Soviet elections. By January 1941 the Soviets had mobilized 14,266 such agitators, "most of whom are locals."[131] They were everywhere. They appeared before film screenings to remind audiences to vote. They visited classrooms and urged children to remind parents "that they have to vote the next day." The masses had to be taught wherever they happened to be, "in the factories, enterprises, villages, and farmsteads of the oblast."[132] Aiming for total participation in the elections, Soviet officials set up agitational collectives and circles for studying Stalin's Constitution and Soviet electoral laws all over the oblast.[133]

When the elections finally took place on January 12, 1941 the Soviets saw them as the regime's first real test in Northern Bukovina. They aced it, achieving a 99.54 percent participation rate in the elections and 98.31 percent votes for the "Communist and non-party bloc," according to their own reports.[134] Even so, Hrushetskyi felt compelled to explain the failure to achieve 100 percent of the vote in Northern Bukovina by saying that Bukovinans were still used to voting techniques from Romanian times.[135] At their first oblast-level party conference, which took place one month after the elections, Soviet officials discussed these shortcomings at length.

The Soviet party state, with its mobilizing, totalizing, pedagogical qualities, had a striking penchant for self-criticism. This inclination—or rather, obsession—came fully into view at the party conference of February 1941. *Obkom* officials criticized Communist Party cadres in the oblast for the low ideological level that had led them to violate party discipline on countless occasions. They were displeased to find that the local alliances Communists had forged relied on complicity in corruption and mutual "violations of work discipline," not on a radically reimagined relationship between state and citizens. Relationships between Communist officials and locals were clientelistic, based on the political capital Communist cadres acquired through "wheelings and dealings with [. . .] property." The Chernivtsi city housing department's head was found to "shamelessly cover up" the absences of his department's employees. Procurators also quietly pardoned people found guilty of absenteeism.[136]

By February 1941 it felt increasingly as if the revolution was coming too slowly to Northern Bukovina. Collectivization was inadequate, and the radio, cinema, and school networks were not expanding fast enough. Many raions still had a low level of "cultural construction." Above all, the Soviet authorities were concerned about the proliferation of enemy elements across the oblast and their infiltration of the party-state apparatus.

## Enemy Elements

That the Soviets did not tolerate any enemy elements was well known. Expecting the worst, many Bukovinans who thought they would be targeted as counterrevolutionary elements tried to flee. Some fugitives "had been told that [the Soviets] would send them into the *kolkhozy*, rape the women, take the men."[137] Others escaped for more particular reasons, such as an inability to make themselves at home in Soviet Northern Bukovina. One man told the guards who caught him crossing the border, "I hate the Ukrainian language, if you want me to stay here [. . .] then it is better that I hang a stone around my neck, I won't stay here, I will go drown myself in the Prut."[138]

After 150 people made a narrow escape to Romania, the Soviet authorities closed border crossings "everywhere 15–20 kilometers from Chernivtsi."[139] They increased the number of border guards, turning the area around the Romanian frontier into a no-man's land, reinforced by barbed-wire fencing, with the ground freshly plowed every day so escapees' footsteps were easily tracked.[140] To strengthen security at the border, in January 1941 the authorities relocated over four hundred families living within 800 meters of the frontier. On moving day, the families were provided "with warm clothing and shoes" and 400 rubles each. One peasant protested that he "would rather have his head cut off than have to move from Prisaka," and another that "we should all be killed on the spot because we are not going anywhere."[141] But they went in the end.

Even after crossing the border to Romania became increasingly difficult, people still tried, both alone and in groups led by hired local guides. Sometimes the guides helped; sometimes they delivered would-be escapees straight into the Soviet authorities' hands.[142] Border guards were instructed to punish all attempts at crossing with arrest and imprisonment, and in some cases by shooting. On April 2, 1941 Stalin wrote to the first secretary of the Communist Party of Ukraine (KP(b)U: Kommunisticheskaya Partiia bolshevikov Ukrainy), Nikita Khrushchev, that "of course, shooting people is permissible, but shooting is not our main work method."[143] More often than not, however, local guards made life and death decisions independently. On April 1, 1941 hundreds of Romanian peasants were marching toward the border with Romania near Fântâna Albă (now Bilia Krynytsia), equipped with icons and crosses, when "all of a sudden they were surrounded by Soviet guards on horses who asked them to go back." When someone at the head of the column shouted "Forward, brothers!" the Soviet guards began firing, killing most and arresting the few survivors.[144] A similar massacre took place near Lunca a few months earlier, when Soviet guards shot escapees and buried the bodies in "pits not far from the Prut."[145]

The difficult crossing left many anti-Soviet elements trapped in Northern Bukovina, amplifying Soviet anxieties about counterrevolutionary elements in the province. Comrade Martynov, head of the oblast NKVD (the secret police: Narodnyi Komissariat Vnutrennikh Del, "the People's Commissariat for Internal Affairs"), described Northern Bukovina as "the basis of all intelligence operations" in the region and estimated that "almost a thousand people are members of anti-Soviet organizations here." Communists were advised to be vigilant and "not to forget for one minute that our oblast is a frontier one."[146]

The elections of January 1941 helped Soviet officials track down counterrevolutionary sentiment and identify "enemy agents," whether "Trotskyites" or "Cuzists," for later liquidation. These included locals who had slipped papers inscribed "Down with the Communists, long live National Socialist Germany, long live Reich Chancellor Adolf Hitler!" into the voting urns. They included skeptical locals like the peasant overheard saying, "If there were five or six people like myself in the village, then we would say these elections aren't right, that we must vote not only for those put forward but for those we want."[147] The lesson the party leadership took was that "the task of the party organization and *raikom* is now to pay special attention to those villages where we had the most votes against our candidates and increase mass-political work there and make sure that enemy agents are liquidated."[148]

In truth, there was little evidence of organized, large-scale anti-Soviet resistance in Northern Bukovina. What the Soviets were registering was growing dissatisfaction, above all with the rapidly deteriorating conditions in the province. In Gertsa/Herţa raion, people complained that "there are enough children's shoes but they are all in the *raitsentr* and they don't ever reach the villages."[149] Many villages suffered from "an insufficient supply of basic products such as salt, kerosene, shoes."[150] From these shortages, some locals derived dramatic conclusions. "The Russian people," one man said, "led by Satan, does not recognize humanity. You think that after all they want to give people food, but no, they do only evil because through them Satan is working."[151] The son of a merchant from a Romanian-speaking district confessed that, months into Soviet rule, he did not see "any difference between feudalism and the socialist state. Under feudalism man was forced to labor and dependent on it, he was almost held captive, and now, under the socialist regime, there is nothing different, man is just as forced to work and just as dependent on labor."[152]

The internal passport system, introduced into Northern Bukovina almost completely by the end of January 1941, allowed the Soviet authorities to keep tabs on "unreliable elements."[153] All individuals over sixteen were now required to "present birth, housing, work certificates, military cards, [and] two photos to obtain a passport."[154] The passports of individuals considered unreliable were marked with "clause 39," while elements whose skills were needed or considered useful to the Soviet economy were also singled out and their mobility curtailed (so that they wouldn't relocate), their passports marked with "clause 40."[155] The Soviets also conferred upon nationality and social origin an immutable quality they had never had before in Bukovina, as these data were recorded on each individual's passport.[156]

Marked and made visible, unreliable elements could be easily arrested, interrogated, and in many cases deported. The Soviets were, of course, not the first to subject Bukovinans to deportations. Whole groups of people deemed unreliable had been deported by Austrian and Russian imperial officials during World War I. Dating back to the Civil War in Russia, deportations were an important element of the Bolsheviks' toolkit as well, allowing them to "foster an idealized image of the politico-social body by excising [. . .] elements determined to be harmful."[157] The Soviets deployed this wartime instrument of social engineering in peacetime and on a whole new scale, deeming this once extraordinary measure indispensable for "pacifying" volatile frontier territories like Northern Bukovina.[158]

In Northern Bukovina, undesirable elements targeted for deportation included relatives of those who had fled to Romania or attempted to cross the border illegally, as well as former Romanian functionaries, members of Romanian political parties, landowners, clergy, and prostitutes.[159] The deportations were carried out in waves between April and June 1941, with the last groups of deportees departing Northern Bukovina just as the German and Romanian troops were coming in.[160] Although the deportations did not target a particular ethnic group, they hit Romanians and Jews hardest.[161] NKVD staff, assisted by locals who were indispensable to the cleansing operations' success, compiled lists of individuals slated for deportation. Ilie Piven, who was deported from Bukovina with his parents, recalled how the NKVD officer who picked up his father told him, "Don't cry, don't wring your hands, it wasn't us who caused this trouble and so on, it was your own people who denounced you for looking askance at Soviet power."[162]

The NKVD would show up in the middle of the night in their notorious black vans, knock on the door, and give deportees minutes to prepare for their long journey. Dumitru Nimigeanu knew the NKVD had begun operations in his village when he heard "from somewhere, from high above us, from the big road, screams; women's and children's voices, shooting, and dogs barking. From another part of the village we could hear awful moaning, horrific shouting, bit by bit stifled." Nimigeanu and his family hid, but when the NKVD found his wife under a pile of hay, he turned himself in. The NKVD, accompanied by the neighbor who had denounced the family, walked them back to their home, which they searched thoroughly for weapons. "Since they did not find any weapons," Nimigeanu recalled, "they chose whatever was most beautiful, thus filling six large sacks and a box with rugs and all kinds of clothing."[163]

Peasants who had never before left their homes could not bear to be parted from their households and animals. Aniţa Nandriş-Cudla, whose family was deported to Omsk, recalled how when the NKVD showed up at her house, she "started shaking, shaking so badly that the teeth in my mouth were clattering, as though it were minus 40 degrees [Celsius]."[164] "The poor women were having a hard time separating from their nest," another survivor remembered. "They were kissing the walls, the doors, kissing the cattle in the barn, crossing themselves, kneeling down, lifting their eyes filled with tears up to the sky."[165] But the worst was yet to come. The deportees faced a long and agonizing journey inside a sealed train with only salted fish, dried bread, and dirty water to eat and drink. Then there was the horrible life awaiting them at their destinations.

At the end of their journey east, Bukovinan deportees were scattered across different oblasts (Krasnoyarsk, Altai, Omsk, Komi), always hundreds of kilometers away from railway lines and raion centers so they could not escape.[166] Some were dropped on the frozen shores of the Ob river, with no roof above their heads. Others were placed in barracks and mud huts without windows and doors, and only a wooden board as furniture.[167] As the Communist cadres in the eastern oblasts admitted, no arrangements were made to accommodate the deportees. They were placed in dwellings with shattered windows and without ovens. Many had no shoes or warm clothing, making it impossible for them to work in winter.[168] Since bread went only to those who worked, many starved.[169] Even getting to work was difficult: Nimigeanu slogged through knee-deep snow for fifteen kilometers daily to reach the *kolkhoz* to which he had been assigned. To satisfy their hunger, the deportees hunted ground squirrels. Some begged or stole, trying to keep themselves and their families alive with fistfuls of wheat snatched while working in the fields.[170] Many Bukovinans died cold and hungry in Siberia. Arcadie Opaiţ's father was too weak to bury his mother and daughter in the frozen ground, so he wrapped their bodies in a rug and took them behind their hut to bury in spring. "When the snow melted, he found nothing, for the wolves had eaten them. Of grandma, there was nothing left but the skull and hip bones, and of my little sister, nothing but a few bones."[171]

## Back "Home to the Reich"

By the end of Northern Bukovina's year-long Soviet experiment, its population had been cleansed not only of "unreliable elements," mostly Romanians and Jews, but of its ethnic German population. Notwithstanding its non-aggression pact with Nazi Germany, the Soviet Union viewed Germans as a potential fifth column. Germany made the Soviets' task easier by removing ethnic Germans from territories newly incorporated into the Soviet Union. Germans in Bukovina (both in the Soviet northern half and the south) were officially not deported, but resettled on a voluntary basis—although in practice, their relocation to the Reich was mandatory. By November 17, 1940 a total of 43,641 Germans had left Northern Bukovina through the "Heim ins Reich Aktion" ("Home to the Reich" initiative).[172] They were followed by more Germans from Southern Bukovina, once Nazi Germany had signed an agreement with Romania on October 22, 1940.[173]

FIGURE 7.3. "Resettlement from southern Bukovina: *Volksdeutsche* wait for the train" (1940): ethnic Germans waiting to board the train that would carry them "Heim ins Reich" (home to the Reich). Courtesy of Bundesarchiv Deutschland.

The Heim ins Reich Aktion was part of the larger Nazi project of remaking Europe, tied up with the mass deportation and annihilation of Jews and Poles from areas of occupied Eastern Europe that Hitler had marked for Germanization.[174] Ethnic Germans from Eastern Europe—*Volksdeutschen,* as the Nazis called them—were to be relocated from areas now within the Soviet sphere of influence to Nazi-occupied lands "cleansed" of their local populations. The mission of the resettled *Volksdeutschen* was to help Germanize these Slavic lands, to integrate them into the greater German *Lebensraum.*

In Northern Bukovina the Heim ins Reich Aktion was completed between September 15 and November 15, 1940 by a mixed German–Soviet resettlement commission also charged with resettling Germans from Bessarabia. The German commission members sent to represent the Reich's interests during the resettlement arrived in Chernivtsi in September as part of a larger delegation of almost 600 people and 250 automobiles, headquartered in the Bessarabian town of Tarutino.[175] Sub-branches of the delegation operated in five major cities across districts with sizable ethnic German populations, including Chernivtsi, where the delegation employed local ethnic Germans to register applicants for resettlement and check they were bona fide Germans.[176]

The resettlement was preceded by protracted negotiations between Nazi Germany and the Soviet Union starting in July 1940. The two sides disagreed over what kind of property resettled Germans should be allowed to take with them and how they should be compensated for property left behind. They also clashed over Germany's request that incarcerated ethnic Germans be allowed to leave. The Soviets insisted that Soviet legislation should be applied to determine what constituted private property, while the Germans tried to minimize how much German property was socialized.[177] Soviet officials undervalued German property to retain as much of it as possible, so they could later redistribute it among poor peasants or absorb it into the collective farm system. German applicants for resettlement tried to preempt the state by selling their cattle and household goods independently.[178] They complained that the Soviets deliberately undervalued their property, putting them in the awkward position of going around "evaluating and haggling for higher prices."[179]

The agreement, finally signed on September 5, 1940,[180] allowed Germans from Northern Bukovina to take "one coat and shoes, only one fur coat and underwear," no more than fifty kilograms per head of family or single person and twenty-five kilograms for each additional member, but no disposable income, silver or gold, documents, or art objects.[181] The Soviets retained a good deal of German property, much of which they wasted, however, through mismanagement and neglect.[182] Officials in Chernivtsi oblast counted 346 homes and German-owned factories that they socialized and 1,028 buildings and 273 hectares of land they recycled for "educational institutions, cultural and social establishments, industry, and [other] organizations."[183] For all this property, the Soviets agreed to compensate the German Reich fully in the next ten years.[184]

Although the Soviet and German delegations were instructed to allow only ethnic Germans to relocate from Northern Bukovina, many non-Germans, both Ukrainians and Romanians, also left Northern Bukovina through the Heim ins Reich Aktion. Applicants were required to prove their German ancestry, but how exactly this was evaluated was determined by delegation members on an individual basis. Local delegation members, including SD-member Rudolf Wagner, stretched the definition to include neighbors, acquaintances, and others whose links to Germanness were tenuous or non-existent.[185] Since in formerly Habsburg Bukovina the German language had remained widely spoken throughout the interwar years and many non-Germans had embraced elements of Austrian-German culture, it was not difficult for non-ethnic Germans to pass for German. But the Bukovinans most devoted to German culture—Chernivtsi's Jews—were not admitted for resettlement, even when married to ethnic Germans. The Soviet authorities were struck by the situation: "the clearly expressed hatred of persons of Jewish nationality is to be numbered among the most obvious violations of the accord on the part of the German delegation."[186]

The Soviet authorities were aware that non-Germans were trying to sneak out of Northern Bukovina by joining the German *Heimkehrer* (homecomers) through subterfuge, including hasty marriages to ethnic Germans. Others, including Ukrainian nationalists, apparently enjoyed the German delegation's protection. One such person was found hiding inside the German National Home in Chernivtsi, where "sick persons are also being held." He was promptly arrested.[187] In total some four thousand Ukrainians, including "many priests, writers, teachers," left Northern Bukovina through the Heim ins Reich Aktion.[188] The German delegation agreed to evacuate Romanians who had not managed to flee but wished to leave from both Northern Bukovina and Bessarabia. Later, some were repatriated to Romania at the Romanian government's expense. The Soviets took a dim view of the German delegation's dealings with locals. They suspected German delegation members and resettlement applicants of espionage, and contemplated recruiting some of them for counterespionage purposes.[189]

The *Heimkehrer* ended up including a motley group of people: German youths with Nazi leanings, Ukrainian nationalists, desperate Romanians, and Germans anticipating the riches they had been promised. Germans had been told to look forward to "neat farmhouses awaiting their owners" and were reassured that "you have always carried Germany in your hearts even if you have never seen your real home."[190] Few knew that those "neat farmhouses" had been the homes of brutally deported or murdered Poles and Jews. To accommodate a family of resettled *Volksdeutschen*, Nazi officials consolidated several such homes and lands, which they otherwise considered too small to be suitable for German ownership. Some resettled Germans were horrified to discover how this property came to them, and refused to move in.[191] The vast majority, stuck in transit camps for months and years, waiting to be assigned properties whose owners could not be expelled fast enough to accommodate them, did not get to the point of having moral qualms.

While waiting, the evacuated Germans were subjected to humiliating racial evaluations that found many of them unfit for settlement in western Poland, as initially planned. Nazi officials complained about the quality of the people from Northern Bukovina, warning local delegation members no longer to accept "foreigners" for resettlement.[192] But the fact was, as German consul Fritz Gebhard Schellhorn noted, that Bukovina's Germans had become ethnically mixed over time, and so "some mishmash" was inevitable.[193] Those who were classified as "less balanced crossbreeds" and deemed insufficiently German were to be settled first in the Reich to be re-Germanized, and then sent to western Poland.[194]

While waiting seemingly forever to "go home," the resettled Germans discovered the heavy price they were expected to pay for the Reich's protection. Their Nazi patrons effectively required them to renounce every ounce of autonomy and freedom they had enjoyed. Applicants who had been put on the resettlement list and changed their minds the very next day were turned down when they asked to be removed from the list. They could not return to Bukovina if they wished to. One German woman from Chernivtsi, with a Jewish husband and a daughter from a previous marriage, was forcibly evacuated even though "she didn't want to register for evacuation to Germany, wishing to remain in Chernivtsi with her second husband."[195] And when German evacuees protested at conditions in their transit camps, Nazi officials sometimes threatened to send them to concentration camps.[196] And so the long history of German life in Bukovina came to an end.

## Anti-imperial Empire

Tens of thousands of Soviet propagandists unleashed on Northern Bukovina recited the principles of Marxism-Leninism, proclaiming Bukovina's liberation the dawn of a new day. Bukovinans had heard something similar before; but although the Soviet regime sounded familiar, it was not the Russian Empire that many knew and remembered from Bukovina's World War I occupations. The new state was an empire too, but one self-defined in anti-imperial terms. Its architects, the Bolsheviks, departed from the old Russian Empire most clearly in their approach to the nationality question: how, that is, they governed the former empire's multiethnic territories.

Formulated by Lenin and elaborated by Stalin, Soviet nationality policy revolved around the principle of national self-determination, which the Bolsheviks fully recognized, including the right to secede (although Lenin could not imagine anyone would ever want to). The policy's ultimate goal was not to promote national self-determination, however, but to eliminate what Lenin saw as nationalism's root causes—political and economic oppression—and thus make nationalism itself obsolete. Differentiating between oppressed and oppressor nations, Lenin argued that in the case of the former, it was necessary to support national movements to speed up the revolutionary process that would eventually lead to socialism.[197] In some cases, this meant the Bolsheviks were required to invent new national languages and cultures.

The Soviet Union was officially established in 1922 as a union of ethnicities, with federalized state structures supplemented by a centralized Communist Party hierarchy. Its composite nature allowed the Bolsheviks to maintain a unitary state by institutionalizing the "national-territorial principle."[198] It also allowed them, ironically, to reconstruct the Russian Empire and expand beyond its former possessions while denying any kind of affinity with it.[199]

Perhaps the most important feature of Soviet nationality policy was *korenizatsiia*: the indigenization policy adopted at the Twelfth Communist Party Congress in 1923. *Korenizatsiia*'s goal was to foster native elites loyal to the Bolsheviks from among the Union's non-Russian populations. The Bolsheviks moreover sought to overcome non-Russians' distrust by "publicly condemning the oppression of non-Russians and acknowledging national languages and cultures."[200] They hoped to use indigenization policies to take the sting out of nationalism by "fostering national cultures and creating national autonomies, national schools, national languages and cadres."[201]

By some accounts, it was while trying to solve the Ukrainian problem that the Bolsheviks developed their policy to its full extent.[202] To integrate Ukraine, with its vast peasant, Ukrainian-speaking population, into their state, the Bolsheviks realized they needed to promote the majority language. In June 1923, they proclaimed Ukrainian the official language of the Ukrainian SSR. After this, all state employees in the Ukrainian SSR were required to learn Ukrainian, as were students and staff in schools and cultural institutions.[203]

At the time, Ukrainians were the largest ethnic group in Europe without a state of their own. Poland's and Romania's large Ukrainian-speaking minorities were subject to discriminatory practices. The Polish government prohibited the use of Ukrainian in state institutions and schools after 1924. Romania put areas inhabited by Ukrainian-speaking majorities under a state of siege and closed Ukrainian cultural organizations and schools.[204] Meanwhile the Soviets offered Ukrainians a state of their own and recognized their right to national culture, albeit, as we shall see, not one defined on their own terms. The Bolshevik approach had a significant coercive side to it as well, evident in the violent extermination of "preliterate" rural Ukrainian culture.[205] During the "struggle for grain" in the 1930s the Soviets had shattered Ukraine's countryside to clear the path for a new urban, Soviet Ukrainian culture to emerge, proletarian and secular.

When they annexed Northern Bukovina in 1940, the Soviets claimed it on Soviet Ukraine's behalf, arguing that the province was indisputably Ukrainian and belonged to the Ukrainian state. Many Ukrainian nationalists agreed with this claim, but it took some imagination to make it persuasive. Soviet officials offered as evidence Northern Bukovina's ethnic composition, which they meddled with, grouping together peoples who had thought of themselves as separate and introducing ethnic distinctions where there had been none before. By the Soviets' count, in 1941 there were 41,866 people in the Chernivtsi raion, 33,872 of whom were Ukrainian. The rest included 4,729 "Moldovans," a category imported from eastern Ukraine, where the Romanian-speaking minority traditionally identified themselves this way: by applying the term to Bukovina's Romanians, Soviet officials aimed to stir up irredentism, especially after the creation of a Moldavian SSR. Hutzuls, a mountain population alternately classified as Ukrainian and Romanian, were now proclaimed indisputably Ukrainian, "for they all speak Ukrainian and differ very little from other [Ukrainians], only based on their way of life."[206]

While redefining Northern Bukovina ethnically, Soviet officials never framed their actions in explicitly ethnic terms. Rather, they deemed Ukrainians victims of capitalist exploitation, an economically and nationally oppressed group that collectively constituted a kind of "surrogate proletariat" for Bukovina.[207] The Soviets attributed the backwardness of Ukrainians in Northern Bukovina to the Romanian government, which "instead of selling them medication [. . .] had sold them vodka." Under the Romanians, Soviet officials reminded Ukrainians, "one could not find a Ukrainian book, newspaper, or a Ukrainian school" and the "Romanian boyars tortured and ruined our people, forbade the Ukrainian word, the Ukrainian song, school, press, theater, and even persecuted Bukovinans for [wearing] Ukrainian national costume."[208]

As the Soviet regime's designated supporters in Northern Bukovina, Ukrainians were encouraged to educate themselves and promoted to positions in the party-state apparatus. Beginning in August 1940, Soviet officials also decreed that "in all civil courts, all trials are to be carried out exclusively in the Ukrainian language."[209] They went out of their way to recruit Ukrainian-speakers, even poorly qualified ones, to attend the university in Chernivtsi.[210] In September 1940 Hrushetskyi ordered that "every measure should be taken to make sure the Ukrainian nationality is better represented among the students," only 2–2.5 percent of whom were Ukrainian, mostly "children of kulaks, priests, landowners."[211] By February 1941, 69.6 percent of local cadres "drawn into the Soviet apparatus" were Ukrainian.[212] To observers such as Carl Hirsch, an engineer from a German-speaking Jewish family in Chernivtsi, it looked as if the Ukrainians were quickly learning to "[align] themselves with the new administration and got some good leadership positions."[213]

Yet promoting the Ukrainian language did not always yield the intended results. Many party-state cadres sent to Northern Bukovina from the eastern oblasts of Soviet Ukraine continued speaking Russian. Many could not speak Ukrainian at all and did not see the point of learning it. While inspecting offices to make sure the language policy was enforced, *obkom* officials observed that many Soviet cadres saw Ukrainian as an inferior, useless language. "There are some bad people who say there is no sense in learning the Ukrainian language," one report noted; as far as they were concerned it was "more useful to learn Russian, because everyone speaks it."[214] The leader of one raion agitation and propaganda branch confessed he spoke Russian because "I am used to speaking only Russian." *Obkom* first secretary Hrushetskyi made phone calls to various institutions in the oblast to "check what language is being spoken," only to discover "that they stubbornly respond in Russian, [. . . which] shows that "in our institutions the dominant language is Russian." This was something Hrushetskyi believed "we need to set right."[215] Even when Ukrainian did make its way into the public sphere, as when Soviet officials renamed streets and shops with Ukrainian names, the language was often riddled with mistakes. The new language policy's enforcers were novices.[216]

The problem was not only with the Soviet apparatchiks, but also with local Ukrainians, many of whom could not take advantage of the perks on offer because they themselves did not speak proper Ukrainian. At the university, Soviet officials had to introduce special courses to teach Ukrainian candidates from Northern Bukovina Ukrainian. Even so, Ukrainian candidates lacked basic literacy skills, which officials ascribed to "the hatred of Ukrainian culture" under Romanian rule, leading to "the complete liquidation of Ukrainian schools."[217] "Young people come to the university," the new Soviet rector explained, "and ask, 'What language will it be in?' 'Ukrainian' [we say]. This is very difficult for them. And indeed, young people don't know the Ukrainian language because under Romanian rule, Ukrainian was taught very little, as a foreign language."[218] Moreover, it proved difficult to persuade "oppressed" Ukrainians to attend the university at all, as many had no interest in applying in the first place.[219] Some Ukrainians, on the other hand, took the new language policies to mean they could do as they pleased merely because they were Ukrainian. Their abuses gave non-Ukrainians the feeling that they were being discriminated against by a regime which, contrary to what it professed, cared more about ethnicity than about qualifications. Romanians protested: "It's a Ukrainian, and nothing more! For [the Soviets] that's sufficient, that he is Ukrainian, and this [policy] takes clearly chauvinistic forms."[220]

Many obstacles that Soviet nationality policy ran up against in Northern Bukovina were due to this misalignment between the Soviet vision of Ukrainian culture and the existing Ukrainian culture that Soviet officials encountered, which had to be redefined, transformed, and reforged to fit the Soviet mold. Soviet cultural officials appropriated elements of Ukrainian tradition in the province and "retrofitted" them to align with the Soviet project.[221] Features of local Ukrainian tradition provided the Soviets with the raw material they needed to construct what was in fact a new Soviet Ukrainian identity in Northern Bukovina, lending it a sense of legitimacy and continuity.

Through this process of recycling and adaptation, the Bukovinan Ukrainian writer Olha Kobylianska was transformed from a little-known local writer into a virtual patron saint of Soviet Ukrainian culture. Born to a Polish- and

German-speaking family in southern Bukovina, Kobylianska came of age under Austrian rule. Educated mostly at home, her first literary attempts, inspired by reading Goethe and Heine, were written in German. She started writing in Ukrainian during the 1890s, following contact with Ukrainian intellectual milieux in Galicia. No longer able to publish in Ukrainian under Romanian rule, she reached out to presses across the Ukrainian diaspora, in western Ukraine and Europe further west, North America, and Soviet Ukraine. Soviet Ukrainian officials published her collected works in more than twenty editions and provided her with a pension for life. In exchange they asked only that she "devote her work to the interests of the working class."[222] Nevertheless, Kobylianska thought of herself as a non-political person. She liked to say that she "never took any part in [. . .]. political life [. . .] because she knew very little about politics, and only used her skills and energy to serve Ukrainian culture."[223] She appreciated the support from Soviet Ukraine, but did not feel ideologically bound by it.

By 1940, sitting back while enjoying the benefits of Soviet patronage was no longer an option for Kobylianska. Coming to rescue her from oblivion, the Soviets found her old and frail, but still expected her full participation in Northern Bukovina's Sovietization. During the preparations leading up to the elections of January 1941, the official oblast newspaper published expressions of approval and legitimizing propaganda under her name, including a call to "the entire people, men and women, of liberated Bukovina to prepare for and carry out elections peacefully: may our native, free land Soviet Bukovina, united with the great family of peoples of the USSR, live and blossom."[224]

Barely a day went by without Kobylianska's name appearing in the local newspaper, whether to denounce the oppression Ukrainians had suffered under Romanian rule or to celebrate Northern Bukovina's Soviet liberation as a miraculous dream come true. "[The Soviet Union's] fierce enemies spoke and wrote completely untrue things about the Bolsheviks, people who lead all workers to a better life," she (apparently) wrote. "I have listened with great enthusiasm to lectures about Shevchenko, Pushkin, Franko [. . .]. I was very happy [to witness] the great flourishing of Ukrainian Soviet culture [. . .]. How many happy minutes have I experienced when the radio broadcast Ukrainian popular songs that one used to be sent to prison for singing."[225]

Kobylianska became an emblem of Soviet Ukrainian culture and a model of *kul'turnost'*. The Soviets never tired of pointing out that, after being forced to leave school early, Kobylianska had "worked on herself [. . .] using all the possibilities [available to her] in the city to improve her cultural level."[226] Soviet authorities named streets and schools after her and staged a jubilee to celebrate her fifty-five years of activity. This was what it was like to be a Soviet writer. The Soviet Union, as Mayhill Fowler writes, "spent an enormous amount of time, money, paper, and bullets on artists."[227] Soviet officials gave writers pensions and houses and apartments, but they also dictated what they could or could not write. And as was likely the case with Kobylianska, they sometimes wrote in their stead, under their names.[228]

So fixated on promoting Ukrainian culture and language was the Soviet regime in Northern Bukovina that it prevented Soviet officials from taking advantage of the support some non-Ukrainians were eager to provide. A good number of Bukovinan Jews were enthusiastic about working with the Soviets. "In our attitude and that of most Jews from Czernowitz," Carl Hirsch recalled that "there were two elements in the positive approach to the coming Soviet rule in Bucovina, one was sympathy to the Soviet experiment [. . .] and the other the fact that in this way we are saved from the coming German rule."[229] Soviet officials, however, found Bukovinan Jews' affection for all things Soviet rather embarrassing. When local Jews began occupying administrative positions in the oblast, more senior party officials worried that this would create an image problem for the regime. One noted that in his raion the Komsomol organization consisted of 456 Ukrainians and 401 Jews, which he found problematic, for "while Ukrainians make up 75 percent of the oblast's population, it turns out that 50 percent [of the work] is done by the Jewish population."[230] Soviet officials therefore sought to limit the number of Jews admitted to positions in the party-state apparatus, even practicing "numerical discrimination against Jewish representation in the Ukrainian National Assembly."[231]

In theory at least, Jews benefited from Soviet nationality policies that granted all ethnic groups in Northern Bukovina equal access to education in their native languages. But it was the Soviets who decided what constituted those native languages. Jews in Northern Bukovina were allowed to study in their own language, but that language was Yiddish—not German, which most Jews in Bukovina spoke.[232] Jews could go to Jewish schools, but they could not decide what was taught there. While Jews had positions within the state apparatus such as they could never have dreamed of holding under Romanian rule, Bundists had to cease their activity and Zionists were interrogated and tortured. Jews who belonged to the wrong socio-economic class—landowners, petty bourgeois—had their belongings expropriated and were deported to Siberia. None other than the anti-Semite Pepe Georgescu recalled how a Jewish shopkeeper who could not decide whether to leave Northern Bukovina was persuaded by his brother that "it would be a mistake to go to Romania, for we won't have any rights there." Only a few months later, the Soviet police "confiscated his house and everything, and sealed the doors."[233] One could be Jewish under the Soviets, in other words, but only on Soviet terms.

At the same time, the Soviets neglected and alienated Northern Bukovina's Romanian-speaking population, or what was left of it after mass flight and deportations. Although they found some collaborators among Romanian-speakers, the Soviets treated Romanians overall as national oppressors. To weaken Romanian claims to Northern Bukovina, the Soviets distinguished between "Moldavians" (whose language was to be rendered in Cyrillic script) and "Romanians," further reducing the already dwindling Romanian population under their rule.

This approach was entirely inadequate. The Soviets had an insufficient number of cadres fluent in Romanian who could carry out propaganda in Romanian-speaking areas such as the Gertsa (Herţa) raion. In November 1940 the regime could count only "seven Communists who mastered the Moldavian and Romanian languages" in the entire oblast.[234] Oblast party leaders suggested that officials in Kyiv should "take some of our party workers who were sent here from Moldova" and use them as agitators in Romanian-speaking districts. "It is true these workers are on a very low level," they admitted, "but we don't have any alternative."[235] Always suffering from a shortage of "Moldavian language"-materials, the Soviets never managed to get a hold on the Romanian-speaking districts of Northern Bukovina, leaving these areas especially vulnerable to "counterrevolutionary propaganda."

---

On June 22, 1941 Nazi Germany launched its attack on the Soviet Union. The operation, code-named Barbarossa, had been in the works since at least December 1940. German and Romanian units crossed into Northern Bukovina between 4 and 5 p.m. German planes bombed the airport in Chernivtsi while the Romanians opened fire on the Soviet border guards at the frontier in Herţa. The Soviets managed to push the Romanian troops back over the course of the following day, even taking a few German and Romanian prisoners.[236]

The authorities in Northern Bukovina set to work reforming their infantry corps for front-line service. Civilians were ordered to stay put and warned that "those who individually evacuated their families will be held responsible." "Under no circumstances should we give in to panic," Hrushetskyi said during a party meeting on June 24.[237] Yet panic prevailed, and people ran in every direction.[238] Within days, tens of families "of military who are at the front, families of Communists who are mobilized into the army and those with many children" were gone.[239] It was evident that the Soviets were losing control over Northern Bukovina. "After a few days," Leopold Hessing recalled, "it became clear that this part of the land would be given up and the troops began withdrawing in great confusion."[240]

Germany's attack on the Soviet Union took few locals by surprise. Many had anticipated it for months. Already during the elections of January 1941 some Bukovinans had been heard saying that the Soviets should allow them to vote not just for candidates to the Supreme Soviet but for the country they wished to join, so sure were they that "the Germans and Romanians will come to liberate the land from Soviet power."[241] People who had lost relatives to the deportations and property to collectivization campaigns were especially eager to see Hitler advancing eastward. They hoped Germany's victory would allow them to live better: "under Hitler we won't be standing in line as much as we are now under Stalin." Some Ukrainians imagined that Hitler would "come with the German army and take Northern Bukovina away and make it a part of the Ukrainian republic and then we will live well."[242] Many wanted revenge.

As the Red Army prepared to withdraw from Northern Bukovina, Soviet officials celebrated the "many volunteers" who joined the army to keep the "fascists" from taking Bukovina.[243] Yet many factory workers and *sovkhoz* (state-run farm) personnel stopped coming to work. Men summoned to military recruitment centers feigned illness or disability. Over 170 men from Berezhnytsia "went into the forest, taking with them horses," among them "the president and secretary of the *selsovet* [village soviet, *silrada* in Ukrainian], both of whom were members of the OUN [Organization of Ukrainian Nationalists]."[244] Across the oblast, Soviet officials discovered "counterrevolutionary papers in Romanian, Ukrainian, and Russian."[245] Deserters were joining partisan gangs, one led by "bandit and Romanian spy Kolotylo" which "grows every day by adding more deserters."[246] The OUN took over Vyzhnytskyi raion, where Kolotylo's band operated, on June 25, instituting a temporary Ukrainian National Committee, setting up institutions and carrying out reprisals against the Jewish population, blamed for Ukrainian nationalists' sufferings under Soviet rule. Soviet officials locked up four active OUN members, eleven people they suspected of espionage, and four Siguranţa (Romanian secret police) agents.[247] But the "counterrevolutionary elements" fought back. Not far from Chernivtsi, on the evening of June 23, a group of "bandits" assaulted the Red Army troops and "tried to take away their weapons."[248] The president of one *selsovet* woke up one night to find his house engulfed by flames.[249]

Holding Northern Bukovina by a thread, the Soviet authorities nevertheless celebrated the anniversary of the province's unification with Soviet Ukraine. Local party organizations summoned peasants and workers "in all villages and factories" to talk about "what Soviet rule did here in one year."[250] But there was little time to talk. On July 4 and 5 the Soviets left Chernivtsi, blowing up buildings behind them.[251] A new revolution, even more devastating for some, was only minutes away.

# 8

# War and Reconstruction

ION ANTONESCU, who single-handedly ran a military dictatorship in Romania after putting down the Legionary rebellion of January 1941, learned of Germany's plans to launch Operation Barbarossa on June 12, 1941, while visiting Hitler in Munich, where he was informed that the Romanian army's main task was to protect the German Army Group South's rear and, above all, to guard the oil fields.[1] Although Hitler gave him the option of waiting, Antonescu agreed to bring Romania into the war immediately. He put at Germany's disposal a sizable army of 587,000, making Romania Nazi Germany's most important partner on the eastern front.[2] Antonescu's decision was both ideological and strategic: he believed it was Romania's mission to defend European civilization against the Bolshevik threat—a mission it could best fulfill alongside Nazi Germany.[3] He was also committed to reversing Romania's territorial losses. Hitler had given him to understand that Germany would reward Romania with "boundless" territorial compensation. Though it effectively became a "satrapy" of Germany, Romania remained fully sovereign: Antonescu was given formal command of the German–Romanian army group that marched on the Soviet Union and retained it for as long as the troops operated on Romanian territory.[4]

Romania joined Nazi Germany's attack on the Soviet Union in the summer of 1941. The Romanian Third Army crossed into Northern Bukovina on July 2, with German advisors, SS and SD officials, and Einsatzgruppen (mobile killing units of the SS) members following shortly thereafter.[5] Because the Romanian troops liberated the province single-handedly, Northern Bukovina remained in Romanian hands. It came under Romanian civilian administration on July 11 and was officially reunified with Romania on July 18. Although the German authorities in what now became once more Cernăuţi offered unsolicited guidance to their Romanian partners, the Romanians were free to govern as they liked. They were neither completely subordinate to Nazi Germany nor merely its imitators.[6] Officially, northern Bukovina was reincorporated into Romania on September 3, 1941, as a part of a larger governorship including both northern and southern Bukovina and the Dorohoi county of historical Moldova.[7]

On returning to northern Bukovina, the Romanian authorities set out to dismantle what the Soviets had done during their brief rule. They hoped to succeed where interwar Romanian governments had failed: in integrating the province definitively into the nation-state. In northern Bukovina and neighboring Bessarabia, they wished to spearhead a national revolution they hoped would eventually spread to the rest of the country. In northern Bukovina, the Romanian authorities found a population thirsty for revenge: in the wake of the Soviet revolution, people were ready to settle scores. People whose family members had been arrested or deported and those who lost their property to collectivization went after the "perpetrators." Locals set about reckoning with other locals, predominantly Jews, accused of supporting Soviet rule, during the brief interregnum between Soviet and Romanian rule. Although they did not orchestrate this violence, the Romanian authorities benefited from it. Moreover, the returning Romanian army was eager to take revenge on the Bukovinans who had chased them out of the province in 1940. They were determined that the people responsible for their humiliating retreat should pay.

Notwithstanding this chaotic and violent beginning, the Romanians had long-term plans for Bukovina. In contrast to the unruly Legionaries, with whom he had been temporarily allied but whom he despised, Antonescu dreamed of an orderly Romania: an authoritarian, "civilized" state that would succeed where interwar Romania had failed. For him, the outbreak of World War II provided an unprecedented opportunity to recast Romania's position in Europe. What he set out to do in northern Bukovina mirrored his vision of a reconstructed Romania.

The Romanians were not alone in recognizing the new possibilities opened up by Nazi Germany's attack on the Soviet Union. Surviving Ukrainian nationalists resurfaced in Bukovina and neighboring Galicia to court German authorities in Bukovina, even though technically the Romanians were sovereign and German officials merely counselors and aides. By steadily demonstrating loyalty to Germany, the Ukrainian nationalists hoped to bring about a new policy toward Ukrainians in Bukovina and elsewhere. The German presence in Cernăuţi broadened their scope for action, allowing the Ukrainians to circumvent Romanian authorities; the Germans even occasionally intervened to reduce the severity of Romanian policies toward Ukrainian irredentists. Yet their attitude toward the Ukrainian national cause remained profoundly instrumental. When the Ukrainians no longer served their purpose, the Germans did not hesitate to discard them.

Germany's priority in the region was to secure access to Romania's oil fields and fold Romania into Nazi Germany's plan for a New Europe purged of Jews.

German officials therefore urged their Romanian allies to pay more attention to the "Jewish question" in Bukovina, instead of focusing on "the Ukrainian problem." Antonescu agreed that Jews—and Ukrainians for that matter—needed to be gotten rid of. Unlike Hitler, he had no elaborate plans for exterminating Romania's Jews. He just wanted them sent east, beyond the Dniester, in what was initially German-occupied territory. In Bukovina, Romanian officials wanted the Jews removed as fast as possible so the work of making the province truly Romanian could begin. In October 1941 they began deporting Jews eastward from Bukovina to Transnistria, hoping to thus resolve interwar Romania's problem: the absence of a Romanian middle-class.

The "Romanianization" process initiated through the deportation of Bukovinan Jews did not have the intended effect. The transfer of Jewish property seized by the Romanian state from the deportees quickly degenerated into a bacchanal of thieving and pilfering. Like the Soviets, who also perfected the art of stealing from themselves, the Romanians pocketed the confiscated goods before an official inventory and redistribution plan could be drawn up. Instead of fostering national unity, as the government had hoped, the influx of stolen Jewish capital sparked new conflicts among Romanians. It alienated them further from an administration that promised much and delivered little and proved itself every bit as corrupt as previous ones. Local Romanians who felt entitled to a better life felt mistreated, despised, and disenfranchised by a new privileged class that, once again, came from Bucharest looking for easy money. Rather than heal the festering wounds that plagued Bukovina's relationship with Bucharest, the Romanianization process thus deepened them further.

In the meantime the deported Jews spent the next couple of years in improvised camps in Transnistria. An area of about forty thousand square kilometers (twenty-five thousand square miles) with a population of 2.3 million people, roughly delimited by the Dniester and Bug rivers, Transnistria until recently had been part of Soviet Ukraine. After August 1941 it was removed from the Wehrmacht's control and placed under Romanian sovereignty, although Germany retained almost all control over communication lines.[8] The Jews there experienced the Holocaust in the form of arbitrary executions and death by starvation, illness, and exhaustion, living in ghettos and camps guarded by Romanian gendarmes and officials, some of them native Bukovinans who shared the Jews' Austrian past and cultural background. Although the Romanian authorities proved unbelievably cruel and callous, more Jews from Bukovina survived in the areas administered by Romanians than in those territories directly under Nazi Germany's jurisdiction. It was the encounter between the two perpetrators, Romania and Nazi Germany, along the Dniester and Bug rivers, in what had once been Soviet Ukraine, that proved deadliest to the victims.

## Revenge

The Soviets had not yet left northern Bukovina when "counterrevolutionary elements," still numerous despite several rounds of purges, came out of the woodwork to launch "revenge attacks against a part of the population which was not just deemed to have collaborated with the Soviets but was held to be directly responsible for the liquidation of national hopes and aspirations."[9] Between June 22 and 30, 1941 the Soviets had arrested 553 of these "elements" in Northern Bukovina, including a hundred members of the OUN (Organization of Ukrainian Nationalists). Some were accused of shooting at the Red Army, others of signaling to German planes. In Chernivtsi, Olena Hermanivna Ridush was arrested for allegedly firing on Red Army soldiers from her roof.[10] The ranks of the OUN, which had played the key role in these "revenge attacks," had been depleted but not destroyed. After Dmytro Yaremchuk, former leader of OUN's branch in Bukovina, had fled to Germany, another local nationalist, Petro Voinovsky, stepped into his role. The organization had survived by infiltrating the Soviet party-state apparatus, and Soviet officials now watched in disbelief as village soviet (*silrada*) heads abandoned their posts and took to the forests, joining Red Army deserters who had also left their units, taking their weapons with them. The OUN had also maintained a sizable presence underground, especially in the Vyzhnytskyi raion.[11] They now resurfaced, attacking Red Army soldiers and NKVD employees, and blowing up phone and railway lines.

Barely had the Red Army retreated than OUN members and unaffiliated locals took advantage of the power vacuum to settle scores with the people they blamed for their sufferings under Soviet rule.[12] As one Ukrainian man from the Kitsmanskyi raion recalled, "after the NKVD left, the village could not go on without shedding blood" because everyone believed "the local corrupt people would have to pay for what they had done." Peasants who had lost their land to collectivization and their families to deportations blamed Jews for their personal tragedy. Years later, Maria Hryvul, a Ukrainian woman from northern Bukovina, still insisted that "there were many Jews" who under the Soviets "went around and listened to what people babbled about and then those cars came and took people to Siberia."[13]

In many small towns, practically all Jews were killed, often before the Romanian troops had arrived.[14] In Stăneştii de Jos, Ukrainians and Romanians shot and beat local Jews to death.[15] In Milie, Jewish "women were stripped completely, carried down the street, and whipped constantly with sticks until they died." Among the victims was the Zionist leader Jakob Geller, who was killed with pitchforks, then cut in half on a sawhorse.[16] The Milie killings were orchestrated and assisted by OUN oblast leader Petro Voinovsky. Local

Legionaries and former Cuzists were also involved, as were Romanian and Ukrainian mayors, schoolmasters, and members of Civic Guards and national committees formed after the Soviets retreated.[17] Locals needed neither formal orders nor sophisticated weapons to start killing their neighbors. Agricultural implements, or whatever was at hand, sufficed.[18] In Jadova Veche Jews had their eyes gouged out.[19] In Bănila pe Siret, a group led by the village mayor killed fifteen Jews and used the blood to grease their wagon axles.[20] In Nepolocăuţi Ukrainians broke into Jewish homes and attacked residents with pitchforks.[21]

In some places the newly arrived Romanian gendarmerie put a temporary stop to the killings. Elsewhere, they joined in, relying on locals to track down Jews and enlisting their help in disposing of bodies. Locals drafted lists of former Soviet activists and people guilty of "Communist ideas and [. . .] an anti-Romanian attitude, being among the first to welcome Bolshevik troops with red silk flags."[22] Ironically, the "culture of denunciation" and "legacy of distrust" the Soviets had bestowed on Bukovinans served the new occupation authorities, who found no shortage of collaborators.[23]

Many locals not directly involved in the murders nevertheless benefited from the victims' property.[24] In Storojineţ, locals helped the Romanian troops massacre over two hundred Jews over two days.[25] In Sniatyn, Romanian troops shot Jews while "peasants on the left shore of the Cheremush began plundering, robbing, murdering."[26] In Ciudei, the plundering was so thorough that, as one survivor recalled, "the windows were gone! The doors were gone! The bricks were missing!"[27] Similarly, in Bilia Krynytsia (Fântâna Albă) "the bandits threw themselves upon the empty homes of agitators and teachers" and, once they occupied the village, "brought with them the former leadership together with a gang of kulaks" who ordered the peasants to "gather all goods from the cooperatives and then turn them over to the authorities." "Once they occupied the villages," a former *raikom* head recalled, "they rang a bell and gathered separately all the men and women and proposed to the soldiers to shoot the men." The men begged for mercy and brought the soldiers "bread and salt," and in this case the soldiers contented themselves with cutting off an old man's beard.[28]

People eager to distract the Romanian authorities' attention from their own pasts made especially eager collaborators. Alexandru Wilentz, who had been a chauffeur for the Soviets in Chernivtsi, became the most trusted person "in the entourage of Commissar Gheorghiu, who carries out the Police and Siguranţa services within the Gouvernement of Bukovina."[29] A Cernăuţi lawyer known to have "glorified Stalin and the Bolshevik regime" and "spoken up against the Romanian state" resurfaced under the Romanians to take a new position at the city hall.[30]

Gendarmes and soldiers who participated in the murders of July 1941 were often motivated by a desire to take revenge on the people they blamed for the Romanian army's shameful retreat from northern Bukovina in 1940.[31] Antonescu himself justified the Romanian troops' actions in northern Bukovina this way when he warned the Romanian Jewish leader Wilhelm Filderman that Jews would be punished for having "spat on our officers, ripped their tunics, torn their uniforms, and wherever possible, clubbed soldiers to death."[32] Many soldiers returned to the places from which they had retreated in the summer of 1940, murdering Jews (much as they had done then) to restore their tarnished honor.[33] In Ciudei, where Romanian soldiers in the Sixteenth Infantry Regiment, led by Valeriu Carp, had left hundreds of Jewish victims in the summer of 1940, they murdered around five hundred more Jews when they returned on July 3, 1941.[34] In Boian, returning soldiers carried out mass shootings and buried victims in mass graves. One survivor recalled seeing local "gentiles through a crack in the attic wall" as they were "dragging the rabbi with the pitchfork stuck in his back."[35] In Rădăuţi, returning Romanian troops destroyed synagogues and made drumskins and shoe padding out of the Torah scrolls they stole.[36] Soldiers and locals alike were motivated by material incentives to perpetrate massacres. They burst into Jewish apartments "under the pretext that they were looking for weapons [and] stole jewelry, clothing, linen, in short everything they could carry."[37] In Cernăuţi, they went "from house to house, taking people out, beating them and shooting them on the spot," and then loading their "jewelry and expensive carpets" onto trucks and touring cars.[38]

Soldiers and gendarmes were told that their task in northern Bukovina was to cleanse the newly liberated territory of enemy elements,[39] through "the extermination on the spot of all Jews in rural areas, enclosing them in ghettos in urban areas, and the arrest of all those suspected of being Communist party members or of having held important functions under Soviet rule."[40] Lacking more specific instructions, soldiers went about these tasks haphazardly and chaotically, continuing what they had started in Jassy earlier.[41] After the Soviets bombed Jassy twice on June 24 and 26, Romanian soldiers and the soldiers of the German Eleventh Army had gone on a rampage, blaming local Jews for signaling to the Soviets. Jews all over Jassy were rounded up and brought to the police headquarters, where several hundred were shot. The survivors were loaded onto freight trains, where they died by the thousand as the trains went back and forth, due to contradictory directives, or waited on the tracks in the scorching summer heat.[42] Antonescu had intervened to end the pogrom in Jassy, but in northern Bukovina he gave no orders to end the looting and shooting. Locals were left to conclude that Romanian soldiers could do as they pleased.

The Romanian soldiers' behavior in Bukovina offended the sensibilities of the German authorities who followed the Romanian army into northern

Bukovina. While the principle was in their view correct, the German Einsatzkommando 10b, based in Cernăuţi's Hotel Pajura Neagră (known to the Germans by its old Habsburg name, the Schwarzer Adler), disapproved of the chaos in which the murders were carried out.[43] Einsatzgruppe D noted in a report from July 21 that "there would be nothing to criticize about the many executions of Jews had the technical preparation and manner of their execution not been inadequate. The Romanians leave the bodies of those who are executed where they fall, without burying them. The Einsatzkommando has enjoined the Romanian police to be more orderly in that regard."[44] Headed by Otto Ohlendorf, Einsatzgruppe D had four executive commandos, with one, Ek 10b, tasked with assisting Romanian soldiers and gendarmerie with cleansing operations in northern Bukovina and Bessarabia.[45] After arriving in Cernăuţi on July 6, Ek 10b, headed by Alois Persterer, operated jointly with the Romanian police and gendarmerie. Persterer also objected to the "unsystematic character" of the cleansing operations, including "a high incidence of acts of pillage and rape committed by Romanian soldiers."[46]

By August 1 the Ek 10b was said to have executed 682 Jews in Cernăuţi and captured fifty Communist functionaries.[47] Among their victims was the chief rabbi, Abraham Mark, arrested and imprisoned in the elevator shaft of the Schwarzer Adler hotel together with Chief Cantor Gurmann, Cantor Tofstein, and another synagogue employee.[48] Ek 10b staff interrogated civilians, using torture and beatings to identify Communists and other enemies.[49] With the information it gathered and that from the archives the NKVD had left behind, they summoned over 1,500 individuals, suspected Communists and partisans, to the Palace of Culture on July 8 for further investigation.[50] Most suspects were released, but a hundred people were marched to a shooting range on the city's outskirts and executed. Only one man was left alive to bury the victims.[51]

The Ek 10b wished the Romanian authorities to focus, chaotically or not, on the "Jewish question" in Bukovina, not the Ukrainian one.[52] That the Romanians did not restrict their thefts and crimes to Jewish victims scandalized the German consul in Cernăuţi, Fritz von Schellhorn, who concluded that "this people [the Romanians] is completely unsuitable for the difficult mission of rebuilding a province that has been more or less ruined."[53] Although their attitude would soon change, German authorities still viewed Ukrainians as useful, and worried that Romanian officials would alienate them with robberies and "mistreatments," as a result of which the city had "suffered much destruction."[54] To divert the Romanians' attention from Ukrainians, Persterer set fire to the Jewish synagogue on Cernăuţi's former Theaterplatz, hoping that a giant fire would show how unpopular the Jews were with the local population.[55] Sidi Gross, who lived across the street from the synagogue, watched it burn to the ground: "a German jeep went up to one side of the temple and an SS officer got out and went inside with a can of petrol and set it on fire."[56]

## Antonescu's Plans

Although the Romanian army's actions during the early days of northern Bukovina's "liberation" from the Soviets seemed to suggest otherwise, Antonescu had long-term plans for the province. They reflected his broader vision for Romania's role in World War II and the country's place in the postwar order. By 1941 it was clear to him that Romania's territorial ambitions could only be achieved in partnership with Nazi Germany.[57] He saw the war as a colossal confrontation between Christian civilization and its Communist destroyers, with Romania in the role of European civilization's defender in the east, a "guardian against barbarians of all sorts."[58] In order to fulfill its historic mission, Antonescu believed the country would have to change on an almost unthinkable scale. "We are one of the poorest countries of Europe," Antonescu lamented in a meeting of the Council of Ministers: "we are poor people in a rich country. Because of our disorganization, because of our sloth, we lost our place as one of the most important countries in Europe."[59] The war would change all this.

For Antonescu, the war provided an unprecedented opportunity to remake Romania into a new state, free of the corruption and incompetence that had afflicted it in the interwar period. It would be militaristic, un-ideological, authoritarian, built on peasant foundations, based on "the primacy of what is Romanian in every domain and [. . .] founded on our agricultural and peasant structure."[60] To succeed where interwar Romania had failed, the new state would resort to extraordinary measures—first and foremost, ethnic cleansing. As Vladimir Solonari has shown, by 1941 Romanians across the political and intellectual spectrum believed that ethnic homogeneity, achieved through ethnic cleansing, was a prerequisite for modernization.[61] Ion Antonescu and his vice-premier Mihai Antonescu looked forward to expelling foreigners from Romania, beginning with the newly liberated provinces. "Bessarabia and Bukovina will experience Titus's policy with regard to certain ethnic groups," Mihai Antonescu thundered in a cabinet meeting on June 14, 1941, "and I assure you not only in respect of the Jews, but of all the nationalities; we will implement a policy of total and violent expulsion of foreign elements."[62] In their speeches before the Council of Ministers, the two Antonescus proposed that Jews and Ukrainians be forcibly relocated beyond Romania's frontiers and interned in labor camps.[63] "I don't know how many centuries must pass," Mihai Antonescu said, "before the Romanian people shall again enjoy such total liberty of action, such an opportunity for ethnic cleansing and national revision [. . . ;] this is a period in which we are masters of our land."[64]

This new Romania would begin in the newly liberated territories of northern Bukovina and Bessarabia. At least until 1943, Antonescu envisioned them as "model provinces," or laboratories for state-building, "cells of experience on which we will construct a new economic and administrative order, which we will then transfer to the rest of the country."[65] "The two provinces," the newspaper *Bucovina* announced in August 1941, "will be the preface to the work of reforming the entire state through a new civil service apparatus conscious of its responsibilities and educated for its great mission."[66] The two provinces' physical separation from the rest of the state by a "wall of impermeability," intended to keep Soviet influence at bay, was an important prerequisite to this work.[67] As spaces of exception, the provinces would constitute for Antonescu's regime an unconstrained domain in which to try its hand at policies not yet feasible elsewhere: to play the "role of demiurge of the new provinces with a purified and re-educated population."[68] If all went well, Cernăuţi (and Chişinău) would come to "personify the soul of Romania, fulfilling a special mission of their own, as border cities."[69]

The work of reinventing Bukovina began with an administrative reform inspired by two German advisors, Karl Pflaumer and Theo Ellgering, among the last Nazi German "experts" to be invited to Bucharest to strengthen Romania's ties with Germany.[70] Drawing on their recent experience in the Alsace borderland, they urged Antonescu to experiment with a more decentralized administration, on the German model.[71] Their recommendations were reflected in a new administrative law, issued on September 3, 1941, that turned Bukovina into a "governorate" (*guvernământ*) of Romania. The law gave the province the status of a juridical person directly subordinated to Antonescu and represented by a governor with the rank of "plenipotentiary of General Ion Antonescu for the administration of Bukovina."[72] All communication between the governorate, headed by General Alexandru Rioşanu (and after his death in August, 1941 by Corneliu Calotescu and Corneliu Dragalina), and the Bucharest ministries would pass through a special body: the Civil Military Cabinet (Cabinetul civico-militar pentru Basarabia şi Bucovina).[73] This was meant to "put an end to the unfortunate practice of creating hierarchies in the Romanian territories and considering the provinces and their rights in an inversely proportional relationship to their distance from the capital."[74]

By granting Bukovina and Bessarabia greater provincial autonomy, Antonescu's administration aimed to correct the interwar state's failed approach to national integration. Bukovina and Bessarabia would not be treated like "colonies," for "nothing enduring can be built [. . .] if we don't let each administrative cell and each corner of the country live its own life."[75] At the same time, Antonescu hoped to consolidate Romania's position internationally by proving its worth as a civilized state.[76] Haunted by a sense of inferiority and frustration with Romania's marginality, the Conducător was determined to "show the country and those abroad that this nation is capable of a different administration, of a different morality, and of a different spirit of sacrifice," and that a Romanian need not be "only an Abyssinian of Europe, but he can also be a German and a Frenchman of Europe."[77] This gave the administrative reform envisioned for Bukovina (and Bessarabia) special urgency. To attract the most skilled functionaries to the newly liberated provinces, the regime offered civil servants perks, including salary increases of up to 30 percent and access to special shops.[78]

Yet before the work of rebuilding Bukovina could begin, the province had to be purged of the dangerous relics of Soviet rule.[79] Romanian soldiers and gendarmes came to northern Bukovina equipped with lists of locals who "had received help from the Soviet state" or "praised and thanked the [Communist] Party and Soviet government and Stalin, and heaped insults upon the Romanian government."[80] One suspect had been quoted in the *Radyanska Bukovyna* newspaper as saying that "under the Romanian boyars, to be able to make a pair of trousers one had to sell two or three hens, while now with one hen one can buy two pairs of trousers."[81] A local priest came under investigation due to his "hostile attitude to Romania," which his denouncer gleaned from statements such as "things weren't so bad under the Russians" or that Romanians in Rădăuţi "had been waiting for the Russians to come."[82]

To prevent former collaborators from infiltrating the new administration, the Romanian authorities formed special "review commissions" to investigate all state employees who wished to work under Romanian rule.[83] By October 25, 1941 the commission had reviewed over 1,800 petitions to return to service; 2,200 additional ones awaited review.[84] Suspected Soviet collaborators were issued with an "unfavorable notice," while the rest received certificates of good behavior. One man prevented from returning to work and facing bankruptcy without a "certificate proving that during the occupation of Cernăuţi by the USSR [he] behaved impeccably" complained that the commission "had given permits to all foreigners but not Romanians like himself," leaving them to "go from door to door trying to obtain a repatriation permit without success."[85]

Suspected Soviet collaborators and Communist sympathizers were to be arrested and confined in internment camps.[86] The purge in southern Bukovina began even before the Romanian army crossed the frontier into Soviet territory. On June 21, 1941 the Conducător ordered the gendarmerie to remove all Jewish men from the Siret-Prut area bordering on Soviet-occupied northern Bukovina to an internment camp in Târgu Jiu. Their families were relocated to nearby towns.[87] Alleged Soviet collaborators from northern Bukovina were later rounded up and interned just outside Cernăuţi, in Sadagura. Among the 2,783 people held there in November 1942 were "1,079 Orthodox and 704 Jews."[88] They included old Communists and former Soviet civil servants from northern Bukovina, such as a former village mayor interned for "taking grain from people and forcing those who didn't have any to buy some and hand it over." For having "contributed to the deportation of many families" under the Soviets and taken possession of "the goods left behind by refugees," Alexei Bodnar was given a one-year sentence in the camp at Edineţi.[89] Between June 1942 and February 1943, almost seven hundred people from Cernăuţi were condemned for "showing favor to the Bolsheviks and a hostile manner with regard to the interests of the state." Bukovinans who had applied for "repatriation" to Soviet-occupied northern Bukovina in 1940 now lost their Romanian citizenship.[90]

Material and cultural traces of Soviet rule were more difficult to remove. Refugees who returned to the homes they had abandoned in a hurry in 1940 discovered that "in Cernăuţi on almost every street mailboxes are painted with the Ukrainian flag."[91] While searching the apartment of one former "Communist partisan" in Cernăuţi, the Romanian police came across a portrait of Stalin behind an icon on the wall. In the city's public library they found "numerous volumes of Russian propaganda, Russian maps, and several statues of Stalin."[92] Interwar Romania's material traces in northern Bukovina, by contrast, seemed negligible. The returning Romanian authorities found one lone statue of a Romanian soldier lying "on a ramp at the train station in Cernăuţi." It was a piece of a larger monument, the rest of which had been "taken by the Russians to places that are still unknown to us today." In its place, the "Bolsheviks had put up Communist posters and a photo of Stalin."[93] The Siguranţa took it upon itself to "collect and destroy all this material so that it should not be hidden and then spread by elements who remained faithful to the Communist regime."[94] By April 1942 the authorities had confiscated 618,000 volumes of Soviet literature and 650 kilograms of printed matter, including "200,000 schoolbooks, 100,000 propaganda books, 100,000 books of literature, 160,000 brochures, 40,000 scientific books, 10,000 military books, 2,000 books of statistics, 1,000 on sports, 1,000 philological, 1,000 juridical, 1,000 dictionaries and encyclopedias, 300 music scores, 500 maps, 250 kg of newspapers, [and] 400 kg of [other] printed material."[95] By May, they had also collected and burnt eight hundred thousand volumes of Soviet literature, saving only a few "for an anti-Bolshevik exhibit."[96]

Romanian officials, though deeply anti-Soviet, were awed by a state that had left so deep an imprint on the province so quickly. In just one year, the newspaper *Bucovina* observed in July 1941, "the Bolshevik regime abolished everything that was Romanian in Bukovina, tore up from the foundations everything that was autochthonous, ruined lives, robbed the population, and took from Bukovina everything that could be transported in one way or another."[97] Governor Calotescu, who took over as head of Bukovina's administration after Rioşanu's death in August 1941, argued that "given the extensiveness of the artistic and theatrical movement in Cernăuţi under the Bolshevik regime," the Romanian administration also had to meet locals' cultural needs.[98] Local officials and notables including priests and teachers and public notaries were invited to form "initiative committees" and found cultural enlightenment institutions in villages lacking them. In a Council of Ministers meeting in March 1942, the Conducător proclaimed that "cultural and national propaganda must be extended to the remotest villages through schools, homes of culture, village libraries, and missionary teams." The "cultural offensive in villages," he insisted, "is very necessary," particularly in the liberated provinces where "parents, brothers, children, and mothers were deported by the Russians and left behind empty homes."[99] By November 1942, fifteen mobile libraries "were going around from village to village, stopping in each for fifteen days."[100] The authorities reopened the theater in Cernăuţi with a new mission to "bring back the flame of Romanian culture and civilization" to northern Bukovina.[101] To restore the province's ties with "the heart of the country," they sent theater troupes around the province on "propaganda tours," promoting "the patriotic idea among the great masses of population, to centers that aren't visited by the usual tours organized by the state and private theaters."[102]

## Ukrainian Dreams

Achieving independent statehood had been the OUN's supreme goal since its founding in 1929. As Stepan Lenkavskyi, the author of the OUN's "Decalogue"—the "Ten Commandments of Ukrainian Nationalists"—put it, "You will attain a Ukrainian state or die in the struggle for it." Its leaders, many of them World War I veterans who recalled earlier struggles for national liberation, envisioned the OUN's task as continuing efforts to forge a unified Ukrainian state.[103] The OUN indeed incorporated many ideological and institutional elements of earlier national independence projects, but with a new twist.[104] OUN leaders blamed past failures on former nationalist leaders' excessive commitment to democracy, as well as poor organizational skills and an inability to gain the local population's trust.[105] The remedy, they believed, was investing in developing a proper Ukrainian military and police and laying the groundwork for the future Ukrainian state's administration.[106]

In 1940 a group of OUN members led by Stepan Bandera split off from the main organization to form the OUN-B. Less compromising than the core organization (OUN-M led by Andrii Melnyk, successor to Yevhen Konovalets), Bandera's group advocated a radical approach to state-building: their state was to be a military-authoritarian dictatorship, anti-capitalist and anti-Marxist: a "natiocracy" (*natsiokratiia*).[107] At their second assembly, in 1939 in Rome, they formulated on August 27 "the leader principle" and called for a state without political parties, achieved through national insurrection or "permanent revolution."[108] For the OUN-B, the priority was to create a Ukrainian state: the movement had to ""invent its state, facilitate its quickest and happiest possible birth, and support it with a firm hand when it begins to rise on its still feeble legs."[109]

There were two sides to the OUN state-building project. On the one hand, the OUN worked to build institutions from the ground up and cultivate new elites by promoting Ukrainian culture, improving literacy among Ukrainians, and cultivating national consciousness through schooling and propaganda. During the power vacuum after the Red Army's retreat from western Ukraine, the OUN quickly set up its own administrative bodies, appointed mayors and police chiefs, and formed its own paramilitary units.[110] In Vyzhnytsia, in northern Bukovina, they formed a Provisional Ukrainian Committee in late June 1941. Led by local OUN member Myroslav Mychkovskyi, this committee was a shadow government which in the long term aimed to achieve co-rule with the Romanian administration.[111] Though militarist, the OUN also recognized the value of cultural efforts and propaganda, especially in territories that had recently experienced Bolshevik rule. They looked to schools to facilitate the state-building project by imparting new values, and to teachers to foster a love of Ukrainian language and culture through cultural enlightenment and literacy campaigns.[112] In a manifesto of October 1941 the OUN-B listed among its aims a campaign "against foreign and enemy songs": "only Ukrainian, Cossack, hunting, national, and patriotic songs" should be sung.[113] Another manifesto appealed to Ukrainian teachers in Bukovina to "bring Ukrainian culture to the people" and make up for the time when "we were compelled to hide from our children the truth about the glorious past of Ukraine" and "poison the minds of children with Jewish internationalism, with love for everything that belongs to Moscow and disgust for our fatherland, language, literature, and culture."[114]

On the other hand, OUN leaders believed that cleansing Ukrainian territories of Soviet collaborators and other enemy elements was also a prerequisite to building a lasting independent state.[115] Since the mid-1930s anti-Semitism and anti-Bolshevism had become increasingly central to OUN ideology.[116] Neither Yaroslav Stetsko, who proclaimed an independent Ukrainian state in Lviv on June 30, 1941, nor Andrii Melnyk ever made a secret of their animosity toward Jews.[117] Both OUN branches espoused an ideology which "took ethnic purity and aggression as the default" and drew "attention to the Ukrainian problem through acts of sabotage." For them, "Jews, Poles, and Russians were all mortal enemies."[118]

Much as Ukrainian nationalists wanted to build a Ukrainian state with their own hands, their earlier failures had taught them that they needed a larger power to partner with them. The Nazi–Soviet war provided the OUN with a perfect opportunity to put their state-building project on the international agenda. With Nazi Germany's support, the OUN hoped to remove the Soviets and carry out a national revolution culminating in the founding of a Ukrainian state. OUN leaders were convinced that, if presented with a *fait accompli*, Nazi Germany would recognize them as the only legitimate representatives of the Ukrainian people. They counted themselves natural partners of Germany, "cofounders of the new order," given Germany's support for the Ukrainian nationalist project during World War I.[119]

German support for the OUN was indeed crucial, especially in the years before Germany's attack on the Soviet Union. The German-occupied General Gouvernement zone in Poland provided Ukrainian nationalists who fled Soviet-occupied Poland with a safe haven to reorganize, rebuild their ranks, and prepare for the upcoming offensive against the Soviets.[120] In turn, Germany relied on the OUN's assistance during the liberation of Soviet-occupied western Ukraine.[121] Ukrainian battalions accompanied the Wehrmacht on their eastward march, "cleansing" the terrain side by side with German soldiers. They drew up lists of enemies to be liquidated or turned over to the Germans.[122] Across the newly liberated territories, OUN leaders organized festivities to welcome the Wehrmacht,[123] from burnings of Soviet books to the writing of letters commending Hitler for returning civilization to Ukraine.[124] In Bukovina they vowed that if Germany guaranteed that "these regions belong to Greater Ukraine," Ukrainian youth would join in Germany's war effort. They believed it was only a matter of time before Germany set up under its patronage "an independent Ukraine that will incorporate eastern Galicia and northern Bukovina." "Ukrainians," they reassured themselves, "will be paid back for their role in the war, with northern Bukovina and Bessarabia." Yet Germany made no explicit promises, offering only vague assurances that "the question will be settled at the end of the war when the political and geographical fate of Europe is decided."[125]

The OUN also put itself at Germany's disposal in Bukovina, even though the German authorities had only a secondary role there. As we saw in chapter 6, during the 1930s Ukrainian nationalism in Bukovina had grown increasingly radical. Frustrated Romanian officials noticed that Ukrainians in Bukovina refused to take the Romanian administration seriously, assuming Romanian sovereignty was temporary.[126] When the Soviet Union annexed northern Bukovina, however, many Ukrainian nationalists fled the province and went to Romania, viewing it as the lesser of two evils.[127] Among them was Orest Zybachynskyi, head of Bukovina's OUN, first arrested in 1937 for passing out irredentist propaganda there.[128]

Once the Romanians reclaimed northern Bukovina in 1941, the Siguranţa kept a close eye on OUN underground members. Dumitru Bendac, head of the "committee of Ukrainian nationalists" in Cernăuţi in 1941 and a former officer in the Austrian army, had "been active in various political organizations with a Ukrainian irredentist character," and toyed with Communism during the interwar period.[129] Mykhailo Kolotylo, a Ukrainian student from the Cernăuţi suburb of Clocucica, was also an old acquaintance of the Siguranţa in Bukovina. In January 1941 the Romanian authorities arrested him and condemned him to fifteen years of forced labor.[130]

Given their tensions with the Romanian authorities, OUN members in Bukovina looked to German officials for protection, even if this further alienated the Romanians. In return for German patronage, Voinovsky approached German officials in Cernăuţi with a plan to "organize the formation of Ukrainians who would be at the service of the German police" and then "leave to enroll in a Ukrainian army."[131] As in Galicia, German officials in Bukovina pursued a divide-and-rule strategy, encouraging conflict between Ukrainians and Romanians.[132] Even though Nazi Germany officially recognized Romania's authority over northern Bukovina at a conference in Piatra Neamţ in June 1941, German officials in Cernăuţi indirectly influenced the course of events in the province. Through their presence and support, they allowed Ukrainian nationalists to circumvent Romanian authority, making their Romanian allies question Germany's commitments and designs for Bukovina. German officials—the Einsatzkommando leadership, SS, and SD members in Cernăuţi—lent Ukrainian nationalists in Bukovina an ear even after Germany had formally rejected the OUN-B's declaration of independence in Lviv in June 1941. For as long as Ukrainian nationalists seemed useful as a counterweight to the Romanians, the German headquarters at the Schwarzer Adler hotel was open for conspiratorial meetings with the OUN.

In turn, OUN leaders courted the Einsatzkommando authorities in Cernăuţi, insisting that their national project was compatible with Nazi Germany's designs for a free Europe: "no nation has more in common with Germany than the Ukrainians."[133] In exchange for helping the German army to cleanse the newly liberated territories of enemy elements, OUN leaders received German documents and uniforms that allowed Ukrainian nationalists to circulate freely between Bukovina and Galicia, carrying out irredentist activities directly under the Romanian officials' noses.[134] As late as January 1942 an OUN leader from Galicia was spotted visiting Cernăuţi using "a German car and identity card issued by the German command in Krakow."[135]

Although Germany denied Ukrainian nationalists the right to build a military and state of their own, the limited German protection they did enjoy in Bukovina permitted them to recruit volunteers for a paramilitary formation: the "Bukovynskyi Kurin." Along with other paramilitary groups, so-called *pokhidni hrupy*, the Bukovina Kurin traveled across Galicia and into eastern Ukraine, leaving behind qualified personnel who would form the nucleus of a future Ukrainian administration and military. More than a hundred volunteers joined the Bukovina Kurin in July 1941, both old OUN members and Ukrainians whose prospects under Romanian rule were, for whatever reason, grim. Antonina Frunza-Ochkinskyi, for instance, had been accused of collaborating with the Soviets in 1940 and faced a possible trial. Called before the village council to account for her involvement with the Komsomol, she crossed the Ceremuş river and joined the Kurin in Stanislaviv.[136] While stopping in Sniatyn for eight days, the Kurin gathered more volunteers, mostly from the Vyzhnytsia (Vijniţa, in Romanian) area.[137] With Petro Voinovsky at its head—"a tall, thickset man with a Cossack mustache, dressed in a strange mix of clothes: high Magyar boots, NKVD breeches, a civilian jacket, without a hat"—the Kurin then proceeded to Horodenka and Kamianets-Podilskyi, and finally to Kyiv, where they may have participated in the massacres at Babyn Yar.[138]

Ukrainian nationalists still used the Schwarzer Adler hotel to organize conspiratorial meetings after the Kurin had left and the SD and Einsatzkommando authorities had relocated to the Kulturpalast in Cernăuţi.[139] The limited German protection OUN members in Bukovina enjoyed emboldened them to question openly Romania's rights to northern Bukovina. Between July and September 1941 the OUN drafted a series of memoranda demanding acknowledgment of northern Bukovina's Ukrainian character and protesting the province's annexation to Romania.[140] The Reich Chancellery received numerous letters concerning northern Bukovina, among them one drafted by Bukovinan Teofil Brândzan that listed "all the wrongs inflicted by the Romanians [on the Ukrainians]" and insisted on "the Ukrainian character of Bukovina."[141] In other memoranda, the OUN noted that "Bukovina was always Ukrainian" and appealed to Germany to "help with the creation of a great nationalist Ukrainian state" and rescue Ukrainians "from the Romanian yoke."[142] Some of these memoranda reached Antonescu's administration in Bucharest, prompting Ion Nistor to draft a reply in which he argued that Ukraine had no place in Hitler's new Europe; but most were directed to the German consulate and authorities in Cernăuţi and Bucharest.

As long as Germans were present—even at a distance—Ukrainian nationalists felt free to defy Romanian authorities in Bukovina. The Ukrainian owner of a train station tavern near the Galician–Bukovinan border used his position to relay instructions from Ukrainian nationalists in Galicia to OUN members in Bukovina. These included warnings to Ukrainians in Bukovina "not to send their children to school but to buy textbooks and books in the Ukrainian language for children to study at home so they can develop national irredentist feelings." The owner of a restaurant in Vijniţa who "used to display the Ukrainian flag but when our troops came pretended to be Romanian" now invited Ukrainians from neighboring villages "to sing Ukrainian songs and toast to the creation of Greater Ukraine."[143] Ukrainian priests who kept "in touch with propaganda centers in Galicia" threatened to "cause a Ukrainian revolt through their activity." One such priest, standing on the frozen Ceremuş river in January 1942, told Ukrainians on both the Galician and Bukovinan shores, "Brothers, do not worry. Soon the Ceremuş will no longer be a frontier and then we will walk together wherever we wish."[144]

The Romanian administration felt German support was making Ukrainians "increasingly impertinent and even threatening toward the Romanian population."[145] Ukrainian was "spoken in public increasingly" in Cernăuţi, in public squares, "as well as in the stores [and] in the streets."[146] When asked a question in Romanian, Ukrainians declined to answer. During Romanian-language masses, they would "start coughing and then leave the church." They came to the city hall in Cernăuţi and insisted on speaking only Ukrainian, even if this meant "going back with their problems unsolved."[147] Some Ukrainians ostentatiously wore their national costumes, "blue and yellow belts and feathers painted in these colors," to set themselves apart from the Romanians.[148] People walked around "with the Ukrainian symbol" pinned on their jackets and business cards inscribed "We create Ukraine or we die trying."[149] Romanian officials thought it likely that Ukrainian nationalists would soon engage in "acts of sabotage or terrorism or revolt."[150]

This surge in Ukrainian irredentism seemed to confirm the wisdom of General Antonescu's plans to take "all Ukrainians, Ruthenians, and Hutsuls who are known to be elements opposed to our interests" over the Dniester and forcibly settle them "in occupied regions in the Ukraine."[151] The German authorities understood that their Romanian allies were "inclined to eliminate Ukrainian elites so that by exploiting current circumstances, they can definitively solve the Ukrainian problem."[152] While Ukrainian nationalists had German protection, however, Romanian officials refrained from taking overly harsh measures. They had no choice but to allow OUN members to cross the border into Galicia, but insisted that those who left formally renounce their Romanian citizenship. If they returned, General Antonescu ordered that they be "arrested and sent to the camps."[153]

Yet it was soon clear that OUN leaders had too much confidence in both Germany's support and in their own popularity.[154] After August 1941 the Wehrmacht began cracking down on the OUN-B, now considered a "partisan group."[155] That fall, they began arresting OUN-B and OUN-M members, and in November they dissolved the Ukrainian National Council in Kyiv, which the Bukovina Kurin had previously recognized as the sole legitimate Ukrainian governing body.[156] In December 1941 the Gestapo arrested and shot Ukrainian nationalists, including many OUN members from Cernăuţi.[157] Following another wave of arrests in Kyiv in 1942, the Bukovynskyi Kurin was liquidated. All Ukrainian militias and paramilitary formations were banned, and Ukrainians appointed by the OUN to administrative positions were replaced with German-appointed staff. Many Ukrainian nationalists continued fighting by the only means still available, as members of *Schutzmannschaften* (native auxiliary police units), if only to prove that they remained a "de facto partner" of Germany.[158] Other members of former militias, including the Kurin, began trickling back into western Ukraine.[159] This narrowing of options was the result of a turn in German policy in Ukraine toward a war of colonial exploitation, an approach modeled by Erich Koch's administration in the RKU (Reichskommissariat Ukraine).

As earlier Nazi plans to cultivate a clientelist relationship with Ukrainians receded, OUN members in Bukovina were left at the mercy of Romanian officials, for whom any form of collaboration with Ukrainians was impossible. In January 1942 the Romanian administration banned "the performance in public locales of Ukrainian, Russian, and Hungarian songs" as well as "Romanian adaptations of Ukrainian songs," threatening that all locales in which such songs were sung would be closed.[160] "Young boys were singing and the gendarmes on one street beat them," one local recalled, "and then they ran into another [street] and continued singing [. . .]—oh, how they beat them."[161] Ukrainian students were now told that "Ukrainians don't have the right to study in middle schools."[162]

Upon discovering letters containing directives to launch a national insurrection and establish OUN rule in northern Bukovina, Romanian officials began rounding up Ukrainians. Twenty-two Ukrainian nationalists from Bukovina were brought before the military tribunal in Jassy in January 1942 and condemned to fifteen years in prison. Among them was Mykhailo Kolotylo, the most prominent OUN-B member in Bukovina. Sick with typhus, Kolotylo was brought to the prison hospital, from where he escaped with the help of a Ukrainian teacher from Bukovina. Disguised "in women's clothing," the two fled the hospital and "crossed all of Romania by cart," escaping to Galicia in June 1942.[163]

By the time he returned to Bukovina in April 1943, to "inspect the situation from a political and organizational point of view," Kolotylo had had a change of heart. He was severely disappointed in Germany which, it was now evident, had no intention of sponsoring an independent Ukraine. After so many of its members had fallen victim to Gestapo-led raids and arrests, the OUN-B redefined itself as an anti-imperialist movement, fighting on behalf of Ukraine and other nations and against both Nazi Germany and the Soviet Union. The OUN-B adopted a resolution to collaborate with other anti-Bolshevik nations, since "fighting against Russian Bolshevism demands the political and military collaboration of all nationalities and states in the name of the idea of liberty, justice, and a just order based on the principle of national sovereignty and the creation of free independent states on the ethnic territory of each nationality."[164] The resolution noted that "all imperialist tendencies must be excluded from this fight," since the only way to prevail over "the age-old enemies of European peace" was to fight "shoulder to shoulder with the other nationalities."[165]

Kolotylo "stopped talking about the establishment of a Ukrainian state under German aegis" and began looking to Romania for an anti-Bolshevik alliance. OUN members in Bukovina were instructed "not to carry out anti-Romanian propaganda, but talk about the common fate of these two peoples, the Bolshevik danger, and the necessity of fighting together against Moscow."[166] In the fall of 1943 Ukrainian nationalists sent a delegation to Bukovina's governor to "demand that a formula of reconciliation between the Ukrainian element and the Romanian state be found."[167] The OUN-B proceeded to hold a conference for "the oppressed people of Eastern Europe and Asia" as part of its effort to recast itself as a broader, anti-imperialist organization.[168] But the partnership it sought with the Romanians was not to be. Kolotylo was arrested again and condemned to twenty-five years' hard labor.

## Deportations

On October 9, 1941 Governor Calotescu issued orders for the entirety of Cernăuţi's Jewish population to relocate to the so-called "lower city"—a small area around the former Judenviertel, an old Jewish neighborhood. Soon to be surrounded by barbed wire, it became the city's Jewish ghetto.[169] By orders of the "higher command of the army," Jews in Cernăuţi were required to move into "a district of the city limited to a few streets."[170] The city authorities had only two days to herd over fifty thousand people into a space designed to hold fifteen thousand, where people would live "in the most precarious conditions of hygiene and public health, of location and food supply."[171] The operation lasted nine hours. Governor Calotescu instituted "a surveillance cordon around the municipality of Czernowitz in order to prevent the Jews from exiting the city" while the ghetto was being formed.[172] The authorities' task was made easier by earlier measures limiting free movement of Jews in Cernăuţi.[173] Beginning on August 1, all Jews in Cernăuţi had been required to wear "a visible white armband with the Jewish star sewn on to it, replete with six corners, in black."[174] That month, travel agencies had been forbidden to issue travel documents or tickets to Jews. Now easy to spot due to the "special sign" they wore, Jews were prohibited from moving between localities.[175]

FIGURE 8.1. Portrait of a young Romanian Jew wearing the yellow star, the day before he was deported to Transnistria; Cernăuţi, October 30, 1940. United States Holocaust Memorial Museum, courtesy of Mark Brandman.

Jewish community leaders were informed of the authorities' plans on the morning of October 9. As the news spread, people ran around collecting their belongings and hurrying into the ghetto "with suitcases, with rucksacks on their backs, with pillows or duvets in their hands, [. . .] with bundles made in a hurry, out of which laundry was hanging and various objects would fall," running in every direction to find accommodation. Not all succeeded. It was a wet, cold fall day and an even colder night, with "penetrating damp, heavy and thin rain," which many ended up spending outside. "Nobody knew exactly where the ghetto was," the Jewish journalist Marius Mircu recalled; "they would run, come back, stepping on each other."[176] Jews living outside the designated area were allowed to take clothing and goods, "as much as they can carry on their backs, both for living in the ghetto and for the evacuation, taking into account that none of them will be returning to their former apartments."[177] Each Jewish family was required to bring along keys to their apartment and an inventory of goods they left behind: "the inventory as well as the keys will be placed inside a closed envelope on which the name and address of the resident will be recorded. The envelope will be handed over upon request, in the ghetto."[178]

By October 15 over three thousand Jews had departed the ghetto on eastbound trains that unloaded their human cargo on the Dniester's banks. Jews from Cernăuţi were joined by thousands from neighboring Storojineţ and the Dorohoi-Rădăuţi region. The task of rounding up the deportees and loading them onto trains fell to the Romanian gendarmerie, headed by General Ioan Topor.[179] "Those singled out for deportation," Cernăuţi's mayor Traian Popovici remembered, "were collected in groups of two thousand, marched through the mud to access ramps at the main railway station, then placed in forty to fifty cars per train under military guard" and "sent to Atachi and Mărculeşti on the banks of the Dniester." There, the deportees were "stripped of whatever they still had including personal identification documents which were destroyed so all trace of them would be lost," after which they were "ferried across, then marched again, barefoot and starving through the mud and mire."[180] The deportation orders came from General Antonescu himself, who claimed they would palliate public resentment against Jews and prevent an outburst of violence that would be more dangerous and harder to control.[181] When some Jews managed to leave the Cernăuţi ghetto, a local government official sounded a similar note: "since the presence of Jews in a state of idleness and freedom presents an outrageous spectacle to true Romanians, I think that [. . .] everything that is of Jewish blood should be in the ghetto; only in this way can we satisfy the Romanian element that had so much to suffer because of these Jews."[182]

These aspirations remained unfulfilled, as the ghetto in Cernăuţi was very soon dissolved, in November 1941, freeing almost twenty thousand Jews. A few days after the deportations began, General Calotescu received a phone call from Ion Antonescu, granting him permission to spare up to twenty thousand Jews whom the administration deemed useful;[183] the city hall would determine which Jews were to receive exemptions.[184] Mayor Traian Popovici, who had taken office in August, and General V. Ionescu instructed Jewish community leaders in Cernăuţi to list the city's Jewish population by profession. They agreed that Jews played a disproportionate role in Bukovina's economy and society, but the ghettoization and deportation orders struck them as barbarous. By Popovici's own account, he warned the governor that "you have no right to take the lives of anyone. How do you wish to be remembered by history, at Robespierre's side? As for me, I do not wish to see history tarnish my name. Think of what you are doing. You still have time."[185] General Ionescu, for his part, claimed that "it would have been better for me not to have come to Bukovina than to witness such barbaric acts." Colonel Gheorghe Petrescu of the Second Section (army counterintelligence) meanwhile admonished them: "I have come here to pull out weeds from your garden, and you are against this?"[186] All in all, the Romanian authorities issued a total of 19,500

FIGURE 8.2. Three young women pose in the Cernăuţi ghetto, 1942–43. United States Holocaust Memorial Museum, courtesy of Erika Neuman Kauder Eckstut.

authorizations for Jews to remain in Cernăuţi, five thousand from the mayor, and the remaining 14,500 from Calotescu.[187] For many Jews, these authorizations were the only hope for survival, a treasure to be acquired at any cost. To increase their chances of acquiring one, many put their names on multiple lists of professions.[188]

The authorizations were likely a concession to the German authorities, especially the German consul in Cernăuţi, Fritz von Schellhorn, who repeatedly warned the Romanian authorities that deporting all Cernăuţi's Jews would have devastating economic consequences, potentially leading to "the total collapse of economic life in Bukovina."[189] An old Nazi who had served as a consul in Bukovina since 1934, Schellhorn agreed with Antonescu that Jews should not be allowed to run the Romanian economy.[190] Yet by October 1941 he had come to "the regrettable conclusion that currently we cannot dispense with the Jews, as they are necessary for the reconstruction of economic life in Cernăuţi."[191] German advisors Pflaumer and Ellgering agreed with Schellhorn's prediction that the wholesale deportation of Jews from Cernăuţi would impoverish the city.[192] Like him, they were concerned about the effect of Bukovina's economic woes on Germany's war effort in the east. Schellhorn and other German officials sought to protect Jews employed by German firms or working in enterprises that benefited the Wehrmacht.[193] Ellgering personally saved the Jewish "master, engineer, and mechanic" of a brewery in Bukovina which supplied the Wehrmacht. He also railed against the Romanian authorities' decision to deport all Jewish workers from a coat factory commissioned to provide the Wehrmacht with eight thousand woolen coats.[194] Economic concerns aside, Schellhorn took a special interest in Bukovina's Jews because they looked Central European. As he wrote to the German Legation in Bucharest in July 1941, in Cernăuţi "there lived above all Austrian Jews who kept their distance from Eastern Jews per se."[195]

Like other German officials in Romania, Schellhorn believed the Romanian authorities' poorly thought-out anti-Jewish measures typified their chaotic approach to governing the newly liberated territories; they seemed bent on mining the provincial economy instead of rebuilding it. They staffed their administration with unqualified personnel, including military staff and individuals from the Old Kingdom "who do not attain the level of the replaced Bukovinans."[196] Locals, Theo Ellgering thought, were undoubtedly superior to their Old Kingdom counterparts; they had not only indispensable legal knowledge, but "an Austrian education," which German officials apparently still respected.[197] Schellhorn agreed that the administrative personnel's incompetence stood in the way of Bukovina's successful reconstruction, as did Bucharest's total disregard for local interests. "On the basis on my experience," he wrote in July 1941, "I can assert that in this country it is extremely difficult to impose order upon authorities of inferior quality."[198] But Schellhorn's complaints and protestations in the end made little difference, especially to the Jewish question. Suspended in November 1941, the deportations were resumed in 1942 with scant regard for their economic consequences. By 1942 Schellhorn's predictions had come to pass, and Bukovina's economy was struggling: "the current situation," he insisted, "could have been avoided by promoting a more rational policy."[199]

Over five thousand more Jews from Cernăuţi were sent to Transnistria in the summer of 1942, in the second large wave of deportations.[200] These resumed on June 7; a thousand more Jews were deported on June 14, and another two thousand on June 28.[201] After the first trains rolled out of Cernăuţi, rumors about the impending deportations spread, and people went into hiding. Gendarmes supplied with lists of names of people to transport to the train station could not find the individuals they were looking for. Some trains left Cernăuţi half empty.[202] Gendarmes then grabbed Jews randomly in the streets "to make sure the wagons wouldn't be left empty like before." Once the trains were filled, they sent the extras back home—recalling them later when it turned out they had overestimated the number of people left on the trains.[203] The victims included not only those who had received authorizations from Mayor Popovici—who had fallen from grace that summer—but also people with authorizations from Governor Calotescu.[204]

## Birds of Prey

When the Jews who had been "collected, evacuated, and stationed" in Dorohoi in preparation for their deportation were finally sent to Transnistria in November 1941, local police reported that "the Romanians will thus regain their ethnic rights, to which they aspired for so long. Their hopes are that the entire Jewish problem in this district will be resolved and the Romanianization that has been awaited for so long will be extended to every domain of public life."[205] By "Romanianization," officials meant the confiscation of Jewish property by the Romanian state. The confiscated property, however, quickly disappeared into the pockets of private individuals. A few hours after the ghetto had been established in Cernăuţi, gentiles streamed in to grab whatever they could lay their hands on, often for laughably low prices: "Christians, profiteers," as Isak Weissglas later recalled, "bought up for next to nothing the poor Jews' last pieces of gold, rings, clothing."[206] The few things people inside the ghetto had managed to salvage slowly disappeared too, bartered for food: "for one kilo of salami one would hand over a manteau, for one kilo of butter you would hand over a complete suit, for a few eggs you would hand over silk shirts."[207]

The scent of these riches attracted gold-diggers and opportunists. Old Kingdom Romanians dropped their lucrative jobs and rushed to Cernăuţi with spacious suitcases to fill with whatever goods fell into their laps. "There were people one would never have suspected of being birds of prey," Mircu wrote, "who left weekly or even more often, on an expedition [...] to Cernăuţi, from where they brought to Bucharest suitcases filled with all kinds of objects such as chandeliers, cutlery, cigarette holders, jewelry, of silver or gold, stolen from Jewish homes, from synagogues, from stores."[208] Civil servants newly arrived from Romania "occupied multiple apartments, houses they found abandoned but furnished with everything necessary."[209] "The ladies who came into the ghetto with simple, used coats would leave with astrakhan furs."[210] Though they preferred to call themselves liberators, locals called them "Californians," because they were like "gold seekers in California, who after having gathered a quantity of gold would leave, having absolutely no interest in what would remain in their wake."[211]

Bukovina's Soviet legacies worked to the gold-diggers' advantage. During their year of rule in northern Bukovina, the Soviets had expropriated, confiscated, and redistributed property. Locals had taken advantage of the regime change to blackmail each other into handing over possessions. One family's maid in Cernăuţi had threatened to turn them in to the NKVD unless they gave her all their money. When the Romanian authorities returned, they searched the maid's house and found the goods she had amassed, "including valuable carpets, [and] a collection of crystal objects."[212] Such experiences were then seen to legitimize the asset grabs the Romanians now carried out, as people sought to enrich themselves with property they claimed had once belonged to them. Two pig merchants and a lieutenant in Bukovina made a fortune visiting local "auction commissions" and amassing goods this way, including 106 large woolen carpets, eleven sewing machines, nineteen large beds, fifty-four chairs, "a lot of dishes," silver forks and knives, and eighty-four quilts, "some of them of very expensive silk." To remove suspicion, the robbers donated 100,000 lei "for the reunification loan" and supplied the Romanian administration with free pigs.[213]

New Romanianization laws further destabilized the concept of private property by making property rights dependent on race. A law from September 1941 stipulated that "the mobile goods of deported Jews are to be considered without an owner and consequently enter into the patrimony of the state."[214] Rural properties confiscated from deported Jews were to be distributed among Romanian peasants.[215] It was also the Romanianization office's task to send "Jews whose residence is demanded by a Christian tenant to live in the Jewish quarter." Cernăuţi's mayor Traian Popovici, who authorized some Jewish families to reclaim apartments confiscated by gentiles, was the exception. "I cannot accept," Governor Calotescu reprimanded him, "that if a Jewish home was assigned to a Christian, you should evacuate the Christian so the Jew can come in [. . .]. The rights of Jews to their residence will be respected to the same extent that the Jews respected the rights of Romanians and the Romanian nation."[216] Calotescu warned other functionaries that they would be "severely punished if they [did] not inform him of illegal interventions on behalf of Jews."[217]

Few people waited for official permission to grab Jewish property. "It wasn't necessary to write a petition," the Jewish journalist Marius Mircu recalled. "You could first occupy the factory or store you liked, and then petition for it."[218] Anything could be claimed for Romanianization, from lightbulbs to underwear. A certain Professor Mandiuc visited his former student Isaak Ehrlich on the eve of Ehrlich's deportation to Transnistria to ask for his overcoat, since "you will all be deported to the Ukraine, and you will not survive. You must give me your coat, I was your professor."[219] The Orthodox Metropolitan of Suceava petitioned Governor Calotescu to "assign part of the bedlinen left after the evacuation of Jews to meet the needs of twenty persons—members of the association of priests."[220] The Gouvernement of Bukovina appropriated "candle-shaped light bulbs" from Jewish synagogues in Cernăuţi for the "chandeliers of the Gouvernement Palace," as well as for Calotescu's private residence.[221] The Suceava police found Jewish residences after deportations completely "ravaged" by "unidentified individuals who went into the homes of evacuated Jews and stole things."[222] Often the guards tasked with protecting confiscated Jewish property themselves broke the seals and pocketed goods. One official used his position to draw up "fictional sale documents" proving that he had "bought furniture from the house that used to be the property of the Jew Moses Snap." In October 1941 an official in Vijniţa, where 90 percent of Jewish residences lay empty, reported that "every day numerous thefts are committed, the majority of them by breaking in through the windows or doors sealed by the local city hall."[223]

Given the speed with which Jewish property disappeared, the Romanian authorities feared that "if we don't proceed to take into custody or sell these homes with all the goods left behind, we will lose many of the things left over from the Jews."[224] "I often blushed when I was informed of the breaking of seals," Governor Calotescu admitted, "the transportation of furniture from one place to another, violations of other people's residences."[225] In Cernăuţi and Bukovina, he said, "a terrible battle is being fought against honor and organization by rascals who want to lay their hands on things and get rich."[226] As "liberators," they felt entitled to lay claim to "a central residence, lush furniture, and everything."[227]

Far from unaware of these facts, General Antonescu in Bucharest sought to weed out corrupt individuals. Governor Calotescu himself was dismissed in March 1945 on corruption charges, but other functionaries found ways to circumvent Antonescu's attempts to enforce discipline. Civil servants defied a ban on administrative staff purchasing land in Bukovina by putting property in their wives' names.[228] Even Romanians who expected to benefit from the restoration of Romanian sovereignty in northern Bukovina ended up falling victim to the new authorities' corruption and greed. Refugees who had fled northern Bukovina in 1940 returned to find "their residences were occupied by functionaries, military, or various persons who neither owned homes nor had lived in Cernăuţi before."[229] German counselor Ellgering recalled "situations in which the refugee without a home was invited by friends to dinner, and there noticed that he was being served on porcelain plates and in crystal glasses that had once belonged to him."[230] Moreover, returning refugees were scandalized to find former Soviet collaborators and Communists who "still remained in place or regained their functions by intervening with influential people."[231] A self-described "good Romanian" informed Bukovina's governor that "being in Cernăuţi to do my Christmas shopping a few days ago, I was greatly amazed to see one of the best known and greatest advocates and agitators of Communism walking down the streets of Cernăuţi." "Mister governor," the plaintiff continued, "we who took refuge, leaving behind the little we had saved through honest work, but which for us is a fortune, we are hurt when we see these scoundrels were not deported to the place they deserve so well."[232]

Romanian refugees who returned to Bukovina expected to be compensated for their sufferings with administrative positions and other favors. Instead, these positions were handed over to Old Kingdom Romanians who had gotten there first. Old resentments returned with a vengeance. As V. Dimitriuc, a former government minister for oil and mining and a native of Bukovina wrote, "the unanimous complaint of all Bukovinans was that they were completely ignored by the administration of Bukovina and can't participate in their own home either in the administration or economic life," even though they were "better prepared than the extremely weak elements coming from the Old Kingdom."[233] Several associations of "Bukovinan volunteers from the war of unification" wrote to Antonescu to demand that "Bukovinans not be excluded from the work of reorganizing this province," because "they are tied body and soul to this corner of the country [. . .], know better than anyone else the surroundings and local needs, and think they have the right to participate in leading the reorganization and reconstruction of Romanian life [there]."[234]

Romanians in Bukovina were also displeased with the pace of Romanianization in the province. The task of undoing the "Jewish economic and social takeover" that allegedly stood in the way of Bukovina's reconstruction fell within the Directorate for Romanianization's purview. Yet here too, Old Kingdom "liberators" were first in line.[235] Even more frustrating to Bukovinan Romanians was the Directorate's lukewarm approach to Romanianization, which seemed to suggest the Romanian state was still too weak to do anything of consequence. On learning that Romanian dignitaries "intervened so that certain Jews of great material status should remain in Bukovina," the Association of War Volunteers in Bukovina denounced these "anti-national acts" in a letter of protest to Mihai Antonescu.[236] Returning Romanian refugees also sent the authorities in Cernăuţi letters of complaint about the fact that "all services in the locality from restaurants, butcher shops, and other enterprises—all staff are only Jews." While "foreigners" got to keep their positions, they complained, "Romanians walk around the streets unable to find any kind of post, since all of them are taken by Jews." As late as 1943 there were complaints that "there exists almost no enterprise that is not dominated either by the Jewish element or the Ukrainian one."[237]

The reality of Bukovina meant that the Directorate for Romanianization's task was in fact an impossible one. Despite their eagerness to purge the province of "foreigners," Romanian authorities found that the Romanian population's economic wellbeing was inextricably bound up with that of Bukovina's Jews.[238] After Cernăuţi's Jews were pushed into a ghetto and deported, food supplies plummeted and prices rocketed, as there were "no Christian merchants to replace them."[239] Three months after the first round of deportations from Cernăuţi had ended, the police reported that "even simple city residents are amazed that there used to be so many professionals among Jews."[240] When Suceava's Jews were deported, the city's economy similarly crashed, "hurting above all Romanians in the city, who due to their precarious material situation didn't have sufficient provisions for an extended period of time."[241] The authorities felt they had no choice but to invite some Jewish professionals to reclaim their posts, "since the situation in this province is completely different from that of the rest of the country" and "the use of Jewish labor is necessary for a certain period of time both for economic development and to instruct new Christian elements that are meant to replace them."[242]

With no middle class of their own, no skilled workers or specialists to take over the positions Jews had held, Romanians in Bukovina were forced to choose between "Jewish" services and no services. As Theo Ellgering noted in October 1942, in places like Rădăuţi and Câmpulung, where "a hundred percent of crafts and commerce were in Jewish hands," one could no longer find "doctors and pharmacists." "All stores where peasants used to buy goods" were now closed, and there were no more tailors, shoemakers, or electricians. No "horseshoes or nails for horseshoes" could be found.[243] Bad as things had been for Romanian peasants, they were now significantly worse. "Villagers say it was hard with the Jews," a procurator from Suceava reported, "but now it's even worse, for nobody takes any interest in them, except for when the state demands their lives to defend its borders, their labor, horses and carts, requisitioning, taxes on their fields, taxes to the state and commune."[244]

## Transnistria

Waves of Jewish deportees crossed into Transnistria during the summer and fall of 1941. Having disposed of them, the Romanian gendarmerie left the deportees unguarded and unprovided for.[245] As more deportees congregated in the Wehrmacht's rear, German authorities grew anxious about the security threat.[246] In August 1941 German border guards began driving Jewish deportee convoys back into Romanian territory.[247] Antonescu ordered them pushed back across the Dniester again. Thousands of Jewish deportees were sent back and forth repeatedly. The Romanian authorities expelled them through Moghilev and Chişinău; the Germans sent them back at Iampol and Kamianets-Podilskyi.[248] Of the twenty-five thousand Jewish deportees the Romanians sent into German-occupied territories across the Dniester in July 1941, only 16,500 returned. The rest were shot by German and Romanian guards and gendarmerie while being shuttled back and forth across the river.[249] Eventually German gendarmes and bridge guards were instructed not to allow Jewish deportees from Romania into German-administered territory under any circumstances. The German authorities closed all major river crossings, including at Moghilev. After Romanian gendarmes rerouted the deportees to the south, the Germans closed the southern crossings too.[250] Unable to rid themselves of the "returned" Jewish deportees, the Romanian authorities concentrated them in transit camps. In Vertujeni, Mărculeşti, Edineţi, and Secureni freshly arrived deportees from Bukovina joined the Jewish inmates awaiting deportation further east.[251]

The pressure on the transit camps was only relieved after the Germans transferred authority over the territory between the Dniester and Dnieper rivers (Transnistria) to Antonescu's administration. According to the Tighina Agreement of August 28–30, 1941 the territory became a zone of Romanian occupation that Antonescu saw as a "holding station" and eventually a "dumping ground" for deportees from Bukovina and Bessarabia.[252] By the late 1941 Transnistria held more than eighty-six thousand Jewish deportees—a population that kept growing.[253] Ideally, these deportees were to be expelled further east into German-occupied territory, enabling the Romanian administration to begin their work of transforming Transnistria into a paragon of Romanian civilization and living proof of Romania's modernity. "We pursue in Transnistria an important political goal," Antonescu said. "We need to demonstrate in the face of history, in the face of humanity, and in the face of even our own country that we are able to administer ourselves."[254]

For the time being, however, expelling the deportees further east was not an option. The Tighina Convention, aside from granting Romania jurisdiction over Transnistria, also established that "the evacuation of Jews across the Bug river is not possible at the moment.[255] Therefore they must be concentrated inside labor camps and put to work until the cessation of hostilities when it will be possible to move them east."[256] Although the Romanians still hoped in the long term to deport the Jews in Transnistria's over two hundred ghettos and camps further east, in the short term they had to keep them there.[257] Yet they had made no preparations to provide food and accommodation for these large numbers.[258] The chief military prosecutor General Topor lamented that "there is no one to guard [the deportees]. There is no one to feed them. Please tell us what to do with these Jews."[259]

Disease spread like wildfire among the deportees, housed in pigsties, barns, and abandoned collective farm buildings with no windows or doors.[260] As Felicia Gininger, a survivor, recalled, "we went to the Dniester to drink water. The water was red with blood. In the river there were corpses."[261] Those who made it across the river were forced to march for many miles to the camps. They were left in open fields in freezing weather to feed on frozen potatoes.[262] On arriving in Iampol, Musja Gottfried was sent to live in a pigsty with Jews who had been deported earlier. She saw a woman lying on the floor, "still alive" but who "could no longer walk and who could also not speak due to fear. The rats were eating a piece of flesh from her body."[263] Another survivor, who landed up in Mărculeşti, recalled how after he lay down on the floor, "mice and rats ran over our heads."[264] A couple of bank officials who had been sent to Transnistria to buy valuables from the deportees attested to the abominable conditions in the camps: "mice swarmed in the thousands down the dirt alleys and through the houses, the flies, in a totally inordinate number, were extremely tiresome" and "the corpses of the deportees were lying everywhere, in cellars, in ditches, in courtyards."[265]

Whether one survived was almost entirely a matter of chance, but the locals' attitude could make the difference between life and death. Some survivors recalled that locals at markets where they went to barter their few remaining possessions sometimes offered help,[266] usually because they "wanted valuables or cheap labor in exchange for clothes, shelter, bedding."[267] Some Bukovinan Jewish women survived by sewing or doing housework for Ukrainians who shared food with them in exchange.[268] Lydia Harnik from Cernăuţi was saved by a Ukrainian Communist who found her lying in a ditch, half-starved, and offered her food and shelter in exchange for German lessons so he could read "Marx and Engels in the original."[269] Cilli Förster, who ended up in the ghetto of Moghilev, remembered that the peasants around were sympathetic but hard to make contact with.[270] There were also instances—perhaps more numerous—when locals were hostile, unwilling to share the little bread they had with the deportees.[271] Sabina Rüber wrote in her diary that a Jewish girl in Moghilev so hungry she could barely walk asked a Ukrainian woman at the market for bread. The woman shooed her away: "Off with you, Juda! Am I to give bread to you?" "The hatred of Jews is in their blood," Rüber concluded, "they cannot drop it, just as the cat can't let go of the mouse." Survivors singled out the Ukrainian militia for their unusual brutality. "We are in the hands of the Ukrainian militia and that is as good as being outlawed," Rüber wrote; "a civilized person cannot even imagine what brutality and cruelty these militiamen are capable of."[272]

It also mattered whether one ended up in a camp run by a ruthless commander or one who could be bribed.[273] Fortunately for the deportees, the Romanian camp administration was filled with individuals who took bribes in exchange for allowing deportees' relatives to send them "money, clothes, and underwear."[274] Typically, local peasant couriers who took letters, money, and food into the camps got to keep 10 percent of the value they transported to Transnistria. If they could present the sender proof that the package had landed in the hands of its intended recipient, they could get an additional 20–30 percent upon their return.[275] Josip Bursuk's family received letters from relatives deported to Transnistria by way of a German officer who "came to their home with letters written in Yiddish so the Germans couldn't read them."[276]

FIGURE 8.3. Map of Transnistria, September 1, 1943, showing the number of Jews per district and locality who had been deported from Bessarabia and Bukovina. United States Holocaust Memorial Museum, courtesy of Romanian National Archives.

Survival rates were higher where food distribution and hygiene were organized by a Jewish ghetto or camp committee.[277] Nowhere were deportees better organized than in Moghilev, which by 1943 had become the largest ghetto in Transnistria.[278] Over half of all Jewish deportees from Bukovina ended up there. Mortality rates were higher in camps such as Pechora and Vapniarka, or the short-lived agricultural camp Scaținęț, where Jewish deportees were fed a soup made of toxic peas that caused paralysis, killing most of them within a month and a half of their arrival.[279] Many Jewish community leaders from Bukovina ended up in Moghilev, including Siegfried Jägendorf, born into an Orthodox Jewish family in Cernăuți and educated in Vienna.[280] An engineer and former director of the German Siemens-Schukert factory in Rădăuți, Jägendorf ended up in Moghilev with some 6,500 Jews deported from Rădăuți in October 1941.[281] He believed the deportees should make themselves useful to the Romanians, who desperately needed a workforce to "rebuild the city, clean up ruins, restore factories and industries destroyed by war and flooding."[282]

Romanian authorities in Moghilev assented to Jägendorf's request to restore an old Soviet iron foundry in the city. For the thirteen thousand Jewish families who worked at the "Turnătoria" producing iron stoves, the foundry was a godsend. As Jägendorf's employees they enjoyed some protection, as the authorities respected his technical expertise.[283] Jägendorf furthermore capitalized, for as long as he could, on the upbringing he shared with the first head of the Romanian administration in Moghilev, a fellow Bukovinan who had also fought in the Austrian army in World War I. Jägendorf did not hesitate to display his status to his fellow deportees. One recalled that "it was not unusual for Jägendorf to arrive at the Turnătoria wearing an expensive new hat or jacket. Every day at lunchtime he would walk to his house and sit down to a good meal, served to him by his wife and the other women in his household." In some deportees' eyes, Jägendorf became morally suspect. While he secured protection and improved living conditions for many deportees' families, he was also a mouthpiece and mediator for the Romanian authorities in Moghilev, doing their bidding by conscripting Jews for forced labor.[284]

Whether one ended up in a camp on the Romanian or German side of the Dniester could also make the difference between life and death. Although Transnistria was technically under Romanian jurisdiction, the German authorities reserved the right to intervene. Periodically, German officials from the Reichskommissariat Ukraine crossed the Bug river into Romanian-occupied territories and rounded up inmates for forced labor on the German side. Few if any of these deportees ever returned. Isak Weissglas, who was interned at the stone quarry camp Cariera de Piatră with his family, witnessed several such raids in the camp run by Romanian officials.[285] The day after the German authorities paid a surprise visit to Cariera de Piatră, Romanian camp officials had to send a group of gendarmes and deportees to the Bug to "fish out the bodies of those killed by the Germans while crossing the river."[286] By November 1943 over 1,500 Jews held in Transnistria had been kidnapped and taken across the Bug. Many were from Cernăuţi and Dorohoi, including the poet Paul Celan's parents.[287] Not knowing what lay in store, and believing they would be safer among people who spoke their language—German—some deportees at Cariera de Piatră, on the Romanian side, fantasized about conditions in German-run camps. Those who could afford it even paid substantial bribes to get camp officials to put them on the list for deportation to the German side.[288]

There were also survivors who owed their lives to the preferential treatment they received from German officials. Selig Ascher Hofer, who had been deported to Moghilev and Şargorod from Cernăuţi, was saved by a German soldier, a fellow Bukovinan who had gone to Germany with the Heim ins Reich

Aktion, then joined the Wehrmacht in its eastward trek, landing up in Transnistria.[289] Hedwig Brenner was also helped by a German officer who provided her with "groceries, bread, soap, and other things" because, like him, she had graduated from the Deutsche Technische Hochschule in Prague in 1936.[290] Romanians were "revolted by German soldiers" who went out of their way to protect Jews.[291]

Some Bukovinan Jews clung to old ideas about the superiority of German culture and civilization despite much evidence to the contrary. Many decades later Rosa Roth-Zuckermann, whose entire family perished in Transnistria, admitted that "until today I will want to believe that no cultivated and truly sensible people took part in these horrors, but only the mob. And the Romanians were in general less civilized and less cultivated."[292] Some Bukovinan Jews came out of the war convinced that "the German language saved us."[293] So strong was the attachment of Cernăuți's Jews to German culture that they could not conceive that what had befallen them had been initiated by the Germans. Manfred Hilsenrath recalled in his memoirs that "German soldiers didn't behave in a hostile way" in Transnistria because they discovered "an entire colony of people who spoke German in the middle of Ukraine."[294] Severin Schrajer, another survivor, confessed that "I cannot hate the Germans even though they exterminated everyone, I cannot hate them, because that would mean hating myself. No one ever understood that on the inside I am a German and only in the documents am I Jewish."[295]

In fact, the deportees' fates were shaped less by the German or by the Romanian authorities than by the interactions between them across the border that demarcated their separate zones of occupation. The two sets of authorities failed to coordinate with and often circumvented each other. Tensions rose when the Romanian authorities, defying explicit German orders, continued expelling deportees across the Bug even as late as the summer of 1942, when five thousand Jews were deported from Cernăuți beyond the river.[296] When the Germans sent the deportees back, Romanian officials concentrated them in transit camps such as Bogdanovca, Acmecetca, and Domanevka. The ban on further expulsions created a "bottleneck" in areas with large populations of ethnic Germans, who now felt threatened by their growing proximity to the disease-ridden deportees.[297] The consequences were disastrous for the Bukovinan Jews caught in between and who had "had taken from them in Ukraine everything they owned. They have nothing available to prepare food, each person cooks in the house where they are staying. There is a shortage of medicines."[298]

Sonderkommando-R, a special detachment sent from Germany in September 1941 to consolidate ethnic German communities in former Soviet territories, alarmed by the threat of contagion, took it upon itself to intercept and divert convoys of Jewish deportees, through murder if necessary.[299] By

December 1941 the Sk-R had shot fifty-two thousand Jews along the Bug, gradually turning from being an ethnic defense organization into a "frontline killing formation."[300] The Romanians continued sending Jewish deportees their way, no doubt to take advantage of their free "services." In February 1942 tens of thousands of Jews were still crossing the Bug into German-occupied territory unaccompanied by Romanian guards.[301] In April Adolf Eichmann warned the Romanian authorities that their disorderly expulsions endangered ethnic Germans in Transnistria and threatened to disrupt the overall flow of deportations across Europe.[302]

Ion Antonescu remained committed to expelling Jews from Bukovina (and Bessarabia), but once it became clear, after the battle of Stalingrad, that Germany might lose the war, he began changing course. In a Council of Ministers meeting on October 13, 1942 Vice-President Mihai Antonescu officially suspended deportations to Transnistria.[303] What precisely caused this sudden turnaround remains unclear.[304] The "commissioner general" tasked with solving Romania's "Jewish question," Radu Lecca, went to Berlin to meet with Eichmann. German officials spurned him, and he returned to Bucharest feeling humiliated. Several official warnings from Britain and the United States, as well as a round of protest letters from the papal nuncio and Swiss chargé d'affaires, gave Antonescu to understand that Romania would pay for its crimes after the war.[305] He had the good sense to temper his anti-Jewish policies and began encouraging Jewish emigration to Palestine and allowing some Jewish deportees in Transnistria to repatriate themselves, beginning in 1943.[306]

Where exactly the "repatriated" deportees were supposed to go was far from clear. Rural areas cleansed of Jews were too dangerous. As one Gouvernement official remarked, locals had a "marked anti-Semitic spirit, especially following the last concessions made to the Jews, the schools, the return from Transnistria."[307] The Jewish Central Office in Bucharest urged the Romanian administration not to send Jewish survivors back to places where "their lives would be under threat, for their goods seem to have been appropriated."[308] Governor Dragalina himself acknowledged that resettling survivors in "rural Bukovina" or in "Moldova or other parts of the country where there are already local Jews" might cause "a series of discontents."[309] Those who made it back to Cernăuți often found strangers living in their apartments and wearing their clothes. Having confiscated not only the deportees' belongings but their entire lives, these people did not take kindly to the survivors' return. So painful was one man's homecoming that he came to regret having survived Transnistria. "What is going on in Bukovina ever since the deportees returned," he wrote, "surpasses everything. This is the first time that I regret we even survived." "One cannot create any kind of coexistence with provocations and terror from the peasant population," he concluded in May 1945.[310]

Besides the terror of living amidst people who hated them, survivors who returned to Bukovina and those who stayed in Transnistria after the Romanian administration's withdrawal faced the terror of another so-called liberation by the Red Army. They did not all survive to experience it, however, for the German Eighth Army murdered people and devastated villages on their retreat through Bukovina. Meanwhile, the incoming Red Army treated all German-speakers it encountered, including Jewish survivors, with suspicion.[311] Meier Teich, who remained in Transnistria after the Romanians abandoned it in February 1944, survived the German retreat only to be imprisoned by the NKVD.[312] The Soviets immediately began recruiting other surviving Bukovinans into the Red Army and sending them back to the front. Many young Jewish survivors who had just returned from Transnistria, traumatized and emaciated, now donned a Soviet uniform and began fighting the Germans. Men and women in northern Bukovina were rounded up in the streets and sent to the Donbas as forced labor in the coal mines. Some survivors were denied entry into Cernăuţi because they lacked identification documents.[313] For many survivors of Transnistria's camps, liberation spelled the beginning of a new era of subjugation.[314]

---

During the weeks leading up to Bukovina's liberation by the Red Army, the Communist underground resurfaced, reinvigorated by a growing number of Bukovinans who joined the partisans. Among them were many Ukrainian nationalists who, disenchanted with both Nazi Germany and their own organization, were leaving the OUN and joining "Communist bands of partisans."[315] While the Germans had proved that they had "no intention to create an independent Ukrainian state," the Soviets still seemed open to collaboration.[316] Ukrainians outside the OUN "express[ed] the opinion that under the Soviet regime they enjoyed all kinds of freedoms, especially cultural ones" and that "back then almost all the leaders used to be Ukrainian."[317] The Soviets had also been dropping parachutists behind enemy lines to "fill the gaps" within partisan ranks "destroyed by the German troops."[318] When the Romanian authorities evacuated northern Bukovina again in March 1944, local Communists hoisted the red flag on top of the city hall in Cernăuţi well before the Red Army arrived.[319]

Once again, Bukovinans had front-row seats for a terrifying spectacle. As the Soviets advanced into Central Europe, people in Cernăuţi would "put their measuring tape to the map and calculate how many kilometers there are from the place where the front had got to and us." "If this arrow [the Soviets] reaches Cernăuţi," General Antonescu warned, "then the front is broken, the gate to

Central Europe is open, and the two branches of the German army—the northern one cut off at the Baltic Sea, the southern one at the Black Sea—will be trapped, and then disaster awaits the Germans."[320] That spring all Cernăuţi watched as large groups of German soldiers, emaciated, exhausted, desperate, retreated through Bukovina, killing and stealing and striking terror into everyone's hearts. Cernăuţi's Jews, including those recently back from Transnistria, "locked themselves up in their houses, cellars, and attics," desperate to save their lives and possessions even if "after four years of hunger and unemployment, nobody had anything left."[321]

As in 1940, the Romanian administration and army were caught unprepared. Even though General Antonescu had considered the possibility of a German defeat since at least 1942, Romania continued fighting loyally on Germany's side. And as in 1940, no provision was made to evacuate the civilian population from northern Bukovina. Most Romanians were left behind, but only in part because the "wagons and personal trains" available for the job were "insufficient to satisfy the needs of the population panicked by the evacuation."[322] Antonescu had decided it was "against our interests" to evacuate the Romanian population from northern Bukovina: keeping northern Bukovina's ethnic makeup intact would permit Romania to lay claim to it at a future peace conference.[323] In January 1944 he instructed Governor Dragalina to keep both people and resources in place, including "all the industry we don't absolutely have to transport to the west."[324] Antonescu also thought Romanians would refuse to leave northern Bukovina because "they don't detach themselves too easily from their homes."[325]

Faced with another Soviet occupation, many Romanians in northern Bukovina were convinced that the Bolsheviks, if they came back, would "exterminate them either by deporting them deep into the Russian steppes or by killing them for having made a pact with the Romanians."[326] Some Bukovinan personalities, including former mayor Traian Popovici, appealed to the authorities to save Romanians through a timely evacuation. In a memorandum from February 1944, they pleaded "that you please embrace warmly our case, ordering that all the necessary, timely measures be taken to evacuate the entire population which by no means wishes to come to a tragic end under the knout of the invading executioner."[327]

Left without official help, Bukovinans began evacuating themselves. They loaded up their belongings on carts and crossed into Romania even though they had little idea where they were headed and how they would fare there. "The Romanian population and functionaries of all kinds," the Cernăuţi police reported in February 1944, "tried by all means to evacuate their movable goods and homes and families into the country's interior."[328] "Heads of institutions," industrialists, and merchants had their possessions transported to the Old

Kingdom for "enormous sums of money."[329] People desperate to leave threatened to "throw themselves into the waters of the Prut" if guards stopped them at the border. Others vowed they wanted to "die with the cross at their heads and not with the Soviet star."[330] The authorities turned a deaf ear to these pleas and did what they had planned, evacuating only themselves. From this experience, many Bukovinans drew the familiar conclusion that Bucharest did not care about them. The botched evacuation proved yet again that "the so-called great work of national reconstruction of this province suffered the most lamentable failures precisely because the Bukovinan element was never listened to."[331] It was yet another tragedy that could have been avoided had Bucharest lent the provinces its ear.

The Bukovinans who ended up in Romania secured some physical safety but were tormented by homesickness and the feeling of being unwanted and looked down upon. They were no longer "locals," but refugees, a burden on the state, begrudged by their hosts. Civil servants who had spent fortunes relocating their families from Bukovina to the Old Kingdom found they "were doomed to starve to death because of the surplus of functionaries" or because "life there was too expensive and the authorities in the Regat didn't offer any help."[332]

Those who stayed behind also understood that their lives would no longer be the same. One Romanian peasant, Paraskiva Moldovan, fearing "mortal danger," tried to cross into Romania with her two children, brother, and husband. The children got sick, so she hid in the forest for two weeks to care for them. When both children perished, she decided to go back home to northern Bukovina. "On the one hand, I was afraid to go back home, because I thought the Red Army would kill me, but on the other hand, I felt so sorry to leave my house and decided to return."[333]

As she and many others soon discovered, returning home was impossible. The war and a new Soviet "liberation" permanently altered Bukovina. To survive, one had to learn how to live in a new place and era, even more ruthless and uncompromising than those that came before.

# Epilogue

BY APRIL 1944, northern Bukovina was once again in Soviet hands. Unlike in eastern Ukraine, where the Soviet regime had time to develop local roots, here the returning Soviets encountered an ambivalent, even hostile population.[1] The Bukovinan branch of the OUN had gone underground but continued to contest Soviet authority. Soviet officials were equally worried about "Cuzists" (supporters of the former National-Christian Defense League, or LANC) and Iron Guardists in Bukovina. Before they could fully reintegrate northern Bukovina into Soviet Ukraine, the authorities needed to bring these hostile elements under control, which they planned to do through a new wave of purges.[2] These reflected the Soviet regime's fear of foreign infiltration as World War II morphed into the Cold War and Stalin grew increasingly worried about perceived Western plans to dominate Eastern Europe.[3] Indeed, in 1946 the Soviets found evidence of American support for nationalist-insurrectionist groups in Ukraine.[4]

The new round of counter-insurgency operations, which were not completed until the early 1950s, were carried out against the backdrop of a difficult postwar reconstruction process. The war brought the resurgence of nationalism across the region and led to the emergence of a "new assertive citizen" who felt entitled to some measure of autonomy in return for the sacrifices made during the war.[5] In many areas of Soviet Ukraine the war had also led to the dissolution of collective farms and the re-emergence of private property.[6] Though tolerated during the war, these developments were now considered destabilizing and targeted for rollback. In 1946 private property was recriminalized, and in 1948 Stalin launched a recollectivization campaign in western Ukraine that led to severe shortages and famine.[7]

At the same time, the Soviets bolstered their claim to western Ukraine through a narrative of the war that emphasized the Red Army's role in liberating this territory from Nazi rule.[8] Other elements of the local experience of war were de-emphasized, including the victimization of Jews and participation of non-Communists in the anti-fascist resistance. In northern Bukovina, the

FIGURE 9.1. Chernivtsi Victory Stele monument to fallen Red Army Soldiers in World War II. Such monuments to Soviet liberation sprung up all over western Ukraine after the war. AlexeIA / Alamy Stock Photo.

Soviets built monuments to the province's liberation by the Red Army. On the side of the road leading from the train station to Chernivtsi's center, they placed a Soviet tank on a pedestal, allegedly the tank General Nikitin drove into Chernivtsi on March 25, 1944. In the city's central park they erected a memorial to General Bobriev and other officers who liberated the province. Later, the authorities commissioned a monument to the Komsomol youth who resisted "the fascists" and were executed by the Romanians in 1942, which they placed in the predominantly Romanian Gertsa (Herţa, in Romanian) district. Soviet generals and members of the local Communist resistance were always the heroes of official Soviet narratives of World War II. Resistance members with foreign-sounding names proved inconvenient and were quickly forgotten about. So was the specificity of Jewish suffering.[9]

Some wartime developments, however, helped the Soviet effort to restore their power and authority in northern Bukovina. As a province of Soviet Ukraine, postwar Bukovina was expected to look and feel Ukrainian—or Soviet Ukrainian, at least. This was a less far-fetched notion in 1944 than it had been in 1940, as the war had made Bukovina more ethnically homogeneous. Over ninety-six thousand ethnic Germans left Bukovina in 1940 through the Heim ins Reich Aktion. Some sixty thousand to eighty thousand Bukovinan Germans were scattered across Europe, many still in displaced persons' camps. Many ethnic Romanians had fled northern Bukovina with the Romanian administration in the spring of 1944, and many more crossed the border into Romania well into 1947, when it was officially closed. From then on, as Marianne Hirsch and Leo Spitzer write, "every departure from Czernowitz was an adventure, an act of outwitting an arbitrary system based on suspicion, intimidation, and punishment, carried out by officials who themselves oftentimes did not believe in the laws they were supposed to enforce."[10]

Almost two thirds of Bukovina's prewar Jewish community perished during the war, yet Jewish survival rates were higher in Bukovina than the rest of Eastern Europe.[11] Some thirty thousand Jews were still alive in Transnistria at the time of liberation, while some seventeen thousand had survived in Chernivtsi. In fact, on arriving, the Red Army was taken aback by how many Jews still lived there.[12] In April 1944 the local party leader Ivan Zeleniuk estimated that Jews still made up 42 percent of Chernivtsi's population. An NKVD report from June 1944 counted 23,213 Jews in Chernivtsi—or 53 percent of the city's inhabitants.[13] Their numbers swelled as more survivors returned from Transnistria, some riding Soviet military trucks or peasant carts, others walking all three hundred kilometers back. Soviet patrols posted on the bridge over the Prut river turned away individuals who lacked identification documents or travel papers.[14] Since most survivors had had these documents confiscated or destroyed, they had to sneak back into Chernivtsi at night.

Although the war had ended, anti-Jewish sentiment persisted and conditions were extremely difficult. Jewish survivors from rural areas could not go home to villages where entire Jewish communities had been destroyed. This was especially the case in regions where the guerrilla war between Ukrainian nationalists and the Soviet authorities was in full swing. Chernivtsi seemed like the safest option, although life there was far from easy. Exhausted and malnourished, survivors stood in line for bread. Things worsened when the Soviets began recruiting "volunteers" to labor in the coal mines of Donbas. People who had barely recovered from the ordeals of Transnistria now feared being picked up in the street and shipped off to do forced labor. Males over

FIGURE 9.2. Marcel Koller posing with three friends from a Young Pioneers school in Cernăuţi after his family's return from Transnistria, 1946. United States Holocaust Memorial Museum, courtesy of Mark Mordechai Koller.

eighteen years of age could be immediately sent back to the front lines to fight the tail end of the war. Amid this chaos, survivors tried to build a community. In 1945 Soviet officials counted no fewer than twenty-four functioning synagogues in the Chernivtsi region, most in the city. That year, a new yeshiva opened in Chernivtsi.[15] But this brief Jewish renaissance could not last.

Soviet officials felt that Chernivtsi's large Jewish presence was at cross purposes with their commitment to giving northern Bukovina a Soviet Ukrainian character. As the titular nationality of Soviet Ukraine, Ukrainians should dominate the oblast's administration and culture. Yet Chernivtsi, its capital, continued to feel "Jewish-German," as Svitlana Frunchak writes.[16] The city's nineteenth-century Austrian architecture had survived the war intact, but even more than that, its large Jewish population continued to speak German. Chernivtsi's German-speaking Jews found themselves in a paradoxical position. Although they were victims of Nazism, speaking German drew the Soviet authorities' suspicion. On August 8, 1945 the Soviet government adopted a resolution allowing northern Bukovinan Jews who had been Romanian citizens before June 1940 to emigrate to Romania. Between February and April 1946 over twenty-two thousand Jews left Northern Bukovina. Though formulated in the language of rights, the resolution was in reality an "eviction" or "expulsion"—the terms the NKVD used to describe it in their internal correspondence.[17] Its objective was to remove as much of the province's prewar Jewish population as possible.

The Jewish emigrés left behind empty apartments and houses, many in highly desirable areas of Chernivtsi. This real estate was soon occupied by Soviet officials who had been eyeing it for a while.[18] The officials who made up the new Soviet administrative apparatus in Northern Bukovina were mostly Ukrainians from the eastern oblasts of Soviet Ukraine, people who identified strongly with the Soviet state and had no direct ties to Bukovina. Many took pride in their role as emissaries of an anti-fascist empire and, as William Risch writes, believed that "the Soviet Union offered the best way of life in the world." Though self-assured, the new arrivals struck old Bukovinans as impoverished, culturally backward, greedy people who were there to pocket whatever they could.

The truth was that most Soviet citizens who came to Chernivtsi were drawn to the city's location and its past. Like Lviv, Chernivtsi offered a "window on the West."[19] Igor Pomerantsev's family moved to Chernivtsi in 1953 from Chita, near Lake Baikal. A Russian-speaker from Crimea, Pomerantsev's father got a job as a writer for the *Radyanska Bukovyna* newspaper. Accustomed to Chita's long, dark nights, young Pomerantsev felt he had just been propelled "from a black-and-white movie into the far Mediterranean." Chernivtsi took his senses by storm: "I did experience a sensual shock in Czernowitz, erotic in its own childish way. I landed up in a colour movie, in a world lit by a dazzling sun, where you almost lost consciousness from the scent of the white blossom—apple, cherry, *marhul*, as they call apricots in Bukovina."[20]

To Pomerantsev and other new arrivals, living in Chernivtsi felt like living abroad while still in the Soviet Union. The city's "foreignness" was amplified by the fact that the Soviets did not erase its architectural heritage. Chernivtsi, Pomerantsev recounts, "was perhaps the only city in Ukraine, and I think the entire Soviet Union, where streets were named after figures like Goethe and Schiller. [. . .] The Soviets didn't change that, they decided to let it be."[21] Instead, they recycled urban space and built around its prewar core. That is not to say they left the city unchanged: they repurposed pre-Soviet buildings and spaces, often to jarring effect. The former Jewish Home of Culture, inaugurated on Czernowitz's Theaterplatz in 1908, was transformed into a textile workers' club. The modern Jewish synagogue (*sinahoha*) nearby became a cinema, jokingly referred to as the *kinahoha*.[22] The former Greek-Oriental cathedral became a crafts museum.[23]

The Soviets superimposed their version of Bukovina's past onto the city through artifacts and monuments that appropriated some elements of local memory while erasing others. They celebrated the local writer Olha Kobylianska as a "defender of the peasantry" and a "humanist," but made no mention of poet Paul Celan.[24] Igor Pomerantsev first heard about Celan from the Ukrainian poet Mykola Bazhan in Kyiv. "My friends and I would devour books, but we were still barbarians," he later wrote. "We had no idea what veins of gold

FIGURE 9.3. After World War II, Chernivtsi's center kept its prewar appearance. The Soviets built a new city around the old one. *Source*: https://czernowitz.ehpes.com/czernowitz8/chernovtsy/index.html.

we were trampling, what priceless ruins we walked over. We were not run-of-the-mill barbarians, of course. We had Russian, American, and French literature in us, but barbarism is the absence of memory, historical, cultural memory." Such erasures were part of the postwar Soviet project of remaking Northern Bukovina's cultural geography. Yet the province's past survived, hidden beneath its new veneer of Soviet culture. The handful of Austrian Jews still living in Chernivtsi in the 1950s gave the city the feeling of a place out of time. They were, Pomerantsev recalled, "unlike anybody else." They wore "battered dark velour hats, grey double-breasted houndstooth coats, worn-out shoes with narrow toes, matte marble-effect cufflinks, and all of their stuff was old, almost ancient [. . .]. For me Czernowitz was always this prehistoric Austrian Jew dumped by a time machine in a Soviet zoo."[25]

At the same time, a new Bukovina and Czernowitz were being born far away, in the memory and imagination of exile. The province and its capital became, in Hirsch and Spitzer's words, "an idea physically disconnected from its geographical location and tenuously dependent on the vicissitudes of personal, familial, and cultural memory."[26] Many Bukovinan Jews who left for Romania, where a Communist regime came to power in 1947, viewed their time there as a temporary stopover on the way to Israel, emigrating to Eretz-Israel with the help of the Joint and Zionist organizations, which operated relatively freely in Romania for the first few years after the war.[27] After 1947, when Romania's borders closed, emigration became much more difficult. Jews had to apply for visas repeatedly and suffered terrible consequences when their applications were denied.[28]

Those Bukovinan Jews lucky enough to make it to Israel struggled to feel at home there. They felt Israel's militant Zionists had little patience with their cultural values and disapproved of their continued attachment to the German language.[29] The writer Aharon Appelfeld, a child survivor from Bukovina, arrived in Palestine in 1946 after a couple of years in displaced persons' camps. He felt homesick and uprooted. The Hebrew language seemed to him "only good for ordering people around" so he resisted learning it and resented those who forced it upon him. At the same time, Appelfeld began forgetting his mother tongue: "My mother tongue, which I greatly loved, died within me after two years in Israel. I tried to revive it in different ways, by reading and even repeating words and sentences, but despite these efforts it still died rapidly." It was only when he joined the New Life Club, an association of Bukovinan and Galician Jewish survivors, that Appelfeld began to feel at home in Israel. And by reading the Galician-born Israeli writer Shmuel Yosef Agnon, he learned "how to carry the native homeland within oneself wherever one went and live fully within it."[30]

Similarly, ethnic Germans who had left Bukovina in 1940 struggled to make themselves at home in West Germany and the Republic of Austria. In cities like Darmstadt and Stuttgart, Bukovinan Germans formed special homeland societies. These *Landsmannschaften* aimed to represent members' interests with regard to German citizenship and financial compensation and to nurture their memories and cultural ties with the *Heimat* in the east. They trod a fine line between helping Bukovinan Germans integrate into their new homeland and allowing them to maintain their sense of distinctiveness. Some of the "repatriated" Germans were convinced that they were in fact "better Germans" than their West German counterparts, simply by virtue of having lived in Bukovina, on the outer edges of Germandom. In keeping with the German Federal Republic's *Ostpolitik*, the *Landsmannschaften* eventually reconciled themselves to the loss of Bukovina and steered their activities in a cultural direction. As Germany committed itself fully to an integrated Europe, some Bukovinan Germans began highlighting Bukovina's Europeanness to stress their own commitment to European values.[31]

## Soviet Collapse and Ukrainian Independence

The winds of change swept through Bukovina again in 1991. The Communist regime in Romania had been toppled two years earlier. When Ukrainians voted for independence in December 1991, the Soviet federal tapestry began unraveling fast.[32] The border between Northern and Southern Bukovina reopened and Bukovinans who had been living under different regimes for almost half a century came back into contact with each other. It soon became clear that Bukovinans under Soviet rule had fared better than those in the south, with residents of this Soviet provincial backwater spared many of the deprivations southern Bukovinans suffered under Nicolae Ceauşescu's dictatorship.[33] Not long after the Soviet collapse, Bukovinan exiles and tourists began streaming into Chernivtsi. They found the city they had left behind almost intact, albeit dusty and disheveled. The Communist project had left a deeper imprint on southern Bukovina's urban makeup. Drab and grey, the town of Suceava bore the marks of Ceauşescu's Chinese- and North Korean-inspired cultural revolution, which had entailed building up Romania's heavy industry and carrying out a vast urban renewal project, often at the expense of pre-Communist architecture.

With the Communist project in tatters and the Soviet Union gone, Bukovinans on both sides of the border anticipated another social revolution. In the north, Ukrainian nationalists, former Soviet dissidents, and ordinary citizens pinned their hopes for prosperity and modernization on Ukrainian independence. Like many post-imperial elites before them, they hoped that by severing the Ukrainian nation-state's ties to the Soviet empire, they could transform it from a "civilizational peripher[y] of the West" into a "sovereign entity able to communicate directly with the larger world."[34] But the improvements they imagined were slow in coming. Though sovereign and independent, Ukraine's cultural and economic ties anchored it in a vast post-Soviet space, and the young state had neither the will nor the resources to detach itself wholly from post-Soviet Russia. Many people across Ukraine still spoke Russian as their primary language, and most were bilingual. Independent Ukraine depended on Russia for patronage and economic aid in the form of heavy energy subsidies, among other things.[35] For the first decade or so after independence, Ukraine was mired in a vicious cycle of post-Soviet corruption.[36] The planned economy gave way to crony capitalism, the *nomenklatura* to the rule of the oligarchs who used government connections to merge "big business and big politics."[37] Imperial collapse and independence brought Ukraine to the brink of bankruptcy.

Ukraine's relationship with its neighbor to the south was relatively peaceful, although occasionally clouded by suspicion. In 1997, the two countries officially recognized each other's borders and signed a treaty of cooperation. Beyond a small nationalist fringe, irredentism and revanchism did not gain much political traction in Romania. Some tensions emerged after Romania revised its citizenship law in 2003 to provide ethnic Romanians living elsewhere with a fast-track to Romanian citizenship. By this point, most East European governments had moved away from old-fashioned territorial revisionism and toward reclaiming lost populations through citizenship policies favoring co-ethnics in neighboring states.[38] The change alarmed Ukrainian officials, some of whom interpreted the new citizenship law as evidence of an incipient Romanian revanchism. Worries about Romania's intentions were projected on the Romanian minority in Northern Bukovina and elsewhere in Ukraine, with Ukrainian officials increasingly worried about Romanians' reluctance to give up speaking Russian and *surzhyk* (a mixture of Romanian and Ukrainian).[39] As independent Ukraine embarked on a state-building-cum-nationalization project, ethnic Romanians in Northern Bukovina feared losing their linguistic and cultural freedoms. Bukovina risked becoming a new source of conflict between Ukraine and Romania.

The cross-border dynamic changed again after Romania joined the European Union in 2007 through the Eastern Partnership Project, which put the line separating EU from non-EU space right in the middle of Bukovina. Southern Bukovinans entered the EU along with Romania; northern Bukovinans under Ukrainian rule remained on the other side of "the golden curtain," confined to a space Russia increasingly regarded as its backyard. The new border deepened disparities between Bukovina's two halves. As EU citizens, southern Bukovinans could access economic opportunities out of reach to their neighbors across the Ukrainian–Romanian border. As the standard and cost of living in the south grew, the border brought economic opportunities for northern Bukovinans in the form of petty trading and smuggling. Many Ukrainian Bukovinans felt ashamed of having to engage in contraband and other illicit activities to make ends meet, and the knowledge that Romania had once been their "poorer neighbor" made it all the more galling.[40] Even more embarrassing was that Bukovinans in Ukraine began searching for whatever traces of Romanian heritage they could find to claim Romanian citizenship. After 2007 Romanian citizenship was a real asset, as it granted Romanian passport holders access to the EU labor market. As late as 2021 a team of Ukrainian and Romanian researchers found that ethnic Romanians in Ukrainian Bukovina identified with the Ukrainian state less than ethnic Ukrainians in southern Bukovina did with Romania.[41]

Although Ukraine remained firmly embedded in the post-Soviet world, the years following the Soviet Union's collapse gave rise to a new Ukrainian middle class that in 2004 challenged the status quo through the Orange Revolution, the first major popular unrest in independent Ukraine. The revolution succeeded in removing some of the "old guard," the "predatory elites" protesters blamed for Ukraine's multiple afflictions.[42] The new elites, however, including President Viktor Yushchenko and prime minister Yuliya Timoshenko, failed to deliver on their promises. For all their talk of "democratization," Ukraine remained internally divided and corrupt. In an ironic twist, Viktor

Yanukovych, removed by the Orange Revolution, won the elections of 2010 and returned to power. These failures notwithstanding, the Orange Revolution put Ukraine on Europe's map just as the EU was launching its eastward expansion project. Although the country's ties with Europe remained tenuous, President Yushchenko never tired of emphasizing that "our path to the future is the one now being allowed by United Europe. We belong to the same civilization as its peoples; we share the same values."[43]

Part of this process of redefining Ukraine as fundamentally European was a new-found respect and admiration for the country's past multiculturalism and ethnic diversity and their rhetorical mobilization to extricate Ukraine from its Soviet and immediate post-Soviet past and link it to Europe. This rhetoric did not reflect the reality of contemporary Ukraine, which was less ethnically and culturally diverse than ever before. According to the census of 2001, Chernivtsi had a population of 236,700: 78 percent were Ukrainian, 11 percent Russian, 6 percent Romanian and Moldavian, and a minuscule percentage Jewish.[44] Ukraine's vaunted multiculturalism was appealing because it let those who felt burdened by the country's provinciality and marginality reimagine the past in order to envision a different future for the country.[45]

Northern Bukovina, especially Chernivtsi, fueled the pro-Western Ukrainian imagination. In 2008, on the city's six hundredth anniversary, Ukrainian officials launched an urban restoration project that highlighted the city's European past.[46] Chernivtsi was by then a backwater town, far from the centers of power and culture, neglected and derelict. Its infrastructure was rapidly decaying, its buildings—once architectural gems—were crumbling. The renovation project was inspired and funded in part by Chernivtsi's diaspora, people who flocked to Bukovina after 1991 looking for traces of the past in "neglected buildings, antique bazaars, and poetry books."[47] Understanding that money could be made from Chernivtsi's "affective register of nostalgic cosmopolitanism," local officials played it up.[48] On Chernivtsi's main street, named Olha Kobylianska after the Ukrainian writer, urban officials installed cobblestones engraved with the city's name in six different languages (Romanian, German, Ukrainian, Russian, Yiddish, and Polish). Local entrepreneurs opened Habsburg-themed restaurants and cafes in the city center. Before long, Emperor Franz Joseph returned to Chernivtsi in the form of a bronze statue in one of Chernivtsi's public parks, across from the former Jesuit church.[49] Gradually, the city began resembling other Central European cities, albeit without the prosperity.[50] The Polish poet Zbigniew Herbert, admiring the city from afar, concluded that Chernivtsi was "in fact the last European city."[51]

State officials and locals treated the city as a "political tableau" upon which they could inscribe their aspirations for the future, unencumbered by any

FIGURE 9.4. Statue of Emperor Franz Joseph in Chernivtsi sprayed with red paint during the period leading up to the Euromaidan revolution that began on November 21, 2013, sparked by President Viktor Yanukovych's decision not to sign the European Union–Ukraine Association Agreement. Around the same time, Russian flags were being painted on trees in Chernivtsi. Photo by author, 2013.

direct memories of the city's past.[52] Their efforts to "resurrect" Chernivtsi's multicultural past entailed a good deal of misremembering and forgetting.[53] Upon revisiting Chernivtsi, Jewish survivors and their descendants were saddened to find the city's large Jewish cemetery neglected and overgrown.[54]

Those who traveled back to former killing sites, ghettos, and camps found no acknowledgement of their past suffering. Hirsch and Spitzer had to walk deep into the woods outside Chernivtsi to find a modest memorial to the hundreds of Jews shot above the Prut's banks in July 1941.[55] Moreover, when a Jewish museum finally opened in Chernivtsi in 2008, the exhibition failed to mention the Holocaust. City officials claimed they wanted the museum to be "about life, not about death"[56]—conveniently allowing them to bypass complicity and guilt. New monuments and plaques celebrating the city's literary past appeared: a statue to the Romanian poet Mihai Eminescu, a monument to the German-language poet Paul Celan.[57]

FIGURE 9.5. The entrance to the old synagogue in Chernivtsi blocked by a wall of bricks (May 2002). Once home to a vibrant Jewish community, Chernivtsi became a kind of Jewish ghost city. Photo by Karel Cudlin, courtesy of the Joint Distribution Committee Archives.

The Meridian poetry festival, named for Paul Celan's speech about his native Czernowitz, set out to save the city through literature.[58] Sponsored by an air-conditioning merchant turned cultural entrepreneur, the festival aimed to revive memories of literary Czernowitz through poetry recitals and conventions in symbolic locations across the city such as the mortuary hall of the abandoned old synagogue, fallen into disrepair.[59] For Igor Pomerantsev, one of the festival's founders, ruins and poetry went hand in hand. "When all around you is falling apart—empires, canons, reputations—who do you rely on, if not yourself? So you become 'subjective' and work with your own 'I.'"[60] Thus poetry was born once more in Chernivtsi.

A new revolution broke out in Ukraine in 2013, shortly after I arrived in Chernivtsi to begin my dissertation research. In November, President Yanukovych suddenly backed out of a planned "Association Agreement" between Ukraine and the EU after meeting with the Russian president Vladimir Putin. News of Yanukovych's turnaround raised a furor in Chernivtsi, especially among students and young professionals. In Kyiv, people streamed onto Maidan Square, just as they had ten years earlier, during the Orange Revolution, to demand Yanukovych's removal. Social media quickly spread news of the protests to the provinces, and within a week or two, the Maidan was metaphorically on fire, as were city squares across Ukraine. In Chernivtsi, protesters gathered around the statue of the Ukrainian poet Taras Shevchenko, across from city hall, wrapping themselves in EU and Ukrainian flags to stay warm. Though few had deep roots in Bukovina, the protesters began invoking the province's "tolerant" Habsburg past to justify their desire for closer ties with Europe. Young Bukovinans boarded trains to Kyiv to join the protesters on the Maidan and were met by security forces using "live ammunition, rubber bullets, tear gas, [and] flash grenades."[61] In February 2014 President Yanukovych fled to Russia, and the protesters occupied several government buildings in Kyiv.

The people in the streets of Chernivtsi, Kyiv, and other Ukrainian cities called their revolution "Euromaidan" or "the revolution of dignity." For them, Europe and dignity, prosperity, the rule of law, democracy were one and the same. In March 2014 Russian forces seized the Crimean peninsula in the south of Ukraine (several hundred kilometers to the south and east of Chernivtsi oblast). Separatists in Luhansk and Donetsk held a referendum for independence. Although Russia supported them through special operatives and proxy forces, Ukraine chose not to respond militarily.[62] European leaders declared support for Ukraine and disapproval of Russia's actions. British foreign secretary William Hague found it "inspiring to see these people standing up for their vision of the future of Ukraine: a free, sovereign, democratic country with much closer ties to the EU and a positive relationship of mutual respect with Russia."[63] At the end of the day, however, pragmatism prevailed. While the United States imposed sanctions on Russia, Western European countries, dependent on Russian gas, felt that their hands were tied. Once again, Ukrainians found themselves separated from "Europe" by a deep, seemingly unsurpassable abyss.

## War All Over Again

When Russia's war on Ukraine began in 2014, it remained confined to the country's eastern territories, and quickly evolved into a frozen conflict. Although the West's initial response to Russian aggression was weak, NATO strengthened its presence in Eastern Europe in the following years as relations with Russia cooled. In 2017 NATO dispatched tank brigades to Poland. In January 2018 the United States imposed sanctions on Russian individuals and companies and approved the sale of anti-tank weapons to Ukraine.[64] Bukovina was far from the front lines, however, and daily life in Chernivtsi was pretty much unchanged. When Kate Tsurkan, a doctoral student at NYU arrived there as a volunteer English teacher in the fall of 2021, she found Chernivtsi slightly expanded to accommodate new waves of refugees from the east. The war had aggravated the city's perpetual lack of funding. Walking through its streets felt to Tsurkan a bit like walking "through a neglected graveyard": "you notice how many of the once magnificent buildings and cobblestone streets are blighted by neglect."[65] In the wake of "the revolution of dignity," city officials had renamed streets that honored Soviet heroes: Dzerzhinskoho, Frunze, Stasiuka. On the spot once occupied by an Austrian monument that was torn down by the interwar Romanian administration, officials had built a Pietà monument commemorating the "Heavenly Hundred" who perished during Euromaidan.[66]

On February 24, 2022 the Russian president Vladimir Putin announced a "special military operation" that was in fact Russia's attempted full-scale invasion of Ukraine. The attack had been predicted by US intelligence, on the basis of satellite images showing evidence of a planned mass invasion. In December 2021 the Russian foreign minister had called for an end to NATO's military activity in Eastern Europe and demanded that Ukraine be banned from joining NATO then or ever. Western officials rejected these demands as a violation of NATO's "open door policy," and warned Ukraine of the impending invasion.[67] Ukrainian president Volodymyr Zelensky brushed off the warning: a Russian invasion seemed too outrageous to imagine.[68] Even more outrageous was Putin's claim that an invasion was required to demilitarize and "denazify" Ukraine and prevent the genocide of ethnic Russians on Ukrainian territory.[69] Yet on February 23 at midnight, as Russian troops began moving toward Ukraine's borders, the Ukrainian parliament declared a state of emergency. Unlike other government members, President Zelensky stayed in Kyiv. Shortly afterward, he posted on Facebook a video in which he declared Ukraine would go on fighting because "this is our land. This is our history." "We are talking about both peace and principles," Zelensky said. "We are talking about justice and international law. About the right to self-determination, the right to decide our own future, the right to security and the right to live without being threatened."[70]

In Chernivtsi, as people watched footage from the frontlines on their cellphones, a wave of refugees streamed in from Kyiv. They were, as Tsurkan recalls, clearly from elsewhere, "because some of their clothes looked more expensive than the knockoff brands that most people here find at the Kalinka bazaar, and so did their cars, which added to the already congested traffic on our broken cobblestone streets."[71] No air strikes hit the city, but people panicked when a Russian missile hit Ivano-Frankivsk's airport, only sixty kilometers away.[72] Thousands of refugees from the areas directly affected by the war flowed into Chernivtsi and crossed the border to Romania. Around eleven o'clock at night an order was issued forbidding men between eighteen and sixty years of age from leaving the country. One Romanian man from northern Bukovina crossed the border hours before President Zelensky issued a general mobilization decree. "The northern Bukovinans are not eager to fight," he told a Romanian journalist. "Apart from those who went to fight in the Donbas in 2014, the rest were never at war, they are afraid of weapons, of shootings. They are not professionals, they have no idea what an army is and what they should do in such a situation. Many decided to leave the country." Romanian officials and locals welcomed the refugees with water, bread, and tea, and offers of accommodation and transport. Yet President Zelensky's call for those who had left to return and defend their country tugged at this refugee: "every one of us has this dilemma in our hearts: whether to return or not." "Ukraine was already in a wretched state, some say, not very developed. After roads, airports, electric stations have been destroyed in this war, what will this country be? It's complicated, misery after misery."[73]

The war did not remain a regional affair for long. A few days into the invasion, the United States and the European Union promised Ukraine hundreds of millions of dollars in arms and humanitarian aid.[74] The crisis took on global dimensions once Russia seized Ukraine's ports and blocked food exports.[75] President Zelensky requested that Ukraine be admitted into the European Union.[76] "Prove that you are indeed Europeans," he said in a video speech to the EU parliament. "And then life will win over death and light will win over darkness."[77] In April 2022, when Ukraine managed to push the Russian army back out of the Kyiv region, it found ample evidence of war crimes: summary executions, torture, rape. On April 18 Russia launched a new offensive in eastern Ukraine, and by May, the Russians had seized the city of Mariupol. Here, too, they deliberately targeted civilians, as seen in the horrendous attack on Mariupol's theater. After a months-long siege of Bakhmut, Russian forces advanced into the northeast in the fall of 2022, annexing Luhansk, Donetsk, Kherson, and Zaporizhzhia. When Putin announced the partial mobilization of reservists, thousands of Russians fled the country.[78] Ukraine launched a long-awaited counteroffensive that met with stiff resistance. By now, the conflict was a war of attrition, with every small territorial gain costing huge amounts in ammunition and lives.[79]

In the summer of 2023 Jeffrey Gettleman and Finbar O'Reilly of the *New York Times* reported from Chernivtsi that "there's not a sandbag, cracked window or soldier in sight, you can almost forget this country is at war." People were still strolling down Chernivtsi's streets lined with confectioners' stores. "Looking up at the intricately made wrought iron balconies, or down at the glossy cobblestone streets," Gettleman and O'Reilly reported, "you might for a moment think you were in Vienna or Paris."[80]

But in fact, the war had arrived in Chernivtsi, too. Every morning, a ceremony to commemorate the war dead was held on the square facing city hall. The police cordoned off the streets for three minutes, while city officials played the nineteenth-century anthem "A Prayer for Ukraine." "People hold their hands over their hearts. Languid, operatic music flows from the loudspeaker positioned on a wrought iron balcony overlooking the cobblestone square."[81] The city had turned into the "back office of war," where materiel for the army was prepared and supplies acquired and shipped to the front lines. Refugees were living in Chernivtsi's garages, parking lots, barns, and the old Soviet Hotel Chernivtsi, repurposed as a displaced persons camp. Volunteers from across Ukraine and abroad had come to Chernivtsi to help the war effort.[82] Moreover, as Gettleman and O'Reilly reminded readers, "Chernivtsi has lost a lot of people, too. Sometimes it buries two young soldiers a day."[83]

As the war dragged on, people grew tired, and the state grew desperate. In the winter of 2023 a lawyer from Chernivtsi reported that she was receiving between thirty and forty calls daily from people being forced into military service, including individuals with medical exemptions. A man called Yefimenko from the Vyzhnytsia district in northern Bukovina was walking to a doctor's appointment when he was picked up and taken to a recruitment center, which he managed to escape that night. Another man from Chernivtsi was seized at work and sent to the front lines, where he died in combat in July 2023. News of his death "sent a chill through the town, fanning residents' fear of being taken from the streets and dying in battle." A soldier working for the recruitment center in Vyzhnytsia admitted that one quarter of the conscripts brought to his center tried to bribe their way out of the draft.[84] In November 2023 the Ukrainian police discovered an illegal group run by a forty-four-year-old man from northern Bukovina that provided "counseling" and "escorting" services to military-aged men looking to cross illegally into Romania at a cost of $3,000–$5,000 per person. For those looking for safer ways to cross the border, "emigration companies" provided applicants for

FIGURE 9.6. City officials removing a statue commemorating Soviet liberation from Chernivtsi in a demonstrative gesture signaling the city's desire to distance itself from Russia (April 2022). Creative Commons Attribution 4.0 International license.

Romanian passports with "archival documents" certifying their Romanian origins.[85] For every tale of heroism and self-sacrifice, there were as many tales of cowardice and corruption. Landlords and corrupt local officials enriched themselves at the expense of refugees and displaced persons.[86] In early 2024 the Chernivtsi Romanian-language paper *Zorile Bucovinei* reported that only two of the twenty-three ambulances donated by the Italian government to Bukovina as humanitarian aid could still be found. Where the other twenty-one were, and who was using them, nobody knew.[87]

## Century of Nomads

Although the place we call Bukovina no longer exists as a political-administrative entity, it is again at the epicenter of a geopolitical revolution. The Russo–Ukrainian war, the largest on the European continent since World War II, has unleashed massive transformations both regionally and globally—many unintended, as so often in the past. Breaking with its postwar pacifism, Germany has ramped up its defense spending and, to Putin's dismay, NATO has expanded further, admitting Sweden and Finland as members.[88] Russian aggression, at least initially, brought Europe together when few Europeans thought this was possible. In France and Germany, Romania and Poland, Europeans everywhere manifested their solidarity with Ukrainians, protesting Putin's "barbarous campaign" and displaying Ukrainian flags and symbols in public.[89] The war radically changed Russian lives, too. Some Russians who prior to the war had found a *modus vivendi* with Putin's regime could no longer do so after the invasion, as Putin tightened his grip on power still further.[90] The war has also had a profound imprint on the global economy, provoking a sharp rise in fuel costs and famine in Africa, among other things.[91] Its consequences are, of course, most severely felt in Ukraine itself. Beyond the vast toll of military dead and wounded on both sides, by the end of 2024 Ukraine had sustained over forty thousand civilian casualties in air strikes and as a result of combat on the ground. At the time of writing, over three years since the beginning of the Russian full-scale invasion, of the country's estimated population of 39 million in 2022, some 3.6 million people have been internally displaced, 6.8 million have fled the country, and 12.7 million are considered to be in need of humanitarian aid.[92] The death and destruction are ongoing. American-brokered peace discussions have made little headway, and although Ukraine recaptured over half of the land it initially lost to Russia in 2022, approximately one fifth of its prewar territory remains in Russian hands.[93]

The war in Ukraine has become not just a battle for territory, moreover, but a crucible for rival visions of Europe's past and future. While Western governments have remained formally committed to Ukraine's cause, they are becoming increasingly divided over how the conflict might be resolved. Some international observers, invoking the Korean model, have urged an expedient peace—even at the cost of Ukrainian sovereignty and aspirations for joining NATO.[94] Others have cautioned that any deal struck with Putin would be fragile and short-lived. The election of Donald Trump as president of the United States in November 2024 made the situation still more volatile, as his administration set about issuing demands for an immediate ceasefire, only to discover that Russia continued "asking for too much." America's perceived retreat from Europe in the aftermath of Trump's election has fueled anxieties across the continent, even as key European allies reaffirm their opposition to Russia's invasion.[95] Meanwhile, a loose coalition of anti-Western actors (China, Iran, North Korea) have been using the war as a pretext to challenge the American-guaranteed post–World War II order; while within Europe itself, far-right, anti-establishment voices are seizing on the opportunity provided by the conflict to revive old territorial claims and foment doubts as to the legitimacy of the whole project represented by the European Union.

In Romania specifically, the ultranationalist Alliance for the Unification of Romanians (Alianţa pentru Unirea Românilor, or AUR), formed in 2019, clamors for the annexation of northern Bukovina and other former Romanian possessions now under Ukrainian sovereignty—in the wake of which, in a domino effect reminiscent of situation regarding Czechoslovakia in 1938, the Hungarian extremist party Mi Hanzák has proceeded to demand Transcarpathia for Hungary.[96] The AUR, a self-described conservative party with a national irredentist agenda, has ties to neo-Legionary groups in Romania. Drawing on a disturbing mix of anti-imperialism, nationalism, and anti-Semitism, it calls for a Europe of nations rather than what it styles "a socialist empire of a federal kind," rejecting multiculturalism, Marxism, and what it portrays as Europe's pollution by "foreign elements."[97] AUR's leader George Simion goes by the title "Căpitan" (captain)—a direct allusion to the interwar Legionary leader Corneliu Zelea Codreanu—and senator Diana Șoșoacă, a former AUR member, quotes from Codreanu's speeches in her parliamentary interventions and recites poems by the Legionary Radu Gyr.[98] Since the beginning of the war, Șoșoacă has agitated for the return of northern Bukovina and Bessarabia from Ukraine to Romania. In March 2023 she drafted a new law on the annexation of formerly Romanian territories from Ukraine. When the Ukrainian Ministry of Foreign Affairs called for sanctions against her, she likened Ukraine to Nazi Germany and declared solidarity with "the oppressed Romanian minority" in Ukraine, who were allegedly being "ethnically purged."[99] Meanwhile, as of May 2025, George Simion had advanced to the second round of the Romanian presidential elections, declaring his goal of "first place for the Romanian people," and promising to soon reveal "how much we have contributed to the war effort in Ukraine, to the detriment of Romanian children and our elderly."[100]

All this must look grim, but unsurprising, to Bukovinans such as the writer Igor Pomerantsev, who sees the present as the continuation of a twentieth century characterized by displacement and homelessness, of people being moved, expelled, and dispensed with. The twentieth century was, as Pomerantsev writes, "a time of nomads, European Bedouins who were looking for refuge."[101] Born in Saratov in 1948, Pomerantsev was himself displaced several times. First his parents moved from the little town of Chita to Chernivtsi. Born in Odessa and Kharkiv, they had ended up near Lake Baikal fleeing the Wehrmacht.[102] Though outsiders to Chernivtsi, the family fit right in. Their Soviet passports listed their nationality as "Jewish." Although citizens of Soviet Ukraine and technically Ukrainian, their mother tongue was Russian. After a run-in with the KGB, who branded him a "dissident," Pomerantsev went into exile in the West, where he worked for the BBC and Radio Free Europe. Now he lives in Prague, where he records his podcast "Humanitarian Corridor," which features interviews with Ukrainian refugees and displaced persons. When an interviewer on Czech television asked Pomerantsev where he felt most at home, he said, "I am a person in transit. I have lived in five countries and half a dozen cities, but I only feel at home in a hotel room."[103] A person with no homeland in the traditional sense of the word, Pomerantsev has found his compatriots amidst the "flood of refugees, political emigrants, just emigrants, displaced persons! I am with them, they are my people! That's why I said and wrote that I may not have a homeland but I definitely have compatriots. And the number of my compatriots is becoming larger."[104]

Pomerantsev would likely have found a "compatriot" in Rosa Roth-Zuckermann, one of the very few residents of old Czernowitz who remained there after World War II. When Marianne Hirsch and Leo Spitzer visited her in 1998, Roth-Zuckermann was living in Ukrainian Chernivtsi surrounded by objects and books from a different time and place. On her mantelpiece, she kept a bust of Emperor Franz Joseph. Next to an Israeli flag was a framed portrait of Franz Joseph's consort, Empress Sissi. Zuckermann lost her entire family in Transnistria. When she returned from the camps, she built a new life in Soviet Ukraine. Although she dreamed of going to Israel, she stayed because her son's life was in Ukraine. She supplemented her meager pension by giving German- and English-language classes to Ukrainian students in her book-filled room, where she sat surrounded by Ukrainian and Romanian classics, and her German favorites Schiller, Heine, Rilke, Mann, Hauptmann, and Keller.[105] "I am a Jew, just as before," she told an interviewer. "I have lived many lives, an Austrian one, a Romanian one, one as a stateless person at the mercy of every blow delivered by fate, a Soviet one and now a Ukrainian life."[106]

Paul Celan's poetry had pride of place in Roth-Zuckermann's library. Like her, Celan lived outside place and time, finding a semblance of home only in language. Tragically, that language was German, tainted by its association with the murder of Celan's parents. Self-exiled in Paris, Celan labored over his poems in "deterritorialized German." This was, in Marjorie Perloff's words, "an eerie, near ghostly language; it is both mother-tongue, and this firmly anchored in the realm of the dead, and a language the poet has to make up, to recreate, to invent, to bring back to life."[107] Other Bukovinans also wrestled with the paradox of language and place wherever they went. The German-Jewish writer Edgar Hilsenrath, who fled Germany in 1938 with his mother to her parents in southern Bukovina and was then deported to Transnistria, remarked while living in the United States, "I don't want to live where I don't feel well, such as America. I can't live in Israel because of the language. I don't want to move again. So Germany remains at least my linguistic homeland."[108] The Bukovinan poet Rose Ausländer, who ended up in West Germany, in a hotel, surrounded by unopened suitcases, liked to call herself "a Jewish Gypsy of the German language."[109] Igor Pomerantsev also struggles with the crisis of writing in Russian, a language he now associates with evil—as do many others, no doubt. "Today death is a master from Russia," he writes, alluding to the famous line in Celan's poem *Todesfuge*: "death is a master from Deutschland."[110] The war, Pomerantsev adds, "is a limit situation not only for the speakers of the language, but also for the language itself."[111]

---

This current moment constitutes a new episode in the long Eastern European saga of imperial conflict, competition, and reinvention told in this book, in miniature, through the story of Bukovina's making and unmaking from the eighteenth century to the present. The region continues to inspire dreams of renewal. Though still peripheral, it periodically resurfaces in Europe's consciousness, demanding attention as the place where the borders of states, cultures, and civilizations are periodically renegotiated.

Telling the story of Bukovina, this microcosm of Eastern Europe, feels especially important now that the region's cultural and physical memory is under threat. This has happened before, of course. Ukrainian state and regional archives, which hold the bulk of the materials on which this book is based, suffered immense losses during World War II. Both the Nazis and the Soviets captured local archives or evacuated and never returned them. Soldiers used documents to make fires and deliberately destroyed materials deemed too dangerous to fall into enemy hands.[112] Since the beginning of the Russo-Ukrainian war in 2014, and especially since 2022, archival collections and cultural sites across Ukraine have been displaced and destroyed. Russian troops stole documents from the Kherson state archives and damaged Kharkiv's Rare Book Library.[113] The archival collections in Chernivtsi are still physically intact, but even more difficult to access than before.[114]

Bukovina's old capital Chernivtsi remains a "palimpsest," a "quotation from another epoch."[115] Bukovina, and Eastern Europe, remain anchored in several eras and places at once. The region preserves within itself a variety of pasts and a variety of imagined futures; a multitude of aspirations and hopes and just as many disillusionments. Its story highlights the fragility of memory and the past's eternal return, not in the sense of endless repetition, but its inescapability. Our story ends here: fittingly, not at a finale, but in the middle of a new episode whose contours we cannot yet know.

# NOTES

## Introduction

1. *Österreichisch-ungarische Monarchie [...]: Bukowina*, 4. For more on the *Kronprinzenwerk*, see Baiersdorf, "*Kronprinzenwerk*"; Bendix, "Cultural Reification."

2. *Österreichisch-ungarische Monarchie [...]: Bukowina*, 3.

3. Franzos, "Karl Emil Franzos," 231.

4. Steiner, *Karl Emil Franzos*, 26.

5. Franzos, "Von Wien nach Czernowitz," 32.

6. Franzos, "Ein Culturfest," 55.

7. Franzos, "Ein Culturfest,"55.

8. Franzos, "Ein Culturfest," 56.

9. Franzos, "Ein Culturfest."

10. Rechter, *Becoming Habsburg*, 3.

11. On other, comparable borderlands around the world, see, for instance, Amrith, *Crossing the Bay of Bengal*; Carrol, *Return of Alsace*; Eckert, *West Germany*; Guidi, *Generations of Empire*; Rogaski, *Hygienic Modernity*; Tagliacozzo, *Secret Trades*; Young, *Japan's Total Empire*; Zanou, *Transnational Patriotism*.

12. On the Annales School's use of the term "longue durée," see Braudel and Wallerstein, "History and the Social Sciences."

13. "States exist in an implicitly competitive universe," writes Charles Maier. Maier, *Leviathan 2.0*, 80; Kazancigil, *State in Global Perspective*, 147.

14. Stanoeva, "Architectural Praxis."

15. Scharr, "Habsburg Cadastral Registration"; Scharr, "Innere Verwaltungsentwicklung"; Scharr, *"Landschaft Bukowina"*; Scharr, *Griechisch-orientalische Religionsfonds.* Hausleitner, *Rumänisierung*. Fisher, *Resettlers and Survivors*. See also the following dissertations: Frunchak, "Making of Soviet Chernivtsi; Lazar, "Czernowitz Jews."

16. Rechter, *Becoming Habsburg*, 2.

17. On the importance of integrating stories of the countryside into larger narratives that tend to focus on cities, see E. Weber, *Peasants into Frenchmen*. Gaëlle Fisher and Maren Röger make a similar point in their overview of historiography on Bukovina, where they argue that the literature's tendency to emphasize Czernowitz at the expense of the surrounding countryside "also somewhat problematically perpetuates the relegation of the countryside and rural populations and their concerns." Fisher and Röger, "Bukovina," 191.

18. For a detailed analysis of how nationalism has led to the compartmentalization of historiography on Bukovina, see Frunchak, "Studying the Land." (This constitutes the first volume

["Essay"] of the monograph series *The Carl Beck Papers in Russian and East European Studies*, no. 2108; the second volume contains one of the most complete bibliographies on Bukovina to date.)

19. For an analysis of similar trends in Galicia, see the final chapters of Wolff, *Idea of Galicia*. Gaëlle Fisher traces the afterlife of the "Bukovina idea" in Fisher, "Looking Forwards"; Fisher, *Resettlers and Survivors*.

20. Kaindl, *Geschichte der Bukowina*, 4.

21. In Bukovina's case, most histories focus on traditionally delimited periods such as the Romanian, the Habsburg, or the Soviet period, or the Holocaust, usually treated separately. The best work on the Soviet period is Svetlana Frunchak's unpublished dissertation: Frunchak, "Making of Soviet Chernivtsi." For the Romanian period, see Hausleitner, *Rumänisierung*. For the Holocaust in Bukovina, see Lazar, "Czernowitz Jews," and the work of Vladimir Solonari, including Solonari, "'Model Province'"; Solonari, "Important New Document."

22. For models of writing about empire not in terms of periphery and center, but as a "web" without clear hierarchies, see Ballantyne, *Entanglements of Empire*; Lester, "Imperial Circuits."

23. Chakrabarty, *Provincializing Europe*.

24. Behrends, "Histories of the Big and Small."

25. Dragostinova, *Cold War*, 7.

26. Case, *Between States*, 4.

27. Hillis, *Children of Rus'*, 15. See also Nemes, *Another Hungary*, 2.

28. Lieven, *Empire*; Adelman, *Sovereignty and Revolution*.

29. K. Clark, *Moscow*, 281.

30. This is alluded to in Bartov and Weitz, *Shatterzone*.

31. On marginality, see Spitzer, *Lives In Between*, 14.

32. Fichman, *Before Memories Fade*, 8.

33. DLA, Gregor von Rezzori, Mappe 1: Texte h. Gespräche, Interviews, "Der Ex-Staatenlose Gregor von Rezzori über Europa als Jugendherberge und seine neuen 'Idiotenführer durch Europas Vaterländer,' Althergebrachte Gemeinplätze durch neue ersetzen." *Die Weltwoche*, 16/17 April, 1997.

34. Menczel, *Trügerische Lösungen*, 9.

35. For a discussion of backwardness in the East European context, see Todorova, "Trap of Backwardness. On the imagining of Eastern Europe as a backward space, see Wolff, *Inventing Eastern Europe*.

36. See, for example, Zahra, *Great Departure*; Silverstein, "Periphery"; or, for a later period, Stanek, *Architecture in Global Socialism*.

37. Wolff, *Idea of Galicia*, 13; Rechter, "Geography is Destiny."

38. Kumar, *Visions of Empire*, 185.

39. Kumar, *Visions of Empire*, 193.

40. Davies, *Russo-Turkish War*, 208; Davison, *Essays*, 29.

41. Weczerka, *Deutschen im Buchenland*, 4–5.

42. J. T. Gross, *Revolution from Abroad*.

43. On Galicia see, for instance, Wolff, *Idea of Galicia*; Bartov, *Anatomy of a Genocide*.

44. On this topic in general, see Hobsbawm and Ranger, *Invention of Tradition*.

45. For a similar case in Galicia of Polish, Ukrainian, and Jewish inhabitants living "side by side for several centuries—weaving their separate tales of the past, articulating their distinctive understanding of the present, and making widely diverging plans for the future," see Bartov, *Anatomy of a Genocide*, 4.

46. On the categories used in the Austrian census and specifics on Bukovina, see Brix, *Umgangssprachen*.

47. Rechter, *Becoming Habsburg*, 326.

48. Masan, "Czernowitz." By 1910, Ruthenians formed 38.38% of Bukovina's population, Romanians 34.38%, Germans 21.24%, Poles 4.55%, Magyars 1.13%, and "others" 0.13%, according to the Austrian census.

49. Leslie, "Ausgleich."

50. Ludwig Adolf Simiginowicz-Staufe was the first local German-language poet of Bukovina, a graduate of the University of Vienna, where he studied history and German studies. Sienerth, "Simiginowicz-Staufe."

51. Simiginowicz-Staufe, *Völkergruppen*, 9.

52. Fischer, *Bukowina*, 123.

53. On "national indifference," see, among others, Zahra, "Imagined Noncommunities"; Zahra, *Kidnapped Souls*; J. King, *Budweisers*; Karch, *Nation and Loyalty*; Bjork, *Neither German Nor Pole*.

54. Rechter, "Geography Is Destiny," 328.

55. Rechter, *Becoming Habsburg*; Leslie, "Ausgleich"; Broszat, "Von der Kulturnation."

56. Felstiner, *Paul Celan*, 10.

57. Franzos, *Aus Halb-Asien*, 3–4.

58. Ausländer, "Alles kann Motiv sein," 107–8.

59. Ausländer, "Erinnerungen," 38–39.

60. Heinzen, "Wo die Hunde," 250.

61. Maier, *Among Empires*, 85.

62. Baud and Van Schendel, "Toward a Comparative History," 215.

63. Spruyt, *Sovereign State*, 35–41.

64. Benton, *A Search for Sovereignty*, 2. See too Kratochwil, "Of Systems"; Agnew, *Reinventing Geopolitics*, 11; Philpott, "Sovereignty," 357.

65. McKeown, *Melancholy Order*, 319.

66. Kashani-Sabet, *Frontier Fictions*, 5; on homeland territoriality, see Shelef, *Homelands*.

67. Hopkins, *Ruling the Savage Periphery*, 7, 17.

68. Dullin, *Frontière épaisse*.

69. On the borderlands of East Central Europe, some excellent examples of this historiographical turn include: Brown, *Biography*; Case, *Between States*; Ciancia, "Borderland Modernity"; Ciancia, *On Civilization's Edge*; Hillis, *Children of Rus'*; Judson, *Guardians*; Kirchner Reill, *Nationalists*; Sammartino, *Impossible Border*; Zahra, *Kidnapped Souls*. For an excellent general analysis of borderlands as a paradigm in Eurasian history, see von Hagen, "Empires, Borderlands, and Diasporas."

70. Bartov and Weitz, *Shatterzone*, 18.

71. Hämäläinen and Truett, "On Borderlands," 341.

72. Bartov and Weitz, *Shatterzone*.

73. J. C. Scott, *Seeing Like a State.*

74. Maier, *Among Empires,* 82.

75. Baud and Van Schendel, "Toward a Comparative History," 236.

76. Bartov and Weitz, *Shatterzone,* 1.

77. For more of this critique, see Cooper, *Colonialism in Question.*

78. David-Fox, *Crossing Borders,* 84.

79. See also Strauss, *State Formation.*

80. Adelman, "Mimesis and Rivalry," 81.

81. For similar cases see, for instance, Dumitru, *State, Antisemitism*; Amar, *Paradox.*

82. For a similar analysis of how war injected ethnic differences and conflict with new meanings, see Bergholz, *Violence.*

83. Vorrath, "On the Margin of Statehood," 90.

84. Strauss, "Regimes," 231.

85. Kotsonis, "Taxes," 230.

86. On how borderlands residents used their geopolitical position to negotiate with states or play them off against each other, see Adelman, "Mimesis and Rivalry," 90.

87. For more on this, see Kohlrausch and Behrends, *Races to Modernity,* 18.

88. Mëhilli, *From Stalin to Mao,* 12.

89. Shmuel Eisenstadt's ideas are discussed in Katzenstein, *Civilizations*; see also Eisenstadt, "Multiple Modernities,"3.

90. On urbanization being coterminous with a civilizing mission, see Osterhammel, *Europe,* 23; Broers, "Cultural Imperialism."

91. On culture as normative concept, see K. Clark, *Moscow,* 45. On various definitions of culture, see Swidler, "Culture in Action"; Sewell, *Logics of History,* 169.

92. On states' urge to improve or "try and fix a deficient population," see Li, *Will to Improve,* 60. See also Bowden, *Empire of Civilization,* 12; Fischer-Tiné and Mann, *Colonialism.* On Poland, see Ciancia, *On Civilization's Edge*; on France, Conklin, *Mission to Civilize.*

93. Reill, *German Enlightenment,* 4.

94. Maier, "Culture of Culture," 18. See also Ingrao, "Problem of 'Enlightened Absolutism.'"

95. Liulevicius, *German Myth,* 21.

96. Kaindl argued this in a variety of publications, such as: Kaindl, "Deutsche Aufgaben"; Kaindl, *Deutsche Siedlung*; Kaindl, *Deutschen in den Donauländern*; Kaindl, *Österreich, Preussen, Deutschland*; Kaindl, *Geschichte der Deutschen.*

97. Numerous articles on Czernowitzers' *Bildungsdrang* appeared in the urban press: see, for instance, "Die Studierwut," *Czernowitzer Tagblatt,* July 14, 1903.

98. The Swiss theologian Karl Barth, quoted in Herdt, *Forming Humanity,* 14.

99. Maier, "Culture of Culture," 18.

100. On the Herderian reinterpretation of culture as pluralistic and unique to every people, see Blanning, *Culture of Power,* 254.

101. For a similar argument, see Judson, *Exclusive Revolutionaries*; Judson, *Habsburg Empire.*

102. On the extreme right's complaints about "politicianism," see Bruja, *Extrema dreaptă,* 101; R. Clark, *Holy Legionary Youth,* 25.

103. David-Fox, *Crossing Borders*, 55, 65.

104. Koselleck, *Futures Past*, 48; Mayer, *Furies*.

105. On historicism in the German Enlightenment, see Reill, *German Enlightenment*; Edelstein, Geroulanos, and Wheatley, "Chronocenosis," 18.

106. Koselleck, *Futures Past*, 37.

107. Edelstein, Geroulanos, and Wheatley, "Chronocenosis," 18.

108. Mayer, *Furies*, 26–27.

109. Walter Benjamin's "Theses on the Philosophy of History," cited in Fritzsche, *Stranded in the Present*, 32.

110. Mayer, *Furies*, 40.

111. Friedjung, *Wir wollten nur das Paradies*, 23–24.

112. The urban press was filled with ruminations on whether Czernowitz had become a great city yet. One especially good example is the "Die kleine Großstadt" series of articles in the March 1914 issues of *Czernowitzer Tagblatt*.

113. On the notion of historical legacy and its significance to the Balkans, see Todorova, *Imagining the Balkans*, 194.

114. Cooper, *Colonialism in Question*, 188.

115. Adelman, "Liberalism," 511; see also Burbank and Cooper, *Empires in World History*.

116. On the nuanced relationship between nationalisms and empire see, among others: Judson, *Exclusive Revolutionaries*; Judson, *Guardians*; Kirchner Reill, *Nationalists*; Kumar, "Nation-States as Empires"; Miller and Berger, *Nationalizing Empires*.

117. See especially Ciancia, *On Civilization's Edge*.

118. Burbank and Cooper, *Empires in World History*, 3.

119. Lieven, "Russian Empire," 626.

120. Rieber, "Sedimentary Society."

121. Alfred Rieber, cited in David-Fox, *Crossing Borders*, 53.

122. Edelstein, Geroulanos, and Wheatley, "Chronocenosis," 4.

123. Edelstein, Geroulanos, and Wheatley, "Chronocenosis," 8, 4.

124. Rezzori, *Mir auf der Spur*, 13–14.

125. M. Berman, *All That Is Solid*, 13.

126. DLA, Gregor von Rezzori, Mappe 1: Texte h. Gespräche, Interviews, "'Ich bin ein lebender Anachronismus.' Warum Gregor von Rezzori als Snob und Lebemann gilt, was er von Feministinnen hält und was ihm 'Heimat' bedeutet." *Süddeutsche Zeitung*, 26/27 November, 1994, 19.

127. Quoted in Britskyi et al., *Bukovyntsi v trahichni roki*, 133.

128. I borrow the term from Gregory Massell: Massell, *Surrogate Proletariat*.

## Chapter 1. The Enlightened State

1. Menczel, *Trügerische Lösungen*, 19.

2. On the partitions, see Snyder, *Reconstruction*, 23–25; Dabrowski, *Poland*, esp. part 3.

3. Vushko, *Politics of Cultural Retreat*, 35.

4. Kann, *History of the Habsburg Empire*, 164.

5. Polek, *Erwerbung*, 25.

6. Davison, *Essays*, 30.

7. Hitchins, *Romanians*, 15.

8. Davies, *Russo–Turkish War*, 208.

9. Polek, *Josephs II. Reisen*, 8.

10. Werenka, *Bukowinas Entstehen*.

11. Roider, "Reform and Diplomacy," 317. As Roider notes, the emperor was especially weary of incorporating territories that would prove expensive to rule after the Habsburg experience in Banat, which the empire had acquired in 1716–18 and considered a "failed experiment."

12. Polek, *Erwerbung*, ix.

13. Dimitrie Cantemir, *Descriptio Moldaviae*, cited in Kohl, *Austria*, 427.

14. Roider, "Reform and Diplomacy," 316.

15. Bidermann, *Bukowina*, 7.

16. Roider, *Baron Thugut*, 39.

17. Davison, *Essays*, 29.

18. Mieg, *Topographische Beschreibung*.

19. Splényi von Mihàldy, *Beschreibung*, vii.

20. Polek, *Joseph's II. Reisen*, 8.

21. Kaps, "Creating Differences," 140.

22. Wolff, *Idea of Galicia*, 13.

23. This process made it "a field of experimentation for the modern territorial state." Scharr, *"Landschaft Bukowina"*, 179.

24. Compare this with the case of Galicia as outlined in Wolff, *Idea of Galicia*, 16.

25. These wars included the War of the Polish Succession (1733–38), the Turkish war of 1737–39, and the War of Austrian the Austrian Succession (1740–48). Szabo, "Cameralism," 2.

26. Kaps, "Creating Differences"; Ingrao, *Habsburg Monarchy*.

27. Judson, *Habsburg Empire*, 28.

28. Ingrao, *Habsburg Monarchy*, 193.

29. Robert Evans, cited in Hochedlinger, "Habsburg Monarchy," 57.

30. Hochedlinger, "Habsburg Monarchy"; H. M. Scott, "Reform," 152–53.

31. Judson, *Habsburg Empire*, 48.

32. H. M. Scott, "Reform," 146; Szabo, "Cameralism."

33. Hochedlinger, "Habsburg Monarchy," 77.

34. Krueger, "Mediating Progress," 51–52.

35. Judson, *Habsburg Empire*, 70.

36. H. M. Scott, "Reform," 157.

37. Ingrao, *Habsburg Monarchy*, 189.

38. Judson, *Habsburg Empire*.

39. Ingrao, *Habsburg Monarchy*, 222.

40. Judson, *Habsburg Empire*, 58.

41. Hochedlinger, "Habsburg Monarchy," 90.

42. Szabo, "Cameralism," 14.

43. Evans, "Culture and Authority," 59.

44. Ingrao, *Habsburg Monarchy*, 170, 176; Vushko, *Politics of Cultural Retreat*, 5.

45. On Sonnenfels and Justi, see Stapelbroek, "International Politics."

46. Seppel, "Introduction," 14.

47. Wakefield, *Disordered Police State*, 33.

48. Raeff, "Well-Ordered Police State."

49. Tribe, "Cameralism," 274.

50. Raeff, "Well-Ordered Police State," 1229.

51. Krueger, "Mediating Progress," 53.

52. Judson, *Habsburg Empire*, 71.

53. Mitchell, *Grand Strategy*, 43.

54. Seegel, *Mapping Europe's Borderlands*. In 1766 Catherine the Great introduced a General Land Survey as part of her larger project of centralizing the Russian state. Later, Russian cartographers produced maps of the theater of war with the Ottomans, which included Bukovina, highlighting Russia's growing interest in the Danubian principalities. In Prussia, just as in the Habsburg monarchy where early maps were drawn by military officers, cartographers were also "agents of expansion." Scharr, *"Landschaft Bukowina"*, 95; Seegel, *Mapping Europe's Borderlands*, 27.

55. Scharr, *"Landschaft Bukowina"*, 105.

56. Splényi von Mihâldy, *Beschreibung*, 118.

57. Kohl, *Austria*, 427.

58. Splény, cited in Kaindl, *Ansiedlungswesen*, 102.

59. Wagner, *Revolutionsjahre 1848/49*, 175.

60. Werenka, *Bukowinas Entstehen*.

61. Kogălniceanu, *Răpirea Bucovinei*, 89, 50.

62. Werenka, "Über die Grenzregulierung."

63. Kann, *History of the Habsburg Empire*, 70–71.

64. Rohrer, *Bemerkungen*.

65. For discussion of the role of frontiers in modern territorial states, see Maier, *Among Empires*, 79; Maier, *Once Within Borders*.

66. Wagner, *Revolutionsjahre 1848/49*, 182.

67. Scharr, *"Landschaft Bukowina"*, 130, 132.

68. Kohl, *Austria*, 430.

69. Scharr, *"Landschaft Bukowina"*, 145.

70. Splényi von Mihâldy, *Beschreibung*, 74.

71. Scharr, *"Landschaft Bukowina"*, 160.

72. Scharr, *"Landschaft Bukowina"*, 148, 153.

73. Bidermann, *Bukowina*, 7.

74. Polek, *Joseph's II. Reisen*, 49.

75. For a fascinating discussion of the early Austrian bureaucracy, see Vushko, *Politics of Cultural Retreat*.

76. Mitchell, *Grand Strategy*, 35.

77. Sugar, *Southeastern Europe*, 140.

78. Panaite, "Legal and Political Status," 28.

79. Hitchins, *Romanians*, 8; Taki, *Russia on the Danube*.

80. Taki, *Russia on the Danube*, 20; Sugar, *Southeastern Europe*, 116.

81. Hitchins, *Romanians*, 12, 14.

82. On Cantemir's alliance with Russia, see Taki, *Russia on the Danube*, 23–26.

83. Philliou, *Biography of an Empire*, 8.

84. Hitchins, *Romanians*, 13.

85. Taki, *Russia on the Danube*, 19.

86. Hitchins, *Romanians*, 26.

87. Philliou, *Biography of an Empire*, 15–16. The *hospodar* Grigore Ghika, for instance, descended from a family of Albanians who had emigrated to Constantinople and become hellenized in the seventeenth century.

88. Philliou, *Biography of an Empire*, 10.

89. Correspondence between Thugut and Kaunitz, cited in Kogălniceanu, *Răpirea Bucovinei.*

90. Splényi von Miháldy, *Beschreibung*, 35, 33.

91. Splény, cited in Grigorovici, *Bucovina*, 283.

92. Splény, cited in Kaindl, *Ansiedlungswesen*, 102.

93. Splényi von Miháldy, *Beschreibung*, 75.

94. See Vushko, *Politics of Cultural Retreat* for discussion of how traditional institutions were similarly not erased in Galicia.

95. Balş, cited in Grigorovici, , 291.

96. Balş, in Grigorovici, *Bucovina*, 291, 334.

97. Kaps, "Creating Differences," 145.

98. Taki, *Russia on the Danube*, 31.

99. Ceauşu, *Un iluminist bucovinean*, 2007.

100. Ceauşu, "Czernowitz und die Rumänen," 71.

101. Scharr, "Innere Verwaltungsentwicklung."

102. Sugar, *Southeastern Europe*, 138, 137.

103. Sugar, *Southeastern Europe*, 138.

104. Ceauşu, "Zur sozioökonomischen Gesamtsituation."

105. H. M. Scott, "Reform," 177–79.

106. Melton, *Absolutism*, 156–57.

107. Justi, cited in Hölzl, "Towards Ecological Statehood," 153.

108. Justi, cited in Melton, *Absolutism*, 155.

109. H. M. Scott, "Reform," 179.

110. Krueger, "Mediating Progress."

111. Ungureanu, "Parzellengrössen."

112. Ungureanu, "Parzellengrössen," 70.

113. Kaps, "Creating Differences," 137.

114. Ceauşu, "Zur sozioökonomischen Gesamtsituation," 20.

115. Scharr, "Habsburg Cadastral."

116. Ungureanu, "Parzellengrössen," 70.

117. Budinszky and Polek, *Bukowina zu Anfang*, 74, 68.

118. For a Romanian history of colonization în Bukovina, see Grigoroviţă, *Din istoria colonizării.*

119. Ceauşu, "Zur sozioökonomischen Gesamtsituation," 17.

120. Splényi von Miháldy, *Beschreibung*, 70.

121. Scharr, *"Landschaft Bukowina"*, 129.

122. Kaindl, *Ansiedlungswesen*, 13.

123. Judson, *Habsburg Empire*, 74; Wickenhauser, *Deutschen Siedlungen*.

124. Scharr, *"Landschaft Bukowina"*, 193.

125. Rechter, "Geography Is Destiny," 326.

126. Scharr, "Entwicklung des 'ländlichen Raumes.'"

127. Bidermann, *Bukowina*, 68–76.

128. Enzenberg, cited in Rechter, *Becoming Habsburg*, 16.

129. See Delfiner, "Jewish Farmers"; Hirsch and Spitzer, *Ghosts of Home*, 26–28.

130. Hitchins, *Romanians*, 41.

131. Splény, cited in Polek, *Anfänge des Volksschulwesens*, 11.

132. Wagner, *Revolutionsjahre 1848/49*, 131.

133. Wagner, *Revolutionsjahre 1848/49*, 132.

134. Wagner, *Revolutionsjahre 1848/49*, 130.

135. H. M. Scott, "Reform," 170–71.

136. Scharr, *"Landschaft Bukowina"*, 159; Leuştean, "Eastern Orthodoxy," 1120.

137. For more on the religious fund, See Scharr, *Griechisch-orientalische Religionsfonds*.

138. Bidermann, *Bukowina*, 21.

139. Woloch and Brown, *Eighteenth-Century Europe*, 240.

140. Ingrao, *Habsburg Monarchy*, 213; Melton, *Absolutism*, 202; Vushko, *Politics of Cultural Retreat*, 75.

141. Melton, *Absolutism*, 210.

142. Prokopowitsch, "Entwicklung," 269.

143. Zieglauer, *Entwickelung*, 4–10.

144. Prokopowitsch, "Entwicklung," 280.

145. Joseph II, cited in Evans, "Culture and Authority," 70.

146. Wagner, *Revolutionsjahre 1848/49*, 132.

147. Prokopowitsch, "Entwicklung," 277.

148. Bendella, *Bukowina*, 10–11.

149. Vushko, *Politics of Cultural Retreat*, 98, 103.

150. Rohrer, *Bemerkungen*, 7.

151. Kohl, *Austria*, 430.

152. Franzos, *Aus Halb-Asien*, 147.

153. Kaindl, *Geschichte von Czernowitz*, 131.

154. Franzos, *Aus Halb-Asien*, 143.

155. Evans, "Culture and Authority," 73.

## Chapter 2. Liberal Empire

1. "Czernowitzer Feiertagsgestalten am Vormittag," in Porubsky, *Czernowitzer Skizzen*.

2. "Kaffeehäusler," in Porubsky, *Czernowitzer Skizzen*.

3. On the *Bildungsbürgertum* in Austria, see Cohen, *Education*.

4. Judson, *Exclusive Revolutionaries*, 121.

5. On the Austrian civilizing mission in Bosnia-Herzegovina, see Hajdarpasic, *Whose Bosnia?*.

6. Judson, *Habsburg Empire*, 279.

7. British liberals similarly contrasted their empire of law and "just governance" with the "rule by the sword" of Muslims, while German liberals promised to bring "representative government, superior civilization, and economic prosperity to non-European peoples in Africa and Asia." Kurlander, "Between Völkisch and Universal Visions," 141. On civilizing missions carried out by non-Western states at their peripheries, see Hirono, *Civilizing Missions*; on non-Western invocations of civilizing missions to justify rule at the periphery, see Fischer-Tiné and Mann, *Colonialism*.

8. Judson, *Habsburg Empire*, 319; Kumar, *Visions of Empire*.

9. Judson, *Exclusive Revolutionaries*, 16–17.

10. Judson, *Habsburg Empire*, 279. For an in-depth exploration of liberal views on education, see Coen, *Vienna*.

11. Kwan, *Liberalism*, 4–6.

12. Kwan, *Liberalism*, 95.

13. Otto Bernhard Friedman, cited in Kwan, *Liberalism*, 11.

14. Kwan, *Liberalism*, 12.

15. Judson, *Exclusive Revolutionaries*.

16. Judson, *Habsburg Empire*, 270; see also Fillafer, "Imperium oder Kulturstaat?," 40.

17. Sperber, *European Revolutions*, 111. For the most recent and comprehensive account of the 1848 revolutions, see C. Clark, *Revolutionary Spring*.

18. Sperber, *European Revolutions*, 42, 21.

19. Wagner, *Revolutionsjahre 1848/49*, 91.

20. For more details on the events of 1848 in Bukovina, see Rechter, *Becoming Habsburg*, 95–96.

21. R. W. Seton-Watson, *History of the Roumanians*, 557.

22. Wagner, *Revolutionsjahre 1848/49*, 83.

23. Kaindl, *Geschichte von Czernowitz*, 60.

24. Wagner, *Revolutionsjahre 1848/49*, 83–84.

25. Kaindl, *Geschichte von Czernowitz*, 60.

26. Wagner, *Revolutionsjahre 1848/49*, 91–97.

27. Judson, *Habsburg Empire*, 190–93.

28. Wagner, *Revolutionsjahre 1848/49*, 86.

29. Shevchenko, *Luk'ian Kobylytsia*.

30. Judson, *Habsburg Empire*, 194.

31. Wagner, *Revolutionsjahre 1848/49*, 89.

32. Judson, *Habsburg Empire*; Sperber, *European Revolutions*, 56.

33. Prokopowitsch, "Entwicklung," 275.

34. Wagner, *Revolutionsjahre 1848/49*, 101–2.

35. Corbea-Hoişie, *Bucovine*.

36. Turczynski, *Geschichte der Bukowina*, 125.

37. Ceauşu, "Czernowitz und die Rumänen."

38. Quoted in Klug, *Ernst Rudolf Neubauer*, 35

39. *Emancipationsruf*, 12, 11.

40. Corbea-Hoişie, *Bucovine*; Judson, *Habsburg Empire*; Ceauşu, *Parlamentarism*, 109.

41. Corbea-Hoişie, *Bucovine.*

42. Žaloba, "Erste Schienenbahnprojekt."

43. Judson, *Habsburg Empire*, 341–42.

44. Judson, *Habsburg Empire*, 346; Prokopovych, *Habsburg Lemberg*, 280.

45. See *Bukowina Portal*, "Digitale Topographie der multikulturellen Bukowina," Orte (https://www.bukowina-portal.de/de/orte): "Erzbischöfliche Residenz" and "Hauptbanhof" (accessed May 7, 2025).

46. Porubsky, *Rund um den Rathausturm*, 8, 10.

47. Josef Burg, "Ich freue mich, dass ich ein jiddischer Schriftsteller bin," in Ranner, Halling, and Fiedler, *". . . und das Herz [. . .]"*, 32.

48. Rein, "Czernowitz und die Deutschen."

49. Heymann, *Crépuscule*, 74.

50. "Das Neue Stadttheater," *Czernowitzer Allgemeine Zeitung*, October 4, 1905.

51. Lihaciu, "Kunst und Kultur, 49.

52. "Das Neue Stadttheater," *Czernowitzer Allgemeine Zeitung*, October 4, 1905.

53. See also Judson, *Habsburg Empire*, 337; Röskau-Rydel, "Staatliche Kulturpolitik," 212.

54. Adolf Hadler so described it in 1844. Lihaciu, "Kunst und Kultur," 55.

55. "Die dunkle Bukowina," *Czernowitzer Tagblatt*, February 12, 1905.

56. Judson, *Habsburg Empire*, 327.

57. Winkler, *Jüdische Identitäten.* Compare this with the case of the Krakow press, described in Wood, *Becoming Metropolitan*, 194.

58. Wood, *Becoming Metropolitan*, 193.

59. Corbea-Hoişie, *Czernowitzer Geschichten*, 119.

60. "Die Stadt," *Czernowitzer Tagblatt*, March 8, 1903.

61. "Die 'enteren' Gründe," *Czernowitzer Allgemeine Zeitung*, January 21, 1904.

62. Franzos, "Von Wien nach Czernowitz," 18.

63. "Die Mission Österreichs," *Czernowitzer Tagblatt*, February 15, 1903.

64. Corbea-Hoişie, *Bucovine*, 45.

65. "Gegen die Verländerung der städtischen Volksschulen Debatte in der Sitzung des Gemeinderates am 15 November 1911," *Czernowitzer Gemeinde-Zeitung* (special edition), November 15, 1911, 6.

66. Aharon Appelfeld, cited in Hirsch and Spitzer, *Ghosts of Home*, 37.

67. Felix Lazar Pinkus called Czernowitz "Jerusalem on the Prut" because it was "the only place on earth in which the emancipation of Jews had gone so far that Jews felt entirely at home." Corbea-Hoişie, "Jüdisches und jiddisches Czernowitz," 67.

68. Masan, "Czernowitz," 26–27.

69. Sha'ari, "Die jüdische Gemeinde."

70. Heymann, *Crépuscule*; Fisher, *Resettlers and Survivors.*

71. "Joseph II: Edict of Tolerance, January 2, 1782," in Bloomberg, *Jewish World*, 56, 54.

72. On the structure and status of the Kultusgemeinde, see Sternberg, *Zur Geschichte der Juden.*

73. Corbea-Hoişie, "Jüdisches und jiddisches Czernowitz," 72; McCagg, *History of Habsburg Jews.*

74. Rozenblit, *Reconstructing*, 31.

75. Sternberg, *Zur Geschichte der Juden*, 8.

76. Corbea-Hoişie, "Jüdisches und jiddisches Czernowitz," 66.

77. Broszat, "Von der Kulturnation."

78. Cited in Perloff, *Edge of Irony*, 133.

79. The argument is also made in Rechter, *Becoming Habsburg*.

80. Mayer Ebner, cited in Broszat, "Von der Kulturnation," 592. For a discussion of the Jewish relationship with the German language, see Aschheim, *Brothers and Strangers*; M. Volovici, *German as a Jewish Problem*.

81. Brodfeld, *Festrede*, 11.

82. Weiser and Fogel, *Czernowitz at 100*. See also Hausleitner, *Rumänisierung*, 77.

83. "Die dunkle Bukowina," *Czernowitzer Tagblatt*, February 12, 1905.

84. Goldsmith, *Modern Yiddish Culture*, 97; Heymann, *Crépuscule*, 177–82; Hirsch and Spitzer, *Ghosts of Home*, 44–47; Roskies, *Bridge of Longing*, 236.

85. Olson, *Nathan Birnbaum*, 188.

86. Franzos, "Karl Emil Franzos," 229.

87. Franzos, *Aus Halb-Asien*, 27.

88. Franzos, Franzos, "Karl Emil Franzos," 229.

89. Corbea-Hoişie, "Jüdisches und jiddisches Czernowitz," 67.

90. Broszat, "Von der Kulturnation," 577; See also Rechter, "Geography Is Destiny."

91. Hirsch and Spitzer, *Ghosts of Home*, 28.

92. Sha'ari, "Die jüdische Gemeinde," 114–15.

93. Kühn, *Dr. Eduard Reiss*.

94. Hirsch and Spitzer, *Ghosts of Home*, 31. See also Masan, "Czernowitz," 31.

95. Mosser, "Das Habsburgerreich," 69, 55–57.

96. Cisleithania was the Austrian portion of the Austro-Hungarian Empire, following the compromise of 1867 which created the dual monarchy of Austria-Hungary. The empire was then divided into two semi-autonomous regions: Cisleithania and Transleithania. Bukovina was among Cisleithania's crown lands.

97. Mischler, "Stellung der Bukowina," 56.

98. Mischler, "Stellung der Bukowina," 44.

99. On the post-emancipation economic problems of Galician peasants, see also Stauter-Halsted, *Nation in the Village*.

100. Bukhovets, "Ekspluatatsiia," 102–3.

101. On Galicia's oil industry, see Fleig Frank, *Oil Empire*.

102. "Die Schulstrafen," *Freie Lehrerzeitung*, March 13, 1909.

103. Kravets, *Narysy z storii*, 26.

104. Ungureanu, *Învățământul primar*, 140–50.

105. Judson, *Habsburg Empire*, 336.

106. Ungureanu, *Invățământul primar*, 140–50.

107. Burger, "Mehrsprachigkeit," 29.

108. Burger, "Mehrsprachigkeit," 100.

109. Grünberg, "Volksschulwesen, 203–5.

110. DAChO, f. 211, op. 1, d. 186, April 1871.

111. *Stenographische Protokolle*, July 23, 1902, VII Sitzung, 265.

112. Ungureanu, *Învăţământul primar.*

113. Prokopowitsch, "Entwicklung"; Ungureanu, *Învăţământul primar*, 60.

114. DAChO, f. 211, op. 1, d. 10349, l. 6, 1909. In many cases, the only way to separate children by language was to teach them in shifts. This method shortened the time they spent in school. In wintertime, Polish-speaking students at a school in Waskoutz had to go home after only two hours of class because it got dark so early.

115. *Stenographische Protokolle*, July 23, 1902, VII Sitzung, 265.

116. Burger, "Mehrsprachigkeit," 100.

117. "Die Wahrheit über die Schulstrafen," *Freie Lehrerzeitung*, April 17, 1909.

118. Ungureanu, *Învăţământul primar*, 57.

119. Note from Governor Bourguignon to all district school councils and the Czernowitz city school council from December 17, 1898, published in *Pädagogische Blätter*, January 10, 1899.

120. "Sind die Schulstrafen notwendig? Eine Stimme aus Lehrerkreisen," *Freie Lehrerzeitung*, September 3, 1911; and "Die Wahrheit über die Schulstrafen," *Freie Lehrerzeitung*, March 20, 1909.

121. "Das Land," *Czernowitzer Tagblatt*, March 11, 1903.

122. Burger, "Mehrsprachigkeit."

123. DAChO, f. 211, op. 1, d. 4326, January 1897.

124. DAChO, f. 211, op. 1, d. 5322, November 1899; "Die Studierwut," *Czernowitzer Tagblatt*, July 14, 1903.

125. "Die Studierwut," *Czernowitzer Tagblatt*, July 14, 1903.

126. DAChO, f. 211, op. 1, d. 8531.

127. "Warnung," *Czernowitzer Tagblatt*, July 12, 1914.

128. Corbea-Hoişie, *Bucovine*, 82.

129. Turczynski, "Czernowitz als Beispiel." For more on the development of Habsburg universities, see Surman, *Universities in Imperial Austria*.

130. Kaler, *Gründung*, 13.

131. Lihaciu, "Kunst und Kultur," 57.

132. For a short overview of the university's history, see Prokopowitsch, *Gründung*.

133. Riedl, "Universität Czernowitz," 381.

134. *Gedenkschrift aus Anlass*, 11.

135. Ceauşu, *Parliamentarism*, 187.

136. Riedl, "Universität Czernowitz," 381.

137. Turczynski, "Czernowitz als Beispiel," 190.

138. Franzos, *Aus Halb-Asien*, 143.

139. Rittershein, "Die Gründungs-Feier," 71.

140. Speech by Constantin Tomaszczuk before the Abgeordnetenhaus, March 26, 1874, cited in Kaler, *Gründung*, 15.

141. Speech by Constantin Tomaszczuk, cited in Kaler, *Gründung*, 44.

142. Lagler, *Landesfeier*, 20.

143. On imperial festivities, jubilees, and commemorations in the Habsburg Empire, see Unowsky, *Pomp and Politics*.

144. Speech by Governor Hyeronimus Alesani, cited in Lagler, *Landesfeier*, 45.

145. Lagler, *Landesfeier*, 45.

146. Speech by Constantin Tomaszczuk, cited in Riedl, "Universität Czernowitz," 382.

147. Libloy, *Festrede*, 6.

148. Cited in Lagler, *Landesfeier*, 5.

149. *K.K. Franz-Josephs-Universität*, 108.

150. Corbea-Hoişie, *Bucovine*, 45.

151. Kellner, *Leon Kellner*, 75.

152. Leuştean, "Eastern Orthodoxy," 1124–26.

153. Ceauşu, *Parliamentarism*, 282.

154. The most numerous *Burschenschaften* were Romanian (Arboroasa, Junimea, Bucovina, Academia ortodoxă, Dacia, Moldova); Catholic German (Frankonia); Ukrainian (Sojuz, Zaporoze, Czornomore); Polish (Ognisko, Lechia); Jewish (Hasmonea, Zephira, Hebronia, Humanitas, Emunah, Heatid); and there were several supranational ones (Austria, Lesehalle, Gothia, Alemannia). Prelitsch, *Student in Czernowitz*, 8. For an overview of Jewish academic associations in Czernowitz, see Roubicek, *Von Basel bis Czernowitz*.

155. DAChO, f. 3, op. 1, d. 4531, l. 29; DAChO, f. 3, op.1, d.4010, October 4, 1875. See also Cândea, *Arboroşenii*; Vitencu, *Cernăuţiul meu*, 75.

156. Turczynski, *Geschichte der Bukowina*, 157.

157. Kindleberger, *Financial History*, 131.

158. Good, *Economic Rise*, 220.

159. Kravets, *Narysy z istorii*, 105.

160. Kravets, *Narysy z istorii*, 78.

161. Marin, *Peasant Violence*, 101.

162. Kravets, *Narysy z istorii*, 73.

163. Botushanskyi, "Stanovishche silskohospodarskikh," 89.

164. DAChO, f. 3, op. 1, d. 5816, l. 15.

165. Botushanskyi, "Bukovynska trudova emihratsiia."

166. DAChO, f. 3, op. 1, d. 5816, l. 244.

167. DAChO, f. 3, op. 2, d. 6288.

168. DACHO, f. 3, op. 1, d. 6639, note from district captain in Kotzman to Bukovina's Landespräsidium, May 12, 1897.

169. DAChO, f. 3, op. 1, d. 5816, l. 60.

170. Alois Riedl, *Organisation der Auswanderung*, cited in Chmelar, *Höhepunkte*, 128.

171. For more on this, see Florea, "Frontiers of Civilization"; Zahra, "Travel Agents on Trial."

172. Zahra, *Great Departure*.

173. On Austrian consuls, see Phelps, *U.S.–Habsburg Relations*, esp. chs 4 and 5.

174. Eduard, Graf Wickenburg, "Zur österreichischen Auswanderung" (On Austrian emigration), *Bukowinaer Post*, June 11, 1914.

175. Botushanskyi, "Bukovynska trudova emihratsiia," 141.

176. Wyman, *Round-Trip*, 51; Morawska, "Labor Migrations," 193.

177. Wyman, *Round-Trip*; Morawska, "Labor Migrations"; and see too other essays in Hoerder and Page Moch, *European Migrants*.

178. For the Ukrainian case, see Martynowych, *Ukrainians in Canada*.

179. On these newcomers to politics, see Judson, *Habsburg Empire*, 300–301.

180. Boyer, *Political Radicalism*, 27.

181. Sartori, *Bengal*, 93.

182. Okey, *Habsburg Monarchy*, 276.

183. Sartori, *Bengal*, 135.

## Chapter 3. National Dreams

1. Later, Iorga wrote a book about the Byzantine empire's cultural and political legacies in the Romanian principalities of Wallachia and Moldavia. Iorga, *Byzantium After Byzantium*.

2. Under the leadership of historian Nicolae Iorga, the League became very active. Its members included intellectuals from both the Old Kingdom and the other side of the Carpathians. Their propagandistic and nationalist activities intensified after 1914, when they sponsored the defection from Austria-Hungary of a number of Romanian writers. Bucur, "Romania."

3. ANIC, fond Xerografii Viena, CCXLII, 27, article from *Românul*, August 20/September 1, 1871.

4. ANIC, fond Xerografii Viena, CCXLII, 27, article from *Românul*, August 20/September 1, 1871. On the celebration at Putna, see too an article by Teodor V. Ştefanelli, "Amintiri despre Eminescu (Serbarea de la Putna, 1871)," in *Junimea literară*, 7/8 (July 8, 1909).

5. Iorga, *Neamul românesc*, 15–16, 22

6. DAChO, f. 3, d. 2, op. 16899, note from Central Commission for Art Historical Monuments, Vienna, August 19, 1896.

7. Iorga, *Neamul românesc*, 22, 30–31.

8. Iorga, *Aportul Bucovinei*.

9. Nistor, "Zur Geschichte," 16, 4.

10. Gavril Rotică, "Cursuri pentru sufletul românesc," *Junimea literară*, September–October 1908.

11. Iorga, *Neamul românesc*, 216.

12. Schorske, *Fin-de-siècle Vienna*, ch. 3.

13. J. King, *Budweisers*, 56.

14. Cohen, *Politics of Ethnic Survival*, 142.

15. J. King, *Budweisers*, 75, 93; Boyer, *Political Radicalism*, 417–18.

16. On the 1907 electoral reform in Austria, see Boyer, *Political Radicalism*, 401.

17. Burger, *Sprachenrecht*, 162–63; Cohen, *Politics of Ethnic Survival*, 217.

18. Leslie, "Ausgleich," 115–16.

19. Nationalism's development in Bukovina generally followed the pattern described in Hroch, *Social Preconditions*. See also Connelly, *From Peoples into Nations*, 126.

20. On the Slavic intellectuals who went to Jena to study and encountered Fichte and Herder's writings, see Connelly, *From Peoples into Nations*, 86.

21. Connelly, *From Peoples into Nations*, 84.

22. Leuştean, "Eastern Orthodoxy," 1125.

23. *Membrii Soțietății pentru cultura*.

24. Hurmuzaki, cited in Ştefan Saghin, "Momentele cele mai remarcabile din viața și activitatea Societății pentru cultura și literatura română în Bucovina," in *Românii din Bucovina*, 27.

25. *Românii din Bucovina*, 10–12.

26. Prokopowitsch, *Rumänische Nationalbewegung*, 10–11; Hitchins, *Idea of Nation*.

27. Burger, "Mehrsprachigkeit."

28. Himka, "Construction of Nationality," 110, 116.

29. Popovych, *Vidrodzheniya*, 18–19.

30. Dobrzhanskyi, "Czernowitz und die Ukrainer."

31. Popovych, *Vidrodzheniya*.

32. Sbiera, "Puterea graiului," 6.

33. *Românii din Bucovina*, 43.

34. Greciuc, *Utracvismul*, 33.

35. Burger, *Sprachenrecht*, 28.

36. Greciuc, *Utracvismul*, 32, 27.

37. For this argument in the Austrian context, see Brix, *Umgangssprachen*, 36; Judson, *Guardians*, 12–13.

38. Burger, *Sprachenrecht*, 10.

39. Burger, "Mehrsprachigkeit," 98; Burger, *Sprachenrecht*, 38.

40. Burger, *Sprachenrecht*, 40–41, 44.

41. Burger, "Mehrsprachigkeit."

42. Brix, *Umgangssprachen*, 61.

43. Stourzh, *Gleichberechtigung*.

44. Brix, *Umgangssprachen*.

45. Brix, *Umgangssprachen*, 397–98.

46. Until the end of 1870s, German remained the main language of instruction even at the Greek-Oriental *Gymnasium* in Suczawa, funded with Greek-Oriental religious funds. Burger, "Mehrsprachigkeit," 104.

47. Aurel Onciul, "Zur Bukowiner Sprachenfrage," *Die Wahrheit*, May 21, 1910, 2–3.

48. Onciul, *Zur österreichischen Frage*.

49. Kaczut, *Reichsgerichtserkenntnis*, 52.

50. DAChO, f. 211, op. 2, d. 1131, l. 2, 2 (ob), petition to k.k. Landesregierung by k.k. Feldmarschall-Leutnant Herr von Chavanne.

51. Himka, "Construction of Nationality."

52. *Stenographische Protokolle*, July 26, 1902, IX Sitzung, 429.

53. Toroutiu, *Românii și clasa intelectuală*, 17.

54. Greciuc, *Utracvismul*, 20–22.

55. DAChO, f. 3, op. 1, d. 11325, l. 3, report from Bukovina's Landesregierungs-Präsidium to Ministry of Interior in Vienna, 1913.

56. Scharr, *Griechisch-orientalische Religionsfonds*, 37.

57. Leuştean, "Eastern Orthodoxy."

58. Scharr, *Griechisch-orientalische Religionsfonds*, 13.

59. On the Orthodox Church in Serbia as an incubator of national memory, see Connelly, *From Peoples into Nations*, 133; Leuştean, "Eastern Orthodoxy," 1127.

60. Scharr, *Griechisch-orientalische Religionsfonds*, 29.

61. Scharr, *Griechisch-orientalische Religionsfonds*, 116, 133.

62. Hakman briefly gave in to appeals to unify Bukovina's Orthodox Church with Transylvania in 1848, but as soon as the emperor suspended the constitution of 1849, he returned to his initial position. Leuştean, "Eastern Orthodoxy," 1128.

63. Leuştean, "Eastern Orthodoxy," 1129.

64. Hitchins, *Orthodoxy and Nationality*, 193.

65. Leuştean, "Eastern Orthodoxy," 1129, 1133.

66. This was especially the case within the Konsistorium, a new entity created in 1869. Leuştean, "Eastern Orthodoxy."

67. Pihuliak, *Gr.-or. Kirchenfrage.*

68. Z. Voronca, *Rutenizarea Bucovinei*, quotation at 22.

69. *Kulturliga für die Bukowina*; DAChO, f. 3, op. 1, d. 4533, May 1881.

70. Scharr, *Griechisch-orientalische Religionsfonds*, 179.

71. ANIC, fond Iancu Flondor, nr. inv. 945, dosar 9/1898, 12, letter to Flondor by Romanian priests in Bukovina Greek-Orthodox archdiocese, October 18/30, 1899. (Double dates here and subsequently refer to Julian/Gregorian calendar respectively.)

72. ANIC, fond Iancu Flondor, nr. inv. 945, dosar 9/1898, 12, letter to Flondor by Romanian priests in Bukovina Greek-Orthodox archdiocese, October 18/30, 1899.

73. *Beitrag zur kirchlichen Frage*, 5–6, 19–20.

74. ANIC, fond Iancu Flondor, dosar 9/1898; fond Xerografii Viena, XXXIII/21 and XXXIII/24.

75. ANIC, fond Xerografii Viena, XXXIII/17, "Abschrift: Resolutionen der Versammlung gr-or. Priester ruthenischer Nationalität, " October 10, 1913.

76. Scharr, *Griechisch-orientalische Religionsfonds*, 181, 205.

77. ANIC, fond Iancu Flondor, nr. inv. 945, dosar 9/1898, 12, letter to Flondor by Romanian priests in Bukovina Greek-Orthodox archdiocese, October 18/30, 1899.

78. ANIC, fond Iancu Flondor, dosar 9/1898, 17, copy of petition to k.k. Apostolische Majestät by representatives of Greek-Orthodox Church in Bukovina, July 4/17, 1911.

79. ANIC, fond Xerografii Viena, XXXIII/22, 5, report from k.k. Regierungsrat and Polizeidirektor Tarangul to k.k. Landespräsidium concerning meeting of Greek-Orthodox clergy in metropolitan residence building, October 2, 1913.

80. ANIC, fond Xerografii Viena, XXXIII/17, 2, Resolutions of assembly of gr.-or. priests of Ruthenian nationality on October 10, 1913.

81. Judson, *Guardians*, 5, 68.

82. Judson, *Guardians*, 92.

83. Zahra, *Kidnapped Souls*, 5.

84. Burger, "Mehrsprachigkeit," 98, 101.

85. "Massgebende Grundsätze über die Frage der Minoritätsschulen und sonstigen sprachlichen Berücksichtigung sprachlicher Minderheiten in den Volksschulen," *Pädagogische Blätter*, June 25, 1899.

86. Burger, *Sprachenrecht*, 29.

87. DAChO, f. 211, op. 1, d. 10349, report by inspectors Pawlitschek and Popowicz concerning inspections of primary schools with Polish language of instruction in Gurahumora district, June 1909. On further drawbacks of the system, see chapter 2, note 114 above.

88. DAChO, f. 211, op. 1, d. 1504, l. 10, report to Ministry of Culture and Enlightenment concerning introduction of Romanian and Ukrainian language courses in high schools in Czernowitz, November 8, 1878.

89. DAChO, f. 3, op. 1, d. 11124, l. 2, complaint against Prof. Eugen Kozak at the Greek-Oriental (Orthodox) theological faculty in Czernowitz, concerning his behavior with Ukrainian students, August 18, 1911.

90. Popovych, *Vidrodzhennya*, 9.

91. For this argument, see also Judson, *Guardians*, 9; Zahra, *Kidnapped Souls*, 12.

92. "Der jüdische Kulturkampf der Schule," *Bukowinaer Volksblatt*, March 30, 1909.

93. DAChO, f. 211, op. 1, d. 3382, statistical report for Greek-Orthodox Oberrealschule, Czernowitz, 1890–91.

94. Greciuc, *Utracvismul*, 8.

95. Ehrlich, *Aufgaben der Sozialpolitik*, 28.

96. *Stenographische Protokolle*, July 23, 1902, VII Sitzung, 270–71.

97. In 1871 only 10.9% of school-aged children in Bukovina went to school; by 1902/3, school attendance had increased to 88%. See Burger, "Mehrsprachigkeit."

98. Burger, "Mehrsprachigkeit "; Burger, *Sprachenrecht*, 131.

99. Burger, "Mehrsprachigkeit," 113.

100. Burger, "Mehrsprachigkeit," 111, 113. First- and second-grade students began attending separate language sections beginning in 1898/99. In 1909/10 the first national classes for the first three grades opened in Czernowitz.

101. DAChO, f. 211, op. 2, d. 704, October 8, 1897.

102. DAChO, f. 211, op. 2, d. 704, text of decisions made by Gemeinderath Czernowitz in meeting of September 28, 1897, conveyed to k.k. Landesschhulrat on October 8, 1897.

103. Judson, *Guardians*, 79.

104. Stauter-Halsted, *Nation in the Village*, 215.

105. Judson, *Guardians*, 74.

106. In Galicia, too, Jews were blamed for bringing about the peasantry's death through alcohol. Struve, "Gentry, Jews, and Peasants," 108–9.

107. Leslie, "Ausgleich," 116.

108. Leslie, "Ausgleich," 120–23.

109. On further divisions within Romanian national parties by 1911, see Hensellek, *Letzten Jahre*, 116.

110. "Trezirea Bucovinei," *Voința poporului*, May 24, 1908 (quoting the Viennese *Reichspost*). For Onciul's role in the Bukovinan Compromise, see Onciul, *Aurel Ritter von Onciul*. For a thorough account of the national compromise in Bukovina, see Stourzh, "National Compromise."

111. Judson, *Guardians*, 13.

112. Burger, *Sprachenrecht*, 190–91. In Moravia, in accordance with the "Lex Perek"—a law promoted by Czech activists aimed at undoing the alleged effects of *Kinderfang* (child capture), whereby German schools took in children who did not speak German to fill places, thus ensuring the schools' survival—children were ascribed a nationality and admitted only to schools whose language of instruction they spoke. See Zahra, *Kidnapped Souls*, 34.

113. J. King, *Budweisers*, 142–43.

114. Burger, *Sprachenrecht*, 203; Leslie, " Ausgleich."

115. Hensellek, *Letzten Jahre*, 10–11, 37.

116. Leslie, "Ausgleich," 126.

117. Across Galicia, Jewish politicians demanded that Yiddish be recognized as an *Umgangssprache*. Similar appeals came from the Bukovinan districts of Wiznitz and Zastawna after the census of 1910. See Brix, *Umgangssprachen*, 396.

118. Olson, *Nathan Birnbaum*, 108.

119. Shanes, *Diaspora Nationalism*, 203.

120. Kupchanko, *Schicksale der Ruthenen*, 45.

121. *Slavisirung der Bukowina*, 18.

122. As in Bohemia, German nationalists in Bukovina mobilized in reaction to the nationalist mobilization of other groups. For the Bohemian case, see Cohen, *Politics of Ethnic Survival*, 26.

123. *Satzungen des Vereines* (pamphlet, Czernowitz university library).

124. Zieglauer, *Festschrift*, 6.

125. Kaindl, "Raimund Friedrich Kaindl," 185.

126. Kaindl, Universität in Czernowitz, 62.

127. Onciul, *Das österreichische Problem*, 1, 5.

128. Niculiţă-Voronca, *Casa naţională*.

129. *Stenographische Protokolle*, October 30, 1908, III Sitzung, IV Session, X Wahlperiode.

130. Niculiţă-Voronca, *Casa naţională*, 4.

131. Niculiţă-Voronca, *Casa naţională*, 5. Compare this with the case of pluralist nationalists discussed in Kirchner Reill, *Nationalists*, 205.

132. *Apel către răzeşii*, 10.

133. Niculiţă-Voronca, *Casa naţională*.

134. Tcaciuc, *Câteva cuvinte*.

135. *Apel către răzeşii*, 31

136. *Niedergang des deutschen Unterrichtes*, 5, 6.

137. Rosenzweig, *Wir Juden*, 10, 14.

138. König, "Geschichte der J.N.A.V. Hasmonaea," 114.

139. Cornis-Pope and Neubauer, *History of the Literary Cultures*, 70.

140. Drozdowski, *Damals in Czernowitz*, 194.

141. Rezzori, *Ermine in Czernopol*, 12.

142. Connelly, *From Peoples into Nations*, 23, 25.

## Chapter 4. Between Worlds

1. AT-OeSTA/KA NL B/8: 2, fol. 1–153, Tatbeschreibung VI, I. Grenzverteidigung gegen Russland vom 6. bis 31. August 1914.

2. Watson, *Ring of Steel*, 310.

3. "Grosse Erfolge unserer Armee westlich und östlich der Weichsel," *Neue Freie Presse*, August 25, 1914, 2.

4. Wiener Library, Ludwig Diesche papers, 0637-Box 1–1581728.

5. Menczel, *Als Geisel*, 25–27.

6. Mason, *Dissolution*, 75–80.

7. Cusco, "Wartime Mobilization," 135.

8. AT-OeSTA/KA NL B/8:2, fols 1–153, "Aus dem Tagebuche des Landesgendarmeriekommandanten Obersten Eduard Fischer," June 17, 1916.

9. Gerwarth, *Vanquished*, 31.

10. Watson, *Ring of Steel*, 158.

11. Narskij, "Reality of War. For more on the eastern front, see Strachan, "Eastern Front"; Showalter, "War in the East." For a comprehensive account of the war in Eastern Europe, see Borodziej and Górny, *Forgotten Wars*.

12. Ther, "Pre-Negotiated Violence."

13. Leonhard, "Legacies of Violence"; Sanborn, "Genesis of Russian Warlordism"; Holquist, "Tools for Revolution." See also Deak and Gumz, "How to Break a State."

14. See Gatrell, "War After the War"; Gerwarth, *Vanquished*.

15. Menczel, *Trügerische Lösungen*, 28.

16. Sukiennicki, *East Central Europe*, 1:97. The first trial took place from December 29, 1913 to March 3, 1914. The second took place on March 9 in Lwów.

17. "Flucht der Brüder Gerowski aus dem Untersuchungsgefängnis," *Czernowitzer Tagblatt*, June 9, 1914.

18. ANIC, Xerografii Viena, XXXIII/27, note from Ministry of External Affairs to Ministry of Interior, April 5, 1913, "Grossrumänische Tendenzen," 2–3.

19. AT-OeSTA/AVA Inneres MdI Präsidium A 2096, Zl 949/27 January 1914, encl. in Zl 4395/1914, letter from Landespräsident of Bukovina to Ministry of Interior, January 19, 1914.

20. AT-OeSTA/AVA Inneres MdI Präsidium A 2096, Zl 3048/21 March 1914, note from Landespräsident of Bukovina to Ministry of Interior, March 14, 1914.

21. AT-OeSTA/AVA Inneres MdI Präsidium, A 2096, Zl 12.535/13, encl. in 12.535/1913.

22. Menczel, *Trügerische Lösungen*, 24–25.

23. J. Weber, *Russentage in Czernowitz*.

24. Menczel, *Als Geisel*, 28.

25. Menczel, *Als Geisel*, 16.

26. Cusco, "Wartime Mobilization," 136. See also Holquist, "Role of Personality."

27. AT-OeSTA/AVA Inneres MdI Präsidium A 2096, Zl 20914/24, October 1917, encl. in Zl 20914/1917, report from head of Bukowina Landesregierung to Präsidium des Ministeriums des Innern.

28. DAChO, f. 3, op. 1, d. 12462, July 21, 1915, report from Kotzman Bezirkmannschaft to k.k. Landesregierungs-Präsidium in Dornawatra, 2.

29. CAHJP, HM 2/8594, December 1, 1914, letter to President of Alliance Israélite from Bucharest office.

30. "Russische Verwaltungskomödie in Czernowitz," *Czernowitzer Allgemeine Zeitung*, August 26, 1917.

31. DAChO, f. 283, op. 1, d. 4, Chancellery of Bukovina's governor, protocol on investigation, December 1, 1914.

32. DAChO, f. 3, op. 1, d. 12462, l. 2, report from Kotzman Bezirkmannschaft to k.k. Landesregierungs-Präsidium in Dornawatra, July 21, 1915.

33. DAChO, f. 3, op. 1, d. 12462, l. 2, note from the administrative authorities of Kotzman/Kitsman district to k.k. Landesregierungs-Präsidium in Dornawatra, July 21, 1915.

34. During the Russian occupation a "special hospital for female illnesses," including "numerous venereal diseases" was opened in Czernowitz. AT-OeSTA/AVA, Inneres MdI Präsidium, A 2096, Zl 23741/ December 3, 1917.

35. An-Sky, *Enemy at His Pleasure*, 9.

36. Gatrell, *Whole Empire Walking*. In the Russian Empire Jews were not allowed to live within fifty kilometers of the western frontier because they were suspected of endangering border security. When Russia suffered military defeats, the high command was allowed to take harsh measures against Jews in the borderlands, attacking individual Jews and confiscating their property, in retaliation for losses.

37. Prusin, *Nationalizing a Borderland*, 27.

38. AT-OeSTA/AVA Nachlässe AN Wassilko I, Abschrift von Ing. Glinski, Seletin, March 22, 1915, 12.

39. AT-OeSTA/AVA Nachlässe AN Wassilko I, Abschrift von Ing. Glinski, Seletin, March 22, 1915, 12.

40. Holquist, "Tools for Revolution," 225.

41. J. Weber, *Russentage in Czernowitz*, 61.

42. DAChO, f. 3, op. 1, d. 12462, "An das k.k. Landesregieruns-Präsidium in Dornawatra," July 21, 1915, 2.

43. Lohr, "Russian Army," 407.

44. AT-OeStA/AVA Nachlässe AN Wassilko I, Karton 1, Konvolut 2, letter from Pihuliak to Wassilko, June 24, 1915.

45. AT-OeStA/AVA Nachlässe AN Wassilko I, Karton 1, Konvolut 2, letter from Pihuliak to Wassilko, June 24, 1915.

46. The most prominent member of this ethnic Romanian family was Nikolai Wassilko (later Mykola Vasylko) (1868–1924). Wassilko, as we have seen, was the most prominent Ruthenian (Ukrainian) politician in Austrian Bukovina. He was a deputy in the provincial Diet and a member of the imperial parliament in Vienna. Initially a member of the Old Ruthenian party, he later represented the Liberal Alliance and the Ukrainian National Democratic Party.

47. AT-OeStA/AVA Nachlässe AN Wassilko I, Karton 1, Konvolut 2, letter from Dmytro Ladygyn, Hilfspriester in Berhometh to Nikolai Wassilko, n.d.

48. AT-OeStA/AVA Inneres MdI Präsidium A 2096, Zl 24694/1917 (February 27, 1917), encl. Zl 24694/1917 from Landesgendarmeriekommando No 15 on Stimmung der Bevölkerung in der Bukowina, by Eduard Fischer.

49. "Russische Verwaltungskomödie in Czernowitz," *Czernowitzer Allgemeine Zeitung*, August 26, 1917.

50. AT-OeSTA/AVA Nachlässe AN Wassilko I, Karton 1, Konvolut 2, "Beiträge zur Kriegsgeschichte der Bukowina."

51. AT-OeSTA/AVA Inneres MdI Praesidium A 2096, Zl 24694/1917 (February 17, 1917), encl. Zl 24694/1917 from Landesgendarmeriekommando No. 15 on Stimmung der Bevölkerung in der Bukowina, by Eduard Fischer.

52. Healy, *Vienna and the Fall*, 149; see also Judson, *Habsburg Empire*, 154–59.

53. Cusco, "Wartime Mobilization," 142.

54. AT-OeStA/AVA Inneres MdI Präsidium A 2096, encl. Zl 15803/1915, "An das k.u.k. Feldgericht des Brückenkopf-Kommandos in Kolomea."

55. Cusco, "Wartime Mobilization," 143.

56. On Austria's transformation from *Rechstaat* into military dictatorship, see Judson, *Habsburg Empire*, 385–417. See also Scheer, *Zwischen Front*.

57. Bălan, *Suprimarea mişcărilor naţionale*, 44.

58. AT-OeSTA/AVA Nachlässe, AN Wassilko I, Karton 1, letter from Erotey Pihuliak to Nikolai von Wassilko, June 24, 1915.

59. Healy, *Vienna and the Fall*, 146.

60. AT-OeSTA/AVA Nachlässe, AN Wassilko I, Karton 1, Konvolut 2, 3, letter from Oberlehrer Yurii Hordiichuk to Wassilko, April 8, 1915, 3, 5.

61. AT-OeStA/AVA Nachlässe AN Wassilko I, Karton 1, Konvolut 2, "Beiträge zur Geschichte der Bukowina."

62. AT-OeSTA/AVA Inneres MdI Präsidium A 2096, Zl 11352, June 3, 1915. Also Zl 13543, June 30, 1915. The letter eventually ended up in the hands of Bukovina's governor, who confirmed that, while the number of deserters reported in it was a wild exaggeration, "there have been some grievances with respect to teachers in Czernowitz" and "a great number of Jews have tried by any means to evade their military duty."

63. ANIC, fond Xerografii Viena, XXXIII/56–62, 4–5, May 20, 1915, petition of Gh. Serbu to k.k. Landespräsident of Bukowina, in response to complaints brought against him. Tarok was a card game played in Central Europe with a pack containing twenty-two tarots, roughly equivalent to modern playing cards.

64. Zombory-Moldovan, *Burning of the World.*

65. AT-OeSTA/AVA Inneres MdI Präsidium A 2096, Zl 24694, encl. Zl 24694/1917, report from Landesgendarmeriekommando No. 15 on mood of the population in Bukovina, by Eduard Fischer, February 17, 1917.

66. AT-OeSTA/AVA Inneres MdI Präsidium A 2096, Zl 3262, February 13, 1915.

67. AT-OeSTA/AVA Inneres MdI Präsidium A 2096, Zl 16594, November 23, 1914, Encl in Zl 17231, December 3, 1914, report on investigation of Vasile Lițu.

68. AT-OeSTA/AVA Inneres MdI Präsidium, A 2096, Zl 14618, October 23, 1914, letter from Landespräsident of Bukovina to Ministry of Interior.

69. AT-OeSTA/AVA Inneres MdI Präsidium, A 2096, Zl 14618, October 23, 1914, letter from Landespräsident of Bukovina Rudolf von Meran to Ministry of Interior.

70. AT-OeStA/KA NL B/8: 2, fols 1–153, Eduard Fischer Diary, July 21, 1916, 103.

71. NoeLA, Zl 2881/ XII e/1918, "Abschrift Leitung der Beschäftigungskurse für Schülerinnen der Bukowinaer Mädchen Lyzeen," Vienna, October 31, 1916, An das Ministerium des Innern; Polizei Archiv Wien, 9029/1914–1915, April 14, 1915, report on mood among refugees from Bukovina and Galicia in Vienna.

72. DAChO, f. 3, op. 1, d, 12706, l. 57, petition to Hohes Präsidium by Ludwig Kuczynski.

73. DAChO, f. 3, op. 1, d. 12706, petition from Elias Wender to the Bukovina Landesregierung, June 5, 1916.

74. Judson, *Habsburg Empire*, 401.

75. Habartová, "Jewish Refugees," 142.

76. AT-OeStA/AVA Nachlässe, AN Wassilko I, Karton 1, Konvolut 2, note on "Flüchtlingsfürsorge," from Baron Stiglitz to Rudolf, Graf von Meran, March 26, 1915, 8. For context on Austrian refugee camps and state-building efforts through refugee policy during the war, see Crețu, "Child Assistance."

77. Dimitrie Marmeliuc, "In preajma unirii: file din carnet," in Nistor, *Amintiri răzlețe*, 209.

78. Hausleitner, "Konfliktfelder," 107–8. Torouțiu, *Poporația.*

79. Romulus Reut, "Die rumänische Kulturliga und die österreichischen Rumänen," *Czernowitzer Tagblatt*, April 12, 1914.

80. Aurel Ritter von Onciul, "Ein österreicher Rumäne gegen die Kulturliga: Äusserungen des Reichsratsabgeordneter Aurel Ritter von Onciul," *Bukowinaer Post*, April 5, 1914.

81. AT-OeSTA/AVA Inneres MdI Präsidium A 2096, Zl 14618, October 23, 1914, copy of "Verfolgung der Bukowiner Rumänen," *Dimineața*, September 2, 1914.

82. AT-OeSTA/AVA Inneres MdI Präsidium A 2096, Zl 14618, October 23, 1914, letter from k.k. Landespräsident to Ministry of Interior.

83. AT-OeSTA/AVA Inneres MdI Präsidium A 2096, Zl 14618, October 23, 1914, Copy of "Verfolgung der Bukowiner Rumänen," from *Dimineața*, September 2, 1914.

84. AT-OeSTA/AVA Inneres MdI Präsidium A 2096, Zl 17501, December 7, 1914, encl. in Zl 17501/1914, letter from Landespräsident of Bukovina to Ministry of Interior.

85. AT-OeSTA/AVA Nachlässe, AN Wassilko I, Karton 1, Konvolut 2.

86. AT-OeSTA/AVA Nachlässe, AN Wassilko I, Karton 1, Konvolut 2, speech in the Reichsrat, October 8, 1912, XLVI Session, 9 Sitzung, Vienna.

87. Eager to benefit from the anti-Russian elements of the Ukrainian movement, the authorities in Vienna and Berlin offered Ukrainian nationalists not only encouragement, but also financial backing. On August 4, 1914, a group of Russian Ukrainian émigrés formed the Union for the Liberation of Ukraine (Soiuz Vyzvolennia Ukrainy) in Lemberg. In May 1915, the General Ukrainian National Council emerged in Vienna. Von Hagen, *War in a European Borderland.*

88. On Austro-Hungarian citizens who fell into Russian hands, becoming prisoners of war—and the politics of POWs—see Rachamimov, *POWs and the Great War.*

89. For more on the Union for the Liberation of Ukraine, see Plokhy, *Gates of Europe*, 203.

90. AT-OeSTA/AVA Nachlässe, AN Wassilko I, Karton I, Konvolut 1, "Die österreichisch-ungarische Monarchie und die ukrainische Frage," June 1916, 6.

91. AT-OeStA/AVA Nachlässe AN Wassilko I, Karton 1, Konvolut 2, Independent Akt, "Die Österreichisch-Ungarische Monarchie und die ukrainische Frage," June 1916, 5.

92. Zeman, *Break-up*, 53.

93. Kauffman, *Elusive Alliance.*

94. Cusco, "Wartime Mobilization," 165, 137. See also Arhire, "Russian–Romanian Diplomatic Negotiations."

95. Cusco, "Wartime Mobilization," 124.

96. J. Weber, *Russentage in Czernowitz*, quotation at 34.

97. AT-OeSTA/AVA Inneres MdI Präsidium A 2096, Zl 15803/1915, encl in Zl 18493/1915, "An das k.u.k. Feldgericht des Brückenkopf Kommandos in Kolomea."

98. DAChO, f. 10, op. 1, d. 846, ll. 65–66, May 26, 1912, "Bericht über die am 23. dm abends im Festsaale der jüdischen Nationalhauses stattgefundene Volksversammlung mit der Tagesordnung 'Bericht über die letzte Tagung des Bukowinaer Landtages.'"

99. SANIC, Xerografii Viena, XXXIV/76–77, April 16, 1918, "Modest Scalat, gewesener Gemeinderat in Czernowitz, politisches Verhalten Abschrift, Czernowitz April 16, 1918"; SANIC, Xerografii Viena, XXXIV/ 87, June 30, 1918, "An den Militäranwalt des k und k Militärkommandanten in Przemysl exponiert in Lemberg," 5.

100. Plokhy, *Gates of Europe*, 202.

101. Cusco, "Wartime Mobilization," 142.

102. AT-OeSTA/AVA Inneres MdI Präsidium A 2096, Zl 23741, December 3, 1917. In May 1917 Doroshenko was replaced with another Ukrainian activist, Oleksandro Lototskyi.

103. AT-OeSTA/AVA Inneres MdI Präsidium A 2096, Zl 23741, December 3, 1917, 23. The revolution also gave a new impulse to the Polish national movement: Russian Poles arrived in Czernowitz, came into contact with local Poles, and set up organizations and events to promote the freedom and independence of Poland.

104. AT-OeSTA/AVA Inneres MdI Präsidium A 2096, Zl 23741/1917 (December 3, 1917), encl. in Zl 23741/1917, note by k.k. Hofrat and Polizeidirektor Tarangul to the Landesregierungs-Präsidium.

105. AT-OeSTA/AVA Inneres MdI Präsidium A 2096, Zl 20914/1917, encl. Zl 20914, October 24, 1917, note from leader of Bukowina Landesregierung to Präsidium of Ministry of Interior.

106. ANIC, fond Xerografii Viena, XXXIV/88–89, July 16, 1918, 3, telegram of Landespräsident in Czernowitz to Minister of Interior.

107. DAChO, f. 3, op. 1, d. 13034, l.1, complaint by Oberlt. Brome, leader of German Kriegsgräberverwaltung in Czernowitz, July 27, 1918. "Marmeladesoldat" was a common insult used by Austrian soldiers against Germans and especially northern German soldiers in World War I. It refers to the fact that German soldiers did not receive rations of butter, only thin marmalade.

108. Judson, *Habsburg Empire*, 421.

109. Cited in Judson, *Habsburg Empire*, 432.

110. Valiani, *End of Austria-Hungary*, 244.

111. AT-OeStA/KA NL B/8: 2, fols 1–153, copy of article from *Czernowitzer Morgenblatt*, November 5, 1918.

112. Valiani, *End of Austria-Hungary*, 9

113. Nistor, *Zece ani*, 179.

114. Nistor, *Amintiri răzlețe*, 184.

115. ANIC, fond Xerografii Viena, XXXIV/95, telegram of Landespräsident in Czernowitz to k.k. Ministry of Interior, state police bureau, on Romanian national assembly in Czernowitz, October 23, 1918.

116. ANIC, fond Iancu Flondor, dosar 19/1918, 41, document without title on formation of Constituent Assembly in Bukovina.

117. Novosivskyi, *Bukovinian Ukrainians*, 156–57. Fearing chaos and anarchy, Bessarabian elites made a similar appeal in January 1918. See Cusco, "Wartime Mobilization," 134.

118. Hausleitner, "Konfliktfelder," 113–14.

119. Ion I. Nistor, "Discursul festiv rostit la congresul general al Bucovinei, Cernăuți Sala Sinodală, 1918, November 28," in Nistor, *Amintiri răzlețe*, 280–82.

120. BAR, Colecția de manuscrise A 218/1, "Procesul verbal asupra Congresului General al Bucovinei, ținut joi la 15/28 noiembrie 1918 in Sala Sinodală din Palatul Metropolitan în Cernăuți, în care s-a hotarât Unirea Bucovinei cu România, dăruit de Ion Nistor, 11/24 Decembrie 1919"; PUL-CR, vol. 6 (1930), 8–9.

121. Ukrainian Delegation, *Notes présentées*, 6.

122. PUL-CR, vol. 6 (1930), 3.

123. At first the Romanians pressurized Austria-Hungary for territorial concessions in return for neutrality—and Germany tried to persuade Austria-Hungary to give in, hoping to thus draw Romania in on the side of the Central Powers.

124. Hitchins and Sharp, *Ionel Brătianu*, 82.

125. Torrey, *Romania and World War I*, 26.

126. Mantoux, *Paris Peace Conference*, 10.

127. PUL-CR, vol 6 (1930), 5.

128. Drăghicescu, *Problèmes nationaux*, 181–82, 212.

129. Petrescu-Comnen, *Great War*, 27.

130. PUL-CR, vol. 6 (1930), 20.

131. Torrey, *Romania and World War I*, 31.

132. Nistor, *Amintiri răzleţe*, 22.

133. Drăghicescu, *Problèmes nationaux*, 188.

134. Headlam, *Memoir*, 136.

135. "Czernowitzer Tagebuch aus der Kriegszeit," *Czernowitzer Tagblatt*, August 15, 1914.

## Chapter 5. "Returning" to Romania

1. Smith, *Sovereignty*, 134; Suveică, *Post-imperial Encounters*, 66.

2. Deak, "Habsburg Empire," 134; Rigó, *Capitalism in Chaos*, 9. Like other successor states, Romania found its newly incorporated cities had "better connections with cities in other countries than with other cities within [its own]." See Ramet, "Interwar East Central Europe, 6.

3. Iordachi, "Continuum," 236.

4. Boia, *În jurul Marii Uniri*, 36.

5. *Bukovina: Handbooks [. . .], No. 6*, 6.

6. Iorga, *Aportul Bucovinei*, 5.

7. "Conferinţa dlui profesor universitar şi fost ministru Ion Nistor," *Glasul Bucovinei*, November 30, 1928.

8. ANIC, fond Ministerul Instrucţiunii şi Artelor, nr. inv. 710, dosar 39/1922, 1, report on promotion of cultural activity in Bukovina.

9. DAChO, f. 213, op. 1, d. 3739, l. 3, Revizoratul şcolar al Jud. Suceava către onoratul Inspectoratul Regiunii XIV şcolare in Cernăuţi, October 17, 1928.

10. On Bukovina's loss of autonomy, see Bruja, *Extrema dreaptă*, 28–29.

11. Pedersen, *Guardians*, 6.

12. Fichman, *Before Memories Fade*, 15.

13. Aldcroft, *Europe's Third World*, 89.

14. Livezeanu, *Cultural Politics*, 11.

15. Weitz, "From the Vienna to the Paris System," 1315.

16. Vasile Grecu, "Tratatul pentru scutul minorităţilor," *Glasul Bucovinei*, June 27, 1922.

17. In Pieter Judson's words, "each of these self-styled nation-states in fact acted like a small empire": cited in Kirchner Reill, *Fiume Crisis*, 17. See also Alexander Motyl's argument about the resurfacing of empires due to persisting power differentials and differences in state structure and capacity: Motyl, "Why Empires Reemerge." For a similar argument outside the European context, see Cooper, *Colonialism in Question*, 156.

18. Wheatley, "Central Europe as Ground Zero," 911.

19. Deak, "Habsburg Empire," 129–30.

20. John Connelly refers to the uniform yellow color of Habsburg administrative buildings in *From Peoples into Nations*, 226. On the resilience of imperial forms and obstacles to nationalization, see also Egry, "Navigating the Straits"; Kirchner Reill, Jeličić, and Rolandi, "Redefining Citizenship."

21. DAChO, f. 12, op. 1, d. 76, l. 1, note from Eighth Division to minister delegate of Bukovina, n.d.

22. DAChO, f. 12, op. 1, d. 76, l. 2, note to Ministry of Interior, Direcţiunea Poliţiei şi Siguranţei Generale, n.d.

23. DAChO, f. 213, op. 1, d. 1556, l. 7, note from Ministry of the Interior to Ministry of Education, n.d. (1923).

24. Drozdowski, "Stadt am Prut," 59.

25. "Şcoala din Bucovina," *Glasul Bucovinei*, December 15, 1918.

26. DAChO, f. 6, op. 1, d. 7, l. 1, 1919, note from the Presidium of Bukovina government: memorandum to all state offices in Bukovina.

27. DAChO, f. 43, op. 1, d. 3510, l. 2, decision concerning transfer of Austrian monuments to the museum in Chernivtsi, 1925.

28. DAChO, f. 43, op. 1, d. 88, l. 1, note from Bukovina Duty Secretariat for internal affairs to the Presidium of the magistrate of Cernăuţi city, February 4, 1919.

29. CAHJP, HM2/8336.5, instructions from city magistrature Czernowitz to all civilian and military authorities and offices, February 20, 1919. For similar activities in interwar Poland, see Ciancia, *On Civilization's Edge*, 539.

30. DAChO, f. 12, op. 1, d. 76, l. 33, Gastwirte-Genossenschaft Gruppe X in Czernowitz, letter to city magistrature, September 30, 1919.

31. "Firmenschilder," *Ostjüdische Zeitung*, January 11, 1924.

32. Speech by Vasile Marcu, February 16, 1920, in Iaţencu and Olaru, *Bucovineni în Parlamentul României*, 105. On the circulation of multiple currencies in post-imperial Fiume, see Kirchner Reill, *Fiume Crisis*, 75.

33. On the integration and nationalization of currencies in interwar Romania, see Rigó, *Capitalism in Chaos*, 180.

34. "Denkmäler, ein Wort an die Bildstürmer," *Ostjüdische Zeitung*, September 26, 1922.

35. DAChO, f. 43, op.1, d. 2732, l. 33, address to Directoratul general pentru culte, Cernăuţi, November 22, 1924.

36. DAChO, f. 43, op.1, d. 2732, l. 62, founding charter for the unification monument in Cernăuţi, November 22, 1924.

37. DAChO, f. 43, op.1, d. 2732, l. 3, "Desvelirea monumentului unirii la 11 Noiembrie 1924"; l. 115, "Programul official al serbărilor pentru desvelirea monumentului unirii la Cernăuţi," November 11, 1924.

38. DAChO, f. 43, op. 1, d. 2732, l. 33, note to Directoratul general pentru culte, Cernăuţi, November 22, 1924.

39. "Die Vereinigung: Zur Enthüllung des Unirea-Denkmals," *Ostjüdische Zeitung*, November 11, 1924.

40. Turczynski, *Geschichte der Bukowina*, 223.

41. Livezeanu, *Cultural Politics*, 17.

42. LBI, Israel Cohen Papers, RG 448-YIVO, series 1, folder 27, "A Stroll Through Czernowitz," 5. *Hakenkreuzler* were members of a postwar Germanophone anti-Semitic organization who adopted the *Hakenkreuz* (swastika) as a symbol.

43. Aurel Morariu, "Studenţimea în serviciul culturii Româneşti," *Glasul Bucovinei*, January 4, 1922, 1.

44. "Die Errichtung des Nationaltheaters in Czernowitz—Aus einem Gespräche mit dem Generaldirektor des Nationaltheaters Professor Dr. Berariu," *Czernowitzer Allgemeine Zeitung*, 5.

45. "Die Theaterfrage," *Czernowitzer Morgenblatt*, January 25, 1922; "Gewaltsame Besetzung des Stadttheaters," *Czernowitzer Morgenblatt*, January 3, 1922, 1.

46. Kittner and Silbermann, *Erinnerungen*, 10–11.

47. ANIC, fond Ministerul Instrucţiunii şi Artelor, nr. inv. 811, dosar 396/1927, report to Ministry of Education on cultural inspections in Bukovina, 10.

48. H. Seton-Watson, *Eastern Europe*, 152.

49. Bruja, "Constituirea Ligii," 11; DAChO, f. 6, op. 1, d. 29, ll. 9–10, report of minister-delegate of Bukovina on his conflict with the general of the Romanian army, Petală.

50. Speech by Teofil Lupu, December 22, 1919, in Iaţencu and Olaru, *Bucovineni în Parlamentul României*, 157.

51. DAChO, f. 118, op. 4, d. 390, l. 4, declaration from Caterina Buliga to general commander of Eighth Division in Cernăuţi concerning accusation against Ladislaus Friedrich for insulting the Romanian state, August 18, 1921.

52. Bruja, *Extrema dreaptă*, 37.

53. "Bucovina în trecut, conferinţa tinuta in Cernăuţi, August 16, 1919," in Iorga, *Conferinţe bucovinene*, 10.

54. "Conferinţa dlui profesor universitar şi fost ministru Ion Nistor," *Glasul Bucovinei*, November 30, 1928.

55. Ion Nistor, "Homo Bucovinensis," *Glasul Bucovinei*, December 11, 1918.

56. "Conferinţa dlui prof univ şi fost ministru Ion I. Nistor," *Glasul Bucovinei*, November 30, 1928.

57. "Wenn einer eine Reise tut . . . ," *Czernowitzer Tagblatt*, January 26, 1919.

58. Speech by Nicolae Carabioschi, February 21, 1920, in Iaţencu and Olaru, *Bucovineni în Parlamentul României*, 144.

59. Speech by Vasile Marcu, January 29, 1920, in Iaţencu and Olaru, *Bucovineni în Parlamentul României*, 103.

60. Speech by Ion Zelea Codreanu, December 11, 1919, in Iaţencu and Olaru, *Bucovineni în Parlamentul României*, 77. Bessarabians voiced many of the same complaints about the Romanian administration's abuses and corruption. See Suveică, *Post-imperial Encounters*, 38.

61. Hitchins, *Rumania*, 410.

62. "Ce trebue să reţină Bucovinenii?," *Bucovina: Ziarul românilor bucovineni*, September 9, 1919.

63. ANIC, fond Iancu Flondor 5 (1908–1922), nr. inv. 945, 288, letter from Mr. Simionovici to Iauncu Flondor on audience with king in Bucharest, March 20, 1919.

64. "V. Gr." [Vasile Greciuc?], "Unire fără autonomie?," *Glasul Bucovinei*, December 1, 1918.

65. "În Bucovina au drept de viaţă şi Bucovinenii," *Glasul Bucovinei*, September 20, 1931.

66. "Turcul te bate—Turcul te judecă: Reflexiuni critice asupra pretinsului nostru regionalism," *Glasul Bucovinei*, October 20, 1931. See also *Memoriul Bucovinei*, a regionalist manifesto published by Nistor's *Glasul Bucovinei*.

67. N. Tatu, "Armonia grupărilor etnice," *Viaţa Bucovinei*, April 15, 1933; Dr. T. Cristureanu, "15 ani dela Unire," *Viaţa Bucovinei*, November 1, 1933.

68. Dr T. Cristureanu, "Regionalism?!," *Viaţa Bucovinei*, 3 (March), 1934, 228.

69. Mazower, "Minorities," 50.

70. Pedersen, *Guardians*, 20.

71. Fink, "Minority Rights," 388, 390; Prott, *Politics of Self-Determination*, 212.

72. Prott, *Politics of Self-Determination*, 213, 221, 217–18.

73. Prott, *Politics of Self-Determination*, 213.

74. UNLAG-LNS-File R564-11-2537-19551—Bucovina—Bucovan Delegation of the Ukrainian National Council, Vienna, note from Elie Semaka, president of the Bukovinan Delegation of the Ukrainian National Council to His Excellency Mr. Secretary General of Society of Nations Sir Eric Drummond, 4.

75. UNLAG-LNS-File R1698-41-40858-40858—Ukrainian minority in Bukovina [Bukowina], petition from Le Comité politique de la Bukovine, Johann Rudnicki, president, to "Monsieur le Secrétaire general de la Société des Nations sir Eric Drummond," December 2, 1924.

76. UNLAG-LNS-File R564-11-2537-19551—Bucovan Delegation of the Ukrainian National Council, Vienna, note from Elie Semaka on behalf of Bukovinan Delegation of Ukrainian National Council to His Excellency Mr. Secretary General of Society of Nations Sir Eric Drummond.

77. UNLAG-LNS-File R1698-41-40858-40858—Ukrainian minority in Bukovina [Bukowina], "Appendice Abrégé de l'histoire de la Buchovine," attached to petition to President of the Council of Nations Hymans by Johann Rudnicki, president of the Comité politique de la Bukovine, 7.

78. UNLAG-LNS-File R564-11-2537-19551—Bucovan Delegation of the Ukrainian National Council, Vienna, note from Elie Semaka on behalf of Bukovinan Delegation of Ukrainian National Council to His Excellency Mr. Secretary General of Society of Nations Sir Eric Drummond, 7–8.

79. UNLAG-LNS-File R1652-41-9428-57537, minutes by Eric Colban on a petition submitted by the Ukrainian National Council, 1927, 1–2.

80. UNLAG-LNS-File R1652-41-9428-57537, Ukrainian National Council's note to the Secretariat General of the Society of Nations in Geneva, Berlin, February 15, 1927.

81. UNLAG-LNS-File R1698-41-40858-40858, petition from the Committee of Bukovina to the president of the Council of Nations Hymans, December 2, 1924, 4–5.

82. UNLAG-LNS-File R1698-41-40858-40858, "Appendice Abrégé de l'histoire de la Buchovine," attached to petition from the Committee of Bukovina to the President of the Council of Nations Hymans, December 2, 1924, 12.

83. UNLAG-LNS-File R1629-41-1481-48068, "Pétition au Secretariat de la Société des Nations à Genève, Mémoire composé et envoyé par le docteur Basile Dutczak, avocat à Cernauti, Bukovine (Roumanie)."

84. UNLAG-LNS-File R564-11-2537-9826, "Document du Conseil R4—Société des nations; Les Ruthenes de Bukovine, Lettre du Comité Carpatho-Russe," December 16, 1920, 3.

85. UNLAG-LNS-File R1698-41-40858-40858—Ukrainian minority in Bukovina [Bukowina], "Le regne arbitraire," translation of article from *Vorwärts*, September 13, 1924, part of "Appendice Abrégé de l'histoire de la Buchovine," attached to petition to President of the Council of Nations Hymans by Johann Rudnicki, president of the Comité politique de la Bukovine, 13–14.

86. UNLAG-LNS-File R1698-41-40858-40858—Ukrainian minority in Bukovina [Bukowina], petition to President of the Council of Nations Hymans by Johann Rudnicki, president of the Comitée politique de la Bukovine, 9. See also File R564-11-2537-19551—Bucovina—Bucovan Delegation of the Ukrainian National Council, Vienna, note from Elie Semaka,

president of the Bukovinan Delegation of the Ukrainian National Council to His Excellency Mr. Secretary General of Society of Nations Sir Eric Drummond, 4.

87. UNLAG-LNS-File R1698-41-40858-40858—Ukrainian minority in Bukovina [Bukowina], petition to President of the Council of Nations Hymans by Johann Rudnicki, president of the Comité politique de la Bukovine, 15, 11, 9. See also File R564-11-2537-19551—Bucovina—Bucovan Delegation of the Ukrainian National Council, Vienna, note from Elie Semaka, president of the Bukovinan Delegation of the Ukrainian National Council to His Excellency Mr. Secretary General of Society of Nations Sir Eric Drummond, 4.

88. UNLAG-LNS-File R1698-41-40858-40858—Ukrainian minority in Bukovina [Bukowina], "Appendice Abrégé de l'histoire de la Buchovine," attached to petition to President of the Council of Nations Hymans by Johann Rudnicki, president of the Comité politique de la Bukovine, 11.

89. UNLAG-LNS-File R1698-41-40858-40858—Ukrainian minority in Bukovina [Bukowina], "Appendice Abrégé de l'histoire de la Buchovine," attached to petition to President of the Council of Nations Hymans by Johann Rudnicki, president of the Comité politique de la Bukovine, 20.

90. UNLAG-LNS-File R564-11-2537-19551—Bucovina—Bucovan Delegation of the Ukrainian National Council, Vienna, note from Elie Semaka, president of the Bukovinan Delegation of the Ukrainian National Council to His Excellency Mr. Secretary General of Society of Nations Sir Eric Drummond, 5.

91. UNLAG-LNS-File R1698-41-40858-40858—Ukrainian minority in Bukovina [Bukowina], "Appendice Abrégé de l'histoire de la Buchovine," attached to petition to President of the Council of Nations Hymans by Johann Rudnicki, president of the Comitée politique de la Bukovine, 18. UNLAG-LNS-File R564-11-2537-19551—Bucovina—Bucovan Delegation of the Ukrainian National Council, Vienna, note from Elie Semaka, president of the Bukovinan Delegation of the Ukrainian National Council to His Excellency Mr. Secretary General of Society of Nations Sir Eric Drummond, 5. Shortly afterward, the Romanian administration dissolved the Ukrainian *Gymnasium* in Wiznitz and transferred its teachers to other parts of Romania. See Semaka's petition, 6.

92. The academic club Sojuz was banned in July 1921, as was the Ruska Besida reading circle in Horishnii Vyzhiv and Putyliv in 1922. See UNLAG-LNS-File R1698-41-40858-40858—Ukrainian minority in Bukovina [Bukowina], petition from Le Comité politique de la Bukovine, Johann Rudnicki President to "Monsieur le Secrétaire general de la Société des Nations sir Eric Drummond," December 2, 1924.

93. UNLAG-LNS-File R1698-41-40858-55597, minute sheet on memorandum by Senator Lukaszewicz from Bukovina, by Céspedes, April 27, 1927.

94. UNLAG-LNS-File R1698-41-40858-55597, speech by Senator Lukaszewicz in the Romanian parliament, *Monitorul Oficial*, December 19, 1926, "Senat Sesiune ordinary 1926–7, sedinta de vinery, 3 Decembrie 1926," 110.

95. UNLAG-LNS-File R1698-41-40858-55597, "Memoriu privitor la şcolile primare cu limba de preparare ucraineană în România" (Senator Lukaszewicz's memorandum concerning Ukrainian-language primary schools in Romania).

96. Duchak (Romanian: Dutceac) argued for more extensive rights for minorities in interwar Romania. See Dutceac, *Minimul drepturilor minorităţilor.*

97. UNLAG-LNS-File R1698-41-40858-55597, minute sheet by M. Colban; and petition "A das Oberlandsgericht Cernăuţi," attached to minute sheet.

98. UNLAG-LNS-File R2126-4-2168-8349, "Annexe A: Loi sur l'enseignement primaire de l'état et l'enseignement normal primaire du Dr. C Angelescu, Ministre de l'instruction publique," 1926, 16, 17.

99. UNLAG-LNS-File R2126-4-2168-8349, "Pétition du Dr. Dutczak au Secretariat de la Société des Nations à Genève—Réclamation composé et envoyé par le docteur Basile Dutczak," May 12, 1928, Cernăuţi, 6, 2.

100. UNLAG-LNS-File R2126-4-2168-2168, "Mémoire sur la situation des Ruthenes en Bucovine" (Romanian Government's response to Dutczak's memorandum), 1–2, 7.

101. For more on minorities who managed to hold on to privileges acquired under Austrian rule even after 1918, see Rigó, *Capitalism in Chaos*, 138, 178.

102. Toroutiu, *Românii şi clasa intelectuală*, 14.

103. LBI, Israel Cohen Papers, RG 448-YIVO, series 1, folder 27, "A Stroll Through Czernowitz," 2.

104. ANIC, fond Ministerul Cultelor şi Instrucţiunii Publice, nr. inv. 2553, dosar 423/1921, 156, note from General Secretariat for Public Education to Directorates of Secondary and Public Schools in Bukovina, November 18, 1920.

105. DAChO, f. 213, op. 1, d. 515, l. 9, note to General Secretariat of Public Education in Cernăuţi, October 2, 1920.

106. R. Clark, "Interwar Romania," 154–55.

107. DAChO, f. 325, op. 1, d. 2128, l. 1, "Şcoala primară com. Cernăuţi Lascăt Luţia către Epitropia Comunităţii Israelite Cernăuţi," July 24, 1928.

108. Vasile Conta, cited in Motta, *Less Than Nations*, 39; Iordachi, *Liberalism*, 360.

109. "Evreii între ei," *Glasul Bucovinei*, April 30, 1930.

110. DAChO, f. 213, op. 1, d. 1542, l. 2, note from Ministry of Education, General Direction of Secondary and Superior Education, to General Directorate for Bukovina (1923).

111. "Die Minoritäten und die Schulfrage. Ergebnis der Schulkonferenz," *Czernowitzer Morgenblatt*, August 1, 1921.

112. Adolf Gabor, "Das hebräische Schulwerk," *Ostjüdische Zeitung*, January 14, 1921; "Die Sprachenlosigkeit des jüdischen Volkes," *Czernowitzer Allgemeine Zeitung*, May 21, 1925, 2.

113. See https://www.bukowina-portal.de/de/ct/195-Franz-Porubsky (accessed May 7, 2025).

114. ANIC, fond Ministerul Cultelor şi Instrucţiunii Publice, nr. inv. 2553, dosar 423/1921, 187, report from Cernăuţi to Ministry of Education on Ukrainian teachers requesting positions in the Old Kingdom, May 17, 1921.

115. AT-OeStA/AVA Unterricht 5C, Zl.14712/1919; Zl. 12231/1919, 28–29.

116. "Moţiunea studenţimii Române in chestia Ehrlich-Last," *Glasul Bucovinei*, March 15, 1921.

117. Fichman, *Before Memories Fade*, 13.

118. Shmueli, *Kind aus guter Familie*, 42.

119. ANIC, fond Ministerul Instrucţiunii, nr. inv. 710, dosar 39/1922, report from Inspectorate of Primary Schools and for Romanian culture in Transylvania, Bukovina, and Bessarabia on inspection of primary schools in Cernăuţi, June 5, 1922.

120. BAR, Arhiva Constantin Angelescu, X, Varia 10.

121. ANIC, fond Ministerul Instrucţiunii, nr. inv. 710, dosar 11/1922, 95, report to Ministry of Education, Inspectorate of Primary Schools and for Promotion of Romanian Culture in Bukovina on inspection of Bukovina district.

122. ANIC, fond Ministerul Instrucţiunii, nr. inv. 811, dosar 396/1927, 9, report to Ministry of Education on cultural inspection of Bukovina in October 1927.

123. For a detailed account of the assault, see Livezeanu, *Cultural Politics*, 84.

124. Hausleitner, *Rumänisierung*, 167.

125. ANIC, fond Ministerul Instrucţiunii, nr. inv. 714, dosar 324/1926, letter from Prof. Diaconescu to Minister of Education, November 10, 1926.

126. UNLAG-LNS-File R1287-19-54009-32214, No. 9 Joint's Memorandum on the Anti-Semitic Movement in Romania, submitted to M. Duca, September 17, 1925, 32, 33, 35.

127. "Die romänische Sprache im Amtsgebrauche," *Czernowitzer Allgemeine Zeitung*, February 28, 1919.

128. "Gegen den jüngsten Sprachenerlass," *Czernowitzer Allgemeine Zeitung*, June 13, 1922.

129. "Der Sprachenerlass—Wo liegt die Wahrheit?," *Czernowitzer Morgenblatt*, July 20, 1922.

130. "Der Sprachenerlass tritt doch in Kraft?" *Czernowitzer Morgenblatt*, July 4, 1922.

131. DAChO, f. 6, op 1, d. 255, l. 1, petition from Dr. Friedrich Kuczynski, March 17, 1919. Only candidates who obtained a grade of one, two, or three were allowed to keep their positions; candidates who obtained a grade of five were promptly dismissed; those who got a four could retake the exam in six months.

132. "Der Sprachenerlass—eine Versammlung der Advokaten," *Ostjüdische Zeitung*, August 15, 1922; "Der Sprachenerlass," *Czernowitzer Morgenblatt*, July 12, 1922.

133. DAChO, f. 12, op. 1, d. 1678, l. 39, "Copie comunicat secretariatul pentru interne Siguranţa Generală, Cernăuţi Direcţia Poliţiei, Divizia a 8a."

134. DAChO, f. 43, op. 1, d. 1163, l. 2, "Prezidiul primăriei Cernăuţi, D-lui Şef al Departmentului III," April 27, 1922.

135. DAChO, f. 15, op. 1, d. 4415, l. 74, note from Ministry of the Interior to prefect of Bukovina.

136. DAChO, f. 15, op. 1, d. 4415, l. 3, note from Ministry of the Interior, Direcţiunea Administraţiei Generale Contencios şi Statisticei, to prefect of Bukovina.

137. DAChO, f. 15, op. 1, d. 4415, l. 76, copy of instructions by Ministry of the Interior to prefectures of Transylvania, Banat, Hungarian territories, and Bukovina, July 18, 1923.

138. DAChO, f. 38, op .2, d. 10187, l. 1, copy of order of Regional Police Inspectorate Cernăuţi, February 4, 1937.

139. DAChO, f. 24, op. 1, d .6, l. 5, "Proces verbal asupra şedinţei Comisiunii de Unificare din 16 iunie 1920," June 16, 1920.

140. DAChO, f. 15, op. 1, d. 4345, report from Aurel Percec, superior administrative counselor replacing prefect of jud. Cernăuţi, regarding Romanian language exams held in the city of Cernăuţi.

141. DAChO, f. 15, op. 1, d. 4345, l. 26, decision of subsecretary of state, Department of Internal Affairs. The decision about which "administrative political functionaries" would have to take the exam lay with the local prefects, who were required to publish the candidates' names beforehand in the local press.

142. ANIC, fond Casa Şcoalelor, nr. inv. 641, dosar 10/1921, 5, copy of decision no. 1358 of January 5, 1921 by secretary of state in the Department of Public Education.

143. DAChO, f. 43, op. 1, d. 7231, l. 3, letter to mayor of Cernăuţi, March 5, 1935.

144. Motta, *Less Than Nations*, 42. On the pogroms, see also Veidlinger, *In the Midst*.

145. Motta, *Less Than Nations*, 54.

146. Iordachi, *Liberalism*, 354, 353.

147. Rozenblit, "Dilemma of Identity," 148.

148. Yavetz, *Erinnerungen*, 141.

149. ANIC, fond Direcţia Generală a Poliţiei, nr. inv. 2349, dosar 1/1920, report from Police Directorate Botoşani to General Directorate of Police, January 9, 1920.

150. "Die Kulturstufe," *Czernowitzer Morgenblatt*, June 2, 1927.

151. LBI, Israel Cohen Papers, RG 448-YIVO, series 1, folder 27, "A Stroll Through Czernowitz," 2–3.

152. Nistor, *Zece ani*, 3.

153. ANIC, fond Direcţia Generală a Poliţiei, nr. inv. 2349, dosar 1/1920, report from Police Directorate Botoşani to General Police Directorate, January 9, 1920.

154. Hausleitner, *Rumänisierung*, 114.

155. UNLAG-LNS-File R1287/19/54009/32214, "Report of the Secretary and Special Delegate of the Joint Foreign Committee on Questions of Jewish Interest at the 5th Assembly of the League, No. 18 (Memorandum submitted to the Joint Foreign Committee, June 30, 1924)," 39. For more on citizenship laws in interwar Romania, see Müller, *Staatsbürger auf Widerruf*.

156. Kirchner Reill, Jeličić, and Rolandi, "Redefining Citizenship," 327.

157. Kirchner Reill, Jeličić, and Rolandi, "Redefining Citizenship," 329–32.

158. UNLAG-LNS-File R1287/19/54009/32214, "Report of the Secretary and Special Delegate of the Joint Foreign Committee on Questions of Jewish Interest at the 5th Assembly of the League, No. 18 (Memorandum submitted to the Joint Foreign Committee, June 30, 1924)," 40 and 41.

159. UNLAG-LNS-File R1287/19/54009/32214, "Jewish Grievances in Romania, no. 6 (Memorandum of the Romanian Government on the Law of Nationality)," 26.

160. UNLAG-LNS-File R1287/19/54009/32214, "Report of the Secretary and Special Delegate of the Joint Foreign Committee on Questions of Jewish Interest at the 5th Assembly of the League, No. 18 (Memorandum Submitted to Joint Foreign Committee, June 30, 1924)," 40.

161. UNLAG-LNS-File R1287/19/54009/32214, "Report of the Secretary and Special Delegate of the Joint Foreign Committee on Questions of Jewish Interest at the 5th Assembly of the League, No. 7 (Counter-Memorandum of the Joint Foreign Committee)," 31–32.

162. UNLAG-LNS-File R1560/39/29135/29135, petition submitted to His Majesty the King of Romania by pensioned officials, widows, and orphans from the Bukovina, 1.

163. UNLAG-LNS-File R1560/39/29135/29135, petition submitted to His Majesty the King of Romania by pensioned officials, widows, and orphans from the Bukovina, 1.

164. UNLAG-LNS-File R1560/39/29135/29135, "Beschwerde der altösterreichischen Zivilpensionisten aus der Bukowina wegen Einstellung ihrer Ruhegenüsse durch die k.rum. Regierung," Vienna, July 1, 1923.

165. UNLAG-LNS-File R1560/39/29135/29135, "Request for Assistance by Natives of Bukovina in Vienna," minutes to Mr. Colban from Dr. Van Hamel, July 20, 1925. Indeed, all

applicants for citizenship in the Austrian Republic were now required to provide proof of German nationality. See Motta, *Less Than Nations*, 59.

166. UNLAG-LNS-File R1560/39/29135/29135, M. Wuorimaa, minute sheet on petitions from Bukowiner Zentralverband, Vienna.

167. UNLAG-LNS-File R1560/39/29135/29135, "Request for Assistance by Natives of Bukovina in Vienna," minutes to Mr. Colban from Dr. Van Hamel, July 20, 1925, 2.

168. UNLAG-LNS-File R1560/39/29135/29135, Mr. Colban's note to M. De Azcarate, July 6, 1925.

169. UNLAG-LNS-File R2119/4/939/12027, "Pétition supplémentaire au Secrétariat Général de la Société des Nations Genève," Vienna, July 8, 1928.

170. UNLAG-LNS-File R2119/4/939/12027, petition to General Secretariat of the Society of Nations in Geneva (French translation) by E. Tattmar and President Fischer, Vienna, May 25, 1928, 1.

171. UNLAG-LNS-File R2119/4/939/12027, "Pétition supplémentaire au Secrétariat Général de la Société des Nations Genève," Vienna, July 8, 1928, 8.

172. UNLAG-LNS-File R2119/4/939/12027, minute sheet to Monsieur Aguirre de Carcer, by M. Céspedes, August 30, 1929.

173. Weitz, "From the Vienna to the Paris System," 1315.

174. DAChO, f. 15, op. 1, d. 5, note from Comandamentul jandarmeriei țării, district Cernăuți to Prefectura Jud. Cernăuți, February 22, 1919.

175. S. Griseanu, "Jos masca!," *Unirea*, September 1, 1920.

176. Hanebrink, *Specter*, 20.

177. "Kriegsschäden-Kriegsleistungen," *Czernowitzer Tagblatt*, January 18, 1919.

178. One Bukovinan deputy in the Bucharest parliament complained that "wagons of bread never make it into Bukovina" because they get stolen or disappear into Ukraine. Speech by Iorgu Toma, January 29, 1920, in Iațencu and Olaru, *Bucovineni în Parlamentul României*, 132.

179. "Die Rückkehr des Ministers dr Nistor von Bukarest," *Czernowitzer Allgemeine Zeitung*, May 21, 1919.

180. ANIC, fond Iancu Flondor 1, nr. inv. 945, dosar 16/1918, report of Reconstruction Department I of k.k. Landesregierung on damages, progress so far, and projected measures concerning reconstruction in Bukovina by Von Rezori, March 27, 1926.

181. Speech by Ion Zelea Codreanu, December 11, 1919, in Iațencu and Olaru, *Bucovineni în Parlamentul României*, 73.

182. Speech by Vasile Bodnărescu, December 13, 1919, in Iațencu and Olaru, *Bucovineni în Parlamentul României*, 69.

183. Hausleitner, "Von der Diskriminierung, 104–5.

184. DAChO, f. 12, op. 1, d. 1, report from Eighth Division to Presidium of Government.

185. DAChO, f. 15, op. 1, d. 5, Circulara către toate prefecturile de județe și expoziturile politice Cernăuți," from Bukovina's Administration, Presidential Bureau of Minister-Delegate, April 24, 1919.

186. S. Griseanu, "Jos masca!" *Czernowitzer Morgenblatt*, September 1, 1920.

187. "Der Belagerungszustand," *Czernowitzer Allgemeine Zeitung*, January 29, 1919.

188. ANIC, fond Iancu Flondor, nr. inv. 945, dosar 32/1919, telegraph of conversation between prime minister and Minister Flondor, 14–15.

189. DAChO, f. 6, op. 1, d. 15, note from commander of Eighth Division General Zadik concerning decisions of minister-delegate of Bukovina, March 31, 1919.

190. Kissman, "Zur Geschichte," 129, 131. For more on the Austrian Social Democratic Party's approach to the nationality problem in the monarchy and their views on national autonomy, see Beneš, *Workers and Nationalism.*

191. Kissman, "Zur Geschichte," 131–38.

192. OeLA, Josef Burg Nachlass, Bestand: VL Josef Burg 117/98, Moysey Loev, "Chernovtsy try pamyatnye daty," *Tshernavitser Bleter*, nos. 62–63 (1999).

193. OeLA, Josef Burg Nachlass, Bestand: VL Josef Burg 117/98, Josef Burg, "Oyf fremde vegn," *Dos Jidisze Wort*, October 22, 1990, no. 21, 35.

194. CAHJP, HM2–8594, October 5, 1930.

195. Kissman, "Zur Geschichte," 141.

196. CAHJP, HM2–8568, September 9, 1936.

197. Hitchins, *Rumania*, 399.

198. H. Seton-Watson, *Eastern Europe*, 213.

199. ANIC, fond Microfilme Communism, Mişcarea socialistă din Bucovina, nr. inv. 2873, rola 373, unit 13, c 59–66, letter by socialist militant to Gheorge Grigorovici criticizing him for speech given in Senate, July 4, 1920.

200. ANIC, fond Microfilme Communism, Uniunea Ţăranilor Revoluţionari din Bucovina, nr. inv. 2196, rola 466, unit 5, c 504–22, "Proiect de program al organizaţiei naţional revoluţionare Vyzvolennia," December 30, 1931; unit 6, c 523–44, "Raport de activitate semnat de biroul provizoriu al organizaţiei Vyzvolennia," December 9, 1932.

201. Fichman, *Before Memories Fade*, 40.

202. Friedjung, *Wir wollten nur das Paradies*, 131.

203. ANIC, fond Microfilme Communism, Comitetul regional Bucovina al Ajutorului Roşu din Romania, nr. inv. 2669, rola 173, unit 1, c 1–6, unsigned manifesto entitled "Tovarăşi şi tovarăşe!" which calls for action against fascism and the war and enumerates some of Ajutorul Roşu's task concerning the above, October 1932.

204. UNLAG-LNS-File R1698/41/40858/55597, "Die Verfolgung der ukrainischen Sozialdemokraten," *Vorwärts*, January 11, 1927, 3.

205. H. Seton-Watson, *Eastern Europe*, 78.

206. Hitchins, *Rumania*, 293.

207. On the idea of an ahistorical peasant culture opposed to corrupt politics and state institutions, see Trencsényi, *Politics of "National Character"*, 22.

208. Hitchins, *Rumania*, 124.

209. Trencsényi, *Politics of "National Character"*, 49.

210. Rothschild, *East Central Europe*, 283.

211. Van Meurs, "Land Reform in Romania," 111; H. L. Roberts, *Rumania*, 111.

212. H. L. Roberts, *Rumania*, 14–15.

213. Bideleux, "Peasantries," 281, 8–9.

214. H. L. Roberts, *Rumania*, 23. For the connections between events in the Russian empire and the Romanian principalities, see Mitrany, *Land and the Peasant*, 100.

215. H. L. Roberts, *Rumania*, 23. See also Mitrany, *Land and the Peasant*, 95–98.

216. H. L. Roberts, *Rumania*, 25, 26.

217. Mitrany, *Land and the Peasant*, 115; H. L. Roberts, *Rumania*, 27–28.

218. H. Seton-Watson, *Eastern Europe*, 78.

219. Mitrany, *Land and the Peasant*, 101–2.

220. Van Meurs, "Land Reform in Romania," 111.

221. On the decree-laws for each province, see Mitrany, *Land and the Peasant*, 111–12.

222. The only exception made was for peasants who temporarily migrated to America. Mitrany, *Land and the Peasant*, 176.

223. Mitrany, *The Land and the Peasant*, 122–25, 154–57.

224. H. L. Roberts, *Rumania*, 36.

225. Mitrany, *Land and the Peasant*, 133–34, 147, 161. To prevent the land reforms from being undone, a new law was issued in 1921, banning the division through inheritance of land below two hectares.

226. H. Seton-Watson, *Eastern Europe*, 90; Van Meurs, "Land Reform in Romania," 112.

227. It was true, meanwhile, that other categories of people besides peasants were entitled to land: these included decorated World War I officers. See Mitrany, *Land the Peasant*, 139.

228. UNLAG-LNS-File R1698/41/40858/55597, "Die Klagen und Forderungen der Ukrainer aus der Interpellation des Abgeordneten Krakalia," *Czernowitzer Deutsche Tagespost*, December 10, 1926, 2.

229. UNLAG-LNS-File R1629/41/48068/1481, "Pétition au Secrétariat de la Société des Nations à Genève, Mémoire composé et envoyé par le docteur Basile Dutczak, avocat à Cernăuţi, Bukovine (Roumanie)," 7.

230. UNLAG-LNS-File R1629/41/48068/1481, "Observations du Gouvernement Roumain," Berne, December 1, 1925, 8.

231. UNLAG-LNS-File R1629/41/48068/1481, "Observations du Gouvernement Roumain," Berne, December 1, 1925, 6, 4.

232. Müller, "Property," 125.

233. UNLAG-LNS-File R1629/41/48068/1481, "Observations du Gouvernement Roumain," Berne, December 1, 1925, 10.

234. Bruja, "Constituirea Ligii," 9–10.

235. Dr. I. Ionaşcu, "Biblioteci populare," *Glasul Bucovinei*, September 24, 1922.

236. Livezeanu, *Cultural Politics*, 52.

237. Similar initiatives to "go to the people" engaged agronomists and ethnographers throughout the interwar period in Eastern Europe. Bideleux, "Peasantries," 285.

238. George Tofan, "Viitoarea şcoală primară II: Ce şcoală ne trebuie," *Glasul Bucovinei*, February 10, 1919.

239. ANIC, fond Casa Şcoalelor, nr. inv. 641, dosar 394/1921, 7–8, statute of Home of Culture, Broşteni.

240. ANIC, fond Liga pentru unitatea culturală a tuturor românilor, nr. inv. 1115, dosar 49/1931–1936, proces verbal, May 18, 1931.

241. ANIC, fond Casa Şcoalelor, nr. inv. 643, dosar 914/1928, 60, letter from rectorate of primary school Valea-Putnei asking for donations. On damage to infrastructure, see Casa Şcoalelor, nr. inv. 642, 316/1923, 235, letter from school inspector of Cernăuţi district regarding lack of public libraries in Cernăuţi, May 30, 1923.

242. ANIC, fond Casa Şcoalelor, nr. inv. 642, dosar 481/1925, 1, letter requesting materials for Prince Carol High school in Gura Humorului, March 6, 1925.

243. ANIC, fond Ministerul Instrucţiunii si Artelor, nr. inv. 712, dosar 129/1924, 77, report on school attendance in Botuşana village, Gura Humorului, December 3, 1924.

244. ANIC, fond Ministerul Instrucţiunii si Artelor, nr. inv. 712, dosar 214/1924, letter on school attendance, from Vultureşti, Vama district, February 7, 1924.

245. ANIC, fond Ministerul Instrucţiunii şi Artelor, nr. inv. 812, dosar 10/1928, report on inspections and cultural conferences held in Bukovina in December 1927, June 11, 1928, 180–82.

246. Newman, "Shades of Empire," 158.

247. Müller, "Statehood," 149–150.

248. H. L. Roberts, *Rumania*, 96, 100.

249. Scurtu, *Democraţia la români*, 293.

250. H. L. Roberts, *Rumania*, 97–99.

251. Solonari, *Purifying the Nation*, 414.

252. Bideleux, "Peasantries," 289.

253. Maner, *Parlamentarismus*, 79.

254. R. Clark, "Images of Crisis," 200.

255. H. L. Roberts, *Rumania*, 130–32.

256. Hitchins, *Rumania*, 368; R. Clark, "Shape of Interwar Romanian History"; R. Clark, "Interwar Romania," 159.

257. Maner, *Parlamentarismus*, 76; Bucur, "Carol II."

258. Hitchins, *Rumania*, 417.

## Chapter 6. Decade of Extremes

1. Mazower, *Dark Continent*, 4. See also S. Berman, *Democracy and Dictatorship*; Capoccia, *Defending Democracy*.

2. C. A. Bejan, *Intellectuals and Fascism*, 12. For more on Eliade and Cioran's generation, see L. Volovici, *Nationalist Ideology*.

3. Iordachi, "Continuum," 263; Călinescu, "1927 Generation"; C. A. Bejan, *Intellectuals and Fascism*, 16.

4. Solonari, *Purifying the Nation*, 21–22.

5. Solonari, *Purifying the Nation*, 30.

6. Bucur, *Eugenics*, 30, 121.

7. Solonari, *Purifying the Nation*, 120, 15–18.

8. Solonari, *Purifying the Nation*, xv; Hausleitner, "Gegen die Zwangsrumänisierung."

9. Boia, *Capcanele istoriei*, 50.

10. Bruja, "Constituirea Ligii," 11–12.

11. Blasen, "Terrorisme légionnaire," 102.

12. ANIC, fond Ministerul Instrucţiunii şi Artelor, nr. inv. 811, dosar 396/1927, 16, report from general inspector of cultural propaganda Radu Cosmin to Minister of Education.

13. Mazower, *Dark Continent*, 19. On the connection between regionalism and voting against the establishment in Bukovina, see Bruja, *Extrema dreaptă*, 81.

14. Bruja, "Constituirea Ligii," 14.

15. Bruja, "Constituirea Ligii," 14, 17–20.

16. Yavetz, "Eyewitness Note," 599.

17. Kaltenbrunner, "Anti-Semitic Violence," 119.

18. Bruja, *Extrema dreaptă*, 28, 115.

19. Hausleitner, "Gegen die Zwangsrumänisierung."

20. Bruja, "Constituirea Ligii," 19, 175.

21. Haynes, "Corneliu Zelea Codreanu."

22. Niculescu Bran, *Mistica rugăciunii*, 116.

23. R. Clark, "Salience," 282; Hitchins, *Rumania*, 404.

24. R. Clark, *Holy Legionary Youth*, 66, 152.

25. Tismăneanu, *Stalinism*, 41.

26. Rothschild, *East Central Europe*, 308.

27. Cârstocea, "Approaching Generic Fascism," 156; R. Clark, "Romanian Right," 193–94.

28. Cârstocea, "Breaking the Teeth," 90.

29. R. Clark, "Salience," 282.

30. R. Clark, "Salience," 276; Iordachi, "Continuum," 241.

31. Cârstocea, "Approaching Generic Fascism," 158.

32. Maner, *Parlamentarismus*, 118.

33. R. Clark, *Holy Legionary Youth*, 139. On Crainic's disenchantment with democracy, see Solonari, *Purifying the Nation*, 27.

34. Cioran, cited in Boia, *Capcanele istoriei*, 71.

35. George Macrin, "Exterminarea bătrânilor," *Însemnări sociologice*, May 1937, 27.

36. Boia, *Capcanele istoriei*, 24.

37. C. A. Bejan, *Intellectuals and Fascism*, 34.

38. The quotation is from a translated excerpt from Cioran's book: Cioran, "Transfiguration of Romania," 359.

39. Cited in Boia, *Capcanele istoriei*, 71. On the existential threat to the nation, see R. Clark, "Romanian Right," 193–94.

40. Bruja, *Extrema dreaptă*, 175–76, 226.

41. Vesper, *Memorii*, 68.

42. Bruja, "Traian Brăileanu," 140.

43. Trebici, "Traian Brăileanu," 386.

44. Lepuş, *Tânăra generaţie interbelică*, 304.

45. Vintilă, "Traian Brăileanu," 496. For more on Brăileanu, see Boia, *Capcanele istoriei*, 103–4.

46. Cited in Bruja, *Extrema dreaptă*, 93–100.

47. George Macrin, "O nouă şcoală românească," *Însemnări sociologice*, June 1935, 16. On the Legionaries' work camps, see Haynes, "Work Camps."

48. George Macrin, "Taberele de muncă—Aspectul politic," *Însemnări sociologice*, August 1935, 21.

49. Bruja, "Traian Brăileanu," 145.

50. Cicerone Mucenic, "Legiunea şi învăţătorii," *Însemnări sociologice*, November 1937, 5–8.

51. George Macrin, "Taberele de muncă - Aspectul politic," *Însemnări sociologice*, August 1935, 20.

52. Ciuntu, *Din Bucovina pe Oder*, 12.

53. Bruja, *Extrema dreaptă*, 101.

54. Ion Turcan, "Câteva date în sprijinul unei probleme," *Însemnări sociologice*, April 1935, 27.

55. Ion Turcan, "Câteva date în sprijinul unei probleme," *Însemnări sociologice*, April 1935, 29.

56. George Macrin, "Taberele de muncă. Aspectul politic," *Însemnări sociologice*, August 1935, 19.

57. Traian Brăileanu, "Elita 'ascetică,'" *Însemnări sociologice*, September 1935, 9.

58. Traian Brăileanu, "Adevărata democraţie," *Însemnări sociologice*, May 1937.

59. Ing. Nicolau-Bîrlad, "Răspunderea generaţiilor," *Însemnări sociologice*, August 1935, 12–14.

60. George Macrin, "Exterminarea bătrânilor," *Însemnări sociologice*, May 1937, 27.

61. Cârstocea, "Approaching Generic Fascism," 159–60.

62. Traian Brăileanu, "Problema muncitorească în lumina doctrinei naţionaliste," *Însemnări sociologice*, June 1935, 25, 30.

63. Traian Brăileanu, "După alegerile din decembrie, 1937," *Însemnări sociologice*, January 1938, 2.

64. Traian Brăileanu, "Uneltiri criminale," *Însemnări sociologice*, September 1937, 2.

65. Traian Brăileanu, "Problema muncitorească în lumina doctrinei naţionaliste," *Însemnări sociologice*, July 1935, 35.

66. Liviu Rusu, "Omul român în lumina de cântec," *Însemnări sociologice*, July 1935, 28. See also R. Clark, *Holy Legionary Youth*, 135.

67. Barbu Sluşanschi, "Ura de clasă şi ura de rasă," *Însemnări sociologice*, May 1937, 13.

68. Barbu Sluşanschi, "Literatura şi societatea românească," *Însemnări sociologice*, April 1935, 19.

69. R. Clark, *Holy Legionary Youth*, 79.

70. Codreanu, cited in Radu, "Peasant Democracy," 49.

71. Lepuş, *Tânara generaţie interbelică*, 311.

72. Sandache, "Le groupe 'Iconar'," 207, 206.

73. Mamina and Scurtu, *Guverne şi guvernanţi*, 100. Vaida himself was a proponent of the *numerus valachicus* and therefore likely sympathized with the Legionaries' nationalist convictions.

74. Mamina and Scurtu, *Guverne şi guvernanţi*, 106.

75. Maner, *Parlamentarismus*, 162, 165–71. Yavetz recalls that "respectable gentlemen" such as Vaida Voevod, Argetoianu, Maniu, Mihalache, and Gh. Brătianu testified in favor of Codreanu's legion. See Yavetz, "Eyewitness Note," 602.

76. Ciuntu, *Din Bucovina pe Oder*, 10.

77. See ANIC, Arhivele Judeţului Ilfov, fond Chestura Poliţiei Cernăuţi, nr. inv. 883, dosar 1/1935, report to Ministry of the Interior, General Directorate of Siguranţa.

78. Ciuntu, *Din Bucovina pe Oder*, 11.

79. Bruja, *Extrema dreaptă*, 157, 175, 247.

80. Bruja, "Conflictele antisemite," 209–10.

81. Bruja, *Extrema dreaptă*, 85.

82. Scurtu, *Democraţia la români*, 77.

83. Kaltenbrunner, "Anti-Semitic Violence," 130.

84. Bruja, *Extrema dreaptă*, 157.

85. Nichifor Robu, cited in Hausleitner, "Gegen die Zwangsrumänisierung," 40.

86. Bruja, *Extrema dreaptă*, 241.

87. Ciuntu, *Din Bucovina pe Oder*, 12.

88. Kissman, "Zur Geschichte," 144.

89. Rybak, *Everyday Zionism*, 230.

90. König, "Geschichte der J.N.A.V. 'Hasmonäa' in Czernowitz," 114; Rybak, *Everyday Zionism*," 12.

91. König, "Geschichte der J.N.A.V. 'Hasmonäa,'" 113.

92. Sternberg, *Zur Geschichte der Juden*, 117.

93. Neuborn, "Jüdisch-nationaler akademischer Leseverein 'Humanitas,'" 120.

94. König, "Geschichte der J.N.A.V. 'Hasmonäa,'" 114.

95. Among them was Hebronia, founded by Bukovinan Jewish students who encountered the Zionist movement at the university in Vienna and who organized this society in Bukovina to continue their activity during the summer holiday See Mosberg, "Geschichte der J.N.A.V. Hebronia," 121. Another organization was Emunah, formed in 1903. It built a sizable Zionist library of publications and newspapers and organized Zionist seminars for Jewish students in Cernăuţi. Sternberg, *Zur Geschichte der Juden*, 118.

96. Kissman, "Zur Geschichte," 145.

97. Mendelsohn, *Jews of East Central Europe*, 189–90; Kissman, "Zur Geschichte," 147–48.

98. Polesiuk-Padan, "Geschichte des 'Haschomer Hazair,'" 147–48.

99. Polesiuk-Padan, "Geschichte des 'Haschomer Hazair,'" 149–50.

100. CZA, Z4\42613–8, letter from Manfred Reifer, Karen Hajessod Cernăuţi, to Dr. Lauterbach, London, December 16, 1926.

101. Shmueli, *Kind aus guter Familie*. Even committed Zionists like Ilana Shmueli's father, who joined a host of Zionist organizations and proudly displayed his convictions even at the risk of falling victim to the brutality of anti-Semitic Romanian students, "never talked about moving to Palestine."

102. Rottner, *Das ethische Seminar*, 16–20.

103. CZA, Z4\42396–250, report by Keren Hajessod, Palestina Grundfonds, Abteilung für Zentraleuropa, April 30, 1922.

104. CZA, Z4\42396–43, Z4\42396–45, "Bericht über die Reise von Hari Kohn und Julius Berger nach Czernowitz," Berlin, May 6, 1923.

105. Theodor Weisselberger, commenting on the lack of unity within the Zionist organization in Bukovina, in "Die XIII. Bukowinaer Zionistische Landeskonferenz. Bericht über die Tagung am 25. December 1932," *Ostjüdische Zeitung*, January 8, 1933.

106. Manfred Reifer, "Volk und Führer: Zum 60 Geburtstag dr Mayer Ebners," *Ostjüdische Zeitung*, October 30, 1932.

107. Ezra Mendelsohn notes that this was a common feature of East European Zionism, which had both a Hebraic, Palestinocentric orientation and was simultaneously focused on "present work," agitating for national and civil rights. See Mendelsohn, *On Modern Jewish Politics*, 57. See also Rybak, *Everyday Zionism*, 14.

108. Mayer Ebner, "Doppelte Nationalität," *Ostjüdische Zeitung*, April 26, 1919.

109. Weinstein, "Juden im Pressewesen."

110. Bruja, *Extrema dreaptă*, 51. "Der Fall: Jüdisches Lyzeum in Czernowitz," *Ostjüdische Zeitung*, December 23, 1931.

111. Davis, *Hungarian Religion*, 90.

112. Speech given by Mayer Ebner in the Romanian Senate on April 10, 1930, featured in "Für die Staatslosen in Rumänien," *Ostjüdische Zeitung*, April 15, 1930. On Mayer Ebner's activity in interwar Romania, see Reifer, *Dr. Mayer Ebner*.

113. "Für die Staatslosen in Rumänien," *Czernowitzer Morgenblatt*, April 15, 1930.

114. "Für die Staatenlosen," *Ostjüdische Zeitung*, September 4, 1932.

115. "Dr. Mayer Ebner's Lebenslauf," *Ostjüdische Zeitung*, October 30, 1932.

116. Mendelssohn, *On Modern Jewish Politics*, 14–15.

117. Mayer Ebner, "Zur Minoritätenfrage in Rumänien. Dr Filderman und das Minoritätenstatut," *Ostjüdische Zeitung*, May 3, 1931.

118. Max Diamant, "Lebensfragen einer Minderheit, zum Besuche Dr Filderman in Czernowitz," *Czernowitzer Morgenblatt*, February 22, 1930.

119. Mayer Ebner, "Zur dritten Invasion der UER in die Bukowina. I. Die Ersten Zwei Invasionen," *Ostjüdische Zeitung*, February 2, 1930.

120. "Zur dritten Invasion der UER in die Bukowina. I. Die Ersten Zwei Invasionen," *Ostjüdische Zeitung*, February 2, 1930; "Lebensfragen einer Minderheit," *Czernowitzer Morgenblatt*, February 26, 1930. On the great diversity among Jewish communities in Greater Romania, see Mendelsohn, *Jews of East Central Europe*, 174.

121. "Vier bewehte Versammlungen in zwei Tagen in Czernowitz," *Czernowitzer Morgenblatt*, April 4, 1929.

122. "Die nationale Schule," *Ostjüdische Zeitung*, May 6, 1921.

123. CAHJP, HM3/1277 (originally DAChO, f. 325, op. 2, d. 392, ll. 1–3), protocol on conference concerning national schools held in hall of Jewish Kultusgemeinde in Cernăuţi, August 22–24, 1926.

124. "Die Schulfrage im Nationalrat," *Ostjüdische Zeitung*, August 30, 1919.

125. "Die nationale Schule," *Ostjüdische Zeitung*, May 6, 1921.

126. Mayer Ebner, "Die Schulfrage im Nationalrat," *Ostjüdische Zeitung*, August 30, 1919.

127. Mendel Kinsbrunner, "Die nationale Schule," *Ostjüdische Zeitung*, August 23, 1919.

128. Mayer Ebner, "Die Nationale Schule," *Ostjüdische Zeitung*, May 6, 1921.

129. Mayer Ebner, "Zur Theaterfrage: Die Juden und das deutsche Theater," August 13, 1922.

130. Mayer Ebner, "150 Jahre Deutschtum in der Bukowina," *Ostjüdische Zeitung*, September 4, 1932.

131. Glass, *Zerbrochene Nachbarschaft*, 367.

132. Meier Teich, the leader of Suceava's Jewish community, didn't hesitate to proclaim his allegiance to German culture. In an article in the *Ostjüdische Zeitung* he wrote, "[W]e are convinced that we Asians, together with the German Asians, at the end and finally will emerge victorious and that the spirit of Isaiah and the kiss of Schiller and Beethoven will continue to live for thousands of years." Cited in Glass, *Zerbrochene Nachbarschaft*, 365.

133. Cited in Glass, *Zerbrochene Nachbarschaft*, 381.

134. Kvitkovskyi, *Bukovyna*, 338; Hausleitner, *Rumänisierung*, 180.

135. At the elections of 1928 the UNP gained one seat in the senate. Kvitkovskyi, *Bukovyna*, 346–47.

136. "Prava ukrainskoi movy v Rumunii," *Chas*, July 24, 1932; "Menshosti v Rumunii," *Chas*, April 27, 1929.

137. "Novyi zamakh proty ukrainskoi movi v shkolakh," *Chas*, August 28, 1920.

138. "V spravi ukrainskikh shkil na Bukovyni," *Chas*, December 1, 1931.

139. Kvitkovskyi, *Bukovyna*, 351–52. On policies on Ukrainian-language education in late 1930s Romania, see Blasen, "Învățământul în limba ucraineană."

140. Cited in Kvitkovskyi, *Bukovyna*, 381.

141. "Za ukrainsku shkolu i ukrainski chytalni," *Chas*, July 16, 1931.

142. Bruja, *Extrema dreaptă*, 42.

143. Brofman and Telefus, "Diialnist Orhanizatsii," 69, 70.

144. Ivanesko, "Partiia 'Vyzvolennia.'"

145. Brofman and Telefus, "Diialnist Orhanizatsii," 72.

146. Ivanesko, "Partiia 'Vyzvolennia.'"

147. "Narodna osvita na Sovitskyi Ukrainy," *Chas*, January 12, 1935.

148. "Politika natsionalnostei na Ukrainy," *Chas*, March 6, 1929; "Chernovetska ukrainka povernula z Radyanskoho Ukrainy," *Chas*, March 6, 1939.

149. "Za ukrainsku shkolu i ukrainski chytalni," *Chas*, July 16, 1931; "Ukrainstvo v Rumania zahrozhene bezhramotnistiu," *Chas*, June 18, 1933; "Bez hramoty hyne natsiya," *Chas*, October 29, 1935.

150. "Ridna mova," *Chas*, September 15, 1932.

151. "Shcho povinen robyty kodzhyi chesnyi Ukrainets," *Chas*, November 16, 1928.

152. "Uchim ukrainskoi movy," *Chas*, March 5, 1931.

153. "Shlyakhom drugikh," *Chas*, January 6, 1929.

154. "Mistse Ukraintsiv sered drugikh natsionalnykh menshostey u Rumunii," *Chas*, January 26, 1929; "Chytaite i peredplachuite hazetu!," *Chas*, March 14, 1929; "Bez ukrainskoi presy nema ukrainskoho hromadyantsva: Rishaimosya, chy hochemo zhyty chy vmyraty," *Chas*, June 15, 1934.

155. ANIC, Arhivele Județului Ilfov, nr. inv. 883, fond Chestura Poliției Cernăuți, dosar 1/1935, letter to "Societatea ucraineană Ajutorul Mutual Winnipeg," June 20, 1935. The *Kultfond* donated money to the Ukrainian theater to keep it from closing down. "Zhertvuite na kultfond," *Chas*, April 4, 1930. A Ukrainian delegate in the Canadian parliament, Mykhailo Lukhovych, visited Chernivtsi in October 1931 to tell Ukrainians about their counterparts, fellow Ukrainians from Bukovina, now living in Canada in villages named after their homes. "Ukrainska hromada v Chernivtsiakh vitae postal M. Lukhovycha," *Chas*, October 11, 1931.

156. Mandryk, "Ukrainskyi natsionalistychnyi," 3–4, 4–5.

157. Kvitkovskyi, *Bukovyna*, 381–82. "Pismo z akademika Smal-Stotskoho pro ukrainskoi vidrodzhennya na Bukovyni," *Chas* January 26, 1929; "Academic Stepan Smal-Stotskyi," *Chas*, January 12, 1935.

158. Mandryk, "Ukrainskyi natsionalistychnyi," 3–4, 11.

159. Mandryk, "Ukrainskyi natsionalistychnyi," 3.

160. ANIC, fond Ministerul Instrucțiunii, al Cultelor și Artelor, nr. inv. 908, dosar 7/1934, 13, report on state of school system in Cernăuți region from February 1934.

161. ANIC, fond Ministerul Instrucțiunii, al Cultelor, și Artelor, dosar 80/1934, report of Court of Appeal, Cernăuți to Ministry of Justice.

162. BAR, Arhiva Constantin Angelescu, X, Varia 11, 6.

163. Zaliznyak was likely named after Ivan Zaliznyak, a Cossack leader from the eighteenth century. The name also alluded to *zalizo*, meaning "iron" in Ukrainian.

164. Motyl, *Turn to the Right*, 154.

165. Zaitsev, "Integral Nationalism," 119–21, 123.

166. Zaitsev, "Integral Nationalism," 123.

167. Hausleitner, "Gegen Zwangsrumänisierung," 40.

168. Motyl, *Turn to the Right*, 143, 166.

169. Mandryk, "Ukrainskyi natsionalistichnyi," 9–10.

170. Shapiro, "Prelude to Dictatorship," 55–56; Scurtu, *Democrația la români*, 60.

171. Hitchins, *Rumania*, 418.

172. Iordachi, "Continuum," 233.

173. Blasen, "Terrorisme légionnaire," 302.

174. Shapiro, "Prelude to Dictatorship," 65.

175. Ciuntu, *Din Bucovina pe Oder*, 13–14.

176. Yavetz, "Eyewitness Note," 606. The Iron Guard was a military wing of the Legion of Archangel Michael, established in 1930. "Iron Guard" and "Legion" are often used interchangeably.

177. Iordachi, "Continuum," 243.

178. Hitchins, *Rumania*, 404; Maner, *Parlamentarismus*.

179. Shapiro, "Prelude to Dictatorship," 50–51.

180. Blasen, *"Primauté [...]"*, 320.

181. Bruja, *Extrema dreaptă*, 55.

182. Shapiro, "Prelude to Dictatorship," 72.

183. New language exams allowed the authorities to purge about 15–20% of minority functionaries in 1934–35. Gábor Egry cited in Blasen, *"Primauté [...]"*, 338–40.

184. Welisch, "Bukovina-Germans," 428.

185. Buchet, "Centrele iredentiste," 312–13.

186. Blasen, *"Primauté [...]"*, 73.

187. LBI, Israel Cohen Papers, RG 448-YIVO, series 1, folder 26, letter from Joint Foreign Committee to Israel Cohen, January 14, 1938.

188. Kehlmann, *So Weit Nach Westen*, 27.

189. Blasen, *"Primauté [...]"*, 39. On the continuous loss of citizenship rights by Jews from Goga's government through the royal dictatorship, see Buchet, "Centrele iredentiste," 16.

190. Hausleitner, "Von der Diskriminierung."

191. LBI, Leopold Hessing Collection, ME 1070, MM II 29 (accessed in digital form), 2.

192. Shapiro, "Prelude to Dictatorship," 80–85.

193. Rothschild, *East Central Europe*, 311.

194. Hitchins, *Rumania*, 420; Maner, *Parlamentarismus*, 254.

195. Hausleitner, *Rumänisierung*, 304.

196. Ciuntu, *Din Bucovina pe Oder*, 16–17, 20.

197. Buchet, "Centrele iredentiste," 306–8.

198. Blasen, *"Primauté [...]"*, 48.

199. Bucur, "Carol II."

200. Buchet, "Centrele iredentiste," 309–10, 303.

201. Hitchins, *Rumania*, 423–24.

202. Blasen, *"Primauté [...]"*, 130–32.

203. R. Clark, "Interwar Romania," 159; Mamina and Scurtu, *Guverne și guvernanți*, 117; Hausleitner, *Rumänisierung*, 306.

204. Bucur, "Carol II," 91.

205. Boia, *Capcanele istoriei*, 113.

206. Solonari, *Purifying the Nation*, 154.

207. Blasen, "Terrorisme légionnaire," 303–4.

208. Iordachi, "Continuum," 305.

209. Flondor, cited in Blasen, *"Primauté [. . .]"*, 28.

210. Solonari, *Purifying the Nation*, 50.

211. Buchet, "Centrele iredentiste," 323, 315.

212. DAChO, f. 26, op. 1, d. 401, l. 3, telephonic note, "extra urgent," from district Suceava to Chestura de Poliţie Cernăuţi, January 17, 1939.

213. Silbermann, "Deutsch," 40.

214. Bruja, *Extrema dreaptă*, 69.

215. Hausleitner, *Rumänisierung*, 316.

216. Kvitkovskyi, *Bukovyna*, 357.

217. Blasen, *"Primauté [. . .]"*, 161; Hausleitner, *Rumänisierung*, 316.

218. Kvitkovskyi, *Bukovyna*, 357.

219. Blasen, *"Primauté [. . .]"*, 194.

220. Ibid., 197–98; Hausleitner, *Rumänisierung*, 314.

221. Blasen, *"Primauté [. . .]"*, 196, 194.

222. S. G. Gross, *Export Empire*, 14; Waldeck, *Athene Palace*, 19.

223. Haynes, *Romanian Policy*, 3.

224. Deletant, *Hitler's Forgotten Ally*, 9.

225. Haynes, *Romanian Policy*, 167.

226. Haynes, *Romanian Policy*, 53–56, 167.

227. Haynes, *Romanian Policy*, 23; Solonari, *Purifying the Nation*, 51–52; Bucur, "Carol II," 114.

228. Haynes, *Romanian Policy*, 10; S. G. Gross, *Export Empire*, 3.

229. S. G. Gross, *Export Empire*, 3.

230. Deletant, *Hitler's Forgotten Ally*, 26.

231. S. G. Gross, *Export Empire*, 16–17, 222, 234.

232. S. G. Gross, *Export Empire*, 7; Waldeck, *Athene Palace*, 56.

233. S. G. Gross, *Export Empire*, 15; 254–55.

234. Glass, *Zerbrochene Nachbarschaft*, 46.

235. Haynes, *Romanian Policy*, 71; Hausleitner, *Rumänisierung*, 182.

236. Glass writes that *Czernowitzer Deutsche Tagespost* "reacted with caution to Hitler's victory." Glass, *Zerbrochene Nachbarschaft*, 361.

237. Hausleitner, *Rumänisierung*, 326.

238. ANIC, Arhivele Judeţului Ilfov, fond Chestura Poliţiei Cernăuţi, nr. inv. 883, dosar 1/1935, petition of Olteanu Pandele to Direcţiunea Generală a Poliţiei de Siguranţă, December 31, 1934.

239. ANIC, Arhivele Judeţului Ilfov, fond Chestura Poliţiei Cernăuţi, nr. inv. 883, dosar 1/1935, 69, report to General Police Directorate Bucharest, November 15, 1935; Kosiul, *Buchenlanddeutschen*, 127.

240. ANIC, Arhivele Judeţului Ilfov, fond Chestura Poliţiei Cernăuţi, nr. inv. 883, dosar 1/1935, 67, report to chief of Siguranţa on investigation of Erwin Millanich on January 12, 1935.

241. Kosiul, *Buchenlanddeutschen*, 145–46.

242. ANIC, Arhivele Județului Ilfov, fond Chestura Poliției Cernăuți, nr. inv. 883, dosar 1/1935, note to Police Directorate Bucharest on investigation of Heier Samuel, November 15, 1935.

243. Hausleitner, *Rumänisierung*, 322–23.

244. Hausleitner, *Rumänisierung*, 320.

245. Hausleitner, "Von der Ansiedlung," 32.

246. Hausleitner, *Rumänisierung*, 322–23.

247. Blasen, *"Primauté [. . .]"*, 99.

248. Kvitkovskyi, *Bukovyna*, 361; Blasen, *"Primauté [. . .]"*, 65.

249. Blasen, *"Primauté [. . .]"*, 161; Haynes, *Romanian Policy*, 71.

250. Solonari, *Purifying the Nation*, 52; Haynes, *Romanian Policy*, 132; Waldeck, *Athene Palace*, 107.

251. Haynes, *Romanian Policy*, 128.

252. Deletant, *Hitler's Forgotten Ally*, 15.

253. Haynes, *Romanian Policy*, 146. On the Wohlthat accords between Germany and Romania, from March 1939, see S. G. Gross, *Export Empire*, 290.

254. Iordachi, "Continuum," 259; Blasen, *"Primauté [. . .]"*, 221.

255. Haynes, *Romanian Policy*, 149.

256. Hausleitner, *Rumänisierung*, 352.

257. Haynes, *Romanian Policy*, 153.

258. On the hybridization of authoritarianism and fascism in interwar Europe, see Baranowski, "Authoritarianism and Fascism," 263.

259. Angrick, *Besatzungspolitik*, 114.

260. Harward, *Romania's Holy War*, 78–79.

261. Ion Antonescu, together with Iuliu Maniu, appeared in court as witnesses for the defense in Corneliu Zelea Codreanu's second trial for treason in May 1938. After Codreanu was convicted and sentenced to ten years' imprisonment, Antonescu was placed under house arrest on King Carol's orders. See Deletant, *Hitler's Forgotten Ally*, 45.

262. Waldeck, *Athene Palace*, 114.

263. Deletant, *Hitler's Forgotten Ally*, 50–51.

264. Solonari, *Satellite Empire*, 14.

265. Waldeck, *Athene Palace*, 178.

266. Radu, *Holocaust in Romania*, 43; Deletant, *Hitler's Forgotten Ally*, 19–20.

267. Deletant, *Hitler's Forgotten Ally*, 2, 109.

268. Deletant, *Hitler's Forgotten Ally*, 59; Solonari, *Purifying the Nation*, 130; Waldeck, *Athene Palace*, 279–84.

269. Ioanid, *Holocaust in Romania*, 46.

270. Angrick, *Besatzungspolitik*, 116; Deletant, *Hitler's Forgotten Ally*, 65.

## Chapter 7. Soviet Utopia

1. "Solntse nad Bukovynoi," *Izvestiya*, July 3, 1940.

2. "Po doroge na Chernovitsy," *Izvestiya*, June 30, 1940.

3. J. T. Gross, *Revolution from Abroad*, 30.

4. A. Popovici, "Ne-au batjocorit," 32.

5. Wortman, *Scenarios of Power*

6. J. T. Gross, *Revolution from Abroad*, 30.

7. "Z informatsii Chernivetskoho povitkomu KP(b)U TsK KP(b)U pro vstanovlennya radyanskoi vlady v pivnichni Bukovyni i pochatok roboty partiinykh i radyanskikh orhaniv," in *Radyanska Bukovyna, 1940–1945*, 27.

8. Levin, *Lesser of Two Evils*, 36; J. T. Gross, *Revolution from Abroad*.

9. Statiev, "Motivations and Goals," 979.

10. Gilburd, *To See Paris*, 5.

11. David-Fox, *Showcasing*, 1–10; Gilburd, *To See Paris*, 2.

12. On the Soviet Union's relationship with the West, see David-Fox, *Crossing Borders*, 67; also Westad, *Global Cold War*, 4.

13. Amar, *Paradox*, 9, 61.

14. Amar, "Sovietization," 34.

15. Amar, *Paradox*, 16, 62.

16. F. Hirsch, *Empire of Nations*, 72; Michaels, "Medical Propaganda," 162.

17. Hoffman, "European Modernity," 246; F. Hirsch, *Empire of Nations*, 62. For more on Soviet state interventionism and its affinities with other modern states, see David-Fox, *Showcasing*, 11.

18. F. Hirsch, *Empire of Nations*, 226.

19. Prusin, *Lands Between*, 125.

20. The classic account of Stalinism as a civilization is Kotkin, *Magnetic Mountain*.

21. On the "all-inclusiveness" of Soviet rule, see Prusin, *Lands Between*, 147; O'Keeffe, *Multiethnic Soviet Union*, 23.

22. F. Hirsch, *Empire of Nations*, 69–72; Kotkin, "Modern Times," 152.

23. Matlock, "Russia, Europe," 236; F. Hirsch, *Empire of Nations*, 9.

24. Hacman, "Aspecte diplomatice," 612.

25. Kotkin, *Stalin*, 681.

26. Liber, *Total Wars*, 204.

27. On the Soviet desire to take revenge for the humiliations suffered in the Polish–Soviet war of 1920, see Dullin, *Frontière épaisse*.

28. Kotkin, *Stalin*, 695.

29. Botushanskyi, *Bukovyna v konteksti*, 588, 590.

30. Kotkin, *Stalin*, 665.

31. J. T. Gross, *Revolution from Abroad*, 9.

32. On deteriorating Soviet–Romanian relations, see Avdeev, *Sovetsko–rumynskie otnosheniia*; on the founding of a Moldavian Autonomous Soviet Socialist Republic on the western border of Western Ukraine to stimulate irredentism among Bessarabians, see C. King, *Moldovans*.

33. Botushanskyi, *Bukovyna v konteksti*, 592, 596.

34. "No. 1: Nota Uryadu SRSR Rumynskomu uryadovi pro provedeniia Bessarabii ta peredachu pivnichnoi Bukovyni radyanskomu Soyuzu," June 26, 1940, in *Radyanska Bukovyna, 1940–1945*, 18–19.

35. Botushanskyi, *Bukovyna v konteksti*, 602.

36. Hausleitner, *"Viel Mischmasch mitgenommen"*, 43; Hausleitner, *Rumänisierung*, 349.

37. Botushanskyi, *Bukovyna v konteksti*, 605.

38. Hausleitner, *Rumänisierung*, 349.

39. Weber and Hecker, *Bukowina im Zweiten Weltkrieg*, 14.

40. Botushanskyi, *Bukovyna v kontektsi*, 607.

41. Hacman, "Aspecte diplomatice," 618.

42. Weber and Hecker, *Bukowina im Zweiten Weltkrieg*, 15.

43. "Nota 28," in Dobre, Manea, and Nicolescu, *Anul 1940*, 60–61.

44. "Nota 20," in Dobre, Manea, and Nicolescu, *Anul 1940*, 41–43.

45. "Nota 14," in Dobre, Manea, and Nicolescu, *Anul 1940*, 30; Botushanskyi, *Bukovyna v konteksti*, 615.

46. "Nota 74," in Dobre, Manea, and Nicolescu, *Anul 1940*, 182.

47. "Nota 2," in Dobre, Manea, and Nicolescu, *Anul 1940*, 3.

48. Botushanskyi, *Bukovyna v konteksti*, 599; "Nota 6," in Dobre, Manea, and Nicolescu, *Anul 1940*, 16–17.

49. Hausleitner, *Rumänisierung*, 336.

50. Botushanskyi, *Bukovyna v konteksti*, 617.

51. "Nota 33," in Dobre, Manea, and Nicolescu, *Anul 1940*, 78–79.

52. "Nota 58," in Dobre, Manea, and Nicolescu, *Anul 1940*, 160.

53. "Nota 33," in Dobre, Manea, and Nicolescu, *Anul 1940*, 82.

54. "Nota 58," in Dobre, Manea, and Nicolescu, *Anul 1940*, 157.

55. This rumor was not confirmed. "Nota 62," in Dobre, Manea, and Nicolescu, *Anul 1940*, 171.

56. Flondor, *Dulce-amar*, 57.

57. "Nota 30," in Dobre, Manea, and Nicolescu, *Anul 1940*, 65–66.

58. "Nota 27," in Dobre, Manea, and Nicolescu, *Anul 1940*, 58–59. Royal residents were appointed according to the new administrative law of August 14, 1938 to represent ministers, supervise functionaries, direct prefects, and command police forces and the gendarmerie in each administrative unit. See Blasen, "Terrorisme légionnaire," 303–4.

59. Hausleitner, *Rumänisierung*, 355; Levin, "Jews and the Inception," 53.

60. "Nota 27," in Dobre, Manea, and Nicolescu, *Anul 1940*, 59.

61. The Romanian military spoke of the "cowardly betrayal by the Jewish population who, upon hearing rumors about the arrival of the Russian army, already donned the red coat of communists subjecting everything Romanian to terror." "Nota 33," in Dobre, Manea, and Nicolescu, *Annual 1940*, 82.

62. "Nota 60," in Dobre, Manea, and Nicolescu, *Anul 1940*, 167.

63. Levin, "Jews and the Inception," 54.

64. "Nota 60" and "Nota 27," in Dobre, Manea, and Nicolescu, *Anul 1940*, 167 and 94.

65. "Nota 115," in Dobre, Manea, and Nicolescu, *Anul 1940*, 279.

66. "Nota 87," in Dobre, Manea, and Nicolescu, *Anul 1940*, 222.

67. "Nota 27," in Dobre, Manea, and Nicolescu, *Anul 1940*, 59.

68. Frunchak, "Making of Soviet Chernivtsi," 140.

69. "No. 15: Z informatsii Chernivetskoho povitkomu KP(b)U TsK KP(b)U pro vstanovlennya radyanskoi vlady v pivnichnii Bukovyni i pochatok roboty partiinykh i radyanskikh orhaniv," in *Radyanska Bukovyna, 1940–1945*, 27.

70. Weber and Hecker, *Bukowina im Zweiten Weltkrieg*, 16; "No. 16: Zakon pro vkliuchennya pivnichnoi chastyny Bukovyni i Khotynskoho, Akermanskoho ta Izmailskoho povitiv Bessarabii do skladu Ukrainskoi Radyanskoi Sotsialistychnoi Respubliki, August 2, 1940," in *Radyanska Bukovyna, 1940–1945*, 33.

71. Kurylo, *Pivnichna Bukovyna*, 135.

72. "No. 47: Z Ukazu prezydii verkhovnoi rady URSR shchodo likvidatsii povitiv i utvorennya raioniv u Chernivetskii oblasti," October 12, 1940, in *Radyanska Bukovyna, 1940–1945*, 67; Weber and Hecker, *Bukowina in Zweiten Weltkrieg*, 16.

73. On the concept of "multiple modernities," both liberal and illiberal (which historians have extended to the Soviet Union), see Eisenstadt, "Multiple Modernities." On the Soviet modernity project, Hoffman, "European Modernity."

74. David-Fox, "What Is Cultural Revolution?," 121. For a different view, see Fitzpatrick, "Cultural Revolution."

75. Slezkine, *Arctic Mirrors*, 254; Hoffmann, *Stalinist Values*, 11.

76. David-Fox, *Showcasing*, 13. In the Russian context, it was the intelligentsia of the nineteenth century that took it upon itself to bring culture to the backward masses. See Boym, *Common Places*.

77. On "cultural war," see Slezkine, "From Savages to Citizens," 64.

78. David-Fox, "What is Cultural Revolution?," 192.

79. Volkov, "Concept of *kul'turnost'*," 212, 215–16; Slezkine, "From Savages to Citizens," 75.

80. Liber, *Total Wars*, 154.

81. "Zavoiuvannia sotsialistychnoi kultury," *Radyanska Bukovyna, 1940–1945*, November 14, 1940.

82. Amar, "Sovietization," 44.

83. Hoffman, *Stalinist Values*, 16; Volkov, "Concept of *kul'turnost'*," 227.

84. On the Bolshevik reading revolution, control of libraries, and reading as a path to *kul'turnost'* see Lovell, *Russian Reading Revolution*, 28.

85. "No. 104: Dovidka viddilu Propahandy ta ahitatsii Chernivetskoho obkomu KP(b)U pro robotu politosvitnikh ustanov oblasti," June 15, 1941, in *Radyanska Bukovina, 1940–1945*, 177.

86. "No. 104: Dovidka viddilu Propahandy ta ahitatsii Chernivetskoho obkomu KP(b)U pro robotu politosvitnikh ustanov oblasti," June 15, 1941, in *Radyanska Bukovina, 1940–1945*, 177.

87. DAChO, f. P1, op. 1, d. 15, l. 33, text of telegram to Stalin, read by secretary of Shevchenko *raikom partii* tov. Kucherenko, December 8–24, 1940.

88. Gilburd, *To See Paris*, 15. The Soviets, Svetlana Boym writes, "taught Marxist-Leninist ideology together with table manners, mixing Stalin with Pushkin." Boym, *Common Places*, 105.

89. On the destruction of old ways of life, see Slezkine, "From Savages to Citizens," 61.

90. See Viola, *War Against the Peasantry*.

91. DAChO, f. P1, op. 1, d. 44, l. 29, stenogram of the first Chernivtsi oblast party conference, February 9–10, 1941.

92. M. Gurin, "Numa în colhoz viaţa îndestulata şi culturală," *Adevărul Bolşevic*, March 7,1941.

93. A similar process, whereby about 30% of land was confiscated and redistributed, took place in eastern Poland. See Prusin, *Lands Between*, 132–33.

94. DAChO, f. P1, op. 1, d. 44, l. 21, official report on the work of the Chernivtsi *obkom* KP/b/U during the first oblast conference of the KP/b/U, February 9, 1941.

95. Kurylo, *Pivnichna Bukovyna*, 137–42.

96. Nimigeanu, *Însemnările*, 29.

97. A. Popovici, "Ne-au batjocorit," 37.

98. Kurylo, *Pivnichna Bukovyna*, 144.

99. DAChO, f. P1, op. 1, d. 62, l. 42, stenogram of meeting of secretaries MK and RK KP/b/U in Chernivtsi oblast, January 16, 1941.

100. DAChO, f. P1, op. 1, d. 11, l. 98, stenogram of meeting with participants in delegation which was at the demonstrations during October festivities in Kyiv, November 21, 1940.

101. DAChO, f. P1, op. 1, d. 72, l. 5, "political information" (*politinformatsiia*), April 14, 1941, Khotyn RK KP/b/U to Chernivtsi *obkom* secretary KP/b/U tov. Hrushetskyi.

102. DAChO, f. P1, op. 1, d. 58, l. 138, stenogram of conference of Chernivtsi *obkom* KP/b/U, May 23, 1941.

103. Levin, "Jews and the Inception."

104. "No. 7: Povidomlennya pro stanovyshche v m. Chernivtsyakh pislya zalyshenniia ioho ocupantamy ta pershi zakhody radyanskoi vlady," July 9, 1940, in *Radyanska Bukovyna, 1940–1945*, 16.

105. DAChO, f. P1, op. 1, d. 28, l. 17, report on the work of Chernivtsi city house of propaganda, October 10, 1940.

106. "Red corners" (*krasnye ugolki*) were special propaganda rooms where party gatherings were held, typically decorated with portraits of Lenin, Stalin, and so on. The concept was a play on the "holy corner" in Russian Orthodox households where the icons were usually displayed.

107. "No. 64: Z dovidki orhanizatsiino-instruktorskoho viddilu Chernivetskoho obkomu KP(b)U pro stan roboty partiinoi orhanizatsii panchishno-trykotazhnoi fabryki No 1," November 27, 1940, in *Radyanska Bukovyna, 1940–1945*, 91.

108. The title "Stakhanovite," derived from the name of Alexei Stakhanov, an exemplary miner in the Donbas region of Soviet Ukraine, was awarded to workers for exceptional productivity, "busting" work quotas or production norms.

109. "No. 64: Z dovidki orhanizatsiino-instruktorskoho viddilu Chernivetskoho obkomu KP(b)U pro stan roboty partiinoi orhanizatsii panchishno-trykotazhnoi fabryki No 1," November 27, 1940, and "No. 86: Z rezolutsii 1-i oblasnoi partiinoi konferentsii Chernivets'koi oblasti," July 10, 1941, in *Radyanska Bukovyna, 1940–1945*, 91 and 138 respectively.

110. Georgescu, *265 de zile*, 14–15.

111. Snyder, *Bloodlands*, 270. Similarly, across Soviet-occupied western Ukraine, locals would "tell and retell stories about the wives of Red Army officers who allegedly attended theaters in nightgowns, believing them to be evening dresses." Plokhy, *Gates of Europe*, 261.

112. Nimigeanu, *Însemnările*, 19.

113. DAChO, f. P1, op. 1, d. 15, l. 21, stenogram of meeting of *obkom* KP/b/U concerning preparations for elections to the Supreme Soviet USSR and Ukrainian SSR, September 26, 1940.

114. Nichita-Toma, "Chinurile și speranțele," 177.

115. Frunchak, "Making of Soviet Chernivtsi," 210.

116. DAChO, f. P1, op. 1, d. 9, l. 7, resolution of the first oblast *aktiv* of Chernivtsi party organization on the report of tov. Hrushetskyi, August 30, 1940: on summary of July plenum Tsk VKP/b.

117. DAChO, f. P1, op. 1, d. 7, l. 23, stenogram of meeting Chernivtsi *obkom* KP/b/U, October 3, 1940. For more on the moral failures that undermined the Soviet civilizing mission, see Amar, "Sovietization," 41–42.

118. "Rishennya TsK KP (b)U pro sklad povitovykh komitetiv KP(b) u radyanskoi Bessarabii i pivnichnoi chastyny Bukovyny," July 4, 1940, in *Radyanska Bukovyna, 1940–1945*, 15.

119. Frunchak, "Making of Soviet Chernivtsi," 155.

120. Frunchak, "Making of Soviet Chernivtsi," 224–26.

121. Frunchak, "Making of Soviet Chernivtsi," 192.

122. DAChO, f. P1, op. 1, d. 58, l. 86, stenogram of conference of Chernivtsi *obkom* KP/b/U.

123. Kotkin, "Modern Times," 131.

124. DAChO, f. P1, op. 1, d. 70, l. 4, special report on the progress of preparations for elections to the Supreme Soviet of Ukrainian SSR and USSR in Chernivtsi oblast, January 8, 1941, to *obkom* KP/b/U secretary tov. Hrushetskyi.

125. DAChO, f. P1, op. 1, d. 44, l. 50, stenogram of first Chernivtsi oblast party conference, February 9–10, 1941.

126. Kurylo, *Pivnichna Bukovyna*, 135.

127. DAChO, f. P1, op. 1, d. 10, l. 47, stenogram of assembly of oblast *partaktiv* which took place on December 11, 1940 in the National Theater in Chernivtsi. In the Khotyn raion, one official reported that "on the day on which the primary party organization was formed not even one party meeting was held" and the party organization could happily go on without responding to any orders from above because "nobody is checking whether they are fulfilled."

128. DAChO, f. P1, op. 1, d. 28, l. 12, report to secretary of Chernivtsi *obkom* KP/b/U on propaganda, August 20, 1940.

129. DAChO, f. P1, op. 1, d. 44, l. 102, stenogram of first Chernivtsi oblast party conference, February 9–10, 1941.

130. DAChO, f. P1, op. 1, d. 15, ll. 23 and 75, stenogram of meeting of *obkom* KP/b/U on preparations for elections to the Supreme Soviet of Ukrainian SSR and USSR, December 8–24, 1940.

131. DAChO, f. P1, op. 1, d. 44, l. 48, stenogram of first Chernivtsi oblast party conference, 9–10 February, 1941. On the Soviet Union as a "propaganda state," see Kenez, *Birth of the Propaganda State*.

132. DAChO, f. P1, op. 1, d. 15, ll. 78 and 3, stenogram of meeting of *obkom* KP/b/U on preparations for elections to the Supreme Soviet of Ukrainian SSR and USSR, 8–24 December, 1940.

133. "Z dovidki Chernivetskoho obkomu KP(b)U tsentralnomu komitetovi KP(b)U pro pidhotovku do vyboriv deputativ u verkhovni rady SRSR i URSR po oblasti," November 14, 1940, in *Radyanska Bukovina, 1940–1945*, 76.

134. DAChO, f. P1, op. 1, d. 62, l. 1, stenogram of meeting of secretaries MK and RK KP/b/U in Chernivtsi oblast from January 16, 1941.

135. DACHO, f. P1, op. 1, d. 15, l. 74, stenogram of meeting of Chernivtsi *obkom* KP/b/U with secretary of *raipartkom*, December 24, 1940.

136. DAChO, f. P1, op. 1, d. 9, ll. 13, 41, and 38, stenogram of the first oblast *aktiv* of Chernivtsi party organization, August 30, 1940.

137. DAChO, f. P1, op. 1, d. 11, l. 94, stenogram of meeting of Chernivtsi *obkom* KP/b/U, November 18, 1940

138. DAChO, f. P1, op. 1, d. 22, l. 1, report from TsK KP/b/U to tov Khrushchev, November 24, 1940.

139. DAChO, f. P1, op. 1, d. 11, l. 93, stenogram of meeting of Chernivtsi *obkom* KP/b/U, November 18, 1940.

140. Nimigeanu, *Însemnările*, 191.

141. DAChO, f. P1, op. 1, d. 67, l. 8, letter from administration of 97th Border Squad NKVD USSR to secretary of Chernivtsi *obkom* Hrushetskyi, and head of Ukrainian NKVD, Chernivtsi oblast Captain Martynov, January 1941.

142. Nimigeanu, *Însemnările*, 19.

143. Quoted in Weiner and Rahi-Tamm, "Getting to Know You," 40.

144. Covalciuc, "Amintiri din vremuri de restrişte."

145. O. Voronca, "Răni ce se vindecă greu."

146. DAChO, f. P1, op. 1, d. 10, ll. 118 and 34, stenogram of assembly of oblast *partaktiv* which took place on December 11, 1940 in Chernivtsi's National Theater.

147. DAChO, f. P1, op. 1, d. 15, l. 56, stenogram of meeting of *obkom* KP/b/U on preparations for elections in January 1941 to the Supreme Soviet USSR and Ukrainian SSR, December 8–24, 1940.

148. DAChO, f. P1, op. 1, d. 62, stenogram of meeting of secretaries MK and RK KP/b/U in Chernivtsi oblast, January 16, 1941.

149. DAChO, f. P1, op. 1, d. 11, l. 91, stenogram of meeting of Chernivtsi *obkom* KP/b/U, November 18, 1940.

150. DAChO, f. P1, op. 1, d. 3, l. 1, ordinance of Chernivtsi *obkom* KP/b/U, November 18, 1940.

151. DAChO, f. P1, op. 1, d. 70, l. 7, special report on preparations for elections to Supreme Soviet USSR and Ukrainian SSR in Chernivtsi oblast, January 8, 1981, to secretary of *obkom* KP/b/U tov. Hrushetskyi.

152. DAChO, f. P1, op. 1, d. 70, l. 9, special report on preparations for elections to Supreme Soviet USSR and Ukrainian SSR in Chernivtsi oblast, January 8, 1981, to secretary of *obkom* KP/b/U tov. Hrushetskyi.

153. Between January and March 1940, over 1,758,000 people in cities and districts of western Ukraine occupied by Soviets had been issued with passports. Weiner and Rahi-Tamm, "Getting to Know You," 16.

154. Weiner and Rahi-Tamm, "Getting to Know You," 16.

155. Frunchak, "Making of Soviet Chernivtsi," 190.

156. On the Soviet passport system, see Zaslavsky and Luryi, "Passport System."

157. Holquist, "State Violence," 25.

158. Statiev, *Soviet Counterinsurgency*.

159. Bugai, *Deportation*, 152.

160. Polian, *Against Their Will*, 122. During June 12–13, 1941 over thirty thousand people were deported from the Moldovan SSR and the Chernivtsi and Ismail oblasts of the Ukrainian SSR to Siberia.

161. Hausleitner, *Rumaenisierung*, 361; Frunchak, "Making of Soviet Chernivtsi," 275; Hirsch and Spitzer, *Ghosts of Home*, 118–19; Prusin, *Lands Between*, 139.

162. Pivin, "Mă doare trecutul," 134.

163. Nimigeanu, *Însemnările*, 43.

164. Nandriş-Cudla, *20 de ani în Siberia*, 56.

165. Nandriş, *Povestea vieţii mele*, cited in Corobca and Covalciuc, *Golgota românească*, 10–11.

166. "Shifrtelegramma o ssyl'nopereselentsakh iz zapadnykh oblastei SSSR," May 21, 1941, in Pasat, *Trudnye stranitsy*, 146.

167. "Dokladnaya zapiska UNKVD o rasselenii i trudovom ustroistve ssyl'noposelentsev v raionakh Novosibirskoi oblasti," September 10, 1941; "Dokladnaya zapiska UNKVD Krasnoyarskogo Kraya o rasselenii ssylnoposelentsev, ikh trudovom i khoziaistvennom ustroistve," September 17, 1941; "Dokladnaya zapiska GULAGa NKVD o rasselenii ssylnoposelentsev, ikh trudovom i khoziaistvennom ustroistve po sostoyanniu na 15/IX - 1941 goda," October 1941; in Pasat, *Trudnye stranitsy*, 177–78, 182, and 187 respectively.

168. "Dokladnaya zapiska UNKVD o trudovom i khoziaistvennom ustroistve ssyl'noposelentsev, rasselennykh o Krasnoyarskom Krae," February 10, 1942, in Pasat, *Trudnye stranitsy*, 196.

169. "Iz dokladnoi zapiski Chanovskogo RO NKVD Novosibirskoi oblasti o snabzhenii ssyl'noposelentsev khlebom," December 13, 1941, in Pasat, *Trudnye stranitsy*, 192.

170. Nimigeanu, *Însemnările*, 59.

171. Opaiţ, "Vânătoare de oameni," 83–84.

172. Hausleitner, *Rumänisierung*, 370; Richter, *Heimkehrer*.

173. Ther, *Dark Side*, 195; Hausleitner *Rumänisierung*, 371. In total, 52,129 Germans left Bukovina.

174. Prusin, *Lands Between*, 135; Hausleitner, *"Viel Mischmasch mitgenommen"*, 3.

175. "Dokladnaya zapiska o rabote sovets'koi komissii po evakuatsii lits nemets'koi natsionalnosti s territorii Bessarabii i Severnoi Bukovyni," September 23, 1940, in Pasat, *Trudnye stranitsy*, 95.

176. The leader of the German resettlement commando in Cernăuţi was SS Standartenführer Horst Hoffmeyer. SS Sturmbannführer Müller from Oldenburg was named 'Gebietsbevollmächtiger' for the resettlement of Germans from Northern Bukovina. Rudolf Wagner, a Bukovinan later known for his monographs on the history of Germans in Bukovina, was responsible for communicating with Soviet commission members. Hausleitner, *Rumänisierung*, 368.

177. "Zapiska o razrabotke dokumentov sovets'koi pravitel'stvennoi delegatsii," July 20, 1940; "Soobshchenie Germans'kogo Posla Shulenburga"; "Dokladnaya zapiska o rabote sovets'koi komissii po evakuatsii lits nemets'koi natsional'nosti s territorii Bessarabii i Severnoi Bukovyni"; in Pasat, *Trudnye stranitsy*, 73–74, 82, and 96 respectively.

178. "Dokladnaya zapiska o khode rabot sovets'koi pravitel'stvennoi komissii po evakuatsii lits nemets'koi natsional'nosti iz Bessarabii i Severnoi Bukovyni," September 26, 1940, in Pasat, *Trudnye stranitsy*, 108.

179. DAChO, f. P1, op. 1, d. 32, l. 27, report on work by Soviet delegation for evacuation of Germans from territory of Chernivtsi oblast.

180. Hausleitner, *Rumänisierung*, 367.

181. "Postavlennie SNK SSSR o rabote sovets'koi delegatsii v smeshannoi komissii po evakuatsii lits nemets'koi natsional'nosti s territorii Bessarabii i severnoi Bukovyni," July 20, 1940, in Pasat, *Trudnye stranitsy*, 78. Germans from Southern Bukovina were allowed to take much more with them.

182. "Dokladnaya zapiska o sostoyannii kolonii i prinyatom imushchestve posle otezda nemetskikh kolonistov v Germaniyu iz Bessarabii i Severnoi Bukovyni," October 25, 1940, in Pasat, *Trudnye stranitsy*, 125.

183. DAChO, f. P1, op. 1, d. 32, l. 27, report on work by Soviet delegation for evacuation of Germans from territory of Chernivtsi oblast, November 19, 1940.

184. Hausleitner, *"Viel Mischmasch mitgenommen"*, 89–90.

185. SD: "Sicherheitsdienst," the Nazi security service, the intelligence agency of the SS (Schutzstaffel), led by Reinhard Heydrich.

186. DAChO, f. P1, op. 1, d. 32, l. 30, report on work by Soviet delegation for evacuation of Germans from territory of Chernivtsi oblast, November 19, 1940.

187. DAChO, f. P1, op. 1, d. 32, ll. 30–31, report on work by Soviet delegation for evacuation of Germans from territory of Chernivtsi oblast, November 19, 1940. On Ukrainian nationalists hidden by Germans, see also Armstrong, *Ukrainian Nationalism*.

188. Kurylo, *Pivnichna Bukovyna*, 399.

189. "Direktiva NKVD USSR o prikaze LP Beriya po aktivizatsii razvedyvatel'noi i kontrarazvedyvatel'noi raboty," August 21, 1940, in Pasat, *Trudnye stranitsy*, 88–89.

190. DAChO, f. P1, op. 1, d. 32, l. 26, report on work by Soviet delegation for evacuation of Germans from territory of Chernivtsi oblast, November 19, 1940.

191. Hausleitner, *"Viel Mischmasch mitgenommen"*, 115.

192. Hausleitner, *Rumänisierung*, 369.

193. Hausleitner, *"Viel Mischmasch mitgenommen"*, 94; Frunchak, "Making of Soviet Chernivtsi," 264.

194. Ther, *Dark Side*, 93.

195. DAChO, f. P1, op. 1, d. 32, ll. 30–31, report on work by Soviet delegation for evacuation of Germans from territory of Chernivtsi oblast, November 19, 1940.

196. Hausleitner, *"Viel Mischmasch mitgenommen"*, 122–23.

197. F. Hirsch, *Empire of Nations*, 32, 27–28.

198. F. Hirsch, *Empire of Nations*, 5.

199. On adopting federalism as a general "principle of relations among the nationalities," see Slezkine, "USSR as a Communal Apartment."

200. Liber, *Total Wars*, 119; O'Keefe, *Multiethnic Soviet Union*, 19. Terry Martin famously likened the Soviet Union's efforts to promote the development of non-Russian nationalities to a kind of "affirmative action" policy. Martin, *Affirmative Action Empire*.

201. Slezkine, "USSR as a Communal Apartment," 420.

202. Hillis, "Intimacy and Antipathy."

203. Liber, *Soviet Nationality Policy*.

204. Liber, *Total Wars*, 90.

205. Liber, *Soviet Nationality Policy*, 125.

206. DAChO, f. R-3, op. 1, d. 35, l. 17, historico-geographical and economic description of Chernivtsi oblast 1941.

207. Massell, *Surrogate Proletariat*, 76.

208. "Rezoliutsiia narady holiv ta sekretariv volosnykh vykonkomiv, silskikh i miskikh rad pro rozpodil pomishchytskikh ta tserkovykh zemel mizh bezzemelnymi ta malozemelnymi selyanami Chernivetskoho povitu," July 11, 1940, in *Radyanska Bukovyna, 1940–1945*, 18.

209. Kurylo, *Pivnichna Bukovyna*, 397.

210. See the guide for candidates to Chernivtsi university under Soviet rule, *Dovidnyk dlya vstupnykiv*.

211. DAChO, f. P1, op. 1, d. 7, l. 22, stenogram of meeting of Chernivtsi *obkom* KP/b/U, September 26, 1940, on preparations for beginning of school year at university.

212. DAChO, f. P1, op. 1, d. 44, l. 40, stenogram of first Chernivtsi oblast party conference, 9–10 February, 1941.

213. C. Hirsch, *Life in the Twentieth Century*.

214. DAChO, f. P1, op. 1, d. 10, stenogram of assembly of oblast *partaktiv* which took place on December 11, 1940 in Chernivtsi national Theater.

215. DAChO, f. P1, op. 1, d. 11, l. 53, stenogram of meeting of *kolektiv* of *obkom*, *gorkom* KP/b/U and *obkom* LKSMU, October 4, 1940.

216. Frunchak, "Making of Soviet Chernivtsi," 243–44.

217. Ivan Hrushetskyi, "Cherhovi zavdannya radyanskoi shkoly i narodnoho vchytelya," *Radyanska Bukovyna*, September 13, 1940.

218. DAChO, f. P1, op. 1, d. 44, l. 80, stenogram of first Chernivtsi oblast party conference, February 9–10, 1941.

219. DAChO, f. P1, op. 1, d. 9, l. 51, stenogram of oblast party *aktiv* in Chernivtsi, August 30, 1940.

220. DAChO, f. P1, op. 1, d. 7, l. 20, stenogram of meeting of Chernivtsi *obkom* KP/b/U, September 26, 1940.

221. For a parallel process in Soviet Lviv, see Amar, *Paradox*, 73.

222. Ladygina, *Bridging East and West*, 13, 196.

223. Quoted in Ladygina, *Bridging East and West*, 197.

224. DAChO, f. P1, op. 1, d. 26, l. 12, report on organizational and mass-agitation work in Chernivtsi oblast for November 20, 1940.

225. "Lyst pysmennytsi O Iu Kobylianskoi do trudyashchykh radyanskoi Ukrainy," *Radyanska Bukovyna*, July 2, 1940, 14.

226. "Slavna dochka Ukrainskoho narodu," *Radyanska Bukovyna*, September 8, 1940.

227. Fowler, *Beau Monde*, 16.

228. For a discussion as to whether Kobylianska actually authored these pieces, see Frunchak, "Making of Soviet Chernivtsi," 186.

229. C. Hirsch, *Life in the Twentieth Century*.

230. DAChO, f. P1, op. 1, d. 58, l. 86, stenogram of conference of Chernivtsi *obkom* KP/b/U, March 24, 1941.

231. Levin, *Lesser of Two Evils*, 59.

232. Hirsch and Spitzer, *Ghosts of Home*, 115; Levin, "Jews and the Inception," 62–65.

233. Georgescu, *265 de zile*.

234. DAChO, f. P1, op. 1, d. 22, l. 1, report from Kiev TsK KP/b/U to tov. Khrushchev, November 24, 1940.

235. DAChO, f. P1, op. 1, d. 11, l. 91, stenogram of meeting of Chernivtsi *obkom* KP/b/U, November 18, 1940.

236. "Z politychnoi informatsii Chernivetskoho obkomu KP(b)U pro stanovishche v m. Chernivtsiakh i oblasti," June 26, 1941, in *Radyanska Bukovyna, 1940–1945*, 188.

237. DAChO, f. P1, op. 1, d. 80, ll. 6 and 2, meeting with secretary *obkom* KP/b/U tov. Hrushetskyi, June 24, 1941.

238. Frunchak, "Making of Soviet Chernivtsi," 282.

239. DAChO, f. P1, op. 1, d. 80, l. 6, meeting with secretary *obkom* KP/b/U tov. Hrushetskyi, June 24, 1941.

240. LBI, Leopold Hessing Collection, ME 1070, MM II 29 (accessed digitally), 12.

241. DAChO, f. P1, op. 1, d. 58, l. 129, stenogram of conference of Chernivtsi *obkom* KP/b/U, April 26, 1941.

242. DAChO, f. P1, op. 1, d. 72, l. 1, report to secretary of RK KP/b/U tov. Zhylenko, Novosyelitsa; on moral-political state of population in Novosyelytsia raion, March 11, 1941.

243. "Korespondentsiia 'Komsomoltsi staiut na zakhyst svoei batkivshchynu,'" June 24 1941 in *Radyanska Bukovyna, 1940–1945*, 186.

244. DACHO, f. P1, op. 1, d. 80, l. 25, "political information" (*politinformatsiia*).

245. DAChO, f. P1, op. 1, d. 76, special report to secretary of Chernivtsi *obkom* KP/b/U Hrushetskyi, June 27, 1941.

246. DAChO, f. P1, op. 1, d. 80, l. 26, report to secretary of Chernivtsi *obkom* KP/b/U tov. Hrushetskyi from Vashkivtsi raikom KP/b/U, June 26, 1941.

247. DAChO, f. P1, op. 1, d. 76, special report to secretary of Chernivtsi *obkom* KP/b/U Hrushetskyi, June 27, 1941.

248. DAChO, f. P1, op. 1, d. 80, l. 25, "political information" (*politinformatsiia*).

249. DAChO, f. P1, op. 1, d. 90, report to secretary *obkom* KP/b/U tov. Hrushetskyi, 23 June, 1941.

250. DAChO, f. P1, op. 1, d. 80, report to secretary *obkom* KP/b/U tov. Hrushetskyi, June 28, 1941.

251. Levin, "Jews and the Inception," 66.

## Chapter 8. War and Reconstruction

1. Deletant, *Hitler's Forgotten Ally*, 78; Weber and Hecker, *Bukowina im Zweiten Weltkrieg*, 32.

2. Ancel, "German–Romanian Relationship: 266–67. See also Bartov, *Eastern Front*.

3. Solonari, *Satellite Empire*, 21; Angrick, *Besatzungspolitik*, 119.

4. Angrick, *Besatzungspolitik*, 128, 130; Deletant, *Hitler's Forgotten Ally*, 127.

5. Weber and Hecker, *Bukowina im Zweiten Weltkrieg*, 41, 33.

6. Solonari, *Purifying the Nation*, 341.

7. Weber and Hecker, *Bukowina im Zweiten Weltkrieg*, 43.

8. Solonari, *Satellite Empire*, 1, 35.

9. Levene, *Crisis of Genocide*, 191.

10. Fostii, "Diialnist OUN," 11–12.

11. Fostii, "Diialnist OUN," 11–12.

12. There was widespread anti-Jewish violence across Eastern Europe in the summer of 1941, especially in territories that experienced Soviet rule for the first time in 1939–40. Himka, *Ukrainian Nationalists*, 199. Over a hundred pogroms took place in East Galicia that summer, resulting in, according to some accounts, as many as twelve thousand Jewish deaths. Lower, "Axis Collaboration."

13. Quoted in Britskyi et al., *Bukovyntsi v trahichni roky*, 135.

14. Geissbühler, *Blutiger Juli*, 64. See also Solonari, "Patterns of Violence"; Dean, *Collaboration*, 20.

15. Ioanid, *Holocaust in Romania*, 99–100.

16. Mircu, *Pogromurile*, 46; Ioanid, *Holocaust in Romania*, 99–100.

17. Marius Mircu, cited in Harward, *Romania's Holy War*, 106. On mayors and schoolmasters' involvement, see Geissbühler, *Blutiger Juli*, 69.

18. Geissbühler, *Blutiger Juli*, 95.

19. Geissbühler, "'He Spoke Yiddish,'" 434.

20. Geissbühler, *Blutiger Juli*, 63–64; Geissbühler, "'He Spoke Yiddish,'" 434.

21. Geissbühler, *Blutiger Juli*, 66.

22. DACHO, f. R-307, op. 3, d. 14, l. 17, note from governor of Bukovina to regional police inspectorate Cernăuţi, June 13, 1942.

23. On the Soviet-induced culture of denunciation, see Berkhoff, *Harvest of Despair*, 55.

24. Solonari, *Purifying the Nation*, 195; Himka, *Ukrainian Nationalists*, 201–3.

25. Geissbühler, "'He Spoke Yiddish,'" 433.

26. CSRJ, Jean Ancel Collection, Testimonies, David Grinberg, 03-1473, 166.

27. Geissbühler, *Blutiger Juli*, 102.

28. DACHO, f. P1, op. 1, d. 80, l. 30, "Soobshchenie sekretarya Glubokskoho raikoma partii tov. Velyko."

29. DACHO, f. 30, op, 4, d, 43, l. 170, copy of note by Special Information Service (Siguranţa), 1941.

30. CSRJ, Jean Ancel Collection, Photocopies Osobyi Arkhiv Moscow, vol. 4, November 17, 1941, 151–52.

31. Solonari, *Purifying the Nation*, 164–65.

32. Cited in Ancel, *History of the Holocaust*, 71.

33. Similar revenge murders were perpetrated in Galicia and Volhynia that summer, in retribution for the NKVD's crimes. Entire Jewish towns were wiped out in Volhynia in retaliation for alleged Jewish cooperation with the Soviets. See Lower, "Pogroms," 217. In Lviv, the incoming German troops, accompanied by Ukrainian battalions, revealed the mutilated, decomposed bodies of political prisoners executed by the departing NKVD, fanning the flames of anti-Semitism and instigating a local pogrom.

34. Ioanid, *Holocaust in Romania*, 96. See also Mircu, *Pogromurile*, 23.

35. Geissbühler, *Blutiger Juli*, 68.

36. Mircu, *Pogromurile*, 54.

37. CSRJ, Jean Ancel Collection, Testimonies, 03-1436, report, "The Fate of the Border Region Jablonitza by Sniatyn in 1941–44 According to Witnesses," by Dr. Getzler, Czernowitz, sent to Prof. Dr. Hermann Sternberg, Tel Aviv.

38. CSRJ, Jean Ancel Collection, Testimonies, David Grinberg, 03-1473, 166.

39. The head of gendarmerie Constantin Vasiliu issued instructions to all gendarmerie units on June 17, 1941 to prepare for cleansing the land of Jews and Communists. Harward, *Romania's Holy War*, 108; Deletant, *Hitler's Forgotten Ally*, 143; Deletant, "Transnistria," 162–63.

40. Deletant, *Hitler's Forgotten Ally*, 143.

41. Angrick, "Im Wechselspiel der Kräfte," 338. On how different gendarmerie majors interpreted orders, see Solonari, *Purifying the Nation*, 176–77.

42. Angrick, *Besatzungspolitik*, 141–45; Ioanid *Holocaust in Romania*, 66, 72; Solonari, *Purifying the Nation*, 167.

43. Angrick, "Im Wechselspiel der Kräfte," 338.

44. Cited in Ioanid, *Holocaust in Romania*, 108.

45. Harward, *Romania's Holy War*, 109; Trașcă and Deletant, *Al III-lea Reich*, doc. 18, July 14, 1941, 198.

46. Ancel, "Romanian Campaigns, 97.

47. Trașcă and Deletant, *Al III-lea Reich*, doc. 30, August 1, 1941, 235; Angrick, *Besatzungspolitik*, 159; Ioanid, *Holocaust in Romania*, 101.

48. Angrick, *Besatszungspolitik*, 150; Mircu, *Pogromurile*, 96.

49. Angrick, *Besatzungspolitik*, 150–52.

50. Mircu, *Pogromurile*, 71.

51. Angrick, *Besatzungspolitik*, 153.

52. Angrick, *Besatzungspolitik*, 149.

53. Trașcă and Deletant, *Al III-lea Reich*, doc. 22, July 26, 1941, 210.

54. Trașcă and Deletant, *Al III-lea Reich*, doc. 16, July 11, 1941, 194.

55. Solonari, *Purifying the Nation*, 182; Angrick, *Besatzungspolitik*, 150.

56. Gross and Wiehn, *Zeitzeugin Sein*, 50–55.

57. Solonari, *Purifying the Nation*, 145–46.

58. Solonari, *Satellite Empire*, 125; Deletant, *Hitler's Forgotten Ally*, 81.

59. Solonari, "'Model Province,'" 475.

60. Deletant, *Hitler's Forgotten Ally*, 69.

61. Solonari, *Purifying the Nation*, 74.

62. Deletant, "Transnistria," 159. By "Titus's policy" Mihai Antonescu referred to the Roman emperor Titus, who destroyed Jerusalem, leading to the dispersal of its Jewish population.

63. As Mihai Antonescu put it, "I am for the forced migration of the whole Jewish population in Bessarabia and Bukovina, which must be expelled over the frontier." Cited in Deletant, "Transnistria," 161. See also Ioanid, *Holocaust in Romania*, 92.

64. Cited in Poliec, *Holocaust*, 19.

65. Solonari, *Purifying the Nation*, 152.

66. *Bucovina*, August 20, 1941.

67. Antonescu, *Pentru Basarabia*, 13.

68. Solonari, "'Model Province,'" 483.

69. Antonescu, *Pentru Basarabia*, 3.

70. Kurt Pflaumer came to Bucharest in February 1941. After serving as head of the civil administration of Alsace, he was by this stage a counselor for matters of domestic administration. See Solonari, *Satellite Empire*, 56–58. Theo Ellgering was located in Cernăuți. See Moraru, *Bucovina*, 40–42.

71. Moraru, *Bucovina*, 45; Solonari, *Purifying the Nation*, 155.

72. Weber and Hecker, *Bukowina im Zweiten Weltkrieg*, 34–35. Only the gendarmerie, schools, railways, and customs were subordinated to Bucharest, other functions being represented by special directorates for administration, finances, agriculture, economy, education,

work and social welfare, transport, health, colonization, and Romanianization. Governor Alexandru Rioșanu died on August 30, 1941. Corneliu Dragalina became governor of Bukovina in 1943. See Ioanid, *Holocaust in Romania*, 141.

73. Solonari, *Satellite Empire*, 58; Moraru, *Bucovina*, 62.

74. Antonescu, *Pentru Basarabia*, 12.

75. Antonescu, *Pentru Basarabia*, 11.

76. Solonari, *Purifying the Nation*, 226.

77. Solonari, "Hating Soviets," 490; Dumitru, *State, Antisemitism*, 226.

78. Solonari, "Hating Soviets," 484.

79. Moraru, *Bucovina*, 39.

80. DAChO, f. 30, op. 4, d. 222, note from General Directorate of Romanian police to Cernăuți's Gendarmerie Inspectorate, March 25, 1942.

81. DAChO, f. 30, op. 4, d. 222, l. 13, "Țăranii se pregătesc pentru sărbătoare" (translation into Romanian of article from "*Bucovina Sovietică*" [= *Radyanska Bukowyna*] of May 10, 1941) in note from regional police inspectorate in Cernăuți to police commissariat in Vășcăuți, March 1942.

82. DAChO, f. 30, op. 4, d. 6, l. 20, "Proces Verbal," June 26, 1942.

83. DAChO, f. 30, op. 4, d. 46, l. 125, "Nota informativă no. 1," March 10, 1942.

84. Moraru, *Bucovina*, 79.

85. DAChO, f. 30, op. 4, d. 2, l. 251, letter from Artemie Baculinschi to Inspector of Gendarmerie, Bukovina, July 1941.

86. Deletant, *Hitler's Forgotten Ally*, 72.

87. Ioanid, *Holocaust in Romania*, 111; Solonari, *Purifying the Nation*, 164–65; Deletant, *Hitler's Forgotten Ally*, 130.

88. YVA, M.52/121, July 5, 1941–October 31, 1942, report from November 1942, 1716.

89. Both cases in DAChO, f. R-307, op.1, d. 1314, ll. 2–4, note to Gendarmerie Inspectorate Cernăuți regarding internments in Edineți camp, December 28, 1942.

90. Moraru, *Bucovina*, 78, 79–80.

91. ANIC, Arhivele Județului Ilfov, nr. inv. 883, 21/1943, copy of report from Regional Police Inspectorate to Comis. Pol. Cozmeni, Orășeni gara, Orășeni bariera, Sadagura, Tg. Nistrului, June 5, 1943.

92. DAChO, f. R-307, op. 1, d. 4079, l. 112, note to Directorate of Education and Cults in Cernăuți, March 7, 1942.

93. DAChO, f. R-307, op. 1, d. 1036, l. 3, note to General Corneliu Calotescu, governor of Bukovina, n.d. (1942).

94. DAChO, f. R-307, op. 1, d. 4079, l. 112, note to Directorate of Education and Cults in Cernăuți, March 7, 1942.

95. DAChO, f. R-307, op. 1, d. 4079, l. 116, report to General Secretariat of Bukovina's Gouvernement Statistical Service, April 21, 1942.

96. DAChO, f. R-307, op. 1, d. 4079, l. 124, note to the Directorate of Labor and Social Insurance Cernăuți, April 17, 1942.

97. *Bucovina*, July 19, 1941.

98. DAChO, f. R-307, op. 1, d. 4, l. 231, report from Bukovina Gouvernement to Presidency of Council of Ministers, Civilian-Military Cabinet, December 13, 1941.

99. I. Manciuc, "Ofensiva culturală la sate," *Bucovina*, March 4, 1942.

100. DAChO, f. R-307, op. 1, d. 2803, l. 2, report on the activity of the Regional Inspectorate for Propaganda for Bukovina from November 15, 1941 through November 15, 1942.

101. "Deschiderea stagiunii Teatrului Național," *Bucovina*, January 12, 1942; "Deschiderea stagiunii oficiale dela Teatrul Național," *Bucovina*, January 16, 1942.

102. "Turneele Teatrului Național," *Bucovina*, January 10, 1942.

103. Himka, *Ukrainian Nationalists*, 122.

104. On the UVO as the direct forerunner of OUN, see Himka, *Ukrainian Nationalists*, 135.

105. Himka, *Ukrainian Nationalists*, 120–23.

106. The OUN's resolve to focus on forming their own military units was especially strong after the its defeat in Carpathian Ukraine. See Duda, *Bukovynskyi kurin*, 57; Bruder, *"Den Ukrainischen Staat [...]"*, 177.

107. Bruder, *"Den Ukrainischen Staat [...]"*, 122, 157.

108. Himka, *Ukrainian Nationalists*, 140; and Rossolinski-Liebe, *Stepan Bandera*.

109. Himka, *Ukrainian Nationalists*, 149.

110. Grelka, *Ukrainische Nationalbewegung*, 247–49; Hausleitner, *Rumänisierung*, 411; Himka, *Ukrainian Nationalists*, 212.

111. Duda, *Bukovynskyi kurin*, 59–61. Although the incoming Romanian troops initially used the Provisional Committee to mediate with the Ukrainians in Northern Bukovina, they soon dismantled all OUN administrative structures. The Provisional Committee outlasted other institutions, but on July 11 it dissolved itself and went underground.

112. Bruder, *"Den Ukrainischen Staat [...]"*, 144, 161.

113. CSRJ, Jean Ancel Collection, Photocopies Osobyi Arkhiv Moscow, vol. 3, 492-1-10, SSI: Nota informativa 1703, October 1941.

114. CSRJ, Jean Ancel Collection, Photocopies Osobyi Arkhiv Moscow, vol. 3, 492-1-10, manifesto to Ukrainian teachers, 55.

115. Rossolinski-Liebe, *Stepan Bandera*, 185; Rossolinski-Liebe, "'Ukrainian National Revolution.'"

116. Himka, *Ukrainian Nationalists*, 153–54, 167–70.

117. Hausleitner, *Rumänisierung*; Rossolinski-Liebe, *Stepan Bandera*, 174.

118. Weiner, *Making Sense of War*, 246.

119. Grelka, *Ukrainische Nationalbewegung*, 247, 379, 240.

120. Some twenty- to thirty thousand Ukrainian activists escaped into the German zone from the Soviet area. See Himka, *Ukrainian Nationalists*, 143, 179; Bruder, *"Den Ukrainischen Staat [...]"*, 114.

121. Grelka, *Ukrainische Nationalbewegung*, 251–52.

122. Bruder, *"Den Ukrainischen Staat [...]"*, 115, 130, 151.

123. Grelka, *Ukrainische Nationalbewegung*, 242–44.

124. Rossolinski-Liebe, *Stepan Bandera*, 233.

125. DAChO, f. R-307, op. 3, d. 4, letter from Regional Police Inspectorate Cernăuți to governor of Bukovina, September 29, 1941.

126. Hausleitner, *Rumänisierung*, 316.

127. The Soviet occupation had the paradoxical effect of removing the more moderate Ukrainian nationalists. See Bruder, *"Den Ukrainischen Staat [...]"*, 133.

128. Fostii, "Diialnist OUN," 1; Hausleitner, *Rumänisierung*.

129. ANIC, Județul Ilfov, nr. inv. 883, 15/1941, report to Chestura de Poliție, Biroul Siguranței Cernăuți from Comis. Circ. I Poliție, November 22, 1941.

130. DAChO, f. 30, op. 4, d. 475, l. 103, "Radiogram from Bucharest" on activity of Ukrainian nationalists.

131. DAChO, f. 30, op. 4, d. 475, l. 101, "Radiogram from Bucharest" on activity of Ukrainian nationalists.

132. Bruder, *"Den Ukrainischen Staat [. . .]"*, 153–55.

133. DAChO, f. R-307, op. 3, d. 4, copy of report by General Directorate of Police, Bukovina, January 12, 1942.

134. Angrick, "Im Wechselspiel der Kräfte," 341.

135. DAChO, f. R-307, op. 3, d. 4, copy of report by General Directorate of Police, Bukovina, January 12, 1942.

136. Duda, *Bukovynskyi kurin*, 67.

137. Fostii, "Diialnist OUN," 13–14.

138. Duda, *Bukovynskyi kurin*, 72–77. The Bukovynskyi Kurin arrived just in time to participate in the Nazi mass murders at Babyn Yar (Russian: Babi Yar), but we do not know for sure whether they did. See Himka, *Ukrainian Nationalists*, 299.

139. Angrick, "Im Wechselspiel der Kräfte," 341.

140. Solonari, *Purifying the Nation*, 183.

141. Duda, *Bukovynskyi kurin*, 63.

142. DAChO, f. 30, op. 3, d. 4, note from Presidency of Council of Ministers to governor of Bukovina. Ukrainian nationalists also disputed Germany's decision to annex Eastern Galicia to the General Gouvernement, which, they argued, kept Ukrainians scattered across different administrations by implicitly resolving Polish–Ukrainian territorial disputes in Poland's favor. See Bruder, *"Den Ukrainischen Staat [. . .]"*, 116, 136; also Grelka, *Ukrainische Nationalbewegung*, 361.

143. DAChO, f. R-307, op. 3, d. 3, "Notă informativă" of Regional Police Inspectorate Cernăuți, December 3, 1941.

144. DAChO, f. R-307, op. 3, d. 3., l. 270, "Notă informativă" of Regional Police Inspectorate Cernăuți, February 5, 1942.

145. ANIC, Arhivele Județului Ilfov, nr. inv. 883, 58/1941, 487, Chestura Poliției Cernăuți, "Notă informativă," October 12, 1941.

146. YVA, M.52/135, 1811.

147. DAChO, f. R-307, op. 1, d. 3, "Notă informativă," Notarul Comunei Cadobești-Cernăuți, February 14, 1942.

148. DAChO, f. 30, op. 4, d. 2, l. 418, report by Secret Service of Presidency of Council of Ministers, August 26, 1941.

149. DAChO, f. R-307, op. 1, d. 104, l. 5, report by Gouvernement of Bukovina, Military Cabinet Cernăuți, April 22, 1942.

150. DAChO, f. R-307, op. 3, d. 4, l. 86, letter from governor of Bukovina, Corneliu Calotescu, to German consul in Cernăuți, November 26, 1941.

151. DAChO, f. R-307, op. 1, d. 3, l. 17, report from Prefecture of Rădăuți district to governor of Bukovina.

152. Trașcă and Deletant, *Al III-lea Reich*, doc. 18, July 14, 1941, 200.

153. ANIC, Arhivele Județului Ilfov, nr. inv. 883, 44/1941, "Circ. I-VI Comis Pol. Cozmeni, Orășeni gară, Sadagura, Zastavna, Herța," December 16, 1941; see also Hausleitner, *Rumänisierung*, 422.

154. On the wishful thinking of Bandera and Stetsko, see Grelka, *Ukrainische Nationalbewegung*, 265–66.

155. Grelka, *Ukrainische Nationalbewegung*, 377–78.

156. In September 1941 Bandera found himself under arrest in Berlin; in January 1942 he was sent to Sachsenhausen concentration camp. See Grelka, *Ukrainische Nationalbewegung*, 388, 415; Duda, *Bukovynskyi kurin*, 86–87.

157. Fostii, "Diialnist OUN," 14.

158. Grelka, *Ukrainische Nationalbewegung*, 383.

159. Duda, *Bukovynskyi kurin*, 90.

160. ANIC, Arhivele Județului Ilfov, nr. inv. 883, 44/1941, report by Chestura Politiei Cernăuți, January12, 1942.

161. Britskyi et al., *Bukovyntsi v trahichni roki*, 79.

162. Iurii Gorbashevskyi, "Ustanovlennia radyanskoi vlady u Pivnichnii Bukovyni i Khotynshchyni ta otsinka ii dialnosti selyanami, Borivtsi Kitsmanskyi raion," in Britskyi et al., *Bukovyntsi v trahichni roki*, 106.

163. Duda, *Bukovynskyi kurin*, 192–93.

164. DAChO, f. 30, op. 4, d. 475, l. 136, OUN brochure, Romanian translation.

165. DAChO, f. 30, op. 4, d. 475, l. 137, OUN brochure, Romanian translation.

166. DAChO, f. 30, op. 4, d. 475, l. 137, OUN brochure, Romanian translation: "Rezoluțiile Conferinței a 31a a organizației Ucrainenilor Naționaliști, Conducerea OUN, 1943," l. 103, "Radiogramă de la București."

167. DAChO, f. R-307, op. 1, d. 1157, l. 2, "Copie Nota: Gruparea ucrainenilor moderați din Bucovina dorește o apropiere din statul român," October 9, 1943.

168. Bruder, *"Den Ukrainischen Staat [. . .]"*, 195.

169. Şiperco, *Holocaust în România*, doc. 53, December 2, 1941, 112–14.

170. ANIC, Arhivele Județului Ilfov, nr. inv. 883, 18/1941, 36, "Circ. I-VI Comis. Pol. Cozmeni, Orășeni, Detaș. Sadagura, Zastavna, Crisceatic, Orășeni bar, Herța."

171. Şiperco, *Holocaust în România*, doc. 53, December 2, 1941, 112. See also Hausleitner, *Rumänisierung*, 396.

172. YVA, P6/67, October 9, 1941, 131; Ioanid, *Holocaust in Romania*, 141, 155–56.

173. Moraru, *Bucovina*, 84.

174. Şiperco, *Holocaust în România*, doc. 37, July 30, 1941, 87. A new ordinance issued in August 1942 required Bukovinan "Jews of any age and sex" to "wear on the left side of their chest, visibly, the distinctive sign of the Jewish star" or risk "internment in a work camp." DAChO, f. R-307, op. 1, d. 3340, Copie ordonanța nr. 42/43, August 24, 1942.

175. ANIC, nr. inv. 883, 18/1941, 36, "Circ. I-VI Comis. Pol. Cozmeni, Orășeni, Detaș. Sadagura, Zastavna, Crisceatic, Orășeni bar, Herța."

176. Mircu, *Pogromurile*, 80.

177. YVA, M 52/131, 1786, October 11, 1941.

178. YVA, P6/667, 135.

179. Deletant, "Transnistria," 170, 165.

180. T. Popovici, *Spovedania/Testimony*, 95.

181. Moraru, *Bucovina*, 111.

182. DAChO, f. R-307, op. 1, d. 102, ll. 346–47, "Referat: Guvernamântul Provinciei Bucovina, Cernăuţi, şeful Biroului 2 Maior," July 5, 1942.

183. Solonari, *Purifying the Nation*, 215.

184. Deletant, "Transnistria," 168.

185. Cited in Ioanid, *Holocaust in Romania*, 155–65.

186. Ioanid, *Holocaust in Romania*, 156.

187. Hausleitner, *Rumänisierung*, 396.

188. Deletant, "Transnistria," 168.

189. Traşcă and Deletant, *Al III-lea Reich*, doc. 54, October 15, 1941, 316.

190. Cremers, "Czernowitz 1941/1942," 463.

191. Traşcă and Deletant, *Al III-lea Reich*, doc. 56, October 16, 1941, 320.

192. Traşcă and Deletant, *Al III-lea Reich*, doc. 57, October 17, 1941, 335.

193. Traşcă and Deletant, *Al III-lea Reich*, doc. 55, October 15, 1941, 318.

194. Traşcă and Deletant, *Al III-lea Reich*, doc. 57, October 17, 1941, 334.

195. Traşcă and Deletant, *Al III-lea Reich*, doc. 23, July 28, 1941, 214; Angrick, "Im Wechselspiel der Kräfte," 343.

196. Traşcă and Deletant, *Al III-lea Reich*, doc. 57, October 17, 1941, 332.

197. Traşcă and Deletant, *Al III-lea Reich*, doc. 22, July 26, 1941, 210.

198. Traşcă and Deletant, *Al III-lea Reich*, doc. 22, July 26, 1941, 211–13.

199. Traşcă and Deletant, *Al III-lea Reich*, doc. 78, April 17, 1942, 415.

200. Moraru, *Bucovina*, 116–17.

201. Hausleitner, *Rumänisierung*, 401.

202. Traşcă and Deletant, *Al III-lea Reich*, doc. 86, June 16, 1942, 436.

203. Traşcă and Deletant, *Al III-lea Reich*, doc. 89, July 3, 1942, 445–47.

204. Traşcă and Deletant, *Al III-lea Reich*, doc. 84, June 9, 1942, 429.

205. DAChO, f. 30, op. 4, d. 16, l. 79, report on popular mood by Suceava police to Regional Inspectorate of Police, November 18, 1941.

206. Weissglas, *Steinbruch am Bug*, 20.

207. Mircu, *Pogromurile*, 85.

208. Mircu, *Pogromurile*, 101–2.

209. ANIC, Arhivele Judeţului Ilfov, nr. inv. 883, 58/1941, "Notă Informativă; Chestura Generală a Poliţiei Cernăuţi," September 9, 1941.

210. Mircu, *Pogromurile*, 85.

211. Dumitru, *State, Antisemitism*, 224.

212. DAChO, f. 30, op. 4, d. 43, l. 365, police report regarding denunciation of Agapia Buga by Mr. and Mrs. Iaslovitz from Cernăuţi.

213. YVA, M.52/46, address to governor from Pretura Plăşii Buceni, by Otto Schlegel, former refugee to Germany, n.d.

214. YVA, M52/44, 905, January 12, 1942.

215. "Proprietăţile evreieşti din Nordul Bucovinei: pe aceste proprietăţi se poate face o nouă colonizare de ţărani români," *Universul*, January 13, 1942, in YVA, M 52/73, 1206–7.

216. DAChO, f. R-307, op. 1, d. 234, letter from governor of Bukovina, Corneliu Calotescu, to mayor of Cernăuţi, December 12, 1941.

217. YVA, M 52/44, letter to governor of Bukovina from delegate of Gouvernement in Oficiul de Locaţiuni, Cernăuţi, November 15, 1942.

218. Mircu, *Pogromurile*, 97.

219. Cited in Hirsch and Spitzer, *Ghosts of Home*, 186.

220. YVA, M.52/50, 966, note to governor from Mitropolia Bucovinei, December 14, 1942.

221. YVA, M.52/68.

222. DAChO, f. R-307, op. 1, d. 3, ll. 77–78, "Poliţia de Reşedinţă Suceava, Buletin de evenimente," October 21, 1941.

223. DAChO, f. R-307, op. 3, d. 3, l. 23, "Copie de pe raportul confidenţial al judecatoriei de pace mixtă Vijniţa (jud. Storojineţ)," October 22, 1941.

224. On the looting and mismanagement of property, see Solonari, *Purifying the Nation*, 261.

225. DAChO, f. R-307, op. 1, d. 4, l. 189, note by Bukovina's governor, Corneliu Calotescu, to Eighth Division, November 29, 1941.

226. ANIC, Consiliul de Miniştri, nr. inv. 3039, 45/1942, 52, "Şedinţa Consiliului de Miniştri; Stenograma şedinţei Consiliului de Miniştri în care Ion Antonescu a expus cele constatate în cadrul inspecţiei făcute în Basarabia, Bucovina, şi Transnistria," April 17, 1942.

227. T. Popovici, *Testimony*, 69.

228. Moraru, *Bucovina*, 178.

229. T. Popovici, *Testimony*, 69.

230. Traşcă and Deletant, *Al III-lea Reich*, doc. 57, October 17, 1942, 338.

231. DAChO, f. R-307, op.1, d. 7, l. 241, "Notă informativă nr. 13," January 13, 1942.

232. DAChO, f. R-307, op. 3, d. 14, l. 22.

233. Cited in Moraru, *Bucovina*, 51–52.

234. DAChO, f. 30, op. 4, d. 3, l. 75, "Notă informativă, Suceava," July 23, 1941.

235. Moraru, *Bucovina*, 171.

236. DAChO, f. R-307, op. 3, d. 4, "Telegramă Mareşal Antonescu," November 3, 1941.

237. DAChO, f. R-307, op. 1, d. 1635, l. 1, note to governor from Regional Police Inspectorate Cernăuţi, August 20, 1943.

238. Solonari, *Purifying the Nation*, 220.

239. DAChO, f. R-307, op. 3, d. 3, l. 122, "Buletin informativ," March 1, 1942.

240. DAChO, f. 30, op. 4, d. 2, report from police of Hotin to regional inspector of police, January 17, 1942.

241. DAChO, f. R-307, op. 3, d. 3, l. 122, "Suceava—Notă informativă."

242. DAChO, f. R-307, op. 1, d. 96, l. 113, "Referat către Dl Guvernator al Bucovinei."

243. Traşcă and Deletant, *Al III-lea Reich*, doc. 57, October 17, 1942

244. Moraru, *Bucovina*, 211.

245. Angrick, *Besatzungspolitik*, 194–95.

246. Deletant, *Hitler's Forgotten Ally*, 150; Angrick, *Besatzungspolitik*, 195–97; Ioanid, *Holocaust in Romania*, 119.

247. Deletant, *Hitler's Forgotten Ally*, 128; Deletant, "Transnistria," 163–64.

248. Angrick, *Besatzungspolitik*, 202.

249. Ioanid, *Holocaust in Romania*, 116.

250. Hausleitner, *Rumänisierung*, 390.

251. Deletant, *Hitler's Forgotten Ally*, 152.

252. On the convention of Tighina and Antonescu's possibly deliberate misunderstanding on how Hitler imagined Romania's role in the region, see Solonari, *Satellite Empire*, 35; also Harward, *Romania's Holy War*, 120; Deletant, "Transnistria," 157; Solonari, *Purifying the Nation*, 204.

253. Solonari, *Purifying the Nation*, 208.

254. Solonari, *Satellite Empire*, 31–32.

255. On the division of responsibilities between Romania and Germany in Transnistria, see Solonari, *Satellite Empire*, 35–37. Romanians oversaw "security, administration and economic exploitation, communication, and transmissions." See Şiperco, *Holocaust în România*, doc. 68, August 30, 1941, 135.

256. Ancel, "Romanian Campaigns," 88.

257. Deletant, *Hitler's Forgotten Ally*, 186.

258. Solonari, *Purifying the Nation*, 201.

259. Ioanid, *Holocaust in Romania*, 124.

260. Deletant, *Hitler's Forgotten Ally*, 186; Nuchim Bendit, "Woran ich mich erinnere," in Finkel and Winkler, *Juden aus Czernowitz*, 34.

261. Felicia Gininger, "Das Erlebte," in Finkel and Winkler, *Juden aus Czernowitz*, 51.

262. Boris Bucharskyi, "Ich bin allein geblieben," in Finkel and Winkler, *Juden aus Czernowitz*, 38.

263. Musja Gottfried, "Ihr Gesicht vergesse ich nie," in Finkel and Winkler, *Juden aus Czernowitz*, 54.

264. Michail Eibschitz, "Vergiss nicht, dich zu rächen," in Finkel and Winkler, *Juden aus Czernowitz*, 44–45.

265. Deletant, "Transnistria," 166–67.

266. Hausleitner, *Rumänisierung*, 408.

267. Ofer, "Life in the Ghettos," 258.

268. Emanuel Druckmann, "Das war eine heilige Hilfe," in Finkel and Winkler, *Juden aus Czernowitz*, 42–43.

269. Lydia Harnik, in Ranner, Halling, and Fiedler, *". . . und das Herz [. . .]"*, 81.

270. CSRJ, Jean Ancel Collection, Testimonies, 03-1444, 241.

271. Hermann Moldower, "Der unvergessene Blutdienstag," in Finkel and Winkler, *Juden aus Czernowitz*, 75.

272. YVA, O.33/6360, diary of Sabina Rüber, March 26, 1942; April 23, 1943.

273. Weissglas, *Steinbruch am Bug*, 96.

274. ANIC, Arhivele Jud. Ilfov, nr. inv. 883, 69/1942, 39, note to Chestura Poliţiei Cernăuţi, by Circ I-VI Poliţie Comis. Pol. Cozmeni, Orăşeni, Detas. Pol. Sadagura, Zastavna, April 14, 1942.

275. ANIC, Archivele Ilfov, nr. inv. 883, 69/1942, "Notă informativă," Chestura Poliţiei Cernăuţi, August 14, 1942.

276. Josip Bursuk, in Ranner, Halling, and Fiedler, *". . . und das Herz [. . .]"*, 34–36.

277. Hirsch and Spitzer, *Ghosts of Home*, 227.

278. Deletant, *Hitler's Forgotten Ally*, 186; On the large number of Jews remaining in Moghilev and orders to evacuate them that were never fulfilled, see Şiperco, *Holocaust în România*, doc. 75, January 10, 1942, 144; On Moghilev as one of the two largest camps in Transnistria, see Hausleitner, *Rumänisierung*, 40.

279. The same happened to internees in the camp at Scaţineţ. See Ioanid, *Holocaust in Romania*, 205.

280. Aron Hirt, in Jägendorf, *Jägendorf's Foundry*, xiv.

281. Jägendorf, *Jägendorf's Foundry*, 25.

282. Şiperco, *Holocaust în România*, doc. 64, December 1941, 132.

283. Jägendorf's employees also produced illegally and sold through the black market various objects such as cigarette lighters, cooking pots, etc. Jägendorf, *Jägendorf's Foundry*, 114.

284. Jägendorf, *Jägendorf's Foundry*, 138, 60; Ofer, "Life in the Ghettos," 265.

285. Weissglas, *Steinbruch am Bug*, 58.

286. CSRJ, Jean Ancel Collection, Testimonies, 03-1127, 22.

287. Ioanid, *Holocaust in Romania*, 190–92.

288. Weissglas, *Steinbruch am Bug*, 45.

289. CSRJ, Jean Ancel Collection, Testimonies, 03-1453, Selig-Ascher Hofer.

290. Brenner and Wollmann-Fiedler, *Czernowitz ist meine Heimat*.

291. ANIC, Arhivele Ilfov, nr. inv. 883, 58/1941, "Notă informativă," Chestura Poliţiei Cernăuţi, October 12, 1941.

292. Rosa Roth-Zuckermann, in Ranner, Halling, and Fiedler, *". . . und das Herz [. . .]"*, 145.

293. Siegmund Meissler, in Ranner, Halling, and Fiedler, *". . . und das Herz [. . .]"*, 117.

294. LBI, Manfred Hilsenrath, "The Story I Was Reluctant to Tell," 74 (accessed digitally).

295. Severin Schrajer, in Ranner, Halling, and Fiedler, *". . . und das Herz [. . .]"*, 169.

296. Finkel and Zebenko, "Über die Orte," 29.

297. Steinhart, *Holocaust and the Germanization*, 114. Sonderkommando-R ended up spreading the typhus epidemic they were supposed to stifle by confiscating the infested victims' clothing and distributing it among the population. See Traşcă and Deletant, *Al III-lea Reich*, doc. 72, February 11, 1942, 390.

298. Deletant, "Transnistria," 164.

299. Harward, *Romania's Holy War*, 138–40; Deletant, *Hitler's Forgotten Ally*, 178–79; Steinhart, *Holocaust and the Germanization*, 10.

300. Steinhart, *Holocaust and the Germanization*, 127–129; 113.

301. Traşcă and Deletant, *Al III-lea Reich*, doc. 74, February 28, 1942, 404.

302. Traşcă and Deletant, *Al III-lea Reich*, doc. 77, April 14, 1942, 412.

303. Deletant, *Hitler's Forgotten Ally*, 209; by then, the administration had already begun opening the camps to aid in the form of food, clothing, and medicines, sent by the deportees' relatives and by Jewish organizations such as the Central Jewish Office, run by Wilhelm Filderman who, for a short while, had been interned in Moghilev; Ofer, "Life in the Ghettos," 244; Hausleitner, *Rumänisierung*, 411–12.

304. Deletant, *Hitler's Forgotten Ally*, 205; Shortly before Antonescu changed his mind, the Romanian administration had agreed to the deportation of all Romanian Jews to Bełżec.

305. Deletant, *Hitler's Forgotten Ally*, 208.

306. Deletant, *Hitler's Forgotten Ally*, 211, 222; Solonari, *Purifying the Nation*, 221; Hausleitner, *Rumänisierung*, 411–12; Deletant, "Transnistria," 179.

307. DAChO, f. R-307, op. 1, d. 1094, l. 2, "Informaţii şi contrainformaţii: Starea de spirit în provincie." The note mentions that "Jewish morale" was high as a result of several "concessions."

Antonescu had allowed some Jews to return from Transnistria and reopened an "Israelite school" in Cernăuţi.

308. YVA, P6/79, 63, November 26, 1943.

309. YVA, P6/79, 73.

310. YVA, P9/10, 36, May 9, 1945.

311. Harward, *Romania's Holy War*, 197; Hirsch and Spitzer, *Ghosts of Home*, 244.

312. Weber and Hecker, *Bukowina im Zweiten Weltkrieg*, 37; Jägendorf, *Jägendorf's Foundry*, 188.

313. Hirsch and Spitzer, *Ghosts of Home*, 236, 229.

314. Himka, *Ukrainian Nationalists*, 120.

315. DAChO, f. R-307, op. 1, d. 1094, l. 9, "Informaţii şi Contrainformaţii: Starea de spirit în provincie."

316. DAChO, f. R-307, op. 1, d. 2381, l. 265, "Inspectoratul General al Jandarmeriei, Inspectoratul Jandarmi Cernăuţi, Serviciul Poliţiei, Studiu sintetic asupra starei de spirit a populaţiei şi problemelor existente pe raza inspectorat jandarmi Cernăuţi, întocmit pe luna noiembrie 1943."

317. DAChO, f. R-307, op. 3, d. 3, l. 255 ob, "Notă informativă."

318. DAChO, f. 30, op. 4, d. 28, l. 14, report from Chestura Poliţiei Cernăuţi to Regional Police Inspectorate Cernăuţi, October 6, 1943.

319. Frunchak, "Making of Soviet Chernivtsi," 306.

320. ANIC, fond Consiliul de Miniştri, nr. inv. 3039, 125/1944, 20, "Şedinţa Consiliului de Miniştri cu guvernatorii privind problema evacuărilor din Basarabia, Bucovina, şi Transnistria, probleme economice şi administrative privind aceste provincii," January 27, 1944. Antonescu's comment at 29.

321. Brenner, Rehn, and Wiehn, *Mein altes Czernowitz*, 110.

322. DACHO, f. 30, op. 7, d. 32, l. 273, report from Chestura Poliţiei Cernăuţi to Inspectoratul Regional de Poliţie Cernăuţi, February 7, 1944.

323. ANIC, fond Consiliul de Miniştri, nr. inv. 3039, 113/1944, 34 ("Stenograma şedinţei Consiliului de Miniştri privind măsuri pentru evacuarea diferitelor departamente din capitală, problema evacuării populaţiei din Basarabia, Bucovina, şi Nordul Moldovei," March 3, 1944.)

324. ANIC, fond Consiliul de Miniştri, nr. inv. 3039, 125/1944, 18 ("Şedinţa consiliului de miniştri cu guvernatorii privind problema evacuărilor din Basarabia, Bucovina şi Transnistria, probleme economice şi administrative privind aceste provincii," January 27, 1944).

325. ANIC, Consiliul de Miniştri, nr. inv. 3039, 113/1944, 34 ("Stenograma şedinţei Consiliului de Miniştri privind măsuri pentru evacuarea diferitelor departamente din capitală, problema evacuării populaţiei din Basarabia, Bucovina, şi Nordul Moldovei," March 3, 1944).

326. DAChO, f. 30, op. 7, d. 32, l. 122, report from police of Hotin to Regional Police Inspectorate Cernăuţi, February 19, 1944.

327. DAChO, f. 30, op. 4, d. 475, l. 13, letter to Marshal Antonescu from members of Bar (lawyers') Association in Cernăuţi.

328. DAChO, f. 30, op. 7, d. 32, l. 273, report on popular mood from Chestura Poliţiei Cernăuţi to Regional Police Inspectorate Cernăuţi, February 7, 1944.

329. DAChO, f. 30, op. 7, d. 32, l. 359, report from police of Hotin to Regional Police Inspectorate Cernăuţi, January 29, 1944.

330. DAChO, f. 30, op. 7, d. 32, report from Police Inspectorate Rădăuţi to Regional Police Inspectorate Cernăuţi, February 19, 1944.

331. DAChO, f. 30, op. 7, d. 32, ll. 92–93, letter to general governor of Bukovina from members of National Council, n.d.

332. DAChO, f. 30, op. 7, d. 32, l. 125, report on public mood in Hotin, n.d.

333. Quoted in Britskyi et al., *Bukovyntsi v trahichni roki*, 153.

## Epilogue

1. On the Soviets' return to Eastern Ukraine, see Weiner, *Making Sense of War*, 310.

2. Taubman, *Nikita Khrushchev*, 94.

3. On the Soviet regime's "intrinsic insecurity," see Mastny, *Cold War*; also G. Roberts, *Stalin's Wars*.

4. Burds, "Early Cold War," 12, 73.

5. Weiner, *Making Sense of War*, 67; Slaveski, *Remaking Ukraine*, 187.

6. Weiner, *Making Sense of War*, 301.

7. Marples, *Stalinism in Ukraine*, 128, 135.

8. Frunchak, "Commemorating the Future," 438.

9. Frunchak, "Commemorating the Future," 440, 444, 448.

10. Hirsch and Spitzer, *Ghosts of Home*, 252.

11. Fisher, *Resettlers and Survivors*, 3.

12. Lazar, "Holocaust Survivors."

13. Frunchak, "Commemorating the Future," 441.

14. Lazar, "Holocaust Survivors," 352–53, 354.

15. Lazar, "Holocaust Survivors," 353–54, 357–57.

16. Frunchak, "Commemorating the Future," 441.

17. Lazar, "Holocaust Survivors," 359, 358.

18. Lazar, "Holocaust Survivors," 443.

19. Risch, *The Ukrainian West*, 84.

20. Pomerantsev, "Czernowitz."

21. Tsurkan, "What Is the Secret."

22. Bernsand, "Returning Chernivtsi."

23. Hirsch and Spitzer, *Ghosts of Home*, 55; see also Heymann, *Crépuscule*.

24. Kyyan, "'To Break Out [. . .].'"

25. Pomerantsev, "Czernowitz."

26. Hirsch and Spitzer, *Ghosts of Home*, xv.

27. In Communist Romania, Bukovinan Jews were also considered politically suspect because they spoke German. See G. Fischer, *Resettlers and Survivors*, 117.

28. See C. Hirsch, *Life in the Twentieth Century*.

29. G. Fischer, *Resettlers and Survivors*, 126.

30. Appelfeld, *Story of a Life*, 109, 111, 152, 187.

31. G. Fischer, *Resettlers and Survivors*, 63, 87, 163.

32. Yekelchyk, *Ukraine*, 57.

33. Tismăneanu and Stan, "Ceaușescu's National Communism," 456.

34. Szporluk, *Russia, Ukraine*, 362.

35. Yekelchyk, *Ukraine*, 59; Merry, "Origins of Russia's War," 31.

36. Wilson, *Ukraine Crisis*, 14–15.

37. Yekelchyk, *Ukraine*, 69.

38. Csergo and Goldgeier, "Kin-State Activism," 115.

39. Koziura, "Memory, Monuments," 173.

40. Cassidy, "Border Crossings," 66–70.

41. Bureiko et al., "Between the Home and Kin-State," 56.

42. Wilson, *Ukraine Crisis*, 39.

43. Viktor Yushchenko, cited in Plokhy, "Epilogue," 433.

44. Frunchak, "Commemorating the Future," 450.

45. Wanner, "Return of Czernowitz."

46. Wanner, "Return of Czernowitz," 218.

47. Koziura, "Spaces of Nostalgia(s)," 225.

48. Wanner, "Return of Czernowitz," 199.

49. Otto von Habsburg, Franz Joseph's heir, was present at the monument's unveiling. See Narvselius and Bernsand, "Lviv and Chernivtsi"; Koziura, "Spaces of Nostalgia(s)," 210.

50. Koziura, "Spaces of Nostalgia(s)," 229.

51. Koziura, "Memory, Monuments," 170.

52. Wanner, "Return of Czernowitz," 202.

53. On the erasure of Jewish life in Galicia, see Bartov, *Erased*, 89; also Bartov, "Eastern Europe."

54. Koziura, "Spaces of Nostalgia(s)," 221.

55. Hirsch and Spitzer, *Ghosts of Home*, 229.

56. Frunchak, "Commemorating the Future," 451.

57. Tsurkan, "Letter from Chernivtsi."

58. Tsurkan, "Letter from Chernivtsi."

59. Bernsand, "Returning Chernivtsi."

60. Pomerantsev, "Czernowitz."

61. D'Anieri, *Ukraine and Russia*, 218.

62. Petraeus and Roberts, *Conflict*, 351.

63. D'Anieri, *Ukraine and Russia*, 223.

64. *Global Conflict Tracker*, "War in Ukraine," March 6, 2024 update.

65. Tsurkan, "Letter from Chernivtsi."

66. Koziura, "Memory, Monuments," 228, 170.

67. *Global Conflict Tracker*, "War in Ukraine," March 6, 2024 update.

68. Petraeus and Roberts, *Conflict*, 355.

69. Petraeus and Roberts, *Conflict*, 365; *Global Conflict Tracker*, "War in Ukraine," March 6, 2024 update.

70. Petraeus and Roberts, *Conflict*, 359.

71. Tsurkan, "Why I Chose to Stay."

72. G. Bejan, "Exclusiv."

73. G. Bejan, "Exclusiv."

74. Wright, "For Ukraine."

75. *Global Conflict Tracker*, "War in Ukraine," March 6, 2024 update.

76. Wright, "For Ukraine."

77. Petraeus and Roberts, *Conflict*, 369–70.

78. *Global Conflict Tracker*, "War in Ukraine," March 6, 2024 update.

79. Petraeus and Roberts, *Conflict*, 394.

80. Gettleman and O'Reilly, "Far from the Front."

81. Gettleman and O'Reilly, "Far from the Front."

82. Zain, "UCSC Alumnus."

83. Gettleman and O'Reilly, "Far from the Front."

84. All cases cited in Gibbons-Neff, "'People Snatchers.'"

85. Andrei, "Ucraina are probleme cu recrutarea"; Păcurar, "Investigație Hotnews.ro." On the Ukrainian police during the Holocaust, see Finder and Prusin, "Collaboration."

86. Tsurkan, "Why I Chose to Stay."

87. "Corupție în Cernăuți!," *Zorile Bucovinei*, March 14, 2024, available at http://zorilebucovinei.com/news/show/5306/ (accessed March 31, 2025).

88. Petraeus and Roberts, *Conflict*, 368. Remnick, "How the War in Ukraine Ends."

89. Wright, "For Ukraine."

90. Gessen, "Russia, One Year After."

91. Petraeus and Roberts, *Conflict*, 361.

92. *UNHCR*, "Emergencies: Ukraine Emergency," https://www.unrefugees.org/emergencies/ukraine/ (accessed May 5, 2025).

93. *Global Conflict Tracker*, "War in Ukraine," May 2, 2025 update.

94. Remnick, "How the War in Ukraine Ends."

95. Walker, "Leaders."

96. Muraru, "Editorial"; Sonko, "Romanian Senator."

97. Lazăr, "Analiză."

98. Muraru, "Editorial."

99. Kiss, "Ucraina anunță sancțiuni."

100. Henley, "Far-right Trump Ally."

101. Kyyan, "'To Break Out [. . .].'" https://www.apofenie.com/interviews/2020/10/1/an-interview-with-igor-pomerantsev.

102. Pomerantsev, "Five Uneasy Pieces."

103. Pomerantsev, "Death Is a Master."

104. Kyyan, "'To Break Out [. . .].'"

105. Hirsch and Spitzer, *Ghosts of Home*, 19.

106. Roth-Zuckermann, "Jüdisches Leben," 263.

107. Perloff, *Edge of Irony*, 129.

108. G. Fischer, *Resettlers and Survivors*, 232.

109. Heymann, *Crépuscule*, 151.

110. Pomerantsev, "Five Uneasy Pieces."

111. Pomerantsev, "Death Is a Master." (The term "limit situation"—German: *Grenzsituation*—deriving from the existentialist writings of Karl Jaspers, refers to potentially transformative extremes of experience.)

112. Tarasiuk, "Working with Archives."

113. Tarasiuk, "Working with Archives"; Ovenden, "Putin's War"; Rail, "'This Is Everyone's Culture.'"

114. Tarasiuk, "Working with Archives."

115. Pomerantsev, "Czernowitz."

# BIBLIOGRAPHY

## Archival Collections

| | |
|---|---|
| ANIC Romania | Arhivele Naționale Istorice Centrale România (Bucharest) |
| AT-OeSTA | Österreichisches Staatsarchiv (Vienna) |
| | AVA Allgemeines Verwaltungsarchiv |
| | KA Kriegsarchiv |
| BAR | Biblioteca Academiei Române (Bucharest) |
| | Arhiva Constantin Angelescu |
| | Colecția de manuscrise |
| CAHJP | Central Archives for the History of the Jewish People (Jerusalem) |
| CSRJ | Center for the Study of Romanian Jews, Hebrew University in Jerusalem |
| CZA | Central Zionist Archives (Jerusalem) |
| DAChO | Derzhavnyi arkhiv Chernivetskoi oblasti (Chernivtsi) |
| DLA | Deutsches Literaturarchiv Marbach (Marbach am Necker) |
| LBI | Leo Baeck Institute, Center for Jewish History Archives (New York) |
| NoeLA | Niederösterreichisches Landesarchiv (St. Pölten) |
| OeLA | Österreichisches Literaturarchiv Wien (Vienna) |
| Polizeiarchiv | Wien (Vienna) |
| PUL-CR | Princeton University Library, Collection of Microfilmed Articles, Pamphlets and Other Materials on Romania |
| UNLAG | United Nations Library and Archives in Geneva |
| YVA | Yad Vashem Archives (Jerusalem) |

## Published Primary Sources

An-sky, S. [Shloyme Zanvl Rappoport]. *The Enemy at His Pleasure: A Journey Through the Jewish Pale of Settlement During World War I.* Translated by Joachim Neugroschel. Metropolitan Books, 2002.

Antonescu, Mihai. *Pentru Basarabia şi Bucovina: Îndrumări date Administrației Desrobitoare.* Bucharest, 1941.

*Apel către răzeşii din satele înstrăinate: Lămuriri asupra originei răzeşilor şi îndemnuri către răzeşii bucovineni de-a se emancipa de influența ruteană, de un Răzeş din Bucovina.* Cernăuţi, 1911.

Appelfeld, Aharon. *The Story of a Life.* Translated by Aloma Halter. Schocken, 2006.

Ausländer, Rose. "Alles kann Motiv sein." In *Ich Fliege auf der Luftschaukel: Europa–Amerika–Europa; Rose Ausländer in Czernowitz und New York*, edited by Helmut Braun. AphorismA, 1994.

Ausländer, Rose. "Erinnerungen an eine Stadt." In *Ich Fliege auf der Luftschaukel: Europa–Amerika–Europa; Rose Ausländer in Czernowitz und New York*, edited by Helmut Braun. AphorismA, 1994.

Avdeev, A. A. *Sovetsko–rumynskie otnosheniia: Dokumenty i materialy*. Mezhdunarodnye otnosheniia, 2000.

Bălan, Teodor. *Suprimarea mişcărilor naţionale din Bucovina pe timpul războiului mondial 1914–1918*. Cernăuţi: Societatea Tipografică Bucovineană, 1923.

*Beitrag zur kirchlichen Frage in der Bukowina: Zwei zeitgemässe Artikel vom Pihuliak und einem gr.-or. Priester*. Czernowitz, 1906.

Bendella, Theophil. *Die Bukowina im Königreiche Galizien*. Vienna, 1845.

Bidermann, Hermann Ignaz. *Die Bukowina unter österreichischer Verwaltung, 1775–1875*. Lemberg, 1876.

Brenner, Hedwig, Marie-Elisabeth Rehn, and Erhard R. Wiehn. *Mein altes Czernowitz: Erinnerungen aus mehr als neun Jahrzehnten 1918–2000*. Hartung-Gorre, 2010.

Brenner, Hedwig and Christel Wollmann-Fiedler. *Czernowitz ist meine Heimat: Unterhaltung mit der Zeitzeugin Hedwig Brenner*. Munda-Verlag, 2009.

Britskyi, P. P., Hanna Skoreiko, Oleg Andriiovych Surovtsev, and Ivan Fostii, eds. *Bukovyntsi v trahichni roky druhoi svitovoi viiny: Statii, spohady, ta dokumenty*. Tekhnodruk, 2013.

Brodfeld, Jose. *Festrede gehalten am heiligen Versöhnungstage des 5. Oktober 1908 im Israel. Gotteshause, Elisabethplatz Nr. 2 anlässlich der in demselben veranstalteten solennen Feier des 60jährigen Regierungsjubiläums Sr. glorreichen kaiserlichen und königlichen Apostolischen Majestät des Kaisers Franz Joseph I von Josef Brodfeld in Czernowitz*. Czernowitz, 1908.

Budinszky, Johann and Johann Polek. *Die Bukowina zu Anfang des Jahres 1783. Nach einer Denkschrift des Mappierungs-Directors J. Budinszky von J. Polek*. Czernowitz, 1894.

*Bukovina: Handbooks Prepared Under the Direction of the Historical Section of the Foreign Office, No. 6*. London (H.M.S.O.), 1919.

Cândea, Romulus. *Arboroşenii: Trădători austriaci şi naţionalişti români*. Cernăuţi, 1937.

Cioran, Emil. "The Transfiguration of Romania." In *Anti-Modernism: Radical Revisions of Collective Identity*, edited by Balázs Trencsényi. Central European University Press, 2014.

Ciuntu, Chirilă. *Din Bucovina pe Oder: Amintirile unui legionar*. Editura Dacia, 1967.

Corobca, Liliana, and Dumitru Covalciuc, eds. *Golgota românească: Mărturiile bucovinenilor deportaţi în Siberia*. Editura Vestala, 2009.

Covalciuc, Vasile D. "Amintiri din vremuri de restrişte." In *Golgota românească: Mărturiile bucovinenilor deportaţi în Siberia*, edited by Liliana Corobca and Dumitru Covalciuc. Editura Vestala, 2009.

Dobre, Florica, Vasilica Manea, and Lenuţa Nicolescu, eds. *Anul 1940: Armata română de la ultimatum la dictat: Documente*. Editura Europa nova, 2000.

*Dovidnyk dlya vstupnykiv do Chernivetskoho derzhavoho universytetu na 1941 rik*. Chernivtsi, 1941.

Drăghicescu, Dimitrie. *Les problèmes nationaux de l'Autriche-Hongrie: Les roumains (Transylvanie, Bucovine, Banat)*. Paris, 1918.

Drozdowski, Georg. *Damals in Czernowitz und rundum: Erinnerungen eines Altösterreichers*. Rimbaud, 2013.

Drozdowski, Georg. "Die Stadt am Prut." In *Europa erlesen: Czernowitz*, edited by Peter Rychlo. Wieser Verlag, 2004.

Dutceac, Vasile. *Minimul drepturilor minorităților naționale în România*. Cernăuți, 1926.

Ehrlich, Eugen. *Aufgaben der Sozialpolitik im österreichischen Osten: Juden- und Bauernfrage*. Munich, 1916.

*Emancipationsruf der Bukowina*. Vienna, 1861.

Fichman, Pearl. *Before Memories Fade: Memoirs*. CreateSpace Independent Publishing Platform, 2005.

Finkel, Jevgenija, and Markus Winkler, eds. *Juden aus Czernowitz: Ghetto, Deportation, Vernichtung 1941–1944; Überlebende berichten*. Translated (from Russian into German) by Kateryna Stetsevych. Hartung-Gorre, 2004.

Finkel, Jevgenija, and Galina Zebenko, "Über die Orte der Massenvernichtung der jüdischen Bevölkerung der Bukowina durch die Faschisten." In *Juden aus Czernowitz: Ghetto, Deportation, Vernichtung 1941–1944; Überlebende berichten*, edited by Jevgenija Finkel and Markus Winkler. Hartung-Gorre, 2004.

Fischer, Eduard. *Die Bukowina: Eine allgemeine Heimatkunde*. Czernowitz, 1899.

Flondor, Sergiu. *Dulce-amar: Povestea unui refugiat din Cernăuți*. Corint, 2017.

Franzos, Karl Emil. *Aus Halb-Asien: Culturbilder aus Galizien, der Bukowina, Südrussland, und Rumänien*. Leipzig, 1876.

Franzos, Karl Emil. "Ein Culturfest." In *Europa erlesen: Czernowitz*, edited by Peter Rychlo. Wieser Verlag, 2004.

Franzos, Karl Emil. "Karl Emil Franzos." In *Die Geschichte des Erstlingswerks: Selbstbiographische Aufsätze; Mit den Jugendbildnissen der Dichter*, edited by Karl Emil Franzos. Leipzig, 1894.

Franzos, Karl Emil. "Von Wien nach Czernowitz." In *Europa erlesen: Czernowitz*, edited by Peter Rychlo. Wieser Verlag, 2004.

Friedjung, Prive. *Wir wollten nur das Paradies auf Erden: Die Erinnerungen einer jüdischen Kommunistin aus der Bukowina*. Böhlau Verlag, 1995.

*Gedenkschrift aus Anlass der Enthüllung des Denkmals für Dr Constantin Tomaszczuk, am 17 October 1897*. Czernowitz, 1897.

Georgescu, Pepe. *265 de zile la Cernăuți 28 iunie 1940–20 martie 1941*. Bucharest, 1942.

Greciuc, Vasile. *Utracvismul sau două limbi de predare la liceele românești din Bucovina*. Cernăuți, 1912.

Grigorovici, Radu. *Bucovina în primele descrieri geografice, istorice, economice și demografice*. Editura Academiei Romne, 1998.

Grigoroviță, Mircea. *Din istoria colonizării Bucovinei*. Editura Didactică și Pedagogică, 1996.

Gross, Sidi and Erhard R. Wiehn. *Zeitzeugin Sein: Geschichten aus Czernowitz und Israel*. Hartung-Gorre, 2005.

Grünberg, Sigmund. "Das Volksschulwesen der Bukowina in seiner historischen Entwicklung und seinem jetzigen Stande," *Österreichisch-ungarische Revue* 5 (1888): 186–227.

Heinzen, Georg. "Wo die Hunde die Namen olympischer Götter trugen." In *Europa erlesen: Czernowitz*, edited by Peter Rychlo, 249–51. Wieser Verlag, 2004.

Hirsch, Carl. *A Life in the Twentieth Century: A Memoir* (unpaginated).1989. Extract only currently available, at https://czernowitz.ehpes.com/czernowitz12/testfile2008/0740.html (accessed May 8, 2025).

Iaţencu, Rodica, and Marian Olaru, eds. *Bucovineni în Parlamentul României întregite/ Bukowiner im Parlament des vereinigten Rumänien*. Editura Academiei Române, 2015.

Iorga, Nicolae. *Aportul Bucovinei la cultura românească*. Cernăuţi, 1925.

Iorga, Nicolae. *Byzantium After Byzantium*. Translated by Laura Treptow. Center for Romanian Studies, 2000 [1935].

Iorga, Nicolae. *Conferinţe bucovinene*. Bucharest, 1919.

Iorga, Nicolae. *Neamul românesc din Bucovina*. Bucharest, 1905.

Jagendorf, Siegfried. *Jagendorf's Foundry: Memoir of the Romanian Holocaust, 1941–1944*, HarperCollins, 1991.

Kaindl, Raimund Friedrich. *Das Ansiedlungswesen in der Bukowina seit der Besitzergreifung durch Österreich mit besonderer Berücksichtigung der Ansiedlung der Deutschen*. Innsbruck, 1902.

Kaindl, Raimund Friedrich. "Deutsche Aufgaben in den Karpathenländern." *Deutsche Arbeit* 14, no. 4 (1914–15): 217–21.

Kaindl, Raimund Friedrich. *Deutsche Siedlung im Osten*. (Der deutsche Krieg 34). Stuttgart, 1915.

Kaindl, Raimund Friedrich. *Die Deutschen in den Donauländern und ihren Nachbargebieten: Ein Sendschreiben an Deutsche und Nichtdeutsche*. Hamm-Westfalen, 1919.

Kaindl, Raimund Friedrich. *Geschichte der Bukowina: Erster Abschnitt; Von der ältesten Zeit bis zur Gründung des Fürstentums Moldau um 1350*. Czernowitz, 1888.

Kaindl, Raimund Friedrich. *Geschichte der Deutschen in Galizien, Ungarn, der Bukowina und Rumänien seit etwa 1770 bis zur Gegenwart* (*Geschichte der Deutschen in den Karpathenländern, Band* 3). Gotha, 1911.

Kaindl, Raimund Friedrich. *Geschichte von Czernowitz von den ältesten Zeiten bis zur Gegenwart; Festschrift zum sechzigjährigen Regierungsjubiläum Kaiser Franz Joseph I. und zur Erinnerung an die erste urkundliche Erwähnung von Czernowitz vor 500 Jahren*. Czernowitz, 1908.

Kaindl, Raimund Friedrich. *Österreich, Preussen, Deutschland: Deutsche Geschichte in grossdeutscher Beleuchtung*. Vienna, 1926.

Kaindl, Raimund Friedrich. "Raimund Friedrich Kaindl." In *Die Geschichtswissenschaft der Gegenwart in Selbstdarstellungen*, volume 1, edited by Sigfrid H. Steinberg, 171–205. Leipzig, 1925.

Kaindl, Raimund Friedrich. "Die Universität in Czernowitz: Ein Wort zur Aufklärung." *Österreichische Rundschau* 11 (1907): 61–65.

Kaler, Kurt. *Die Gründung der k.k. Franz-Josephs-Universität in Czernowitz im Jahre 1875*. Vienna, 1917.

Kehlmann, Heinz. *So weit nach Westen: Von Czernowitz nach New York*. Rimbaud, 2004.

Kellner, Anna. *Leon Kellner: Sein Leben und Sein Werk*. Vienna, 1936.

Kittner, Alfred, and Edith Silbermann. *Erinnerungen 1906–1991*. Rimbaud, 1996.

*Die K.K. Franz-Josephs-Universität in Czernowitz im Ersten Vierteljahrhundert Ihres Bestandes: Festschrift*, edited by the Akademischen Senate. Czernowitz, 1900.

Klug, Alfred. *Ernst Rudolf Neubauer: Der Mann und das Werk*, volume 1. Czernowitz/Cernauti, 1931.

Kogălniceanu, Mihail. *Răpirea Bucovinei, după documente autentice*. Editura Domino, 1999.

Kohl, Johann Georg. *Austria: Vienna, Prague, Hungary, Bohemia, and the Danube; Galicia, Styria, Moravia, Bukovina, and the Military Frontier*. London, 1844.

*Eine Kulturliga für die Bukowina: Offene Antwort auf die Rede des Dr. Popovici in der rumänischen Kulturliga in Bukarest*. Czernowitz, 1903.

Kupchanko, Hryhorii. *Die Schicksale der Ruthenen*. Leipzig, 1887.

Kurylo, Volodymyr Mykhailovych. *Pivnichna Bukovyna, ii mynule i suchasne*. Karpaty, 1969.

Kvitkovskyi, Denys. *Bukovyna: ii mynyle i suchasne*. Vyd-vo "Zelena Bukovyna," 1956.

Lagler, Heinrich. *Die Landesfeier der hundertjährigen Vereinigung des Herzogthums Bukowina mit dem österrechischen Kaiserstaate und der Eröffnung der k.k. Franz-Josefs-Universität im Czernowitz [. . .]*. Czernowitz, 1875.

*Die Lemberg-Czernowitz-Jassy Eisenbahn: Separat-Abdruck aus dem "Sonn- und Feiertags-Courier"*. Vienna, 1872.

Libloy, Friedrich Schuler von. *Festrede zur Eröffnungsfeierlichkeiten der k.k. Franz-Josephs Universität in Czernowitz am 4 Oktober 1875*. Czernowitz, 1875.

Lihaciu, Ioan-Constantin. "Kunst und Kultur im alten Czernowitz: Zum kreativen Milieu einer Provinzmetropole." In *Mythos Czernowitz: Eine Stadt im Spiegel ihrer Nationalitäten*, edited by Martin Pollack. Deutsches Kulturforum östliches Europa, 2008.

*Membrii Soţietăţii pentru cultura şi literatura română în Bucovina*. Cernăuţi, 1884.

*Memoriul Bucovinei*. Cernăuţi, 1931.

Menczel, Philipp. *Als Geisel nach Sibirien verschleppt*. Berlin, 1916.

Menczel, Philipp. *Trügerische Lösungen: Erlebnisse und Betrachtungen eines Österreichers*. Stuttgart, 1932.

Mieg, Friedrich von. *Topographische Beschreibung der Bukowina, mit militärischen Anmerkungen*. Czernowitz, 1897.

Mircu, Marius. *Pogromurile din Bucovina şi Dorohoi*. Bucharest, 1945.

Mischler, Ernst."Die Stellung der Bukowina im Staatshaushhalte," in *Mitteilungen des statistischen Landesamtes des Herzogtums Bukowina* (1). Czernowitz, 1892.

Nandriş, Gheorghe. *Povestea vieţii mele*. Editura Universităţii Lucian Blaga, 2015.

Nandriş-Cudla, Aniţa. *20 de ani în Siberia: Destin bucovinean*. Humanitas, 1991.

Nichita-Toma, Felicia. "Chinurile şi speranţele unui român bucovinean." In *Golgota românească: Mărturiile bucovinenilor deportaţi în Siberia*, edited by Liliana Corobca and Dumitru Covalciuc. Editura Vestala, 2009.

Niculiţă-Voronca, Elena. *Casa naţională: Conferinţă ţinută în 9 Decemvrie 1894 în folosul fondului pentru clădirea unui palat naţional*. Cernăuţi, 1894.

*Der Niedergang des deutschen Unterrichtes im ruthenischen Theile der Bukowina* (offprint from the *Bukowinaer Post*, nos. 943–46, July 1900). Czernowitz, 1900.

Nimigeanu, Dumitru. *Însemnările unui ţăran deportat din Bucovina*. Editura Vestala, 2006.

Nistor, Ion. *Amintiri răzleţe din timpul unirii: 1918*. Cernăuţi, 1938.

Nistor, Ion. *Zece ani dela unirea Bucovinei: 1918–1928*. Cernăuţi, 1928.

Nistor, Ion. "Zur Geschichte des Schulwesens." In *XLVIII. Jahresbericht der gr-or Ober-Realschule in Czernowitz: Veröffentlicht von der Direktion am Schlusse des Schuljahres 1911/12*. Czernowitz, 1912.

Onciul, Aurel Ritter von. *Das österreichische Problem*. Vienna, 1905.

Onciul, Aurel Ritter von. *Zur österreichischen Sprachenfrage*. Vienna, 1898.

Opaiţ, Arcadie. "Vânătoare de oameni." In *Golgota românească: Mărturiile bucovinenilor deportaţi în Siberia.*, edited by Liliana Corobca and Dumitru Covalciuc. Editura Vestala, 2009.

*Die österreichisch-ungarische Monarchie in Wort und Bild; auf Anregung und unter Mitwirkung des Kronprinzen Erzherzog Rudolf: Bukowina*. Vienna, 1899. Available at https://austria-forum.org/web-books/kpwde20de1899onb (accessed May 6, 2025).

Pasat, V. I. ed. *Trudnye stranitsy istorii Moldova: 1940–1950e gg*. Terra, 1994.

Pihuliak, Hierotheus. *Die gr.-or. Kirchenfrage in der Bukowina und die Jungruthenen: kritische Beleuchtung der Brochure: Beitrag zur kirchlichen Frage in der Bukowina*. Czernowitz, 1906.

Pivin, Ilie. "Mă doare trecutul ca o rană deschisă." In *Golgota românească: Mărturiile bucovinenilor deportați în Siberia.*, edited by Liliana Corobca and Dumitru Covalciuc. Editura Vestala, 2009.

Polek, Johann. *Die Anfänge des Volksschulwesens in der Bukowina: Ein Beitrag zu einer Geschichte der Bukowinaer Militaerverwaltung*. Czernowitz, 1891.

Polek, Johann. *Die Erwerbung der Bukowina durch Österreich*. Czernowitz, 1889.

Polek, Johann. *Joseph's II. Reisen nach Galizien und der Bukowina und ihre Bedeutung für letztere Provinz*. Czernowitz, 1895.

Popovici, Aurel. "Ne-au batjocorit veneticii și cozile de topor." In *Golgota românească: Mărturiile bucovinenilor deportați în Siberia*, edited by Liliana Corobca and Dumitru Covalciuc. Editura Vestala, 2009.

Popovici, Traian. *Spovedania/Testimony*. Fundația Dr. W. Filderman, 2001.

Popovych, Omelian. *Vidrodzheniya Bukovyni: Spomyni*. Lviv, 1933.

Porubsky, Franz, *Czernowitzer Skizzen: Betractungen*, edited by Raimund Lang. Traditionsverband Katholische Czernowitzer Pennäler, 2001.

Porubsky, Franz. *Rund um den Rathausturm und den Prut*. Czernowitz, 1906.

Prelitsch, Hans. *Student in Czernowitz: Die Korporationen an der Czernowitzer Universität*. Landsmannschaft der Buchenlanddeutschen, 1961.

*Radyanska Bukovyna, 1940–1945: Dokumenty i materialy*. Naukova Dumka, 1967.

Ranner, Gertrud, Axel Halling, and Anja Fiedler, eds. *". . . und das Herz wird mir schwer dabei": Czernowitzer Juden erinnern sich*. Deutsches Kulturforum Östliches Europa, 2009.

Rezzori, Gregor von. *An Ermine in Czernopol*. New York Review Books Classics, 2011.

Rezzori, Gregor von. *Mir auf der Spur*. Bertelsmann, 1997.

Richter, Hans. *Heimkehrer: Bildberichte von der Umsiedlung der Volksdeutschen aus Bessarabien, der Dobrudscha, dem Buchenlande und aus Litauen*. Berlin (Zentralverlag der NSDAP), 1942.

Riedl, Franz Hieronymus. "Die Universität Czernowitz als Völkerverbindende Institution 1875–1919: Festvortrag auf der Universitäts-Jubiläumsfeier der Landsmannschaft der Buchenlanddeutschen am 15. Mai 1970 zu Regensburg." In *Alma Mater Francisco Josephina: Die deutschsprachige Nationalitäten-Universität in Czernowitz, Festschrift zum 100 Jahrestag ihrer Eröffnung 1875*, edited by Rudolf Wagner. Verlag Hans Menschendörfer, 1975.

Rittershein, Gottfried Ritter von. "Die Gründungs-Feier der Czernowitzer Universität." In *Alma Mater Francisco Josephina: Die deutschsprachige Nationalitäten-Universität in Czernowitz, Festschrift zum 100 Jahrestag ihrer Eröffnung 1875*, edited by Rudolf Wagner. Verlag Hans Menschendörfer, 1975.

Rohrer, Joseph. *Bemerkungen auf einer Reise von der türkischen Gränze über die Bukowina durch Ost- und Westgalizien, Schlesien und Mähren nach Wien*. Scherer, 1989.

*Românii din Bucovina: Privire scurtă asupra desvoltarii lor pe terenul cultural și economic dela încorporarea Bucovinei la monarhia austro-ungară, 1775 până la 1906: compusă și redactată cu ocaziunea "Expozitiunei generale române din 1906*. Cernauți, 1906.

Rosenzweig, Leon. *Wir Juden: Betrachtungen und Vorschläge von einem Bukowina Juden*. Zurich, 1883.

Röskau-Rydel, Isabel. "Staatliche Kulturpolitik und bürgerliches Engagement im österreichischen Galizien von 1772 bis Mitte des 19 Jahrhunderts." In *Kulturpolitik und Theater: Die kontinentalen Imperien in Europa im Vergleich*, edited by Philipp Ther. Oldenbourg Wissenschaftsverlag, 2012.

Roth-Zuckermann, Rosa. "Jüdisches Leben in der Sowjetunion: Gespraech mit Markus Winkler." In *An der Zeiten Ränder: Czernowitz und die Bukowina: Geschichte, Literatur, Verfolgung, Exil*, edited by Cecile Cordon and Helmut Kusdat. Theodor Kramer Gesellschaft, 2002.

Rottner, Eli, *Das ethische Seminar in Czernowitz: Die Wiege des internationalen Constantin-Brunner-Kreises*. E. Rudnicki, 1973.

*Satzungen des Vereines der christlichen Deutschen in der Bukowina*. Czernowitz, n.d.

Sbiera, Ion G. "Puterea graiului național." In *Prelegeri publice poporale ținute în erna 1883/84 de către membrii Soțietății pentru cultura și literatura română în Bucovina*. Cernăuți, 1884.

Shmueli, Ilana. *Ein Kind aus guter Familie: Czernowitz 1924–1944*. Rimbaud, 2006.

Silbermann, Edith. "Deutsch—die Muttersprache der meisten Bukowiner Juden." In *An der Zeiten Ränder: Czernowitz und die Bukowina: Geschichte, Literatur, Verfolgung, Exil*, edited by Cécile Cordon and Helmut Kusdat. Theodor Kramer Gesellschaft, 2002.

Simiginowicz-Staufe, Ludwig Adolf. *Die Völkergruppen der Bukowina: Ethnographisch-culturhistorische Skizzen*. Czernowitz, 1884.

Şiperco, Andrei, ed. *Holocaust în România: Soarta evreilor din Basarabia, Bucovina și Transnistria 1941–1942; Documente*. Universității din București, 2005.

*Die Slavisirung der Bukowina im XIX Jahrhundert als Ausgangspunkt grosspolnischer Zukunftspolitik: Ethnographische und politische Betrachtungen*. Vienna, 1900.

Splényi von Miháldy, Gabriel. *Beschreibung der Bukowina*. Czernowitz, 1893.

*Stenographische Protokolle des Bukowinaer Landtages*. Czernowitz, 1902 and 1908.

Tcaciuc, Nicolae. *Câteva cuvinte despre românii rutenizați din nordul Bucovinei*. Cernăuți, 1926.

Torouțiu, Ilie. *Poporația și clasele sociale din Bucovina*. Bucharest, 1916.

Torouțiu, Ilie. *Românii și clasa intelectuală din Bucovina: Notițe statistice*. Cernăuți, 1911.

Trașcă, Ottmar and Dennis Deletant, eds. *Al III-lea Reich și Holocaustul din România, 1940–1944: Documente din arhivele germane*. Editura Institutului Național pentru Studierea Holocaustului din România "Elie Wiesel," 2007.

Ukrainian Delegation at the Paris Peace Conference, *Notes présentées par la délégation de la République ukrainienne à la Conférence de la paix à Paris*. Paris, 1919. Available at http://archive.org/details/notesprsente00pariuoft (accessed May 9, 2025).

Vesper, Iulian. *Memorii*. Editura Saeculum, 1999.

Vitencu, Dragoş. *Cernăuțiul meu*. Complexul Muzeal Bucovina, 2008.

Voronca, Octavian. "Răni ce se vindecă greu." In *Golgota românească: Mărturiile bucovinenilor deportați în Siberia*, edited by Liliana Corobca and Dumitru Covalciuc. Editura Vestala, 2009.

Voronca, Zaharia. *Rutenizarea Bucovinei*. Cernăuți, 1904.

Wagner, Rudolf, ed., *Die Revolutionsjahre 1848/d49 im Königreich Galizien-Lodomerien (einschließlich Bukowina): Dokumente aus österreichischer Zeit*. Verlag "der Südostdeutsche," 1983.

Waldeck, R. G. *Athene Palace: Hitler's "New Order" Comes to Rumania*. University of Chicago Press, 2013 [1942].

Weber, Julius. *Die Russentage in Czernowitz: Die Ereignisse der ersten und zweiten russischen Invasion*. Czernowitz, 1915.

Weissglas, Isak. *Steinbruch am Bug: Bericht einer Deportation nach Transnistrien*. Literaturhaus Berlin, 1995.

Werenka, Daniel. *Bukowinas Entstehen und Aufblühen: Maria Theresias Zeit*. Vienna, 1892.

Werenka, Daniel. "Über die Grenzregulierung der Bukowina zur Zeit der Vereinigung mit Österreich," *Jahrbuch des Bukowiner Landes-Museums* 3 (1895): 25–140.

Wickenhauser, Franz Adolf. *Die deutschen Siedelungen in der Bukowina*. Czernowitz, 1887.

Yavetz, Zvi. *Erinnerungen an Czernowitz: Wo Menschen und Buecher lebten*. C. H. Beck, 2007.

Žaloba, I. V. "Das erste Schienenbahnprojekt für die Bukowina (1843)." *Südostdeutsches Archiv* 42 (1999): 41–46.

Zieglauer, Ferdinand von. *Die Entwickelung des Schulwesens in der Bukowina seit der Vereinigung des Landes mit Österreich (1774–1899)*. Czernowitz, 1899.

Zieglauer, Ferdinand von. *Festschrift herausgegeben aus Anlaß der Enthüllung einer Büste Kaiser Joseph II. im Garten des Deutschen Hauses in Czernowitz*. Czernowitz, 1903.


## *Newspapers and Journals*


*Adevărul Bolşevic*
*Bucovina Sovietică*
*Bucovina: Ziarul românilor bucovineni*
*Bukowinaer Post*
*Bukowinaer Volksblatt*
*Chas*
*Czernowitzer Allgemeine Zeitung*
*Czernowitzer Deutsche Tagespost*
*Czernowitzer Gemeinde-Zeitung*
*Czernowitzer Morgenblatt*
*Czernowitzer Tagblatt*
*Dimineaţa*
*Dos Jidisze Wort*
*Freie Lehrerzeitung*
*Glasul Bucovinei*
*Însemnări sociologice*
*Izvestiya*
*Junimea literară*
*Neue Freie Presse*
*Ostjüdische Zeitung*
*Pädagogische Blätter*
*Radyanska Bukovyna*
*Românul*
*Tshernavitser Bleter*
*Unirea*
*Universul*
*Viaţa Bucovinei*
*Voinţa poporului*
*Die Wahrheit*
*Zorile Bucovinei*


## Secondary Sources


Adelman, Jeremy. "Liberalism and Constitutionalism in Latin America in the 19th Century." *History Compass* 12, no. 6 (2014): 508–16.

Adelman, Jeremy. "Mimesis and Rivalry: European Empires and Global Regimes." *Journal of Global History* 10, no. 1 (2015): 77–98.

Adelman, Jeremy. *Sovereignty and Revolution in the Iberian Atlantic*. Princeton University Press, 2009.

Agnew, John A. *Reinventing Geopolitics: Geographies of Modern Statehood*. Department of Geography, University of Heidelberg, 2001.

Aldcroft, Derek H. *Europe's Third World: The European Periphery in the Interwar Years*. Ashgate, 2006.

Amar, Tarik Cyril. *The Paradox of Ukrainian Lviv: A Borderland City between Stalinists, Nazis, and Nationalists*. Cornell University Press, 2015.

Amar, Tarik Cyril. "Sovietization as a Civilizing Mission in the West." In *The Sovietization of Eastern Europe: New Perspectives on the Postwar Period*, edited by Balázs Apor, Peter Apor, and E. A. Rees. New Academia Publishing, 2008.

Amrith, Sunil S. *Crossing the Bay of Bengal: The Furies of Nature and the Fortunes of Migrants*. Reprint edition. Harvard University Press, 2015.

Ancel, Jean. "The German–Romanian Relationship and the Final Solution." *Holocaust and Genocide Studies* 19, no. 2 (2005): 252–75.

Ancel, Jean. *The History of the Holocaust in Romania*. University of Nebraska Press and Yad Vashem, 2011.

Ancel, Jean. "The Romanian Campaigns of Mass Murder in Transnistria, 1941–42." In *The Destruction of Romanian and Ukrainian Jews During the Antonescu Era*, edited by Randolph Braham. Social Science Monographs, 1997.

Andrei, Veronica. "Ucraina are probleme cu recrutarea: În Bucovina a fost prinsă o bandă care făcea trafic de persoane în străinătate." *Ziare.Com*, "Actualitate," November 20, 2023. https://ziare.com/ucraina/ucraina-razboi-rusia-invazie-recrtuatre-contrabanda-1837168 (accessed March 31, 2025).

Angrick, Andrej. *Besatzungspolitik und Massenmord: Die Einsatzgruppe D in der südlichen Sowjetunion 1941–1943*. Hamburger Edition, 2003.

Angrick, Andrej. "Im Wechselspiel der Kräfte: Impressionen zur deutschen Einflussnahme bei der Volkstumpolitik in Czernowitz vor 'Barbarossa' und nach Beginn des Überfalls auf die Sowjetunion." In *NS-Gewaltherrschaft: Beiträge zur historischen Forschung und juristischen Aufarbeitung*, edited by Alfred Bernd Gottwaldt, Norbert Kampe, and Peter Klein. Edition Hentrich, 2005.

Arhire, S. "The Russian–Romanian Diplomatic Negotiations Between 1914 and 1916 for Romania's Entry into the First World War." *Bylye Gody* 54, no. 4 (2019): 1907–17.

Armstrong, John A. *Ukrainian Nationalism*. Third edition. Ukrainian Academic Press, 1990.

Aschheim, Steven E. *Brothers and Strangers: The East European Jew in German and German Jewish Consciousness, 1800–1923*. University of Wisconsin Press, 1982.

Baiersdorf, Paul. "*Kronprinzenwerk* and the *Nationalitätenproblem* in Austria-Hungary." *East Central Europe* 32, nos. 1–2 (2005): 239–47.

Ballantyne, Tony. *Entanglements of Empire: Missionaries, Maori, and the Question of the Body*. Duke University Press Books, 2014.

Baranowski, Shelley. "Authoritarianism and Fascism in Interwar Europe: Approaches and Legacies." *The Journal of Modern History* 94, no. 3 (2022): 648–72.

Bartov, Omer. *Anatomy of a Genocide: The Life and Death of a Town Called Buczacz*, 2018.

Bartov, Omer. "Eastern Europe as the Site of Genocide." *The Journal of Modern History* 80, no. 3 (2008): 557–93

Bartov, Omer. *The Eastern Front, 1941–45: German Troops and the Barbarisation of Warfare*. Second edition. Palgrave in association with St. Antony's College, Oxford, 2001.

Bartov, Omer. *Erased: Vanishing Traces of Jewish Galicia in Present-Day Ukraine*. Princeton University Press, 2007.

Bartov, Omer, and Eric D. Weitz. *Shatterzone of Empires: Coexistence and Violence in the German, Habsburg, Russian, and Ottoman Borderlands*. Indiana University Press, 2013.

Baud, Michiel, and Willem Van Schendel. "Toward a Comparative History of Borderlands." *Journal of World History* 8, no. 2 (1997): 211–42.

Behrends, Natalie. "Histories of the Big and Small: An Interview with Mark Mazower." Toynbee Prize Foundation, February 20, 2019. https://toynbeeprize.org/posts/mark-mazower/ (accessed March 26, 2021).

Bejan, Cristina A. *Intellectuals and Fascism in Interwar Romania: The Criterion Association*. Palgrave Macmillan, 2019.

Bejan, Gabriel. "Exclusiv—Mărturia unui român din Ucraina care a fugit de război în România: "Nord-bucovinenii nu prea sunt dispuși să lupte. Mulți habar nu au ce este o armă."" *HotNews.ro*, February 25, 2022, https://www.hotnews.ro/stiri-razboi_ucraina-25390653-exclusiv-marturia-unui-roman-din-ucraina-care-fugit-razboi-romania-nord-bucovinenii-nu-prea-sunt-dispusi-lupte-multi-habar-nu-este-arma.htm (accessed March 31, 2025).

Bendix, Regina. "Ethnology, Cultural Reification, and the Dynamics of Difference in the *Kronprinzenwerk*." In *Creating the Other: Ethnic Conflict and Nationalism in Habsburg Central Europe*, edited by Nancy Wingfield. Berghahn Books, 2005.

Beneš, Jakub S. *Workers and Nationalism: Czech and German Social Democracy in Habsburg Austria, 1890–1918*. Oxford University Press, 2017.

Benton, Lauren A. *A Search for Sovereignty: Law and Geography in European Empires, 1400–1900*. Cambridge University Press, 2010.

Bergholz, Max. *Violence as a Generative Force: Identity, Nationalism, and Memory in a Balkan Community*. Cornell University Press, 2016.

Berkhoff, Karel C. *Harvest of Despair: Life and Death in Ukraine under Nazi Rule*. Harvard University Press, 2004.

Berman, Marshall. *All That Is Solid Melts into Air: The Experience of Modernity*. Reissue edition. Penguin Books, 1988.

Berman, Sheri. *Democracy and Dictatorship in Europe: From the Ancien Régime to the Present Day*. Oxford University Press, 2019.

Bernsand, Niklas. "Returning Chernivtsi to the Cultural Map of Europe: The Meridian Czernowitz International Poetry Festival." *East European Politics and Societies and Cultures* 33, no. 1 (2019): 238–56.

Bideleux, Robert. "The Peasantries and Peasant Parties of Interwar East Central Europe." In *Interwar East Central Europe, 1918–1941: The Failure of Democracy-Building, the Fate of Minorities*, edited by Sabrina P. Ramet. Routledge, 2020.

Bjork, James. *Neither German nor Pole: Catholicism and National Indifference in a Central European Borderland*. University of Michigan Press, 2008.

Blanning, T.C.W. *The Culture of Power and the Power of Culture: Old Regime Europe 1660–1789*. Oxford University Press, 2003.

Blasen, Philippe Henri. "Învățământul în limba ucraineană din Bucovina în timpul dictaturii regale (1938–1940)." *Archiva Moldaviae* 13, no. 13 (2021): 135–69.

Blasen, Philippe Henri. "Terrorisme légionnaire et ordonnances antisémites: La Région Suceava d'octobre 1938 à septembre 1940." *Archiva Moldaviae* 10, no. 10 (2018): 301–40.

Blasen, Philippe Henri. *La "primauté de la nation roumaine" et les "étrangers": Les minorités et leur liberté du travail sous le cabinet Goga et la dictature royale (décembre 1937–septembre 1940)*. Casa Cărții de Știință, 2022.

Bloomberg, Jon. *The Jewish World in the Modern Age*. KTAV Publishing House, 2004.

Boia, Lucian. *Capcanele istoriei: Elita intelectuală românească între 1930 și 1950*. Revised and enlarged edition. Humanitas, 2012.

Boia, Lucian. *În jurul Marii Uniri de la 1918: Națiuni, frontiere, minorități*. Humanitas, 2017.

Boot, Max. "A Resilient Ukraine Faces Defeat if U.S. Aid Falters." *Council on Foreign Relations*, February 17, 2024. https://www.cfr.org/in-brief/resilient-ukraine-faces-defeat-if-us-aid-falters (accessed March 31, 2025).

Borodziej, Włodzimierz, and Maciej Górny. *Forgotten Wars: Central and Eastern Europe, 1912–1916*. Cambridge University Press, 2021.

Botushanskyi, Vasyl Mefodiiovych. "Bukovynska trudova emihratsiia v kintsi XIX na pochhatku XX st." *Istorychni doslidzhenniia* 1 (1975): 136–45.

Botushanskyi, Vasyl Mefodiiovych. *Bukovyna v konteksti yevropeiskykh mizhnarodnykh vidnosyn: Z davnikh chasiv do seredyny XX st.* Ruta, 2005.

Botushanskyi, Vasyl Mefodiiovych. "Stanovishche silskohospodarskikh robitnykiv pivnichnoi Bukovyni na pochatku XX st." *Ukrainskyi istorychnyi zhurnal* 5 (1973): 89–94.

Bowden, Brett. *The Empire of Civilization: The Evolution of an Imperial Idea*. Reprint edition. University of Chicago Press, 2014.

Boyer, John W. *Political Radicalism in Late Imperial Vienna: The Origins of the Christian Social Movement, 1848–1897*. University of Chicago Press, 1981.

Boym, Svetlana. *Common Places: Mythologies of Everyday Life in Russia*. Harvard University Press, 1995.

Braudel, Fernand, and Immanuel Wallerstein. "History and the Social Sciences: The *Longue Durée*." *Review (Fernand Braudel Center)* 32, no. 2 (2009): 171–203.

Brix, Emil. *Die Umgangssprachen in Altösterreich zwischen Agitation und Assimilation: Die Sprachenstatistik in den zisleithanischen Volkszählungen, 1880 bis 1910*. Böhlau Verlag, 1982.

Broers, Michael. "Cultural Imperialism in a European Context? Political Culture and Cultural Politics in Napoleonic Italy." *Past & Present* 170, no. 1 (2001): 152–80.

Brofman, M. I., and A. M. Telefus. "Diialnist Orhanizatsii 'Vyzvolennia' na Bukovyni." *Ukrainskii istoricheskii zhurnal* 6 (1965): 69–72.

Broszat, Martin. "Von der Kulturnation zur Volksgruppe: Die nationale Stellung der Juden in der Bukowina im 19. und 20. Jahrhundert." *Historische Zeitschrift* 200, no. 1 (1965): 572–605.

Brown, Kate. *A Biography of No Place: From Ethnic Borderland to Soviet Heartland*. Harvard University Press, 2005.

Bruder, Franziska. *"Den ukrainischen Staat erkämpfen oder sterben!": Die Organisation Ukrainischer Nationalisten (OUN) 1929–1948*. Metropol, 2007.

Bruja, Radu Florian. "Conflictele antisemite din Bucovina, în vara anului 1930." *Studia et Acta Historiae Iudaeorum Romaniae* 12 (2015): 201–12.

Bruja, Radu Florian. "Constituirea Ligii Apărării Național Creștine în Bucovina, 1923–1926." *Arhivele totalitarismului* 19, no. 1–2 (2011): 8–22.

Bruja, Radu Florian. *Extrema dreaptă în Bucovina*. Editura Cetatea de Scaun, 2012.

Bruja, Radu Florian. "Traian Brăileanu: Life Marks of a Legionary Ideologist." *Valahian Journal of Historical Studies* 11 (2009): 139–49.

Buchet, Constantin. "Centrele iredentiste ucrainene si România (1920–1940)." In *Relații româno-ucrainene: Istorie și contemporaneitate*, edited by Irina Liuba Horvat. Muzeul Sătmărean, 2019)

Bucur, Maria. "Carol II of Romania." In *Balkan Strongmen: Dictators and Authoritarian Rulers of South Eastern Europe*, edited by Bernd J. Fischer. C. Hurst & Co., 2007.

Bucur, Maria. *Eugenics and Modernization in Interwar Romania*. University of Pittsburgh Press, 2010.

Bucur, Maria. "Romania: War, Occupation, Liberation." In *European Culture in the Great War: The Arts, Entertainment, and Propaganda 1914–1918*, edited by Aviel Roshwald and Richard Stites. Cambridge University Press, 1999.

Bugai, N. F. *The Deportation of Peoples in the Soviet Union*. Nova Science Publishers, 1996.

Bukhovets, I. O. "Ekspluatatsiia pravoslavnoho tserkvoiu selyan pivnichnoi Bukovyni kinets XVIII—Pochatok XX St." *Ukrainskyi istoricheskii zhurnal* 3 (1985): 101–4.

Burbank, Jane, and Frederick Cooper. *Empires in World History: Power and the Politics of Difference*. Princeton University Press, 2011.

Burds, Jeffrey. "The Early Cold War in Soviet West Ukraine, 1944–1948." *The Carl Beck Papers in Russian and East European Studies*, no. 1505 (January 2001).

Bureiko, Nadiia, Teodor Lucian Moga, Alexandra Gheorghiu, and Bogdan-Constantin Ibănescu. "Between the Home and Kin-State: Self-Identification and Attachment of Ukrainians and Romanians in the Ukrainian-Romanian Borderland of Bukovina." *Problems of Post-Communism* 68, no. 1 (2021): 53–65.

Burger, Hannelore. "Mehrsprachigkeit und Unterrichtswissen in der Bukowina 1869–1918." In *Die Bukowina: Vergangenheit und Gegenwart*, edited by Ilona Slawinski and Joseph P. Strelka. Peter Lang AG, 1995.

Burger, Hannelore. *Sprachenrecht und Sprachengerechtigkeit im österreichischen Unterrichtswesen: 1867–1918*. Verlag der Österreichische Akademie der Wissenschaften, 1995.

Călinescu, Matei. "The 1927 Generation in Romania: Friendships and Ideological Choices (Mihail Sebastian, Mircea Eliade, Nae Ionescu, Eugène, Ionesco, E. M. Cioran)." *East European Politics and Societies* 15, no. 3 (2001): 649–77.

Capoccia, Giovanni. *Defending Democracy: Reactions to Extremism in Interwar Europe*. Johns Hopkins University Press, 2007.

Carrol, Alison. *The Return of Alsace to France, 1918–1939*. Oxford University Press, 2018.

Cârstocea, Raul. "Approaching Generic Fascism from the Margins: On the Uses of 'Palingenesis' in the Romanian Context." In *Beyond the Fascist Century: Essays in Honour of Roger Griffin*, edited by Constantin Iordachi and Aristotle Kallis. Springer International Publishing, 2020.

Cârstocea, Raul. "Breaking the Teeth of Time: Mythical Time and the 'Terror of History' in the Rhetoric of the Legionary Movement in Interwar Romania." *Journal of Modern European History* 13, no. 1 (2015): 79–97.

Case, Holly. *Between States: The Transylvanian Question and the European Idea During World War II*. Stanford University Press, 2013.

Cassidy, Kathryn. "Border Crossings, Shame and (Re-)Narrating the Past in the Ukrainian–Romanian Borderlands." In *Migrating Borders and Moving Times: Temporality and the Crossing of Borders in Europe*, edited by Hastings Donnan, Madeleine Hurd, and Carolin Leutloff-Grandits. Manchester University Press, 2017.

Ceaușu, Mihai Ștefan. "Czernowitz und die Rumänen." In *Czernowitz: Die Geschichte einer ungewöhnlicher Stadt*, edited by Harald Heppner. Böhlau Verlag, 2000.

Ceaușu, Mihai Ștefan. *Un iluminist bucovinean: boierul Vasile Balș: 1756–1832*. Junimea, 2007.

Ceaușu, Mihai Ștefan. *Parlamentarism, partide și elită politică în Bucovina Habsburgică (1848–1918): Contribuții la istoria parlamentarismului în spațiul central-est European*. Junimea, 2004.

Ceaușu, Mihai Ștefan. "Zur sozioökonomischen Gesamtsituation der Bukowina im Vormärz vom Josephinischen Kataster 1786 bis 1848." In *Der Franziszeische Kataster im Kronland Bukowina/Czernowitzer Kreis (1817–1865): Statistik und Katastralmappen*, edited by Kurt Scharr, Helmut Rumpler, and Constantin Ungureanu. Böhlau Verlag, 2015.

Chakrabarty, Dipesh. *Provincializing Europe: Postcolonial Thought and Historical Difference.* Princeton University Press, 2007.

Chmelar, Hans. *Höhepunkte der österreichischen Auswanderung: Die Auswanderung aus den im Reichsrat vertretenen Königreichen u. Ländern in den Jahren 1905–1914*. Verlag der Österreichischen Akademie der Wissenschaften, 1974.

Ciancia, Kathryn. "Borderland Modernity: Poles, Jews, and Urban Spaces in Interwar Eastern Poland." *The Journal of Modern History* 89, no. 3 (2017): 531–61.

Ciancia, Kathryn. *On Civilization's Edge: A Polish Borderland in the Interwar World*. Oxford University Press, 2020.

Clark, Christopher. *Revolutionary Spring: Europe Aflame and the Fight for a New World, 1848–1849*. Crown, 2023.

Clark, Katerina. *Moscow, the Fourth Rome: Stalinism, Cosmopolitanism, and the Evolution of Soviet Culture, 1931–1941*. Harvard University Press, 2011.

Clark, Roland. *Holy Legionary Youth: Fascist Activism in Interwar Romania*. Cornell University Press, 2015.

Clark, Roland. "Images of Crisis, the Press and the Rise of Fascism." In *Conservatives and Right Radicals in Interwar Europe*, edited by Marco Bresciani. Routledge, 2020.

Clark, Roland. "Interwar Romania: Enshrining Ethnic Privilege." In *Interwar East Central Europe, 1918–1941: The Failure of Democracy-Building, the Fate of Minorities*, edited by Sabrina P. Ramet. Routledge, 2020.

Clark, Roland. "The Salience of 'New Man' Rhetoric in Romanian Fascist Movements, 1922–44." In *The New Man in Radical Right Ideology and Practice, 1919–1945*, edited by Jorge Dagnino, Matthew Feldman, and Paul Stocker. Bloomsbury, 2018.

Clark, Roland. "The Shape of Interwar Romanian History." *Journal of Romanian Studies* 3, no. 1 (2021): 11–42.

Coen, Deborah R. *Vienna in the Age of Uncertainty: Science, Liberalism, and Private Life*. University of Chicago Press, 2008.

Cohen, Gary B. *Education and Middle-Class Society in Imperial Austria: 1848–1918*. Purdue University Press, 1996.

Cohen, Gary B. *The Politics of Ethnic Survival: Germans in Prague, 1861–1914*. Purdue University Press, 2006.

Conklin, Alice L. *A Mission to Civilize: The Republican Idea of Empire in France and West Africa, 1895–1930*. Stanford University Press, 1997.

Connelly, John. *From Peoples into Nations: A History of Eastern Europe*. Princeton University Press, 2020.

Cooper, Frederick. *Colonialism in Question: Theory, Knowledge, History*. University of California Press, 2005.

Corbea-Hoișie, Andrei. *La Bucovine: Eléments d'histoire politique et culturelle*. Institut d'études slaves, 2004.

Corbea-Hoișie, Andrei. *Czernowitzer Geschichten: Über eine städtische Kultur in Mittelosteuropa*. Böhlau Verlag, 2003.

Corbea-Hoişie, Andrei. "Jüdisches und jiddisches Czernowitz." In *Mythos Czernowitz: Eine Stadt im Spiegel ihrer Nationalitäten*, edited by Harald Heppner. Deutsches Kulturforum östliches Europa, 2008.

Cornis-Pope, Marcel, and John Neubauer. *History of the Literary Cultures of East-Central Europe: Junctures and Disjunctures in the 19th and 20th Centuries.* John Benjamins Publishing, 2006.

Cremers, Hartwig. "Czernowitz 1941/1942—der Einsatz des deutschen Konsuls Fritz Schellhorn für die Juden/Czernowitz 1941/42—the Efforts of the German Consul Fritz Schellhorn for the Jews." *Südost-Forschungen* 73, no. 1 (2014): 444–73.

Creţu, Anca Maria. "Child Assistance and the Making of Modern Refugee Camps in Austria-Hungary During the First World War." *Central European History* 55, no. 4 (2022), 510–27.

Csergo, Zsuzsa, and James M Goldgeier. "Kin-State Activism in Hungary, Romania, and Russia: The Politics of Ethnic Demography." In *Divided Nations and European Integration*, edited by Tristan James Mabry. University of Pennsylvania Press, 2013.

Cusco, Andrei. "Wartime Mobilization of Ethnicity, Shifting Loyalties, and Population Politics in the Borderlands of Nationalizing Empires: Reshaping Bessarabia and Bukovina, 1914–1919," in *Imperial Designs, Postimperial Extremes: Studies in Interdisciplinary and Comparative History of Russia and Eastern Europe*, edited by Andrei Cusco and Victor Taki. Central European University Press, 2023.

Dabrowski, Patrice M. *Poland: The First Thousand Years.* Northern Illinois University Press, 2014.

D'Anieri, Paul J. *Ukraine and Russia: From Civilized Divorce to Uncivil War*. Cambridge University Press, 2019.

David-Fox, Michael. *Crossing Borders: Modernity, Ideology, and Culture in Russia and the Soviet Union.* University of Pittsburgh Press, 2015.

David-Fox, Michael. *Showcasing the Great Experiment: Cultural Diplomacy and Western Visitors to the Soviet Union, 1921–1941.* Oxford University Press, 2012.

David-Fox, Michael. "What Is Cultural Revolution?" *The Russian Review* 58, no. 2 (1999): 181–201.

Davies, Brian L. *The Russo-Turkish War, 1768–1774: Catherine II and the Ottoman Empire.* Bloomsbury Publishing, 2016.

Davis, R. Chris. *Hungarian Religion, Romanian Blood: A Minority's Struggle for National Belonging, 1920–1945.* University of Wisconsin Press, 2019.

Davison, Roderic H. *Essays in Ottoman and Turkish History, 1774–1923: The Impact of the West.* University of Texas Press, 2013.

Deak, Istvan. "The Habsburg Empire." In *After Empire: Multiethnic Societies and Nation-Building; The Soviet Union and the Russian, Ottoman, and Habsburg Empires*, edited by Karen Barkey and Mark von Hagen. Westview Press, 1997.

Deak, John, and Jonathan E. Gumz. "How to Break a State: The Habsburg Monarchy's Internal War, 1914–1918." *American Historical Review* 122, no. 4 (2017): 1105–36.

Dean, Martin. *Collaboration in the Holocaust: Crimes of the Local Police in Belorussia and Ukraine, 1941–44.* Macmillan, 2000.

Deletant, Dennis. *Hitler's Forgotten Ally: Ion Antonescu and His Regime, Romania 1940–1944.* Palgrave Macmillan, 2006.

Deletant, Dennis. "Transnistria and the Romanian Solution to the 'Jewish Problem.'" In *The Shoah in Ukraine: History, Testimony, Memorialization*, edited by Ray Brandon and Wendy Lower. Indiana University Press, 2010.

Delfiner, Henry. "Jewish Farmers in the Bucovina: 1780s to 1848." *East European Quarterly* 24, no. 4 (1991): 529–37.

Dobrzhanskyi, Oleksandr. "Czernowitz und die Ukrainer." In *Czernowitz: Die Geschichte einer ungewöhnlichen Stadt*, edited by Harald Heppner. Böhlau Verlag, 2000.

Dragostinova, Theodora K. *The Cold War from the Margins: A Small Socialist State on the Global Cultural Scene*. Cornell University Press, 2021.

Duda, Andrii. *Bukovynskyi kurin v boiakh za ukrainsku derzhavnist: 1918, 1941, 1944*. Nakladom T-va "Ukrainskyi narodnyi dim v Chernivtsiakh," 1995.

Dullin, Sabine. *Frontière épaisse: Aux origines des politiques soviétiques*. EHESS, 2014.

Dumitru, Diana. *The State, Antisemitism, and Collaboration in the Holocaust: The Borderlands of Romania and the Soviet Union*. Cambridge University Press, 2016.

Eckert, Astrid M. *West Germany and the Iron Curtain: Environment, Economy, and Culture in the Borderlands*. Oxford University Press, 2021.

Edelstein, Dan, Stefanos Geroulanos, and Natasha Wheatley. "Chronocenosis: An Introduction to Power and Time." In *Power and Time: Temporalities in Conflict and the Making of History*, edited by Dan Edelstein, Stefanos Geroulanos, and Natasha Wheatley. University of Chicago Press, 2020.

Egry, Gábor. "Navigating the Straits: Changing Borders, Changing Rules and Practices of Ethnicity and Loyalty in Romania After 1918." *The Hungarian Historical Review* 2, no. 3 (2013): 449–76.

Eisenstadt, Shmuel, "Multiple Modernities," in *Multiple Modernities*, edited by Shmuel N. Eisenstadt. Transaction Publishers, 2002.

Evans, R.J.W. "Culture and Authority in Central Europe, 1683–1806." In Evans, *Austria, Hungary, and the Habsburgs*. Oxford University Press, 2008.

Felstiner, John. *Paul Celan: Poet, Survivor, Jew*. Yale University Press, 1995.

Fillafer, Franz Leander. "Imperium oder Kulturstaat? Die Habsburgermonarchie und die Historisierung der Nationalkulturen im 19. Jahrhundert." In *Kulturpolitik und Theater: Die kontinentalen Imperien in Europa im Vergleich*, edited by Philipp Ther. Oldenbourg Wissenschaftsverlag, 2012.

Finder, Gabriel N., and Alexander V. Prusin. "Collaboration in Eastern Galicia: The Ukrainian Police and the Holocaust." *East European Jewish Affairs* 34, no. 2 (2004): 95–118.

Fink, Carole. "Minority Rights as an International Question." *Contemporary European History* 9, no. 3 (2000): 385–400.

Fischer-Tiné, Harald, and Michael Mann. *Colonialism as Civilizing Mission: Cultural Ideology in British India*. Anthem Press, 2004.

Fisher, Gaëlle. "Looking Forwards Through the Past: Bukovina's Return to Europe After 1989–1991." *East European Politics and Societies and Cultures* 33, no. 1 (2019): 196–217.

Fisher, Gaëlle. *Resettlers and Survivors: Bukovina and the Politics of Belonging in West Germany and Israel, 1945–89*. Berghahn Books, 2020.

Fisher, Gaëlle, and Maren Röger. "Bukovina: A Borderland Region in (Trans-)National Historiographies After 1945 and 1989–1991." *East European Politics and Societies and Cultures* 33, no. 1 (2019): 175–95.

Fitzpatrick, Sheila. "Cultural Revolution in Russia 1928–32." *Journal of Contemporary History* 9, no. 1 (1974): 33–52.

Fleig Frank, Alison. *Oil Empire: Visions of Prosperity in Austrian Galicia*. Harvard University Press, 2007.

Florea, Cristina. "Frontiers of Civilization in the Age of Mass Migration from Eastern Europe." *Past & Present* 258, no. 1 (2023): 115–150.

Fostii, Ivan. "Diialnist OUN na Bukovyni u 1940–1941 rr." *Z arkhiv VChUK-GPU-NKVD-KGB*, no. 2/4 (13/15) (2000). Pdf available (in Ukrainian) https://chtyvo.org.ua/authors/Fostii_Ivan/Diialnist_OUN_na_Bukovyni_u_1940-1941/ (accessed March 31, 2025).

Fowler, Mayhill C. *Beau Monde on Empire's Edge: State and Stage in Soviet Ukraine*. University of Toronto Press, 2017.

Fritzsche, Peter. *Stranded in the Present: Modern Time and the Melancholy of History*. Harvard University Press, 2004.

Frunchak, Svitlana. "Commemorating the Future in Post-War Chernivtsi." *East European Politics and Societies* 24, no. 3 (2010): 435–63.

Frunchak, Svitlana. "The Making of Soviet Chernivtsi: National 'Reunification,' World War II, and the Fate of Jewish Czernowitz in Postwar Ukraine." Unpublished PhD dissertation, University of Toronto, 2014. Available at https://tspace.library.utoronto.ca/handle/1807/65701 (accessed March 26, 2025).

Frunchak, Svitlana. "Studying the Land, Contesting the Land: A Select Historiographic Guide to Modern Bukovina: Volume 1: Essay," *The Carl Beck Papers in Russian and East European Studies*, no. 2108 (December 2011).

Gatrell, Peter. "War After the War: Conflicts, 1919–1923." In *A Companion to World War I*, edited by John Horne. Wiley-Blackwell, 2010.

Gatrell, Peter. *A Whole Empire Walking: Refugees in Russia during World War I*. Indiana University Press, 1999.

Geissbühler, Simon. *Blutiger Juli: Rumäniens Vernichtungskrieg und der vergessene Massenmord an den Juden 1941*. Ferdinand Schöningh, 2013.

Geissbühler, Simon. "'He Spoke Yiddish like a Jew': Neighbors' Contribution to the Mass Killing of Jews in Northern Bukovina and Bessarabia, July 1941." *Holocaust and Genocide Studies* 28, no. 3 (2014): 430–49.

Gerwarth, Robert. *The Vanquished: Why the First World War Failed to End*. Reprint edition. Farrar, Straus and Giroux, 2017.

Gessen, Keith. "Russia, One Year After the Invasion of Ukraine." *The New Yorker*, February 21, 2023. https://www.newyorker.com/news/essay/russia-one-year-after-the-invasion-of-ukraine (accessed March 31, 2025).

Gettleman, Jeffrey, and Finbarr O'Reilly. "Far from the Front," *The New York Times*, July 17, 2023. Available at https://www.nytimes.com/2023/07/17/world/asia/chernivtsi-western-ukraine-aid.html (accessed March 31, 2025).

Gibbons-Neff, Thomas. "'People Snatchers': Ukraine' Recruiters Use Harsh Tactics to Fill Ranks." *The New York Times*, December 15, 2023. Available at https://www.nytimes.com/2023/12/15/world/europe/ukraine-military-recruitment.html (accessed March 31, 2025).

Gilburd, Eleonory. *To See Paris and Die: The Soviet Lives of Western Culture*. Harvard University Press, 2018.

Glass, Hildrun. *Zerbrochene Nachbarschaft: Das deutsch-jüdische Verhältnis in Rumänien, 1918–1938*. R. Oldenbourg, 1996.

*Global Conflict Tracker*, "War in Ukraine," https://cfr.org/global-conflict-tracker/conflict/conflict-ukraine (regularly updated).

Goldsmith, Emanuel S. *Modern Yiddish Culture: The Story of the Yiddish Language Movement.* Expanded edition. Fordham University Press, 1997.

Good, David F. *The Economic Rise of the Habsburg Empire, 1750–1914*. University of California Press, 1984.

Grelka, Frank. *Die ukrainische Nationalbewegung unter deutscher Besatzungsherrschaft 1918 und 1941/42*. Harrassowitz, 2005.

Gross, Jan Tomasz. *Revolution from Abroad: The Soviet Conquest of Poland's Western Ukraine and Western Belorussia*. Expanded edition. Princeton: Princeton University Press, 2002.

Gross, Stephen G. *Export Empire: German Soft Power in Southeastern Europe, 1890–1945*. Cambridge University Press, 2016.

Guidi, Andreas. *Generations of Empire: Youth from Ottoman to Italian Rule in the Mediterranean.* University of Toronto Press, 2022.

Habartová, Klára. "Jewish Refugees from Galicia and Bukovina in East Bohemia during World War I in Light of the Documents of the State Administration." *Judaica Bohemiae* 43, no. 1 (2007): 139–66.

Hacman, Serghei. "Aspecte diplomatice ale problemei Basarabiei şi Bucovinei în relatiile internaţionale (1940)." *Apulum* 34, no. 1 (1997): 611–20.

Hajdarpasic, Edin. *Whose Bosnia?: Nationalism and Political Imagination in the Balkans, 1840–1914*. Cornell University Press, 2015.

Hämäläinen, Pekka, and Samuel Truett. "On Borderlands." *Journal of American History* 98, no. 2 (2011): 338–61.

Hanebrink, Paul A. A *Specter Haunting Europe: The Myth of Judeo-Bolshevism*. Harvard University Press, 2018.

Harward, Grant T. *Romania's Holy War: Soldiers, Motivation, and the Holocaust.* Cornell University Press, 2021.

Hausleitner, Mariana. "Gegen die Zwangsrumänisierung: Die Kooperation von Bukowiner Deutschen, Juden und Ukrainern in der Zwischenkriegszeit." *WerkstattGeschichte*, no. 32 (November 2002), 31–43.

Hausleitner, Mariana. "Konfliktfelder zwischen Rumänen und Ukrainern in der Bukowina zwischen 1910 und 1920." In *Mutter: Land—Vater: Staat: Loyalitätskonflikte, politische Neuorientierung und der Erste Weltkrieg im österreichisch-russländischen Grenzraum*. Verlag Friedrich Pustet, 2017.

Hausleitner, Mariana. *Die Rumänisierung der Bukowina: Die Durchsetzung des nationalstaatlichen Anspruchs Grossrumäniens 1918–1944*. R. Oldenbourg, 2001.

Hausleitner, Mariana. *"Viel Mischmasch mitgenommen": Die Umsiedlungen aus der Bukowina 1940*. De Gruyter Oldenbourg, 2018.

Hausleitner, Mariana. "Von der Ansiedlung bis zur Umsiedlung: Institutionen und Akteure der Deutschen in der Bukowina." In *Danubia Carpathica*, vol. 10 (57): *Bukowina-Deutsche. Erfindungen, Erfahrungen und Erzählungen einer (imaginierten) Gemeinschaft seit 1775* 57. De Gruyter Oldenbourg, 2021.

Hausleitner, Mariana. "Von der Diskriminierung zur Vertreibung: Nichtrumänen in der Bukowina zwischen 1918 und 1944." In *An der Zeiten Ränder: Czernowitz und die Bukowina; Geschichte, Literatur, Verfolgung, Exil*, edited by Cécile Cordon and Helmut Kusdat. Theodor Kramer Gesellschaft, 2002.

Haynes, Rebecca. "Corneliu Zelea Codreanu: The Romanian 'New Man.'" In *In the Shadow of Hitler: Personalities of the Right in Central and Eastern Europe*, edited by Rebecca Haynes and Martyn C. Rady. I.B. Tauris, 2011.

Haynes, Rebecca. *Romanian Policy Towards Germany, 1936–40*. St. Martin's Press, 2000.

Haynes, Rebecca. "Work Camps, Commerce, and the Education of the 'New Man' in the Romanian Legionary Movement." *The Historical Journal* 51, no. 4 (2008): 943–67.

Headlam, James Wycliffe. *A Memoir of the Paris Peace Conference, 1919*, edited by Agnes Headlam-Morley, Russell Bryant, and Anna. Cienciala. Methuen, 1972.

Healy, Maureen. *Vienna and the Fall of the Habsburg Empire: Total War and Everyday Life in World War I*. Cambridge University Press, 2004.

Henley, Jon. "Far-right Trump Ally Secures Decisive Win in First Round of Romania's Presidential Election Rerun." *The Guardian*, May 5, 2025. Available at https://www.theguardian.com/world/2025/may/04/ultranationalist-wins-first-round-of-romanias-rerun-presidential-election (accessed May 10, 2025).

Hensellek, Thomas. *Die letzten Jahre der kaiserlichen Bukowina: Studien zur Landespolitik im Herzogtum Bukowina von 1909 bis 1914*. Diplomarbeiten Agentur, 2011.

Herdt, Jennifer A. *Forming Humanity: Redeeming the German "Bildung" Tradition*. The University of Chicago Press, 2019.

Heymann, Florence. *Le crépuscule des lieux: Identités juives de Czernowitz*. Stock, 2003.

Hillis, Faith. *Children of Rus': Right-Bank Ukraine and the Invention of a Russian Nation*. Cornell University Press, 2013.

Hillis, Faith. "Intimacy and Antipathy: Ukrainian-Russian Relations in Historical Perspective." *Kritika* 16, no. 1 (2015): 121–28.

Himka, John-Paul. "The Construction of Nationality in Galician Rus': Icarian Flights in Almost All Directions." In *Intellectuals and the Articulation of the Nation*, edited by Ronald Grigor Suny and Michael D. Kennedy. University of Michigan Press, 2001.

Himka, John-Paul. *Ukrainian Nationalists and the Holocaust*. Books on Demand, 2021

Hirono, Miwa. *Civilizing Missions: International Religious Agencies in China*. Palgrave Macmillan, 2008.

Hirsch, Francine. *Empire of Nations: Ethnographic Knowledge and the Making of the Soviet Union*. Cornell University Press, 2005.

Hirsch, Marianne, and Leo Spitzer. *Ghosts of Home: The Afterlife of Czernowitz in Jewish Memory*. University of California Press, 2011.

Hitchins, Keith. *The Idea of Nation: The Romanians of Transylvania, 1691–1849*. Editura științifica și enciclopedică, 1985.

Hitchins, Keith. *Orthodoxy and Nationality: Andreiu Şaguna and the Rumanians of Transylvania, 1846–1873*. Harvard University Press, 1977.

Hitchins, Keith. *The Romanians, 1774–1866*. Oxford University Press, 1996.

Hitchins, Keith. *Rumania, 1866–1947*. Oxford University Press, 1994.

Hitchins, Keith, and Alan Sharp. *Ionel Brătianu: Romania*. Haus Publishing, 2011.

Hobsbawm, E. J., and Terence Ranger, eds. *The Invention of Tradition*. Cambridge University Press, 1992.

Hochedlinger, Michael. "The Habsburg Monarchy from Military-Fiscal State to Militarization." In *The Fiscal-Military State in Eighteenth-Century Europe: Essays in Honour of P.G.M. Dickson*, edited by P.G.M. Dickson and Christopher Storrs. Ashgate, 2009.

Hoerder, Dirk, and Leslie Page Moch, eds. *European Migrants: Global and Local Perspectives.* UPNE, 1996

Hoffmann, David L. "European Modernity and Soviet Socialism." In *Russian Modernity: Politics, Knowledge, Practices,* edited by David L. Hoffmann and Yanni Kotsonis. Palgrave Macmillan, 2000.

Hoffmann, David L. *Stalinist Values: The Cultural Norms of Soviet Modernity, 1917–1941.* Cornell University Press, 2003.

Holquist, Peter. "The Role of Personality in the First (1914–1915) Russian Occupation of Galicia and Bukovina." In *Anti-Jewish Violence: Rethinking the Pogrom in East European History,* edited by Jonathan Dekel-Chen, David Gaunt, Natan M. Meir, and Israel Bartal, 52–73. Indiana University Press, 2010.

Holquist, Peter. "State Violence as Technique: The Logic of Violence in Soviet Totalitarianism." In *Landscaping the Human Garden: Twentieth-Century Population Management in a Comparative Framework,* edited by Amir Weiner, 19–45. Stanford, Calif.: Stanford University Press, 2003.

Holquist, Peter. "Tools for Revolution: Wartime Mobilization in State-Building, 1914–1921." *Ab Imperio* 2001, no. 4 (2015): 209–27.

Hölzl, Richard. "Towards Ecological Statehood?: Cameralism and the Human–Nature Interface in the Eighteenth Century." In *Cameralism and the Enlightenment: Happiness, Governance and Reform in Transnational Perspective,* edited by Ere Nokkala and Nicholas B. Miller. Routledge, 2019.

Hopkins, B. D. *Ruling the Savage Periphery: Frontier Governance and the Making of the Modern State.* Harvard University Press, 2020.

Hroch, Miroslav. *Social Preconditions of National Revival in Europe: A Comparative Analysis of the Social Composition of Patriotic Groups Among the Smaller European Nations.* Cambridge University Press, 1985.

Ingrao, Charles W. *The Habsburg Monarchy, 1618–1815.* Third edition. Cambridge University Press, 2019.

Ingrao, Charles W. "The Problem of 'Enlightened Absolutism' and the German States." *The Journal of Modern History* 58 (December 1986): 161–80.

Ioanid, Radu. *The Holocaust in Romania: The Destruction of Jews and Gypsies Under the Antonescu Regime, 1940–1944.* Ivan R. Dee, 2008.

Iordachi, Constantin. "A Continuum of Dictatorships: Hybrid Totalitarian Experiments in Romania, 1937–44." In *Rethinking Fascism and Dictatorship in Europe,* edited by António Costa Pinto and Aristotle Kallis. Palgrave Macmillan, 2014.

Iordachi, Constantin. *Liberalism, Constitutional Nationalism, and Minorities: The Making of Romanian Citizenship, c. 1750–1918.* Brill, 2019.

Ivanesko, M. I. "Partiia 'Vyzvolennia' ta ii mistse v istorii Bukovyny." *Ukrainskii istoricheskii zhurnal* 2 (1989): 36–43.

Judson, Pieter M. *Exclusive Revolutionaries: Liberal Politics, Social Experience, and National Identity in the Austrian Empire, 1848–1914.* University of Michigan Press, 1996.

Judson, Pieter M. *Guardians of the Nation: Activists on the Language Frontiers of Imperial Austria.* Harvard University Press, 2006.

Judson, Pieter M. *The Habsburg Empire: A New History.* Harvard University Press, 2016.

Kaltenbrunner, Andreea. "Anti-Semitic Violence in Eastern Romania: The National Christian Party's Congress, 8 November 1936." *Contemporary European History* 33, no. 1 (2024): 117–36.

Kann, Robert A. *A History of the Habsburg Empire, 1526–1918*. University of California Press, 1980.

Kaps, Klemens. "Creating Differences for Integration: Enlightened Reforms and Civilizing Missions in the Eastern European Possessions of the Habsburg Monarchy (1750–1815)." In *Enlightened Colonialism: Civilization Narratives and Imperial Politics in the Age of Reason*, edited by Damien Tricoire. Springer International Publishing, 2017.

Karch, Brendan. *Nation and Loyalty in a German-Polish Borderland: Upper Silesia, 1848–1960*. Cambridge University Press, 2018.

Kashani-Sabet, Firoozeh. *Frontier Fictions: Shaping the Iranian Nation, 1804–1946*. Princeton University Press, 2011.

Katzenstein, Peter J., ed. *Civilizations in World Politics: Plural and Pluralist Perspectives*. Routledge, 2009.

Kauffman, Jesse. *Elusive Alliance: The German Occupation of Poland in World War I*. Illustrated edition. Harvard University Press, 2015.

Kazancigil, Ali. *The State in Global Perspective*. Gower, 1986.

Kenez, Peter. *The Birth of the Propaganda State: Soviet Methods of Mass Mobilization, 1917–1929*. Cambridge University Press, 1985.

Kindleberger, Charles P. *A Financial History of Western Europe*. Taylor & Francis, 2005.

King, Charles. *The Moldovans: Romania, Russia, and the Politics of Culture*. Hoover Institution Press, 2000.

King, Jeremy. *Budweisers into Czechs and Germans: A Local History of Bohemian Politics, 1848–1948*. Princeton University Press, 2018.

Kirchner Reill, Dominique. *The Fiume Crisis: Life in the Wake of the Habsburg Empire*. Harvard University Press, 2020.

Kirchner Reill, Dominique. *Nationalists Who Feared the Nation: Adriatic Multi-Nationalism in Habsburg Dalmatia, Trieste, and Venice*. Stanford University Press, 2012.

Kirchner Reill, Dominique, Ivan Jeličić, and Francesca Rolandi. "Redefining Citizenship After Empire: The Rights to Welfare, to Work, and to Remain in a Post-Habsburg World." *The Journal of Modern History* 94, no. 2 (2022): 326–62.

Kiss, Robert, ed. "Ucraina anunță sancțiuni împotriva Dianei Șoșoacă. Reacția senatoarei: "Cum își permite?" *DIGI24.ro*, March 24, 2023. https://www.digi24.ro/stiri/actualitate/politica/ucraina-anunta-sanctiuni-impotriva-dianei-sosoaca-reactia-senatoarei-cum-isi-permite-2293511 (accessed March 31, 2025).

Kissman, Joseph. "Zur Geschichte der Jüdischen Arbeiterbewegung 'Bund' in der Bukowina." In *Geschichte der Juden in der Bukowina: Ein Sammelwerk* (2 vols), edited by Hugo Gold, vol. 1. Edition "Olamenu," 1958.

Kohlrausch, Martin, and Jan C. Behrends. *Races to Modernity: Metropolitan Aspirations in Eastern Europe, 1890–1940*. Central European University Press, 2014.

König, Adolf. "Geschichte der J.N.A.V. 'Hasmonäa' in Czernowitz." In *Geschichte der Juden in der Bukowina: Ein Sammelwerk* (2 vols), edited by Hugo Gold, vol. 1. Edition "Olamenu," 1958.

Koselleck, Reinhart. *Futures Past: On the Semantics of Historical Time*. Translated by Keith Tribe. Columbia University Press, 2004.

Kosiul, Willi. *Die Buchenlanddeutschen*. Shaker Media, 2017.

Kotkin, Stephen. *Magnetic Mountain: Stalinism as a Civilization*. University of California Press, 1997.

Kotkin, Stephen. "Modern Times: The Soviet Union and the Interwar Conjuncture." *Kritika* 2, no. 1 (2008): 111–64.

Kotkin, Stephen. *Stalin: Waiting for Hitler, 1929–1941*. Penguin Press, 2017.

Kotsonis, Yanni. "Taxes and the Two Faces of the State Since the Eighteenth Century." In *State Formations: Global Histories and Cultures of Statehood*, edited by John L. Brooke, Julia C. Strauss, and Greg Anderson. Cambridge University Press, 2018.

Koziura, Karolina. "Memory, Monuments, and the Project of Nationalization in Ukraine: The Case of Chernivtsi." In *The Burden of the Past: History, Memory, and Identity in Contemporary Ukraine*, edited by Małgorzata Głowacka-Grajper and Anna Wylegała. Indiana University Press, 2020.

Koziura, Karolina. "The Spaces of Nostalgia(s) and the Politics of Belonging in Contemporary Chernivtsi, Western Ukraine." *East European Politics and Societies and Cultures* 33, no. 1 (2019): 218–37.

Kratochwil, Friedrich. "Of Systems, Boundaries, and Territoriality: An Inquiry into the Formation of the State System." *World Politics* 39, no. 1 (1986): 27–52.

Kravets, M. M. *Narysy z istorii selyanstva pivnichnoi Bukovyni na pochhatku XX stolittya*. Vinnytsia, 1998.

Krueger, Rita A. "Mediating Progress in the Provinces: Central Authority, Local Elites, and Agrarian Societies in Bohemia and Moravia." *Austrian History Yearbook* 35 (2004): 49–80.

Kühn, Franka. *Dr. Eduard Reiss: Der erste jüdische bürgermeister von Czernowitz, 1905–1907*. Hartung-Gorre Verlag, 2004.

Kumar, Krishan. "Nation-States as Empires, Empires as Nation-States: Two Principles, One Practice?" *Theory and Society* 39, no. 2 (2010): 119–43.

Kumar, Krishan. *Visions of Empire: How Five Imperial Regimes Shaped the World*. Princeton University Press, 2017.

Kurlander, Eric. "Between Völkisch and Universal Visions of Empire: Liberal Imperialism in *Mitteleuropa*, 1890–1918." In *Liberal Imperialism in Europe*, edited by Matthew P. Fitzpatrick, 141–165. Palgrave Macmillan, 2012.

Kwan, Jonathan. *Liberalism and the Habsburg Monarchy, 1861–1895*. Springer, 2013.

Kyyan, Dmytro. "'To Break Out of This Kingdom of Cooked Mirrors': An Interview with Igor Pomerantsev." *Apofenie*, October 2, 2020. Available at https://www.apofenie.com/interviews/2020/10/1/an-interview-with-igor-pomerantsev (accessed March 31, 2025).

Ladygina, Yuliya. *Bridging East and West: Ol'ha Kobylians'ka, Ukraine's Pioneering Modernist*. University of Toronto Press, 2019.

Lazăr, Mihnea. "Analiză: Ce este, de unde vine şi ce vrea AUR, partidul de extremă dreapta care a ajuns de la puţin peste zero la pragul electoral." *DIGI24.ro*, December 6, 2020. https://www.digi24.ro/stiri/actualitate/politica/ce-este-de-unde-vine-si-ce-vrea-aur-partidul-de-extrema-dreapta-care-a-ajuns-de-la-putin-peste-zero-la-pragul-electoral-1413193 (accessed March 31, 2025).

Lazar, Natalya. "Czernowitz Jews and the Holocaust: Anti-Jewish Violence, Ghettoization and Interethnic Relations in a Multi-Ethnic City, 1941." Unpublished PhD dissertation, Clark University, 2014.

Lazar, Natalya. "Holocaust Survivors and Soviet Policies in Postwar Chernivtsi, 1944–1946." *Revista de istorie a evreilor din România* 1, no. 16–17 (2016): 350–60.

Leonhard, Jörn. "Legacies of Violence: Eastern Europe's First World War: A Commentary from a Comparative Perspective," in *Legacies of Violence*, edited by Jochen Böhler, Włodzimierz Borodziej, and Joachim von Puttkamer. De Gruyter, 2014.

Lepuş, Miruna. *Tânăra generație interbelică: Grupul Criterion, tinerii avangardiști, tinerii de la Sburătorul, gruparea Iconar ș.a.* Editura Vremea, 2015.

Leslie, John. "Der Ausgleich in der Bukowina 1910: Zur österreichischen Nationalpolitik vor dem Ersten Weltkrieg." In *Geschichte zwischen Freiheit und Ordnung: Gerald Stourzh zum 60. Geburtstag*, edited by Emil Brix, Thomas Fröschl, and Josef Leidenfrost. Verlag Styria, 1991.

Lester, Alan. "Imperial Circuits and Networks: Geographies of the British Empire." *History Compass* 4, no. 1 (2006): 124–41.

Leuștean, Lucian N. "Eastern Orthodoxy and National Indifference in Habsburg Bukovina, 1774–1873." *Nations and Nationalism* 24, no. 4 (2018): 1117–41.

Levene, Mark. *Crisis of Genocide, Volume 2: The European Rimlands 1939–1953*. Oxford University Press, 2014.

Levin, Dov. "The Jews and the Inception of Soviet Rule in Bukovina." *Soviet Jewish Affairs* 6, no. 2 (1976): 52–70.

Levin, Dov. *The Lesser of Two Evils: Eastern European Jewry under Soviet Rule, 1939–1941*. Jewish Publication Society, 1995.

Li, Tania. *The Will to Improve: Governmentality, Development, and the Practice of Politics*. Duke University Press, 2007.

Liber, George. *Soviet Nationality Policy, Urban Growth, and Identity Change in the Ukrainian SSR, 1923–1934*. Cambridge University Press, 1992.

Liber, George. *Total Wars and the Making of Modern Ukraine, 1914–1954*. University of Toronto Press, 2016.

Lieven, D.C.B. *Empire: The Russian Empire and Its Rivals*. Yale University Press, 2001.

Lieven, D.C.B. "The Russian Empire and the Soviet Union as Imperial Polities." *Journal of Contemporary History* 30, no. 4 (1995): 607–36.

Liulevicius, Vejas Gabriel. *The German Myth of the East: 1800 to the Present*. Oxford University Press, 2011.

Livezeanu, Irina. *Cultural Politics in Greater Romania: Regionalism, Nation Building, and Ethnic Struggle, 1918–1930*. Cornell University Press, 1995.

Lohr, Eric. "The Russian Army and the Jews: Mass Deportation, Hostages, and Violence During World War I." *The Russian Review* 60, no. 3 (2001): 404–19.

Lovell, Stephen. *The Russian Reading Revolution: Print Culture in the Soviet and Post-Soviet Eras*. MacMillan, 2000.

Lower, Wendy. "Axis Collaboration, Operation Barbarossa, and the Holocaust in Ukraine." In *Nazi Policy on the Eastern Front, 1941: Total War, Genocide, and Radicalization*, edited by Alex J. Kay, David Stahel, and Jeff Rutherford. Boydell & Brewer, 2012.

Lower, Wendy. "Pogroms, Mob Violence and Genocide in Western Ukraine, Summer 1941: Varied Histories, Explanations and Comparisons." *Journal of Genocide Research* 13, no. 3 (2011): 217–46.

Maier, Charles S. *Among Empires: American Ascendancy and Its Predecessors*. Harvard University Press, 2006.

Maier, Charles S. "The Culture of Culture: Toward a German Variant of Performative Democracy." *German Politics and Society* 20, no. 2(2002): 14–25.

Maier, Charles S. *Leviathan 2.0: Inventing Modern Statehood.* Harvard University Press, 2014.

Maier, Charles S. *Once Within Borders: Territories of Power, Wealth, and Belonging since 1500.* Harvard University Press, 2016.

Mamina, Ion, and Ioan Scurtu. *Guverne și guvernanți, 1916–1938.* Silex, 1996.

Mandryk, M. "Ukrainskyi natsionalistychnyi rukh 1920–30-kh rr na Pivnichnyi Bukovyni u svitli rumunskikh arkhivnykh dokumentiv." *Ukrainskyi vyzvolnyi rukh* 3 (2004): 87–96.

Maner, Hans-Christian. *Parlamentarismus in Rumänien (1930–1940): Demokratie im autoritären Umfeld.* R. Oldenbourg, 1997.

Mantoux, Paul. *Paris Peace Conference, 1919: Proceedings of the Council of Four, March 24–April 18.* Droz, 1964.

Marin, Irina. *Peasant Violence and Antisemitism in Early Twentieth-Century Eastern Europe.* Palgrave Macmillan, 2018.

Marples, David. R. *Stalinism in Ukraine in the 1940s.* St. Martin's Press, 1992.

Martin, Terry. *The Affirmative Action Empire: Nations and Nationalism in the Soviet Union, 1923–1939.* Cornell University Press, 2001.

Martynowych, Orest T. *Ukrainians in Canada: The Formative Period, 1891–1924.* Canadian Institute of Ukrainian Studies, University of Alberta, 1991.

Masan, Oleksandr. "Czernowitz im Vergangenheit und Gegenwart." In *Czernowitz: Die Geschichte einer ungewöhnlichen Stadt,* edited by Harald Heppner. Böhlau Verlag, 2000.

Mason, John. *The Dissolution of the Austro-Hungarian Empire, 1867–1918.* Longman, 1997.

Massell, Gregory J. *The Surrogate Proletariat: Moslem Women and Revolutionary Strategies in Soviet Central Asia, 1919–1929.* Princeton University Press, 1974.

Mastny, Vojtech. *The Cold War and Soviet Insecurity: The Stalin Years.* Oxford University Press, 1998.

Matlock, Jack. "Russia, Europe, and 'Western Civilization.'" In *The Cultural Gradient: The Transmission of Ideas in Europe, 1789–1991,* edited by Catherine Evtuhov. Rowman & Littlefield, 2003.

Mayer, Arno. *The Furies: Violence and Terror in the French and Russian Revolutions.* Princeton University Press, 2000.

Mazower, Mark. *The Dark Continent: Europe's Twentieth Century.* Knopf, 1999.

Mazower, Mark. "Minorities and the League of Nations in Interwar Europe," *Daedalus* 126, no. 2 (1997): 47–63.

McCagg, William O. *A History of Habsburg Jews, 1670–1918.* Indiana University Press, 1992.

McKeown, Adam. *Melancholy Order: Asian Migration and the Globalization of Borders.* Reprint edition. Columbia University Press, 2011.

Meek, James. "Two Armies in One." *London Review of Books,* vol. 46, no. 4 (February 22, 2024). Available at https://www.lrb.co.uk/the-paper/v46/n04/james-meek/two-armies-in-one (accessed March 31, 2025).

Mëhilli, Elidor. *From Stalin to Mao: Albania and the Socialist World.* Cornell University Press, 2017.

Melton, James Van Horn. *Absolutism and the Eighteenth-Century Origins of Compulsory Schooling in Prussia and Austria.* Cambridge University Press, 1988.

Mendelsohn, Ezra. *The Jews of East Central Europe Between the World Wars.* Indiana University Press, 1987.

Mendelsohn, Ezra. *On Modern Jewish Politics*. Oxford University Press, 1993.

Merry, Wayne. "The Origins of Russia's War in Ukraine: The Clash of Russian and European 'Civilizational Choices' for Ukraine." In *Roots of Russia's War in Ukraine*, edited by Elizabeth A. Wood, William Pomeranz, E. Wayne Merry, and Maxim Trudoliubov. Woodrow Wilson Center Press, 2016.

Michaels, Paula A. "Medical Propaganda and Cultural Revolution in Soviet Kazakhstan, 1928–41." *The Russian Review* 59, no. 2 (2000): 159–78.

Miller, Alexei, and Stefan Berger, eds. *Nationalizing Empires*. Central European University Press, 2014.

Mitchell, A. Wess. *The Grand Strategy of the Habsburg Empire*. Princeton University Press, 2018.

Mitrany, David. *The Land and the Peasant in Rumania: The War and Agrarian Reform (1917–21)*. Humphrey Milford, Oxford University Press, 1930.

Moraru, Pavel. *Bucovina sub regimul Antonescu (1941–1944)*. Prut Internaţional, 2004.

Morawska, Ewa. "Labor Migrations of Poles in the Atlantic World Economy, 1880–1914." In *European Migrants: Global and Local Perspectives*, edited by Dirk Hoerder and Leslie Page Moch. UPNE, 1996.

Mosberg, Josef "Geschichte der J.N.A.V. 'Hebronia' in Czernowitz." In *Geschichte der Juden in der Bukowina: Ein Sammelwerk* (2 vols), edited by Hugo Gold, vol. 1. Edition "Olamenu," 1958.

Mosser, Alois. "Das Habsburgerreich als Wirtschaftsraum unter besonderer Berücksichtigung der östlichen Karpatengebiete." In *Die Bukowina: Vergangenheit und Gegenwart*, edited by Ilona Slawinski and Joseph P. Strelka. Peter Lang AG, 1995.

Motta, Giuseppe. *Less Than Nations: Central-Eastern European Minorities After WWI*. Cambridge Scholars Publishing, 2013.

Motyl, Alexander J. *The Turn to the Right: The Ideological Origins and Development of Ukrainian Nationalism, 1919–1929* (East European Monographs 65). *East European Quarterly* (distr.by Columbia University Press), 1980.

Motyl, Alexander J. "Why Empires Reemerge: Imperial Collapse and Imperial Revival in Comparative Perspective." *Comparative Politics* 31, no. 2 (1999): 127–45.

Müller, Dietmar. "Property Between Delimitation and Nationalization: The Notion, Institutions and practices of Land Proprietorship in Romania, Yugoslavia and Poland, 1918–1948." In *Property in East Central Europe: Notions, Institutions, and Practices of Landownership in the Twentieth Century*, edited by Hannes Siegrist and Dietmar Müller. Berghahn Books, 2015.

Müller, Dietmar. *Staatsbürger auf Widerruf. Juden und Muslime als Alteritätspartner im rumänischen und serbischen Nationscode: Ethnonationale Staatsbürgerschaftskonzepte 1878–1941*. Harrassowitz Verlag, 2005.

Müller, Dietmar. "Statehood in Central, Eastern, and South-Eastern Europe." in *The Routledge History Handbook of Central and Eastern Europe in the Twentieth Century*, edited by Włodzimierz Borodziej, Stanislav Holubec, and Joachim von Puttkamer. Routledge, 2020.

Muraru, Alexandru. "Editorial: Coloana a V-a. Sau cum AUR, Simion, Şoşoacă şi alţii au devenit agenţi subversivi care submineazǎ solidaritatea naţională din interior." *DIGI24.ro*, February 16, 2024. https://www.digi24.ro/opinii/agora-digi/coloana-a-v-a-sau-cum-aur-simion-sosoaca-si-altii-au-devenit-agenti-subversivi-care-submineaza-solidaritatea-nationala-din-interior-2689531 (accessed March 31, 2025).

Narskij, Igor. "The Reality of War and the War Experience of Russian Soldiers on the Russian Western Front, 1914–1915," in *The Forgotten Front: The Eastern Theater of World War I, 1914–1915*, edited by Gerhard Paul Gross and Janice W. Ancker. The University Press of Kentucky, 2018.

Narvselius, Eleonora and Niklas Bernsand. "Lviv and Chernivtsi: Two Memory Cultures at the Western Ukrainian Borderland." *East/West* 1, no. 1 (2014): 59–84.

Nemes, Robert. *Another Hungary: The Nineteenth-Century Provinces in Eight Lives*. Stanford University Press, 2016.

Neuborn, Erich, "Jüdisch-nationaler akademischer Leseverein 'Humanitas.'" In *Geschichte der Juden in der Bukowina: Ein Sammelwerk* (2 vols), edited by Hugo Gold, vol. 1. Edition "Olamenu," 1958.

Newman, John Paul. "Shades of Empire: Austro-Hungarian Officers, Frankists, and the Afterlives of Austria-Hungary in Croatia, 1918–1929," in *Embers of Empire: Continuity and Rupture in the Habsburg Successor States After 1918*, edited by Paul Miller and Claire Morelon. Berghahn Books, 2018

Niculescu Bran, Tatiana. *Mistica rugăciunii şi a revolverului: viaţa lui Corneliu Zelea Codreanu*. Humanitas, 2017.

Novosivskyi, Ivan M. *Bukovinian Ukrainians: A Historical Background and their Self-Determination in 1918*. Association of Bukovinian Ukrainians, 1970.

Ofer, Dalia, "Life in the Ghettos of Transnistria." *Yad Vashem Studies* 25 (1996): 229–74.

O'Keeffe, Brigid. *The Multiethnic Soviet Union and Its Demise*. Bloomsbury Academic, 2022.

Okey, Robin. *The Habsburg Monarchy: From Enlightenment to Eclipse*. St. Martin's Press, 2001.

Olson, Jess. *Nathan Birnbaum and Jewish Modernity: Architect of Zionism, Yiddishism, and Orthodoxy*. Stanford University Press, 2013.

Onciul, Aurel Constantin. *Aurel Ritter von Onciul und der Nationale Ausgleich in der österreichischen Bukowina: Eine wissenschaftliche Dokumentation*. Arvo, 1999.

Osterhammel, Jürgen. *Europe, the "West" and the Civilizing Mission*. German Historical Institute, 2006.

Ovenden, Richard. "Putin's War on Ukrainian Memory." *The Atlantic*, April 23, 2023. Available at https://www.theatlantic.com/ideas/archive/2023/04/russia-war-ukraine-occupation-libraries-archives/673813/ (accessed March 31, 2025).

Păcurar, Bogdan, ed. "Investigaţie Hotnews.ro: Cum se obţine cetăţenia română cu acte false, pe axa Ucraina–România." *DIGI24.ro*, January 3, 2024. https://www.digi24.ro/stiri/actualitate/investigatie-hotnews-ro-cum-se-obtine-cetatenia-romana-cu-acte-false-pe-axa-ucraina-romania-2636575 (accessed March 31, 2025).

Panaite, Viorel. "The Legal and Political Status of Wallachia and Moldavia in Relation to the Ottoman Porte." In *The European Tributary States of the Ottoman Empire in the Sixteenth and Seventeenth Centuries*, edited by Gábor Kármán and Lovro Kunčević, 9–42. Brill, 2013.

Pedersen, Susan. *The Guardians: The League of Nations and the Crisis of Empire*. Oxford University Press, 2015.

Perloff, Marjorie. *Edge of Irony: Modernism in the Shadow of the Habsburg Empire*. The University of Chicago Press, 2016.

Petraeus, David, and Andrew Roberts. *Conflict: The Evolution of Warfare from 1945 to Ukraine*. Harper, 2023.

Petrescu-Comnen, Nicolae. *The Great War and the Romanians: Notes and Documents on World War I*. Center for Romanian Studies, 2000.

Phelps, Nicole M. *U.S.–Habsburg Relations from 1815 to the Paris Peace Conference: Sovereignty Transformed*. Cambridge University Press, 2013.

Philliou, Christine May. *Biography of an Empire: Governing Ottomans in an Age of Revolution*. University of California Press, 2011.

Philpott, Daniel. *Revolutions in Sovereignty: How Ideas Shaped Modern International Relations*. Princeton University Press, 2001.

Plokhy, Serhii. "Epilogue. The EuroRevolution: Ukraine and the New Map of Europe." In *Ukraine and Europe: Cultural Encounters and Negotiations*, edited by Giovanna Brogi Bercoff, Marko Pavlyshyn, and Serhii Plokhy. University of Toronto Press, 2017.

Plokhy, Serhii. *The Gates of Europe: A History of Ukraine*. Basic Books, 2015.

Polesiuk-Padan, Jaakow. "Geschichte des 'Haschomer Hazair' in der Bukowina." In *Geschichte der Juden in der Bukowina: Ein Sammelwerk* (2 vols), edited by Hugo Gold, vol. 1. Edition "Olamenu," 1958

Polian, P. M. *Against Their Will: The History and Geography of Forced Migrations in the USSR*. Central European University Press, 2004.

Poliec, Mihai I. *The Holocaust in the Romanian Borderlands: The Arc in the Romanian Borderlands*. Routledge, 2019.

Pomerantsev, Igor. "Czernowitz—Reminiscences of a Drowned Man," *Hungarian Review*, July 8, 2014. Available at https://hungarianreview.com/article/20140706_czernowitz_reminiscences_of_a_drowned_man/ (accessed March 31, 2025).

Pomerantsev, Igor. "Death Is a Master from Russia." Translated by Frank Williams. *The Oxonian Review*, August 9, 2022. Available at https://oxonianreview.com/articles/death-is-a-master-from-russia (accessed March 31, 2025).

Pomerantsev, Igor. "Five Uneasy Pieces." *European Review of Books*, November 22, 2023. Available at https://europeanreviewofbooks.com/five-uneasy-pieces/ (accessed March 31, 2025).

Prokopovych, Markian. *Habsburg Lemberg: Architecture, Public Space, and Politics in the Galician Capital, 1772–1914*. Purdue University Press, 2009.

Prokopowitsch, Erich. "Die Entwicklung des Schulwesens in der Bukowina." In *Buchenland: Hundertfünfzig Jahre Deutschtum in der Bukowina*, edited by Franz Lang. Verlag des Südostdeutschen Kulturwerks, 1961.

Prokopowitsch, Erich. *Gründung, Entwicklung, und Ende der Franz-Josephs Universität in Czernowitz*. Piepersche Buchdruckerei und Verlaganstalt, 1955.

Prokopowitsch, Erich. *Die Rumänische Nationalbewegung in der Bukowina und der Dako-Romanismus: Ein Beitrag zur Geschichte des Nationalitätenkampfes in Österreich-Ungarn*. Verlag Hermann Böhlaus Nachf., 1965.

Prott, Volker. *The Politics of Self-Determination: Remaking Territories and National Identities in Europe, 1917–1923*. Oxford University Press, 2016.

Prusin, Alexander V. *The Lands Between: Conflict in the East European Borderlands, 1870–1992*. Oxford University Press, 2010

Prusin, Alexander V. *Nationalizing a Borderland: War, Ethnicity, and Anti-Jewish Violence in East Galicia, 1914–1920*. University of Alabama Press, 2005.

Rachamimov, Alon. *POWs and the Great War: Captivity on the Eastern Front*. Berg, 2002.

Radu, Sorin. "Peasant Democracy, or What It Was Like to Practice Politics in the Countryside of Romania Between the Two World Wars." In *Politics and Peasants in Interwar Romania: Perceptions, Mentalities, Propaganda,* edited by Sorin Radu and Oliver Jens Schmitt, 25–58. Cambridge Scholars Publishing, 2017.

Raeff, Marc. "The Well-Ordered Police State and the Development of Modernity in Seventeenth- and Eighteenth-Century Europe: An Attempt at a Comparative Approach." *The American Historical Review* 80, no. 5 (1975): 1221–43.

Rail, Evan. "'This Is Everyone's Culture': Ukraine's Architectural Treasures Face Destruction." *The New York Times,* March 11, 2022. Available at https://www.nytimes.com/2022/03/11/travel/ukraine-architecture-war.html (accessed March 31, 2025).

Ramet, Sabrina. "Interwar East Central Europe, 1918–1941: The Failure of Democracy-Building, the Fate of Minorities: An Introduction." In *Interwar East Central Europe, 1918–1941: The Failure of Democracy-Building, the Fate of Minorities,* edited by Sabrina P. Ramet. Routledge, 2020.

Rechter, David. *Becoming Habsburg: The Jews of Austrian Bukovina, 1774–1918.* Littman Library of Jewish Civilization in association with Liverpool University Press, 2013.

Rechter, David. "Geography Is Destiny: Region, Nation, and Empire in Habsburg Jewish Bukovina." *Journal of Modern Jewish Studies* 7, no. 3 (2008): 325–37.

Reifer, Manfred. *Dr. Mayer Ebner: Ein jüdisches Leben.* Olympia, 1947.

Reill, Peter Hans. *The German Enlightenment and the Rise of Historicism.* University of California Press, 1975.

Rein, Kurt."Czernowitz und die Deutschen." In *Czernowitz: Die Geschichte einer ungewöhnlicher Stadt,* edited by Harald Heppner. Böhlau Verlag, 2000.

Remnick, David. "How the War in Ukraine Ends." *The New Yorker,* February 17, 2023. https://www.newyorker.com/news/the-new-yorker-interview/how-the-war-in-ukraine-ends (accessed March 31, 2025).

Rieber, Alfred J. "The Sedimentary Society." *Russian History* 16, no. 2/4 (1989): 353–76.

Rigó, Máté. *Capitalism in Chaos: How the Business Elites of Europe Prospered in the Era of the Great War.* Cornell University Press, 2022.

Risch, William Jay. *The Ukrainian West: Culture and the Fate of Empire in Soviet Lviv.* Harvard University Press, 2011.

Roberts, Geoffrey. *Stalin's Wars: From World War to Cold War, 1939–1953.* Yale University Press, 2007.

Roberts, Henry L. *Rumania; Political Problems of an Agrarian State.* Yale University Press, 1951.

Rogaski, Ruth. *Hygienic Modernity: Meanings of Health and Disease in Treaty-Port China.* University of California Press, 2004.

Roider, Karl A. *Baron Thugut and Austria's Response to the French Revolution.* Princeton University Press, 2014.

Roider, Karl A. "Reform and Diplomacy in the Eighteenth-Century Habsburg Monarchy." In *State and Society in Early Modern Austria,* edited by Charles W. Ingrao. Purdue University Press, 1994.

Roskies, David. *A Bridge of Longing: The Lost Art of Yiddish Storytelling.* Harvard University Press, 1996.

Rossoliński-Liebe, Grzegorz. *Stepan Bandera: The Life and Afterlife of a Ukrainian Nationalist; Fascism, Genocide, and Cult.* Ibidem-Verlag, 2014.

Rossoliński-Liebe, Grzegorz. "The 'Ukrainian National Revolution' of 1941: Discourse and Practice of a Fascist Movement." *Kritika* 12, no. 1 (15, 2011): 83–114.

Rothschild, Joseph. *East Central Europe Between the Two World Wars*. University of Washington Press, 1974.

Roubicek, Fritz. *Von Basel bis Czernowitz: Die jüdisch-akademischen Studentenverbindungen in Europa*. Öesterreichischen Verein für Studentengeschichte, 1986.

Rozenblit, Marsha. "The Dilemma of Identity: The Impact of the First World War on Habsburg Jewry." In *The Habsburg Legacy: National Identity in Historical Perspective*, edited by Ritchie Robinson and Edward Timms. Edinburgh University Press, 1994.

Rozenblit, Marsha. *Reconstructing a National Identity: The Jews of Habsburg Austria During World War I*. Oxford University Press, 2004.

Rybak, Jan. *Everyday Zionism in East-Central Europe: Nation-Building in War and Revolution, 1914–1920*. Oxford University Press, 2021.

Sammartino, Annemarie H. *The Impossible Border: Germany and the East, 1914–1922*. Cornell University Press, 2014.

Sanborn, Joshua A. "The Genesis of Russian Warlordism: Violence and Governance during the First World War and the Civil War." *Contemporary European History* 19, no. 3 (2010): 195–213.

Sandache, Cristian. "Le groupe 'Iconar' et le mouvement legionnaire—Sequences." *Codrul Cosminului* 14 (December 2008): 205–13.

Sartori, Andrew. *Bengal in Global Concept History: Culturalism in the Age of Capital*. University of Chicago Press, 2009.

Scharr, Kurt. "Die Entwicklung des 'ländlichen Raumes' am Beispiel der Ansiedlerorte Fontinaalba und Klimoutz." In *Der Franziszeische Kataster im Kronland Bukowina/Czernowitzer Kreis (1817–1865): Statistik Und Katastralmappen*, edited by Kurt Scharr, Helmut Rumpler, and Constantin Ungureanu. Böhlau Verlag, 2015.

Scharr, Kurt. *Der griechisch-orientalische Religionsfonds der Bukowina 1783–1949: Kontinuitäten und Brüche einer prägenden Institution des Josephinismus*. Böhlau Verlag, 2020.

Scharr, Kurt. "The Habsburg Cadastral Registration System in the Context of Modernization." In *Property in East Central Europe: Notions, Institutions, and Practices of Landownership in the Twentieth Century*, edited by Dietmar Müller and Hannes Siegrist. Bergahn Books, 201.

Scharr, Kurt. "Die innere Verwaltungsentwicklung der Bukowina 1775–1918: Beharrlichkeit alter und Heranwachsen neuer politischer Strukturen." *Jahrbücher für Geschichte Osteuropas* 55, no. 2 (2007): 100–116.

Scharr, Kurt. *"Die Landschaft Bukowina": Das Werden einer Region an der Peripherie 1774–1918*. Böhlau Verlag, 2010.

Scheer, Tamara. *Zwischen Front und Heimat: Österreich-Ungarns Militärverwaltungen im Ersten Weltkrieg*. Peter Lang, 2009).

Schorske, Carl E. *Fin-de-siècle Vienna: Politics and Culture*. Vintage Books, 1981.

Scott, H. M. "Reform in the Habsburg Monarchy, 1740–90." In *Enlightened Absolutism: Reform and Reformers in Later Eighteenth-Century Europe*, edited by H. M. Scott. Macmillan, 1990.

Scott, James C. *Seeing Like a State: How Certain Schemes to Improve the Human Condition Have Failed*. Yale University Press, 1999.

Scurtu, Ioan. *Democrația la români: 1866–1938*. Humanitas, 1990.

Seegel, Steven. *Mapping Europe's Borderlands: Russian Cartography in the Age of Empire*. University of Chicago Press, 2012.

Seppel, Marten. "Introduction: Cameralism in Practice." In *Cameralism in Practice: State Administration and Economy in Early Modern Europe*, edited by Marten Seppel and Keith Tribe. Boydell & Brewer, 2017.

Seton-Watson, Hugh. *Eastern Europe Between the Wars, 1918–1941*. Cambridge University Press, 1945.

Seton-Watson, R. W. *A History of the Roumanians*. Cambridge University Press, 2015 [1934].

Sewell, William H. *Logics of History: Social Theory and Social Transformation*. University of Chicago Press, 2005.

Sha'ari, David. "Die jüdische Gemeinde von Czernowitz." In *Czernowitz: Die Geschichte einer ungewöhnlicher Stadt*, edited by Harald Heppner. Böhlau Verlag, 2000.

Shanes, Joshua. *Diaspora Nationalism and Jewish Identity in Habsburg Galicia*. Cambridge University Press, 2012

Shapiro, Paul. "Prelude to Dictatorship in Romania: The National Christian Party in Power, December 1937–February 1938." *Canadian-American Slavic Studies/Revue canadienne-americaine d'études slaves* 8, no. 1 (1974): 45–88.

Shelef, Nadav G. *Homelands: Shifting Borders and Territorial Disputes*. Cornell University Press, 2020.

Shevchenko, F. P. *Lukiian Kobylytsia: Z istorii antifeodalnoi borotbi Bukovini v pershii polovino XIX st*. Vid-vo Akademiï nauk Ukr. RSR, 1958.

Showalter, Dennis. "War in the East and the Balkans, 1914–1918," in *A Companion to World War I*, edited by John Horne. Wiley-Blackwell, 2010.

Sienerth, S. "Simiginowicz-Staufe, Ludwig Adolf." In *Österreichisches Biographisches Lexikon 1815–1950* [*ÖBL*], vol. 12. Verlag der Österreichischen Akademie der Wissenschaften, 2005.

Silverstein, Sara. "The Periphery Is the Centre: Some Macedonian Origins of Social Medicine and Internationalism." *Contemporary European History* 28, no. 2 (2019): 220–33.

Slaveski, Filip. *Remaking Ukraine After World War II: The Clash of Local and Central Soviet Power*. Cambridge University Press, 2021.

Slezkine, Yuri. *Arctic Mirrors: Russia and the Small Peoples of the North*. Cornell University Press, 1994.

Slezkine, Yuri. "From Savages to Citizens: The Cultural Revolution in the Soviet Far North, 1928–1938." *Slavic Review* 51, no. 1 (1992): 52–76.

Slezkine, Yuri. "The USSR as a Communal Apartment, or How a Socialist State Promoted Ethnic Particularism." *Slavic Review* 53, no. 2 (1994): 414–52.

Smith, Leonard V. *Sovereignty at the Paris Peace Conference of 1919*. Oxford University Press, 2018.

Snyder, Timothy. *Bloodlands: Europe Between Hitler and Stalin*. Basic Books, 2012.

Snyder, Timothy. *The Reconstruction of Nations: Poland, Ukraine, Lithuania, Belarus, 1569–1999*. New edition. Yale University Press, 2004.

Solonari, Vladimir. "Hating Soviets—Killing Jews How Antisemitic Were Local Perpetrators in Southern Ukraine, 1941–42?" *Kritika* 15, no. 3 (2014): 505–33.

Solonari, Vladimir. "Important New Document on the Romanian Policy of Ethnic Cleansing During World War II." *Holocaust and Genocide Studies* 21, no. 22 (2007): 268–97.

Solonari, Vladimir. "'Model Province': Explaining the Holocaust of Bessarabian and Bukovinan Jewry." *Nationalities Papers* 34, no. 4 (2006): 471–500.

Solonari, Vladimir. "Patterns of Violence: The Local Population and the Mass Murder of Jews in Bessarabia and Northern Bukovina, July–August 1941." *Kritika* 8, no. 4 (2007): 749–87.

Solonari, Vladimir. *Purifying the Nation: Population Exchange and Ethnic Cleansing in Nazi-Allied Romania*. Johns Hopkins University Press, 2010.

Solonari, Vladimir. *A Satellite Empire: Romanian Rule in Southwestern Ukraine, 1941–1944*. Cornell University Press, 2019.

Sonko, Alona, ed. "Romanian Senator and Nationalist Party Leader Wants to Help Russia Carve Up Ukraine." *NV: The New Voice of Ukraine*, "Nation," January 29, 2024. https://english.nv.ua/nation/romanian-mp-declares-his-wish-to-annex-parts-of-ukraine-50388015.html (accessed March 31, 2025).

Sperber, Jonathan. *The European Revolutions, 1848–1851*. Cambridge University Press, 2005.

Spitzer, Leo. *Lives In Between: The Experience of Marginality in a Century of Assimilation*. Hill & Wang, 1999.

Spruyt, Hendrik. *The Sovereign State and Its Competitors: An Analysis of Systems Change*. Princeton University Press, 1996.

Stanek, Łukasz. *Architecture in Global Socialism: Eastern Europe, West Africa, and the Middle East in the Cold War*. Princeton University Press, 2020.

Stanoeva, Elitza. "Architectural Praxis in Sofia: The Changing Perception of Oriental Urbanity and European Urbanism, 1879–1940." In *Races to Modernity: Metropolitan Aspirations in Eastern Europe, 1890–1940*, edited by Martin Kohlrausch and Jan C. Behrends. Central European University Press, 2014.

Stapelbroek, Koen. "The International Politics of Cameralism: The Balance of Power and Dutch Translations of Justi." In *Cameralism and the Enlightenment: Happiness, Governance and Reform in Transnational Perspective*, edited by Ere Nokkala and Nicholas B. Miller. Routledge, 2019.

Statiev, Alexander. "Motivations and Goals of Soviet Deportations in the Western Borderlands." *Journal of Strategic Studies* 28, no. 6 (2005): 977–1004.

Statiev, Alexander. *The Soviet Counterinsurgency in the Western Borderlands*. Cambridge University Press, 2010.

Stauter-Halsted, Keely. *The Nation in the Village: The Genesis of Peasant National Identity in Austrian Poland, 1848–1914*. Cornell University Press, 2001.

Steiner, Carl. *Karl Emil Franzos, 1848–1904: Emancipator and Assimilationist*. Peter Lang, 1990.

Steinhart, Eric Conrad. *The Holocaust and the Germanization of Ukraine*. Cambridge University Press, 2015.

Sternberg, Hermann. *Zur Geschichte der Juden in Czernowitz*. Olamenu, 1962.

Stourzh, Gerald. *Die Gleichberechtigung der Nationalitäten in der Verfassung und Verwaltung Österreichs*. Verlag der Österreichischen Akademie der Wissenschaften, 1985.

Stourzh, Gerald. "The National Compromise in the Bukovina 1909/1910." In *From Vienna to Chicago and Back: Essays on Intellectual History and Political Thought in Europe and America*, edited by Gerald Stourzh. University of Chicago Press, 2007.

Strachan, Hew. "The Eastern Front: Geopolitics, Geography, and Operations," in *The Forgotten Front: The Eastern Theater of World War I, 1914–1915*, edited by Gerhard Paul Gross and Janice W. Ancker. The University Press of Kentucky, 2018.

Strauss, Julia. "Regimes and Repertoires of State Building: The Two Chinas and Regime Consolidation in the Early 1950s." In *State Formations: Global Histories and Cultures of Statehood*, edited by John L. Brooke, Julia C. Strauss, and Greg Anderson. Cambridge University Press, 2018.

Strauss, Julia C. *State Formation in China and Taiwan: Bureaucracy, Campaign, and Performance*. Cambridge University Press, 2020.

Struve, Kai. "Gentry, Jews, and Peasants: Jews as Others in the Formation of the Modern Polish Nation in Rural Galicia During the Second Half of the Nineteenth Century." In *Creating the Other: Ethnic Conflict and Nationalism in Habsburg Central Europe*, edited by Nancy M. Wingfield. Berghahn Books, 2003.

Sugar, Peter F. *Southeastern Europe Under Ottoman Rule, 1354–1804*. University of Washington Press, 1977.

Sukiennicki, Wiktor. *East Central Europe During World War I: From Foreign Domination to National Independence*, edited by Maciej Siekierski. 2 vols. East European Monographs, 1984.

Surman, Jan. *Universities in Imperial Austria: A Social History of a Multilingual Space*. Purdue University Press, 2018.

Suveică, Svetlana. *Post-imperial Encounters: Transnational Designs of Bessarabia in Paris and Elsewhere, 1917–1922*. De Gruyter Oldenbourg, 2022.

Swidler, Ann. "Culture in Action: Symbols and Strategies." *American Sociological Review* 51, no. 2 (1986): 273–86.

Szabo, Franz A. J. "Cameralism, Josephinism, and Enlightenment: The Dynamic of Reform in the Habsburg Monarchy, 1740–92." *Austrian History Yearbook* 49 (2018): 1–14.

Szporluk, Roman. *Russia, Ukraine, and the Breakup of the Soviet Union*. Hoover Institution Press, Stanford University, 2000.

Tagliacozzo, Eric. *Secret Trades, Porous Borders: Smuggling and States Along a Southeast Asian Frontier, 1865–1915*. Yale University Press, 2005.

Taki, Viktor. *Russia on the Danube: Empire, Elites, and Reform in Moldavia and Wallachia, 1812–1834*. Central European University Press, 2021.

Tarasiuk, Maryna. "Working with Archives amid a War: Experience of a Ukrainian PhD Student." *Visible Ukraine*," November 28, 2023. https://visibleukraine.org/story/working-with-archives-amid-a-war-experience-of-a-ukrainian-phd-student/ (accessed March 31, 2025).

Taubman, William. *Nikita Khrushchev: The Man and His Era*. Yale University Press, 2000.

Ther, Philipp. *The Dark Side of Nation-States: Ethnic Cleansing in Modern Europe*. Berghahn Books, 2014.

Ther, Philipp. "Pre-Negotiated Violence: Ethnic Cleansing in the Long First War." In *Legacies of Violence: Eastern Europe's First World War*, edited by Jochen Böhler, Włodzimierz Borodziej, and Joachim von Puttkamer. De Gruyter, 2014.

Tismăneanu, Vladimir. *Stalinism for All Seasons: A Political History of Romanian Communism*. University of California Press, 2003.

Tismăneanu, Vladimir, and Marius Stan, "Ceaușescu's National Communism as National Stalinism." In *The Routledge Handbook of Balkan and Southeast European History*, edited by John Lampe and Ulf Brunnbauer. Routledge, 2020.

Todorova, Maria. *Imagining the Balkans*. Updated edition. Oxford University Press, 2009.

Todorova, Maria. "The Trap of Backwardness: Modernity, Temporality, and the Study of East-ern European Nationalism." *Slavic Review* 64, no. 1 (2005): 140–64.

Torrey, Glenn E. *Romania and World War I: A Collection of Studies*. Center for Romanian Studies, 1998.

Trebici, Vladimir. "Traian Brăileanu. Omul și Profesorul." *Revista română de sociologie* 10, no. 3–4 (1999): 383–88.

Trencsényi, Balázs. *The Politics of "National Character": A Study in Interwar East European Thought*. Routledge, 2012.

Tribe, Keith. "Cameralism and the Science of Government." *The Journal of Modern History* 56, no. 2 (1984): 263–84.

Tsurkan, Kate. "Letter from Chernivtsi: Ukraine's Ultimate Literary Capital." *New East Digital Archive*, September 28, 2021. https://www.new-east-archive.org/features/show/13153/letter-from-chernivtsi-ukraine-literary-capital (accessed March 31, 2025).

Tsurkan, Kate. "What Is the Secret of Chernivtsi?: A Conversation with Ihor Pomerantsev." *Los Angeles Review of Books*, December 26, 2022. Available at https://lareviewofbooks.org/article/what-is-the-secret-of-chernivtsi-a-conversation-with-igor-pomerantsev (accessed March 31, 2025).

Tsurkan, Kate. "Why I Chose to Stay in Ukraine." *The New Yorker*, March 30, 2022. Available at https://www.newyorker.com/culture/personal-history/why-an-american-writer-chooses-to-stay-in-ukraine (accessed March 31, 2025).

Turczynski, Emanuel. "Czernowitz als Beispiel einer Integrativen Universität." In *Die Teilung der Prager Universität 1882 und die intellektuelle Desintegration in den böhmischen Ländern: Vorträge der Tagung des Collegium Carolinum in Bad Wiessee vom 26. bis 28. November 1982*. Oldenbourg Verlag, 1984.

Turczynski, Emanuel. *Geschichte der Bukowina in der Neuzeit: Zur Sozial- und Kulturgeschichte einer mitteleuropäisch geprägten Landschaft*. Harrassowitz, 1993.

Ungureanu, Constantin. *Învățământul primar din Bucovina: (1774–1918)*. Civitas, 2007.

Ungureanu, Constantin. "Parzellengrössen und agrarische Besitzstrukturen in der Bukowina nach den Grundparzellen-Protokollen des Franziszeischen Katasters." In *Der Franziszeische Kataster im Kronland Bukowina/Czernowitzer Kreis (1817–1865): Statistik Und Katastralmappen*, edited by Kurt Scharr, Helmut Rumpler, and Constantin Ungureanu. Böhlau Verlag, 2015.

Unowsky, Daniel L. *The Pomp and Politics of Patriotism: Imperial Celebrations in Habsburg Austria, 1848–1916*. Purdue University Press, 2006.

Valiani, Leo. *The End of Austria-Hungary*. Knopf, 1973.

Van Meurs, Wim. "Land Reform in Romania—A Never-Ending Story." *SEER* 2, no. 2 (1999): 109–22.

Veidlinger, Jeffrey. *In the Midst of Civilized Europe: The Pogroms of 1918–1921 and the Onset of the Holocaust*. Illustrated edition. Metropolitan Books, 2021.

Vintilă, Alexandru-Ovidiu. "Traian Brăileanu, Grupul de la Cernăuți și revista *Însemnări sociologice* (Debutul unor Dezbateri)." *Revista română de sociologie* 23, no. 5–6 (2012): 483–501.

Viola, Lynne. *War Against the Peasantry, 1927–1930: The Tragedy of the Soviet Countryside*. Yale University Press, 2005.

Volkov, Vadim. "The Concept of *kul'turnost'*: Notes on the Stalinist Civilizing Process." In *Stalinism: New Directions*, edited by Sheila Fitzpatrick. Routledge, 2000.

Volovici, Leon. *Nationalist Ideology and Antisemitism: The Case of Romanian Intellectuals in the 1930s*. Pergamon Press, 1991.

Volovici, Marc. *German as a Jewish Problem: The Language Politics of Jewish Nationalism*. Stanford University Press, 2020.

Von Hagen, Mark. *War in a European Borderland: Occupations and Occupation Plans in Galicia and Ukraine, 1914–1918*. Herbert J. Ellison Center for Russian, East European, and Central Asian Studies, University of Washington, 2007.

Von Hagen, Mark. "Empires, Borderlands, and Diasporas: Eurasia as Anti-Paradigm for the Post-Soviet Era." *The American Historical Review* 109, no. 2 (2004): 445–68.

Vorrath, J. "On the Margin of Statehood? State–Society Relations in African Borderlands." In *Understanding Life in the Borderlands: Boundaries in Depth and in Motion*, edited by William I. Zartman. University of Georgia Press, 2010.

Vushko, Iryna. *The Politics of Cultural Retreat: Imperial Bureaucracy in Austrian Galicia, 1772–1867*. Yale University Press, 2015.

Wakefield, Andre. *The Disordered Police State: German Cameralism as Science and Practice*. University of Chicago Press, 2009.

Walker, Shaun. "Leaders of UK, France, Germany, and Poland to Visit Ukraine in Joint Show of Support." *The Guardian*, May 9, 2025. Available at https://www.theguardian.com/world/2025/may/09/leaders-of-uk-france-germany-and-poland-to-visit-ukraine-in-joint-show-of-support (accessed May 10, 2025).

Wanner, Catherine. "The Return of Czernowitz: Urban Affect, Nostalgia, and the Politics of Place-Making in a European Borderland City," *City & Society* 28, no. 2 (2016): 198–221.

Watson, Alexander. *Ring of Steel: Germany and Austria-Hungary at War, 1914–1918*. Allen Lane, 2014.

Weber, Eugen. *Peasants into Frenchmen: The Modernization of Rural France, 1870–1914*. Stanford University Press, 1976.

Weber, Hermann, and Hellmuth Hecker. *Die Bukowina im Zweiten Weltkrieg: Völkerrechtliche Aspekte der Lage der Bukowina im Spannungsfeld zwischen Rumänien, der Sowjetunion und Deutschland*. Forschungstelle für Völkerrecht un ausländisches öffentliches Recht der Universität Hamburg, 1972.

Weczerka, Hugo. *Die Deutschen im Buchenland*. Holzner, 1955.

Weiner, Amir, *Making Sense of War: The Second World War and the Fate of the Bolshevik Revolution*. Princeton University Press, 2001.

Weiner, Amir, and Aigi Rahi-Tamm. "Getting to Know You: The Soviet Surveillance System, 1939–57." *Kritisetka* 13, no. 1 (2012): 5–45.

Weinstein, Elias. "Juden im Pressewesen der Bukowina." In *Geschichte der Juden in der Bukowina: Ein Sammelwerk* (2 vols), edited by Hugo Gold, vol. 1. Edition "Olamenu," 1958.

Weiser, Kalman, and Joshua A. Fogel, eds. *Czernowitz at 100: The First Yiddish Language Conference in Historical Perspective*. Lexington Books, 2010.

Weitz, Eric D. "From the Vienna to the Paris System: International Politics and the Entangled Histories of Human Rights, Forced Deportations, and Civilizing Missions." *The American Historical Review* 113, no. 5 (2008): 1313–43.

Welisch, Sophie A. "The Bukovina-Germans in the Interwar Period." *East European Quarterly* 14, no. 4 (1980): 423–37.

Westad, Odd Arne. *The Global Cold War: Third World Interventions and the Making of Our Times*. Cambridge University Press, 2005.

Wheatley, Natasha. "Central Europe as Ground Zero of the New International Order." *Slavic Review* 78, no.4 (2019): 900–911.

Wilson, Andrew. *Ukraine Crisis: What It Means for the West*. Yale University Press, 2014.

Winkler, Markus. *Jüdische Identitäten im kommunikativen Raum: Presse, Sprache und Theater in Czernowitz bis 1923*. Edition Lumière, 2007.

Wolff, Larry. *The Idea of Galicia: History and Fantasy in Habsburg Political Culture*. Stanford University Press, 2012.

Wolff, Larry. *Inventing Eastern Europe: The Map of Civilization on the Mind of the Enlightenment*. Stanford University Press, 1994.

Woloch, Isser, and Gregory S. Brown. *Eighteenth-Century Europe: Tradition and Progress, 1715–1789*. W. W. Norton & Co., 2012.

Wood, Nathaniel D. *Becoming Metropolitan: Urban Selfhood and the Making of Modern Cracow*. Northern Illinois University Press, 2010.

Wortman, Richard. *Scenarios of Power: Myth and Ceremony in Russian Monarchy from Peter the Great to the Abdication of Nicholas II*. Abridged paperback edition. Princeton University Press, 2006.

Wright, Robin. "For Ukraine, Far Too Little, Too Late." *The New Yorker*, February 27, 2022. Available at https://www.newyorker.com/news/daily-comment/for-ukraine-far-too-little-too-late (accessed March 31, 2025).

Wyman, Mark. *Round-Trip to America: The Immigrants Return to Europe, 1880–1930*. Cornell University Press, 1996.

Yavetz, Zvi. "An Eyewitness Note: Reflections on the Rumanian Iron Guard." *Journal of Contemporary History* 26, no. 3/4 (1991): 597–610.

Yekelchyk, Serhii. *Ukraine: What Everyone Needs to Know*. Second edition. Oxford University Press, 2020.

Young, Louise. *Japan's Total Empire: Manchuria and the Culture of Wartime Imperialism*. University of California Press, 1999.

Zahra, Tara. *The Great Departure: Mass Migration from Eastern Europe and the Making of the Free World*. W. W. Norton & Co., 2016.

Zahra, Tara. "Imagined Noncommunities: National Indifference as a Category of Analysis." *Slavic Review* 69, no. 1 (2010): 93–119.

Zahra, Tara. *Kidnapped Souls: National Indifference and the Battle for Children in the Bohemian Lands, 1900–1948*. Cornell University Press, 2008.

Zahra, Tara. "Travel Agents on Trial: Policing Mobility in East Central Europe, 1889–1989." *Past & Present* 223, no. 1 (2014): 161–93.

Zain, Haneen. "UCSC Alumnus at the Forefront of Humanitarian Efforts in Ukraine" *UC Santa Cruz Newscenter*, November 16, 2023. https://news.ucsc.edu/2023/11/peter-gelpi.html (accessed March 31, 2025).

Zaitsev, Oleksandr. "Integral Nationalism in the Absence of a Nation-State: The Case of Ukraine." In *Conservatives and Right Radicals in Interwar Europe*, edited by Marco Bresciani. Routledge, 2020.

Zanou, Konstantina. *Transnational Patriotism in the Mediterranean, 1800–1850: Stammering the Nation*. Oxford University Press, 2019.

Zaslavsky, Victor, and Yuri Luryi. "The Passport System in the USSR and Changes in Soviet Society." *The Soviet and Post-Soviet Review* 6, no. 1 (1979): 137–53.

Zeman, Z.A.B. *The Break-up of the Habsburg Empire, 1914–1918: A Study in National and Social Revolution*. Oxford University Press, 1961.

Zombory-Moldovan, Bela. *The Burning of the World: A Memoir of 1914*. Translated by Peter Zombory-Moldovan. New York Review of Books, 2014.

## *Websites and Web Journals*

*Apofenie*: https://www.apofenie.com/
*The Atlantic*: https://www.theatlantic.com/
*Bukowina Portal*: https://www.bukowina-portal.de
*Council on Foreign Relations*: https://www.cfr.org/
*DIGI24.ro*: https://www.digi24.ro/
*The Guardian*: https://www.theguardian.com/
*Global Conflict Tracker*: https://www.cfr.org/global-conflict-tracker/
*HotNews Romania*: https://www.hotnews.ro/
*Hungarian Review*: https://hungarianreview.com/
*New East Digital Archive*: https://www.new-east-archive.org
*The New Voice of Ukraine*: https://english.nv.ua/
*The New York Times*: https://www.nytimes.com/
*The New Yorker*: https://www.newyorker.com/
*The Oxonian Review*: https://oxonianreview.com/
*UNHCR*: https://www.unrefugees.org/
*Visible Ukraine*: https://visibleukraine.org/

# INDEX

Note: page numbers followed by "f" and "n" refer to figures and endnotes, respectively.

## A NOTE ON THE TYPE

This book has been composed in Arno, an Old-style serif typeface in the classic Venetian tradition, designed by Robert Slimbach at Adobe.